THE ULTIMATE ENCYCLOPEDIA OF

GOLF

THIS IS A CARLTON/HODDER & STOUGHTON BOOK

Revised edition 1996, 1997

10 9 8 7 6 5 4 3 2 1

A CIP catalogue record for this book is available from the British Library

ISBN 0 340 70749 6

Project Editor: Martin Corteel
Project Art Editor: Paul Messam
Picture Research: Sharon Hutton
Designer: Simon Wilder
Production: Sarah Schuman

Printed and bound in Dubai

Hodder and Stoughton Ltd
A division of Hodder Headline PLC
338 Euston Road
London NW1 3BH

To Ray
Pat + Claire 10/01/98

THE ULTIMATE ENCYCLOPEDIA OF

GOLF

The definitive illustrated guide to world golf

Revised and updated edition

Ted Barrett & Michael Hobbs

CARLTON

Hodder & Stoughton

ACKNOWLEDGEMENTS

The authors would like to thank the USGA for permission to use their Centennial Logos (*see* page 198), and for the co-operation of their Technical and Library Support staff at Far Hills, New Jersey. Thanks are also due to John Glover, R&A Rules Secretary, Touche Rosse, Michael Harvey, chairman of the trustees of the Golf Course Wildlife Trust, Richard Doyle-Davidson and Juliette Brindley of the Wentworth Club, Phillips Auctioneers of Chester and "Joe the Pro" Hardwick, lately of Royal Hong Kong Golf Club.

PREVIOUS PAGE: PIN HIGH AT SHENZHEN *Fred Couples, who with Davis Love III triumphed for the United States in the 1995 World Cup, the first major event ever held in mainland China*

CONTENTS

GARY PLAYER *South African golfing legend*

AUGUSTA'S 12TH *Play it well and say "Amen"*

EXCLUSIVE EQUIPMENT *A Ryder Cup golf bag*

7 FOREWORD BY NICK PRICE

8 THE EARLY HISTORY OF GOLF
Looks at the royal and ancient origins of the game.

14 THE GREAT CHAMPIONSHIPS
Describes the highlights four "Majors" and the Ryder Cup and gives coverage of British and American amateur championships, the Walker Cup, Women's PGA Tour, the European PGA Tour and other principal golf events.

54 GOLF AROUND THE WORLD
The development of golf around the globe, from the strongholds of the United States and Great Britain, to the newly emergent nations of Europe, the Far East and Africa.

85 LEGENDS
Pays tribute to 11 of golf's all-time greats, plus the Great Triumvirate of Taylor, Vardon and Braid.

110 THE GREAT GOLFERS
Profiles 200 of golf's famous names from Amy Alcott to Fuzzy Zoeller.

153 THE GREAT HEAD-TO-HEADS
Looks at 10 of golf's epic encounters, encompassing Francis Ouimet's unlikely triumph against Harry Vardon in the 1913 US Open and Nick Faldo's domination of Greg Norman on the final day of the 1996 Masters.

164 THE FAMOUS COURSES
Pays homage to 24 places of golfing pilgrimage, from the storm-tossed shores of Turnberry in Scotland to the flower bedecked fairways of Augusta, Georgia.

190 THE GOLF INDUSTRY
Reviews the operation of the multi-million-pound golf business, and assesses golf's impact on the environment, for good or ill.

204 THE RULES OF GOLF
Describes how the rules of golf were devised and subsequently amended and how the etiquette of the game survives.

212 THE HISTORY OF THE SWING
Analyses the technological advances and innovations in technique that have had a significant impact on the development of the game.

218 GOLF EQUIPMENT
Showcases the balls and clubs that have been integral to the development of the game, and takes a look at the fashions of the fairway.

228 GOLF CULTURE AND GOLF POLITICS
Celebrates the fans who pack the galleries worldwide, and investigates the racial and gender discrimination that has bedevilled the game.

237 SCANDALS, DISASTERS AND TROUBLE-MAKERS
Recalls the chastening moments when misfortunes have been suffered or when the game has fallen into disrepute.

242 GOLF ECCENTRICS, COURSE CURIOSITIES AND BIZARRE HAPPENINGS
Looks at the some of the outlandish characters and quirky episodes in the history of golf.

248 CHRONOLOGY
The milestone events in golfing history, at a glance.

250 INDEX

FOREWORD BY NICK PRICE

In July 1994 I experienced my greatest thrill in golf, winning the Open Championship at Turnberry. It was a dream come true, especially after coming so close at Royal Troon in 1982 and at Royal Lytham in 1988. Standing at the prize-giving with both hands on that famous old claret jug was a feeling that is difficult to put into words. Then, a few weeks later, I managed to sustain my good play and concentration by capturing my second US PGA Championship in the heat of Southern Hills in Tulsa, Oklahoma.

There's no doubt about it, winning one of the four major championships is the goal of every professional golfer. Becoming a major champion is the greatest reward one can pay oneself for all the practice and hard work put in over the years. There is nothing like winning and while I might experience those moments of glory, so can the average player by winning his or her club championship, medal event or company match play tournament. That is what makes golf the great game it is.

Even when golfers are not swinging away on the fairways, they love reading about the game, which brings me to this book. Within its pages it covers the world game in such depth that it will provide all golfers with many hours of great reading. If you are looking for the game's early history, facts about the great championships, the game's legends, the great courses and players, even bizarre happenings, it's all here. For me, it really is the *Ultimate* Encyclopedia of Golf, and I hope you enjoy it.

Nick Price
Orlando, Florida

THE EARLY HISTORY OF GOLF

Golf belongs to the group of sports best described as target ball games. This also includes snooker, pool, ten-pin bowling, bowls, pétanque, croquet, curling and several varieties of billiards. Yet it stands proudly apart from them all, for only golf can claim to be both Royal and Ancient.

Eleven years before his death in 1513 during the disastrous Scottish defeat at Flodden, James IV of Scotland, known as "James of the Iron Belt", had golf clubs made by a Perth artisan whose usual stock in trade was bows and arrows. More clubs and balls were bought the following year, for a match with the Earl of Bothwell.

These purchases by James, the record of whose golf transactions is the earliest historical evidence of a golfer's name, were utterly at variance with previous royal attitudes to golf. In the previous century several bans on "fute-ball, golfe and uther sik unproffitable sportis" were imposed by the Scottish parliament, the last as late as 1491.

The reasoning behind the bans was that time wasted on "the green" – the old Scots term for a course, and not just the putting surface, hence greenkeeper and Green Committee – should have been spent in mastering the martial arts, the better to discomfort the English.

Yet this game despised by the Scottish leadership has conquered, half a millennium later, vast areas of land in every continent, and, like football, the allegiance of millions. The English have never quelled the Scots half as effectively as this Scottish game has colonized the five continents.

ROMANTIC RECONSTRUCTION *Forestier's 1905 impression of Mary Queen of Scots at St Andrews, 1563*

The relatively sudden change of heart in the Stuart camp followed close upon James's marriage to the daughter of Henry VII of England. The royal alliance did not, as Flodden and the Jacobite uprisings of the eighteenth century attest, mean the immediate end of war between the two nations, but longer spells of peace and prosperity supervened.

Moreover, for more than 180 years – until William of Orange replaced James II of England – there was an unbroken line of royal Stuart golfers, including Mary Queen of Scots, who may or may not have been insensitive enough to have played golf shortly after the murder of her husband Darnley, but whose reputation has suffered ever since from the suspicion that she did. Mention of William, who, like the Hanoverians who followed him on the English throne, was no golfer, reopens the great debate as to whether the game is utterly Scottish, or an adaptation of pastimes like *kolven*, popular in Holland, or *chole*, from Belgium and northern France, or *jeu de maille*, a pursuit of Louis XIV. *Jeu de maille*, however, contains even fewer of the essential elements of golf than *kolven* which, as clearly shown in a Rembrandt

KOLVEN ON ICE *Usually playing indoors, Dutch kolf players used frozen rivers, too, as shown in this painting by Dutch artist Hendrik Averkamp*

drawing, was played with a ball the size of a cricket ball, usually in a courtyard or on a frozen river, or even in churches in the days before pews. The object was to drive the ball against a mark or post.

Chole, which dates from at least as early as the middle of the fourteenth century, was a cross-country event, with the target a distant door or pillar. *Chole* still survives in Belgium, and in France by the name of *soule*. Golf historian Robert Browning believes *chole* may have been brought back and adapted to Scottish usages by Scots fighting on the side of the French in the Hundred Years' War after Henry V's victory at Agincourt. *Chole* had hockey-like features absent from golf, since a player was at liberty to hit his opponent's ball into trouble if he had failed to hit the target within the number of strokes he had declared. This rule of *chole*, benefiting the *chole* player's opponent or "*decholeur*", is directly opposed to the principle that the golfer, and never his opponent, shall enjoy the exclusive, unhindered and uninterrupted right to strike his own ball. This principle has stood the test of time throughout the long history of golf, and has been a major factor in preserving the civility of the game.

There are pictures, dating from the early seventeenth century, showing the playing of *kolven* and *chole* that are highly convincing arguments that these games are the forerunners of golf. On the other hand, golfers must have been active, to the annoyance of the Scottish parliament, well before that body first banned the sport in the middle of the fifteenth century (indeed St Andrews claimants back-date the sport to the twelfth century); since Scotland was not rich in graphic art in that era, all we know for certain is that golf was being played two centuries before *kolven* pictures were being painted. Moreover, there is no known form of the Scottish word golf that begins with a "k" sound.

The novelist Sir Walter Scott doubted that the word golf came from the verb "to gowff", meaning to hit. Others theorize that the verb derived from the game. The correlation between verb and game seems too close and too clear, however, to be mere coincidence.

Another possible origin for the game of golf from nearer home is shinty, but no recorded variant of this ancient Celtic hockey-like game has ever included mention of putting a ball into a hole, though in an early sixteenth-century German book of religious and sporting illustrations on vellum there is a depiction of a child apparently putting a ball into a depression. These fragmentary clues, like the club-swinging figure in a stained glass window in Gloucester Cathedral in England (dating from the middle of the fourteenth century), provide no definite answers, and Andrew Lang, the poet who leads the great roll of golf's literati, put the Scots' points of view succinctly with his dictum that "Clearly, kolf is no more golf than cricket is poker."

Putting the ball into the hole is the crucial, and some would say, diabolical, contribution of golf to the cross-country target ball game. The other contribution which can be seen in courses throughout the world is the nature of the Scottish landscape over which golf was developed. Great sums of money have been spent in the United States and Japan, to name only two countries, on earth-moving carried out frequently on a vast scale in order to replicate in turf and sand the characteristic features of natural Scottish courses – formed by wind and water and the depredations of domestic and wild animals.

The world-wide spread of golf received a racing start when Elizabeth I died without issue, and the Stuarts assumed the English throne in 1603 in the person of James I of England and VI of Scotland. He was the son of Mary Queen of Scots and the unfortunate Lord Darnley, and great-grandson of Margaret Tudor. Margaret was the English wife of James IV, none other than our first (known) golfer.

No doubt exists that James I was a powerful influence in favour of golf. Though a century had passed since the Scottish ban on golf had been lifted, James I was moved to make his view known that the common people's right to enjoy sport on Sunday was to be respected, as long as religious observances had been completed first. Charles I repeated this sentiment a few years later. James I, Charles I and II and James

COCKED HATS AND CRAVATS *Four gentlemen golfers, vintage 1798, at St Andrews, complete with tail-coats and caddies*

II all golfed, and so did Bonny Prince Charlie, who succeeded James II as pretender to the throne of England.

Many a 40-shilling fine was imposed on those who persisted in playing "in tyme of sermonis" – notably in Scotland, where the kirk looked down upon such flibbertigibbet behaviour. Despite these hindrances, golf flourished, like cricket, in all classes of the community. Early in James I's reign, bishops, noblemen, and folk of every rank were busy on Scottish links, while James's two sons were making golf fashionable south of the border by taking it up at their father's behest. The eldest son Henry died at 18, the second son Charles surviving to succeed to the crown, only to lose his head after the Civil War. Charles was golfing on Leith Links, near Edinburgh, on the day he received the news of a rebellion in Ireland.

The Restoration of the Monarchy in 1660 brought royal golfers into play again, the most notable being James, Duke of York, later James II. His example is being keenly followed by Andrew, the present Duke. James is credited with setting up and playing in the first international match, partnered by a Scottish shoemaker named Patersone, who was no novice at the tee. This Scottish team of Stuart and shoemaker beat two English noblemen, and Patersone was rewarded with enough cash to build a house in Cannongate, Edinburgh (which stood until 1961).

Not until the middle years of the following century did golf take the next great step forward. The engine of golf's further development was the social device of the club, until then strictly a political entity. No matter how powerful the ruling bodies of the game, no matter how rich the professional tours become, it is the club that remains the beating heart of the game.

A golf course was just that, a place where people could play golf. They did not pay for the privilege: there was no one to pay, no committee, and no greenkeeping costs, since the land over which the game took place was common land, untended apart from grazing animals and rabbits and the more damaging attentions of wind and tide. The links at St Andrews in Fife had since 1552 been given under licence by Archbishop Hamilton for free and unfettered use of citizens at football, golf and other games. That was the only formal convention.

The rules under which people played were a matter of local custom, on-the-spot agreements and wagers. Score cards were yet to be thought of. All golf was of the match play variety, and handicaps a rudimentary give and take between individuals, be they dukes or cobblers. Leading players were, however, already sufficiently celebrated to be the subject of poetry. The next step was to see who was the best player of all.

The defining moment came in 1744, when a group of players, "gentlemen of honour" it goes without saying, well known on Leith Links, presented a petition to the City of Edinburgh to provide a prize for the winning player in an open competition. This was granted in the shape of a Silver Club, by the magistrates, who were quick to indemnify themselves, after the fashion to be expected from careful guardians of public funds in those days, from any further expenditure which might be incurred in running the competition.

The new trophy was carried on the appointed day through the streets of Edinburgh, to the tuck of drums. The entry (of 10) was in the event strictly a local one. An Edinburgh surgeon named John Rattray came out on top, and repeated the dose the following year. The poet Mathison had a year earlier sung of "Rattray for skill ... renowned".

This man of medicine was certainly a cool hand. He went at Bonny Prince Charlie's behest to the aid of the wounded in the

Young Pretender's army during the second Jacobite rebellion of 1745. Owing perhaps to the leading Edinburgh golfers having a heavy presence in the law – they still do – he was not arraigned for treason as he might well have been. His escape has been attributed mainly to the efforts of Duncan Forbes of Culloden, which only goes to show what useful contacts can be made at golf clubs, since Forbes was himself a "Gentleman Golfer". After Rattray's second victory the aftermath of the Jacobite troubles prevented further competition for the Silver Club for two years.

Ten years after the Edinburgh initiative, 22 "Noblemen and Gentlemen" of St Andrews subscribed for a Silver Club of their own. As at Edinburgh, competition for the silver trophy was the only cement binding together the group of local players. The winner each year was captain of the group, and entrusted with the resolution of any disputes between players. Not for another 80 years did the St Andrews men have a regular meeting place, and even then they shared it with the local Archers' Club.

A second key date in the slow, piecemeal development of the idea of a club came in 1764 when, with no sign as yet of the hoped-for challenge for the Silver Club from other parts of Britain, the Edinburgh men moved to restrict entry to competition to "admit such Noblemen and Gentlemen as they approve to be members of the Company of Golfers". The cornerstone of the Honorable Company of Edinburgh Golfers had been laid 20 years earlier, and thus in 1994 the Company celebrated their 250th anniversary – 10 years before their rivals in St Andrews are at liberty to do so.

Edinburgh also scored a first in the matter of setting up a code of rules. This they did in 1744, to govern play for their Silver Club, though it is possible that the players at Leith had already put together a rudimentary list of do's and don'ts. The St Andrews men, following suit in 1754, were to abide by a similar codification, employing the principles of simplicity and brevity.

Today's mighty tomes detailing definitions and settling abstruse queries are a world away from the 13 rules issued in 1754: "back to basics" is an inadequate description. The first of the 13 makes strange reading to the modern golfer, since it directs that the player must tee off within a club's length of the hole, which gives an immediate and daunting idea of what the putting surfaces must have been like in the mid-eighteenth century. The main burden of the other 12 rules is "Play it as it lies", except when the player's ball comes to rest against his opponent's, or is unplayable in "water or watery filth", in which latter case the player may lift his ball, but must allow his opponent a stroke. Removing "stones, bones, or any break-club for the sake of playing your ball" was forbidden, except "upon the fair green, and that only within a club length of your ball". Putting green standards obviously improved over the next hundred years, and needed to be protected, because half-way through the nineteenth century Rule 1 was relaxed to the extent that the ball was allowed to be teed as much as six club lengths from the hole.

All these early rules were, as has been indicated, for match play. Once stroke play became widespread – and stroke play has always been the most popular form of the game in America – the need arose for exact definitions as to what constituted, to give an obvious example, an unplayable ball. A competitor at stroke play needed to know precisely whether the circumstances involved a penalty or not. Otherwise it would be impossible for him to continue his round and complete his card.

A century after the first simple codification of the rules, an attempt by the St Andrews club to define "unplayable" required almost as many words as the whole of the original 13 rules. The process of devoting further words to this intractable problem has used up a quantity of ink since then.

With the Leith Links deteriorating as the city pressed in upon them, the Honourable Company had to move, initially to Musselburgh, while the duties of regulators and adjudicators were assumed little by little by St Andrews. Finally they were shared by the United States Golf Association, and in 1951 a conference made the first real attempt to provide a code for golf worldwide. In doing so, it also got rid of the hated stymie.

Within a few years, the irresistible attractions of golf were spreading south of the border. Just as with the two pioneer Scottish clubs, the presentation of a trophy in 1766 set Blackheath golfing activities in motion in Kent, to the south of London. Not surprisingly, Blackheath's foundation owed much to the presence of expatriate Scots. Such men were often prime movers in helping the game spread further afield.

It did so with great rapidity, and in 1810 came the first mention of a women's competition, at Musselburgh. There had already been reports of Scottish officers playing in New York, and of the formation (1786) of a club in South Carolina, though the game was slow to take root in the United States, a process which took more than another

APPROVED DRESS *Lemuel Francis Abbott's painting of Blackheath captain William Innes, and caddie*

hundred years, and was pre-dated by the founding of Royal Montreal in 1873.

Golf had already followed the Union flag to Calcutta in 1829, and Bombay in 1842. Conversely, though the British began business in Hong Kong in the 1840s, golf did not flower there until 1889. Nor did it make the short journey to the Continent until 1856, when Pau in the shadow of the Pyrenees was founded for holiday visitors. Scottish soldiers of the Duke of Wellington's Peninsular Army are said to have played at Pau in 1814, some of them returning 20 years later on holiday – which places them among the very first of the great army of golf tourists, though many English players belonged to the leading Scottish clubs, and journeyed north for their regular silver club and gold medal meetings.

Australia joined the throng in 1870, with the Royal Adelaide Club, and South Africa in 1885, with the Royal Cape Club.

The rate of golf course construction in the British Isles was prodigious in Victorian times, mostly with horse, cart and shovel. The railways helped, from St Andrews to Blackheath, and from Sheringham, where the line ran within a few feet of the 17th green, to Aberdovey in west Wales, and from Ganton in Yorkshire to Lytham in Lancashire, where there were also gas trams on a line that was later electrified.

Course building reached a feverish pitch in the 1890s, as proved by the number of clubs celebrating their centenaries in the last decade of the present century. Curiously, there had been little golf in Ireland before the boom of the '90s, though Belfast set up their club in 1881. Unsurprisingly it was a Scot, Sir David Kinloch, who brought the game to Dublin.

The popularity of the game had greatly increased because it was given a focus by two competitions. 1860 saw the staging of what has gone down to history as the first "Open" Championship, though as we shall see in the next chapter it was not Open at all, and the crucial value of the events of that year took many years to make themselves apparent. Second, 25 years later, came what eventually was styled as the Amateur Championship, which meant that for players both paid and unpaid there was a summit to strive toward.

Among the catalysts leading to the foundation of golf's first major championship was Blackheath's victory, gained by George Glennie and Lieut. J. C. Stewart, in the Inter-Club Foursomes of 1857, a competition suggested by the Prestwick club. This constituted the first Championship Meeting to be played at St Andrews, and the host club were beaten finalists. The St Andrews club had assumed authority as the game's law-givers, and their decision to cut the number of holes on their course from 22 to 18 made 18 the magic number world-wide.

Significantly the winning pair in 1857 were both Scots; Glennie's natural talent was such that when he was studying at St Andrews University his fellows insisted he should play with only one club. He still won.

The following year a singles event was held, attracting a field of 28 from which the publisher, Robert Chambers, emerged victorious. In 1859 another publisher, Robert Clark, who wrote about golf, was much fancied to win, but a big hitter called George Condie strolled to the title 6 & 5.

These three competitions were amateur, but the leading players were celebrated in newspaper reports and verse, and attained the status of national sporting heroes.

The links were the haunt of a great variety of folk quite apart from the gentlemen amateurs, some of whom played in tall hats – a powerful inducement to keep the head still – and their caddies, whose name, it seems clear, derives from the French word *cadet*. This was the term used to describe the young French noblemen who came to Edinburgh with Mary Queen of Scots when she returned after her years at the French court.

Scottish humour, ever sardonic, extended the usage to mean something less complimentary, and in a classic sequence of semantic change, the meaning of *cadet* journeyed by way of "hanger-on" and "odd jobber" to "porter". Latterly, over the last two centuries, the word has slowly gone up-market again, certainly in the world of the major tours, to mean well-paid golf-bag carriers who keep their player dry when it is wet, watered when it is dry, fed when hungry, and well supplied with advice at all times on how far it is to the hole, which way the wind is blowing, and exactly how far the next putt will

THE FIRST NO. 1 *Allan Robertson (bare-headed, seventh from left), the first acknowledged champion, at St Andrews circa 1853*

OPEN FOR BUSINESS *Members gather outside the newly-constructed Royal & Ancient clubhouse*

swing on its way to the hole.

Many wanderers across the courses were simply out to take the air; others kicked a ball about, or flew kites. Soldiers drilled, horses were raced, cricket matches were played: but on the days of big challenge matches, sometimes with hundreds of pounds at stake, crowds surrounded the growing band of professionals. They got much closer to the action than would be countenanced today. The classlessness of the game, at least in Scotland, is indicated by the story of the caddie who, when he judged that spectators were getting a little too close, grabbed one, who happened to be a magistrate, by the ear, and invited him to stick his nose into the hole, so that he could *feel* the ball was there.

After the success of the events they had set in motion in 1857–59, the innovative members of Prestwick turned their attention to the professionals, many of whom started their golfing life as caddies.

It hardly needs saying that the professionals around the middle of the nineteenth century could not make a living from tournament winnings alone: there was no programme of events, and what money they won with their clubs, which they usually fashioned themselves, came from challenge matches for cash.

Club-making, which in the early days seemed to become the natural fiefdom of bow-makers, was, along with the manufacture of feathery golf balls and teaching, the staple source of income of the early Victorian professional. This state of affairs continued long after the establishment of the first regular Open events.

Allan Robertson, the first golfer to beat 80 at St Andrews, was accepted as the leading player of the day. With his assistant Tom Morris, Robertson ran a thriving feathery-ball business out of the window of their workshop, which was the kitchen of Robertson's house. Stuffing a top hat full of feathers into a leather casing was a job for an expert, though even the best could manage no more than three balls a day.

The era of the feathery, preceded almost certainly by lathe-turned wooden balls as used in such games as *chole*, ended, to Robertson's dismay, with the development of the solid gutta-percha ball during the last years of his life: he died in 1859, aged only 44. The popularity of the cheaper "gutty" must have been an especially severe shock to Robertson, because the family feathery trade had been in existence for so long, run by his grandfather Peter and father Davie before him. The gutty was a solid ball made from the juice of the Malayan percha tree and, unlike the feathery, could be remoulded when damaged – the feathery simply burst open when mistreated, especially in wet weather.

Moreover, the Robertson and Co. output is reckoned to have been well in excess of 2,000 featheries a year. At half a crown each (12.5 pence in sterling metric terms, or about 20 US cents) that came to an annual revenue of about £300, a fair sum in the mid-nineteenth century. The high cost of a feathery in the last days of its dominance no doubt kept many would-be golfers off the course. Robertson proved himself the complete professional, for after first declaring of the new projectile, "It's nae gowff", he reacted positively to the playing problems set by the new ball, which was much less responsive and more difficult to get into the air than the feathery. He made much greater use of the mid and short irons to fly the ball to the target. Pitching had previously been performed with wooden clubs. Never a long hitter, Robertson obeyed the first rule of golf: he kept the ball in play, and used his new iron technique to get close to the hole with his approach shots.

His death posed the question: who is champion now? Prestwick provided a way of finding out in October, 1860, with the game's first formal competitive tournament at stroke play, what we know as The Open. The golfing calendar has for nearly a century been dominated by this and three other majors: two of them, both amateur events, were replaced as social changes reshaped golf. How appropriate that the youngest of the majors, the Masters, is the first great international event of the year.

THE GREAT CHAMPIONSHIPS

With the increasing popularity of golf throughout the twentieth century, four championships have so captured the imagination of players and public alike that they have become known as the majors. The four majors march through the calendar nowadays like this: Masters (held in April), United States Open (in June), British Open (in July) and US PGA (in August) ... *nowadays* because the majors used to be the two Opens and the British and American Amateur Championships, while other tournament organizers style their events as "the fifth major".

DELAYED DOUBLE (left) *Greg Norman welcomes back the Open Championship trophy with a kiss at Royal St George's, Sandwich, in 1993;* (opposite) *Curtis Strange lands a second US Open in a row in 1989, at Oak Hill, Rochester*

After Bobby Jones won all four majors in 1930 it gradually became clear that changes were necessary. They did not occur overnight. When Ben Hogan, uniquely, won the first three of the "modern" majors in 1953, the fourth, the US PGA, was out of reach because it clashed with the British Open. It was a decade later before the idea of a latter-day Jones to hit all four targets in a season seized many minds. The Masters, the youngest major and the only one always played on the same course, got the nod from players, public and Press despite the misgivings of its creator, Jones. Carefully engineered attempts to invent a fifth major have failed. In other words, the majors have a life of their own ...

NIKE

THE MASTERS

GRAND SLAMMER *J.A.A. Berrie's 1930 portrait of Bobby Jones*

It took a long time for the full effects of the years 1930–34 to register upon the world of golf. Indeed, things were never the same again from the moment Bobby Jones, at the age of 28, retired from competitive golf. He had no more peaks to climb after 1930, when he exceeded even the massive expectations of his adoring public on both sides of the Atlantic by winning in one season all four of what were then accepted as the four major championships – the British and United States Opens, and the Amateur championships of the same two countries.

It is difficult for a golf fan under 80 who has not skimmed the contemporary media to take on board the scale of the adulation, respect, affection and general awe commanded by Jones, even before the Grand Slam, a term taken from the game of bridge by his biographer, O. B. Keeler. Jones's fame eclipsed that of such outstanding professionals as Walter Hagen and Gene Sarazen. Besides, they could not play for the two amateur titles, and though the Professional Golfers Championship, founded in 1916, was gaining in importance, its quality was never franked by the presence of the undisputed top golfer of the day, Jones.

Three years after Jones retired, Johnny Goodman won the United States Open. No amateur has won it since, or won any other major. So the amateur titles rapidly lost their honoured position at the topmost level of the game. Playing in high-class amateur golf cost money, and there was little about in the depths of the Depression, as President Franklin Roosevelt began his efforts to revive the nation.

Another major, open to paid and unpaid, was needed, and there was more than a touch of poetic justice in the fact that the greatest amateur of all, Jones, provided it, unknowingly, in 1934. His offering was a uniquely lovely course and an event which admitted pros and amateurs, and would, in time, slot into the calendar alongside the two main Opens and the PGA Championship, which was to move into the top bracket of competition now that the amateur challenge had faded.

Jones had decided to return to his law practice on retirement and to make some money with instructional films and books. He also intended to fulfil a long-held ambition: to found a golf club with a superior course, somewhere near his home in Georgia, which his golfing friends could join. A year before his retirement, Jones had spoken on the subject with Dr Alister Mackenzie at Pebble Beach during the Amateur Championship, in which Jones was beaten by Goodman from Nebraska. Mackenzie had turned, during the First World War, from doctoring to a camouflage unit, and later took up course architecture. He and Jones sought a different marque of course, one which Mackenzie characterized as "adventurous". With the assistance of a New York businessman, Clifford Roberts, who had started out as a suit salesman and enjoyed golf trips to Georgia and friendship with Jones, Thomas Barrett, of the Augusta Chamber of Commerce, the journalist Grantland Rice and several financiers, the project took a big step forward when Barrett suggested the purchase of what had been one of the first nurseries in Georgia, Fruitlands.

Jones fell in love with the site at once. "It seemed that this land had been lying here for years waiting for someone to lay a golf course upon it." The money for the purchase was obtained piecemeal – this was so soon after the Wall Street crash of 1929 that some of his backers were still strapped for ready cash.

Once the purchase had been underwritten, however, more cash flowed in from all over the world to meet building costs. It was built to Mackenzie's design in about a year, incorporating the latest in irrigation systems. Augusta National, as it was to be called, was right up to date in this regard. Jones struck a great many balls to verify shot values around the hilly lay-out, which was designed with massive fairways and greens, little rough and few bunkers. Instead of these, mounds were used to produce a rolling topography much after the style of Jones's beloved St Andrews with its seaside humps and hollows. One of the underlying aims had been to produce a course which would look far more difficult than it really was. Jones wanted all his friends, expert or not, to enjoy the course.

By the time the first Augusta National Invitation was issued in 1934, the final touch had been added – that every hole should be named after a blossom, and decorated with that blossom, among others.

The idea that this was no more than a jolly spring meeting for Jones's friends at the close of the professional winter tour lasted no time at all. No one knows if Roberts had a long-term vision of Augusta as a world-class event, but his promotional skills and the box office appeal of Jones did the trick with bewildering speed. Roberts made a fuss of the Press, always a good Public Relations move, and paid old-time pros to sit around in front of the clubhouse. He later hit a promotional jackpot by enrolling Eisenhower as a member: schmaltz, class and flowers make a potent mixture. Roberts persuaded Jones to play in the first and (as it turned out) only Augusta Invitation event. That followed a get-together for members and friends (a few members had started to play on the course at the end of 1932), at which, at Rice's behest, Roberts and Jones were to be given *carte blanche* to run Augusta National.

Jones did not like the idea of calling the Invitation event the Masters, deeming it presumptuous. However, as soon as the notion that the competition might have been called the Masters got out to the Press, they immediately adopted the name, though the official programme made no mention of "Masters". Many years went by before Jones joined the general acceptance of the title, and indeed before entry

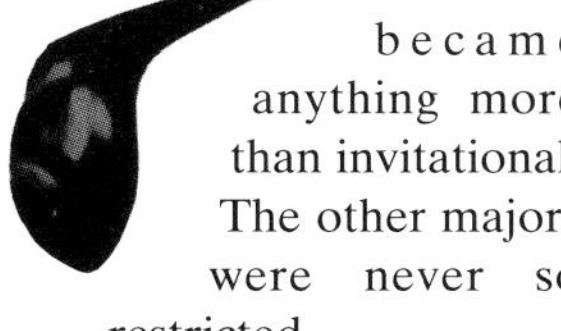

became anything more than invitational. The other majors were never so restricted.

Jones finished 10 shots behind the first winner, Horton Smith, one of the very few players who had beaten Jones in his climactic year of 1930. Yet Jones as usual got more column inches!

The only leading player missing from the field in the first year was Gene Sarazen, who was playing on a tour of South America. He made up for his initial absence in a big way in 1935. He needed three birdies to catch Craig Wood, who had finished with 282. He got the three shots he needed in a flash by holing his four-wood second shot at the par five 15th. Walter Hagen, in a piquant pairing with Sarazen, and Jones, as a spectator, were among the few witnesses of the shot "heard round the world", the description given to it by the media.

Sarazen parred 16, 17 and 18, and as usual when a player is overtaken by such a cruel stroke as Sarazen's, Wood lost the play-off. No one, not the big three of the '60s, Palmer, Nicklaus and Player, nor even Ballesteros, specialist in the spectacular, has topped Sarazen's Masterly touch. Smith won again in 1936, by which time the title Masters was, for all but Jones, set in stone. More Masterly golf, with the new shafts of steel, came from Texan Byron Nelson, who set new standards in 1937 with a flying start of 66, hitting every green in regulation figures (except the par fives, which he reached in two). Still they poured out of Texas: stars like three-time winner Jimmy Demaret, Ralph Guldahl and Ben Hogan helped ticket sales to soar, and yet another, Lloyd Mangrum, shook the Masters firmament, but not the eventual winner, Demaret, with a scintillating opening round of 64 in 1940.

Amazingly, though Jones's golf was on the decline, the same could seldom be said right up to the Second World War of the space newspapers reserved for his rounds. All this finished after Nelson's second Masters in 1942, when the club was wound down for the duration, with cattle keeping the grass short, and profit made from turkey farming. Private contributions from rich members revived the club and course, improved the clubhouse, and got things rolling once Jones, Snead, Hogan and company got out of uniform.

The Masters was still far short of the riches it has attained in the television age. Yet the strong flavour of exclusivity it has always had began to work in its favour more and more, aided by the flowering of Ben Hogan as the first great post-war player. His astonishing recovery from dreadful road crash injuries in 1949 added to the public sense of wonder at his achievements. He lost by a stroke to Herman Keiser in 1946, was within a stroke of the best four-round total in winning his first Masters in 1951, and beat it by five shots with 274 two years later, when he went on to win both the big Opens.

Hogan's quality was succeeded just at the right moment for Augusta by the irrepressible showmanship of a player born to be a television star, for Arnold Palmer won his first Masters (1958) in the early days of sports coverage on the box. He perfectly complemented Roberts's relentless eye for detail and flair for presenting the players as stars upon a green and flowery stage which might have been invented for television.

The exclusive nature of the Masters has been enhanced (and since aped elsewhere) by the outward symbol of success: the symbolic green jacket, made of a specially reserved cloth, that can be worn only by club members and Master golfers. Only the champions may wear it off the course, and only as long as they remain champion and provided it is not demeaned by its use for commercial purposes.

Roberts made sure the course was so policed and roped off that there was space around the players (and no reporters inside the ropes). There is always more room for the players in another important sense: in 1994, for example, only 51 players qualified for the final 36 holes when José-Maria Olazabal got his first green jacket out of a total entry of 86. Nearly twice as many play in most top-line pro events.

Roberts, who was laid low by a terminal illness and died by his own hand in 1977, made the Masters ticket by far the most difficult to obtain in world golf. He was not the most popular of golf's dictators, but proved a truth that many a club should heed: committees are frequently not the best government.

Roberts's skill was to present world-class golf with an amateur, country club ethos in many subtle

FAME AT A STROKE *Gene Sarazen, remembered for his double eagle*

cobra

ways, for little is made of mundane items like money, though plenty of it is available for the leading finishers. Entry is no longer solely a matter of invitation, and the highly successful gain entry whether the club likes it or not. All the same, for the first 38 years no black player was admitted to the Masters, though such men as Charlie Sifford, in 1973, had performed as well as many white players who had gained a place. But he did not get enough points on a scale Roberts had developed, and was excluded despite grumbles from US congressmen. Next year Lee Elder won the Monsanto Open, and cut the Augustan knot for black players. Black *caddies* have always been the norm at Augusta.

Palmer's four Masters triumphs were trumped by Jack Nicklaus's six, the last, in 1986, a tonic to every golfer over 40. Gary Player, thrice a winner, was, in 1961, the first non-American to succeed at Augusta. It was 19 years before another foreigner followed suit – the Spaniard Severiano Ballesteros, who began an unprecedented European domination of an American event. Five European wins in the 1980s (Ballesteros 2, Bernard Langer, Sandy Lyle and Nick Faldo) have been followed up by Faldo, completing a rare treble, Ian Woosnam, Langer (again), and Olazabal.

Faldo's first two Masters were gained at the second extra hole, which is Augusta's 11th, against Scott Hoch in 1989 and Raymond Floyd the following year. Floyd had proved a most convincing of champions in 1976. He was the outright leader after every round, beating Ben Crenshaw by eight strokes. His total of 271 equalled the record set in 1965 by Nicklaus, who was joint third to Floyd, 11 strokes adrift.

A few weeks before Floyd's 271, Eldrick Woods first saw the light of day in Cypress, California: 21 years on, he shrugged off a first nine holes of 40 and lived up his nickname "Tiger" by displacing Ballesteros (23 when he first donned the green jacket) as the youngest winner. So huge was this particularly aggressive young Tiger's hitting off the tee that most of his approaches were made with no more than a wedge. By these unprecedented methods, he posted a new low score of 270, 18 under par, and a record winning margin of 12 strokes over Tom Kite. All this at his first attempt as a professional to win a "major".

For a nation riven by racialism, the most shattering aspect of his stunning victory was his status as the only black winner of a major ... 50 years after Jackie Robinson became the first black major league baseball player – and was vilified by white supremacists, who subjected him and his family to insults, and were, some thought, a stress factor in Robinson's early death. By the same token, Woods' plans to make the game more accessible to young blacks (he had started swinging a club at 18 months) would be vastly more difficult to bring to fruition than his own extraordinary talents.

His win silenced those who had ridiculed Nicklaus's predictions that Woods would win as many Masters and he and Palmer together – 10. Whatever Woods' future might be, and Cary Middlecoff thought his swing might lead to back strain, he had brought fresh wonders to light on what has become the most prominent and distinctive of the game's stages. Whoever wins, press, public and TV lap it up. It is hard to resist the thought that Jones's ability to make things happen has been transferred to the course that was his last rich gift to golf.

Defeat seems crueller here, notably Greg Norman's second extra hole loss to Larry Mize's giant chip-in. It is doubtful whether this was more distressing for Norman than his last day collapse and loss of his 54-hole lead of six strokes against a relentless Faldo in 1996. Cruellest of all was the play-off with Bob Goalby that was denied to Roberto de Vicenzo in 1968 because he signed for a shot more than he had taken. "I am a stupid", said the Argentine, whose courteous acceptance of his fate must have charmed Jones. A spinal illness kept the founder of Augusta from the Masters for the last three years of his life, ended by an aneurysm in 1971.

YOUNGEST MASTER *Nick Faldo helps Tiger Woods into his green jacket*

FINISHING OFF *(Opposite) Nick Faldo driving for his third Masters*

Masters results at Augusta National, Georgia

Year	Winner	Runner-up	Score
1934	H Smith	C Wood	284
1935	G Sarazen	C Wood	282
	WON PLAY-OFF 144 TO 149		
1936	H Smith	H Cooper	285
1937	B Nelson	R Guldahl	283
1938	H Picard	R Guldahl	285
1939	R Guldahl	S Snead, W Burke, W Lawson Little	279
1940	J Demaret	L Mangrum	280
1941	C Wood	B Nelson	280
1942	B Nelson	B Hogan	280
	WON PLAY-OFF 69 TO 70		
1943–45	No tournament		
1946	H Keiser	B Hogan	282
1947	J Demaret	B Nelson, F Stranahan	281
1948	C Harmon	C Middlecoff	279
1949	S Snead	J Bulla, L Mangrum	282
1950	J Demaret	J Ferrier	283
1951	B Hogan	S Riegel	280
1952	S Snead	J Burke, Jnr	286
1953	B Hogan	P Oliver, Jnr	274
1954	S Snead	B Hogan	289
	WON PLAY-OFF 70 TO 71		
1955	C Middlecoff	B Hogan	279
1956	J Burke, Jnr	K Venturi	289
1957	D Ford	S Snead	283
1958	A Palmer	D Ford, F Hawkins	284
1959	A Wall, Jnr	C Middlecoff	284
1960	A Palmer	K Venturi	282
1961	G Player	A Palmer, C Coe	280
1962	A Palmer	G Player, D Finsterwald	280
	WON PLAY-OFF 68 TO 71 TO 77		
1963	J Nicklaus	A Lema	286
1964	A Palmer	D Marr, J Nicklaus	276
1965	J Nicklaus	A Palmer, G Player	271
1966	J Nicklaus	T Jacobs, G Brewer	288
	WON PLAY-OFF 70 TO 72 TO 78		
1967	G Brewer	R Nichols	280
1968	R Goalby	R de Vicenzo	277

Year	Winner	Runner-up	Score
1969	G Archer	T Weiskopf, W Casper, G Knudson	281
1970	W Casper	G Littler	279
	WON PLAY-OFF 69 TO 74		
1971	C Coody	J Miller, J Nicklaus	279
1972	J Nicklaus	T Weiskopf, B Crampton, R Mitchell	286
1973	T Aaron	J C Snead	283
1974	G Player	D Stockton, T Weiskopf	278
1975	J Nicklaus	J Miller, T Weiskopf	276
1976	R Floyd	B Crenshaw	271
1977	T Watson	J Nicklaus	276
1978	G Player	R Funseth, H Green, T Watson	277
1979	F Zoeller	T Watson, E Sneed	280
	WON PLAY-OFF AT SECOND EXTRA HOLE		
1980	S Ballesteros	G Gilbert, J Newton	275
1981	T Watson	J Nicklaus, J Miller	280
1982	C Stadler	D Pohl	284
	WON PLAY-OFF AT FIRST EXTRA HOLE		
1983	S Ballesteros	B Crenshaw, T Kite	280
1984	B Crenshaw	T Watson	277
1985	B Langer	C Strange, R Floyd, S Ballesteros	282
1986	J Nicklaus	T Kite, G Norman	279
1987	L Mize	S Ballesteros, G Norman	285
	WON PLAY-OFF AT SECOND EXTRA HOLE		
1988	S Lyle	M Calcavecchia	281
1989	N Faldo	S Hoch	283
	WON PLAY-OFF AT SECOND EXTRA HOLE		
1990	N Faldo	R Floyd	278
	WON PLAY-OFF AT SECOND EXTRA HOLE		
1991	I Woosnam	J-M Olazabal	277
1992	F Couples	R Floyd	275
1993	B Langer	C Beck	277
1994	J-M Olazabal	T Lehman	279
1995	B Crenshaw	D Love III	274
1996	N Faldo	G Norman	276
1997	T Woods	T Kite	270

US OPEN

Late twentieth-century competitive golf is dominated by the professionals, but the amateurs of America were the fashionable end of the game as the US golf boom throbbed into action in the last decade of the nineteenth century. All the same, early attempts to stage both Amateur and Open Championships were a shambles. Neither the United States Golf Association (USGA) nor the US PGA recognize, as some record books do, the 1894 affair at the St Andrew's Club, in New York City's Bronx, won by Willie Dunn from Musselburgh at match play against fellow Scot Willie Campbell by two holes. This is not surprising, because the USGA was not founded until the winter of 1894, by representatives of St Andrew's and four other clubs, Chicago, Newport, Shinnecock Hills and The Country Club, Brookline.

Their primary purpose was to decide when, where and on what basis the Amateur and Open titles were to be decided. For the first three years both were played at the same time and course; the USGA's first choice was Newport's nine-holer, in September, 1895, but the double-header was put off until the following month because of a clash with the America's Cup yacht races, which says a good deal about golf's standing at the time.

Moreover, the Open was relegated to a one-day, 36-hole affair to follow the three-day Amateur event, won from a field of 32 by Charles Macdonald, founder of the Chicago club. Most early American pros hailed from Scotland; their throaty accents were difficult to understand. Many had started out as caddies, and they had a reputation, deserved or not, as hard drinkers: they were not about to be admitted to the cream of East Coast society.

So Macdonald's victory was considered to be of far greater import than that gained on October 4 by Harold Rawlins, at 19 the youngest of all US Open champions. This Englishman, recently arrived to become assistant at the Newport club, scored 173 (91, 82) with a gutty ball, and won $150, a $50 gold medal and the Open Championship Cup for his club. He had beaten nine other pros and one amateur.

Though the US Open was dominated by Scottish and English pros until the 1911 victory of Johnny McDermott from Atlantic City, it quickly became the one to win for paid or unpaid Americans, and there were some highly resourceful unpaid swingers about. The elevation of the pro to teacher, writer of instructional books and designer and endorser of all manner of golf gear and clothing made it, above all others, the crown that bestowed the Midas touch.

Modern pros have a true-blue amateur, Francis Sales Ouimet from Boston, to thank for putting golf on the front page. His defeat of a formidable English pair in Harry Vardon and Ted Ray in a play-off for the 1913 Open that lit the touch-paper of a further American golf explosion: and Ouimet was merely the scout, not the Seventh Cavalry.

It says much for the easy assumption of his prolonged status as American Sporting Hero grade one by Ouimet's modern counterpart, Arnold Palmer, that although he won the US Open once only, with his most

ON TARGET *Jack Nicklaus putting towards his first major win, in the 1962 play-off with Arnold Palmer at Oakmont*

cavalier finish, he was the first of golf's major tycoons. Within 10 years of his victory at Cherry Hills in 1960, Palmer's businesses had an annual turnover in excess of $15 million.

By contrast, Willie Anderson, four-time winner from North Berwick in Scotland, died at 31, some said because he drank too much. Anderson would strike a bizarre figure on the course today, for he deployed a flat swing with a bent left elbow. Although no one has equalled Anderson's feat of a hat-trick of Opens, from 1903 to 1905, his record of four victories is shared by an illustrious threesome in Bobby Jones, Ben Hogan and Jack Nicklaus, all giants of the game and all totally different from each other in style and temperament.

Jones, the southern gentleman, with degrees in mechanical engineering, literature and law, and with more victories than any other amateur, added to his four US Opens two lost play-offs, a second place and (at 19 years of age) joint fifth. Apart from his saving shot from the sand at Royal Lytham's 17th in 1926, the most remarkable of his career must surely have been at Interlachen, during the third leg of his 1930 Grand Slam, when he was five shots ahead with 18 holes to play. A miscue on the long 9th hole in the second round proved a godsend: although he almost topped his second shot, his ball, instead of diving into the lake guarding the green, skipped across it, ducks and drakes fashion, and was eventually holed for a birdie four.

Hogan, almost universally recognized as the purest striker of the ball in golf history, gained all his Opens in a time span of only six years. He would certainly have earned a fifth and perhaps even a sixth US Open had his life at the top not been limited by the aftermath of the 1949 road crash injuries from which he recovered by a great effort of will to win his second Open in 1950, the Golden Jubilee of the Championship. Even more remarkably, though every step of the extra 18 holes must have been a challenge, he triumphed in a play-off, scoring 69 against Lloyd Mangrum's 73 and George Fazio's 75. Mangrum would have come closer, with 71, had he not picked up his ball to blow a fly off it, incurring a two-stroke penalty.

Further Open successes followed in 1951 and 1953, when Hogan led after every round, a feat unequalled since 1921, and finished (at Oakmont!) with three threes, a par and two birdies. He lost a play-off in 1955, and was joint second the following year.

Of the ones that got away, none would have caused him more regret than the 1960 Open, for it came close to his 48th birthday, and offered the juicy possibility of upstaging two young tigers in one fell swoop, none other than Palmer and Nicklaus. Hogan required pars on the 71st and 72nd holes for 280, which would have equalled Palmer's winning score. He scored a six and a seven, four over. A fired-up Palmer ravenous for success might have been more than even Hogan could manage in a play-off, but the prospect of two generations in mortal combat is, to say the least, enticing.

Nicklaus, who had set an amateur scoring record of 282 in achieving second place at Cherry Hills, went one better in 1962, and won his fourth Open 18 years later. How typical of Nicklaus's career, high level from the first, that his first professional win should be in the 1962 Open at Oakmont. He was a little over 22; best of all, perhaps, it was gained at the expense of Arnold Palmer in a play-off.

Nicklaus was surely the best heeled as a youngster of all the professional giants of the US Open, for his father was a well-to-do owner of pharmacies. Financial security for Nicklaus did not mean security for his opponents: his single-minded pursuit of excellence and major titles has no parallel in golf's history.

While Nicklaus hit the target with his first professional attempt at the Open, Andy North has won only three titles, the first a PGA Tour event in 1977. The other two are US Opens, similar victories in that his final round in each case, at Cherry Hills in 1978 and Oakland Hills in 1985, was a nervous 74.

It seemed for some time at Oakland Hills that the first Open win by an Asian, Tze-Chung Chen from Taiwan, was about to burst on the world of golf. But a double hit at a crucial juncture led to a final 77, after rounds of 65, 66, 69. Even then he was only one shot away from a tie with North.

By contrast, David Graham played a final round to win in 1981 at Merion that was almost without flaw. He strode past George Burns to become the first Australian to win the title, and the first foreigner since Tony Jacklin 11 years earlier. He missed one fairway, the first, and that by not very much: he still birdied that hole, and his final 67 gave him a total of 273, one more than Nicklaus's record Open score, set at Baltusrol the previous year. The round suited Graham's character: straight-backed, very correct in his manner.

His error-free round was succeeded 12 months later by a Tom Watson coup to rob Nicklaus of a coveted fifth Open. Watson's chip at Pebble Beach's short 17th recalls the defining moment of Sarazen's career, his double eagle to turn the 1935 Masters upside-down. Before long Watson was writing a book on the

STRAIGHT AND NARROW *David Graham kept it on the hard-to-find fairways for his 1981 victory at Merion*

short game: how to get "up and down". He showed the world how on the Californian clifftops. Needing a birdie to get past Nicklaus, he overshot the 17th but, from dense semi-rough, he told his caddie he would hole a chip shot – and did hole it, the ball running in downhill from a cuppy lie: a triumph of nerve and touch, for as Bobby Jones once wrote, "the delicate shot, if it fails, fails completely". Watson laid up at the long last hole, but still got a birdie to win by two.

Lack if a first British win since Jacklin's seven-stroke triumph has not been for want of trying by England's Nick Faldo and Scotland's Colin Montgomerie. Faldo lost by four shots in the 1988 play-off at Brookline to Curtis Strange, who won again in 1989 to land the first Open double sinceHogan in 1950–1. Faldo also came close in 1990, sharing third place with Billy Ray Brown, a stroke behind the playoff pair of Hale Irwin and Mike Donald. Irwin won – his third title.

Since Graham's marvellous round, no foreigner had stormed the USGA's most closest guarded citadel – until Ernie Els, the immensely powerful South African, at 24 years of age beat off Loren Roberts and Montgomerie in a sweltering 1994 Oakmont at the second extra hole of a sudden-death play-off after a tie with Roberts in the 18-hole play-off round which is a feature of this championship.

Three years later Els was champion again, shaking off Montgomerie with a daring iron close to the water at the back of the perilous 17th at Congressional – 480 yards, yet a par four! Neither the Scot, nor the reigning British Open champion Tom Lehman, matched Els' decisive par. Indeed, Lehman's approach found the lake. So Els and Montgomerie, watched by President Clinton, became the first non-Americans to lay claim to undisputed first and second places since the early years of the century. It was the Scot's third top three finish.

The 1997 Open dispelled the pipe-dreams of a Grand Slam of Masters champion, Tiger Woods, 10 shots adrift. It also suggested that many newly attracted spectators were ignorant of the game's etiquette.

COREY THE CONQUEROR *Pavin celebrates his Shinnecock Hills victory*

Over the years the Championship has been given an added spice by the USGA's policy of setting courses that stretch nerves and (some say) exact undue punishment for off-line shots. This was perfectly illustrated in 1995, when Corey Pavin's winning score was a level-par 280 at Shinnecock Hills. Not every critic – or golfer – is in love or agreement with the way US Open greens are cut to lightning speed and the rough is encouraged to the extent that recoveries are often a matter of damage-control rather than par-saving. This, say the USGA's detractors, gives safety-first golfers an undue advantage. This view was widely expressed when Sam Parks, known only in the immediate catchment area of the 1935 Open course, Oakmont in Pennsylvania, won with the only sub-300 score – 299. Parks's stroke average of 74.75 rather bore out cynical comment that Parks could score 75 on any course, but that that was about the sum of his abilities. For all that, Open courses, even justifiably feared Oakmont, have on occasion received rough treatment, notably Johnny Miller's final 63 at that very course in 1973.

Of the current players Els, his long-hitting perfectly complemented by a mature touch at close range, is the best bet to put up a stern chase of the four-time winners of the US Open, especially as he has determined to concentrate on the most demanding tour, that of the American PGA.

US Open Championship Results

Year	Winner	Runner-up	Venue	Score
(36 holes till 1898)				
1895	H Rawlins	W Dunn	Newport, RI	173
1896	J Foulis	H Rawlins	Shinnecock Hills, NY	152
1897	J Lloyd	W Anderson	Chicago, IL	162
1898	F Herd	A Smith	Myopia, MA	328
1899	W Smith	G Low, V Fitzjohn, W H Way	Baltimore, MD	315
1900	H Vardon	J H Taylor	Chicago, IL	313
1901	W Anderson	A Smith	Myopia, MA	331
	WON PLAY-OFF 85 TO 86			
1902	L Auchterlonie	S Gardner, W J Travis	Garden City, NY	307
1903	W Anderson	D Brown	Baltusrol, NJ	307
	WON PLAY-OFF 82 TO 84			
1904	W Anderson	G Nicholls	Glen View, IL	303
1905	W Anderson	A Smith	Myopia, MA	314
1906	A Smith	W Smith	Onwentsia, IL	295
1907	A Ross	G Nicholls	Philadelphia CC, PA	302
1908	F McLeod	W Smith	Myopia, MA	322
	WON PLAY-OFF 77 TO 83			
1909	G Sargent	T McNamara	Englewood, NJ	290
1910	A Smith	J J McDermott MacDonald Smith	Philadelphia CC, PA	298
	WON PLAY-OFF 71 TO 75 TO 77			
1911	J J McDermott	M J Brady G O Simpson	Chicago, IL	307
	WON PLAY-OFF 80 TO 82 TO 85			
1912	J J McDermott	T McNamara	Buffalo, NY	294
1913	F Ouimet	H Vardon, T Ray	Brookline, MA	304
	WON PLAY-OFF 72 TO 77 TO 78			
1914	W Hagen	C Evans Jnr	Midlothian, IL	290
1915	J D Travers	T McNamara	Baltusrol, NJ	297
1916	C Evans Jnr	J Hutchison	Minikahda, MN	286
1917-18	No championship			
1919	W Hagen	M J Brady	Brae Burn, MA	301
	WON PLAY-OFF 77 TO 78			
1920	T Ray	H Vardon, J Burke, L Diegel, J Hutchison	Inverness, OH	295
1921	J Barnes	W Hagen, F McLeod	Chevy Chase, MD	289
1922	G Sarazen	J L Black	Skokie, Glencoe, IL	288
1923	R T Jones Jnr	R A Cruickshank	Inwood, NY	296
	WON PLAY-OFF 76 TO 78			
1924	C Walker	R T Jones Jnr	Oakland Hills, MI	297
1925	W Macfarlane	R T Jones Jnr	Worcester, MA	291
	WON PLAY-OFF 147 TO 148			
1926	R T Jones Jnr	J Turnesa	Scioto, OH	293
1927	T Armour	H Cooper	Oakmont, PA	301
	WON PLAY-OFF 76 TO 79			
1928	J J Farrell	R T Jones Jnr	Olympia Fields, IL	294
	WON PLAY-OFF 143 TO 144			
1929	R T Jones Jnr	A Espinosa	Winged Foot, NY	294
	WON PLAY-OFF 141 TO 164			
1930	R T Jones Jnr	MacDonald Smith	Interlachen, MN	287
1931	B Burke	G Von Elm	Inverness, OH	292
	WON SECOND 36-HOLE PLAY-OFF 148 TO 149: FIRST TIED AT 149			
1932	G Sarazen	T P Perkins, R Cruickshank	Fresh Meadow, NY	286
1933	J Goodman	R Guldahl	N. Shore, IL	287
1934	O Dutra	G Sarazen	Merion CC, PA	293
1935	S Parks	J Thomson	Oakmont, PA	299
1936	T Manero	H Cooper	Baltusrol, NJ	282
1937	R Guldahl	S Snead	Oakland Hills, MI	281
1938	R Guldahl	D Metz	Cherry Hills, CO	284
1939	B Nelson	C Wood, D Shute	W. Conshohocken, PA	284
	WON PLAY-OFF 138 TO 141			
1940	W Lawson Little	G Sarazen	Canterbury, OH	287
	WON PLAY-OFF 70 TO 73			
1941	C Wood	D Shute	Colonial, Ft Worth, TX	284
1942-45	No championship			
1946	L Mangrum	B Nelson,V Ghezzi	Canterbury, OH	284
	WON PLAY-OFF 72 TO 73			
1947	L Worsham	S Snead	St Louis, Clayton, MO	282
	WON PLAY-OFF 69 TO 70			
1948	B Hogan	J Demaret	Riviera, L Angeles, CA	276
1949	C Middlecoff	C Heafner, S Snead	Medinah, Chicago, IL	286
1950	B Hogan	L Mangrum, G Fazio	Merion, PA	287
	WON PLAY-OFF 69 TO 73 TO 75			
1951	B Hogan	C Heafner	Oakland Hills, MI	287
1952	J Boros	P Oliver Jnr	Northwood, Dallas, TX	281
1953	B Hogan	S Snead	Oakmont, PA	283
1954	E Furgol	G Littler	Baltusrol, NJ	284
1955	J Fleck	B Hogan	Olympic, CA	287
	WON PLAY-OFF 69 TO 72			
1956	C Middlecoff	B Hogan, J Boros	Oak Hill, Rochester, NY	281
1957	R Mayer	C Middlecoff	Inverness, OH	282
	WON PLAY-OFF 72 TO 79			
1958	T Bolt	G Player	Southern Hills, OK	283
1959	W Casper	B Rosburg	Winged Foot, NY	282
1960	A Palmer	J Nicklaus	Cherry Hills, CO	280
1961	G Littler	R Goalby, D Sanders	Oakland Hills, MI	281
1962	J Nicklaus	A Palmer	Oakmont, PA	283
	WON PLAY-OFF 71 TO 74			
1963	J Boros	J D Cupit, A Palmer	Brookline, MA	293
	WON PLAY-OFF 70 TO 73 TO 76			
1964	K Venturi	T Jacobs	Congressional, MD	278
1965	G Player	K D G Nagle	Bellerive, MO	282
	WON PLAY-OFF 71 TO 74			
1966	W Casper	A Palmer	Olympic, CA	278
	WON PLAY-OFF 69 TO 73			
1967	J Nicklaus	A Palmer	Baltusrol, NJ	275
1968	L Trevino	J Nicklaus	Oak Hill, Rochester, NY	275
1969	O Moody	D Beman, A Geiberger, B Rosburg	Cypress Creek, TX	281
1970	A Jacklin	D Hill	Hazeltine, MN	281
1971	L Trevino	J Nicklaus	Merion, PA	280
	WON PLAY-OFF 68 TO 71			
1972	J Nicklaus	B Crampton	Pebble Beach, CA	290
1973	J Miller	J Schlee	Oakmont, PA	279
1974	H Irwin	F Fezler	Winged Foot, NY	287
1975	L Graham	J Mahaffey	Medinah, Chicago, IL	287
	WON PLAY-OFF 71 TO 73			
1976	J Pate	A Geiberger, T Weiskopf	Duluth, GA	277
1977	H Green	L Graham	Southern Hills, OK	278
1978	A North	J C Snead, D Stockton	Cherry Hills, CO	285
1979	H Irwin	J Pate, G Player	Inverness, OH	284
1980	J Nicklaus	I Aoki	Baltusrol, NJ	272
1981	D Graham	W Rogers, G Burns	Merion, PA	273
1982	T Watson	J Nicklaus	Pebble Beach, CA	282
1983	L Nelson	T Watson	Oakmont, PA	280
1984	F Zoeller	G Norman	Winged Foot, NY	276
	WON PLAY-OFF 67 TO 75			
1985	A North,	D Watson, D Barr, T-C Chen	Oakland Hills, MI	279
1986	R Floyd	L Wadkins, C Beck	Shinnecock Hills, NY	279
1987	S Simpson	T Watson	Olympic, CA	277
1988	C Strange	N Faldo	Brookline, MA	278
	WON PLAY-OFF 71 TO 75			
1989	C Strange	I Woosnam, M McCumber, C Beck	Oak Hill, Rochester, NY	278
1990	H Irwin	M Donald	Medinah, Chicago, IL	280
	WON PLAY-OFF AT FIRST EXTRA HOLE AFTER TIE (74) OVER 18 HOLES			
1991	P Stewart	S Simpson	Hazeltine, MN	282
	WON PLAY-OFF 75 TO 77			
1992	T Kite	J Sluman	Pebble Beach, CA	285
1993	L Janzen	P Stewart	Baltusrol, NJ	272
1994	E Els	L Roberts, C Montgomerie	Oakmont, PA	279
	18-HOLE PLAY-OFF SCORES: ELS 74, ROBERTS 74, MONTGOMERIE 78; ELS BEAT ROBERTS AT SECOND EXTRA HOLE OF SUDDEN-DEATH PLAY-OFF.			
1995	C Pavin	G Norman	Shinnecock Hills, NY	280
1996	S Jones	T Lehman, D Love	Oakland Hills, MI	278
1997	E Els	C Montgomerie	Congressional, MD	276

BRITISH OPEN

Considering that the British Open Championship is a movable feast, it ranks as one of the best organized major sporting events in the world, though it is, perforce, not nearly as well travelled as the US Open, which has visited nearly 50 courses across the North American continent. The Open has drifted into the doldrums from time to time. Nowadays such a fate for the oldest of the major championships (founded 25 years before the second championship to be accepted as a major meeting, the British Amateur), is unimaginable. Attendance often soars past 20,000 a day, a huge tented village offers golf gear, food and drink, and media coverage is massive, notably on television, for which the BBC will continue to provide live coverage in Britain, at least until 2001.

All this stems from the idea put forward by Prestwick Golf Club in 1860 to find a successor to the late, great Allan Robertson. Only eight players competed for the red morocco Championship Belt put up by Prestwick for competition over three rounds of the club's 12-hole course. Willie Park from Musselburgh won from seven rivals (all pros, so this was not technically an Open at all), but the early history of the Open, which involved amateurs from 1861 onwards, is dominated by Tom Morris, runner-up in this first event, and his son, also called Tom, whose brilliant scoring in 1870 was not bettered until 1904. After Old Tom won for the fourth time, Young Tom achieved a hat-trick of Opens, and so took the Belt outright before going on to win for the fourth time in succession, a record still, and becoming the first holder of the present trophy, a silver claret jug, in 1871.

Sport knows no more poignant story than the death of Young Tom in 1875, heartbroken after the death of his wife in childbirth while he and his father were playing Willie and Mungo Park in a challenge match at North Berwick across the Firth of Forth. Old Tom's assessment of his son's golf skills was that he could never cope with young Tom, though he could with Robertson, which rather demolishes the legend of Robertson's invincibility.

It is well documented that Young Tom had no weakness in his game. A long hitter with uncanny touch on and round the green, he had a full house of talents that has never been paralleled, except possibly by Bobby Jones. Sixty golfing societies put together the fund to erect a fine monument to Young Tom in St Andrews Cathedral yard.

His father lived until 1908. "A legend in his own lifetime" could truly be said of Old Tom, for many years greenkeeper of the Old Course. He played in every Open until 1896, a year that linked two golfing eras . . . the year of Harry Vardon's first victory.

Before the golfing giant of America was fully awake, three British champions (16 Opens between them) ruled the roost in the years before the First World War. Harry Vardon edged in 1914 to his record sixth Open, upstaging J. H. Taylor and James Braid (five each). Of the moderns, Tom Watson has come closest to emulating Vardon.

Two names are inseparable from an account of the resurgence of the Championship over the last 35 years: Keith MacKenzie, who officiated as Royal and Ancient Club secretary for the last time in 1983 before Michael Bonallack took over, and Arnold Palmer. The strength of US golf since the First World War has meant that when a representative entry has failed for whatever reason to cross the Atlantic, the British Open's significance has been much diminished.

The persistence of the Great Depression, fewer events on the US PGA tour, and less prize money, meant that few Americans could afford to participate after the early 1930s, as evidence the string of British winners following the almost unbroken run of American champions from 1921, including such box office favourites as Walter Hagen, Gene Sarazen and Bobby Jones. In 1937, however, when the US Ryder Cup team was in Britain, Henry Cotton proved his world class.

KNICKERBOCKER GLORY *Harry Vardon won his sixth Open in 1914*

Sam Snead, who won the first Championship after the 1940–45 hiatus, found that the prize money (about $600) did not cover his expenses. The fact that he at first mistook the stark topography of St Andrews, the scene of his only major Open success (for he invented one unlikely method after another to miss out on his own national Open), for an abandoned golf course may have put him in the right frame of mind to overcome any nerves.

South Africa and Australia provided the stars of the 1950s, in Bobby Locke and Peter Thomson respectively, Locke having surprised

LOCAL HERO *Henry Cotton halts US Open run in 1934*

the American pros by winning sackfuls of money from them, a spree which was restricted after the US PGA banned him from their events in 1949 for allegedly failing to honour playing contracts.

The exception to this southern hemisphere to-ing and fro-ing provided one of the Open's defining moments: a player of legendary skill focusing his powers on a difficult course, and getting the better of it a little more each day.

This was Ben Hogan's one attempt on the Open. Not a man given to adulterating golf with sentiment, he had won the 1953 Masters and the US Open, and no one had ever won these two and the British Open in one season. The thought must also have occurred, as it did in times past to Walter Hagen and Bobby Jones, that he must prove his standing in the game's history by winning in Britain.

He could hardly have chosen a more difficult challenge. His preparations for Carnoustie were thorough; he spent a fortnight sizing up this longest of Open courses, which the R&A dropped from the Open circuit after 1975, but which is to be used again in 1999. His attitude was characteristically taciturn, but more forthcoming with the Press than his laconic legend suggested. His four rounds demonstrated that he could harness the accuracy of his striking to any course, no matter how different from the lay-outs he was used to; in any case, his mastery of long, low shots controlled with a touch of fade was ideal for Carnoustie.

He scored 73, 71, 70, 68, and won by four shots from four players, Frank Stranahan, an American amateur, Antonio Cerda from Argentina, Thomson and Dai Rees. Roberto de Vicenzo was another stroke adrift, and the only other notable American in the field, Lloyd Mangrum, was 19 behind Hogan. Mangrum was used to trailing the new Open Champion by this time. He had been third to Hogan in the Masters – but eight strokes in arrears; and third in the US Open – nine behind. He cannot have enjoyed Carnoustie much, joking that the undulating fairways had made him feel seasick.

Hogan promised to come back to defend his title, but he never did. It would have been difficult to top his performance in any case: it was his last major success, and a date clash with the US PGA Championship meant he was ruled out of that. The clash demonstrates that the four modern majors were not yet seen as the four premier events in world golf. When Gary Player took his first major at Muirfield in 1959, the American challenge was non-existent.

The following year Arnold Palmer, who like Hogan in 1953 had already won the Masters and US Open, came, saw, but did not conquer in the golfing sense, finishing second to Kel Nagle in the Centenary Open. Instead, he captivated the British public, and won the next Open at Birkdale, where his 73 in the worst of a gale in the second round fitted his publicity: heroic. He seemed to have scored 72, but called a penalty stroke on himself on his assertion that his ball moved in the sand at the 16th. Next year he won again at Troon, where he established a record aggregate of 276 and won by six strokes.

The trickle of US participation did not immediately become a flood, but by the mid 1960s Palmer's initiative, followed by that of Jack Nicklaus, a winner at Muirfield in 1966, had ensured that the winner of the Open was again unarguably at the very top of his profession.

Thus the victory of Tony Jacklin in 1969 at Lytham by two shots from Bob Charles, the first and only left-hander to win, in 1963, raised the British game as nothing else could – barring, perhaps Jacklin's victory in the US Open in 1970. Jacklin's win had foreign players like Nicklaus, Orville Moody, Thomson, Nagle, Gay Brewer, Bert Yancey, Gary Player, Billy Casper, Ray Floyd and Lee Trevino all labouring in the Briton's wake.

His final drive to the tough-to-locate 18th fairway ("a corker", said Henry Longhurst, a favourite commentator in the United States just as in Britain) summed up the confidence and precision of his game as his greatest opportunity beckoned. He put his second shot just inside that of playing partner Charles as if to rubber-stamp his win.

Next year came the bitter disappointment of a thunder and lightning interrupted first round at St Andrews, where Jacklin quickly holed three birdies plus an eagle two at the ninth. Starting home with another birdie, his luck ran out when a shout of "Fore" put him off his stroke, and he fired his ball into a gorse bush. Play was suspended, and next day the magic had gone, Jacklin finishing in "no better" than 67.

His anguish was minor compared to that suffered at the climax of this Championship by Doug Sanders, whose restricted swing still sent the ball a fair distance. On the 72nd hole came the moment every golfer longs for and dreads: a downhill four-footer for the Open. Disappointingly, he interrupted his routine to pick up some minute object. Instead of starting again, he putted, and the ball, as so often on the green named after Old Tom Morris, second Open Champion, drifted marginally right.

JACKLIN'S YEAR *A rare British winner beat a world-class field in 1969*

More eyebrow-raising stuff came the next day in a play-off with Nicklaus, who drove *through* the 385-yard 18th, but still managed to chip back and hole his birdie putt to gain a second Open by a stroke from oh-so-nearly man Sanders.

Jacklin was in the same doleful situation in 1972, Lee Trevino's luck being thoroughly in at Muirfield when a series of iffy shots turned up trumps, notably his chip in for his par at the 71st hole after missing the green with his fourth shot.

Turnberry 1977 is a popular choice as the most thrilling Open of all, as Tom Watson and Nicklaus both broke the aggregate record, and Watson took the title by a stroke. Spain's Severiano Ballesteros (even if his routes to Lytham's greens in 1979 tended to be circuitous) and Gary Player were the only players to break the American run of success that followed Jacklin's Open and persisted until a great sea change took place at the Open in the mid-1980s.

Willie Auchterlonie (1893) was the last home-based Scot to win the Open, but Sandy Lyle, a Scottish international, although living south of the border, redressed the balance a little in favour of the land that gave golf to the world by winning at Royal St George's in 1985. A fluffed chip from the side of the 72nd hole could have been expensive, as Payne Stewart, seldom far from the leaders in recent British Opens, and David Graham were chasing hard. Errors crept in, however, and Lyle, waiting in the clubhouse, found his final 70 (par) was just good enough.

Turnberry in 1986 was not about to provide the low-scoring conditions that the Watson-Nicklaus show had featured in 1977. The weather was brutal, the rough seemingly bottomless, and Greg Norman needed every ounce of his strength and deter-mination to keep afloat as his tee-off times condemned him to endure the worst of the weather on day three. A 69 as Turnberry relented on the last day gave him a five-shot margin.

More severe weather at Muirfield the following year brought the long-awaited Nick Faldo victory that seemed sure to follow his brilliant amateur career. Faldo was single-minded and brave enough to spend years remodelling his swing, and the fruits of this intense effort were a secure method that enabled him to par every hole of his fourth round and hold off Paul Azinger, who faltered at the last.

Faldo dominated the Open at St Andrews in 1990 with a record aggregate 270 and a five-shot win over Zimbabwe's Mark McNulty and the persistent Payne Stewart. Faldo's third Open, at Muirfield two years later, was a nerve-shredding affair after he started 64 ("best round of my life", said Faldo), 66 = 130, equalling the 36-hole record.

Yet he seemed to have thrown the title away as he started for home on the final day, and was overtaken by American John Cook, who, fatally, returned the compliment by missing a tiny birdie putt on the 17th, and dropping a shot at the 18th. Faldo, behind him, was carrying out his last-ditch task of "playing the best four holes of my life". In this critical situation two birdies and two pars was winning effort.

Scoring reached a new low – 267, 13 under par – at St George's in 1993 as Faldo chased Norman home, Stewart finished with a fruitless 63, and the Australian's final round of 64, a prodigy of accurate driving, earned a two-shot win from the Englishman.

A monstrous eagle putt on the 71st at Turnberry helped Nick Price edge out Jesper Parnevik for the 1994 title, and ease the pain of two earlier near-misses. Conversely, Costantino Rocca's 60-foot birdie putt, improbably holed from the Valley of Sin on the 72nd at St Andrews in 1995, led only to a play-off defeat by John Daly. Tom Lehman's victory in 1996, founded on a 64 in the third round, continued American dominance, but it was a first for US professsionals at Lytham. Between Daly's win and 1997, the first prize cheque doubled to £250,000.

"THE GREATEST" *Sarazen's view of Greg Norman's Open win at Sandwich*

British Open Results

Year	Winner	Runner-up	Venue	Score
(36 holes until 1892)				
1860	W Park	T Morris Snr	Prestwick	174
1861	T Morris Snr	W Park	Prestwick	163
1862	T Morris Snr	W Park	Prestwick	163
1863	W Park	T Morris Snr	Prestwick	168
1864	T Morris Snr	A Strath	Prestwick	167
1865	A Strath	W Park	Prestwick	162
1866	W Park	D Park	Prestwick	169
1867	T Morris Snr	W Park	Prestwick	167
1868	T Morris Jnr	R Andrew	Prestwick	157
1869	T Morris Jnr	T Morris Snr	Prestwick	154
1970	T Morris Jnr	R Kirk, D Strath	Prestwick	149
1871	No championship			
1872	T Morris Jnr	D Strath	Prestwick	166
1873	T Kidd	J Anderson	St Andrews	179
1874	M Park	T Morris Jnr	Musselburgh	159
1875	W Park	B Martin	Prestwick	166
1876	R Martin	D Strath	St Andrews	176
	STRATH REFUSED TO PLAY OFF			
1877	J Anderson	R Pringle	Musselburgh	160
1878	J Anderson	R Kirk	Prestwick	157
1879	J Anderson	J Allan, A Kirkaldy	St Andrews	169
1880	R Ferguson	P Paxton	Musselburgh	162
1881	R Ferguson	J Anderson	Prestwick	170
1882	R Ferguson	W Fernie	St Andrews	171
1883	W Fernie	R Ferguson	Musselburgh	159
	WON PLAY-OFF 158 TO 159			
1884	J Simpson	D Rolland, W Fernie	Prestwick	160
1885	R Martin	A Simpson	St Andrews	171
1886	D Brown	W Campbell	Musselburgh	157
1887	W Park Jnr	R Martin	Prestwick	161
1888	J Burns	D Anderson, B Sayers	St Andrews	171
1889	W Park Jnr	A Kirkaldy	Musselburgh	155
	WON PLAY-OFF 158 TO 163			
1890	J Ball	W Fernie	Prestwick	164
1891	H Kirkaldy	A Kirkaldy	St Andrews	166
1892	H H Hilton	J Ball, H Kirkaldy, A Herd	Muirfield	305
1893	W Auchterlonie	J E Laidlay	Prestwick	322
1894	J H Taylor	R Rolland	St George's	326
1895	J H Taylor	A Herd	St Andrews	322
1896	H Vardon	J H Taylor	Muirfield	316
	WON PLAY-OFF 157 TO 159			
1897	H H Hilton	J Braid	Hoylake	314
1898	H Vardon	W Park Jnr	Prestwick	307
1899	H Vardon	J White	St George's	307
1900	J H Taylor	H Vardon	St Andrews	309
1901	J Braid	H Vardon	Muirfield	309
1902	A Herd	H Vardon, J Braid	Hoylake	307
1903	H Vardon	T Vardon	Prestwick	300
1904	J White	J H Taylor, J Braid	St George's	296
1905	J Braid	R Jones, J H Taylor	St Andrews	318
1906	J Braid	J H Taylor	Muirfield	300
1907	A Massy	J H Taylor	Hoylake	312
1908	J Braid	T Ball	Prestwick	291
1909	J H Taylor	J Braid, T Ball	Deal	295
1910	J Braid	A Herd	St Andrews	299
1911	H Vardon	A Massy	St George's	303
	WON PLAY-OFF AT 35TH HOLE			
1912	E Ray	H Vardon	Muirfield	295
1913	J H Taylor	E Ray	Hoylake	304
1914	H Vardon	J H Taylor	Prestwick	306
1915-19	No championship			
1920	G Duncan	A Herd	Deal	303
1921	J Hutchison	R H Wethered	St Andrews	296
	WON PLAY-OFF 150 TO 159			
1922	W Hagen	G Duncan, J Barnes	St George's	300
1923	A G Havers	W Hagen	Troon	295
1924	W Hagen	E R Whitcombe	Hoylake	301
1925	J Barnes	E Ray, A Compston	Prestwick	300
1926	R T Jones Jnr	A Watrous	Lytham	291
1927	R T Jones Jnr	A Boomer, F Robson	St Andrews	285
1928	W Hagen	G Sarazen	St George's	292
1929	W Hagen	J Farrell	Muirfield	292
1930	R T Jones Jnr	Macdonald Smith L Diegel	Hoylake	291
1931	T Armour	J Jurado	Carnoustie	296
1932	G Sarazen	Macdonald Smith	Prince's	283
1933	D Shute	C Wood	St Andrews	292
	WON PLAY-OFF 149 TO 154			
1934	T H Cotton	S F Brews	St George's	283
1935	A Perry	A H Padgham	Muirfield	283
1936	A H Padgham	J Adams	Hoylake	287
1937	T H Cotton	R A Whitcombe	Carnoustie	290
1938	R A Whitcombe	J Adams	St George's	285
1939	R Burton	J Bulla	St Andrews	290
1940-45	No championship			
1946	S Snead	A D Locke, J Bulla	St Andrews	290
1947	F Daly	R W Horne, F R Stranahan	Hoylake	293
1948	T H Cotton	F Daly	Muirfield	284
1949	A D Locke	H Bradshaw	St George's	283
	WON PLAY-OFF 136 TO 147			
1950	A D Locke	R de Vicenzo	Troon	279
1951	M Faulkner	A Cerda	Portrush	285
1952	A D Locke	P W Thomson	Lytham	287
1953	B Hogan	F R Stranaham, A Cerda, P W Thomson, D J Rees	Carnoustie	282
1954	P W Thomson	A D Locke, S Scott, D J Rees	Birkdale	283
1955	P W Thomson	J Fallon	St Andrews	281
1956	P W Thomson	F van Donck	Hoylake	286
1957	A D Locke	P W Thomson	St Andrews	279
1958	P W Thomson	D C Thomas	Lytham	278
	WON PLAY-OFF 139 TO 143			
1959	G Player	F van Donck, F Bullock	Muirfield	284
1960	K D G Nagle	A Palmer	St Andrews	278
1961	A Palmer	D J Rees	Birkdale	284
1962	A Palmer	K D G Nagle	Troon	276
1963	R J Charles	P Rodgers	Lytham	277
	WON PLAY-OFF 140 TO 148			
1964	A Lema	J Nicklaus	St Andrews	279
1965	P W Thomson	B Huggett, C O'Connor	Birkdale	285
1966	J Nicklaus	D C Thomas, D Sanders	Muirfield	282
1967	R de Vicenzo	J Nicklaus	Hoylake	278
1968	G Player	J Nicklaus, R J Charles	Carnoustie	289
1969	A Jacklin	R J Charles	Lytham	280
1970	J Nicklaus	D Sanders	St Andrews	283
	WON PLAY-OFF 72 TO 73			
1971	L Trevino	Liang Huan Lu	Birkdale	278
1972	L Trevino	J Nicklaus	Muirfield	278
1973	T Weiskopf	N C Coles, J Miller	Troon	276
1974	G Player	P Oosterhuis	Lytham	282
1975	T Watson	J Newton	Carnoustie	279
	WON PLAY-OFF 71 TO 72			
1976	J Miller	J Nicklaus, S Ballesteros	Birkdale	279
1977	T Watson	J Nicklaus	Turnberry	268
1978	J Nicklaus	S Owen, R Floyd, B Crenshaw, T Kite	St Andrews	281
1979	S Ballesteros	B Crenshaw, J Nicklaus	Lytham	283
1980	T Watson	L Trevino	Muirfield	271
1981	W Rogers	B Langer	St George's	276
1982	T Watson	P Oosterhuis, N Price	Troon	284
1983	T Watson	H Irwin, A Bean	Birkdale	275
1984	S Ballesteros	B Langer, T Watson	St Andrews	276
1985	S Lyle	P Stewart	St George's	282
1986	G Norman	G J Brand	Turnberry	280
1987	N Faldo	R Davis, P Azinger	Muirfield	279
1988	S Ballesteros	N Price	Lytham	273
1989	M Calcavecchia	G Norman, W Grady	Troon	275
	WON PLAY-OFF OVER FOUR HOLES			
1990	N Faldo	M McNulty, P Stewart	St Andrews	270
1991	I Baker-Finch	M Harwood	Birkdale	272
1992	N Faldo	J Cook	Muirfield	272
1993	G Norman	N Faldo	St George's	267
1994	N Price	J Parnevik	Turnberry	268
1995	J Daly	C Rocca	St Andrews	272
	WON PLAY-OFF OVER FOUR HOLES			
1996	T Lehman	M McCumber E Els	Lytham	271

US PGA

Rodman Wanamaker is a name that does not loom large in the minds of most followers of golf, yet he set in motion the Championship which is today the fourth "major" in the world game...not only fourth in the golfing calendar (except for an unpopular and short-lived February experiment in Florida in 1971) but also ranked fourth in most people's estimation behind the two Opens and the Masters.

This does not mean it is the easiest to win, since the ranking US professionals are involved. While Australians and South Africans have done the trick, Europe-based players have found the going tough, though moves have been made in recent years to make the US PGA and US Open more accessible to leading foreign players and so more representative of the world game.

The genesis of the US PGA Championship stemmed from attempts to better the lot of club professionals who, during the first years of the twentieth century, were about as far removed from the millionaire status of today's tour stars as were most operators of small retail businesses of the time. They were in an even worse plight in many ways, since they were not able to command the merchandise they wanted but were supplied by middlemen who reaped the profits and paid the pro a pittance for manning his shop. Many clubs even took the profit from the sale of golf balls.

Rodman Wanamaker was himself in the business of selling, in New York, and a keen golfer. It did not take a genius to see that the professionals needed organizing, and, slowly, regional groups were formed, leading to a national Professional Golfers Association, to whom Wanamaker presented a trophy for a national professional championship. The name Wanamaker is still there on the trophy.

The man himself did well out of the deal, getting the concession to sell golf gear more cheaply than the pros could in their shops. His greatest service to the professional game was to be the prime mover in calling the first founding meeting of the Association, at a luncheon at a New York club on January 17, 1916. Now the professionals had a voice, and an event of their own.

The first winner was born in Britain, as were most of the early winners of the US Open. Long Jim Barnes, whose nickname "Long" was on account of his great length off the tee, came from Lelant, in Cornwall. He beat a Scot, Jock Hutchison, at Siwanoy Country Club, Bronxville, New York, by one hole in the final of what was, for many years, a match play event.

Owing to the war, the second US PGA Championship was not played until 1919, when Barnes won again against Fred McLeod at the Engineers Club, Long Island. McLeod was Scottish also, from North Berwick, and already a US Open winner. For many years, and long after the Second World War, McLeod, who was as short in stature as Barnes was tall, formed the traditional starting twosome in the Masters with Hutchison, who was from St Andrews, and finally got his hands on the Wanamaker Cup, a mighty piece of silverware, in 1920. He defeated a talented English pro, John Douglas Edgar, from Newcastle-upon-Tyne, in the first US PGA played outside New York, at Flossmoor, Illinois.

BOGEY BEATEN *Leo Diegel ended Walter Hagen's 22-match unbeaten run*

Three of American golf's big "names" now took over, for Walter Hagen (for five years), Gene Sarazen (two) and Leo Diegel (two) won the right to look after Wanamaker's gift throughout the rest of the 1920s (and Sarazen won again in 1933).

To tell the truth, Hagen did not look after the trophy all that well. He could not recall where he had left it ("In a taxi?" he pondered), after Diegel's 1928 victory at Baltimore Country Club. It was not located until 1930, parcelled up in a Detroit factory.

Hagen's record in Open championships either side of the Atlantic attests to his stroke-play ability, but he was surely of all golfers who ever lived the most richly endowed with every match play talent. Having become champion at the expense of the inaugural winner, Barnes, in 1921, Hagen did not defend in 1922, but from the time he lost the 1923 final (at the 38th hole) to Sarazen, Hagen was unbeaten till Leo Diegel gained revenge in the third round in 1928 for many Hagen defeats.

One of Hagen's victims, Wild Bill Mehlhorn, must have feared the worst after Hagen's first tee shot against him in the 1925 final, for it went into the hole. Mehlhorn went down 6 & 5.

US PGA FOUR-TIMER *Walter Hagen beating Joe Turnesa to complete a perfect record 1924–1927*

US PGA Results

Year	Winner	Runner-up	Venue	Score
(match play until 1958)				
1916	J Barnes	J Hutchison	Siwanoy, NY	1 hole
1917-18	No championship			
1919	J Barnes	F McLeod	Engineers, NY	6 & 5
1920	J Hutchison	J D Edgar	Flossmoor, ILL	1 hole
1921	W Hagen	J Barnes	Inwood, NY	3 & 2
1922	G Sarazen	E French	Oakmont, PA	4 & 3
1923	G Sarazen	W Hagen	Pelham, NY	38th hole
1924	W Hagen	J Barnes	French Lick, IN	6 & 4
1925	W Hagen	W E Mehlhorn	Olympic Fields, IL	6 & 5
1926	W Hagen	L Diegel	Salisbury, NY	4 & 3
1927	W Hagen	J Turnesa	Dallas, TX	1 hole
1928	L Diegel	A Espinosa	Five Farms, MD	6 & 5
1929	L Diegel	J Farrell	Hillcrest, CA	6 & 4
1930	T Armour	G Sarazen	Fresh Meadow, NY	1 hole
1931	T Creavy	D Shute	Wannamoisett, RI	2 & 1
1932	O Dutra	F Walsh	St Paul, MN	4 & 3
1933	G Sarazen	W Goggin	Blue Mound, WI	5 & 4
1934	P Runyan	C Wood	Buffalo, NY	38th hole
1935	J Revolta	T Armour	Twin Hills, OK	5 & 4
1936	D Shute	J Thomson	Pinehurst, NC	3 & 2
1937	D Shute	H McSpaden	Oakmont, PA	37th hole
1938	P Runyan	S Snead	Shawnee, PA	8 & 7
1939	H Picard	B Nelson	Pomonok, NY	37th hole
1940	B Nelson	S Snead	Hershey, PA	1 hole
1941	V Ghezzie	B Nelson	Cherry Hills, CO	38th hole
1942	S Snead	J Turnesa	Atlantic City, NJ	2 & 1
1943	No championship			
1944	R Hamilton	B Nelson	Manito, Spokane, WA	1 hole
1945	B Nelson	S Byrd	Morraine, Dayton, OH	4 & 3
1946	B Hogan	E Oliver	Portland, OR	6 & 4
1947	J Ferrier	C Harbert	Plum Hollow, MI	2 & 1
1948	B Hogan	M Turnesa	Norwood Hills, MO	7 & 6
1949	S Snead	J Palmer	Hermitage, VA	3 & 2
1950	C Harper	H Williams Jnr	Scioto, Columbus, OH	4 & 3
1951	S Snead	W Burkemo	Oakmont, PA	7 & 6
1952	J Turnesa	C Harbert	Big Spring, KY	2 & 1
1953	W Burkemo	F Torza	Birmingham CC, MI	2 & 1
1954	C Harbert	W Burkemo	Keller, St Paul, MI	4 & 3
1955	D Ford	C Middlecoff	Meadowbrook, MI	4 & 3
1956	J Burke	T Kroll	Blue Hill, Boston, MA	3 & 2
1957	L Hebert	D Finsterwald	Miami Val., Dayton OH	2 & 1
1958	D Finsterwald	W Casper	Llanerch, PA	276
1959	B Rosburg	J Barber, D Sanders	St Louis Pk, MI	277
1960	J Hebert	J Ferrier	Firestone, Akron, OH	281
1961	J Barber	D January	Olympia Fields, IL	277
	WON PLAY-OFF 67 TO 68			

Year	Winner	Runner-up	Venue	Score
1962	G Player	B Goalby	Aronimink, PA	278
1963	J Nicklaus	D Ragan	Dallas Athletic, TX	279
1964	B Nichols	A Palmer, J Nicklaus	Columbus, OH	271
1965	D Marr	W Casper, J Nicklaus	Laurel Valley, PA	280
1966	A Geiberger	D Wysong	Firestone, Akron, OH	280
1967	D January	D Massengale	Columbine, Denver, CO	281
	WON PLAY-OFF 69 TO 71			
1968	J Boros	R J Charles, A Palmer	Pecan Valley, TX	281
1969	R Floyd	G Player	NCR, Dayton, OH	276
1970	D Stockton	R Murphy, A Palmer	Southern Hills, OK	279
1971	J Nicklaus	W Casper	PGA National, FL	281
1972	G Player	T Aaron, J Jamieson	Oakland Hills, MI	281
1973	J Nicklaus	B Crampton	Canterbury, OH	277
1974	L Trevino	J Nicklaus	Tanglewood, NC	276
1975	J Nicklaus	B Crampton	Firestone, Akron, OH	276
1976	D Stockton	R Floyd, D January	Congressional, MD	281
1977	L Wadkins	G Littler	Pebble Beach, CA	282
	WON PLAY-OFF AT FIRST EXTRA HOLE			
1978	J Mahaffey	J Pate, T Watson	Oakmont, PA	276
	WON PLAY-OFF AT SECOND EXTRA HOLE			
1979	D Graham	B Crenshaw	Oakland Hills, MI	272
	WON PLAY-OFF AT THIRD EXTRA HOLE			
1980	J Nicklaus	A Bean	Oak Hill, NY	274
1981	L Nelson	F Zoeller	Atlantic Ath Club, GA	273
1982	R Floyd	L Wadkins	Southern Hills, OK	272
1983	H Sutton	J Nicklaus	Riviera, Los Angeles, CA	274
1984	L Trevino	L Wadkins, G Player	Shoal Creek AL	273
1985	H Green	L Trevino	Cherry Hills, CO	278
1986	R Tway	G Norman	Inverness, Toledo, OH	276
1987	L Nelson	L Wadkins	PGA National, FL	287
	WON PLAY-OFF AT FIRST EXTRA HOLE			
1988	J Sluman	P Azinger	Oak Tree, Edmond, OK	272
1989	P Stewart	A Bean, M Reid, C Strange	Kemper Lakes, IL	276
1990	W Grady	F Couples	Shoal Creek, AL	282
1991	J Daly	B Lietzke	Crooked Stick, IN	276
1992	N Price	J Cook, N Faldo, G Sauers, J Gallagher Jnr	Bellerive, St Louis, MO	278
1993	P Azinger	G Norman	Inverness, Toledo, OH	272
	WON PLAY-OFF AT SECOND EXTRA HOLE			
1994	N Price	C Pavin	Southern Hills, OK	269
1995	S Elkington	C Montgomerie	Riviera, Los Angeles, CA	267
	WON PLAY-OFF AT FIRST EXTRA HOLE			
1996	M Brooks	K Perry	Valhalla, KY	277
	WON PLAY-OFF AT FIRST EXTRA HOLE			

In addition to self-confidence, and the ability to scrape a way out of trouble and slot the most daunting putt, Hagen's armoury included a smile that must have seemed crocodile-like to his opponents.

It didn't always work: before getting down to a 20-foot putt at a critical moment in the third round of the US PGA in 1928, he turned and directed the full force of one of these smiles at Diegel, a frequent victim of his match playing ability. Hagen holed the putt, but Diegel, though he had lost an early four-hole lead and was clearly shaken, managed to survive. He went on to record a crushing final win against Al Espinosa (6 & 5), and followed up the following season with a 6 & 4 victory over Johnny Farrell, one of the few to have beaten Bobby Jones over 36 holes ... for the US Open too.

There was no suggestion at first that the US PGA was a "major" title. The leading amateurs of the day were still to be reckoned with as the elite of golf. Between 1913 and 1933 the two big Opens were won by an amateur on 11 occasions.

Tom Creavy, like John Daly in 1991, was among the most surprising winners of a national championship. He won the US PGA in 1931, aged 20, beating Denny Shute at Wannamoisett, Rhode Island, in the final, and two other Open champions on the way to it. He lived until 1979, but illness restricted his golf after he reached the last four in 1932 and the last eight in 1933, and finished eighth in the Open of 1934.

The US PGA Championship remained a match play event until 1958, providing in 1942, soon after Pearl Harbor, Sam Snead's first national title. He was able to play only because he persuaded his recruiting officer to let him enlist a few days late so that he could compete at Seaview, Atlantic City, where he beat Jim Turnesa 2 & 1.

The Second World War caused only one year's inaction, for Bob Hamilton beat Byron Nelson at Spokane, Washington, in 1944, and the following year Nelson was back to regain the title he first won in 1940, at Snead's expense. The US PGA was also Ben Hogan's first national title, and with the growth of the PGA Tour, and the absence of amateurs good enough to beat the pros, the event grew in importance.

Americans love the pencil and card game, and in its new guise as a medal competition (from 1958) the US PGA gained more and more attention. It also caused agonized disappointment as Arnold Palmer took the place of Hogan in the nation's high regard, for this is the one major Palmer did not win. He certainly tried hard, finishing joint second in 1964, 1968 and 1970.

Discounting early immigrant winners like Barnes, Hutchison, Tommy Armour and (in 1947) the Australian Jim Ferrier, long based in the United States and a heavy money-winner on the PGA Tour, the first foreign winner was Gary Player in 1962 on the occasion of the US PGA's only visit to Aronomink, Pennsylvania. Three years later, by winning the US Open, Player became, with Sarazen and Hogan, the third golfer to have won the modern quartet of majors. Jack Nicklaus made it a foursome when he became Open champion at Muirfield in 1966. Australia's David Graham beat Ben Crenshaw in a play-off only after an excruciating 72nd hole at the difficult Oakland Hills course near Detroit in 1979.

He began with a misplaced drive, and an over-strong approach. Two indifferent chips and a missed putt left him wanting a downhill putt to equal Crenshaw's 272. He holed it, and then made two lengthy putts to keep the sudden-death play-off going to the third hole, which he birdied for victory.

The suspense attached to John Daly's 1991 triumph, his first on the PGA Tour, started for this Californian-born long hitter from Arkansas before he even reached Crooked Stick, Indiana, to which the Championship was making its first visit. He was ninth "reserve" in line for a place in the event, and got in because Nick Price departed to be with his wife, who shortly afterward gave birth to Gregory, their first child. Daly, 25, decided to take a chance and make the seven-hour drive to Crooked Stick before he knew of Price's decision.

His gamble paid off. After two rounds he led on a 7,289-yard course he had never seen before. Daly, known to about one golf fan in a million, was a huge hit with the media, gaining instant fame as "Wild Thing" with his fulsome swing and 300-yard plus drives, not to mention sand wedges that flew 150 yards. His winning total of 276, three strokes ahead of Bruce Lietzke, also owed a good deal to a sharp short game. He received a 10-year exemption on the Tour, life-time US PGA exemption, and a $230,000 (£137,000) start towards finishing 17th on the 1991 money list. Naturally, he was also voted Rookie of the Year.

Price was back for the 1992 US PGA at Bellerive, with his caddie Jess "Squeaky" Medlen, whom Daly had taken over the previous year in Price's absence. Price, a Zimbabwean who come close to "major" fame in the British Opens of 1982 and 1988, won by three shots, and repeated the dose, this time by six shots, two years later at Southern Hills, Tulsa, a month after his Open at Turnberry. His second US PGA put him at the head of the Sony World Rankings. At Tulsa, at the age of 37, Price set new US PGA scoring standards. His 269 (11 under par) beat Bobby Nichols's 1964 record by two shots.

Price's first nine in the final round ruled out much chance of excitement later on, as he reached the turn in 32, but three birdies on the back nine were cancelled out by three bogeys, which cost Price his chance of taking Nicklaus's championship record winning margin which stands at seven shots. Despite these blemishes no one got to within three shots of Price. Proof of Arnold Palmer's lasting popularity came on the eve of the Championship, when Palmer, making his 37th and final appearance in the US PGA, which he never won, was presented with the PGA of America Distinguished Service Award. Daly failed to qualify by a stroke: he confessed to a couple of shanks and said, "Now I know how amateurs feel."

His disputes with other players, officials and his girlfriend, and the need to attend a drying-out clinic robbed the Tour of the full range of the star qualities of one of the longest hitters the game has known.

Between Price's twin triumphs, which meant that "Squeaky" had carried for three winners in four years, came a most popular win by Paul Azinger. The New Englander beat Greg Norman in a play-off at Toledo, making the Australian the unhappy owner of a unique record: he has lost play-offs for all four majors. In the 1986 event (also at Toledo), he lost the championship when playing partner Bob Tway birdied the 72nd hole out of a bunker.

Price's second US PGA was the last stage in the breaking of a mighty mould: for the first time since the US PGA and Masters became majors, not one had been won by a native of the United States.

An American full-house looked likely in 1995, as Ben Crenshaw, Corey Pavin and John Daly won the first three majors. But the USPGA champion Steve Elkington, although a Houston resident was born in Australia. His play-off birdie cost Scotland's Colin Montgomerie his first major; their 72-hole totals of 267 were the lowest in a major championship played in the US.

Mark Brooks scored another first-hole sudden-death win in 1996, as local hero Kenny Perry suffered one disaster after another at the long and difficult 18th at Valhalla, Kentucky ... which Brooks birdied.

ZINGER'S BIG DAY *Paul Azinger with the Wanamaker Trophy after his play-off win over Greg Norman*

RYDER CUP

From the first Ryder Cup match between the United States and Britain up to the first between the US and Europe, the American advantage in points scored, in 22 matches, surpassed three figures. In the first eight US vs. Europe Cup meetings, total American advantage was 12 points. The improvement was not immediate, for Europe did not get into gear until their third outing, and in the last seven matches the Europeans have actually outscored the Americans by four points.

Even the most rock-ribbed European (Community) sceptic could not discount the value to the Ryder Cup and golf in general of the European connection, which was first mooted seriously at the last "old style" Cup match at Lytham. The late Earl of Derby, who was President of the PGA, discussed the idea with Jack Nicklaus, Henry Poe, Lord Derby's opposite number at the US PGA, and senior British professional Neil Coles.

In 1979, at The Greenbrier, West Virginia, with Severiano Ballesteros and Antonio Garrido of Spain in the team led by John Jacobs, a leading figure in the creation of the European Tour, the new series began – not too well, as it turned out, for the brand new team of Europe.

Europe's "banker", Ballesteros, ran into a jinx, in the smooth-swinging shape of Larry Nelson, to whom he lost in singles and three times in partnership with Garrido, though the Spaniards did beat Fuzzy Zoeller and Hubert Green. All told, the result was dustier than the usual one.

The second European match, at Walton Heath, was dominated by an American side which many good judges believe to have been the equal of any sent forth by the US PGA. Moreover Europe, again led by Jacobs, were handicapped by the absence of Ballesteros and Tony Jacklin, who was less than pleased that Mark James was chosen in his stead. The Spaniard was demanding appearance money in Europe; there was talk of his resigning his European Tour membership. On this basis European professional sentiment opposed his selection.

PADDLING PRO *Torrance in trouble, but he rallied to land the 1985 glory blow*

Non-selection of the two players, who alone in the European ranks had won major championships in Britain and the United States, was an even bigger mistake in hindsight than it seemed at the time. This was the team in which Bernhard Langer, Scotland's Sam Torrance, José-Maria Canizares and Manuel Pinero were all making their first appearances. All were to play a part in European victories, and the missing pair's experience might have inspired these new boys to even greater heights. Dave Marr, a US PGA Championship winner whose salty comments in beguiling Texan drawl are a feature of television coverage, was non-playing captain of this daunting aggregation of talent, who were five points ahead when the singles began: Lee Trevino (beat Sam Torrance 5 & 4), Tom Kite (beat Sandy Lyle, who was six under par at the time, at the 16th), Bill Rogers (current Open champion, halved with Bernard Gallacher), Larry Nelson (beat Mark James to make his Cup record played nine, won nine), Ben Crenshaw (beat Des Smyth 6 & 4), Bruce Lietzke (halved with Langer), Jerry Pate (lost 4 & 2 to Pinero), Hale Irwin (beat Canizares one hole), Johnny Miller (lost to Nick Faldo 2 & 1), Tom Watson (lost to Howard Clark 4 & 3), Raymond Floyd (beat Peter Oosterhuis one hole), and Jack Nicklaus (beat Eamonn Darcy 5 & 3). This brought up a final score of $18^1/_2$ to $9^1/_2$.

At the PGA National, Palm Beach Gardens, Florida, in 1983, Europe came within a putt or two of beating the US on their own soil. Even in the days when there were

AGAINST THE ODDS *Despite being dogged by a variety of problems, Europe took the Cup for a third time at Oak Hill in 1995*

only 12 points at stake, Britain and Ireland had never got closer than a four-point deficit in America. To start with, strength in depth and depth of experience were at last approaching American standards … but not yet quite close enough, it transpired.

There was certainly experience at the helm, where non-playing captain Jacklin was getting powerful support from his top-of-the-draw men. Nick Faldo was fulfilling his early promise, and won three times out of four in company with Langer. He also beat Jay Haas. After an initial stumble, Masters champion Ballesteros partnered new boy Paul Way to two wins and a half. Then, after being three up against Fuzzy Zoeller, he had to claw his way back to a half, notably with a wood shot from a bunker that impressed many witnesses as the best shot they had ever seen. It was certainly among the most daring.

PLUCK OF THE IRISH *Eamonn Darcy earned the crucial point in 1987*

Hearts pounded faster on both sides as, in the last three matches, Brown easily beat Raymond Floyd, but Lanny Wadkins was relentlessly cutting back Canizares's three-hole lead, and Gallacher was in a pressure cooker of a match against Watson. Wadkins's pitch almost to "gimme" range at the 18th squeezed a half out of Canizares, and Gallacher said later of his four-footer for a half against Watson, after both men had fluffed their first chip at the 17th: "I still think to this day that I hit a good putt. There was a subtle break but I missed and that was it, two and one." And that was it, 14½ to 13½ for the United States, a score that sold any number of tickets for the 1985 battle at British PGA HQ, the Belfry.

This new course, not far from the heart of Britain's motorway system, had several holes that were, in the view of some critics, not good enough for a Cup match. Moreover the flat terrain restricted spectators' view of play. Nevertheless 27,000 of them celebrated a victory for Europe, with Concorde flying over the course in a roaring celebration of European togetherness not yet achieved by the European Commission in Brussels.

The Belfry does have a finish made for shredding the nerves of all but the bravest. The long dog-leg 17th, to an elevated green, is followed by a final par four where both first and second shots have huge water hazards, the second demanding accurate judgment of length because the green has three tiers.

A five-point win for Europe was promise of giant gates for future Cup matches, and total vindication for the words of Jack Nicklaus almost a decade earlier: "It is vital to widen the selection procedures if the Ryder Cup is to continue to enjoy its past prestige."

In the British Isles the Cup had never lost its prestige, for it still attracted wide media coverage and big attendances even when the US were handing out hidings every two years. This was because opportunities to see the leading American players were limited, and for the most part eagerly taken up. However, the American media and golf-going public were low-key on the Cup matches while they were so one-sided. Three US defeats in 56 years, and two of those having come in the first four matches, did little to build up suspense.

But it is not true of golf that it is better to travel hopefully than to arrive, because when the European team "arrived" at the Belfry in 1985 the whole Ryder Cup ethos, not to mention its attractions to sponsors, was elevated to Open Championship standards and, in the opinion of some, even beyond.

The players are not paid, yet zealously husband selection points, or failing these, cultivate the good opinion of their captains, giving rise to jokes about how sycophantic macho players can be towards the captain if they are on the edge of Cup selection. Lanny Wadkins, the 1995 US captain and among the most combative yet outgoing of players, has expressed mock surprise at how nicely his fellows behaved towards him from the time of his appointment. The pattern of team selection has been similar for both sides – most of the team chosen strictly on performance in official Tour events, the last few places filled by the captain's choices. Dispossessing the American team, led by non-playing Lee Trevino, of the Cup for the first time since Dai Rees scored his greatest triumph as player and leader in 1957 at Lindrick was achieved at last with gratifying ease at the Belfry. Here, Europe performed the rare feat of winning the singles by three points after finishing four-balls and foursomes two ahead. Ironically, the two leading European players of the era barely contributed in singles, Faldo losing to Hubert Green and Ballesteros halving with Tom Kite.

It was now that the new-found strength in depth came to the aid of Jacklin in his second stint as captain, for Pinero gave Europe a flying start on the final day by beating Lanny Wadkins, and Lyle, Langer, Torrance and Clark made a clean sweep of the middle four matches in the singles order.

To Torrance fell the great moment: his opponent Andy North put his drive into the water at the 18th, Sam Torrance hit a vast distance into position A, and sank the birdie putt offered by his accurate approach.

Concorde took the British team to Ohio for the 1987 match, Jacklin having insisted that all of the European planning for the defence of the Cup should be top bracket.

The excitement around Muirfield Village, Jack Nicklaus's pet exercise of his architectural career, was not merely intense over the last couple of hours; it was almost insupportable. The Ryder Cup, 1980s style, had been given the imprimatur of live coverage by US television, a complete reversal of previous media disinterest. An all-ticket crowd of 25,000 was another reward for the success of the Nicklaus European initiative.

Ballesteros and José-Maria Olazabal netted three points out of four, and Faldo and Woosnam dropped only a half point out of four, in the process beating Wadkins and Masters champion Larry Mize after falling four holes behind. Lyle and Langer also contributed three points. So Europe led by five as the singles began; but the match was far from decided.

America won five and halved one of the top eight singles, Andy Bean beginning the rally with a last hole victory over the previously unbeaten Ian Woosnam. It was with considerable relief that Jacklin took in the sight of what looked like the world's happiest golfer, by name Eamonn Darcy, repeatedly shaking his fist after holing a testing downhill putt to beat Crenshaw by one hole. On the American side, Nelson suffered his first defeats, three of them, in 13 starts, and Nicklaus's score as captain was now one win, one defeat. This was the first time America had lost a home Ryder Cup match.

The Ryder Cup fortunes of the two captains had never lacked dramatic qualities, notably in the only halved series of the US vs. Britain and Ireland series, in 1969 at Birkdale, where 16–16 was the result under the ruling 32-match format. After getting his four on the final green from three feet, Nicklaus gave an 18-inch putt to Jacklin which brought up the tied score, saying that he was sure Jacklin would have holed it, "but I was not prepared to see you miss". Jacklin, the Open champion, was not to see Nicklaus and Co. beaten for many years. The 32-match format gave Jacklin two singles against Nicklaus, and he had halved one and won the other.

Beating the leading golfer of the age was given to few in match play. Nicklaus won 17 Cup matches and lost eight, two of them on the same day to Brian Barnes in the 1975 Ryder Cup at Laurel Valley.

The next Ryder extravaganza at the Belfry in 1989 went all the way through hours of tension to a final cliff-hanging and decisive moment: a Cup-saving long iron shot across the lake at Belfry's finishing hole that Christy O'Connor Jr will never forget, nor the multitudes who saw him . . . the television audience was estimated at 200,000,000.

Europe, without Sandy Lyle at his own request owing to lack of form, were two clear as the singles began. Paul Azinger and Chip Beck, both making their first Cup appearances, rapidly evened the score against the seasoned Ballesteros and Langer. They had already gained two points in two starts as partners. Prospects now began to look bleak, with Mark James the only leader lower down the order. He beat Mark O'Meara at the 16th, and Olazabal and Ronan Rafferty fought back to right the ship. The crux of the matter came with that O'Connor shot to foil Fred Couples, and Canizares' cool long putt on the last, where, as it turned out, Ken Green three-putted the Cup away.

A draw at 14 each fired the Americans to prepare a hot welcome in 1991 for the team led by Jacklin's successor, Bernard Gallacher, at a new lay-out on Kiawah Island, South Carolina. The media hyped "The War on the Shore", a phrase which was anathema to traditionalists and and not too well received by the players.

Again the tension was almost beyond bearing, especially as this time the reckoning was 8–8 with the singles to come, which had so often produced a final day bonanza for the Americans. Only 11 singles were to be played, since Steve Pate, bruised in a car crash the previous Wednesday, had played in one four-ball, with Corey Pavin, and lost, and now withdrew. So a half was agreed with David Gilford. Pate had been due originally to play Ballesteros, who had dropped only half a point throughout – a good switch for US captain Dave Stockton.

Azinger and Beck were again the US singles heroes, as were Pavin, Couples and Wadkins, though an effective first appearance was made by Paul Broadhurst for Europe, and Colin Montgomerie too, for he got a half against Mark Calcavecchia by winning all of the last four holes. This time the clincher was not a long iron, but a not very long putt. Langer, who had come back from behind against Hale Irwin, faced it for par and a win and a tied match, for Irwin had already bogeyed. He missed, right edge, and – to a mighty roar – the Cup was held aloft by Stockton.

The 1993 meeting was again at the Belfry, but the 1997 European staging was earmarked for Spain, whose players had done so much to bring a new vitality to Ryder Cup play. Tom Watson took up the American leadership with Raymond Floyd, captain when they were beaten in 1989, in the team; for Europe, Gallacher led again, and had problems. Ballesteros asked to

MEASURING UP *Chip Beck figured it right at Kiawah Island in 1991*

THIRD TIME LUCKY *Bernard Gallacher's golden reward for persistence*

be dropped from his partnership with Olazabal on the grounds of loss of form, though the pair had won twice in three starts. Gallacher, controversially, conceded to him. Joakim Haeggman joined Olazabal, and they lost. Sam Torrance was side-lined by a poisoned toe.

Gallacher was buoyed up by a wonderful display by new Cup selection, Midlander Peter Baker, who had little sleep, because of his daughter's illness, before he beat Corey Pavin on the final day. But elsewhere in singles the old American magic worked again, despite a stunning hole-in-one by Faldo in holding Azinger.

The odds looked forbidding at 5/2 against in 1995 as Gallacher tried for a third time to lead Europe to victory in at Oak Hill, Rochester, in New York State. Ballesteros was off his game: Olazabal withdrew with foot trouble. Faldo's second marriage was breaking up. To the 10 automatic sections, Gallacher added Woosnam and Faldo. American captain Wadkins chose Curtis Strange, without a win since his second US Open in 1989, and Fred Couples as his final two. This proved to have deep consequences.

Ballesteros the legend achieved more than Ballesteros the golfer: his Svengali-of-the-Fairways act on day one was clearly a factor in stirring David Gilford to great things, and the pair of them beat Brad Faxon and Peter Jacobsen 4 & 3. But in the last fourball on the eve of the singles, the US went 9–7 ahead when Pavin, outstanding for his team with four wins in five outings as befits a national champion, struck a paralysing blow by holing a chip at the 18th against Faldo and Langer.

Stunned as the Europeans must have been that night, all was cheers, and much champagne next evening as Gallacher's side took the Sunday singles 7½–4½, and the Cup 14½–13½. Howard Clark beat Jacobsen, helped by a hole in one (Rocca had aced in Saturday's foursomes), Torrance beat Loren Roberts, Montgomerie was never behind against Crenshaw, Mark James and Gilford won also, but the crucial match was the 10th, Faldo versus his old nemesis, Strange.

The American was one up on the 17th tee, but level on the 18th. Here Faldo's 93-yard pitch and 4-foot putt left Strange (like Crenshaw) without a win in three outings, to Wadkins' dismay. "Should have picked Janzen," said the hindsight experts. Ireland's Philip Walton got the final point needed to take the Cup back across the Atlantic, Jay Haas conceding the decisive putt on the 18th.

Europe's selection method of 10 players gaining a place on the basis of points won in Tour events, plus two captain's choices, came under fire as Faldo and Jesper Parnevik prospered on the US PGA tour, and Woosnam talked of joining. What if more players were high on the US money list, and clearly worthy of selection? Would it then be that rewarding stay-at-homes for loyalty was more important than picking the best available talent? Plans to ballot the members about 1997 selection were abandoned. Legal opinion was that any player hopeful of ninth or tenth place would go to law if the system was changed in midstream. Seve Ballesteros, captain for Valderrama in 1997, was nettled at being left with only two "picks". The problem will not go away.

Year	Venue	United States	GB and I
1927	Worcester, MA	9½: W Hagen	2½: T Ray
1929	Moortown, Leeds	5: W Hagen	7: G Duncan
1931	Scioto, Columbus, OH	9: W Hagen	3: C A Whitcombe
1933	Southport and Ainsdale, Lancashire	5½: W Hagen	6½: J H Taylor*
1935	Ridgewood, NJ	9: W Hagen	3: C A Whitcombe
1937	Southport and Ainsdale	8: W Hagen*	4: C A Whitcombe
1939-45	No matches		
1947	Portland, OR	11: B Hogan	1: T H Cotton
1949	Ganton, Yorkshire	7: B Hogan*	5: C A Whitcombe*
1951	Pinehurst, NC	9½: S Snead	2½: A J Lacey*
1953	Wentworth, Surrey	6½: L Mangrum	5½: T H Cotton*
1955	Thunderbird Club, CA	8: C Harbert	4: D J Rees
1957	Lindrick, Notts	4½: J Burke	7½: D J Rees
1959	Eldorado CC, CA	8½: S Snead	3½: D J Rees
1961	Lytham, Lancs	14½: J Barber	9½: D J Rees
1963	Atlanta, GA	23: A Palmer	9: J Fallon*
1965	Royal Birkdale, Southport	19½: B Nelson*	12½: H Weetman*
1967	Houston, TX	23½: B Hogan*	8½: D J Rees*
1969	Royal Birkdale, Southport	16: S Snead*	16: E C Brown*
1971	St Louis, MO	19: J Hebert*	13: E C Brown*
1973	Muirfield, Scotland	19: J Burke*	13: B J Hunt*
1975	Laurel Valley, PA	21: A Palmer*	11: B J Hunt*
1977	Lytham, Lancs	12½: D Finsterwald*	7½: B Huggett*
		United States	**Europe**
1979	The Greenbrier, WV	17: W Casper*	11: J Jacobs*
1981	Walton Heath, Surrey	18½: D Marr*	9½: J Jacobs*
1983	PGA National, FL	14½: J Nicklaus*	13½: T Jacklin*
1985	The Belfry, West Midlands	11½: L Trevino*	16½: T Jacklin*
1987	Muirfield Village, Columbus, OH	13: J Nicklaus*	15: T Jacklin*
1989	The Belfry, West Midlands	14: R Floyd*	14: T Jacklin*
1991	Kiawah Island, SC	14½: D Stockton*	13½: B Gallacher*
1993	The Belfry, West Midlands	15: T Watson*	13: B Gallacher*
1995	Rochester, NY	13½: L Wadkins*	14½: B Gallacher*

(* = non-playing)

BRITISH AMATEUR CHAMPIONSHIP

Allan MacFie was the first British Amateur champion, but never attained the fame of Horace Hutchinson (more properly Horatio Gordon Hutchinson), whom he he beat in the inaugural final at Royal Liverpool's course, Hoylake. Hutchinson won the second and third finals, the third against John Ball. The Hoylake-bred Ball was accounted the greatest of them all long before 1912, when he won his eighth title, which is still a record.

In any case the first Championship, organized by the Royal Liverpool, was not recognized as official until 1920, when the Royal & Ancient finally took over full control of the event; Hutchinson was also a celebrated writer on golf and other sports.

In 1995 the R & A, who like the USGA have a well-developed sense of tradition, marked the 100th Amateur by bringing the event back to its Hoylake birthplace. Besides, Michael Bonallack, secretary of the R&A, is the most successful living competitor in the Amateur, with five titles, including a hat-trick in 1968–70.

Before the turn of the century the entry had reached 100, and by 1958 almost 500. Lower and lower handicaps were demanded to keep down the flood of would-be competitors. In 1983, 36-hole qualifying was introduced, the leading 64 reverting to match play over four days.

Bonallack's feat in the days of greatly increased competition from a world-wide entry is at least the equal of John Ball's achievements, in the days when a small handful would meet year after year in the closing stages of the Championship. Indeed, from 1887 to 1895 either Johnny Laidlay or Ball or both figured in every final. At the same time, Ball was the first Englishman (in 1890) and another amateur, Harold Hilton, two years later, the second, to win the Open.

Freddie Tait, a long hitter who managed to play golf with an extraordinary regularity considering his position as an officer in the Black Watch, might well have emulated Hilton, but in 1900, aged 30, he was killed leading his men against the Boers at Koodoosberg.

HOYLAKE TRIUMPH *Michael Bonallack lifts his fourth title in 1969*

The British Amateur was to attract a growing number of Americans, but the first to win, Walter Travis, in 1904, did not improve transatlantic golf relations. Ironically, the cause of the rift was that Travis, a triple US Amateur champion, won with a brand new putter, adopted in desperation for the Amateur at Royal St George's because, during his preparations for the event, his putting, his greatest strength, suddenly "went off".

But the instrument he chose was looked upon by the British establishment as unfair. It was called a Schenectady putter, invented and patented by Arthur Knight of that particular New York city, and had its shaft attached to the middle of a mallet-shaped head.

No one had ever seen putting such as Travis now deployed against one opponent after another, beating Hilton and Hutchinson in turn to reach the final, where he won at the 33rd against Ted Blackwell, who towered above and outhit Travis throughout. Travis relished a victory which was received with a minimum of applause, which cannot have surprised him, for he felt he had not been accorded the usual courtesies, particularly in the matter of clubhouse facilities and an effective caddie.

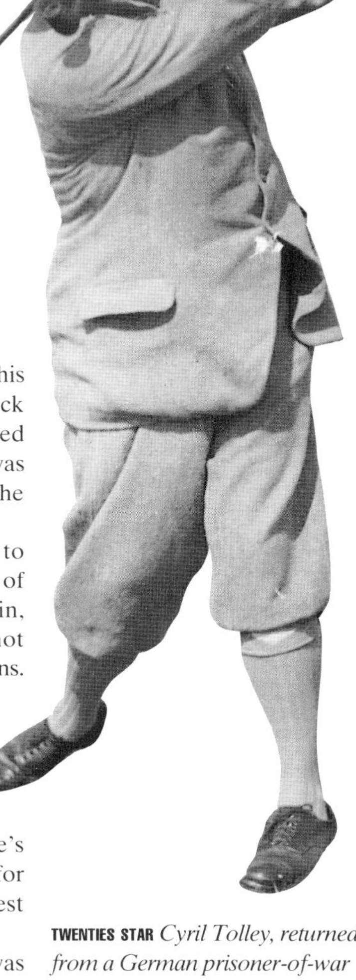

TWENTIES STAR *Cyril Tolley, returned from a German prisoner-of-war camp to capture his first Amateur title*

The Travis Schenectady, centre-shafted wand of victory, though approved by the USGA, was banned by the R&A, though not, contrary to popular legend, directly as a result of Travis's 1904 victory. The ban was imposed in 1910, and even then only after Nga Motu GC, New Zealand, asked if a small croquet mallet was legal. No, said the R&A. Not until mid-century was such a weapon unbanned. Ben Hogan used the same type in his one (triumphant) tilt at the British Open in 1953.

From 1920, when the Championship resumed after the war, it became far more difficult to put together even as few as two wins,

British Amateur Championship Results

Year	Winner	Venue
1885	A F McFie	Hoylake
1886	H G Hutchinson	St Andrews
1887	H G Hutchinson	Hoylake
1888	J Ball	Prestwick
1889	J E Laidlay	St Andrews
1890	J Ball	Hoylake
1891	J E Laidlay	St Andrews
1892	J Ball	St George's
1893	P C Anderson	Prestwick
1894	J Ball	Hoylake
1895	L M B Melville	St Andrews
1896	F G Tait	St George's
1897	A J T Allan	Muirfield
1898	F G Tait	Hoylake
1899	J Ball	Prestwick
1900	H H Hilton	St George's
1901	H H Hilton	St Andrews
1902	C Hutchings	Hoylake
1903	R Maxwell	Muirfield
1904	W J Travis	St George's
1905	A G Barry	Prestwick
1906	J Robb	Hoylake
1907	J Ball	St Andrews
1908	E A Lassen	St George's
1909	R Maxwell	Muirfield
1910	J Ball	Hoylake
1911	H H Hilton	Prestwick
1912	J Ball	Westward Ho!
1913	H H Hilton	St Andrews
1914	J L C Jenkins	St George's
1915-19	*NO CHAMPIONSHIP*	
1920	C Tolley	Muirfield
1921	W I Hunter	Hoylake
1922	E Holderness	Prestwick
1923	R H Wethered	Deal
1924	E Holderness	St Andrews
1925	R Harris	Westward Ho!
1926	J Sweetser	Muirfield
1927	Dr W Tweddell	Hoylake
1928	T P Perkins	Prestwick
1929	C Tolley	St George's
1930	R T Jones Jnr	St Andrews
1931	E Martin Smith	Westward Ho!
1932	J De Forest	Muirfield
1933	Hon. M Scott	Hoylake
1934	W Lawson Little	Prestwick
1935	W Lawson Little	Lytham
1936	H Thomson	St Andrews
1937	R Sweeney Jnr	St George's
1938	C R Yates	Troon
1939	A T Kyle	Hoylake

Year	Winner	Venue
1940-45	*NO CHAMPIONSHIP*	
1946	J Bruen	Birkdale
1947	W P Turnesa	Carnoustie
1948	F R Stranahan	St George's
1949	S M McCready	Portmarnock
1950	F R Stranahan	St Andrews
1951	R D Chapman	Porthcawl
1952	E Harvie Ward	Prestwick
1953	J B Carr	Hoylake
1954	D W Bachli	Muirfield
1955	J W Conrad	Lytham
1956	J C Beharrell	Troon
1957	R Reid Jack	Formby
1958	J B Carr	St Andrews
1959	D R Beman	St George's
1960	J B Carr	Portrush
1961	M F Bonallack	Turnberry
1962	R D Davies	Hoylake
1963	M S R Lunt	St Andrews
1964	G J Clark	Ganton
1965	M F Bonallack	Porthcawl
1966	R E Cole	Carnoustie
1967	R B Dickson	Formby
1968	M F Bonallack	Troon
1969	M F Bonallack	Hoylake
1970	M F Bonallack	Newcastle, Co. Down
1971	S N Melnyk	Carnoustie
1972	T Homer	St George's
1973	R Siderowf	Porthcawl
1974	T Homer	Muirfield
1975	M M Giles	Hoylake
1976	R Siderowf	St Andrews
1977	P McEvoy	Ganton
1978	P McEvoy	Troon
1979	J Sigel	Hillside
1980	D Evans	Porthcawl
1981	P Ploujoux	St Andrews
1982	M Thompson	Deal
1983	A P Parkin	Turnberry
1984	J-M Olazabal	Formby
1985	G McGimpsey	Dornoch
1986	D Curry	Lytham
1987	P M Mayo	Prestwick
1988	C Hardin	Porthcawl
1989	S Dodd	Birkdale
1990	R Muntz	Muirfield
1991	G Wolstenholme	Ganton
1992	S Dundas	Carnoustie
1993	I Pyman	Portrush
1994	L James	Nairn
1995	G Sherry	Hoylake
1996	W Bladon	Turnberry

and Ball's eight began to look as unrepeatable as time has proved it to be. Cyril Tolley, an England international for a quarter of a century, managed two wins. He and Robert Gardner relaunched the Amateur with a 37-hole cliff-hanger of a final at Muirfield. Both men had survived war service (Tolley, who won the Military Cross, was a POW).

Three thousand cheered as Tolley birdied the extra hole, for amateur golf was thoroughly fashionable, and was to become the more so with the advent of Bobby Jones, though he won the Amateur only once, in his Grand Slam year of 1930, beating Roger Wethered in the St Andrews final. His closest call came against Tolley, whose extra-hole luck was out this time, Jones going through with the aid of a stymie which was, as Jones himself said, "a cruel way to lose".

William Lawson Little followed Jones's Grand Slam with two "Little Slams" in 1934 and 1935, capturing both the US and British Amateurs twice. Six American victories in the British Amateur between the wars was succeeded by five more in seven years immediately following the Second World War. Even when James Bruen, the Irish Ryder Cup player, won in 1946, he had to beat an American, Bob Sweeney, to do it. So did Sam McCready, another Belfast golfer, in 1949, holding off Willie Turnesa, the 1947 champion, 2 and 1 at Portmarnock.

Joe Carr carried on the Irish tradition with three wins, but since the war there has been an even stronger American tradition, which lasted until 1983 and was unbroken except in 1963: that is, whenever the US Walker Cup team was, at four-year intervals, visiting Britain, there was an American winner of the Amateur.

On six occasions – 1947, 1951, 1959, 1967, 1971 and 1979 – *both* finalists were American. None of Bonallack's five wins came in years of American Cup visits, but he did win the English Championship five times, shooting a 61 at Ganton, Yorkshire in 1968.

Since Jay Sigel's win over Scott Hoch in 1979, another change has come over the Amateur, for continental invaders from France (1981), Spain (1984), Sweden (1988) and Holland (1990) have replaced US winners. Otherwise it has been British Isles players only, with Gary Wolstenholme gaining a measure of personal satisfaction by beating Bob May of the successful 1991 Walker Cup team 8 and 6 at Ganton.

Bonallack is sure of the best Amateur final he has ever seen, and he should know: it was played in 1993 at Portrush in Ireland, Yorkshire's Iain Pyman beating Kent's Paul Page at the 37th hole.

CUP CONSOLATION *Gary Wolstenholme was a comfortable winner at Ganton*

US AMATEUR CHAMPIONSHIP

The first United States Amateur Championship started three days before the nation's first Open, and play lasted three times as long, a pecking order that was not quickly disturbed. Across the Atlantic the Open pre-dated the Amateur by a quarter of a century, and rapidly became the Holy Grail for all golfers.

ARNIE'S FIRST BIG ONE *Palmer in quarter final action in his first national title triumph, the US Amateur of 1954*

There is a direct personal link between the US Amateur and the British Open. Old Tom Morris, winner of four Opens, coached the first winner of the American Amateur, a well-built, self-willed Chicagoan named Charles Blair Macdonald. He had first fallen in love with golf in Scotland as a student at St Andrews in the 1870s, and in the early 1890s built the Chicago club, then a much improved 18 holes at Wheaton, a Chicago suburb.

Macdonald had first come to the public's notice in his campaign to become American Amateur champion. Since golf lacked a national authority, the clubs of Newport, Rhode Island, and St Andrew's, New York, put on "Championships" in 1893 and 1894.

Macdonald came second in both, but discounted the quality both of the venues and of his opponents. He was an influential man, a stockbroker on the New York exchange, but the game was clearly in need of leadership a little less egotistical than his. So the US Golf Association came into being at the end of 1894, and the first president, Theodore Havemeyer, a sugar baron, gave an extra veneer of authority to the inaugural Amateur starting on September 1, 1895, by donating a championship trophy.

Macdonald won it, easily.

UNIQUE DOUBLE *Young Chick Evans took the US Open and Amateur in 1916 – a record*

His victim in the final, by 12 and 11, at Newport, was Charles Sands, who preferred lawn tennis. Although Macdonald went on to perform great service as a USGA committee man and (unpaid) course designer, his fame was as nothing compared to that of Walter J. Travis, the champion in 1900, 1901 and 1903.

Travis came from Australia as a child and did not take up golf until he was 35. At 37 he reached the semi-final of the US Amateur, and the following year, 1900, he won it. He was also second in the 1902 US Open.

Travis was a short hitter but a devastating putter. His most celebrated single feat was his British Amateur title, his last major win, in

1904. His "trade-mark" was his eternal black cigar.

Travis's victory on foreign soil, for the British title, was answered seven years later by Harold Hilton, who had two British Opens to his credit. Having won the British Amateur in 1911, he went for the transatlantic double at the age of 42. He strolled through the early rounds, but Fred Herreshoff took Hilton to the 37th hole in the final before surrendering.

Ouimet's Amateur title in 1914 sounds pallid after his 1913 giant-killing in the US Open, but it had been the great ambition of his life to lift the Amateur. For a former caddie like Ouimet, or a caddie like Chick Evans who graduated to the Stock Exchange to finance his golf, the Amateur was still the thing.

Evans followed recovery-expert Jerome Travers's record fourth Amateur success with a unique double in 1916. First he recorded a total of 286 to win the US Open at Minikahda, Minnesota, a figure not beaten for 22 years. Three months later Evans beat Bob Gardner in the Amateur final at the Merion course in Pennsylvania. Gardner had got into the last four by virtue of a 5 and 3 victory over a 14-year-old from Georgia playing in his first USGA championship. This was R. T. (Bobby) Jones Jnr, five times a winner between 1924 and 1930.

Only one man had two wins in the 1930s, William Lawson Little, but he added the novelty of winning the British Amateur in the same years, 1934 and 1935.

With Jones's retirement, and the fitful but sure growth of the professional tour, the fascination of the amateur game began to fade. After the war, the names of the outstanding professional players Byron Nelson, Ben Hogan and Sam Snead dominated the sports pages, and with the coming of television the process accelerated.

Gene Littler, Arnold Palmer and Jack Nicklaus used the Amateur as a stepping-stone to wealth, yet the continuing high standards of the amateur game in the US were never more clearly demonstrated than at Broadmoor, Colorado, in 1959, when Charles Coe, at 35 twice a winner, took Jack Nicklaus, then a student at Ohio State University, to the 36th hole of the final. The winner

US Amateur Championship Results

Year	Winner	Venue
1895	C B Macdonald	Newport, RI
1896	H J Whigham	Shinnecock Hills, NY
1897	H J Whigham	Chicago, IL
1898	F S Douglas	Morris County, NJ
1899	H M Harriman	Onwentsia, IL
1900	W J Travis	Garden City, NY
1901	W J Travis	Atlantic City, NJ
1902	L N James	Glen View, IL
1903	W J Travis	Nassau, NY
1904	H Chandler Egan	Baltusrol, NJ
1905	H Chandler Egan	Wheaton, IL
1906	E M Byers	Englewood, NJ
1907	J D Travers	Cleveland, OH
1908	J D Travers	Garden City, NJ
1909	R Gardner	Wheaton, IL
1910	W C Fownes Jnr	Brookline, MA
1911	H H Hilton	Apawamis, NY
1912	J D Travers	Wheaton, IL
1913	J D Travers	Garden City, NY
1914	F Ouimet	Ekwanok, VT
1915	R Gardner	Detroit, MI
1916	C Evans	Merion, PA
1917-18	*NO CHAMPIONSHIP*	
1919	S D Herron	Oakmont, PA
1920	C Evans	Engineers Club, NY
1921	J Guilford	Clayton, MO
1922	J Sweetser	Brookline, MA
1923	M R Marston	Flossmoor, IL
1924	R T Jones Jnr	Merion, PA
1925	R T Jones Jnr	Oakmont, PA
1926	G von Elm	Baltusrol, NJ
1927	R T Jones Jnr	Minikahda, MN
1928	R T Jones Jnr	Brae Burn, MA
1929	H R Johnson	Del Monte, CA
1930	R T Jones Jnr	Merion, PA
1931	F Ouimet	Beverley, IL
1932	C R Somerville	Baltimore, NJ
1933	G T Dunlap	Kenwood, OH
1934	W Lawson Little	Brookline, MA
1935	W Lawson Little	Cleveland, OH
1936	J W Fischer	Garden City, NY
1937	J Goodman	Portland, OR
1938	W P Turnesa	Oakmont, PA
1939	M H Ward	Glen View, IL
1940	R Chapman	Winged Foot, NY
1941	M H Ward	Omaha, NE
1942-45	*NO CHAMPIONSHIP*	
1946	S E Bishop	Baltusrol, NJ
1947	R H Riegel	Pebble Beach, CA
1948	W P Turnesa	Memphis, TN
1949	C R Coe	Rochester, NY
1950	S Urzetta	Minneapolis, MN
1951	W J Maxwell	Saucon Valley, PA
1952	J Westland	Seattle, WA
1953	G Littler	Oklahoma City, OK
1954	A Palmer	Detroit, MI
1955	E Harvie Ward	Richmond, VA
1956	E Harvie Ward	Lake Forest, IL
1957	H Robbins	Brookline, MA
1958	C R Coe	San Francisco, CA
1959	J Nicklaus	Broadmoor, CO
1960	D R Beman	St Louis, MO
1961	J Nicklaus	Pebble Beach, CA
1962	L E Harris Jnr	Pinehurst No. 2, NC
1963	D R Beman	Des Moines, IO
1964	W C Campbell	Canterbury, OH
1965-73 DECIDED BY STROKE PLAY		
1965	R Murphy	Southern Hills, OK
1966	G Cowan	Merion, PA
1967	R Dickson	Broadmoor, CO
1968	B Fleisher	Columbus, OH
1969	S N Melnyk	Oakmont, PA
1970	L Wadkins	Portland, OR
1971	G Cowan	Wilmington, DE
1972	M M Giles	Charlotte, NC
CHAMPIONSHIP REVERTED TO MATCH PLAY		
1973	C Stadler	Inverness, OH
1974	J Pate	Ridgewood, NJ
1975	F Ridley	Richmond, VA
1976	B Sander	Bel-Air, CA
1977	J Fought	Aronomink, PA
1978	J Cook	Plainfield, NJ
1979	M O'Meara	Canterbury, OH
1980	H Sutton	Pinehurst, NC
1981	N Crosby	Olympic, CA
1982	J Sigel	Brookline, MA
1983	J Sigel	North Shore, IL
1984	S Verplank	Oak Tree, OK
1985	S Randolph	Montclair, NJ
1986	S Alexander	Shoal Creek, AL
1987	W Mayfair	Jupiter Hills, FL
1988	E Meeks	Hot Springs, VA
1989	C Patton	Merion, PA
1990	P Mickelson	Cherry Hills, CO
1991	M Voges	Honours Course, TN
1992	J Leonard	Muirfield Village, OH
1993	J Harris	Houston, TX
1994	T Woods	Sawgrass, FL
1995	T Woods	Newport, RI
1996	T Woods	Portland, OR

SOMETHING TO SING ABOUT *Bing Crosby's youngest son, Nat, was US Amateur champion in 1981*

was about to begin a run of second/fourth/first in the US Open. At 19 years and eight months Nicklaus was the second youngest Amateur champion being three months older than Robert Gardner when he won half a century earlier.

Eight years of stroke-play format, begun with Bob Murphy's win at Southern Hills, Oklahoma, in 1968 (including a win by Lanny Wadkins in 1970), were abandoned in 1973, when more future PGA stars began to take the title, notably Craig Stadler, Jerry Pate, John Cook, Mark O'Meara and Hal Sutton.

In 1981 a stir was caused by a famous name from quite another sphere: Crosby. The singer's son Nathaniel, aged 19, won at Olympic, San Francisco, close to his home. Bing, who once got down to a handicap of two, and attracted a huge crowd when he tried for the British Amateur at St Andrews and birdied two of the first three holes, did not live to see Nat's triumph. He died in 1977 after playing a round in Spain in company with Manuel Pinero.

1981 was Nathaniel Crosby's sole moment of glory: Jay Sigel, champion for the next two years, was far more consistent. When he won in 1982 at Brookline, he was 38, twice as old as Crosby had been the previous year.

A hand injury 20 years earlier dissuaded Sigel from a professional career, and in any case he earned a living in insurance. His services to US golf are legion, and recently took a new turn when he began to coin money on the Senior PGA Tour, winning $1 million in 1996 alone, culminating in the $280,000 first prize in the Tour Championship at Myrtle Beach.

Phil Mickelson, a left-hander who hits long and chips with a velvet touch from the tightest lies, was 1990 champion and within a year, still an amateur, won a PGA tournament at Tucson. Even cynics were ready to believe that here at last was the next great American player.

Mickelson was soon supplanted as "the next great" by a tall, slim Californian of mainly Afro-American and Thai blood, Eldrick Woods, nick-named "Tiger" by his father Earl, a Vietnam veteran, in honour of a South Vietnamese comrade, Lt. Col Nguyen (Tiger) Phong. Young Tiger, the first black to win the US Amateur title in the 94 years of the event, was also the youngest champion at 18 in 1994, having made, aged five, his début as a TV golfer. Precocious is an inadequate term for Woods. He followed up with three US Junior titles: next came an unprecedented hat-trick in the Amateur. A 66 in the 1996 British Open at Lytham is reputed to have convinced Woods that professional golf should cut short his college career.

HIGH HOPES *Phil Mickelson, America's answer to golf's only other world-class left-hander, Bob Charles*

WALKER CUP

By the time the first professional international for the Ryder Cup was played between the two countries, the amateurs had already met four times for the Walker Cup.

This particular Cup competition has been over the years the most difficult of the four major trophies to prise out of American hands. The deep US reserve of amateur talent has been so well organized, coached and led as to win 30 of the 34 matches. Not until the 32nd match did the Americans lose at home, though they were held to 12–12 at Baltimore in 1965.

William Fownes, U.S Amateur champion in 1910, took a team to Hoylake for an informal international on the eve of the 1921 British Amateur Championship. Fownes's team won 9–3.

The R&A sent an official team to the National Golf Links of America at Southampton in New York State to compete for the Walker Cup, presented by a president of the USGA, in 1922. With Fownes at the helm once more, the US sent the R&A select home 8–4 losers. The visitors were handicapped; their captain, Robert Harris, was indisposed and unable to play. Bernard Darwin of *The Times*, who had made the trip as a reporter, took over as captain, and won his single 3 and 1 against Fownes, though Darwin was three down to his opposite number when they stood on the fourth tee.

WILLIAM FOWNES JNR *First US captain, seen here at Oakmont in 1920*

WALKER TRIO *(L–R) Marvin Ward, Reynolds Smith and Johnny Goodman*

Eight more US Cup victories followed, in which the leadership was passed on to Robert Gardner to Bobby Jones to Francis Ouimet. These three held most of the cards, with such men as Chick Evans and Johnny Goodman, both winners of the US Open, to call upon.

The US, after five big wins in a row, looked certain to get through the 1930s unbeaten ... until, in the 10th Walker Cup match, at St Andrews in 1938, Ouimet's team, which included American Amateur champion Goodman and the outstanding Marvin Ward, fell to a side coached by Open champion Henry Cotton and led by John Beck, who refined the selection process with painstaking trials.

Though James Bruen from Belfast gained only half a point, in the top foursome with Harry Bentley, and lost his single, he was the life and soul of the party for the home team. He and Bentley got their half with an inspirational rally; they were three down at lunch, after which they toured the Old Course in about four under par to hold John Fischer and Charles Kocsis.

The US, a point behind in foursomes, were unable to gain the five singles they needed to keep their hands on the Cup. Indeed they lost the singles (5–3) for only the second time in the series.

The Second World War meant that the Walker Cup remained under Royal & Ancient care for nearly a decade. The series was resumed in 1947 with a return to American dominance.

Signs of a challenge to US superiority were few. Ronnie White, from Wallasey on Merseyside, had a fine record with six wins from 10 appearances between 1947 and 1955, but the Americans had almost a monopoly of the won/lost credit balances

The matches of the 1950s never produced a winning US margin of less than three points in a 12-match format. Worse was to come in 1961 with an 11–1 defeat at Seattle.

In terms of cash and time, being a top-class amateur was becoming ever more expensive in Britain. A change of format in 1963 increased the matches to 24, but did not alter the result, though that was in doubt until the second day at Turnberry, an improved performance by Britain and Ireland thrillingly maintained at Baltimore in 1965.

There was plenty of fresh blood in the side ... Gordon Cosh, Rodney Foster, and Clive Clark all in their twenties, teenager Peter Townsend, and Gordon Clark, just into his thirties. Townsend won three points out of four, defeating Billie Joe Patton, who was playing in his last Walker Cup, finishing with an 11–4 record. Britain and Ireland led 10–5, and one match halved, as the final singles began.

GIANT INSPIRATION *Gordon Sherry holes for a birdie at the 17th*

Only Cosh won as America hit back hard, Edgar Tutweiler, at 46 the only American unbeaten throughout, setting the pace with a winning rally against Ronnie Shade. Nothing routine about the climax though, in which Clive Clark had to hole a 34-foot putt to halve with John Mark Hopkins and tie the whole match ... and this Clark did. He and Townsend soon turned pro, and that was the extent of British pretensions to victory for six years, when a second win was gained.

Like the first it came at St Andrews, where the key in 1971 was the final singles series, won 6-2 by the team led by Michael Bonallack, five times British Amateur champion, whose record as captain (two matches, one win) is much superior to his playing record of eight wins in 25 matches. A supremely brave and accurate three-iron approach shot to the Road Hole green (the 17th) was the decisive blow. David Marsh struck it to go dormie against Bill Hyndman, who lost at the next ... his one defeat, against six wins, in five Cup appearances.

Many of the best US amateurs tend to stay amateur, leavening the youthful ambition of the products of collegiate competition. This is certainly borne out by the record defeat inflicted by the US in 1993, 19-5 at Interlachen, Minnesota. The experience of players such as local hero and Walker Cup debutant John Harris, 41, and Jay Sigel, 49, in his ninth Cup match, and Danny Yates, 43, was crucial.

How then to explain the third defeat of the US in 1989 (in Georgia too) by another youthful British selection, in which only Peter McEvoy, in his fifth match, and Garth McGimpsey, in his second, had played Cup golf before?

McEvoy, than whom no more determined amateur breathes, certainly did his bit, winning more than losing. Most crucial were the misadventures of Sigel, in his seventh Cup match for the US, who lost after a series of most un-American chip shots against Jim Milligan in the final single.

Despite a saturated second day, nearly 10,000 fans trudged around Royal Porthcawl in south Wales to see Interlachen avenged, 14–10, by a side inspired by Britain's amateur champion, Gordon Sherry, and a steadfast first day victory over the (then) double US champion Tiger Woods by former British champion Gary Wolstenholme. The Irish pair of Padraig Harrington and Jody Fanagan were, uniquely, 100% in foursomes. David Howell, who holed the Cup-clinching putt, was unbeaten, and soon winning sizeable cheques on the European PGA Tour. Replacing such talent in 1997 against a vengeful US would obviously take some doing.

IN CREDIT *Peter McEvoy, more wins than losses in the first-ever Britain & Ireland away win in Georgia in 1989*

Walker Cup Results

Year	Venue	GB & I	United States
1922	National Links, Southampton, NY	**4:** R Harris (ill: acting captain B Darwin)	**8:** W Fownes
1923	St Andrews	**5½:** R Harris	**6½:** R Gardner
1924	Garden City, NJ	**3:** C Tolley	**9:** R Gardner
1926	St Andrews	**5½:** R Harris	**6½:** R Gardner
1928	Chicago, IL	**1:** Dr W Tweddell	**11:** R T Jones Jnr
1930	R St George's	**2:** R H Wethered	**10:** R T Jones Jnr
1932	Brookline, MA	**2½:** T A Torrance	**9½:** F Ouimet
1934	St Andrews	**2½:** Hon M Scott	**9½:** F Ouimet
1936	Pine Valley, NJ	**1½:** Dr W Tweddell	**10½:** F Ouimet
1938	St Andrews	**7½:** J B Beck	**4½:** F Ouimet
1947	St Andrews	**4:** J B Beck	**8:** F Ouimet
1949	Winged Foot, NY	**2:** P B Lucas	**10:** F Ouimet
1951	Birkdale	**4½:** R H Oppenheimer	**7½:** W P Turnesa
1953	Kittansett, MA	**3:** A A Duncan	**9:** C R Yates
1955	St Andrews	**2:** G A Hill	**10:** W C Campbell
1957	Minikahda, MN	**3½:** G H Micklem	**8½:** C R Coe
1959	Muirfield	**3:** G H Micklem	**9:** C R Coe
1961	Seattle, WA	**1:** C D Lawrie	**11:** J Westland
1963	Turnberry	**10:** C D Lawrie	**14:** R S Tufts
1965	Baltimore, MA	**12:** J B Carr	**12:** J W Fischer
1967	St George's	**9:** J B Carr	**15:** J W Sweetser
1969	Milwaukee, WI	**11:** M F Bonallack	**13:** W J Patton
1971	St Andrews	**13:** M F Bonallack	**11:** J M Winters
1973	Brookline, MA	**10:** D M Marsh	**14:** J W Sweetser
1975	St Andrews	**8½:** D M Marsh	**15½:** E Updefraff
1977	Shinnecock Hills, NY	**8:** A C Saddler	**16:** L W Oehmig
1979	Muirfield	**8½:** R Foster	**15½:** R Siderowf
1981	Cypress Point, CA	**9:** R Foster	**15:** J Gabrielsen
1983	Hoylake	**10½:** C W Green	**13½:** J Sigel
1985	Pine Valley, NJ	**11:** C W Green	**13:** J Sigel
1987	Sunningdale	**7½:** G C Marks	**16½:** F Ridley
1989	Peachtree, GA	**12½:** G C Marks	**11½:** F Ridley
1991	Portmarnock	**10:** G MacGregor	**14:** J Gabrielson
1993	Interlachen, MN	**5:** G MacGregor	**19:** M M Giles
1995	Royal Porthcawl	**14:** C Brown	**10:** D Gray

WOMEN'S CHAMPIONSHIPS

The ambitions of the Ladies' Professional Golf Association of the United States know few bounds. Their collaboration with the state of Florida in general and the City of Daytona Beach in particular, involving more than 4,000 acres, is not intended merely to provide a two-course backdrop to their new headquarters (until 1989 the LPGA were based in Texas). Their aim is to create a full-scale resort, with residential and commercial property.

Millions of dollars are being devoted to improving links between the main LPGA offices and its Academy and Teaching Complex with Interstate highway 95.

Main beneficiary of LPGA prosperity in 1996 was a 21-year-old Australian, Karrie Webb, who was the first LPGA or PGA rookie to top $1 million in a season, though Tiger Woods reached a million in five months after his August, 1996, US Tour début.

The existence of these massive investments and prizes owes much to the Women's PGA pioneers (vintage 1944) such as Hope Seignious, Betty Hicks and Ellen Griffin, and those of the LPGA which replaced the WPGA in 1950. The LPGA owed much to the organizing flair of Fred Corcoran, who made optimum use of the skills and attention-getting exploits of such players as Babe Zaharias and Patty Berg.

GRACEFUL PIONEER *Lady Margaret Scott, three times the British champion*

The sheer scale of the fixture and prize structure of the world's five major women's tours (US, European, Asian, Japanese and Australian) gives the lie to Horace Hutchinson's patronizing advice to women golfers eager to set up the Ladies' Golf Union of Britain, the world's first women's national organization.

Pioneering Ladies

Writing in April, 1893, to Blanche Martin, who was to become Union treasurer, Hutchinson, one of the leading amateurs of late Victorian times, issued what might today be termed a triple whammy. Women were, he pontificated, incapable of pushing any scheme to success: they would soon quarrel. Secondly, they would never get through a single ladies' championship with credit. Thirdly, they were unfitted for golf because they were incapable of lasting through two rounds of a long course in a day.

Regardless, within a few weeks of the receipt of his letter the LGU was formed and the first British Women's Amateur Championship completed at St Anne's. Lady Margaret Scott, aged 18, won, and did so again twice. Contrary to Hutchinson's expectations, Lady Margaret could not only propel the gutty ball close to 150 yards, despite the long skirts she wore, but also excite the admiration of seasoned male pros at the graceful way in which she did so.

Her third win was followed by the first women's international, in which England beat Ireland. This match might have afforded Hutchinson minor consolation, since several hurry-ups had to be issued to players by the secretary, Issette Pearson, to get to the tee on time, a happening which may have been connected with a dance that lasted deep into the previous night.

Ninety-five years later, in November 1990, the Solheim Cup match between the US and Europe at Lake Nona, in Florida, the inaugural US vs. Europe professional international, demonstrated that the women's game was entering its most sophisticated era. The trophy is named after Karsten Solheim, the engineer who built a club-making empire, most famously with his distinctive Ping putter.

The US won it 11–4, with one match halved, but fears that this was to become another one-sided series like the Walker Cup were dispelled by Europe's 10–5 victory, with three matches halved, at Dalmahoy in Scotland in 1992.

The Cup had speedily become a compelling contest. There was some hand-wringing over the fact that Dalmahoy had received such poor media coverage, particularly on television, but it was clear to officials that the fixture would be a money-making event which would prove a magnet to the media in the future, and to sponsors.

So it proved in 1994 when the Greenbrier, in Virginia, provided a second US victory, 13–7, watched by enormous galleries in stark contrast to the meagre admissions achieved by the first Cup match. Big galleries followed the 1996 event too. The Americans, led by Judy Rankin, achieved the first away Cup win, at St Pierre in Wales, and went 3–1 ahead in the series by a score of 17–11, a huge margin considering that Europe led 9–7 on the final morning. US Open champion Annika Sorenstam was Europe's only undefeated player.

International competition

Persistent is an inadequate term to describe America's pioneer of international team golf for women, Margaret Curtis. The game was in her blood, and that of her sister, Harriot: they were nieces of Lawrence Curtis, who had much to do with the formation of The Country Club at Brookline, Massachusetts, was present at the meeting that formed the USGA in 1894, and became the second USGA president.

Margaret, a woman of energy, compassion and considerable organizing skill, was engaged before the First World War in social service and relief work. During the war, and for six years afterwards, she worked in France for refugees under the banner of the Red Cross.

The idea of a US vs. GB match had been born, in the mind of the British LGU secretary, Issette Pearson, as early as 1898. The visits of Margaret, Harriot and several other prominent US women golfers to British events in 1905 and 1907 (the year when Margaret beat Harriot in the US Amateur final) brought the first international closer, but the 1909 offer from the USGA of a cup for such a match was not taken up by the LGU. Nor were two unofficial matches followed up : in 1907 England beat America 6–1, and in 1911 Britain won 7–2 against "American and Colonial".

Financial considerations defeated initiatives for an international series in the 1920s. A guarantee of $5,000 per match by Margaret Curtis in 1928, and a third unofficial match in 1930 were not in themselves enough to start the transatlantic golf ball rolling, but perhaps they gave officialdom the necessary nudge ... for in 1931, the year of the first official women's international (between Britain and France for the Vagliano Cup), the LGU and USGA agreed to biennial matches. The idea was to involve France – all comers if possible – but that option was never adopted.

Fifteen thousand turned up on May 21, 1932, at Wentworth, southwest of London, to see the American tourists, who were led by Marion Hollins and included the outstanding US golfer of the era, Glenna Collett Vare. She and Opal Hill beat the British captain, Joyce Wethered, and Wanda Morgan in foursomes, all of which the US won.

Wethered beat Collett Vare 6 and 4 in singles, but despite further victories by Enid Wilson over Helen Hicks and Diana Fishwick over Maureen Orcutt the Curtis Cup, a silver Revere bowl donated by the Curtis family, went back to the US, by 5–3, with one match halved. The cup is inscribed with the hope that it would stimulate friendly rivalry between the golfers of many lands, but it has remained a two-sided event from that day in May, 1932.

Collett Vare captained a successful defence at Chevy Chase in 1934, and the whole match was halved four years later, thanks to a huge putt by Jessie Valentine on her debut for Britain and Ireland.

SISTERS ARE DOING IT FOR THEMSELVES *Harriot Curtis – a doughty golf pioneer*

REVENGE IS SWEET *Laura Davies and her fellow 1994 Solheim Cup winners*

The US kept defeat at bay until 1952 at Muirfield, where Elizabeth Price, a diabetes sufferer, took the deciding match. Her opponent, Grace DeMoss, unaccountably lost all semblance of form at the 14th, after she had hit straight down the middle and seemed sure to win as Price ran into bunker trouble. Instead DeMoss was racked by an attack of the sockets, repeatedly catching her ball with the bottom of the shaft instead of the blade. She took six to reach the green. Price took full advantage, winning the next also and putting stone dead at the 16th to complete a 5–4 win for her team.

Polly Riley was the inspiration of the US team that wrested back the Cup at Merion, Pennsylvania, two years later. Then Britain and Ireland managed a four-year tenure of the Cup by winning 5–4 at Prince's in Kent in 1956 and halving the 1958 event at Brae Burn, Massachusetts, Frances Smith beating Polly Riley at the penultimate hole to tie the match. No visiting team, amateur or professional, had done so well in America.

There followed 26 years of US domination, the longest one-sided run yet, but suggestions that European players should be brought in to redress the balance have fallen on stony ground, certainly as far as the Americans are concerned. A resounding 13–5 victory by the Great Britain and Ireland side so meticulously prepared for the Cup match of 1986 by their captain, Diane Bailey, put an end to the run of 13 US victories. The win, achieved at Prairie Dunes, Kansas, was another first against the US, who in more than 60 years had never lost a home match to a visiting international side, male or female, pro or amateur.

ALL SMILES *Betty Jameson shows off the US Amateur trophy*

Bailey completed an unprecedented double by leading Britain and Ireland to another win at Royal St George's in 1988, but the US replied in some style in 1990 with a 14–4 trouncing at Somerset Hills, New Jersey. After this Vickie Goetze, the 1989 Amateur champion, summed up the appeal of the Curtis Cup with her remark that she had never been so nervous as when standing on the first tee with her partner Anne Sander at the start of play ...and it wasn't even her tee shot.

Caroline Hall's fine four iron to the last hole of the last match at Royal Liverpool against Goetze was the key for the 1992 repatriation of the Cup for Britain and Ireland, who brought the Cup back with them in 1994 thanks to a tied match at Ooltewah, Chattanooga, Tennessee, with Janice Moodie providing the last hole heroics.

Another US defeat – still only the sixth against 20 wins – followed in 1996 at Killarney. Julie Hall, twice British Champion, made her last appearance. She played in five Cup matches and was only once on the losing side – yet she failed to win a point this time. Scotland's Alison Rose got all four, and had the honour of hitting the Cup-winning stroke. Part of the US strength in the 1960s and 1970s derived, according to Anne Sander, from the long service and hence experience of such players as herself and JoAnne Gunderson. Moreover, US losses to the professional game were relatively small in those years.

The sea change that has come over the Curtis series since the mid-1980s, with the US holding the Cup for only two years in a decade, suggests that American losses to the LPGA are becoming heavier. Consider these five golfers who played only one Curtis Cup match apiece, and who have earned more than $15 million between them as LPGA members: Patty Sheehan, leading the way with more than $5 million, Dottie Pepper, Brandie Burton, Juli Inkster and Danielle Ammaccapane.

Stars of the US Tour

Men pros had long since outclassed the amateurs when American women were struggling to set up a professional circuit in the late 1940s. In the women's game, the amateurs were not only dominant, but fashionable, indeed glamorous. The "bewitching blonde" Edith Cummings, winner of the 1923 Amateur, was reputed to be the model for one of F. Scott Fitzgerald's beautiful high-society women in his novel *The Great Gatsby*. Another lissome blonde golfer, Betty Jameson, took the Amateur in 1939 and 1940, and won the Western Open both as an amateur and as a pro. She was the first to break 300 for 72 holes in any tournament, her 295 taking the 1947 US

US Women's Open Results

Year	Winner	Year	Winner
1946	Patty Berg	1971	JoAnne Carner
1947	Betty Jameson	1972	Susie Berning
1948	Babe Zaharias	1973	Susie Berning
1949	Louise Suggs	1974	Sandra Haynie
1950	Babe Zaharias	1975	Sandra Palmer
1951	Betsy Rawls	1976	JoAnne Carner
1952	Louise Suggs	1977	Hollis Stacy
1953	Betsy Rawls	1978	Hollis Stacy
1954	Babe Zaharias	1979	Jerilyn Britz
1955	Fay Crocker	1980	Amy Alcott
1956	Kathy Cornelius	1981	Pat Bradley
1957	Betsy Rawls	1982	Janet Anderson
1958	Mickey Wright	1983	Jan Stephenson
1959	Mickey Wright	1984	Hollis Stacy
1960	Betsy Rawls	1985	Kathy Baker
1961	Mickey Wright	1986	Jane Geddes
1962	Murle Breer	1987	Laura Davies
1963	Mary Mills	1988	Liselotte Neumann
1964	Mickey Wright	1989	Betsy King
1965	Carol Mann	1990	Betsy King
1966	Sandra Spuzich	1991	Meg Mallon
1967	Catherine LaCoste (Amat.)	1992	Patty Sheehan
1968	Susie Berning	1993	Lauri Merten
1969	Donna Caponi	1994	Patty Sheehan
1970	Donna Caponi	1995	Annika Sorenstam
		1996	Annika Sorenstam

SOLHEIM STALWART *Dottie Pepper was a key figure in the 1994 and 1996 United States Solheim Cup triumphs*

RECORD SHATTERING DEBUT *Nancy Lopez standing over a putt in 1978*

TOUR TREASURE *Babe Zaharias was a central figure in the LPGA's success*

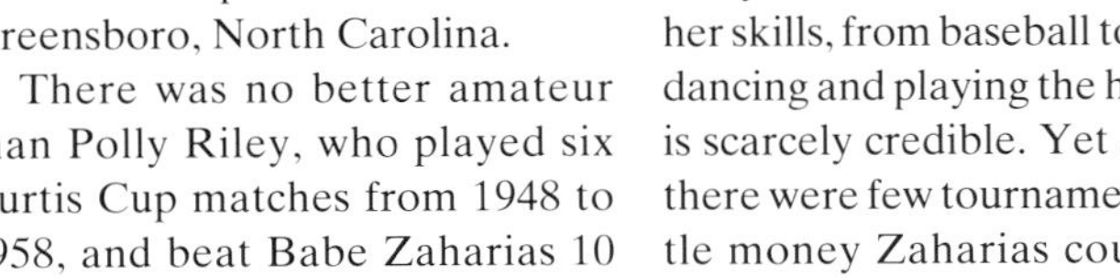

Women's Open at Starmount, Greensboro, North Carolina.

There was no better amateur than Polly Riley, who played six Curtis Cup matches from 1948 to 1958, and beat Babe Zaharias 10 and 9 in the 36-hole final of the 1948 Texas Open. When the LPGA got started in 1950 after the fade-out of the WPGA, Riley won their first tournament, the Tampa Open.

All the same, Zaharias was the glittering star of the early years of the LPGA. The tour, with such players as Patty Berg to back her up, would doubtless have become prosperous without her, eventually, but she was the catalyst to its more rapid development.

Fame followed Zaharias around, starting from her two 1932 Olympic gold medals and one silver in athletics (as Mildred Didrickson before her marriage to George Zaharias). At 16, she could reputedly drive a golf ball more than 250 yards, but she did not take the game at all seriously until she was 23. The range of her skills, from baseball to ballroom dancing and playing the harmonica, is scarcely credible. Yet as a golfer there were few tournaments and little money Zaharias could try for after she had been reported for breaking the amateur status rules and designated a pro by the USGA, a decision which Jack Burke termed "the dirtiest deal I've heard of in a long time".

Her strength was her strength, and after taking a raft of amateur titles when her status was restored, Zaharias turned pro again (voluntarily, upon accepting an offer of $300,000 to make golf films), and proceeded to outhit every rival.

She is also reputed to have commanded bigger fees than Ben Hogan in exhibition matches. Her appearance in LPGA events was a guarantee of public interest.

She tended to be a prima donna, using her fame to get her own way, which irritated rivals, but they had much to thank her for as sponsors, especially makers of products that interested women, recognized the attractions of women's golf. At the same time the emerging talents of Louise Suggs, Betsy Rawls and Peggy Kirk enlivened competition. A decade after that amateur victory by Polly Riley in the LPGA's first event, the tour prize money was $200,000, and events numbered 26.

The supreme stylist Mickey Wright, then Nancy Lopez, were the next dominating figures.

Though Kathy Whitworth achieved a career record of 88 tournament wins between 1959 and 1991, the immediate and lasting impact of Lopez had a publicity value second only perhaps to that of Zaharias. Lopez, second in the Open as an amateur, took nine events in 1978, her first full year on the Tour, including five in a row. This galvanized the golfing public, sent gate receipts soaring, and earned for Lopez simultaneous Rookie of the Year and Player of the Year awards.

The professional women's set of majors has varied over the years with the nature of sponsorship. There have not always been four. Two players have managed a seasonal sweep of the available majors, Zaharias with the three available in 1950 (US Open, Titleholders and Western Open), Sandra Haynie with the two on offer in 1974, the US Open and LPGA title.

Pat Bradley came closest to the current feminine version of Bobby Jones's Impregnable Quadrilateral. She won the 1986 LPGA title, the du Maurier Classic, and the Nabisco Dinah Shore, but finished third in the Open to Jane Geddes. Bradley, a former skiing instructor, has constructed an LPGA record of marvellous consistency, with over $5 million in official prize money. She has 13 times finished in the top ten money-winners, and was No. 1 in 1986 and again, with $763,118, in 1991. Not surprisingly, in that year

AYATO OKAMOTO *From Hiroshima, she has won 17 times on the LPGA tour, earning over $2.7 million*

she was also leader in three other categories, achieving 21 top ten finishes in 26 starts, the best scoring average and 314 birdies.

Patty Sheehan, the first double Open winner in 1992, with the US title at Oakmont, Pennsylvania, and the British at Woburn, has managed to reach six figures in prize money annually since 1981.

The late Dinah Shore added to her fame as a singer by becoming the Bing Crosby, so to speak, of women's professional golf. Her tournament, richly sponsored by Colgate, who also owned the Ram golf company, began in 1972 at Palm Springs, California, and attracted plenty of Shore's Hollywood and music-business friends, in the tradition of Crosby's celebrity "Clambake" event on the Monterey courses. Like the Masters, this major is always played at the same venue, Mission Hills in California, at which the 1991 winner Amy Alcott jumped into the lake with Dinah.

The success of Chako Higuchi, an LPGA champion, and Ayako Okamoto, 1987 Player of the Year, gained the attention of Japanese sponsors: these and other supporters swelled average tournament purses from $30,000 in the early 1970s until it was nudging $700,000 in 1997 when total purse offered by the LPGA reached $30 million.

The Tour has unearthed heart-warming stories of struggles against ill fortune, none more remarkable than that of Martha Nause. She won the LPGA title in 1994 by a shot in Ottawa, with four birdies in the last seven holes to beat her playing partner Michelle Gann by a stroke. Nause, 39, from Wisconsin, had just spent a year recovering from an infection causing nerve damage in her ear, destroying her sense of balance. "I had to hold on to things to walk. I couldn't drive a car at all," Nause explained.

Her doctor said she should consider never playing again. Nause's feeling was that she had everything needed to be a winner, and proved it. Betsy King, who had lost the two-stroke lead she held when the final round started, no doubt admired Nause's feat, but must have breathed a sigh at her own joint fourth place, because she needed only one more win to enter the LPGA Hall of Fame, 30 being the required figure. This she achieved in 1995.

The European tour

European women began breaking into the rich, charmed circle of the US Tour. Laura Davies, Annika Sorenstam (in 1995), and Liselotte Neumann all became US Open champions within a decade and in 1996 they looked down on the rest of the world from the head of the Ping Rankings. Davies, LPGA Player of the Year in 1996, scored a first in 1996 by competing creditably in a Queensland skins game against Tom Watson, Peter Senior and John Daly – out-hitting the first two on occasion.

The European women's tour was a good deal slower achieving rich and piping times than the American. Total prize money, nearly £3 million ($4.5 million) is still only about one-eighth of the US figure. The first British Women's Open in 1972, won by Jenny Lee Smith, now a golf-gear entrepreneur, post-dated the American version by a quarter century. It was not played at all in 1983, for lack of a sponsor. Since 1987 it has been safe-guarded under the banner of Weetabix.

Sponsorship has generally been hard to come by from the inception of the European tour, when prize money totalled £80,000. Cathy Lewis, the first winner of the tour's inaugural Order of Merit, earned £2,494.50. These relatively meagre pickings did not suggest to the best amateurs that turning pro would make their fortunes. Early standards of play were patchy, and helped depress the number of tournaments from an initial 18 to 10 in 1982.

Prize-money climbed back to £2.2 million ($3,410,000) in 1995, when the Tour visited 14 countries, staging 18 events. In 1996 the schedule of events grew to 22. Other signs of prosperity were Amex "headline" sponsorship, the need for a qualifying school, and live coverage of the 1996 Solheim Cup – on both sides of the Atlantic.

British Women's Open

Year	Winner
1976	Jenny Lee Smith
1977	Vivien Saunders
1978	Janet Melville
1979	Alison Sheard
1980	Debbie Massey
1981	Debbie Massey
1982	Marta Figueras-Dotti
1983	*NO COMPETITION*
1984	Ayako Okamoto
1985	Betsy King
1986	Laura Davies
1987	Alison Nicholas
1988	Corinne Dibnah
1989	Janet Geddes
1990	Helen Alfredsson
1991	Penny Grice-Whittaker
1992	Patty Sheehan
1993	Karen Lunn
1994	Liselotte Neumann
1995	Karrie Webb
1996	Emilee Klein

WORLDWIDE WINNER *Liselotte Neumann, showing off the British Open trophy at Woburn in 1994, earned richly on the US, European and Asian tours*

US PGA TOUR

Now the powerhouse of world golf, the American PGA Tour in its early, cash-strapped, play-it-by-ear days had need of the spirit of the frontiersman. There were huge distances to cover, usually by automobile, cheap lodgings to find if prize money had been elusive of late, and even if it hadn't in most cases. Tournaments were loosely organized (golfers who got there first teed off first), and players had to have other sources of income because prize money was short, and the available cash did not go far down the list of also-rans.

Since the tour began as a winter event in Florida, Texas and other southern states, the players could combine playing for prize money with a club job in the north during the months when play was difficult or impossible, and custom at professional shops correspondingly light. The tournaments, often at tourist resorts, were usually sponsored by the local chamber of commerce, for the results would be reported in the great cities of the north-eastern seaboard and middle west, giving publicity at a reasonable rate to the fact that where the golfers were, there the sun was. Chilly northerners were made well aware of the best places to take vacations.

There was, if your imagination is allowed to run riot for a moment, a touch of the western gambler/gunslinger about the early tour pro, travelling from town to town chancing his luck. Wild Bill Mehlhorn, whose father had left Germany rather than join the ranks of Kaiser Wilhelm's army, kept dollars in his pocket by giving lessons *en route* to the winter tour, and selling magazine subscriptions.

There is a restless streak in many Americans; many are forever ready to up sticks and seek a new job in the next state, or the next but one time zone.

Besides, the living from a pro's shop was not all that magnificent. Ability to teach the game was not always accompanied by marketing skills, which were the forte of the suppliers of golf clubs, clothing and the like. These middlemen made it a hard life for many club pros, and clubs were wont to command profits on ball sales, the pro's main stock-in-trade.

Hence the establishment in 1916 of the US Professional Golfers Association, which was and is basically an organization to protect the interests of the club pro. This was to be a certain source of friction when tour players grew away from their shop counters and club-repairing, became "names" and wanted privileges the PGA would not grant, of which more later.

A good many British prejudices still ruled in America, inimical to professional golf, for the amateur was still king, and the paid man looked down upon. Pros in England commanded a good deal more respect (but not yet entrée to club-

WILD BILL MEHLHORN *Nicknamed for his brilliant scoring bursts, not for his temper, he was a Tour pioneer who often finished high in the US Open*

houses) thanks perhaps to the mighty reputations, in technique and competitive drive, of players such as Harry Vardon and J. H. Taylor, first and second in the 1900 US Open, and the excitements of watching money matches. What a treat for the Scottish islanders of Islay to watch Vardon and Taylor vs. James Braid and Alex Herd in an international four-ball on the newly consecrated Machrie course.

Tournament life took a different route in the United States. The PGA gave the pros a peg to hang their season on (Open Championship apart) with the US PGA Championship, for which the first (1916) winner, Jim Barnes, received $500 – about what Vardon would get in a big money challenge match in the old country. The US PGA and Open were far from becoming the central events in a well-ordered tour, the growth of which began haphazardly in the Sunbelt of the south immediately around the turn of the century, with prize money reaching three figures in Florida resorts. No detailed chronology exists of how it began, except to say that winter tournaments in California, Texas and Florida in the early 1920s were crucial elements.

Amateur events were held at the resorts long before the First World War, and pro events grew up alongside, usually with less notice being taken of them by the Press.

The power of the pro

What the pro game needed was a hero. Amateurs in particular and US golf in general certainly found a hero at the 1913 Open in Francis Ouimet. Walter Hagen almost achieved that status in the same championship, but fell just short of the epoch-making play-off in which Ouimet beat Ted Ray Vardon and. Such was his confidence that he might well have surprised all three; 12

MIGHTY HITTER *"Long" Jim Barnes left his native Cornwall to win the 1921 US Open by 9 shots*

months later Hagen *was* Open champion, and became leader in the considerable task of transforming the golf pro into an envied, though not always prosperous – or admired – but not always respected, pillar of society.

There is little difference between Hagen's role and that of the touring pro of today, except that he depended less on prize money (there wasn't much, and he sometimes gave it away) and more on exhibition matches. He played such a match rather than defend his first US PGA title, and attracted thousands of spectators to hundreds of his one-day appearances at a dollar or so admission when a dollar was a dollar. He had the happy knack of being able not only to impress the galleries with his golf but to entertain them with a line of chat that would have ensured success as a stand-up comedian.

This stroll-around comedian created his own lucrative theatre of the open air, aided by players such as Gene Sarazen, just out of his teens and winner of the Open and US PGA titles in 1922. This was the US PGA Hagen had passed up to play in an exhibition, so another exhibition, a challenge match between the pair, was set up, expansively billed as being for the Golf Championship of the World: hype is a new word, but not a new phenomenon.

Sarazen, two down after the first two rounds at Oakmont, Pennsylvania, was in pain before the final holes at the palatial Westchester-Biltmore Country Club in New York. In wind and rain Sarazen struggled on, overtook Hagen, and next day had an emergency operation to have his appendix removed. His prize was $2,000, Hagen's $1,000: win-

"FATHER OF THE PGA TOUR" *Bob Harlow (extreme left) with members of the losing 1929 Ryder Cup US team.*

ning the US Open was not worth $1,000 until 1929.

One rock upon which the PGA Tour was founded was the Texas Open, founded in 1923 by businessmen in San Antonio. The total purse was a record at $5,000. Another Tour foundation stone was laid three years later by the Los Angeles Junior Chamber of Commerce: this one worth $10,000. A year later other Californian cities organized pro events. The tour was now getting into some kind of order, the players starting in the west early in the New Year, moving east to Texas and Florida, then up the east coast to spring and summer events.

Total prize money of $77,000 was available in 1928. This supported a growing band of men who depended almost entirely on their playing, rather than pro-shopkeeping, skills. Walter Hagen was no longer the one and only touring pro. But of central organization was there none, until a succession of newspapermen, who had every reason to want the tour to expand, took a hand. Of these the most influential was Bob Harlow, son of a Congregationalist minister. Unsurprisingly, he was also Hagen's manager.

No man has a better claim than Harlow to be the chief begetter of the PGA Tour, though his main difficulty was ... the PGA. Like those before him who had tried to bring order to the tour, he wanted to supplement his income from newspaper articles, and as agent for Hagen and other leading players, with a salary or commission for putting tournaments together and persuading sponsors to part with cash.

He at length got a $100 a week salary, but in 1932 was sacked by the PGA, some of whose officials looked upon touring pros as a pampered, footloose gang of opportunists, who unjustly commanded too many choice club pro jobs on the basis of their playing prowess. Ostensibly he was dismissed because he was spending too much time on his extra-tour activities.

Maybe, but it was Harlow who rationalized the tour with a showman's flair. He used every contemporary method of advertising to publicize tournaments, issued lists of tournament pairings and tee-times (no first come first served with Harlow), got golf gear makers to buoy up prize money when local sponsors were short of promotional dollars, issued orders of merit, encouraged club volunteers to help in running tournaments (they still do), and in his first year almost doubled the tour purses.

When the PGA re-employed Harlow in 1933, the economy had become chronically sick, yet he invented the minimum purse and worked out a system by which the best players were exempted from qualifying. Already the players, avid for more cash and freedom from the PGA and its club-pro fixation, were looking at ways to set up a rival organizational shop of their own.

Another journalist, Fred Corcoran, was next to ride the tour tiger, beginning in 1936 at $5,000 a year ... golf had moved on quite a way. A born publicist, he improved information services for the public, with coloured scoreboards, and brought a greater range of sponsors, including financial firms and airlines, into play.

The final rift between the PGA and the players widened to involve threats of boycott in the 1960s. Though the sums pocketed by the leading performer on Tour had declined radically at times in the depressed 1930s, better times, looser corporate purse-strings and the sheer quality of pros such as Ben Hogan, Sam Snead and Byron Nelson made life easier for tour managers as peace broke out in 1945. The advent of the greatest crowd pleaser since Hagen, Arnold Palmer, taken together with the advent of televised golf, changed many things. Television started with local coverage of the 1947 US Open at St Louis, Missouri, and soon progressed, under the influence of George S. May, promoter of the Tam O'Shanter National (*sic*) Open in Chicago to national coverage.

The Midas touch

May's tournament in particular and golf in general had a golden stroke of luck in 1953. May was not present when ABC television offered national coverage for $32,000. Chet Posson, May's assistant, took a chance and accepted. May, a management consultant in a big way of business, said when he heard what Posson had done: "I don't care if it costs us a million. Do it!"

So more people – an estimated two million – saw the Tam O'Shanter of 1953 than had witnessed any previous event in golf history: lo and behold, Lew Worsham won it with a 135-yard wedge approach shot to the final green. It went in ... an eagle two. In a flash Chandler Harper, who had finished and must have counted the $25,000 first prize as good as in his bank account, had lost by a stroke. Worsham's shot, which also brought him a contract for 25 exhibitions at $1,000 each, is said to have caused early television couch potatoes to fall off their couches.

Television gave golf the Midas touch. It enabled prize money to double in 10 years from $6.7 million in 1970. In 1995, the tour purse reached $62.25 million. Sponsors could now use golf to hit consumers right across the nation. Golf's top man (Palmer) in 1963 took $128,230. The first recorded leading money winner, Paul Runyan in 1934, had earned $6,767.

The leading post-war players would soon be thinking airplane instead of automobile. The younger ones, many of them not long out of college, had no knowledge of mending clubs and selling chocolate bars across the counter. Once television rights began to swell, tour pros could not see why the PGA should get much of what their skill alone, as they saw it, was channelling into the prize pot.

GOLF'S GIFT TO TV *Lew Worsham (second left) astounded viewers with his eagle in the 1953 Tam O'Shanter event*

Boycott threats by the touring pros in 1967 were followed by an overt move for independence ... an announcement that the breakaway American Professional Golfers had a $3.5 million tour programme for 1969. In this particular poker game the PGA held two pairs, the touring pros held a royal flush, and a gun to the head of the PGA. Without the leading players, which now included Jack Nicklaus, a prime mover in the negotiations with Gardner Dickinson, television and sponsors didn't fancy PGA golf at all: only Sam Snead stuck by the old regime.

So the players became free men, their Magna Carta granted unconditionally under what was no more than a convenient fiction, the creation of a new PGA division. Harlow would have enjoyed living at this hour, but he died in 1954, still married to his golf reporting career. He would have been totally at ease with the fact that golf is the only sport whose professionals run their own events. In recent years the PGA Tour players have even built their own courses. Needless to say, no other professional group in the world of sport owns the bricks and mortar, so to speak.

Next comes the 1998 opening of their world golf village, close to PGA headquarters, in Florida, near Jacksonville. A world golf museum, with a wide-ranging and unifying Hall of Fame concept with separate areas for PGA and LPGA, stands alongside a 300-seat theatre, conference centre, a major hotel, and 54 holes of golf – not to mention thousands of homes, the last word in shopping malls, a spa, and a Mayo Clinic facility. The PGA is not going to be left behind by the LPGA down the coast. A World Golf Library will emphasise an educational, not to say missionary zeal.

There is no "them" (the bosses) and "us" (the players) about golf, a schism which has of late been so costly to baseball, even to the extent of the loss of the 1994 World Series. Moreover, hockey players were off the ice for half the 1994–95 season.

There was a lasting bitterness between the club pros and tour players after the split. Club-makers MacGregor, it was reported, got requests from club pros to remove Jack Nicklaus's name from their products. They perhaps forgot that Nicklaus, Palmer and Co. have enticed battalions of their fans to buy golf gear in pro shops across the world. A further upsurge in US Tour prosperity coincided with Tiger Woods' arrival and his ambition to bring golf to an even wider public, playing and watching. During his third victory of 1997, the Byron Nelson Classic, which attracted double the previous best ticket sales, Tim Finchem, the Tour Commissioner, had glad news for the new Masters champion and his fellow pros: new TV contracts would help to quadruple revenue in four years, ensuring *average* purses of $3 million.

Leading US Tour money-winners

Year	Winner	($)	Year	Winner	($)
1934	Paul Runyan	6,767	1965	Jack Nicklaus	140,752
1935	Johnny Revolta	9,543	1966	Billy Casper	121,944
1936	Horton Smith	7,682	1967	Jack Nicklaus	188,998
1937	Harry Cooper	14,138	1968	Billy Casper	205,168
1938	Sam Snead	19,534	1969	Frank Beard	164,707
1939	Henry Picard	10,303	1970	Lee Trevino	157,037
1940	Ben Hogan	10,655	1971	Jack Nicklaus	244,490
1941	Ben Hogan	18,358	1972	Jack Nicklaus	320,542
1942	Ben Hogan	13,143	1973	Jack Nicklaus	308,362
1943	*NO STATISTICS COMPILED*		1974	Johnny Miller	353,021
1944	Byron Nelson	*37,967	1975	Jack Nicklaus	298,149
1945	Byron Nelson	*63,335	1976	Jack Nicklaus	266,438
1946	Ben Hogan	42,556	1977	Tom Watson	310,653
1947	Jimmy Demaaret	27,936	1978	Tom Watson	362,428
1948	Ben Hogan	32,112	1979	Tom Watson	462,636
1949	Sam Snead	31,593	1980	Tom Watson	530,808
1950	Sam Snead	35,758	1981	Tom Kite	375,698
1951	Lloyd Mangrum	26,088	1982	Craig Stadler	446,462
1952	Julius Boros	37,032	1983	Hal Sutton	426,668
1953	Lew Worsham	34,002	1984	Tom Watson	476,260
1954	Bob Toski	65,819	1985	Curtis Strange	542,321
1955	Julius Boros	63,121	1986	Greg Norman	653,296
1956	Ted Kroll	72,835	1987	Curtis Strange	925,941
1957	Dick Mayer	65,835	1988	Curtis Strange	1,147,644
1958	Arnold Palmer	42,607	1989	Tom Kite	1,395,278
1959	Art Wall	53,167	1990	Greg Norman	1,165,477
1960	Arnold Palmer	75,262	1991	Corey Pavin	979,430
1961	Gary Player	64,540	1992	Fred Couples	1,344,188
1962	Arnold Palmer	81,448	1993	Nick Price	1,478,557
1963	Arnold Palmer	128,230	1994	Nick Price	1,499,927
1964	Jack Nicklaus	113,284	1995	Greg Norman	1,654,959
			1996	Tom Lehman	1,780,159

* War bonds

EUROPEAN PGA TOUR

Leading European Tour money-winners

Year	Winner	(£)	Year	Winner	(£)
1962	Peter Thomson	5,764	1980	Greg Norman	74,829
1963	Bernard Hunt	7,209	1981	Bernhard Langer	95,991
1964	Neil Coles	7,890	1982	Sandy Lyle	86,141
1965	Peter Thomson	7,011	1983	Nick Faldo	140,761
1966	Bruce Devlin	13,205	1984	Bernhard Langer	160,883
1967	Gay Brewer	20,235	1985	Sandy Lyle	254,711
1968	Gay Brewer	23,107	1986	Seve Ballesteros	259,275
1969	Billy Casper	23,483	1987	Ian Woosnam	439,075
1970	Christy O'Connor	31,532	1988	Seve Ballesteros	502,000
1971	Gary Player	11,281	1989	Ronan Rafferty	465,981
1972	Bob Charles	18,538	1990	Ian Woosnam	737,977
1973	Tony Jacklin	24,839	1991	Seve Ballesteros	790,811
1974	Peter Oosterhuis	32,127	1992	Nick Faldo	1,220,540
1975	Dale Hayes	20,507	1993	Colin Montgomerie	798,145
1976	Seve Ballesteros	39,504	1994	Colin Montgomerie	877,135
1977	Seve Ballesteros	46,436	1995	Colin Montgomerie	1,038,718
1978	Seve Ballesteros	54,348	1996	Colin Montgomerie	875,146
1979	Sandy Lyle	49,233			

Much the same club vs tour pro shenanigans took place on the European Tour, which was not established until the early 1970s, but has grown a great deal more quickly than the pioneering US Tour did.

John Jacobs became Tournament Director-General of the PGA in 1971 – it was renamed the European Tournament Players' Division in 1972 – since when the prize money has soared from £250,000 to more than £19 million. Ken Schofield, current executive director, succeeded Jacobs in 1975, and though his claim that the European Tour matches its US counterpart in depth is scarcely tenable, prize money at high-season European Tour events is at about £700,000. The Labour Government's decision, on assuming power in 1997, to ban tobacco sponsorship of sport in Britain did not greatly threaten professional golf, which had only one such sponsor in their calendar

The extension of the Tour to take in events in Asia and the southern hemisphere is not to the taste of every European Tour member. Events in far-off places provide winter opportunities to earn cash and Ryder qualifying points. Since room must be found for the host tours' members, fewer places are available to European Tour members. Out of the original field of 156 for the South African Open in 1997, almost two-third were non-Europeans.Though the title went to a PGA European Tour member, Fijian Vijay Singh, it did not assuage the feeling among Europeans who could not compete, that those who could gained an advantage in the Volvo rankings.

All of which underlines what kick-started the US Tour in the first place: its own winter venues, facilities Europe does not possess.

FOUR TIMER *Colin Montgomerie was leading money-winner on the European Tour in 1996 for the fourth year in succession*

OTHER PRINCIPAL GOLF EVENTS

Amazingly, not only junior extensions have been grafted on to the organization of the two major tours: even greater success has been achieved by the return of senior players to regular competition in their own tour. Fred Raphael, producer of the popular "Shell's Wonderful World of Golf" series, was mustard keen to make Sam Snead's idea of an old timers' circuit work. Some players were fearful that they would not look good in their (relative) old age. This did not apply to Snead, of whom Raphael said: "He knew he was going to play well." Snead did, and, partnered by Gardner Dickinson, won the inaugural event in 1978.

This celebration of mature talents was made into a smash hit by Roberto de Vicenzo and Julius Boros the following year, when they scored in an event named "Legends of Golf". They beat Art Wall and Tommy Bolt in a spectacular low-scoring six-hole play-off that suggested that old golfers do not fade away; they just get more cunning.

Besides, Arnold Palmer, still the darling of the galleries, reached 50 in 1979, his fourth year without a win on the main tour. A four-event Senior Tour was organized in 1980, and the age limit later dropped to 50, and Senior success was assured. Its practitioners are earning far more money than they ever did on the PGA Tour itself 30 years or more ago. Lee Trevino earned $3.4 million on the regular tour in 20 years, $7.5 million in five years with the Seniors.

Significantly, the great players of the post-war period have cleaned up most prize money on the Senior Tour, their nerve and the security of their technique overcoming the penalties of age. Jack Nicklaus won six times in his first three Senior years, including two US Senior Opens. Trevino won seven events and more than $1 million in his first year. Ray Floyd put one over on young and old with a victory on the regular tour and the Senior in the same season.

Next item on the Senior agenda is a Ryder Cup for the over-50s. It can scarcely fail, for nothing seems to dilute the eagerness of sponsors to involve themselves in the game.

Hence, after a full 10 months of weekly chances to win "official money" in PGA tournaments, plus further cash and glory on offer in the Masters and the US Open, American Tour players and their peers from other tours look forward to an unbroken series of extra earning opportunities reaching all the way to Christmas and beyond.

Some brave spirits, like José-Maria Olazabal of Spain, prefer family pursuits and will not play as the holiday approaches; others head for an international event such as the Kapalua International, Hawaii, and there are specials events for the superstars, such as the Skins Game, and the Grand Slam. Skins are played by four golfers, with prizes available on every hole, which can be won by one of the quartet outscoring the other three. If the hole is halved, the players progress hole by hole, with the eventual prize money increasing hole by hole, until someone does come out on top. Six-figure sums can rest on one hole.

The Grand Slam involves the winners of the four major championships: in 1994 Nick Price won two, the Open and the US PGA, so Greg Norman was invited to Poipu Bay, Hawaii, as an alternate, since he was second only to Price in the Sony Rankings of world golf. Ernie Els (US Open Champion) and Olazabal (Masters Champion) were the other two players. Norman scored 136 for $400,000 and a $5,000 gold Rolex watch, Price 139 for $250,000, Els 143 for $200,000, Olazabal 144 for $150,000.

Sun City, near Johannesburg, was first to dangle a $1 million prize carrot, though the so-called "World Championship" in Jamaica just before Christmas, was not to be sniffed at: prizes totalled $2.5 million. The event was strictly for the successful – winners of specified events through the year, and was terminated in 1995.

Yet another "World" event, Gene Sarazen's World Open, first played at The Legends, Atlanta, Georgia, in November 1994, offers

FOUR MAJORS *(from left) Fuzzy Zoeller, Jack Nicklaus, Arnold Palmer and Tom Watson before the 1985 "Skins"*

GLOBE TROTTERS *Phil Mickelson (known to some as the next Ben Crenshaw) watches as Ernie Els tees off in the 1993 Dunlop Phoenix in Japan*

$2 million in prizes. Els won it in 1994, but the New Zealander Frank Nobilo thoroughly upstaged the South African by finishing top the next two years, a lucrative apprenticeship for his membership of the US PGA Tour beginning in 1997. He soon forced his way into the winner's circle at Greensboro.

Alternatively, lords of the links can jet off to Japan, where the Tour begins with the $1.5 million Sumitomo Visa Taiheiyo Masters, followed by the $2 million Dunlop Phoenix, Japan's richest event. Johnny Miller won it first, in 1974, since when 12 other Americans have triumphed, but only two Japanese – Tommy Nakajima in 1985 and the ruler of the Japanese circuit, Jumbo Osaki, with a record last round of 65 to beat Tom Watson by a stroke in 1994. The Japanese Open has seldom been won by a foreigner. Seve Ballesteros did so twice (1977 and 1978).

Then there are the Australasian and Asian honey-pots to think about. The Australian Open (which Jack Nicklaus has won six times, Gary Player seven) dates back to 1904, but the depression years of the late 1980s hit the Australian circuit harder than most. Prize money recovered by the end of the 1994–95 season to A$6.9 million (about £3.4 million, or $5.2 million).

The South African Open, first played in 1903, is older than that of Canada, Australia or New Zealand. Brothers Sid and Jock Brews had dominated South African golf for many years until Bobby Locke won the Amateur and Open in the space of a few days in 1935. He won the Open eight times more – twice as an amateur – and Gary Player has triumphed on 13 occasions.

Ernie Els and Wayne Westner's domination of the World Cup at Cape Town, in 1996 underlined South Africa's re-emergence into world golf after the long reign of apartheid. The Republic provides regular stops on the European Tour – but then so do Australia, Qatar and Malaysia.

World Match Play Championship Results

Played at Wentworth, Virginia Water, Surrey, England

Year	Winner and Result	
1964	Arnold Palmer bt Neil Coles	2 & 1
1965	Gary Player bt Peter Thomson	3 & 2
1966	Gary Player bt Jack Nicklaus	6 & 4
1967	Arnold Palmer bt Peter Thomson	1 hole
1968	Gary Player bt Bob Charles	1 hole
1969	Bob Charles bt Gene Littler	37th
1970	Jack Nicklaus bt Lee Trevino	2 & 1
1971	Gary Player bt Jack Nicklaus	5 & 4
1972	Tom Weiskopf bt Lee Trevino	4 & 3
1973	Gary Player bt Graham Marsh	40th
1974	Hale Irwin bt Gary Player	3 & 1
1975	Hale Irwin bt Al Geiberger	4 & 2
1976	David Graham bt Hale Irwin	38th
1977	Graham Marsh bt Ray Floyd	5 & 3
1978	Isao Aoki bt Simon Owen	3 & 2
1979	Bill Rogers bt Isao Aoki	1 hole
1980	Greg Norman bt Sandy Lyle	1 hole
1981	Seve Ballesteros bt Ben Crenshaw	1 hole
1982	Seve Ballesteros bt Sandy Lyle	37th
1983	Greg Norman bt Nick Faldo	3 & 2
1984	Seve Ballesteros bt Bernhard Langer	2 & 1
1985	Seve Ballesteros bt Bernhard Langer	6 & 5
1986	Greg Norman bt Sandy Lyle	2 & 1
1987	Ian Woosnam bt Sandy Lyle	1 hole
1988	Sandy Lyle bt Nick Faldo	2 & 1
1989	Nick Faldo bt Ian Woosnam	1 hole
1990	Ian Woosnam bt Mark McNulty	4 & 2
1991	Seve Ballesteros bt Nick Price	3 & 2
1992	Nick Faldo bt Jeff Sluman	8 & 7
1993	Corey Pavin bt Nick Faldo	1 hole
1994	Ernie Els bt Colin Montgomerie	4 & 2
1995	Ernie Els bt Steve Elkington	3 & 1
1996	Ernie Els bt Vijay Singh	3 & 2

GOLF AROUND THE WORLD

Arnold Palmer says: "If we had the ability to look into the future we would see golf as the biggest participation sport in the world without question." A long way to go then, Arnie, since FIFA believes there are more than 200 million soccer players whereas the largest golfing nation, the United States, has less than an eighth as many players. On the other hand, golf has scarcely started yet in China and Russia ...

THE UNITED STATES

Golf's growth in the United States since the immediate post-war years has been approximately eightfold in numbers of players. There were an estimated 3.2 million golfers in the US in 1950, playing on some 5,000 courses. The US National Golf Foundation's 1997 figures are: 24.7 million players on 15,703 courses.

Golf is now available to US golf enthusiasts 24 hours a day thanks to the new television Golf Channel, with which Arnold Palmer is inevita-bly associated. (He remains one of golf's biggest earners, with a finger in a great many commercial pies, including items you might expect, like lawn mower and golf club manufacture, and others that you might not, such as batteries for hearing aids.)

Transmitted from Orlando in Florida, the Golf Channel is getting figures of two million viewers per day, and as more channels take a feed from this cable service, it could reach nine million, and no doubt will at the June–August seasonal peak of interest.

The number of players is, however, not as impressive as it looks at first sight, suggesting as it does that around 10 per cent of Americans are regular golfers. Half the 24.7 million, says the National Golf Foundation, are "recreational golfers" playing between one and seven rounds a year. The "core" golfers, ranging from regular, serious and intense to just plain fanatical, are far less numerous: 80 per cent of the rounds, it is believed, are played by 20 per cent of the players.

This gives a clue as to how America deploys such a depth of playing strength from youth to Ryder Cup level, for that 20 per cent represents a fair number of determined, regular low-handicap players ... and the USGA's handicap system is not a provider of ego-massage or free hand-outs.

Averaging out the cost of a round, from the most exclusive and rarefied clubs to public pay and play courses, gives a figure of about $60. It should be noted that while the US remains a bulwark of free enterprise there are the best part of five thousand more public than private clubs. Here is another of the great strengths of American golf, buttressed as it is by the national golf association's Public Links Championships for men and women.

About one golf ball a year is sold for every one of those 24.7 million players, be they two or two hundred rounds a year players. The price of a golf ball has not increased in real cost over the years, for while the retail price index has been increasing fourfold, a three-ball sleeve has advanced from $3.75 to $8.50.

Ball sales offer a significant exception to economic orthodoxy, for when unemployment is high, sales of this luxury item increase: "At last," many of the jobless must console themselves, "now for a round away from all those weekend crowds."

The average price of a golf club is between $50 and $75, and new equipment tycoons have appeared

MAGNIFICENCE AT MONTEREY *One of golf's greatest holes – the par five 18th at Pebble Beach*

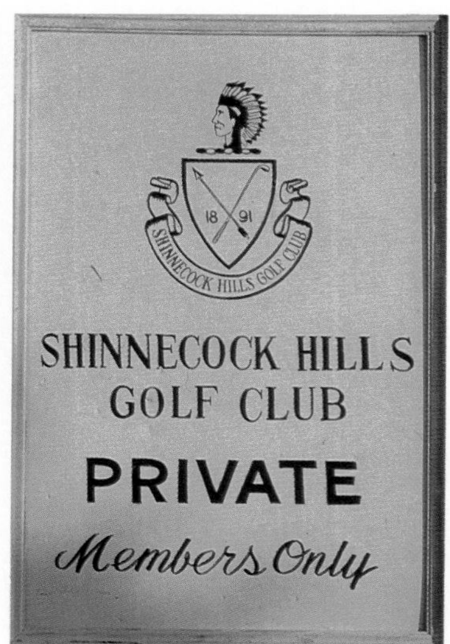

EXCLUSIVE SHINNECOCK *Members only, but US Open host, 1995*

to take large slices of the market once dominated by Spalding and Wilson. Quite apart from Japanese makers, a cobbler turned engineer, Karsten Solheim, still reputedly a shaky 20-handicapper, has built from his Arizona base a club business with his Ping designs which has placed him among the 400 richest men in the US.

After Solheim rang the bell with a Ping, the latest big hit (literally) on the scene has been made by another career-switcher, this time Ely Callaway, formerly prominent in the textile and wine business. His "big is beautiful" philosophy of club-making has rocketed his company into the top 10 of club-makers world-wide.

An apple for the teacher with the best credentials in recent years, David Leadbetter, will not do, for his advice and coaching cost upwards of $300 a session, and a few days' tuition (conservative estimate only) 10 times as much at a fashionable (sunny) resort in Florida, the Carolinas or the rest of the Sunbelt.

The hotter the better for the caddie cart rental business, for one busy resort club can make a million dollars on rentals in a year. The concept appears to be no older than 1930: Curtis Willock, came up with it at Pasadena, California. He was chairman of the Greens Committee at Annandale GC, and he had a wooden leg. Ben Delanty, manager of Pasadena Power Department, made a three-wheel vehicle, each wheel driven by a battery-powered electric motor.

No developments appeared over the next 18 years until the first patent "Arthritis Special" from R. J. Jackson, a Texas oil man, with a cart developed from a three-wheel vehicle built to take spare parts to aircraft on airfields. "Smokey and smelly" was the reaction to the early petrol-engined caddie carts.

Not until improved batteries were available did the caddie cart come into great public favour. They became more and more fashionable, thanks especially to the influence of cart-drivers such as President Eisenhower, Bing Crosby and Bob Hope, whose preference was for a vehicle equipped with a long nose, ski-jump shaped like his own: a million carts were touring US courses by the mid-1990s.

For about $15,000 (a little under £10,000), the golfer in search of total style on wheels can purchase one of the carts made by the Classic Golf Car Company of Princeton, Minnesota. Each is hand built to the style of classic US roadsters of the early 1930s, and exudes not a little of the aura of *The Great Gatsby*.

Caddie carts as prizes in amateur events in California elicited the attention of the USGA Amateur Status Committee. Unlimited use was, they held, a violation and would involve the prize-winner being declared a professional because the cart would be worth more than the amateur prize limit of the day. It would be acceptable if no legal possession of the cart were involved. A compromise was reached: the lucky winner could use the cart only 17 times.

A game slow to start

All this prosperity and the development of a professional circuit paying telephone numbers in prize money had started fitfully and taken something like a century and a half to show much acceleration. A colonial governor named William Burns, who died in 1729, had nine "gouffe" clubs. One was an iron, the estimated value of which was two pounds, worth a small fortune now.

The first mention of golf in American literature was by a Dr Benjamin Rush, in his *Sermons to Gentlemen upon Temperance and Exercise*. It is known that not all golfers are devotees of Temperance, but Rush's recommendation of golf as a healthy pursuit cannot be faulted: it comes as no surprise to discover that Dr Rush studied medicine at Edinburgh.

The first golf club in North America was almost certainly in South Carolina in 1786, and, like the club at Savannah, Georgia, it followed the Scottish pattern of having a social side to club affairs: that is known from advertisements of the time. Although the Carolina club faded from view before the turn of the century – Savannah did not – at about the time of hostilities between Britain and the new United States. Yet there must have been lively interest in 1743, the date of documents relating to the import of 96 clubs and 432 balls from Leith to Charleston, South Carolina, which would have meant no less than £54 for the balls alone, a tidy sum then.

In New York, Maryland, Virginia and Georgia hesitant starts were made on the game, but all came to very little until the last decade of the nineteenth century, despite the efforts of American golf's most steadfast and undeflectable pioneer.

Charles Blair Macdonald, who was to be America's first amateur champion, was only 16 years old when he crossed the Atlantic in 1872 aboard the last of the old side-

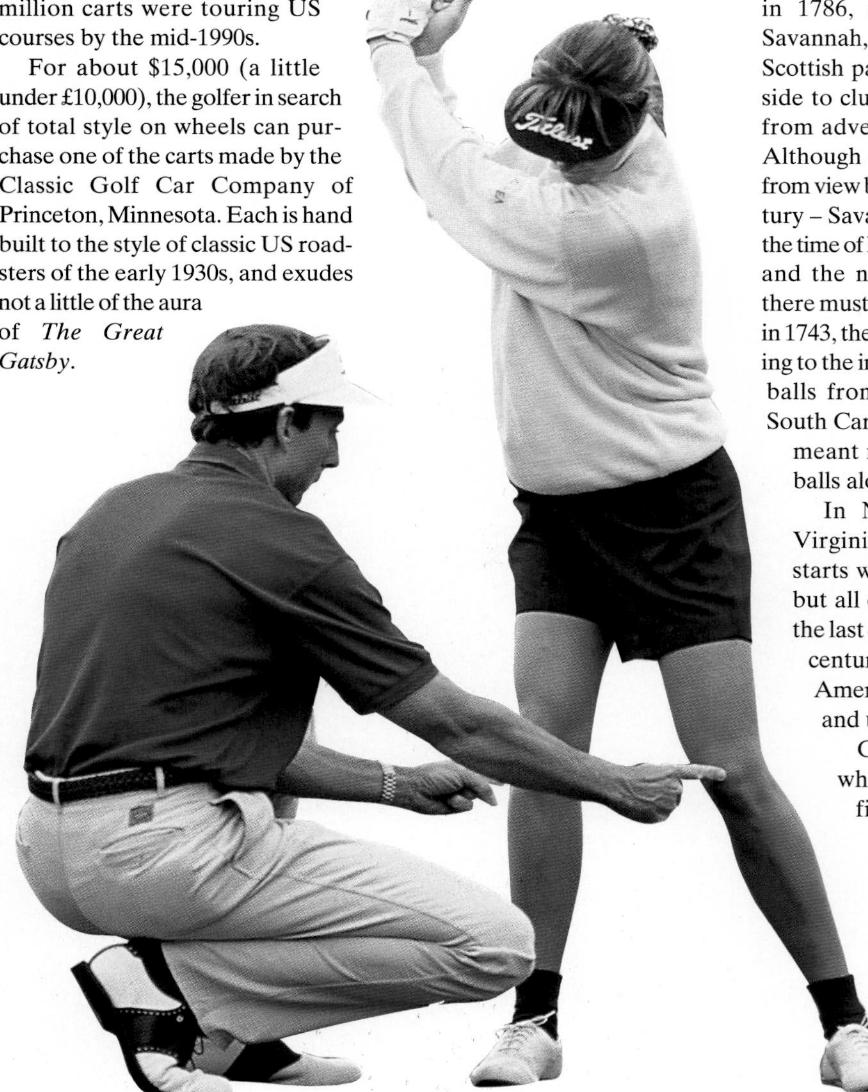
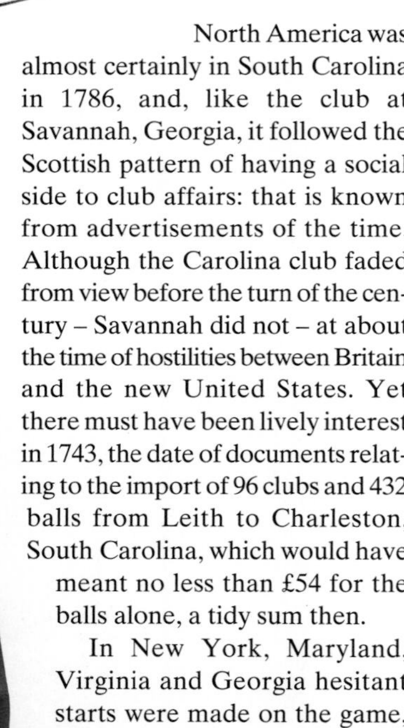

COSTLY GURU *David Leadbetter with pointers about posture*

wheel steamers to make the trip, the Cunard Line's *Scotia*. The voyage, undertaken because he was to continue his education at St Andrews University, took nine days to Queenstown (now Cóbh) in Ireland, whence Macdonald went on to visit the Blarney Stone. Kissing it cannot greatly have improved his powers of persuasion, to judge from his subsequent brushes with authority.

He went on to Musselburgh, just east of Edinburgh in Scotland, to stay with the mother of an old family friend. Here Macdonald first came into contact with golf. It was the heyday of the Scottish professionals. He watched them and the (amateur) red coats and the "leisurely loungers" on Musselburgh Common.

Young Tom Morris had not long ago won his fourth Open title, but golf seemed "tiddle-de-winks" to Macdonald, who thought it a slow, stupid game for old men; he had never come into contact with a sport that was not strenuous or violent before. Once Macdonald touched the golf game, however, he was lost, greatly attracted by its code of honour, and the discipline of "play it as it lies".

His grandfather took him to see Old Tom, who sold him clubs and provided a locker in his shop – no juniors were allowed in the R&A Clubhouse. St Andrews had few tourists, but plenty of golfers and not a few intellectuals, including John Stuart Mill, Thomas Carlyle, Charles Kingsley and Anthony Trollope.

Macdonald watched or played with many of the leading golfers of this golden age, though he did not follow Old Tom's example of bathing in East Bay's chilly waters. Macdonald and two other amateurs had the privilege of discovering that their best ball did not prevail against Young Tom's skill. So back to Chicago Macdonald went, filled with zeal. He set out a rudimentary course back home: the holes were cans left behind by the soldiers at Camp Douglas. He ran into a brick wall of indifference in a city ruined by market crash and fire. These were hard times; the news of Young Tom's death at the end of 1875 had scarcely improved Macdonald's spirits.

THEY LIKED IKE *Former US President Dwight Eisenhower at Wentworth, 1962: he played "fairly well"*

The World's Fair of 1893 in Chicago and the enterprise of two Scots from the industrious town of Dunfermline, close to the Firth of Forth, succeeded where Macdonald had failed. One of his greatest friends suddenly changed his mind after years of indifference to the game after the Fair had brought a number of young English businessmen, who were golfers, into town.

One of the Dunfermline pair, John Reid, was a leader among six citizens of Yonkers, New York, who in 1888 set up the St Andrew's Golf Club. These were the days of endless labour for low wages, and precious little opportunity for most folk for exercise or enjoyment. Racing, boxing and baseball were on the rise, cycling too, but for the generality active sport was not an option. It was badly needed, and in fresh air too, for the majority of Americans now lived in towns, and the pollution from domestic and factory chimneys was well advanced.

Lockhart starts the drive

The mighty engine of US productivity was just moving into high gear, with the vision of Henry Ford, Thomas Edison and Andrew Carnegie at the controls, and the Wright brothers looking wonderingly at birds in flight.

Wealth would produce leisure, and Robert Lockhart, who had been at school with Reid, imported the means to brighten that leisure. He had obtained them, six golf clubs and two dozen guttie balls, on a trip to Scotland to do with his linen merchant's business, from none other than Macdonald's supplier, Old Tom Morris.

Lockhart tried them out on what is now Riverside Drive, on New York's Upper West Side. A mounted policeman was watching, and jumped down to have a go. His first effort was (according to Lockhart's son) long and straight, but he could not repeat the feat, and departed, his beginner's luck used up. Where New York's finest faltered, Reid's St Andrew's six went on to glory, for their's is the club with the oldest continuous existence in the United States.

They cannot boast the longest history in North America: Montreal founded a golf club in 1873. Clearly the extended British influence there must have played a part, compared with the antipathy to many things British revived by the War of 1812. Three holes in a pasture opposite Reid's house in Yonkers was the extent of their first sporting domain. The first game on February 22, 1888, was between Reid and John Upham, for the pioneers had only the six clubs. There followed weeks of enforced inaction because of snow. When the weather cleared, they had obtained enough clubs for all to play, and quickly determined that their first course was inadequate. Their first "clubhouse" was a wooden table (two boards set upon two barrels) to bear their drinks.

On November 14 of the same year the St Andrew's Golf Club of Yonkers on Hudson was formed at Reid's house. Lockhart was elected as first member, Reid as president. Before 1888, according to the doyen of American golf writers, Herbert Warren Wind, there were fewer than a dozen golfers in the United States.

The St Andreans of the New World did not stay for long at their second course, a six-holer. They moved instead to another six-holer on steeply sloping ground four blocks north in an apple tree orchard, inevitably becoming known as the Apple Tree Gang.

This move, to a spot with a fine view of the Hudson River and New Jersey, was enforced by the extension through their old course of Palisades Avenue, which ran parallel to North Broadway.

The Saints, as they came also to be known, were treated with the same derision as early English golfers, among whom Horace Hutchinson has described how he and his fellows were regarded as indulging in a "harmless form of imbecility".

Ignorance about the game as the St Andrew's men golfed indomitably onwards, bringing down predictions of hell-fire on their heads from ministers of religion aghast at their habit of playing on Sundays, was still almost as deep in America as it had been at the 1845 publication of *Hoyle's Games*. The name is that of the eighteenth-century Englishman Edmond Hoyle, who in 1740 wrote *A Short Treatise on Whist*.

According to Hoyle in 1845, golfers used light balls when playing with the wind, heavy ones against it, a notion that would intrigue today's Rules Committees. Hoyle's 266 pages included only two on golf, compared to six on breeding game cocks and organizing cock fights.

St Andrew's accommodation at their new third course, which was set up in a day without the loss of a single apple tree, was relatively extensive, a bench around an apple tree serving as the clubhouse, food and drink hanging from its branches. One of these branches is now in the R&A Clubhouse at St Andrews in Fife; another is in the present US St Andrew's clubhouse.

The apple trees dotted about the course made the ability to loft the ball essential. Knowing nothing of the treeless, moonlike terrain of links in Scotland, Americans new to golf thought trees were indispensable obstacles in true golf.

By 1894, St Andrew's had competition. There were a number of clubs in and around New York and Newark in New Jersey by the mid-1890s. John Reid and company had really started something.

The resort of Newport, Rhode Island, soon had a country club and course, financed by some of the giants of contemporary society, among them John Jacob Astor and Cornelius Vanderbilt. Up in Maine, rich vacationers from Boston and New York were enjoying wild and lovely Mount Desert Island where, near the port of Bar Harbour, stand the wooded slopes of Kebo Valley, third oldest US course. An extra spring-time hazard here is ferocious black flies.

A wind-blown course was built on Long Island at Shinnecock Hills. At first there was a men's course, and nine holes for women members (of which St Andrew's had none in the early days). This form of discrimination was not liked, and the women's course was incorporated with the men's. Moreover, it had a splendid clubhouse designed by no less than Stanford White. Judge O'Brien, on his first round at Shinnecock, said it was not a golf course at all … "because it had no apple trees over which to loft and play".

Charles Macdonald had designed the only 18-hole course in the country in Chicago, which opened in 1895, then another nearby at Wheaton, which had the first artificial watering systems for greens – all 18 of them. Macdonald would never accept fees for his many course designs.

American golf was able to claim another first in course care, when in 1925 the Brook Hollow Country Club in Dallas, Texas, installed a complete fairway irrigation system.

St Andrew's members, intent on a nine-holer equal to those of their New York rivals, had to move north again, three miles further out of town, just as thousands were going the other way on to Manhattan Island. Their new home was at Grey Oaks, on a 100-acre farm site, where their first nine-holer was laid out:

YONKERS 1888 *(L to R) Harry Holbrook, Alexander Kinnan, John Upham and John Reid*

GOLFING MAN OF STEEL *Andrew Carnegie in his cottage near St Andrew's, NY, 1911*

seven holes had a stone wall running across them. By taking possession of the former farmhouse they had a clubhouse with walls and a roof – and a ghost, the legacy, it was said, of a violent death on the premises.

The list of members lengthened rapidly at Grey Oaks: it included such luminaries as Oliver Harriman, Stanford White, Henry Taft and Andrew Carnegie, who was of the opinion that golf was "the indispensable adjunct of high civilization".

Civilization and the country club

Talking of which, that peculiarly American institution, the country club, was reaching the heights of fashion in the last 20 years of the nineteenth century. Henry James the novelist described the country club as America's only contribution to civilization. It certainly contributed to the development of golf, absorbing the game as one of its members' pleasures along with lawn tennis.

There was no one for tennis among John Reid's friends, who were busy trying to make best use of the same sharply bent left elbow and sweeping, slashing flat swing as the original St Andreans had found effective on their wind-swept links. Reid's clubs were typical of the era back in Scotland. His driver had a long nose, a thick neck, a longer shaft than the modern club, and a fairly massive sole plate.

He and his friends also took on the red coat tradition (and painted the Grey Oaks clubhouse red also). But red coats, decorated with brass buttons and the cross of St Andrew in silver, did not last long in the United States as a general rule, since casual wear was a near essential in summer heat. Besides, unlike coats it did not hamper the swing, nor did sweaters in winter.

The St Andrew's club was not to stay at Grey Oaks for long, moving two miles further out again in 1897 to an undulating site at Mount Hope, where it cost $1,500 to lay out the course, and $65,000 to provide a new clubhouse, for which Carnegie guaranteed the mortgage. He built a home for himself nearby, steel-shuttered, for he was not popular with his steel workers.

It is said that on the day he sold his company for a quarter of a billion dollars, he parred the fifth hole for the first time. Later a friend, hearing of the deal, commented that he had been hearing great things of him. Carnegie's reply reveals that he had his priorities right: "How did you know I had a par on the fifth today?"

Carnegie, like Reid and Lockhart, came from Dunfermline, the son of a poor weaver, who brought his family to Pittsburgh in 1848. His enthusiasm for golf has a late echo now in Scotland, where he luxuriously refurbished Skibo Castle, near Dornoch, and built a nine-hole course. There he was able to call upon J. H. Taylor for instruction. Skibo is now being developed into a highly exclusive private club, with an updated 18-hole course, by Peter de Savary, whose greatest claim to sporting fame was in a determined but unsuccessful bid for yachting's America's Cup. Fire damaged the castle early in 1995, but Mr de Savary still contrived to get the club open on time.

The Yonkers players' new course in 1897 employed a Scottish professional, Sam Tucker, brother Willy being its first greenkeeper. He helped to construct the course to a design by Henry Tallmadge, a St Andrew's founding member. Willy later designed courses himself, thoroughly absorbed the American enthusiasm for technical improvement, and became a turf expert, putting down the Yankee Stadium playing surface and the original lawn tennis courts at Forest Hills. The Tallmadge/Tucker course is still in use, though it has had a face-lift by way of a Jack Nicklaus re-design.

Transport was ever a problem for the golfer. Before the automobile became widely accessible, St Andrew's members got out of the train five miles north of their club's birthplace at Yonkers, and had to scramble for horse buses and coaches. From New York to Hong Kong the same sort of thing was beginning to happen across the face of the globe.

Shinnecock stole a march on St Andrew's in one particular. It was the first club to be incorporated. It rapidly became a haunt of the élite. Golf was gaining public approval at an extraordinary rate after the years of nil progress that had so disheartened Macdonald.

In 1895 the Christmas message from the *New York Times* was: "In the history of American field sports there can be found no outdoor pastime that developed and attained such popularity in such a relatively short period of time as the game of golf."

The process was accelerated in the next two years by the opening of the nation's first public course, Van Cortland Park, New York City, in 1896, and the launch of the first US golf magazine, *Golf*, in 1897. Also in 1897, Yale got ahead in academia by winning the first collegiate golf championship.

From a state of golf course famine in the early 1890s, it took little over 30 years to reach relative plenty. By 1927 there were 400 courses in Metropolitan New York alone, 200 in the Chicago area, and 4,000 in the US as a whole, against 1,500 in Britain.

In the beginning, women's golf was more of a social occasion than a hard-fought contest to which any great sporting prestige could be attached. Besides, it was known that British champions, like Lady Margaret Scott, were capable of scores 20 shots better than the US pioneers.

The players' outfits were exhaustively described in the Press; the best golfers were already looking around for styles which would least hamper their play. Intricate styles, though sure to attract newspaper attention, seemed to equal high scores. Reports included the names of socially prominent spectators, such as Mrs John Jacob Astor.

Hundreds of spectators crowded on to the Ardsley Club course by the Hudson River for the 1898 Amateur Championship, when Beatrix Hoyt, herself a society girl, secured her third title in a row, hitting accurately to strategies indicated by her caddie, W. H. Sands, an Ardsley member.

The first stirrings of golf among the women of America, apart from the fading echoes of the clubs in the southern states, came sometime after an 1877 article in Frank Leslie's *Popular Monthly* exhorting American womanhood to give golf a chance, if only to "escape from the wearisome monotony of croquet". Golf would be a welcome addition to the meagre list of outdoor sports available to women.

No one took much notice of this, but a little progress was made in 1889, when a mixed foursome was played at St Andrew's. The original male golfers, Reid and Upham, took part. Carrie Low was Reid's partner in a victory over Upham and Mrs Reid.

Another nudge was given by Florence Boit, who had learned the game with Britons at Pau in France, and brought her clubs home to Massachusetts. But, consternation, no courses around Boston, so a start was made by turning the lawns of neighbours and relatives into pitch-and-putt holes. Laurence Curtis of The Country Club, Brookline, was impressed, and suggested the club should take the game up. It has hosted two US Opens, and will stage the 1999 Ryder Cup.

The time of the missionaries

The time was ripe, the St Andrew's club concluded in their splendid new club, to learn from the home of golf. They suggested that a score or so of clubs should contribute $80 each for expenses plus $20 a week salary to Harry Vardon and James Braid, who would then travel to the US to play exhibition matches on an eight-week tour.

It didn't happen, but American golf, now off and running, was speedily conceived as a business opportunity as well as a sport. Among the earliest sporting goods makers to turn their attention to the upwardly-rocketing golf business were A. G. Spalding and Bros Company, founded in 1876 by Albert Goodwill Spalding, a first-class major league pitcher, to make baseballs. Spalding were eager to push their Vardon Flyer guttie ball, and saw a Vardon tour as a sure-fire marketing opportunity.

How utterly right the company were. Vardon's tour began in February, 1900. He was Open Champion at that date, and interrupted his American tour to go back to Britain to defend his title. He lost it to Taylor at St Andrews but, on returning to the US, won the Open at Chicago, relegating Taylor to second place. Vardon, champion by two strokes, could afford to smile about missing his ball altogether when he was a mite casual over a tiny putt on the final green. The best score by an American was 10 shots worse.

The previous five Opens had been won by two Englishmen and three Scots, all based in the US, so Vardon was the first player to take the trophy abroad. It has been a rare accomplishment this century. (Vardon's record in three attempts on the US Open is played three, winner once and runner-up twice.)

Vardon was in the best form of his life in 1900, his perfect timing and awesome accuracy inspiring players all over the US – for there was a club in every state by this time, and more than 200,000 players. He lost only one singles match on his tour, and as he usually played against the best ball of two or three other players, his record of 13 defeats in 87 matches speaks for itself on an itinerary of 20,000 miles.

WILLIAM HOWARD TAFT
Presidential preacher of golf gospel

But as it transpired, the Vardon Flyer had appeared as the guttie era was drawing to its close. Two years before the Vardon tour the Haskell three-piece ball, based on the resilience of rubber bands wound under tension, had been patented, a type that would soon command the market.

Another champion came from over the water to charm American galleries in 1903. This one had red hair and the pale complexion that goes with it, and had "made a lifelong study of the second shot". Rhona Adair from Portrush had been unbeatable since 1900 in her native Irish championship, and won the British title in 1900 and again in 1903.

Plenty of practice, and in particular her mastery of the half- or punch-shot approach, a useful talent at breezy Portrush, had brought her to the top in Britain. In the US she beat a strong field at Merion from which only the champion, Bessie Anthony, was missing.

Her public utterances, mainly in exclusive *Illustrated Sporting News* articles, were careful and diplomatic: she proved an accurate talent spotter, praising the potential of Margaret Curtis, who was just out of her teens, and, nearly 30 years before the first Curtis Cup match, she possibly whetted American appetites for battle by predicting that a team of the best British players would trounce an American team. Possibly she was right – at the time.

She gave credit, in total refutation of Horace Hutchinson's 1893 opinions, to the "army of women golfers ... increasing every year" for being "above the petty squabbles and jealousies which are frequently met with at large gatherings of women".

In 1893, the year of the foundation of the Ladies' Golf Union in Britain, American women staked a claim for golfing emancipation. The women of Morristown in New Jersey set up a golf course of their own.

The opening was at least a social triumph, even though Mrs Arthur C. James whiffed the first shot. The Marquise de Talleyrand-Périgord of Paris and Prince Rospoli, mayor of Rome, and Princess Rospoli were among those present, along with many of the wealthy residents of the leafier New York suburbs.

The club's male associate members, who would have been cheered on by Horace Hutchinson, held that the women officers of the club could not adequately handle the business of the club. Early in 1895 these men obtained control of Morris County, some said by influencing the votes of those of their wives who were members. So the administration soon became all male.

There was a odd sequel: Morris County hosted the second US Women's Amateur Championship. Beatrix Hoyt won, her prize the trophy donated by Robert Cox, of Edinburgh in Scotland, on condition that the 1896 Championship be played at Morris County, where he had helped to lay out the course.

Most trophies are much of a muchness: Cox's slim and elegant silver gift is worthy of close examination, if only for its charming coloured panels of golf scenes.

AUGUSTAN INTIMATES *Cliff Roberts and Dwight Eisenhower, 1957*

Hail to the (golfing) chief

Golf's history is replete with royal patrons. In 1909 the game recruited its first major Republican figure, in more ways than one. William Howard Taft was elected US President as Republican candidate in 1909. He weighed well over 200 pounds. He had been captivated by the game since 1896. He commended golf in an electioneering speech in 1908 to folks in California as being "full of moments of self-abasement, with only a few moments of self-exaltation. And we Americans, who are not celebrated for our modesty, may find such a game excellent training."

The media were quickly on to this Presidential enthusiasm, in which he was hampered by putting problems. Nothing disturbed his love of the game, not even the arrival of a foreign head of state in the Capitol. "I'll be damned if I will give up my game to see this fellow," said he, and persevered with his round with the self-possession of a latter-day Drake.

Taft's preaching of the golf gospel came at the same time as American golf was coming of age. Tom MacNamara's final round of 69 earned him second place in the 1909 US Open, the highest finish yet achieved by a native-born American.

While Taft was still in office, Johnny McDermott became the first native US Open champion in 1911, and won again in 1912, and while Taft later took up duties as Chief Justice of the Supreme Court, Francis Ouimet beat the best Britain could offer in 1913.

Coincidences no doubt, but Taft had done no harm to golf's social acceptability. Presidents Wilson and Harding followed Taft's lead. Harding, who gave a trophy for the Amateur Links Championship, declared: "It used to be thought that golf was a game for the elderly, but the beauty of golf is that everybody can play it."

Franklin Delano Roosevelt's golf was cut short by polio, but the line of White House golfers continued through Dwight Eisenhower, John Kennedy, Richard Nixon, Gerald Ford, George Bush and Bill Clinton. Of these it was Eisenhower who, despite his lack of prowess, had the highest profile.

Between the presidency of Taft and that of Eisenhower, the story of golf in America is of the tour professional's gradual climb to supremacy over the amateur as the sport's leader, and America's speedier progress to supremacy over other golfers worldwide. In 1922, only 11 years after the first American-born player won the US Open, Walter Hagen won the British Open. That same year, he became the first professional to set up a company under his own name to make golf clubs.

Not only was the professional game gaining more headlines than the amateur, especially after Bobby Jones retired. The professionals, the vast majority of them native-born between the wars, were light years away, in public perception, from the flock of Scots who had manned professional shops and won the US Open year after year before the McDermott/Ouimet/Hagen years ... Scots whose brogue was seldom more than semi-intelligible. Many were accused of having too great a liking for the wine of that country.

Most of all, the professional game had Hagen, said by Gene Sarazen to be golf's greatest showman. He was certainly the first true tournament professional. Sarazen did well out of the new social chic and earning power of the the pro, and after his Open/US PGA double of 1922 got himself into the headlines by beating Hagen in the final of the next US PGA Championship, winning at the 38th hole thanks to a tree which prevented his ball from going out of bounds. At the end of the decade, and despite the deepening economic depression, Sarazen won the biggest first prize yet offered, $10,000 in the Agua Caliente Open at Tijuana, Mexico.

Just as the abolition of tax on newspapers allowed the popular Press in Britain to reach the working classes and become a potent force in popularizing football and cricket, golf's quick progress in the US was greatly fostered by newspapers and magazines. This was despite a reluctance on the part of tournament officials to grant working facilities or much information

USGA EXECUTIVE COMMITTEE 1916 *President Frank Woodward seated centre*

on the state of play to reporters.

Typically, Clifford Roberts gave the media "free" lunches and good facilities at the Masters, well aware that tournament golf, like all top-class sport, cannot exist without extensive coverage. All was light and joy as long as commentators toed the line of Augustan propriety, i.e., no mention on television of filthy lucre prize money. One commentator was banned for years for saying that a "mob" encircled the final green, and another one for saying that the bumpy fairways "look suspiciously like body bags".

Prominent among the early writers was Englishman Jim Whigham, Charlie Macdonald's son-in-law, twice a winner of the US Amateur title. Magazines started to appear around the turn of the century. Walter Travis was first editor of *The American Golfer*, started in 1907. Ever increasing demand for tournament news and golf instruction meant there seemed always to be room for one more publication. Bob Harlow started the weekly *Golf World* in 1947, which included international golf news, and in 1959 *GOLF Magazine* appeared, tackling the question of how good, or how bad, was Ike's game. *GOLF*'s circulation in the 1990s is in the high six figures range: *GOLF* and *Golf Digest*, started as a throwaway magazine in Chicago in 1951, are the leading US golf publications.

Like Bob Harlow, Fred Corcoran combined public relations and writing with his administrative pioneering labours for the PGA and LPGA. Grantland Rice and O. B. Keeler (Bobby Jones's biographer) were the best-known writers of the inter-war years, since when Herbert Warren Wind of the *New Yorker* has become the doyen of golf writers and Herb Graffis, who wrote a PGA history, earned a place in the World Golf Hall of Fame.

Radio reporters, meanwhile, found it difficult to get near enough to the action to see what was going on, and far enough away to be inaudible to players. TV solves such problems.

USGA takes helm from start

Though the R&A received its Royal warrant in 1834, and was accepted at the time as authoritative on golf and its rules, nearly a century passed before it took over full responsibility for the organization of the major British Championships.

In contrast, the USGA was founded, first and foremost, to run the men's and women's amateur events, as well as the men's Open, and this it did within 12 months of its foundation (but only just, for the Women's Amateur was not contested until November of 1895). It also took over the women's Open when requested (by the LPGA) in 1953, the year of the eighth Women's Championship. The USGA remains active in almost every facet of the game.

The USGA soon had to make its first decision when the inaugural Amateur Championship began in 1895. It was one of the Association's least controversial decisions, forbidding Richard Peters to putt with a pool cue on the Newport greens. Joe Davis, the late world billiards and snooker champion, was sometimes heard to regret this decision when he played in British Press Golfing Society events.

The USGA's history has been riven with disputes about amateur status, in the view of many causing unnecessary friction by too unforgiving a reading of the definition of amateur. On the other hand, amateur golfers have always been nearer a Corinthian state of true-blue no-pay-for-play than those who for so long persisted with the label, amateur, top class rugby union for example. The relevant USGA/R&A definition of an amateur golfer is "one who plays the game as a non-remunerative or non-profit-making sport".

Countless words have been printed and spoken and battles fought over the boundaries between pro and amateur. One *cause célèbre* concerned the banishing of Francis Ouimet, Open hero of 1913, to the professional ranks in 1916: his crime was to have opened a sporting goods business. He had been in the business, working for a Boston firm, Wright and Ditson, before his Open win gave him instant fame, proved that Americans could play at the highest level, and demonstrated that the game was for the man on the Boston omnibus, who worked for a living, just as much as for the country club set.

The USGA president at the time was Frank Woodward, a stickler for a strict interpretation of the status rule. The decision was thought unfair, since Ouimet had been in the sports goods business before the 1913 Open. Thanks in part to the opposition of the Western GA, the decision was rescinded in time for Ouimet to play in the first post-war Amateur in 1919.

Ten years before that, caddies, caddie masters and greenkeepers aged over 16 were deemed to be professionals. Attitudes slowly changed, to the extent that the age limit was 18 from 1930, and 21 from 1945. In 1963, the age limit was rescinded.

Amateur status rules were strengthened because of clubs and colleges enrolling good players with offers of entrance fees and the like. The thinking of the ruling body on this is clearly demonstrated by the decision that Charles Rymer, 1985 Junior champion, should be allowed honorary membership of Tega Cay, South Carolina, as long as no time limit was placed on membership. The awarding of entry fees as prizes, even if they are no more than the amateur prize limit ($500), is a violation.

A major change came when college golfers were allowed to accept scholarships without prejudice to their amateur status. Many foreign student golfers have benefited from the decision. College staff may give golf instruction yet stay amateur as long as the instruction takes up less than 50 per cent of their working hours.

Acceptance of golf equipment from a manufacturer is forbidden, and so is payment of expenses by anyone except family or legal guardian, with exceptions such as for team competitions and young players under 19 or until shortly after graduation. The career of the outstanding US amateur of the 1950s, Harvie Ward, was blighted by the expenses trap.

IMPORTANT ADDRESSES

United States Golf Association, Far Hills, New Jersey 07931

Ladies Professional Golf Association, 2570 W International Speedway Blvd, Suite B, Dayton Beach, Florida 32114-1118

PGA of America, Box 109601, 100 Avenue of the Champions, Palm Beach Gardens, Florida 33418

PGA Tour, 112 TPC Blvd, Ponte Vedra Beach, Florida 32082

CANADA

Few of the leading golfers of the world have not tried for or won the Canadian Open, though Canada itself is still without a winner of a "major". Apart from the British and US Opens, it is the only current tour event listed by the US PGA that dates from before the First World War; that is, long before the US Tour was up and running.

Nor did a Canadian win an American Tour event until 1955, when Al Balding from Toronto did so in the Mayfair Inn Open. He won again, three times, in 1957.

His greatest feat was yet to come, for at the age of 44 Balding, partnered by George Knudson, from Winnipeg, carried off the World Cup at Olgiata, in Rome, beating Lee Trevino and Julius Boros of the US into second place. Balding was leading individual into the bargain, 14 under par.

Team golf is evidently Canada's forte, for further World Cup wins came in 1980 (Dan Halldorson, another Winnipeg man, and Jim Nelford, a right-handed golfer from Vancouver who putts left-handed) and 1985 (Halldorson again, and Dave Barr).

Barr, like Nelford a British Columbian, was top individual in the World Cup won by the US in 1983, then carried on the team-play torch to St Andrews in the 1994 Alfred Dunhill Cup. Barr, 44, and two journeyman pros, Ray Stewart and Rick Gibson, beat a thoroughly up-market US trio of Tom Kite, Curtis Strange and Fred Couples 2–1 in the final. Stewart had never won a significant pro event, and after six years on the US Tour switched to the Asian circuit. Gibson lives in Manila, and has two wins on the Japan circuit.

To say that Canada shook one and all is a considerable understatement. Starting at 28-1 against, and still 7-2 when the final started, Canada had never got past the last 16 before, and in previous years had been obliged to qualify to reach that point, staged always at St Andrews from the inaugural Dunhill Cup of 1985. This time they did not have to qualify, but progressed into the semi-finals from their group of four (made up by Zimbabwe, Germany and section favourites Sweden) by the narrowest of margins.

CANADA'S WEE MIRACLE WORKER *Marlene Streit at Wentworth in 1959*

SWILKEN CELEBRATIONS *Canada's 1994 Dunhill Cup victors at St Andrews*

During the 40-50 mph gales of the first day, when the average group score was 78, Canada lost to Sweden 2–1, Gibson slumping to Anders Forsbrand 85 to 81. Barr lost too, but had only one reverse thereafter, in the semi-finals against US Open Champion Ernie Els, beating Nick Price, Bernhard Langer and, in the final, Fred Couples. Barr's win over Langer was crucial: if the German had holed his 15-foot putt on the 18th in the decisive match, Zimbabwe would have qualified to meet South Africa, who were beaten by virtue of Gibson and Stewart both getting around the Old Course in 70.

Satellite television covered the event: no Canadian journalist did, which rather sums up Canada's *sotto voce* golf history. That is said to have begun with officers of General James Wolfe's army playing on the Plains of Abraham near Quebec during the British campaign to expel the French from Canada. Victory there cost Wolfe his life, and his opposite number, Montcalm, was killed also.

Golf was also played at Halifax, Nova Scotia, 200 years ago, organized and continuous club existence beginning at Montreal in 1873. Quebec (1874) and Toronto (1875) quickly followed. Montreal and Quebec scored another North American first for Canada by holding the first inter-club match in the hemisphere. The Royal Canadian GA was founded in Ottawa in 1894, contemporaneously with the USGA, when there were only 10 clubs. These swelled to 34 by 1914, and 30 of these are still extant. Canada's PGA was founded in 1911, five years before the US PGA.

The Canadian Women's Amateur title was the target of more anointed heroines of the game in the early days than the Open was of male stars. Dorothy Campbell from North Berwick, first to win the Amateur title of Britain and the US in the same year, landed a hat-trick in the Canadian Amateur (1910–12) and the English champion Cecil Leitch gained the title in 1921.

These feats were modest compared to the achievements of Canada's little giant, Marlene Streit, née Stewart, from Alberta.

Long winters are undoubtedly an obstacle to the acquisition of golf skills in Canada, though the beauty of the courses there is unmatched. That by the Bow River, overlooked by the Banff Springs Hotel, is a prime example, while two further west at Kananaskis, in Alberta, near the site of the Winter Olympics of 1988 in and around Calgary, have a grandeur all their own.

It is something of a curiosity that only Arnold Palmer, and not Jack Nicklaus and Gary Player of the 1960s "big three", has won the Canadian Open (Palmer's first professional victory). One of the very few Englishmen to win the Canadian Open, much revived by Seagram's sponsorship in 1936 after the event showed signs of flagging in the wake of the Depression, is Peter Oosterhuis (1981).

Another Englishman, born in Newcastle-upon-Tyne in 1884, John Douglas Edgar, strolled in 16 strokes clear in 1919. He won again, in a play-off against Tommy Armour (a pupil of his) and Charles Murray, the following year. However, in 1921, this brilliant stylist, tipped to soar to the summit of his profession, met with his still unexplained death in the streets of Atlanta.

IMPORTANT ADDRESS

Royal Canadian Golf Association,
Golf House, RR No. 2 Oakville, Ontario,
L6J 4Z3

GREAT BRITAIN AND IRELAND

From the £40 million ($63 million) London club, designed by the Jack Nicklaus organization, to the lawn mowers of Niddry Castle in Scotland, golf is in a healthy state of growth in Britain and Ireland. Lawn mowers? Certainly – being pushed up the fairways by members, their wives marching behind with rakes.

Niddry, in the Lothian district near Edinburgh, has progressed since then, and deploys more appropriate machinery. The community effort that produced the Niddry course has been replicated in a number of Scottish regions, with especial emphasis on the more northerly districts of the Highlands and Islands.

Scotland, as befits the land that gave birth to the game, has a ratio of courses to population, one to 13,000, challenged only in Australasia. This happy circumstance for golfers in Scotland extends to one course for 600 people on the Isle of Arran off the west coast.

The Scottish Golf Union has encouraged and guided the building of courses to provide an extra attraction for tourists: more than 10 million visit Scotland each year. Pressure on golf facilities south of the border, and their cost, make a Scottish holiday most attractive to English golfers. In south-east England, the course/population ratio reaches one to 43,000.

Nine-hole courses have been and are being built in beguiling areas, notably Ullapool, Dunvegan (on the lovely island of Skye near to the centuries-old stronghold of the MacDonald family), and Eriskay, a tiny island just to the south of South Uist. Members supply labour in the building of the Inverrary nine-holer community project. Lochgilhead's course has been enlarged from nine to 18 holes.

The most westerly point of mainland Britain, the wild and beautiful Ardnamurchan, acquired a course through a low-handicap cousin of the Scottish Golf Union's secretary, Ian Hume. Finding the journey to the nearest course a chore, he persuaded a local farmer to turn some of his land into a course.

The farmer's caravan site is well patronized in summer, when the long northern days almost banish night, and the project went ahead, and Hume's cousin, a teacher, provides instruction for local youngsters in the royal and ancient game.

Scottish golfers affiliated to the national union number 193,000; juniors total 27,000. There are 518 affiliated clubs, 428 courses – some have playing rights on more than one course.

The English Golf Union has 1,715 affiliated clubs, 20 per cent of them public courses, with 674,260 members, and here too there is much development in progress. (It should be noted that the membership figures of the four home unions [England, Ireland, Scotland and Wales] do not take account of pay-and-play golfers on private and public courses, or society members playing "away". Women golfers are affiliated, through their clubs, to the LGU and women's unions.)

At least 100 courses are under construction or having radical extensions built most of the time; 500 course projects have planning permission, but from past experience it is unlikely that a sizable percentage of them will go ahead. At any particular time there can be more than 30 or 40 courses built and waiting to open. On the same basis, 50 others can have been completed, and have applied for affiliation, and 20 more constructed but not yet applicants to join the EGU. In a phrase, the situation is fluid. Yet the pressure on facilities seldom lessens. About 25 per cent of courses are public.

New and ambitious resort type lay-outs have proved more prone to cash crises soon after opening than courses which do not have other businesses linked to them – luxury hotels, health clubs and the like. Belton Woods Hotel and Country Club at Grantham, in Lincolnshire, birthplace of that stalwart of private enterprise, Margaret Thatcher, cost £20 million and was sold for much less to the De Vere hotel group after running into difficulties. Slaley Hall in Northumberland, a superb project, of championship standard and used for pre-qualifying rounds for would-be European Tour card-holders, suffered much the same type of misfortune.

Remembering that the (Nicklaus designed) London club, which is in Kent, south of the Thames and just off the M25 London Orbital motorway, cost £40 million, and that there is a finite number of players that can use the club's two courses, and hence subscriptions and green fees that a

THE OLD... *John Taylor, captain of the Honorable Company...*

AND THE NEW... *Jack Nicklaus's Heritage Course at the London Club, just south of the Thames at Ash in Kent, close to the M25: this is the par 4 12th*

course can bear, it is clear that the early financial return and, looking ahead, even the mature return, from such an expensive enterprise might disappoint. Then there is the ever present threat of the weather closing the course down for a fortnight, say, so chopping 5 per cent from annual revenue.

While this is a bugbear that any new capital project must face, costly golf infrastructure must be built and then maintained, and the burden absorbed of that highly expensive endeavour, growing good grass and keeping it in order.

By contrast, the ingenious golfers of the Hereford/Wales borders built a course at Ross-on-Wye, which is in the English county of Herefordshire, at a bargain price, to replace the nine-hole course the club had used since 1903. The club, re-sited beside the M50 motorway, has a highly convenient slip road now almost on the clubhouse doorstep five miles north of Ross.

Albert Evans, who played for Wales for 30 years until 1961, and Bill Bishop were among the small group who eyed a tract of just over 100 thickly wooded acres, some of it marshy, all of it little better than scrubland. They received a good deal of advice to the effect that a golf course could not be built there. Undaunted, the intrepid members relied on self-help and the first nine holes were completed in 1964 with no more heavy equipment than a £150 tractor and a £300 tipping trailer, plus a contractor's caterpillar to pull out tree roots. Costs were defrayed in part by selling wood for pea-sticks and head-stakes; no wastrels at Ross.

Members cut more costs by tramping up and down with baskets clearing a few acres on the site that were afflicted by stones. Once swathes had been cut through the scrub, the architect Ken Cotton could see the lie of the land and set out the holes. Cultivation was by discs and harrowing, Evans himself doing much of the seeding. By 1966–67 the course was ready, at the astoundingly low total cost, including clubhouse, of a little over £40,000 (around $80,000 at the time).

All this, by the way, is no pitch and putt, but a serious set of 18 holes, much used for top-class competition. The last three holes – down, up, and down again – are apt to prove to the complacent the truth of the old golfing saw that "Two up and three to play never saw the light of day."

Over the border, Wales itself has expanded steadily: 94 clubs in the Union in 1955, growing fourfold in membership to more than 55,000 members and more than 140 clubs. Which is perhaps why Wales captured the European youth crown. Ireland has added 60 clubs to their roster in as many years to 1994, when the membership of the country's 321 clubs first exceeded 100,000: another 75,000 also play.

Women's golf can report even greater growth, the Ladies' Golf Union total of affiliations topping 200,000, against 146,000 25 years ago.

A social and gastronomic game

Clubs are the backbone of golf, the muscle and sinew of the national associations, but their creation in eighteenth-century Scotland was not indiscriminately welcomed. *The Golf Book of East Lothian* considered that the old free and easy days, when all classes mingled on the links, had been destroyed by the institution of the clubs. First The Gentlemen Golfers of Edinburgh, secondly the St Andrews men, allowed only members to play in the big event of the year, the Silver Club.

What the clubs did not have was permanent premises, or anything faintly resembling a clubhouse, except perhaps that food and drink was served at their tavern meeting-places. Until their Golf House was built in 1768, Leith players ate at Luckie Clephan's tavern.

Silver Club days were followed by

members taking dinner together, a habit taken up fortnightly at Bailie Glass's at St Andrews, where a player was called to account for withdrawing from the Silver Club event, and then not dining with his associates. Dinner cost one shilling per member, whether he sat down at table or was absent. Meals were substantial and drinking was on a generous scale: three-bottle men were proud of their ability to take their liquor.

There was also pride in club uniform, which was changed now and then, but ever colourful, replete with brass buttons, silver badges, velvet capes and other fancies. These grew more and more elaborate in the nineteenth-century, and such dress was obligatory. Finally the Puritan ethic, or perhaps simple parsimony, arrested this trend, and tweed jackets and knickers were the dress for much of the first 50 years of the Open Championship era.

The idea of the Silver Club winner automatically taking the captain's role was no longer appropriate as club life grew more complicated. It became less important for the captain to be the best player, and more useful for him to be a businesslike leader. Captaincy became elective although, after the example set by the Royal & Ancient Club, captains world-wide drive themselves into office. The ritual on the 1st hole of the Old Course, where the caddies scramble to retrieve the captain's drive and claim a reward, remains of the old system under which members could win the captaincy.

Westward Ho! club got rid of the old system the year after Horace Hutchinson, aged 16, won the club's gold medal and the captaincy, to sustain which his elders evidently and understandably considered Hutchinson unready.

The North Devon links of Westward Ho! was but one conduit of the spread of the Scottish game into England; the most royal was James I of England and VI of Scotland, whose sons probably played in the royal parks. The first club was Blackheath, to the south of London; though the most important, in view of its contribution to the amateur game, was undoubtedly the Royal Liverpool Club at Hoylake in Cheshire on the north-west coast, close to major centres of British industrial and commercial might at Liverpool and other Lancashire towns.

There is little doubt that Blackheath, the first club formed south of the border, began in 1766 in the same way as the early Scottish clubs, when Henry Foot presented a Silver Club (in Blackheath's case a Silver Driver), to the Honourable Company of Golfers at Blackheath. Not until 1818 did a second English club appear, at Manchester, a club which, unlike Blackheath and Liverpool, has not had a continuous existence.

Westward Ho! certainly has, from the time the course was set out by the elder Tom Morris, then working at Prestwick, in 1863. Play began that year and the Royal North Devon Club was founded in 1864, the first set up by English-born golfers. Blackheath had strong Scottish connections.

Hoylake, which was to be the site of the Liverpool, later Royal Liverpool, Club from 1869, had an earlier sporting existence as the racecourse of the Liverpool Hunt Club. Racing continued there into the 1870s, but the fame of the warren at Hoylake was to be founded on the quality of the amateur golfers who

YOUNG SCOTS GUN *Andrew Coltart at Tanah Merah, one of the European Tour's far-flung stop-offs*

learned to play on it, its major part in launching the Amateur Championship, and not least its popularity as an Open course. That privilege has now been lost to it because Hoylake lacks space to house the ever growing facilities offered to the public. Hoylake also staged the first matches between Britain and the US (the 1921 forerunner of the Walker Cup), and the first home international, against Scotland. Contrary to American experience, innovation in Britain has almost always been club-driven.

At the instance of J. Muir Dowie a meeting was held in 1869 in the Royal Hotel, Hoylake. The decision was taken to found a golf club, and this was done a month later. The club was based on the Royal Hotel, and rejoiced in advisers and course designers with impeccable credentials ... Robert Chambers, winner of the forerunner of the Amateur Championship, and Old Tom Morris's brother George, whose son Jack Morris quickly became the first professional. It is safe to say that no club has ever produced amateurs who achieved such frequent major honours as those achieved by John Ball and Harold Hilton.

Yet a third Hoylake player, Jack Graham, a sporting all-rounder of many talents, was leading amateur in the Open five times before the First World War. He reached the Amateur Championship semi-finals four times, and was held by many to be inferior in very few particulars to Ball or Hilton, added to which he was a considerable Rugby Union player with Liverpool. Graham was killed in action serving with the Liverpool Scottish, at Hooge, in 1915.

Hoylake Opens featured the first won with the Haskell rubber-cored ball, by Sandy Herd in 1902, and the first won by a foreigner, Arnaud Massy in 1907. Massy rushed home to France with the trophy to see his baby daughter, to whom his Scottish wife had given birth during Open Championship week. He named the newcomer Hoylake.

AMATEUR POWERHOUSE *Royal Liverpool, whose Ball and Hilton are, with Bobby Jones, the only amateurs to win the Open*

Titleist
BLACK

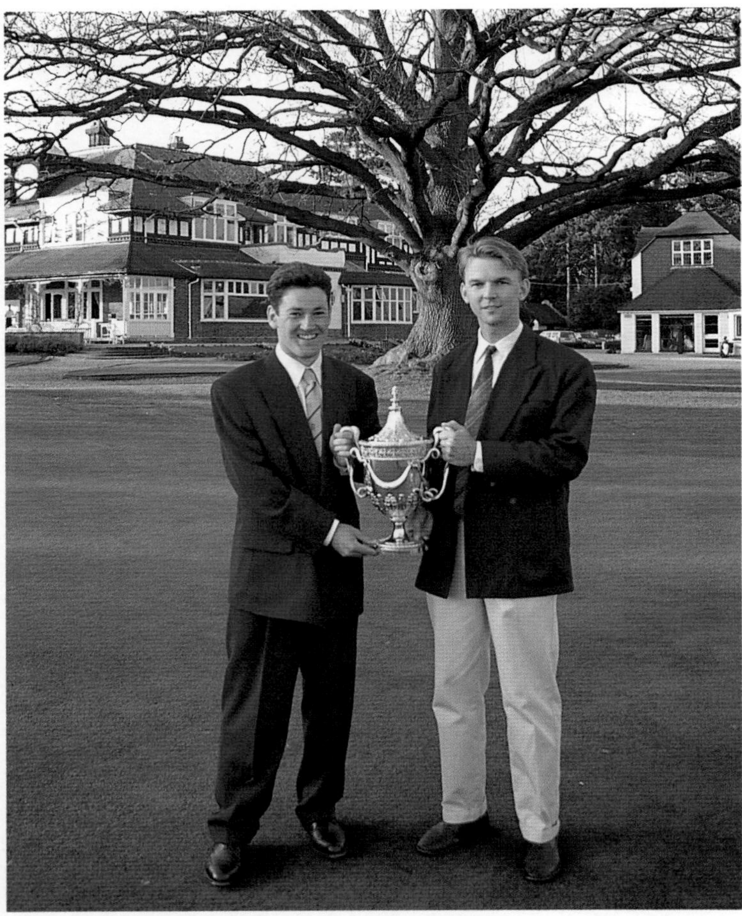

SUNNINGDALE FOURSOMES, 1993 *Lee James and (right) Andy Beal with trophy*

"J.H." organizes the pros

A young pro called Tom Williamson received a job offer in a letter from the secretary of Notts GC in 1896, towards the end of a quarter century of surging club growth. There were less than 100 clubs in Britain in 1875, 1,300 in 1900. His wages were to be five shillings a week, a couple of dollars or so, and he was to take all profits from making, mending, and selling clubs and balls. (This last, as we have seen, was more than many US club pros were offered).

In return, Williamson (whose sister was stewardess) was to coach at 1s 6d. a round, supervise clubhouse security, manage the caddies, run the draw for Medal competitions, and work for eight hours a week on course maintenance. This was, the letter made clear, a temporary and experimental engagement, which might become a permanence. Williamson took it, for 54 years, and there were others like him, including men who knew little about golf, but developed what aptitude they had for the game, and taught themselves club repair and the like as they went along.

The first pros at English clubs had been mostly Scots, as they were to be in America, but by 1900 half the 300 or so pros at English clubs were English. J. H. Taylor, born to the wife of a working man in the village of Northam, overlooking the links of Westward Ho!, had three Opens to his name in 1901 when he emerged as the man to unite and lead his fellow professionals.

Many of them were suffering because club members were cutting them out of the circuit of equipment supply, buying direct from factory sources. Scottish professionals had already begun to flex their muscles. In 1892 the Open was switched to the Honourable Company's new Muirfield course, thus cutting out Musselburgh, and ending the long-established three-way roster of the Opens, which had been circulating between St Andrews, Prestwick and Musselburgh for 20 years. The business, and particularly the golfing, community of Musselburgh were appalled at the potential loss of trade, and they put together £100 prize money to hold their own Open, three times the cash on offer in the 1891 Open. The Honourable Company recognized that this was no idle threat, and responded by raising the Muirfield purse to £110. So the warring pros held their meeting after Muirfield (won, ironically, by an amateur, Hilton) and so had £210 in their sights in all.

Further discontents were expressed as the Open prize money was not regularly increased, and Taylor, while advocating moderation, determined to organize his fellows. Hilton's own *Golf Illustrated* opened the pros' case in a leading article.

Thereafter progress was rapid. Regional then national unity as the Professional Golfers' Association was the pattern, with a £1 membership subscription for pros, half that for assistants. Protection of trade interests, setting up competitions and a Benevolent Fund were among the aims. A professional tournament was quickly organized, with a mere £15 available in prize money, at Tooting Bec. Taylor won. That club and the competition no longer exist, except that the Tooting Bec Cup goes each year to the PGA member with the lowest round in the Open.

Taylor was elected chairman, and there was also the recruitment of a most valuable ally of golf, when Arthur James Balfour, soon to become Prime Minister as head of the Conservative Party, agreed to become PGA President. Balfour was throughout his life a staunch friend of, propagandist for and keen participant in the game, and his soubriquet as Father of English Golf was thoroughly earned.

There were no straight political battle lines indicated here, though, for Balfour, productively for the game of golf, had a foot in both professional and amateur camps. The Kent seaside club, Littlestone, had a foot in both parties, for at one time the Liberal Prime Minister, Henry Asquith, was their captain, and Balfour, Leader of His Majesty's Opposition, their president. The Littlestone course, incidentally, was remodelled in the 1920s by Dr Alister MacKenzie, co-designer with Bobby Jones of Augusta National.

The PGA's next problem was the furore over the coming of the Haskell ball, with which Sandy Herd had won the Open in 1902, when the PGA membership was nation-wide, reaching 300, including an Irish section. Midland PGA members wanted the guttie as the prescribed tournament ball, but, fatally for its chances of success, their resolution gave the new ball a sparkling, if unintended, endorsement. It said: "Competitors should be on an equal footing so far as the ball is concerned." This was an unwitting coded statement meaning, "The Haskell is best" – which it was, and opposition to it faded, though not instantly.

The PGA broke new ground with the incorporation, in 1921, of the Professional Golfers' Co-operative Association. The 1920s was a period in which the making of clubs moved from pro shops to small, then major, factory units, and the shortage of hickory and ever greater demand for clubs hastened the dominance of the steel shaft despite the misgivings of many British pros. The USGA's 1926 acceptance of steel came three years before the R&A followed suit, without consulting the PGA, who had earlier opposed the move which, in an era of golf boom, was inevitable.

The boom was reflected in a modest increase in tournaments. By 1924 there were five major pro events each with four-figure purses. Unmistakable signs appeared in the PGA (now with more than 1,000 members) of a schism between ambitious young members with tournament aspirations, and the traditional club pros, who looked upon the PGA as their shield and comforter, not primarily as a seeker after tournament sponsors.

So the American experience of tour vs. club pro was mirrored in Britain and Ireland, and the discontent grew more acute in the 1950s, when the tournament programme and purses declined, just when television in America was revealing golf's full potential, and prize money was sky-rocketing. The growth in PGA membership overall in the 16 years from 1975 to 1990 is astounding. Including overseas membership, which increased rapidly with British pros taking jobs on the Continent, there was a 38.8 percent rise. The 1994 total was 4,902.

Progress was slow until the 1960s, when prize money increased more rapidly, thanks in part to the improved cash allotted to the 1960 Open, the date of the arrival in Britain of Arnold Palmer. All the same it was not until 1976 that the tournament players gained autonomy, with the foundation of the Tournament Players' Division.

The full-time amateur arrives

Amateur golf has changed radically over the last 20 years, moulded afresh by two major influences. First, Henry Cotton, knighted just before his death in 1987, was influential in setting up the Golf Foundation, for which clubs raise money to pay for professional tuition for youngsters, who mature to scratch and better at an ever earlier age. County and international teams now seem to be manned entirely by players whose average age hardly seems out of the teens.

They eye the second great influence, the chimera of riches on the European Tour – chimera because, for all but a tiny percentage, starting places on the Tour are unattainable, especially now that they are fought for by so many Continental players, and ones from even further afield. Parents' support allows the creation of a new class of amateurs, whose description seems almost a contradiction in terms: the full-time amateur.

The route from amateur to pro goes through two channels. Every autumn, hundreds of players go through the wringer of the Qualifying School. Even those who obtain one of the handful of tour cards and prosper, describe the process as the most nerve-racking of their lives. Players can keep their amateur status if they fail in the first section of qualifying, but once they have struck a shot in the final series they are professionals, though there is always an option to apply for reinstatement in the future.

The second channel is through the Challenge Tour, which is proving a better test of potential than the Qualifying School. In recent years the top 10 who qualified from the Challenge Tour did better on the main Tour than the School Qualifiers (the top 15 qualify now). There are three "minor" tours for aspiring young British pros, if that word can properly be applied to such a programme as the (former) Gosen Tour, which under its new sponsor will have a prize fund of £305,000. The other two are the Hippo tour, and the British Professional Golf Tour, run by the PGA, with 10 events in 1997.

The competitive amateur scene, despite these professional attractions, is ever more crowded in Britain. J. H. Taylor, as he proved by his pioneering work with the PGA, was a far-sighted individual, but he was well wide of the mark in his *Taylor on Golf* at the beginning of the century. He wrote: "County golf, I regret to say, appears only too likely to die a more or less natural death."

The county game was born in 1894, with the foundation of the Hampshire Union. Yorkshire was quick to follow, and despite Taylor's doleful view of their future, the two counties have survived to play a centenary match: 'prospered' is more accurate, since Yorkshire have frequently been national champions or top of the Northern Counties League. Hampshire, though often dominant among southeastern counties, did not achieve the national title until 1996 – four years after Hampshire's women first stormed the heights.

Every county in England plays in the English Golf Union's County Championship, in which qualifying meetings for the North, Southeastern, Southwestern and Midlands counties produce four teams for the autumn finals. Moreover, every county in England is represented in the six English leagues, playing at weekends, and two Welsh counties, Glamorgan and Gwent, are members of the Channel League, along with five southwestern English counties. This system is replicated in the rest of Wales, in Scotland and in Ireland.

GOLD VASE *Van Phillips and (right) Charlie Challen were joint winners, 1993*

Activity has intensified in the nineties. Surrey's secretary, Mike Ashton, points out that on 80 days a year a Surrey team is playing or a county championship is in progress. Since fixtures are few over four winter months, there is action on one day in three in the season, and national events often rob county captains of their best players.

All these competitions are run under the general guidance of the national Unions, whose accent, like that of the PGA, is more and more on training. The professional version of the Golf Foundation, started in 1952, were the training courses begun in 1961. Former tournament players, notably Tom Jones of Maesdu in Wales, instructed assistant pros not just in the primary pursuit of lower scores, but in how to run a shop profitably, how to mend clubs, and how to coach members. A few months after leading Europe to Ryder Cup success at Oak Hill, Bernard Gallacher became the first professional to be appointed president of the Foundation – from which he received tuition as a teenage member of Bathgate, near Edinburgh.

The European Tour has its Apollo Week: this is a winter break at San Roque in southern Spain that is anything but leisurely for the young card-carrying pros who attend this finishing school of golf. (Talking of school, one in Leicestershire named "playing golf with the family" as the second most frequently used excuse for truancy.)

Experts on the mental and physical fitness aspects of the game are available at San Roque for consultation, and John Jacobs, among other coaches, passes on his views on the swing. The sponsors are represented too, by an executive who explains what is expected from the players in return for the cash injected by industry and commerce. Chief tour referee John Paramor outlines his job (learn the definitions and all will be revealed, rules-wise, is his creed), guidance is given as to how to choose a manager, and there is plenty of practice time.

British newspapers have of recent years conceived sponsorship for competition at schools level as good for

PERILOUS PAR 3 *The 12th at the English Golf Union's new home, at Woodhall Spa, Lincolnshire*

prestige, even if they do not noticeably boost circulation. The scheme run by *The Daily Telegraph* has progressed from a holiday event at a few seaside courses to an event attracting 25,000 country-wide, finishing with a final in Georgia. Peter Oosterhuis, Peter Townsend and Ian Woosnam are successful professionals from among former competitors.

EGU set up new golf academy

Woodhall Spa has no peer among the world's inland courses. The decision of the English Golf Union to buy it and move their headquarters there, in the wide open spaces of Lincolnshire, has gladdened the hearts of the nation's amateur golfers. The potential it holds for the good of the English game is considerable.

Woodhall Spa is, as the name suggests, a place where the waters can be taken, but the quality of the course has meant that the excellent hotel accommodation nearby has been taken up more and more by golf visitors. The EGU spent many hours thumbing through course-sale literature, and visiting courses on the market, before deciding on developing Woodhall Spa.

To help them in their final choice they had a trusted adviser to rely on in Neil Hotchkin, owner, and son of the designer of Woodhall Spa, and a leading amateur golf administrator for many years. Hotchkin has run Woodhall Spa in the way you would expect from a champion of the principles of amateurism.

EGU plans for Woodhall are expansive. The overall cost of their scheme is £8 million ($12,800,000), including the purchase of 180 additional acres. The required site had to be at least 300 acres and, if possible, up to 500, because of the following facilities alongside the championship course: a second course, training centre (with driving range, short game practice area, including bunkers and putting greens), and either a par three course or training holes; EGU administration offices and conference room, amalgamated with a clubhouse for 200 people, on a common site.

The cash (supplemented by a £650,000 – $1,075,000 grant from the National Lottery) will come from a bank loan to be repaid by raising subscriptions from £1 to £3 ($1.60 to $4.80). This would be a small price to pay for the range of facilities offered by the plan, for the Welsh subscription is £4 ($6.40), and the Irish £4.50 ($7.20). Amateurs in developing golf nations such as France and Spain would think this a bargain: they pay £27.50 ($44.00) and £30 ($48.00) respectively.

By the time the EGU moved from Leicester to the new headquarters at Woodhall Spa in 1996, the National Lottery also made more than £2million available for 10 other golf projects. The Woodhall Spa plan may prove a solution to a problem which, given the increasing volume of course traffic year by year, may become chronic: seven clubs approached to stage EGU controlled tournaments in future years refused to make their courses available. Possession of Woodhall Spa, and a "spare" course close by, would obviate that poser for the EGU.

The cumulative coaching efforts of the EGU, PGA, and the Golf Foundation and the opportunities created by sponsors' money for junior events have all played their part in European and in particular British struggles to turn the tide of American supremacy over the past couple of decades.

Golfers on the eastern side of the Atlantic should also be grateful to reformers who after years of frustration achieved a major improvement in the British game, the introduction of the 1.68 inch ("American-size") ball in place of the traditional 1.66. Much credit is due to them for their part in making the Ryder, Curtis and Walker Cups, among other events, less US-dominated than they were for half a century.

Leonard Crawley was a member of a Walker Cup team that defeated the Americans (1938) when such a feat was almost as rare as hen's teeth. Later, his reports on the game from hither and yon would often include a lament that the 1.68 ball required purer striking, but was much more obedient to correct technique. American mastery of this meant that their leading players had an inbuilt advantage over their rivals. Moreover, even an indifferent player could appreciate that the 1.68 putted better – and many a Cup match had been lost to deadly US holing-out. It was difficult for mid-to long-handicap players, Crawley agreed, to appreciate all the advantages of the 1.68 ball, but that did not invalidate the case for its adoption.

Bill Tillman, an up-market furniture maker, decided to do something about it. The main obstacles to change were ball manufacturers, unenthusiastic at the thought of retooling, and the game's administrators, luke-warm to the 1.68. As a good-class amateur Tillman played in Bing Crosby's "Clambake" at Pebble Beach and got a close-up view of the superior method (and scoring) of US professionals.

Tillman had in any case been convinced by Doug Sanders, so adept as a manoeuvrer of the ball, that British golf would never thrive if the 1.66 era continued. Thus was born the Tillman Trophy, "Large Ball Open Amateur 72 Holes"; still going strong and a magnet for ambitious amateurs. Its conditions of play began: "The tournament shall be played by Stroke Play using the 1.68 size ball"... Early winners, over some of Britain's premier courses, included Philip Parkin, Peter Baker and Ernie Els, whose careers were not noticeably damaged by the experience.

IMPORTANT ADDRESSES

Royal & Ancient Golf Club, St Andrews, Fife, Scotland KY16 9JD

English Golf Union, The Broadway, Woodhall Spa, Lincs LN10 6PU

Irish Golf Union, Glencar House, 81 Eglington Road, Donnybrook, Dublin 4

Scottish Golf Union, The Cottage, 181a Whitehouse Road, Barnton, Edinburgh EH4 6BY

Welsh Golfing Union, Powys House, Cwmbran, Gwent NP44 1PB

AUSTRALIA

SOUTHERN (AUSTRALIAN) BEAUTY *The 18th hole at Royal Adelaide*

One Australian in 30 belongs to a golf club and, of the other 29, a couple probably play public courses. Australian golf history rather resembles the US story, in that after a fitful start (even golf tends to come second to a gold rush) all is now enthusiasm, powerfully fanned ever since the late 1970s by Greg Norman. Symbolic of Australia's devotion to golf is the New South Wales GC's Botany Bay lay-out at the 1770 landfall of Captain Cook, first Englishman to set foot in Australia. There are upwards of 1,400 courses.

The *Colonial Times* of Tasmania carried a report in 1827 that two young men, Scots of course, were playing golf there. Bothwell GC in the Tasmanian Midlands became the first club, founded by Alex Reid, who arrived in 1829, needless to say from Scotland.

The Royal Adelaide club, founded in South Australia in 1870, claims to be Australia's oldest in continuous existence. Golfers in Victoria, settled 50 years later than Sydney, are, however, among the world's most cossetted. The capital, Melbourne, itself has 60 clubs; 70 per cent of the the state's population of 4.5 million live there, a quarter of the nation's total. Only a 30-minute drive away lies the Port Phillip Bay "Sand Belt". Here, as on the Ayrshire coast of Scotland, is one fine golf course after another: Royal Melbourne, Victoria, Metropolitan, Kingston Heath, Commonwealth and Huntingdale. The latter is the home of the Masters, which Norman has won six times, and which was designed by an Englishman, Charles Alison, who never visited the site itself.

Deep bunkers and lightning fast greens are specialities hereabouts. Royal Melbourne's West Course and Kingston Heath are designs of Dr Alister Mackenzie, of Cypress Point and Augusta fame. Golf at these premier courses is costly: Royal Melbourne fees are just over a hundred US dollars. The clubs are also exclusive: often the visitor must be the guest of a member.

Yet there are more than 350 courses in Victoria serving about 150,000 golfers, splendid public courses among them, such as Yarra Bend, where the green fee is Aus$15 (less than £7, or nearly $11).

Asian golfers have the opportunity to join with the locals in buying into new developments in share schemes. The National at Cape Schank, Victoria, was the first in 1985 to raise finance in this way, selling at A$6,000 (£2,727/$4,227), but raising share prices later: they are worth double the initial price now. Members also pay an annual subscription of A$1,400 (£636/$986).

Japanese companies have put together a much costlier development at Terrey Hills near Sydney, opened in 1994 and quickly included on the Australian pro circuit.

Robert Allenby is Australia's brightest hope to take the place of Greg Norman. Allenby finished third in the 1996 Volvo rankings of the European PGA Tour although a September car crash cut his season short. Despite a fractured sternum, he travelled to Valderrama for the Tour's October finale. Allenby played the one shot he needed to qualify for a £75,000 bonus – which he gave to cancer charities. Norman's popularity is not so widely celebrated as it once was, possibly owing to his move to Florida, which led to a new nickname for the Great White Shark … the Great White Fish Finger.

Controversy is inescapable for Norman, especially when the vexed question of appearance money comes up – and yet he proved at Adelaide that he is value for such payments. Crowds tend to be smaller on the first two days of a tournament. Without Norman in 1995 the four-day total was 6,200, with him at the Ford Open in 1996, 21,000 spectators came on the first two days.

£75,000 SHOT *Robert Allenby's only stroke at Valderrama in 1996 was a painful affair*

IMPORTANT ADDRESS

Australian Golf Union, Golf Australia House, 155 Cecil Street, South Melbourne, Victoria 3205

NEW ZEALAND

New Zealand golf, of which Charles Richie Howden, a Scot, is the father, began in Dunedin. After various course moves, the club settled down, red coats and all, with Fogarty's pub as a base. Fogarty's went bust, and *all* the members' clubs were sold for one pound. Howden found them a year later, twisted and useless.

Christchurch revived things, helped by the presence of several Westward Ho! men. Edmund Wilder, fearful perhaps of another Fogarty experience, made a course on his own estate, where he played in blazer, jodhpurs and puttees.

Howden, after a trip abroad, came back to restart Dunedin in 1889, and in 1893 the Amateur Championship began. It was the second in any British colony, India pre-dating it in 1892. It was won by a recently arrived Presbyterian minister, J. A. Somerville, from Scotland.

Soon Hugh Macneil of Otago won it, and lifted the Australian version too. The Maori golfer Kurupo Tareha was the first native New Zealander to win: legends have grown about the long hitting of his son, Kapi.

New Zealand teams held their own against Australia in the six-match Kirk-Windeyer series, which ended at three-all.

Growth was phenomenal after 1945, with 10 per cent in a year not uncommon in the 1950s, when golf's first world-class left-hander Bob Charles was making his presence felt, beating Peter Thomson in the New Zealand Open when the Australian was working towards his British Open Championship hat-trick.

Golf course construction boomed, and New Zealand's one course for 10,000 people is the best per capita in the world of a major golf-playing nation. A fine record in the Eisenhower Trophy for amateur teams completes the picture: Maori Phil Tataurangi could claim in 1992 to be the world's leading amateur. He posted the lowest individual score as New Zealand won the Eisenhower in Vancouver from the US. Another member of the side, Michael Campbell, is making a name on the major tours.

IMPORTANT ADDRESS

New Zealand Golf Association, PO Box 11842, Dominion Sports House, Mercer Street, Wellington

MAORI MOVERS *Michael Campbell (left), moving from the European to the US Tour, has made his his mark. Philip "Spud" Tataurangi (far left) was best individual when New Zealand won the Eisenhower Trophy in Canada in 1992*

EUROPE

The golf bug crossed 3,000 miles of ocean and, with an ease no invading army could hope to achieve, rapidly assumed occupation of a vast acreage of North America. So why did the 20-odd miles of the English Channel delay golf's conquest of the Continent for so long? After all, the Scots and the French have often shared political and religious causes.

Yet the explosion of interest on the Continent over the last 15 years, with prodigies of course building in the 1980 and 1990s, comes nearly a century after the United States began the same process. Two reasons spring to mind: first, golf, like cricket, spreads fastest where English is spoken. Second, lack of local heroes: before 1979 only one Continental, France's Arnaud Massy, had won a major Open (1907).

FRANCE

Recent up-tempo building has been most marked in France, which can, however, claim to have the oldest club on the Continent, Pau. This is said to be a hangover from the Peninsular War, when Wellington's officers played there in 1814. What is far more certain is that Britons on holiday, including reportedly two of those pioneering officers, founded the club itself in 1856.

Yet France could boast fewer than 200 courses in 1987. The number has raced past 400 not far into the last decade of the century, by the end of which scores, perhaps hundreds, more will have opened. The cliffs of Dover are visible from the Wimereux course near Calais, and it has been said that another of the French clubs closest to England, Hardelot, is also the nation's best, with echoes of The Berkshire thanks to its splendid stands of trees. Needless to say, though worth remembering as an additional plus point in favour of golf in France, is that the food in French club restaurants is, well, French.

France's fast rate of course building is being imitated elsewhere, despite the handicap carried by Alpine courses in particular that because of the weather they are forced to close in winter, usually from November to March.

THE LOW COUNTRIES

In Belgium, whose former monarch Leopold was certainly the most skilful of all Royal golfers, courses have doubled in number since the late 1980s, and are not frighteningly expensive, a happy state of affairs encouraged also by the French authorities, with an eye to augmenting the vast flow of tourists from Britain and America in particular. Also, hotels and guest houses often arrange discounted fees with local courses.

LETHAL LOVELY *Hardelot, on the French coast near Boulogne, has charm, and a fiendish finish at the 17th and 18th*

GALLERY FEVER *Seve Ballesteros, outstayed by Eduardo Romero in this 1991 Spanish Open play-off at Club de Campo, took his third title there in 1995*

It is surprising the boom took so long, as Flory van Donck was a leading player in the 1950s, being nine times in the top ten in the British Open, including twice runner-up – to Peter Thomson and Gary Player. Holland is another late-comer to whole-hearted commitment to golf, despite Dutch claims to have invented the game. The coastal belt offers ideal links country, opportunities well taken by The Hague, frequent and fearsome home of the Dutch Open, and Noordwijk. Courses have increased in number by more than a third since the mid-1980s.

The impetus for this relatively belated activity must have to do, to some degree, with Ryder Cup successes since 1979, when the contest became US vs. Europe rather than US vs. Britain and Ireland. True, the European Tour's solid progress and the world-class scoring needed to win its tournaments have had their effect.

SPAIN

Wreathed in glory above these corporate successes stand Continental Europe's three Ryder regulars and Masters champions, Bernhard Langer, José-Maria Olazabal and golf's erstwhile leading box-office banker, Seve Ballesteros. How often the trio must be blessed by golf entrepreneurs, club secretaries and professionals (a great many of them with English and Scottish names) all over Europe.

Spain, however, must be excepted from the list of countries whose golf boom is of most recent vintage. Once jet aircraft brought British holiday-makers within three hours of so of the Costas, particularly the Costa del Sol, and the Algarve in Portugal, course building took off.

Being first in the field is not always a boon, and by the 1980s, golf in the Iberian peninsula had run into problems, some of them of local manufacture to do with soaring green fees and the level of service by course staff; some relating to the saturation of the facilities.

First tees were beginning to take on the look of London suburban municipal courses at sunrise in summer. It was often unwise, especially during British winters, not to be part of an organized golf trip with guaranteed access and tee-times.

The pressure, and prices, have gone down since, and there is no ducking the fact that the quality of many Iberian courses is unequalled anywhere, notably the pride and joy of the tin magnate Jaime Ortis Patino, Valderrama. This Robert Trent Jones design is a short drive from Gibraltar reaching its greatest days with the Ryder Cup match in 1997, which means that the Volvo Masters, climactic event of the European Tour, had to find a new home. Montecastillo, near Jerez, designed by Jack Nicklaus, was the 7,024-yard choice.

PORTUGAL

Portugal's oldest club, at Oporto, is a direct outcome of the British liking for port. A nine-holer was laid out near this north-western Portuguese harbour in 1890 by drink-trade Britons.

Penina, the first course of the Algarve, was a, perhaps *the*, key trend-setter for Portugal and Spain. Henry Cotton, the designer, was its life, soul, mordant wit and influential teacher. A massive programme of tree-planting on what was a featureless paddy-field in the 1960s, helped Penina to acquire maturity, fame and many imitators in short order.

Apart from a short period during the Portuguese revolution following Salazar's long, repressive regime, Penina with its luxurious hotel has occupied an enviable position among resorts for the well-heeled – and has often staged the Portuguese Open.

GERMANY AND AUSTRIA

Germany and Austria are other late-comers to the latest golf boom. One of Langer's early experiences in search of golf fame explains a lot. He was told by a career guidance officer that there was no such calling as that of a golf professional. The game was very much for the well-off when he was born, but recent construction, especially of nine-hole courses as in Holland, has opened the door wide. Germany had 60 courses 35 years ago, but now has more than 300, a fair proportion coming with a rush over the past decade: many more are planned or being built.

Austria too, though on a smaller scale, has joined the rush to be on the rota of European Tour stops. Club names have a splendid resonance: for example Golf Club Bad Kleinkirchheim-Reichenau.

RUSSIA

Russia as golfing territory performs well up to its reputation as an enigma wrapped in mystery. Golf started there in 1895 economically and well, with a half guinea entrance fee at the Mourino Club, St Petersburg (annual subscription £2. 12s. 6d.), by a small village 12 miles from the then capital. All the winners' names that have come down to us were British.

The revolution was not kind to golf: surely no pastime, except perhaps polo, smacks more of royalty and the middle and upper classes. No course of any kind existed for long after the Second World War, despite the zeal of Bindari Pasha, Egypt's minister to Russia, which raised only incredulous stares from collective farmers who watched him, complete with plus fours and caddie, whacking white spheres about a field in 1949.

By 1974, Robert Trent Jones was commissioned to build a course on a site 15 minutes from Moscow's Red Square, following keen lobbying by US lumberman Robert F. Dwyer, a member of the USGA Executive Committee. There was something of the humorous spirit of the *Inspector General* in the lack of progress on this project. Next Armand Hammer, another US magnate, this time in the oil business, seemed to have interested Party Secretary Brezhnev.

Progress has been made with a Harold Swan course at Yalta, and the Swedes, thanks to the initiative of ice hockey giant Sven Tumba, got moving with a nine-holer near the Swedish and German embassies. Here John Fite, head pro at Claremont GC, Oakland, California, came to teach; his son was studying on a year's exchange visit at St Petersburg.

In 1992, the Russian Golf Association was founded and four years later the Sovereign Russian Open, a European Challenge Tour event, was played at the Moscow Country Club, whose bourgeois connotations surely sound the final knell of communism. Carl Watts's victory, worth nearly £10,500, was gained over a course which Watts said was "the best we have played on the Challenge Tour" (despite the fourth round being rained off).

BERNHARD LANGER *The toast of Europe with Seve and Olly, photographed in action in 1994*

COTTON'S KINGDOM *The ninth at Penina in Portugal, before one of the game's most charming hotels*

REST OF EUROPE

Italy, with courses of outstanding beauty, Switzerland, Denmark and Sweden were into action much sooner, and so purposefully have Swedes coached and built (well over 200 courses, mostly in the south) that it would be a brave man who gave long odds against a Swedish man winning a major before the 21st century dawns, Liselotte Neumann having already done the trick for the ladies with the US Open. Groups of golfers are put together during national service in Sweden, so that military and sports training can go hand in hand.

Danish golf has a friendly, family feeling: the author remembers the opening of the second nine holes at the Storstrommen Golfklub, on the easterly island of Falster, redolent with the succulent aroma of a wild pig roasting on a spit.

The former communist bloc is a different proposition entirely. To begin with, the promising tourist-golf possibilities of the former Yugoslavia remain unrealized owing to the chaos of war, though the European Women's Tour has operated successfully in Slovenia.

Even where there was a welcome locally for golfers in Iron Curtain days, as in Czechoslovakia, there was little movement until the second Prague spring. The author recalls the disappointment of the European Press Golf Association, whose meetings were attended by scores of journalists from all over Europe, when visas were not forthcoming for all of their number: so no one went. In President Vaclav Havel's more welcoming days the European Tour itself became a visitor, though the 1994 Chemapol Trophy Czech Open tournament at Marianske Lazne in the newly created Czech Republic was savaged by frost. Per-Ulrik Johansson won over 63 holes.

SECOND CUP SWEDE *Per-Ulrik Johansson became the second Swede to play in the Ryder Cup in 1995*

IMPORTANT ADDRESSES

Austrian Golf Federation, Haus des Sports, Prinz-Eugen-Strasse 12, A-1040 Vienna
Belgian Royal Federation of Golf, Chemin de Baudemont 23, 1400 Nivelles
Czech Golf Federation, Erpet Golf Centre, Strakonica 510, 150 00 Prague
Danish Golf Union, Idratteas Hus, 2605, Brondby
Finnish Golf Union, Radiokatu 12, SF-00240 Helsinki
French Golf Federation, 69 Avenue Victor Hugo, 75783 Paris, Cedex 16
German Golf Association, Postfach 2106, 6200 Wiesbaden
Hellenic Golf Federation, PO Box 70003, Glyfada, Athens
Iceland Golf Union, Sport Centre, 104 Reykjavik
Italian Golf Federation, Viale Tiziano 74, 00196 Rome
Luxembourg Golf Union, c/o GC Grand Ducal, 1 Route de Treves, 2633 Senningerberg
Netherland Golf Federation, PO Box 221, 3454 ZL De Meern
Norwegian Golf Union, Hauger Skolevei 1, 1351 Rud
Portuguese Golf Federation, Rua General F. Martins 10 Miraflores, 1495 Alges
Slovenian Golf Association, c/o GC Bled, C. Svobede 13, 64260 Bled
Spanish Golf Federation, Capitan Haya 9-5 Dcha, Madrid 28020
Swedish Golf Federation, PO Box 84, S-182 11 Danderyd
Swiss Golf Association, En Ballegue, Case Postale CH-1066, Epalinges, Lausanne

SOUTH AMERICA AND THE CARIBBEAN

PARAGUAY

Incredible is a frequently misused word. Yet when Raul Fretes, unranked, from Paraguay, beat Colin Montgomerie, then 17th in the Sony Rankings, in the first round of the 1993 Dunhill Cup at St Andrews, it was difficult to object to Fretes's summing-up, "very incredible".

The Paraguayan trio of Carlos Franco, his brother Angel and Fretes had defeated Scotland (Montgomerie, Sam Torrance and Gordon Brand Junior) 2–1 at the home of golf, and in a totally un-Paraguayan style freezing wind too. Brand was the Scots' only winner, beating Angel. "They will not believe this at home," said Fretes. "It is very unreal to me."

Paraguay has fewer golfers than many a single club in Britain has members, and was credited with having fewer clubs (four) than St Andrews, let alone Scotland.

There are only a couple of dozen pros in Paraguay. Six of them are Carlos and Angel Franco and their four brothers. Carlos and Angel are not unused to winning. Both have finished at the head of the Order of Merit of the South American Tour, which was launched in 1991, and Carlos also topped the Asian Order.

Paraguay also beat Wales 2–1, but did not reach the last four because they lost 2–1 on the second day to the team which eventually went on to win the Cup, the USA – far from a disgrace.

The following year Canada's feat in beating the US in the final was hailed as the greatest upset since, well, since Scotland beat Paraguay on the first day, Andrew Coltart doing well in Torrance's place. He beat Fretes at the 19th.

ARGENTINA

Unless the Carlos brothers mount a complete take-over, Argentina will continue to be thought of as Latin America's strongest golfing nation, who look to Edwardo Romero to do great deeds. His compatriot Vicente Fernandez, despite being born with one leg shorter than the other, has seldom been out of the top 40 on the European Tour since the mid-1970s: his fifth win on the Tour, in the 1992 Murphy's Open, was by virtue of an 87-foot birdie putt up the The Belfry's huge triple-tier 18th green.He has since prospered on the US Senior Tour.

Like South America's best player of all, Roberto de Vicenzo, Fernandez is a multiple winner of Argentine and Brazil titles, though not such a dominant player as was Antonio Cerda in the 1950s. Cerda was top World Cup individual in 1953, and second to Max Faulkner by two shots in the 1951 British Open. José Jurado came even closer for Argentina in 1931, when a topped shot on the 71st hole into a Carnoustie stream led to his finishing a shot behind the champion, Tommy Armour.

BRAZIL

Brazil has an unusual claim to golf fame: a hat-trick of Brazilian Open wins was completed in 1961 by the

87-FOOT PUTT = £92,660 *Vicente Fernandez watches his Murphy Open winner drop at The Belfry*

American Bob Falkenburg, who had caused something of a furore when winning the Wimbledon lawn tennis title in 1948. In that era when "play shall be continuous" was rigorously enforced, he regathered his strength by lying down now and then on the hallowed Centre Court turf.

The best native Brazilian players have been Mario Gonzales and his son Jaime, who played on the US and European Tours, but never won.

MEXICO

Victor Relagado from Tijuana did manage to win on the US Tour, but the most noteworthy of Mexican golf happenings is also the most tragic. Willie Smith, who won the US Open in 1899 by 11 strokes, still a record, was from Carnoustie, like his brother Alex who also won the US Open. They are the only brothers to do so, and their brother Macdonald is celebrated as being the best player never to win a major event. Willie died after being found in the cellar of the Mexico City club where he was serving as a pro. The building had been shelled during the Mexican Revolution of 1914–15.

UNREAL FEELING *Raul Fetes of Paraguay helped shock Scotland in the Dunhill*

THE CARIBBEAN

The Bahamas and Bermuda, where the golf tradition is very strong, not to mention Caribbean Islands such as Puerto Rico and Dominica, offer a (much used) sunny escape route for US and Canadian golfers, though the spotlight of publicity had been on Jamaica in the nineties, because of the Johnnie Walker World Championship at Tryall, which has now been discontinued

Barbados has one of the most luxurious and fashionable of the golf/hotel complexes in the world, at Sandy Lane (sited on the sought-after western coast), where the course has been renovated and extended with an extra nine holes in a £3 million ($4,650,000) development. A Sandy Lane round costs £75 ($116.25) including caddie cart, but if you can afford Sandy Lane Hotel rates, the golf is free.

To tempt even more players from cooler climes, an old Barbados sugar plantation is being turned into a £300 million ($465 million) project. Royal Westmoreland will eventually be a mix of residential (380 homes) and sports facilities around a Robert Trent Jones course. A US Senior tournament, or regular tour event is the eventual aim, since it is difficult to see how another tournament on the lines of the Johnny Walker or Sun City event can be shoe-horned into the golfing year between the end of the regular season and Christmas. But if the European Tour can take in Manila, why not Barbados?

TRYALL JAMAICA *Johnny Walker World title, 1993*

IMPORTANT ADDRESSES

South America and Central America

Argentine Golf Association, Corrientes 538, Piso 11, 1043 Buenos Aires
Bolivian Golf Federation, Casilla de Correo 6130, La Paz
Brazilian Golf Federation, Rua 7 de Abril, 01044 São Paulo
Chilean Golf Federation, Casilla 13307, Correo 21, Santiago
Colombian Golf Union, Carrer 7A, 72-64 of Int. 26 Apartado Aereo 90985, Bogotà
Ecuador Golf Federation, Casilla 521, Guayaquil
Mexican Golf Association, Cincinnati, No. 40-104, Mexico 18, DF
Paraguay Golf Association, Casilla de Correo 302, Asunción
Peru Golf Federation, Casilla 5637, Lima
Uruguay Golf Association, Casilla 1484, Montevideo
Venezuela Golf Federation, Local 5, Avda. Avila, La Florida, Caracas 1050

The Caribbean

Bahamas Golf Federation, PO Box N4568, Nassau
Barbados Golf Association, c/o Sandy Lane GC, St James
Bermuda Golf Association, PO Box HM 433, Hamilton HM BX
El Salvador Golf Federation, Apartado Postal 631, San Salvador
Jamaica Golf Association, Constant Spring GC, PO Box 743, Kingston 8

ASIA AND THE FAR EAST

THE ASIAN TOUR

The quickening pulse of economic development on the western side of the Pacific Rim is being reflected as the millenium approaches by enormous changes and expansion in golf. First and foremost is the progressive unification of rival professional tours after years of turf wars.

Asian professionals had for years been frustrated by the fact that outsiders had dominated their Order of Merit. Taiwanese players had prospered until non-Asians began taking the lion's share of prize-money. There was no clear career structure for Asian players such as existed within the US and Europe. There the tours had gone from strength to strength, given extra impulsion by the enthralling personality duels of the Palmer–Player–Nicklaus era. By comparison the Asian circuit stagnated. Founded in 1962 as the Far East Circuit, it was administered by an amateur organization of representatives from member nations. These flaws were exemplified in the Asian pros' eyes by the fact that Frankie Minoza of the Philippines was the only Asian golfer to finish at the head of the Asian Tour's Order of Merit in the six years ending 1994. The Tour seemed to them to be a fragmented circuit co-ordinated outside Asia by non-Asians, largely for the benefit of non-Asians.

In 1994 the Asian Professional Golfers' Association decided to launch the rival Omega Asian PGA Tour starting midway in 1995: 18 events paid out prize-money of $5 million/£3.2 million. The Order of Merit leader was Taiwan's Lin Keng-chi, by a whisker from Boonchu Ruangkit, the veteran Thai.

Omega expanded the following year, to 24 events in 13 countries with prize money rising by nearly $2 million (£1.3 million). Significantly the Epson Singapore Open became the first of the region's national Opens to switch from the Asian Tour to Omega, which also absorbed the Sabah Masters and Volvo China Open. Part of the agreement with the Volvo event was that the APGA would not stage any events during the previous two weeks, when there were four 36-hole tournaments in southern China. Nurturing the game in China with these mini-events would clearly be helped by the presence of Omega Tour players.

Four new events were created for Omega's second year and the 1997 schedule will include the Open Championships of Myanmar (Burma) and Vietnam. There is joint sanction, with the Australasian PGA Tour, for the Dunhill Masters, at Royal Hong Kong, and the Players Championship in Queensland.

"Foreigners" still win on the Omega Asian Tour, but Wook-soon Kang (Korea) led the rankings into 1997 – and amateur Hong Chia-yuh took the 1996 Asian Tour's $275,000 China Open by a record 12 strokes.

Japan's Isao Aoki, second in the 1980 US Open to Nicklaus, and Taiwanese Mr Lu, second in the 1971 British Open, are the only Asian players to come close to a major title (although Tiger Woods' mother is from the Far East).

A YEN FOR GOLF

Japanese pros make lots of money as soon as they get anywhere near the top of their own Order of Merit, and seem disinclined for the most part to seek wider fame. Joe (the Pro) Hardstaff, who retired in 1995 after serving as Royal Hong Kong's pro since 1965 (Mr Lu preceded him there), puts it this way: "They don't travel well." Language and food are particular difficulties. Coach David Leadbetter believes their practice facilities are inadequate, leading to inferior iron play.

There is certainly no financial compulsion for them to travel: it is a chauffeur-driven life for the best of them at home tournaments. Masashi "Jumbo" Ozaki was highest placed, at 38th, of six Japanese players in Nick Price's 1994 Open at Turnberry. Apart from these there

BATTERY GOLFERS *Tokyo's three-tiered Shiba driving range. Despite such facilities, David Leadbetter thinks scope for practice in Japan is inadequate*

ABOVE: HIGH-RISE BACKDROP *Tom Watson defends his Hong Kong Open title in 1993*

RIGHT: SINGAPORE SWINGS *Tanah Merah, with 3,000 members, hosted a European Tour event in 1996*

was not one player from Asia.

Ozaki won the Japan Open a few weeks later, earning 18 million yen, about £120,000 – and £10,000 more than Price earned at Turnberry. Ozaki stood 11th in the Sony World Rankings at the time: none of his colleagues in the Sony Top 30 was in opposition. Japanese purses exceed European Tour rewards. Despite this, none of the Japanese events is included in the Sony Rankings top-40 rated tournaments.

An Englishman, Arthur Groom, "Father of Japanese Golf", chose a spectacular site for the first course in Japan in 1903, a four-hole affair near the summit of Mount Rokko, extended to 18 holes within a year. Groom died after a fall on his way down from the course 14 years later. There were 70 courses by 1934. Tokyo GC was the nation's first, in 1914, to be founded by locals.

Shortage of suitable terrain – Groom's mountainside venture has perforce been followed, expensive as it is, many times – inflates membership fees and subscriptions to the scale of international telephone numbers, and drives Japanese players to fly abroad to buy memberships and courses.

The military regime that led Japan into war in the 1930s was as bad for golf as the communists in Europe; golf was a subversive (US/British) activity. The American military had the opposite effect during the years of occupation, and it cannot be long (though planning authorities not unreasonably oppose the proliferation of courses in some areas) before courses exceed the 2,000 mark.

For all that, golfers short of a few billion yen are struggling. Top club corporate memberships are bought and sold through brokers at six-figure (sterling) terms. Even the moderately rich must be content with golf range golf, like the Shiba, a three-tiered range in Tokyo. Some are perched on top of office blocks.

THE FAR EAST

Costly golf is not confined to Japan. The Pacific Ring is as vibrantly expansive in golf as in most other human activities. However, the richest areas, like Singapore and Hong Kong, are also, not unnaturally, the most restricted for course-worthy land in an era of golf boom.

Singapore's *GOLF* magazine lists 14 private clubs (the island is about the size of the Isle of Man). This includes the Singapore Island Country Club, with four 18-hole courses, 6,000 members, an entrance fee of $137,175 and where a round with a caddie (A, B, or C class) costs in excess of $155. As in Japan, prices vary on a lively market. Then there is the Fairway Country Club – a driving range, where 100 balls will cost $2.74 … not at all expensive by western standards – but a membership fee of nearly $5,000 is payable first.

Also listed are 43 clubs in neighbouring Batam and Malaysia, including Kukup on the south-western tip of the Malaysia peninsula, close to Singapore. These get crowded too, though prices have not attained Singapore levels in general. Kukup has three nine-hole loops (with another to come), a sports centre, a children's miniature course and Kids' Village, six tennis courts, a Conference Centre and restaurant (over a lake), a driving range (with

a pond in front of the bays to help quell golfer's hydrophobia), and an island putting green. To join costs a Malay $11,817 (£7,385) a player from another country $17,724 (£11,078), and then there is a fee of $64 (£40) to pay for a round at the weekend.

A brigadier-general drove the Kukup venture forward, and the Royal Thai Army Course at Bangkok is subsidized by the military, its two courses kept parade-ground neat. A twosome playing a weekend round including caddies would fork out 1,500 baht (£38/$59). There is even a golf resort on the River Kwai: tourists can ride on the Death Railway.

Hong Kong, like Singapore, must look outward to extend its golfing facilities. The Hong Kong Club, with three courses on the New Territories at Fanling (the home of the charmingly named charitable organization the Fanlingerers, which formerly accrued funds for the war-blinded, and now does so for Cheshire Homes) has 600 registered caddies. That speaks volumes as to the heavy use to which the courses are put, involving well over 10,000 players in the week, including 100 Japanese a day. Also busy is the club's other course on Hong Kong Island itself, Discovery Bay.

Corporate memberships have risen in price from about $1,286 in 1970 to more than $1.5 million. It is small wonder then that Hong Kong magazines advertise opportunities to buy into courses in Australia. They also pinpoint Shenzhen, "the only golf club in China close to Hong Kong". Shenzhen's Mission Hills club (designer Jack Nicklaus) broke new ground in 1995 as the first in China to host the World Cup.

FLOURISHING PHUKET *Blue Canyon Golf Club in Thailand, staged the newly created Honda Classic*

CHINA AND INDIA

Admission to Mission Hills for the World Cup was HK$10 (less than £1), the same as a day's wage for the 1,600 labour force that put Nicklaus's course together: the 35-mile six-lane road to it cost £750 million ($1.185 billion). Fred Couples and David Love III won for the US. Their prize of $200,000 each plus Love's individual $100,000 was not dissimilar to the cost of a corporate membership at the club. Sam Torrance lost a ball to a souvenir hunter, which was costly, since he and Andrew Coltart finished third for Scotland a stroke behind Australia. China's pair finished 27th, only five behind England.

Many Hong Kong residents attended, clearly far better informed on golf than the locals but, if only because Den Xiaoping's son-in-law visits the club, golf in China has prospects. Many more courses are on the way in the land that Napoleon promised would surprise the world.

The polite Chinese should be hot on etiquette: relations have eased somewhat since the Treaty of Nanking, in which the Imperial Chinese Government agreed not to refer routinely to Westerners in official documents as "barbarians".

By contrast, India is ancient golfing country. Royal Calcutta (1829) is the oldest club outside the British Isles. Royal Bombay dates from 1842. So, midway through the nineteenth century, England and India had the same number of clubs. India was not represented at Shenzhen, and pickings for India pros are slim. There are a mere 130 courses, many run by the Army, so dreams of cricketing fame are more appropriate on the sub-continent.

A chink of light at last illumined Myanmar (Burma) golf as 1996 began, when Boonchu Ruangkit, from Thailand, an ex-kick boxer, took the inaugural $150,000 Myanmar Open. Besides, there are thought to be 20,000 players in Myanmar.

IMPORTANT ADDRESSES

Asia-Pacific Golf Confederation, 52, 1st Floor, Jalan Hang, Lekiu 50100, Kuala Lumpur

Asia Golf Tour Inc, 8, 2a 8th Floor, Jaya Shopping Centre, Jalau Seiuaugat, 46100 Petaling Jaya, Selauger, Malaysia

China Golf Association, 75 Lane 187, Tunhau S Road, Taipei, Taiwan 10647

Hong Kong Golf Association, Suite 1420, Princes Building, 10 Chater Road, HK

Indian Golf Union, Tata Centre (3rd Floor), 43 Chowringhee Road, Calcutta 700071

Indonesian Golf Association, c/o Bank Bumi Daya, Jin Imam Bonjol 61-PO Box 106, Jakarta Pusat

Japan Golf Association, 606-6th Floor, Palace Building, Marunouchi, Chiyoda-ku, Tokyo

Korean Golf Assocation, 13th Floor, Manhattan Building, 36-2, Yeo-Eui-Do-Dowg, Yeong Deung Po-Ku, Seoul

Malaysian Golf Association, 12a Persiaran Ampang, 55000 Kuala Lumpur

Pakistan Golf Federation, PO Box 1295, Rawalpindi

Philippines Golf Association, 209 Administration Building, Rizal Memorial Sports Complex, Vito Cruz, Manila

Singapore Golf Association, Thomson Road, PO Box 0172, Singapore 9157

Sri Lanka Golf Union, 2 Gower Street, Colombo 5, Sri Lanka

Thailand Golf Association, Railway Training Centre, Vibhavadee Rangsit Road, Bangkok 10900

THE MIDDLE EAST

Courses are few in the Middle East. Israel's lone gem is at Caesarea, the port Herod built and named for Augustus Caesar. The course is not long, but picturesque, and a perfect holiday set-up, especially for its proximity to a Dan Hotel, some of the best of Mediterranean beaches, and a splendid Roman aqueduct and theatre. The southern Israeli resort of Eilat plans a course, but water engineering difficulties are great there, and as yet the project is not far advanced.

Such problems have been solved in the United Arab Emirates sufficiently well to reach a standard which satisfies the officials of two professional tours, for golf hereabouts, founded on oil money, scored a double in 1995. The European Tour again visited the Emirates Course, and the Dubai Creek course of the Dubai Yachting and Golf Club was on the schedule of the new Asia PGA Tour. Next date to be inscribed on the Gulf golf calendar was 1998, the launch date of the $1 million Qatar Masters on the Doha course - immediately after the Dubai Classic. This new European Tour event is a coup for the Emir, Sheik Hamad Bin Khalifa Al Thani, marking the golden jubilee of golf in Qatar.

TAKING SHAPE *Dubai Creek golf course and marina*

DESERT VICTORY *Robert Green moves towards his first significant title – on the Emirates Course in a play-off with Greg Norman and Ian Woosnam*

AFRICA

SOUTH AFRICA

The Bedford Club of Cape Province, founded in 1892, was granted permission in a municipal minute "to make a golf links... provided the holes were covered with large flat stones". Despite this insensitive request, the club prospered by 1896 to the extent of being able to employ a pro named Johnstone, for two weeks at £2 a week.

Golf began in South Africa with the Royal Cape club at Wynberg. Five years later the powerful engine of Transvaal golf, the Johannesburg club, was formed, with John Tudhope as the head of affairs. The club inaugurated the Transvaal Golf Union, which for the first 20 years of its existence was run exclusively by Johannesburg members.

Six years later, for their involvement in the Jameson Raid which foreshadowed the Boer War, the club president, Sir Lionel Phillips, was sentenced to death and the club captain, H. Becker, imprisoned.

A hundred years later and there is a million dollar first prize on offer at the Sun City course designed by Gary Player in Bophuthatswana alongside a hotel, casino and entertainment complex out of Las Vegas by Walt Disney, you might say. Spectacular is the name of the Sun City game, which has a backdrop of the Pilanesberg Game Reserve.

The original name of the site, Letsatsing, means "sun", and the Sun City Classic began in December of 1979. Two years later the first $1 million (now £645,000) prize was offered. International stars performed on stage and on course at Sun City, yet the South African game itself was becoming isolated.

Visiting players were excluded from golf in many countries after their names had appeared in newspaper reports as having played, for example, on the Sunshine Tour in South Africa and subsequently put on a blacklist by the United Nations Anti-Apartheid Committee. South African teams vanished from the World Cup and similar events. Where the professional game was powerful enough and there was no governmental action in the relevant territory, South African players could and did play.

Black players' careers were stunted, and there were well documented cases of out and out cruelty in areas of particularly stony apartheid rule. Sewsunker Sewgolum, of Indian parentage, distinguished himself as the only first-class player to operate with left hand below right on all clubs, a practice seldom adopted except as a cure for putting horrors. He won the Dutch Open three times, but was seldom allowed to play in his native land.

Gary Player followed another Transvaaler, Bobby Locke, putter without peer, as South Africa's shorts-odds prospect wherever he teed off. Player said after winning his second US PGA title (while protected by armed police because of extremist threats) that he was encouraging excellent young black players. One, Vincent Tshabalala, a Bantu, obliged by winning the French Open. He later refused selection for the World Cup, believing it would suggest he condoned apartheid, and then was refused entry to the South African Open.

South Africa's return to the world stage of golf coincided with the rise of another of her sons, Nick Price from Durban, to the head of the world rankings. Clearly Ernie Els, who won his first major, the US Open title, in 1994, is a good bet to succeed him but may have to wait awhile as Price celebrated his 40th birthday by racking up a second then two first places in the three tournaments staged in the Republic in conjuction with the European Tour. Els and Wayne Westner put a gloss on South Africa's return to team events by romping 18 shots clear of Tom Lehman and Steve Jones, of the US, in the World Cup at Erinvale, near Cape Town, in 1996.

Another golfer of whom the South African PGA have high hopes is black, set free at last with others of his race to follow their golfing stars now that his country has been readmitted to the full range of world sport. Mawonga Nomwa, 24, a former caddie from Soweto who started playing at 14, got through in 13th place at the Tour Qualifying School of 1994, when he turned pro. He went on to earn his first cheque early in 1995, in 29th place in the Masters at Sun City's "Lost City" course. He finished three over par, but, significantly, he made great progress over the crucial last nine holes, where most tournaments really begin, coming home in 32 with four birdies.

WAYNE WESTNER *World Cup triumph with Ernie Els*

THE SAFARI CIRCUIT

The lovely Nairobi courses at Karen (where screaming, mocking monkeys and the possibility lurking in the mind that there might be a cobra or two about are good tests of concentration) and flowery Muthaiga, where some of the events dramatized in the film *White Mischief* occurred, are splendid touristic adjuncts to the game parks, and the holiday courses on the north African littoral grow in popularity.

The Safari Circuit, across the continent from Nigeria to Kenya, has been a fine proving ground for young pros: Sandy Lyle, among others, gained his first tournament success there. The Kenya Open, at Mathaiga, and the Ivory Cost Open at Abidjan have become the opening events of the buoyant European Challenge Tour, which has proved to be the prime admission point for players aspiring to the major PGA Tour.

IMPORTANT ADDRESSES

Botswana Golf Union, PO Box 1362, Gaborone
Ghana Golf Association, PO Box 8, Achimola
Kenya Golf Union, PO Box 49609, Nairobi
Malawi Golf Union, PO Box 1198, Blantyre
Namibian Golf Union, PO Box 2989, Windhoek 9000
Nigeria Golf Union, National Sports Commission, Surulere, PO Box 145, Lagos
Sierra Leone Golf Federation, Freetown GC, PO Box 237, Lumley Beach, Freetown
South African Golf Federation, PO Box 391994, Bramley, South Africa 2018
Swaziland Golf Union, PO Box 1739, Mbabane
Tanzania Golf Union, PO Box 2569, Dar es Salaam
Uganda Golf Union, Kitante Road, PO Box 2574, Kampala
Zaire Golf Federation, BP 1648, Lubumbashi
Zambian Golf Union, PO Box 31943, Lusaka
Zimbabwe Golf Association, PO Box 3327, Harare

LEGENDS

In golf, as in other sports, the epithet "legendary" is over-used and much devalued, having been applied to almost every player who has savoured victory at the highest level. But at the summit of the game there is a small elite group whose golfing exploits make them worthy recipients of exaggerated and romanticized praise. Most of all, their game did not wilt when they neared the winning post.

SEVERIANO BALLESTEROS

Blessed with a supreme natural talent, the man from Pedrena is beloved of the fans in the gallery worldwide. The winner of five "Majors", three Opens and two Masters, Seve has a greater and more imaginative range of shots than anyone else in golf today.

BEN HOGAN

Hailing from Dublin, Texas, Ben Hogan became the dominant player in world golf in the immediate aftermath of the Second World War. His long game had an accuracy which has probably never been matched.

ARNOLD PALMER

One of the few men in sport who can boast an army, Arnold Palmer was the first golfer of the television age. Not one of golf's stylists, the pugnacious Pennsylvanian won the acclaim of the crowd for his whole-hearted commitment and his bold stroke play.

LEE TREVINO

Gloriously unorthodox, Lee Trevino was at his peak in the early 1970s. The wisecracking Mexican-American remains a highly successful and very popular performer on the Seniors Tour.

NICK FALDO

Though his sometimes unsmiling persona has not always endeared him to the media, Nick Faldo's single-minded dedication to his craft has ensured that he is frequently "the man to beat", as witness his sixth major at Augusta in 1996.

BOBBY JONES

In 1930 Bobby Jones came as close to achieving golfing invincibility as is humanly possible when he performed the Grand Slam. On retiring from championship golf, he built a course at Augusta, Georgia, and founded a golfing institution – the Masters

GARY PLAYER

A dedicated practiser and fitness fanatic, Gary Player had no rivals as golf's greatest world traveller. For much of the 1960s, the South African was one of the few overseas golfers to win regularly in the United States. His ninth major was the 1978 Masters.

THE TRIUMVIRATE

J. H. Taylor, Harry Vardon and James Braid were exact golfing contemporaries who together took no fewer than 16 of the Open championships between 1894 and 1914.

WALTER HAGEN

Ever a man to enjoy life, Walter Hagen won the US Open in 1914 and 1919 and was a relentless acquirer of trophies in the 1920s and '30s. His ability to extricate himself from the deepest trouble was his hallmark. He was also the first full-time tournament professional.

JACK NICKLAUS

An impetuous power-player who evolved into a cautious perfectionist, Jack Nicklaus was undoubtedly the world's greatest golfer in the 1960s and '70s, was still a leading contender in the 1980s and remains a doughty competitor in the 1990s.

GENE SARAZEN

A diminutive figure with an idiosyncratic style, Gene Sarazen's made a dramatic entrance into the golfing scene when he won the US Open and the US PGA as a 20-year-old. After a nine-year gap, he enjoyed a second purple patch, winning the British Open and US Open in 1932, the US PGA in 1933 and the Masters in 1935.

TOM WATSON

Tom Watson made his majestic mark on the game in the late 1970s and early 1980s with five British Open victories between 1975 and 1983, wresting away from Jack Nicklaus the crown of the world's greatest golfer.

SEVE BALLESTEROS

THE NATURAL FROM SPAIN

Severiano Ballesteros makes the rest of a golf field look like a collection of cart-horses. The glory of his game is his golf swing and the poise and rhythm of the follow-through.

But there is a contradiction. Watch the man on a practice ground or playing a competitive round: he is all worry and rehearsal. He frequently remarks on his dislike of the state of his game and is seldom happy with the position of his club at the top of the backswing.

With the driver in particular he has often been crooked but long; now he is crooked and, by the standards of today, not particularly long. But other wizardries remain, not least his natural genius at those trouble shots – from deep rough, woodland or bushes – that his wayward driving forces him to play.

Ballesteros himself admits his short game isn't as good as when he first appeared on the golf scene in 1976. However, his putting abilities do not seem impaired. From long range he usually coasts the ball to the hole-side and seldom misses those decisive short putts. When he is bunkered beside a green, it is hardly worth watching – you know the ball will finish stone dead. From other trouble spots in this scoring zone, he has greater range of shot and imagination, still, than anyone else in the game.

Love in the press tent

It is no surprise that such a natural talent emerged young with his challenge, at 19, for the 1976 Royal Birkdale Open. Few paid much attention when he tied for the first-round lead with a 69. Who was he? How did you pronounce his name? Interviewed in the press tent afterwards, Seve declared he might take 80 if the wind got up the next day. That remark may have been the beginning of the love affair that the Press have had with Ballesteros – particularly in Britain – throughout his career.

The next day, another 69 gave him a two-stroke lead. Could this very young unknown win? It was not to be, though he held the same margin over Miller after the third day's play. On the last day, however, Miller took the lead quickly while Ballesteros had more than his usual ration of wild tee shots. A late burst allowed him to finish second and he knew he was on his way.

It was only a matter of time before he won the Open, which he did at Lytham in 1979, cementing his growing fame for wild play in his final round by carving his drive into BBC vehicles and, of course, recording a birdie on the hole. When it was all over, his playing partner, Hale Irwin, remarked that he could not understand how anyone could finish as Open champion after so much bad driving.

Seve had still to prove himself in the USA. It didn't take him long: in the 1980 Masters his start of 66, 69, 68 gave him a seven-stroke lead going into the final round. At one point he increased that to ten before some embarrassing play from the 11th to 13th. Easing up, he won in some comfort.

There was the same four-stroke margin in 1983, this time largely because of a blistering start in his final round – birdie, eagle, par, birdie and out in 31. There were no real alarms and he finished by chipping in for a par on the last after roaring through the green with his second and then misjudging his third.

The following year came his second Open title, at St Andrews. It saw some of the steadiest play the Spaniard has produced. Through the rounds par followed par but birdies were few. By generally choosing to go left from the tee to avoid trouble he was leaving himself more difficult lines into the greens. On the 71st hole, he again went well left into the rough, giving himself little chance of hitting, let alone holding, the green. But that is what he did. A birdie putt at the relatively easy last hole then saw him home by two from Watson and Langer.

A fourth Open to cap his 1988 flourish is doubtful, but his Ryder Cup heroics received reward with captaincy at Valderrama in 1997, with a little more power than Gallacher. He is determined to play but, if forced to withdraw through loss of form, has the extra privilege of choosing his replacement – giving him a third captain's pick.

> **“Seve's got shots the rest of us don't even know.”**
>
> *Ben Crenshaw*

Career Milestones

1957 *Born Pedrena, northern Spain.*
1976 *Wins first Tour event, Dutch Open, aged 19.*
1979 *First Spaniard to win the British Open and first Continental European since Arnaud Massy in 1907.*
1980 *First European to win the Masters and, at 23, the youngest champion.*
1983 *A second Masters title.*
1984 *His second British Open title, distinguished by steady play.*
1988 *Third British Open title, defeating Nick Faldo and Nick Price with a final-round 65 – "the best round of my life".*

LYTHAM 1988 *Ballesteros played the round of his life*

NICK FALDO

THE MODERN HOGAN

Nick Faldo, despite an already successful career, famously decided in the mid-1980s that he needed to totally remodel his swing, and went on to become the best golfer in the world.

Faldo first came into the public eye in 1975, when he won the British Youths' Open Amateur Championship and the English Amateur. He turned professional the following year and his first tournament win came in 1977. That year saw another boost to his career when he formed a good partnership with Peter Oosterhuis and also beat Tom Watson – a Watson still with the glow of the Masters and the Turnberry Open Championship about him – in the singles of the Ryder Cup at Royal Lytham and St Anne's.

Determined to be one of the great players of golf's history, and conscious that his swing was not sufficiently reliable under pressure, Faldo astutely chose David Leadbetter as his coach. The swing that emerged after much tutelage took time to work. Faldo won in 1984 but no more successes came his way until the Spanish Open of 1987, the year that saw his arrival as a world figure. Faldo's 68 in the first round of the British Open saw him very well placed, despite the fact that the Australian Rodger Davies held the lead with a 64. Few saw him as a real threat, but Faldo's second-round 69 brought him level. His 71 in the next round put him a short head behind leader Paul Azinger, just a stroke behind.

> **“The one man Greg Norman didn't want to see in his rearview mirror was Nick.”**
>
> *Colin Montgomerie, after the US Masters in 1996.*

Faldo's final round is already part of the golfing legend for in misty, chilly weather he parred every single hole. In the end, he won because of Paul Azinger's failing. With a three-stroke lead and nine to play, he faltered with bogeys on the last two holes. Faldo did not, and his play on the difficult final hole was exemplary – a good drive, an excellent five-iron to the front of the green and two putts.

America is converted

However, his reputation wasn't yet made in the USA. Many thought all those 18 pars could hardly be inspirational golf. Winning the Masters in 1989 changed that, although he had an apparently disastrous third round when he took 77, which dropped him five strokes behind the leader Ben Crenshaw. His putting had been rather poor.

It was very different on the final day. On the 1st hole he got the ball in from about 20 yards and was on his way and reached the turn in 32. Birdies accumulated on the back nine on the 13th, 14th and 16th, where he holed a putt with an almost impossible amount of break. Another from long range followed on the 17th and he finished in 65 to tie with Scott Hoch, who then proceeded to assist Faldo to his second major win. On the first play-off hole Hoch missed from about two feet and a grateful Faldo birdied the next for the title. When it was all over it seemed that Faldo had birdied almost everything in the final hours.

Millionaire golf

Faldo's best year was in 1990, when he came close to equalling Ben Hogan's 1953. First there was another Masters. After rounds of 71 and 72, a 66 then put him in third place, three shots adrift of Raymond Floyd, and a final round of 69 was good enough to force a playoff with the overnight leader. The second hole was again decisive as Floyd put his second shot into the water and that was that. Only Jack Nicklaus, in 1965–66, had won two straight Masters.

In the US Open that same year, he missed the play-off by one shot. Soon it was time to go to St Andrews, where he played his most devastating golf ever. Four majors in the record books. By now Faldo was a millionaire many times over, and his rise to pre-eminence had done much to win Leadbetter his reputation as the new guru of golf.

Muirfield in 1992 saw some silly betting, but Faldo did seem invincible at 130 for 36 holes. When John Cook overtook him on the final, day, Faldo recovered with “the best four holes of my life,” including two birdies, gaining his fifth major. Another staunch finish, against Curtis Strange in the 1995 Ryder Cup was instrumental in Europe's victory. Faldo added a sixth major, his third US Masters at Augusta in 1996, capitalizing on Greg Norman's Sunday afternoon collapse with a best-of-day 67.

Career Milestones

1957 *Born Welwyn Garden City, Hertfordshire.*
1977 *First professional tournament victory, the Skol Lager event.*
1987 *British Open champion at Muirfield.*
1989 *First Masters win.*
1990 *Repeats Masters victory and wins his second British Open title.*
1992 *Wins third British Open Championship.*
1996 *Overtakes Greg Norman for third Masters title.*

KEEPING IN LINE
Fanny Sunnesson helps Faldo read putts

WALTER HAGEN

"EDDIE – HOLD THE FLAG, WILL YOU?"

Walter Hagen probably got more enjoyment from his career in top golf then any great player before or since – and only Jones and Nicklaus won more majors. The above remark came during a social round of golf with Edward, Prince of Wales, soon to be, briefly, Edward VIII. It shows how much Hagen felt at ease with everyone, from kings and presidents to ordinary followers of golf.

Hagen had come to the top very quickly. He played the 1912 Canadian Open and finished 11th. Asked at his home club how he had done, Hagen replied, "I lost." This was an early variation on his famous adage that no one remembers who finished second. He lost again in the 1913 US Open, finishing a stroke behind the play-off between Vardon, Ray and Ouimet. The following year, 1914, was better. He began the US Open with a record 68 and held on to win. He lost some of his career in the war years but won the US Open again in 1919. He was ready to spread his wings further afield and prove himself in the British Open.

Cocking a snook

Hagen arrived at Deal for the 1920 event. Since, as a professional, he was not allowed to enter the clubhouse, he hired a limousine, had his chauffeur park it in front of the clubhouse and enjoyed the contents of his hamper, quite likely prepared by the Ritz Hotel in London. It was a typically grand gesture from a man who enjoyed cocking a snook, but Hagen's play did not impress the spectators nearly as much. He came in 53rd of the 77 qualifiers.

He realized that, to compete more effectively on links courses, he must learn the pitch and run. Having done so, he enjoyed a great run in the British Open during the 1920s. After being sixth the following year, he won in 1922, was second the next year and won again in 1924. For his next entries through to 1929 he was third, first and first. With that last victory, he was nearly finished with the Open.

In the US Open, he was far less successful in the 1920s, not adding to his two titles. The fact that Bobby Jones was always in the field had a great deal to do with this.

But Jones as an amateur was not eligible for the matchplay US PGA, and Hagen proceeded to compile perhaps the greatest run of success of anyone in a major championship. In 1916 he reached the semi-finals and next played in 1921, when he won. His next appearance was in 1923, when he lost a fiercely contested match to Gene Sarazen in the final. Then came his unparalleled run of four in a row, which involved 22 successive match wins.

Nerveless nipper and putter

The strength of his game was from, say, 100 yards in. He was a short pitcher of excellence, could nip the ball off the sand nervelessly when in a greenside bunker and was the best putter in the business. Hagen's long game was less impressive. Not particularly long off the tee, his swaying swing was perhaps the cause of wildness. However, when surveying a shot from wild country he had the sang-froid to be able to say: "Well, I put it there." And then his recovery shots were as fabled as those of Seve Ballesteros later.

By the end of the 1920s, Hagen had taken 11 major titles and was close to entering his 40s. His tally of majors could well have been higher: he did not have the chance to compete in the Masters, which began in 1934, until his best days lay well behind him. To some extent he may have lost his appetite for centre-stage and by this time his name was easily big enough for him to spend much time on exhibition tours world-wide where he could both enjoy himself and make the money he needed to support his luxurious lifestyle. Hagen had a great capacity for enjoyment and only a brief interest in family life, though he was much addicted to the company of attractive women and kept a little black book to record their phone numbers around the world.

He fulfilled his ambitions. Perhaps he didn't passionately desire the major and tournament titles he amassed over the years. They were the means to an end: enjoying life. As he used to say: "I didn't want to be a millionaire. I just wanted to live like one."

WALTER HAGEN
Matchless nerves

Career Milestones

1892 *Born Rochester, New York.*
1914 *Wins first US Open.*
1919 *Second US Open title.*
1921 *Begins a sequence of five US PGA titles from 1921 to 1927.*
1922 *First victory in the British Open Championship.*
1924 *Second victory in the British Open .*
1927 *Captain of the winning US Ryder Cup team in inaugural match against Britain.*
1928 *Third victory in the British Open.*
1929 *Fourth victory in the British Open and losing Ryder Cup Captain.*
1931 *Successful Ryder Cup Captain.*
1933 *Ryder Cup Captain for the fourth time, and second time on the losing side.*
1935 *Third victory as Ryder Cup Captain.*
1937 *Ryder Cup Captain for sixth time, first victory for away team.*

"Never hurry, never worry, and don't forget to stop and smell the roses on the way."

Walter Hagen

BEN HOGAN

LONG GAME, GRAND SLAM

Ben Hogan had a long game the accuracy of which has probably never been matched. The man's shots seemed always to home in on the flag. It then became almost a matter of the luck of the bounce if they stuck a little too short or skidded through a little too far. But, as legend has it, they were always on line.

In his peak years, Hogan was almost as accurate with the driver but never a supreme putter. His method was perhaps too mechanical so that he always lacked real delicacy of touch. But, like his nearest modern counterpart, Nick Faldo, he could stuff the ball into the hole from six feet and under.

At the outset, there were many years of failure, but Hogan was persistent. He first played the US Tour in 1931 and, from time to time, for several years afterwards. There was little if any sponsorship in those far-off years. Hogan would do odd jobs, save up the dollars and then play for as long as the money lasted. He won virtually no prize money. In 1937 he did win some money and, the following year, his first event, a fourball. He was already 34 years old.

The legend is born

But 1940 saw the beginning of the Hogan legend. He won the North and South event over Pinehurst 2 and was on his way.

Then came the war, with Hogan becoming a dominant player, playing 39 events in 1941 and being only once out of the top five. The reasons for this astonishing improvement were that he had become a good short-range putter and had trained himself on the practice ground to shorten the length of his backswing, which had been absurdly beyond the horizontal. His long game immediately became more consistent.

After the war, he emerged as a supreme talent, with 21 wins in the first two seasons, which included the 1946 PGA Championship. He was by no means satisfied. Hogan was aiming at the consistency which leads to greatness. Over the winter of 1947–48 he worked on changing his low drawing hook into a slice. Although he succeeded, he lost much of his length. But the ball finished on the fairway, Hogan's main aim. That slice quite quickly became a slight fade. The length was little altered and the shape of shot was consistent. You rule out the trouble along the left and then have the whole of the fairway to aim at. Hogan won his first US Open.

> **"I'm glad to have brought this monster to its knees."**
>
> *Ben Hogan after winning the US Open at Oakland Hills in 1951*

From smash to slam

But Fate had a trick up its sleeve. Early in 1949, Hogan was very severely injured in a road accident. Many thought he would never play again and he was indeed out of the game for nearly a year. When he returned, walking was an agony and he had to restrict himself to just a few events. The majors became his aim though he had to exclude the US PGA, then a 36-hole match play event, because he knew his legs wouldn't take him around that many holes in a day.

Having missed the 1949 US Open, Hogan took the title on three of his next four entries. His winning last-round 67 at the spectacularly difficult Oakland Hills course in 1951 was, he thought, the best round he ever played. His last US Open win came in 1953, his greatest year, when he also took his second Masters and won the British Open on his only entry to complete the modern Grand Slam.

TRIUMPH AT WENTWORTH *Ben Hogan in 1956*

It was thought at the time that Hogan would go on winning the majors as long as he wanted to. As Hogan himself said, desire was what counted. But he was wrong. Hogan kept both desire and will, but his putting stroke went. He developed what is variously called "the twitch", "the jerks" or "the yips". In one US Open, when still in contention on the final green, he was noticed apparently trying out a variety of putting methods on the edge of the green. A friend later commented on this. Hogan explained that he hadn't been trying to find a stroke that would hole a putt but one that would make missing look respectable.

After 1953, Hogan went into a slow decline, but remained a force to be reckoned with until towards the end of the 1960s.

Career Milestones

1912 *Born Dublin, Texas.*
1938 *First tournament win, Hershey Fourball.*
1946 *The US PGA became his first major title.*
1947 *Victorious Ryder Cup Captain.*
1948 *Wins his first US Open title and second US PGA in a double-major year.*
1949 *Involved in serious car crash, but recovers enough to be non-playing Ryder Cup Captain for victorious match at Ganton, Yorkshire.*
1950 *Second US Open title.*
1951 *Wins both the Masters and the US Open.*
1953 *Wins the Masters, the US Open and the British Open (on his only entry).*
1967 *Non-playing Ryder Cup Captain as USA wins in his home state of Texas.*

BOBBY JONES

THE EMPEROR WHO HAD HAD ENOUGH

Bobby Jones achieved a success rate that was, and remains, beyond compare. In his whole quite brief career he played only 52 tournaments, either amateur or professional, and won 23 of them. Jones played just a handful of events a year and otherwise played his friendly club fourballs at weekends, took the winter of Atlanta off and then warmed up in the spring with some practice shots. On average, that was his golfing year. Yet on that very limited golfing diet he could quickly fire himself up and, usually, go out and win a major championship.

GRAND SLAM *Jones (left) with the four major trophies and his biographer*

By around the age of 20, Jones was already nearly the golfing phenomenon of the age and there could have been few who doubted that he would become the greatest golfer ever. In that decade up to 1930 he provided the proof. Then the question was "Who has a chance of beating Bobby?" In fact, quite a few did over the years – but no one ever beat him twice. Such a great player as Walter Hagen never won a British or US Open when Jones was competing.

It all took off in 1923 when he won his first major, the US Open. This despite completing his final round bogey, bogey, double bogey. It was probably nerves – or was there a flaw in Jones's armour in that he tended to let up when in a commanding position? He was clearly better when under the whip.

That came in the play-off against Bobby Cruickshank. At the last he had to risk all to win, needing to hit a long iron from a sandy lie over water to the green – or play short of the hazard for safety, with the likelihood of having to play another 18 holes. Jones went for the bold shot and played it to perfection.

With the knowledge that he had it in him to win a major, Jones was on his way. In the US Amateur, for instance, from 1924 to 1930, he won five of his seven entries and was runner-up once. In those days, moreover, there were no temptations from lucrative professional tours. There was no money there until much later. So amateurs kept their status and the strength of fields was much greater than today.

In the US Open, Jones's four victories still give him a share of the record. In the other years between 1922 and 1930 he finished 11th – a dismal failure in Jones's terms – was second twice, and lost two play-offs.

His record in the British Open was the most remarkable of all. He first appeared in 1921 when aged 19. After two rounds he was four behind the leaders but then had a disastrous 46 to the turn at St Andrews, double-bogeyed the next two holes – and tore up his card.

He did not appear again in a British Open until 1926. As it was a Walker Cup year, his travelling expenses were paid and the US team then went on to compete in the Amateur. Miffed at not winning, and wanting to show the British what he was made of, Jones decided to stay on for the Open at Royal Lytham and St Anne's. He won, in the end as a result of a cracking mid-iron to the heart of the 71st green from a sandy lie in the rough.

Though he couldn't really afford the trip, Jones felt he had to return for the St Andrews Open the following year. A champion owed it to the public to defend his title. He won comfortably this time with a record score and no theatricals necessary.

Transatlantic Double Whammy

His final Open appearance was at Hoylake in 1930. Again he won, despite once dropping eight shots in the space of three holes and, in his final round, once taking five more to get down when being just short of a par five in two. 1930 was the miracle year, with Jones winning the Amateur and Open Championships of both Britain and America. He had had a hunch that this might just be possible, and in the winter had taken the unusual step, for those days, of trying to keep fit.

Shortly after the completion of the never-to-be-repeated Grand Slam at Merion in 1930, Jones decided to retire. Alexander the Great always felt that his empire could be even bigger. Jones felt that there were no more fields left to conquer.

Instead, he designed some of the best iron clubheads ever, and was instrumental in the design of the Masters Tournament and of the Augusta course. With his amateur status gone, he also made a lot of money from his golf fame.

Career Milestones

- **1902** *Born in Atlanta, Georgia.*
- **1923** *First US Open win.*
- **1924** *First US Amateur win.*
- **1925** *Wins US Amateur.*
- **1926** *US Open, British Open.*
- **1927** *Second British Open, third US Amateur.*
- **1928** *Fourth US Amateur.*
- **1929** *Third US Open.*
- **1930** *US Open, British Open, British Amateur, US Amateur.*
- **1934** *Plays in his invitational tournament at the course he designed at Augusta, which quickly becomes known as the Masters.*

> **"I'd run into Bobby, and he would absolutely annihilate me. You have no idea how good Bobby was."**
>
> *Francis Ouimet*

JACK NICKLAUS

THE COURSE MANAGER WHO CHANGED

Jack Nicklaus knew he was comfortably the best there was and, many would say, played too cautiously. If he had a weakness, it was arrogance. He knew he ought to win and didn't want to let the others in through playing bold shots which could have gone wrong. Safety was almost always his watchword.

That is, until the final round, with Nicklaus, say, a few strokes behind in a major championship and no longer anything to lose. Then, for his last-round tee shots, he would leave the long irons in the bag. At Muirfield in 1966, he manoeuvred his way around, mostly playing the irons from the tee for placement and avoiding the hayfields along the fairways. He won. Several years later, at the same course, he arrived as both Masters and US Open champion. To achieve the modern Grand Slam (Masters, US Open, British Open and US PGA in the same year) was a serious possibility.

HIS LAST MAJOR? *Nicklaus after winning the 1986 Masters*

Charge of the late brigade

Nicklaus, with a round to play, lay six strokes behind the leader, Lee Trevino. Now he would have to go for everything. For a while, it all came off. About two holes behind, Trevino and Jacklin heard the roars come back to them as the Nicklaus birdies mounted. He was out in 32 and then birdied the next two holes. Suddenly he was in the lead. But there were no more birdies and one dropped shot meant, in the end, that Nicklaus – despite his fine 66 – finished a shot behind Trevino's winning total. He had left it too late.

> **“Jack is playing an entirely different game, and one which I'm not even familiar with.”**
>
> *Bobby Jones, watching Nicklaus win the 1965 Masters*

There were many of these magnificent last-round charges in both major championships and tournament play, but it makes one wonder how much greater his record might have been if he had attacked from the very first shot in the first round. Instead, Nicklaus usually played a cautious game. He analyzed a course and, particularly from the tee to the fairway, concentrated on placement. Even if the green was an open target, he would often not go for the flag but aim for a safer area of the green. From that point on he felt confident that the piston-like action of his putting stroke would not let him down. Indeed he has been one of the most nerveless putters of all.

The wonder of the age

Like Jones about 40 years before, Nicklaus (with two US Amateurs under his belt and a near miss in the 1960 US Open) was quickly recognized as a rising star. He truly became one with his first professional season win in the 1962 US Open, which included the added drama of beating the great Arnold Palmer in an 18-hole play-off.

Despite the overwhelming popularity of Arnold Palmer, Nicklaus soon became the new wonder of the age and easily the dominant golfer on the world scene. In 1963, his potential stature was confirmed when he added both the Masters and the US PGA to his record.

When he won the 1965 Masters, breaking the Hogan scoring record by three strokes, winning by a record nine strokes and including a single round of 64, Bobby Jones was moved to remark that his performance was "the greatest in golf history".

Nicklaus had undoubtedly become the greatest golfer in the world, and his dominance lasted from the early 1960s until, you could say, 1977, when Tom Watson managed – just – to beat Nicklaus in both the Masters and the Open. He was the new Number 1.

Even so, Nicklaus was not to be out of the reckoning for a good many years to come. In 1980 he came back from his worst year to take both the US Open and the US PGA. In 1982 he came agonizingly close to adding a record-breaking fifth US Open to his record at Pebble Beach, only foiled by Watson's little pitch from greenside rough on the 71st which astonishingly went into the hole. He had one more major in him, surging up the field over the last nine holes with one of his greatest charges to win the 1986 Masters. Not until early 1996 did Nicklaus so much as hint at the possibility of his calling a halt to his scarcely credible sequence of appearing in 138 majors in a row.

Career Milestones

1940 *Born Columbus, Ohio.*
1956 *Wins Ohio Amateur Championship at age 16.*
1959 *First US Amateur Championship at 19.*
1961 *US Amateur champion for second time.*
1962 *Wins first US Open, defeating Arnold Palmer in play-off at Oakmont.*
1963 *Two-time major winner, taking both the Masters and US PGA.*
1965 *Second victory in Masters.*
1966 *Completes Grand Slam of all four majors when he follows a third Masters victory with his first British Open.*
1967 *Second victory in US Open.*
1970 *British Open Champion for the second time.*
1971 *Second US PGA .*
1972 *Another two-major year with victories in the Masters and US Open.*
1973 *Wins his 15th major, a third US PGA title.*
1975 *His fourth two-major season, as in 1963, taking the Masters and US PGA.*
1978 *Becomes British Open Champion for the third time at St. Andrews*
1980 *His fifth two-major year: a fourth US Open win and fifth US PGA title.*
1983 *Winning Ryder Cup Captain.*
1986 *Aged 46, wins his record sixth Masters.*
1987 *Losing Ryder Cup Captain, as USA goes down 13–15 on the course he built.*
1996 *Won 100th tournament with a closing 65, and made the cut in all four majors.*

ARNOLD PALMER

BATTLING ARNIE THRILLS HIS ARMY

Arnold Palmer had a style of play that was largely responsible for his unique charisma. He has always made the game seem a battle against the golf course. Spectators at an event and the television viewers at home loved to see him play and even today, when he is well into his 60s, many would rather see him open a soft drink can than others hole a full bunker shot.

Top players have mostly hit the ball very hard, but that has often been disguised by a rhythmic swing with the real acceleration coming only in the strike area, followed by a finish that is poised and sometimes elegant. Not so with Arnold. The take-away is quite fast, and after impact the club is flung towards the sky. Sometimes it can look more like a boxer throwing a knock-out punch.

It may not look pretty, but it does look very forceful indeed – and it worked. Palmer is one of the best drivers of a golf ball the game has seen. The method worked equally well for the long and medium irons, usually full shots. However, Palmer was never up with the best when he had to play, for example, a finessed wedge or a gentle eight-iron. Giving the ball a good smash has always been his territory.

Attacking the hole

At his best, the same applied to his game around and on the greens. The aim wasn't to get the shot stone dead, but to hole it. This was especially true of his putting. Many concentrate on trying to achieve perfect pace, so that the ball gently drops into the hole. Not Palmer in the great years. He gave it a firm rap. If he missed, there was no problem with the return from four feet or so.

With the wear of the years, Palmer became less confident. Arguably his long game actually improved, but his putting in particular was increasingly cautious. Instead of aiming to bang it into the hole, he began to want to be sure of getting down in two. He also partly abandoned his policy of always going for the flag – and never mind the penalties for failure – in favour of more percentage shots.

A second important element of his appeal is his expressive face. Spectators always felt they could feel what Arnie was going through. Joy, amusement, anger, disappointment, amazement, ecstasy and even depression – all were on view.

Although Palmer had won two Masters by April 1960, his legend really began with the 1960 US Open in June. He went into the final round six strokes behind the leader, but thought that a 65 might still swing things his way. Out in 30, he parred his way home while his two closest rivals, the aging Ben Hogan and young Jack Nicklaus, faltered.

Instantly, he had the reputation of being the man who could mount a last-round charge to victory, and it remained with him throughout his main career, even though it was by no means entirely true. Palmer was probably better at seizing an early lead and then keeping his nerve right through to the finish.

> **“He comes onto a tee looking like a prize fighter climbing into the ring ready for a world championship bout.”**
>
> *Charles Price, US golf writer*

ARNOLD PALMER *The face always shows his feelings*

Career Milestones

1929 *Born Latrobe, Pennsylvania.*
1954 *US Amateur Champion, after which he turns professional.*
1955 *First professional win, the Canadian Open.*
1958 *Wins his first major, the Masters.*
1960 *Two majors in the year, the Masters and US Open.*
1961 *Wins British Open Championship.*
1962 *Two more majors, a third Masters and second British Open Championship.*
1963 *Becomes the last Ryder Cup Captain to play in the event, leading the USA to a 23–9 victory.*
1964 *Wins his fourth, and last, Masters.*
1975 *Ryder Cup Captain for the second time, this time in his home state.*

Blazing a British trail

In Britain, he transformed the Open Championship almost overnight from a slightly parochial affair which interested few Americans (in 1960 the dominant force in world golf) into a major event on the world scene. He came second in that centenary Open and then won the next two years, producing his greatest major championship performance in the Troon Open of 1962. US entries gradually grew from that period onwards, and a great debt is owed to Palmer for the fact that the Open Championship field is more representative of world talent than the other three majors.

The appeal of Arnold Palmer continues, even though it is over 30 years since he last won a major. Unlike most modern professionals, Palmer can repair as well as swing a club. His industry and skills have expanded into club and course design. He is also a most capable pilot. He was playing again just weeks after undergoing 1997 surgery for prostate cancer and still attracting huge galleries.

GARY PLAYER

THE GREAT PRACTISER

Gary Player could hole a chip or bunker shot or play a ball dead by the holeside. No fluke was involved. The results were achieved only with remorseless practice. For both these shots Player has a method which may be unique. The stroke is a downward stab.

His short game has remained Player's greatest strength over a career which has lasted about 40 years, more than 25 of those seeing him contend for and win major championships. Yet when he first arrived in Britain in the mid-1950s he was advised by professionals of the time to give up the game as a livelihood, go back to South Africa and just play for fun. Opinion was that Gary had a hooker's grip, that his swing was too flat and he lacked rhythm and feel for the game. Perhaps unnoticed was the effectiveness of that stab on the shot shorts. You could say he was the first great golfer to expect to get down in two more once he was near the green.

> **"You know, it's truly amazing. The more I practise, the luckier I get."**
>
> *Player, answering taunts that he was a lucky golfer*

A regime for length

Another first for Player was the emphasis he put on physical fitness and diet. Before his time, most golfers considered that just playing the game was enough to keep you in trim. The same was largely true of eating and drinking. Moderation was good enough.

Player being a small man, one of the main aims of his fitness regime was to increase his length from the tee. Compared to a Nicklaus, hitting a wedge for his second shot on a long par four, he found himself using a medium iron. Player once said he had gained about 25 yards from his healthy foods and strenuous exercise. Though those yards were undoubtedly important, far more significant was his will to win. As someone else said: "Gary just likes beating people."

He began doing that in the mid-1950s and by 1958 had become one of the rare overseas golfers to win in the USA. But his breakthrough to the status of a golfer to be reckoned with on the world scene came in 1959 when he won the Open Championship at Muirfield. Successes in the Masters and the US PGA followed in the early 1960s, and his victory in the 1965 US Open made him one of the happy band to complete the slam of all four majors. Even more, with Nicklaus and Palmer, he was a founder member of what came to be known as the Big Three. The advertising and sponsorship money poured in.

In his native South Africa, with the decline of Bobby Locke, Player was by far the dominant golfer. But he had to be an international golfer, and over the years has probably clocked up more air mileage than anyone else. The United States was his main arena, but he also made annual appearances in Britain and played in Australia often enough to take their Open seven times. In Britain he jointly holds the records of winning the World Matchplay Championship five times and the Open on three occasions. His 1959 success at Muirfield was perhaps a little lucky, as those in pursuit defeated themselves. At Carnoustie in 1968, however, he had to battle head-to-head with Jack Nicklaus. Six years later, at Royal Lytham and St Anne's, he gave one of his finest performances with much use of his one-iron in the strong wind.

Career Milestones

1935 *Born Johannesburg, South Africa.*
1958 *Earns his first US Tour win.*
1959 *Wins his first major, the British Open Championship.*
1961 *Collects the Masters.*
1962 *Wins his third major, the US PGA.*
1965 *Takes the US Open to become only the fourth player to win all four majors.*
1968 *Wins his second British Open Championship.*
1972 *Wins his sixth major, the US PGA.*
1974 *Wins two majors in the year, the Masters and British Open Championship.*
1978 *Wins his ninth major, the Masters at age 42.*

Player masters green

Perhaps his finest hour, however, came at Augusta in 1978, when Player was becoming a figure of the past. Entering the final round of the Masters, he was seven behind leader Hubert Green. His outward nine in 34 was good but seemed unlikely to affect the outcome of the tournament. But his second half did. With six birdies, he was home in 30. Player's remarkable 64 – one of the greatest final rounds in major championship golf – gave him victory when Hubert Green missed a short putt on the last green.

Perhaps that was Player's last hurrah, but he is still competitive on the US Senior Tour and in recent years has represented South Africa on the nation's return to international team golf in the Alfred Dunhill Cup at St Andrews.

PUNCHING HIS WEIGHT *Gary Player at Muirfield in 1972*

GENE SARAZEN

THE SHORTEST CHAMPION

Gene Sarazen had a career that fell into two distinct and highly successful phases – the second culminating in the achievement of the first professional Grand Slam.

First came a change of name. Born of Italian immigrant stock, he decided that Eugene Saraceni, while fine for a violinist, didn't sound right for a 17-year-old who wanted to be a professional golfer. So he went into his career as Gene Sarazen.

By the time the 1922 US Open came around, though he had won a tournament, he was very little known – not surprising at 20 years and four months of age. At the end of that week at Skokie, Illinois, he'd become a national figure on the golf scene. Sarazen closed with a 68 to win – at the time the lowest final round recorded to win a championship .

In the same year, he also won the US PGA and beat Walter Hagen in a challenge match for the "The World Championship". In the following year, he again beat Hagen, this time in the final of the US PGA, then played as match play.

Getting to grips

Suddenly, Sarazen seemed to be the dominant player. However, Hagen was far from finished and Jones was emerging as the golfer who could beat them all. Sarazen also began to experience technical problems. His swing was compact and powerful (especially so for a man of only 5 feet 3 inches, the shortest of major champions) but his grip was laughable by modern teaching standards. With the left hand, he could see four knuckles and explained that there were advantages: the left wrist didn't break down when almost side on to the line of fire.

There was an even more weird feature of his grip: his left thumb played no part but flapped in the air. Sarazen also, like Jack Nicklaus, used the relatively rare interlocking grip, where the little finger of the left hand is fitted between the index and middle finger of the right.

The fast reactions of extreme youth, it could be argued, could cope with these unorthodoxies but, after the first flush of success, Sarazen did not maintain his pace. He could win tournaments from time to time, but the majors were beyond his grasp.

Inventing the sand wedge

He entered his second phase. By the late 1920s and early 1930s he was winning good tournament money, featuring often in the majors, and was only narrowly defeated, 1 down, in the final of the 1930 US PGA.

He was a potentially great player once again – and then also had a revolutionary idea. During this time even players of true excellence had trouble with bunker shots. Today most would prefer to have a good lie in a greenside bunker rather than a good grassy lie from the same distance. The lofted clubs of the day were not effective. Because they bit into the sand, the only way to use them was either to flick the ball off the surface or explode it out, hitting behind the ball and then down and through.

Sarazen decided that what was needed was a clubhead that would glide through the sand, slicing underneath the ball, instead of digging in. So he took a club with a broad sole and added lead solder to raise the height of the rear. After much experimenting and test driving he had cracked the problem. Future players would be able to aim at getting near the flag from a greenside bunker instead of just being content to get their ball out of the hazard.

Sarazen himself was on his way to more major championships and had a glorious 1932, first winning the British Open at Prince's, Sandwich, in 1932 by five strokes and then, a fortnight after, the US Open.

A year later, he took the US PGA for the third time but his most mystical achievement came in the second – and his first – Masters. With no apparent chance of catching Craig Wood, he suddenly holed a four-wood second shot at the par-five 15th, in front of just a handful of spectators. Sarazen had drawn level and went on to win the play-off the next day.

In 1940 he lost a play-off for the US Open and continued to play on the US Tour. Much later he still had a couple of spectacular shots left. On day one of the 1973 Open at Troon he holed in one with a five-iron shot on the Postage Stamp hole (the 8th). The next day he missed the green and was bunkered. No great problem: he holed his shot from the sand.

RYDER CUP PRIDE *Sarazen was always at his best in match play*

Career Milestones

1902 *Born Harrison, New York.*
1922 *Aged just 20 wins two majors, the US Open and US PGA.*
1923 *Retains his US PGA Championship.*
1932 *After a nine-year gap, wins British Open Championship and US Open.*
1933 *Wins his third US PGA.*
1935 *Wins the second (his first) Masters, thanks to double eagle at 15th.*

> **"Perhaps the reason why it all seemed so easy in 1922 was that I had no idea at the time how difficult the things I was accomplishing really were."**
>
> *Gene Sarazen*

LEE TREVINO

UNORTHODOX CAN WORK

Lee Trevino is an odd-looking golfer indeed, but at his peak around the early 1970s this effervescent Mexican-American could beat the best. Trevino's method centres on having a hooker's grip with his left hand and then doing a variety of things to ensure that he plays with a slice. It seems Trevino never was willing to change his grip and so he had to produce counter-measures to avoid a right-to-left shape of shot.

For a start, he takes up the classic slicer's stance, very open to his target line. The club is then taken away on an outside path, but eventually is inside to out in the impact area. To stop that clubhead being shut at impact, Trevino drives strongly with his legs and also pulls the club through with his left side and arm. But really there's more to it than that. Ben Hogan once remarked that he liked watching Trevino because he worked his hands so beautifully through the ball. Trevino is very controlled in the strike zone and has great feel for how his swing is working.

Even though his swing proved effective, no one praised it as he took centre stage. It was described as being that of a weekend hacker and "more suitable for scything grass with".

Difficult hacker to beat

In his 20s, Trevino served in the US armed forces overseas and returned to work in local golf. He did not attempt to qualify for the US Tour. However, he did play in the 1966 US Open. His 54th position made no headlines, but it was a respectable performance when he had previously done little more than win the Texas State Open, which was not a Tour event. The following year, he gave it another go and came in fifth. Again no headlines, but it gave Trevino the feeling of certainty that he could compete with the best.

He proved it at Oak Hill in 1968 when he destroyed Bert Yancey in head-to head play over the final round to win by four, the first man to break 70 in all four rounds of a US Open. Some thought this was a fluke win, that Trevino had happened to hit peak form for one week, and that this was his first and also his last tournament win. In fact he was off on a great career.

In retrospect, his peak years ran from his US Open victory to around the mid-1970s, though he remained a player to be reckoned with for long after that, his last major victory coming with the US PGA as late as 1984. Again, at Shoal Creek, all his rounds were below 70.

Partly through his consistency, Trevino always won very large amounts of money on the US Tour and never had a bad year. For a time he seemed a likely rival to Jack Nicklaus for world supremacy. After being leading money-winner on the US Tour in 1970, he went on to have an even better year in 1971. In the space of five weeks he took the US Open, the Canadian Open and the Open Championship. And in the US Open he had beaten Jack Nicklaus in a play-off. In 1972, he again beat Jack Nicklaus – and Tony Jacklin – for the British Open Championship. But Nicklaus continued on his winning ways while Trevino's peak years were already over. No threat to Nicklaus for supremacy in world golf, he continued to pile up tournament victories.

Office gossip – and a windfall

Trevino is unusual in his relationship with spectators. Most players look as if they are having rather a bad day at the office. Sometimes they are anguished, at other times distressed, pained or just plain bored. Trevino, uniquely, is always full of chat. He does quiet down when in contention, but not completely.

For a time during the 1980s he seemed to be losing interest in tournament golf. In the sunset of a great career he was perhaps thinking more of TV, company days and the like. But the Senior Tour came as a gift when he reached 50. Since then, he has been the most effective competitor, aided considerably by a Nicklaus who does not care to play often. But, as the money pours in, Trevino probably doesn't mind in the least.

Career Milestones

1939 *Born Dallas, Texas.*
1967 *Wins his first tournament, the Hawaiian Open.*
1968 *Wins US Open.*
1971 *Wins his second US Open and follows it with British Open Championship.*
1972 *Successfully defends British Open Championship.*
1974 *Wins his fifth major, the US PGA.*
1984 *Wins his second US PGA eight years after being seriously injured by a bolt of lightning at Western Open.*
1985 *Losing Ryder Cup Captain at the Belfry.*

“You don't know the meaning of pressure until you play for five bucks with two bucks in your pocket.”

Trevino

LEE TREVINO *Always a wonderful player from sand*

THE TRIUMVIRATE

TWENTY YEARS OF DOMINANCE

J. H. Taylor, Harry Vardon and James Braid were exact golfing contemporaries who together, astonishingly, took no fewer than 16 of the Open Championships between 1894 and 1914.

J. H. Taylor emerged first, winning the Open in 1984 and 1985. For a brief spell, having set new standards, he was thought almost invincible. Taylor's style was to stand flat-footed and give the ball a thump, with most of the power appearing to come from his forearms. Two features which distinguished his play were low flight – which helped him to be a great player in high winds – and his ability to impart fizzing backspin with his mashie (about a five-iron). This enabled him to be perhaps the first player to go directly for the flag and stop the ball quickly. One wonders how he would have used modern wedges.

IN HIS SUNDAY BEST *Taylor after his first British Open win*

James Braid was a formidable golfer by the late 1890s; his first Open win, however, was a little overdue when it came in 1901. He then became the dominant member of the Triumvirate, his fifth success in the Open in 1910 putting him temporarily ahead of his two rivals and also making him the first man to win five Opens. He then lost form to some extent. Of the three, Braid, in his best years, was very likely the best putter and the longest hitter, with a flailing lash of a swing.

> **" From 1894 to 1914, they were to rule the world of golf far more completely than did Arnold Palmer, Jack Nicklaus and Gary Player half a century later. "**
>
> *John Hopkins, golf writer*

Harry Vardon, technically, was the most revolutionary of the Triumvirate. He is sometimes supposed to have invented the "Vardon grip" – where the little finger of the right hand overlaps the index finder of the left. In fact, this method of holding the club had been used a few years earlier by the famous Scottish amateur Johnny Laidlay – and perhaps others. Both Taylor and Braid used the same grip, and it was named after Vardon simply because he became the most famous and the most imitated of the Triumvirate.

Vardon's swing was far more revolutionary than his grip. Compared with the conventional "St Andrews swing", which involved a wide stance and a flat path back and through, producing a low flight, Vardon's swing path was very much higher, and the downswing was also naturally much steeper. The result was the high flight which made him consistent at holding fairways and greens and was particularly useful when the ground was hard. It was soon apparent that no one could equal Vardon when it came to playing wooden club shots to the flag, while his driving accuracy became legendary.

Harry Vardon arrived in 1896, first defeating Taylor by 8 and 7 in a match at Ganton and then defeating him for the Open title after a 36-hole play-off. For a few years Vardon was nearly invincible, and by 1903 he had won his fourth Open title.

Then he was afflicted by tuberculosis (and poor putting). He continued to be a great player, but the Open eluded him until 1911. In 1914 he won again, becoming the first and still the only man to win the Open Championship six times.

Today, the Open tallies are usually regarded as the measure of these great players. The other tournaments they played in the same period have become forgotten events. However, the results of recent research by Peter Lewis, director of the British Golf Museum, are revealing. In this period, Vardon won 52 events, 34 per cent of all those he entered, while he topped 50 per cent for first and second places. In his most dazzling period, he won 17 out of 22 tournaments and was second in the others! This is dominance of a kind that only Byron Nelson was able to achieve in later years.

Braid had 34 victories and Taylor 32, but they were a step below Vardon. In his best year, 1898, Vardon won ten times, whereas the other two never bettered four in any one year.

Career Milestones

JAMES BRAID
1870 *Born in Earlsferry, Fife.*
1901 *Wins his first British Open Championship.*
1905 *Collects his second British Open Championship.*
1906 *Successfully defends his British Open Championship.*
1908 *Takes his third British Open Championship in four years.*
1910 *After another year's gap, wins a record fifth British Open Championship.*

J. H. TAYLOR
1871 *Born in Northam, Devon.*
1894 *Wins his first British Open Championship.*
1895 *Successfully defends his British Open Championship.*
1900 *Wins his third British Open Championship.*
1909 *Wins his fourth British Open Championship.*
1913 *Equals the record of Braid and Vardon as he wins his fifth British Open.*
1933 *Captains Great Britain Ryder Cup team to victory.*

HARRY VARDON
1870 *Born in Grouville, Jersey.*
1896 *Wins his first British Open Championship.*
1898 *Collects his second British Open Championship.*
1899 *Successfully defends his British Open Championship.*
1900 *Goes to America and wins US Open.*
1903 *Emulates the record of three others with his fourth British Open Championship.*
1911 *Equals Braid 's record as he wins his fifth British Open Championship.*
1914 *Wins his record sixth British Open Championship.*

TOM WATSON

THE FRESH-FACED KID FROM KANSAS CITY

Tom Watson made his majestic mark on the game with five British Open victories in only nine entries, and wrested away from Jack Nicklaus the crown of the world's leading golfer.

Watson is no longer a kid but he is still fresh-faced and still lives in Kansas City. To remain faithful to roots is unusual among professional golfers. Americans tend to flock to the temperate climes of, say, Florida or California, but Tom Watson, on the other hand, has remained in his home area of Kansas, relishing the challenge of winter golf with his friends – usually not professional golfers.

Early in his career (he turned professional in 1971) Watson earned the reputation of being a "choker", a man who was found wanting when the pressure was on. That was first turned around when he won the 1974 Western Open, shortly after having "choked" in the US Open, blowing a one-stroke lead he held going into the final round with a disastrous 79.

The Open road

It was the British Open Championship that began to establish him as a force to be reckoned with. In 1975 he arrived unheralded at Carnoustie, having finished poorly in both the Masters and US Open, and without even the time to play a full practice round. Eyes were on others as Watson went quietly about his business. He was hardly noticed by the television cameras until he holed a long birdie putt on the final hole to set a target which no one could better. However, one matched it, Jack Newton, but Watson narrowly won the 18-hole play-off the following day.

This success sparked winning ways, and he soon became the dominant player on the US Tour, being five times leading money-winner in the period 1977 to 1984. It quickly came to seem that this might be the man who would dethrone Jack Nicklaus as World Number 1. Psychologically, that came in the 1977 British Open at Turnberry, when, playing the last two rounds head to head, Watson became champion when some great play brought a one-stroke margin over Nicklaus.

Watson was now the man to beat in this event. His next success was even more emphatic. He swept into a comfortable lead at Muirfield after a 64 in the third round and cruised home by four strokes.

Troon in 1982 saw tougher going for Watson. There were others, such as Nick Price and Bobby Clampett, who "ought" to have won. As he said: "I didn't win it. It was given to me." Even so, it was Watson who produced a steady final round and a firm few closing holes while the others faltered.

It was a different story at Royal Birkdale the following year. Several players subdued the course, which was not playing at its most difficult. In the final round Watson lost his narrow lead and didn't regain it until he birdied the 16th. He came to the last, a long four, needing a par to win. The way he achieved it was classic. First he banged a long drive down the middle and he followed up with a superb long iron to the heart of the green. That was that.

Elusive victory

With five Open Championships to his credit in only nine entries, Harry Vardon's record six victories were nearly in his grasp and he was ready to make that mark at St Andrews in 1984. However, a loose long iron to the 71st hole (the 17th) finally killed his chances.

Like Tony Jacklin after his 1972 Open disaster, Tom Watson has not been quite the same man since. He is still a threat in majors, and his first US win in nine years, at the 1996 Memorial Tournament, was hugely popular.

His long game remains imperious but his short game – especially his putting – is not what it was. At his peak, Watson used to give the hole a chance, with a firm rap. If he went a few feet past he was confident he could hole the return. In more recent years he has been far more tentative. There are still the good days with low scoring but as he approaches the later 40s, he is less able to maintain his form through four rounds.

PUTTING PROBLEMS *Watson studies a 1996 Open green at Oakland Hills*

Career Milestones

1949 *Born Kansas City, Missouri.*
1974 *First US Tour win, the Western Open.*
1975 *Wins his first major, the British Open Championship.*
1977 *Wins two majors, the Masters and British Open Championship.*
1980 *Collects his third British Open Championship.*
1981 *Wins his second Masters title.*
1982 *Has another two-major year, the US Open and British Open Championship.*
1983 *Joins Peter Thomson as a five-time modern British Open Champion.*
1993 *Successful Ryder Cup Captain, as the US win at the Belfry.*

> **"I think we are paid far too much. We are not worth it."**
>
> *Tom Watson*

THE GREAT GOLFERS

Every era produces its great golfers. These are the men and women who have captivated the gallery down the years not merely with their play but by their charisma. They drew spectators who may personally have had only the most rudimentary golfing talent, but who were awe-struck by the skills of their idols. Here is a selection of 200 of the greatest of them all.

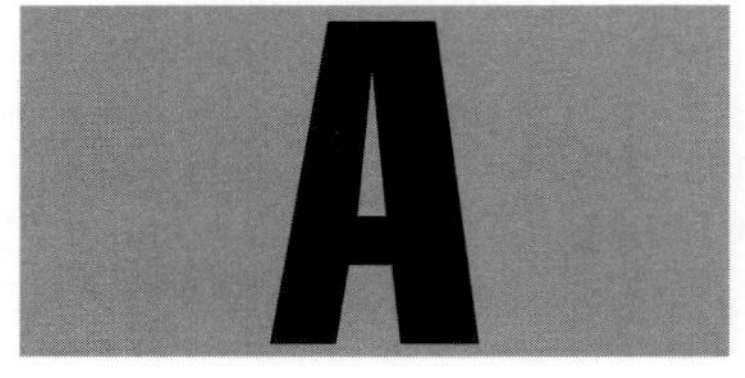

Amy Alcott

Born: February 22, 1956
Kansas City, Mo, USA

At club level many women golfers take the club back much too far and then have to waste effort in lifting it back again to a horizontal position. Alcott is the reverse. The club goes back little beyond shoulder height and she then delivers a very firm blow indeed. The short backswing, if not taken to extremes, can be an aid to consistency, and over a long professional career of about 20 years she has indeed always performed well from week to week, though her career may now be on the wane. In her first 15 years on the LPGA Tour, she was never worse than 18th on the money list and often did a great deal better than that, five times finishing in the top five. Her tournament wins are also impressive. Between 1975 and 1991 she amassed 29 wins, of which five rank as majors: three Dinah Shores, one Peter Jackson plus the 1980 US Women's Open. Her best years were 1979, 1980 and 1984, with four wins in each of these years. Perhaps her outstanding achievement was her US Women's Open victory. Her 280 aggregate was then a record for the event and saw her home by a remarkable nine-stroke margin.

AMY ALCOTT *Short swing can work*

Peter Alliss

Born: February 28, 1931
Berlin, Germany

This is a man who likes talking, and does it incomparably well. Apparently it all began when a BBC producer heard him keeping his fellow tour players in uproar on a journey back to England from Ireland. An invitation followed for him to make a few comments on the air about a tournament round he had just completed and how the course was playing. In due course this led on to television commentary immediately after his main playing career ended in 1969. Peter is now regarded as comfortably the world's best golf commentator and has been voted, in Britain, the best sports commentator. As a professional golfer, he never quite fulfilled his potential, though he was very good indeed, winning some twenty important events during the 1950s and 1960s, including three successive events in Europe in 1958. He was selected for every Ryder Cup team bar one between 1953 and 1969, and also played ten times for England in the World Cup. Alliss was one of the longest and most consistent hitters in the game and was also very tidy around the green. But his putting became his Achilles heel. He had begun with a highly unorthodox grip – but it worked. He was advised to change it, and did, never to be the same player again.

Willie Anderson

Born: circa 1880
North Berwick, Scotland

In the US Open, Anderson set two records that have still to be surpassed. In 1905 he won his fourth championship, a record since equalled only by Bobby Jones, Ben Hogan and Jack Nicklaus – but even they couldn't go on to a fifth title. Anderson also won three of his titles in a row, an achievement which might have been matched by Ben Hogan – winner in 1948, 1950 and 1951 – but for his severe car accident early in 1949. Anderson had a very high performance level in the US Open, for besides his victories he had one second place, one third, two fourths and three fifths. In a relatively short career – he died at the age of 30 – Anderson was nearly always in contention in this championship. He had numerous successes in local tournaments, most of which have disappeared into unrecorded history, as well as a remarkable four wins in the Western Open, which in those days ranked second only to the US Open. Anderson is unusual in that his victories came with two different kinds of ball, the gutta percha and the rubber core. He had a flat swing, with a good deal of bend in the left arm, and opponents thought his greatest strength was an unflappable temperament.

Isao Aoki

Born: August 31, 1942
Abiko, Chiba, Japan

Aoki is one of the most unlikely looking great players, for he uses a remarkably – now unfashionably wristy – technique for both full shots and the short game. In his putting stroke, where he is one of the best performers ever, he uses a centre-shaft putter with the toe of the club cocked high in the air – and raps it into the hole. He is one of the rare Japanese golfers to come close to winning a major championship. This is because the Japan Tour is very lucrative indeed, so few trouble themselves to play on other tours. Aoki does, and in 1994 he won well over $500,000 on the US Senior PGA Tour. He has been leading money winner in Japan five times and has won more than fifty times in both his home country and worldwide.

ISAO AOKI *Playing at St Andrews, 1990*

He is the only Japanese to have won on four different tours – Japan, Australia, Europe and the USA. Perhaps his greatest international success came in the 1980 US Open, where he broke the scoring record with rounds of 68, 68, 68, 70 and still finished a couple of strokes behind Nicklaus. He won the 1978 World Matchplay title at Wentworth and the 1983 European Open, while his third-round 63 in the 1980 Open Championship at Muirfield equalled the lowest ever shot in the event.

George Archer

Born: October 1, 1939,
San Francisco, Ca, USA

Archer is one of the players who must rejoice that the Senior Tour has become such a great commercial success. In the 1990–94 period, he has averaged over $750,000 per year and has twice got very near to the million mark. In just a few years he has piled up 15 victories, already a little better than he did on the main tour, with 12 wins between 1965 and 1984. One of these was a major, the 1969 Masters, where he began with a very good first round of 67 and held on to win by a single stroke. The greatest strength of his game is his putting, where he must surely be ranked in, say, the top half a dozen of modern times. From his great height of 6 feet 5½ inches he crouches low over the ball and then gets himself even nearer by gripping well down the handle of his putter. Besides his highly unusual set-up to the ball for putting, Archer likes to feel that he is guiding the putter with his left hand, while the right is what gives him feel for pace. Playing in the 1980 Heritage Classic he set a tour record by taking only 94 putts for the four rounds.

Tommy Armour

Born: September 24, 1895
Edinburgh, Scotland

Tommy Armour won three major championships. First came the US Open of 1927, when he holed a putt of 10 feet or so on the last hole to tie Harry Cooper and then beat him in a close-fought play-off. Armour's effort had been particularly fine because he had scattered shots in his fourth round and needed an excellent last four holes to draw level. His next win was in the 1930 US PGA, where he had a narrow victory in the final over Gene Sarazen. But the prize he really sought was the British Open, and he won it, against the odds, at Carnoustie in 1931, producing a very good final round while others threw it away. By this time Armour was already on his way out, suffering from the putting "yips", a term he himself invented. When he retired from the game he became a very highly paid teacher and best-selling author of instruction books. Armour achieved the reputation of being a superb iron player. Tommy himself thought he was a better wooden club player and that it was his positioning from the tee which gave him easier shots into greens. Perhaps that is why the woods he is said to have originally designed are much sought after today. Tommy is also remembered for the immortal reply he gave when challenged about his notoriously slow play: "Whoever said golf was supposed to be played fast?"

PAUL AZINGER *A crowd favourite at Kiawah Island in the 1993 Ryder Cup*

Paul Azinger

Born: January 6, 1960
Holyoke, Ma, USA

"When you're 33 you don't expect anybody to tell you that you've got cancer. I was in my prime. I felt bullet-proof." Before 1993, Azinger was possibly the man in American golf thought most likely to become a superstar. In a seven-year winning run from 1987 on the US Tour he had four times been in the top four money winners and never lower than 11th. In 1993 he took the US PGA Championship. Then, following the best season of his professional career, Azinger was informed that a troublesome problem in the shoulders was in fact lymphoma in the right shoulder-blade. Happily, good performances from late 1994 onwards seem to indicate both recovery from the disease and a return to golf form. However, he is not a dominant figure and may be influenced by the memory of his failure in the British Open at Muirfield in 1987. That is the one Nick Faldo won because Azinger dropped shots at both of the last two holes to let Faldo in. However he has also had plenty of successes. The most dramatic came in the 1993 Memorial Tournament, when he holed out from a greenside bunker to win by a stroke from Corey Pavin.

Ian Baker-Finch

Born: October 24, 1960
Nambour, Australia

At Birkdale in the 1991 British Open, all the talk concerned whether or not Seve Ballesteros could perform on the final round and win. Meanwhile, no one was paying much attention to Baker-Finch. They soon were, after he birdied five of the first seven holes and played the first nine in 29, a very rare feat indeed. He finished with a 66, to win by two strokes. Much earlier he had looked a champion – at St Andrews in 1984, when rounds of 68 and 66 gave him a three-stroke lead. A 71 then left him tied for the lead with Tom Watson, but a disaster at the 1st hole in the final round damaged his confidence. Playing to the green, his ball twisted back into the Swilcan Burn which fronts it. And that was that. He managed to break 80, but only by a single stroke. His next real attempt at an Open title came in 1990 when a third-round 64 took him into a tie for second place, with Nick Faldo five strokes ahead. Faldo did not falter. Baker-Finch won a US Tour event in 1989 and was consistently successful in his homeland, Japan and Europe, until back and shoulder injuries and eye surgery in 1994 led to missed cuts galore: 1997 opened no more happily with disqualification for signing for an incorrect score.

John Ball

Born: December 24, 1861
Hoylake, England

This player has a very strong claim to be considered the greatest amateur of all time – as long as one excepts Bobby Jones. But even Jones did not win as many amateur championship titles in Britain and the United States as did Ball, who totalled eight in Britain between 1888 and 1912 and was also the beaten finalist twice. He did not compete at all in America. During his peak years in the 1890s he was fully capable of competing with the very best professionals. In 1890 he became the first Englishman to win the Open Championship, which he achieved at Prestwick as a result of extremely consistent play. In the next few years he was a man to watch out for, but was very likely far more interested in the Amateur Championship, as he may well have preferred the matchplay format and also the camaraderie of those he knew the best. Ball was not renowned as a putter, and his great strength was the accuracy of his long shots up to the flag. In this respect, he was a revolutionary player. Before his great days, all had been content to aim for the green. Ball wanted to be close to the flag.

BRIAN BARNES *Senior tour offer*

Severiano Ballesteros

see Legends pp 86–87

Miller Barber

Born: March 31, 1931
Shreveport, La, USA

Barber's money-winning achievements show how important the Senior US Tour can be. He has won close on $3½ million as one of the more effective performers, with 24 victories between 1982 and 1989. He twice led the money list and eight times finished inside the top 10. The end of 1994 saw him tieing with Lee Trevino with 24 wins, but Trevino will undoubtedly move far ahead. Barber was also extremely effective on the main US Tour, which he joined in 1959, going on to win 11 times. He played in two Ryder Cup matches, in 1969 and 1971. During the period from 1963 to 1978 he was never out of the top 40 money winners and was 12 times in the top 25. Barber seldom featured strongly in the major championships though he did equal the Masters record low round with a 64 in 1979. His best chance of victory in a major came in the 1969 US Open, which he led by three with the final round to play. However, he then fell away with a round of 78 to finish in only sixth position. Barber's swing is highly unorthodox but has worked well for him, as even a very eccentric swing can when the oddities have become more ingrained than the orthodox.

Brian Barnes

Born: June 3, 1945
Addington, England

Regarded as one of golf's eccentrics, Barnes has been known to wear shorts, smoke a pipe and drink copious quantities of canned beer when out playing a tournament. Some would say that this player's greatest achievements came in the Ryder Cup, where he was in every team from 1969 to 1979. In the 1975 event he beat Jack Nicklaus twice in singles in one day. He has also made many appearances for Scotland in both the World Cup and the Double Diamond event. The winner of nearly 29 professional tournaments, he probably had his finest hour in the 1981 Tournament Players' Championship when he had a last round of 62 which got him into a play-off, which he then won. He is a powerful player using a short backswing, followed by a lunge at the ball. He might have become a great player if he had won an Open Championship early in his career, when he had the potential. Now his main playing career has long seemed over, and he has appeared more interested in running a golf club, but he has been seen again in tournament play in recent years. He made a winning start on the Senior tour.

Jim Barnes

Born: 1887
Lelant, England

Nicknamed "Long Jim" because of his 6 feet 3 inch height, Barnes emigrated from his native Cornwall in 1906 to San Francisco. In 1913 he tied for fourth place in the US Open and the following year achieved the first of three victories in the then very important Western Open. Even more significant was his victory in the first ever US PGA Championship of 1916. He also won the first post-war event in 1919, and was to reach two more finals, in 1921 and 1924, each time losing to Walter Hagen. His greatest triumph came in the 1921 US Open. His opening 69 gave him the lead and he drew away round by round, eventually finishing with what remains a record nine-stroke margin. Though Barnes became an American citizen, he still liked to return to Britain, where he tied for second place in the 1922 Open and won in 1925 in the infamous Prestwick event. It was thought that Macdonald Smith had been cheated of victory because of crowd disturbances during his final round. Barnes played in what some consider the first Ryder Cup in 1926, but was ruled out afterwards because he was not a native-born American.

Andy Bean

Born: March 13, 1953
Lafayette, USA

Is golf good for the health? In the case of professionals it's rather doubtful. Constant practice imposes stress on certain body parts, particularly the lower back and the left wrist. Andy Bean was once a real prospect for superstardom, and also physically strong enough to bite golf balls in half. He had enormous

ANDY BEAN *Could bite a golf ball in half, but his back is weaker than his jaw*

power and very good touch around the greens. In recent years, however, he has been plagued by medical problems and of late has had resort to the Qualifying School and the Nike Tour. His best years came in the period 1978 to 1986, when on five occasions he was in the top seven of US Tour money winners. In much the same period he accumulated all his 11 wins. Bean was a Ryder Cup player in 1987, when he had a notable victory against Ian Woosnam in his singles match. He had also played for the USA against Japan in 1984. Since those days, however, his game has declined sharply. In 1994 he entered 19 tournaments and only three times made money, finishing 253rd on the US money list, his worst ever placing. It could well be that he has it in him yet to make a come-back. If not, he has still won over $3 million.

Frank Beard

Born: May 1, 1939
Dallas, Tx, USA

Beard won 11 titles on the US Tour between 1963 and 1971 and was leading money winner in 1969. He once came close to a US Open title, in 1975, when he was in the lead after the third round but then finished disastrously. His 78, after he had finished with two bogeys, left him a stroke away from the play-off between John Mahaffey and Lou Graham. In his best years, Beard was always regarded as being somewhat colourless. Perhaps this was a reflection of his strictly businesslike attitude to the life of a professional golfer. However, Beard is also a man of other parts. His book *Pro*, published in 1970, is still the most perceptive account of what living on the US Tour is really like. When his competitive days on the tour came to an end, he continued to practise his writing skills, mainly as a columnist in a golf magazine. He produced a follow-up to *Pro* in 1992, in which he did the same job for the Senior Tour. On this tour he was quite successful, his best year coming in 1990, when he won over $300,000. However, having probably started to lose interest, he is now concentrating on television work.

Chip Beck

Born: September 12, 1956
Fayetteville, USA

Undoubtedly the highlight of Beck's career is the 59 he scored in the third round of the Las Vegas Invitational at Sunrise Golf Club in October 1991. That made him the second player, after Al Geiberger, to break the magic 60 in a US Tour event. He went out in 29, starting at the 10th, with seven birdies, and the other nine holes were just as eventful. The birdies continued to flow in, and at the last of his holes he fired in an eight-iron shot to about three feet and then completed the job. That meant a total of 13 birdies and no dropped shots – and a reward of $500,000. Beck had a quiet start to his US Tour career in 1979 and did not begin to make real money until 1983. His first big year was 1987, though he had still to win. In 1988 he rectified that with two victories. His closest approach to a major came in the 1993 Masters, when he finished second to Bernhard Langer but four strokes behind. Some observers considered that he had been mentally ready to settle for second place. However, in the Ryder Cup that same year he came from three down with five to play to defeat Barry Lane by one up.

CHIP BECK *At the 1991 Ryder Cup*

Deane Beman

Born: April 24, 1938
Washington, DC, USA

Beman succeeded Joseph Dey as commissioner of the PGA Tour in 1974 and held that position for twenty years. He earned a reputation for being an excellent administrator but also made a few enemies. Perhaps ready for a change after such a long time, he joined the Senior US Tour mid-way through the 1994 season, but made few entries and little impact. However, Beman had already shown potential by qualifying to play in the British Open and finished only a shot behind champion Gary Player in the Senior British Open at Turnberry in 1991. He had put himself through an energetic practice regime to get his game back into trim. His best golf was probably played as an amateur. He represented his country four times each in the Eisenhower Trophy and the Americas and Walker Cups. More significantly, he won the British Amateur in 1959 and the US Amateur twice – 1960 and 1963. Later he left a highly paid insurance brokerage job at the age of 29 to compete on the main US Tour from 1967 to 1974, when he won four events as well as finishing as runner-up in the 1969 US Open.

Patty Berg

Born: February 13, 1918
Minneapolis, Mn, USA

Berg reached the final of the US Women's Amateur on her first entry in 1935. She was there again two years later, but had to wait until 1938 for her first victory. A hugely successful amateur golfer, she won something like 40 events before turning professional just before the Second World War. Together with Babe Zaharias and Betty Jameson, she was one of the three founder members of the fledgling US Women's Tour, which took off properly in 1948, and in which she became a dominant force. In 1946, she had won the first Women's Open, then match play, and went on to win what was billed as the World Championship in 1953, 1954, 1955 and 1957. She was also leading money winner in 1954, 1955 and 1957. This meant that she was the first woman to pass $100,000 in career money winnings. Berg also set the low round record, 64, in 1952 which stood for 12 years until it was beaten by Mickey Wright. Having first won a professional tournament in 1941, she won her last more than 20 years later in 1962, bringing her total to 57. Her last entry came in 1980.

Tommy Bolt

Born: March 31, 1918
Haworth, USA

Bolt was a sublime striker of a golf ball and in his peak years was thought to have the most fluid golf swing in the game. However, he was a rather poor putter – the worst, he was known to claim, among his playing contemporaries. Temperamentally he could handle his bad putting, believing that the good putters were inferior players who didn't appreciate what the game of golf was all about – excellence in the shots through the green. Here Bolt excelled, but earned his "Thunderbolt" nickname through his quite frequent losses of temper when such a shot didn't come off. Clubs would be snapped over the knee or hurled to the heavens. Though already a professional for a few years, Bolt didn't join the US Tour until 1950, at the age of 32. However, he went on to win 11 tour events between 1953 and 1961, and four others of significance but not then regarded as official. His most important victory was in the 1958 US Open, which he took by four strokes from the very young Gary Player. Bolt also had a run at the Masters, in 1952, but his putting again let him down – he three-putted three of the last four greens and came in third.

Michael Bonallack

Born: December 31, 1934
Chigwell, England

Bonallack is one of just three candidates for the title of "Greatest British Amateur Ever", the others being John Ball and Harold Hilton. However, with his consecutive wins in 1968, 1969 and 1970 he achieved something that even they had not managed in the British Amateur. Bonallack had also won this event in both 1961 and 1965. Sometimes uncertain in the long shots, Bonallack was unexcelled even by his professional contemporaries at the short game in general and, particularly, at putting. Asked about his method in this department he declared that he "willed the ball into the hole". A more obvious feature was the way he spread his feet wide and crouched over the ball, a style uncommon nowadays but not earlier this century. Bonallack was indeed a master of the short game. During one of his five wins in the English Amateur Championship, one final came his way despite the fact that he missed 22 greens and still managed to get down in two more. Later, he went into golf administration, and since 1983 he has had one of the key roles in world golf as secretary of the R&A.

Julius Boros

Born: March 3, 1920
Fairfield, USA

Boros was one of those golfers who look more relaxed than they really are. Fearful of becoming locked over the ball, he evolved a method to avoid this. He would walk casually up to his ball, shuffle his feet into his stance – and then swing. It worked so well that people thought that this was the way the game should be played. Boros was a late developer, not giving up accountancy for professional tournament play until the age of thirty. Then he immediately contended for the US Open in 1950 and was fourth the following year. In 1952 he bested the great Hogan comfortably, having trailed him by four strokes after 36 holes. If this was a surprise victory, his win in 1963 was something of a shock to Boros himself. His 76 in the third round did his chances little good, and a 72 in the afternoon round, leaving him nine over par, merely suggested he would get a reasonable pay-cheque in a very high-scoring event. But no one beat that score, and in the 18-hole play-off the following day Boros's 70 was good enough to beat Arnold Palmer by six and Jacky Cupit by three. His other major was the 1968 US PGA at the age of 48, which made him the oldest winner of a major championship.

Pat Bradley

Born: March 24, 1951
Westford, USA

Now probably a little past her best, Pat Bradley was for long one of the very top players on the US LPGA Tour. She first won in 1976, and her 31st victory came in 1995. From 1976 to 1991 she recorded 12 placings in the top six money winners and had just one bad year, the result primarily of hyperthyroidism. She has won six LPGA events which count as majors – two du Maurier Classics, one Nabisco Dinah Shore, one Peter Jackson Classic, an LPGA Championship and the 1981 US Women's Open. Her greatest money-winning year came in 1991, when she took home more than $750,000 and was first on the money list. She had the same placing in 1986, but 1991 was easily her best year. She had four victories, increasing her total to 30, and thus earning a place in the US LPGA Hall of Fame. That same year she also won the Rolex Player of the Year award and the Vare Trophy (for best scoring average) for the second time in her career. Aided by the yearly increases in prize money, Bradley was the first woman golfer to surpass, in turn, career winnings of $2 million, $3 million and $4 million and is now past $5 million.

PAT BRADLEY *A consistent performer*

Harry Bradshaw

Born: October 9, 1913
Delgany, Ireland

In 1949 Bradshaw was playing the Open Championship in Sandwich and in contention after a first-round 68 and at the peak of his form. Playing the 5th in the second round, he found his ball resting against broken glass. He thought he was very likely entitled to a free drop, but was unsure. Nowadays any professional would automatically call for an official ruling. Bradshaw, however, decided to play the ball as it lay, was hit by flying glass and moved the ball less than twenty yards. He took six instead of the par four which had been likely. Worse, he was upset and his normally superb putting stroke was far less sure for the rest of his round of 77. The next day he had recovered his composure, and with rounds of 68 and 70 he went on to tie with South African Bobby Locke – only to be totally outplayed in the play-off. Bradshaw was never again to be in real contention for an Open. His greatest achievement, in partnership with Christie O'Connor, was to win the World Cup, in which, despite being affected by the high altitude, he was individually second. He made three Ryder Cup appearances, and among other successes recorded two wins in one of the most important tournaments of the day, the Dunlop Masters.

James Braid

see Legends pp 106–07

GORDON BRAND JNR *Swing trouble*

Gordon Brand Junior

Born: August 19, 1958
Kirkcaldy, Scotland

Brand's outstanding amateur career was followed by more-or-less instant success as a professional golfer. In his first year on the European Tour, 1982, he won twice and finished seventh on the money list. However, he was unable to maintain his pace the following year. Some said he was striving for too much length on his tee shots when not naturally a long hitter. Perhaps he was listening to too much wise advice and becoming confused. Happily he was soon back on the winning path, and 1984 saw him win two more tournaments and again finish seventh on the money list. Since then, Brand became consistently successful on the European Tour. Until 1995, when he slipped to 88th after another (unsettling) swing change late in 1994 - he had never been below 34th on the money list and had eight placings in the top 12. He has played in three Ryder Cup teams – 1987, 1989 and 1993 – and represented Scotland nine times in the

Dunhill Cup at St Andrews and seven times in the World Cup. His most remarkable performance came during the 1993 season, when he led in the European Open at the East Sussex National from start to finish and sailed to victory by the unusual margin of seven strokes.

Jack Burke

Born: January 29, 1923
Fort Worth, Tx, USA

Winning a sequence of events on the US Tour – or indeed any other tour – is very difficult indeed. That is why the achievements of Byron Nelson are regarded as so phenomenal. Burke had his winning streak in 1952, when in just over three weeks he won four events. It wasn't the stuff of Byron Nelson, whose 11 wins in a row will surely never even be approached, but Burke was hailed as the wonder of the age. Was he going to be better than Nelson? Better than Hogan? The answer was certainly no, for Burke was never quite as good again. However, he had many high achievements ahead of him. The one that secured him a place in golfing legend was his victory in the 1956 Masters. As they entered the final round, amateur Ken Venturi was eight strokes better than Burke's aggregate but, in bad weather, Burke played a well-managed 71 while the amateur staggered in with an 80. Burke also won the US PGA that year and was voted Player of the Year. Burke won a total of 15 events on the US Tour and played on five Ryder Cup teams, captaining his country in both 1957 and 1973.

Dick Burton

Born: October 11, 1907
Darwen, England

Burton's greatest achievement came in the last Open Championship to be played before the Second World War. At St Andrews he had rounds of 70, 72, 77 and 71 to win by two strokes from the American Johnny Bulla. Burton's play on the final hole particularly impressed all who witnessed it. The 350-yard 18th on the Old Course must be one of the easiest climaxes in championship golf. The only real danger for the tee shot is to hit a hotel or golf clubhouse along the right and go out of bounds. Most players, in conditions where they think they have no chance of reaching the green, play safe and aim left. Burton, however, hit his drive tight along the railings to the right. Though dangerous, this gives the best line into the green. It was almost all over. He flicked a short iron to holeable distance and then, as his putt went on line, casually tossed the club to his caddie. Because of the war, he was Open champion for the longest spell of anyone – seven years. Alas, again because of the war, he made little money from his win. Burton had two other high placings in the championship, and set a record for tournament scoring with rounds of 68, 66, 64 and 68 – 266.

Mark Calcavecchia

Born: June 12, 1960,
Laurel, USA

This player's best years to date came between 1987 and 1990, when he was always in the top 10 on the US money list. In the same period he also had five of his seven wins on that tour. However, a greater claim to fame is his victory in the 1989 British Open Championship at Royal Troon. Here, he was always in touch with the leaders but never looked a likely winner until, in his final round, he first holed a long putt on the 11th and then lobbed a shot from a bank into the hole on the next. His round brought him a play-off with Wayne Grady and Greg Norman, who had come storming through the field. In the four-hole play-off Norman took an early lead but dropped a shot on the penultimate hole. The last was a disaster for him as he first drove into a fairway bunker he believed he could not reach, and then went out of bounds through the green. Calcavecchia, on the other hand, hit a much poorer drive but into a reasonable position and then ripped a five iron to about seven feet and birdied for victory. This must have been a consolation for his defeat by Sandy Lyle in the Masters the previous year, when with Calcavecchia readying himself for a play-off, Lyle played his famous long bunker shot, holed the putt, and was champion.

Dorothy Campbell

Born: 1883
Edinburgh, Scotland

In the early years of this century, Dorothy Campbell was arguably the best woman golfer in the world. In 1909 she became the first woman to win both the British and US titles in the same year and remains one of only three to do so. Later she became the first woman to complete the Grand Slam of British, US and Canadian titles. A Scottish international, she also played twice for Britain against the USA and it is estimated that she won in excess of 750 prizes during her career. Early in her golfing career, Campbell won the Scottish Championship three times (1905, 1906 and 1908). Emigrating to Canada on her marriage, after winning the British Ladies title in 1909 and 1911, she won the Canadian in the three years 1910 to 1912 and added a third US championship in 1924. On moving to America at a time when British players were still the best in the world, she won numerous state and regional titles. It was there that a moment's inattention cost Dorothy Campbell (by then Hurd) her life. She was standing on a railway line when she failed to notice an oncoming train and was killed, at the age of 63 in 1945.

José-Maria Cañizares

Born: February 18, 1947
Madrid, Spain

Cañizares joined the European Tour in 1971. He recorded his first win in Italy in 1972, but no more until 1980, when he won twice. His peak years came in the 1980s, when he was six times amongst the top 11 on the money list and collected most of his seven wins on the European Tour. (He has also won significant events in Kenya and Spain.) Cañizares holds a share in the European Tour nine holes scoring record – 27 – while his lowest round is a 61. When he is hot, he is really hot. One of his most memorable moments came when he won a decisive Ryder Cup singles at the Belfry in 1989. Ironically, there is little doubt that captain Tony Jacklin had placed him in the middle of his singles line-up because he was thought likely to lose. (The strong men were positioned at the head and tail of the order.) He has played in four Ryder Cup teams and also won the individual prize in the 1984 World Cup. There are also four Dunhill Cup appearances on his record to add to his selection as one of the pair in eight World Cup finals. He remains an effective player in mainstream golf, but is no longer a likely winner unless everything goes his way one week.

JOSÉ MARIA CAÑIZARES *A very long career*

Joanne Carner

Born: April 4, 1939
Kirkland, USA

Nicknamed today "Big Momma" and earlier "The Great Gundy" (which referred to her maiden name of Gunderson), Carner compiled one of the great records in amateur golf. Starting with the USGA Girls title in 1956, she went on to win the US Amateur five times – 1957, 1960, 1962, 1966 and 1968 – and then turned professional after winning an LPGA event as an amateur in 1969. She was immediately successful, but her best years came in the period 1974 to 1984, when she was never worse than ninth on the money list, headed it three times and was second or third on another four occasions. She added the US Women's Open to her list of majors in 1971 and had a repeat victory in 1976. The first of these wins meant that she became – and remains – the only woman to win the USGA Girls title, the US Amateur and the US Open. On the US LPGA Tour, she won 42 times between 1970 and 1985, and though she is now in her mid-forties she has second-place finishes to her credit and is still a possible winner. She also wins her fair share of prize money despite a fairly limited playing schedule. In 1994 she was a very popular captain of the US Solheim Cup team – and a victorious one.

Joe Carr

Born: February 18, 1922
Dublin, Ireland

Carr is one of the greatest amateurs from the British Isles ever. With his vast hitting and tremendous recovery powers, he is also one of the few British players to prosper in the US Amateur, where he reached the semi-final stage in 1961. In his native Ireland his record was outstanding. Besides a host of regional successes he also won the Irish Closed Amateur Championship on six occasions and the Irish Open Amateur four times – 1946, 1950, 1954 and 1956. Even more significant were his performances in Britain and abroad. In the British Amateur he had a formidable record, winning in 1953, 1958 and 1960. On two occasions he beat leading American amateurs in the final at a time when they were normally superior. He played in every Walker Cup team from 1947 to 1965, captaining the side on the last occasion. He was then non-playing captain for the next match. Carr made a limited number of entries in professional tournaments and was second in the 1959 Dunlop Masters, which was then one of the most prestigious events in Europe. He also came quite close to the centenary British Open, entering the final round just two strokes behind the leader.

BILLY CASPER *An all-time great putter*

Billy Casper

Born: June 24, 1931
San Diego, Ca, USA

Casper was a phenomenally successful golfer on the US Tour, though somewhat prosaic in style compared with his charismatic contemporary Arnold Palmer. Casper's aim was to get his ball into the fairway and then find the green. Thereafter, he knew he was just about the best putter around, albeit an unusually wristy one. As a competitor in the majors, his most dramatic moments came in the 1966 US Open. With nine holes to play, Arnold Palmer held a seven-stroke lead. It was all over, it seemed; Billy Casper was merely playing for second place. But Palmer then began to cast strokes to the wind while Casper plodded methodically on. In the end Palmer had to hole a testing putt just to tie with Casper. It was a similar story in the 18-hole play-off. At the halfway point Palmer led by four but again collapsed, giving Casper his second US Open. His first in 1959 had also been remarkable: he used only 112 putts in his four rounds. Casper's other major victory came in the 1970 Masters, and he also took a total of 51 events on the US Tour. Only five players have won more.

Bob Charles

Born: March 14, 1936
Carterton, New Zealand

It is an oddity of golf history that the greatest left-handed golfer ever is naturally right-handed. He began playing left-handed purely because his parents played that way around and had some spare clubs. It took Bob Charles a long time to make up his mind to become a professional – six years after he won the 1954 New Zealand Open. Thereafter he was soon winning in both Europe and the USA. On the main US Tour he won five times and had eight wins in Europe. Putting excellence has always been central to his success and particularly led to his greatest triumph, the 1963 British Open Championship, when he averaged 30 putts per round. He then went on to destroy American Phil Rodgers in the 36-hole play-off. However, his peak success came as a senior golfer in the USA. From his debut year of 1986 until 1993 he was always at least in the top 10 money winners and topped the list in both 1988 and 1989. In 1993, while finishing second, he won over $1 million. He has 22 victories on this tour and among other successes has twice become the Senior British Open Champion in 1989 and 1993.

Howard Clark

Born: August 26, 1954
Leeds, England

Blessed with one of the best swings in British golf, Clark has probably not done his talents full justice, though he came back to form in 1994 and captained the England team in the Dunhill Cup. Before this his game appeared to be in decline, partly perhaps owing to an elbow injury. He had been a consistent performer from 1976 to 1989, with his best years being 1978 and the period 1984 to 1986. Clark has been very successful in team events, playing in six Ryder Cup teams from 1977 to 1995 and representing England in several World Cups. In 1985, he was the individual winner. He has also made five Dunhill Cup appearances. In addition, he has won 12 times on the European Tour, once winning two in a row. His most prestigious win was the PGA Championship at Wentworth in 1984. He had to wait six years to add his sixth Ryder Cup appearance to his fifth, but the match at Oak Hill greatly revived his reputation. His singles point at the expense of Peter Jacobsen was crucial to European victory, and achieved with the help of a hole in one at the short 11th. It was, he said, the first good six iron he hit all week.

Neil Coles

Born: September 26, 1934
London, England

Coles turned professional at the age of 16. Seven years on, he started to make his mark, and from 1961 began a run of astonishing consistency. From then until 1980 he was never worse than 12th on the money list, was leader twice and second once. He finished in the top six on 12 occasions. But he was not merely a money winner. At a time when the tournament schedule was limited and based largely in Britain, he racked up 28 wins. Coles is proba-

HOWARD CLARK *Achieved a great comeback in the 1995 Ryder Cup*

bly the best British player since the war never to have come really close to an British Open Championship title. However, he did very well on occasion, coming third as early as 1961. A relatively poor last round at Carnoustie in 1975 saw him fall away from strong contention. In 1973, by contrast, he played one of his best rounds, a 66, but had gone out too far behind to have any real chance. He tied second. Apart from his having played in the most Ryder Cup matches in his eight appearances, his proudest achievements are probably his victories in the Match Play Championship (three times), the Dunlop Masters and the PGA Championship. He has won nine times on the Senior Tour, still competes regularly, and is chairman of the board of directors for the PGA European Tour.

Glenna Collett (Vare)

Born: June 20, 1903
New Haven, Ct, USA

Glenna Collett was perhaps the greatest American woman amateur ever, her record of six victories in the US Amateur is approached only by Joanne Carner. Her wins in the US Amateur came in 1922, 1925, 1928, 1929, 1930 and 1935. She was runner-up in 1931 and 1932, and on four occasions was medallist (the leading stroke play qualifier for the match play stages). In her career, over a period of 18 years she won a total of 49 leading amateur events. These included the French title in 1925 and the Canadian in 1923 and 1924. Early on she was a keen baseball player, and this may have helped with her muscle development, for she hit her tee shots a very long way indeed. At the age of 18 she struck one drive which was measured at a little over 300 yards – and this with grace and precision rather than brute force. During her peak years, her only rival on the world scene was Joyce Wethered, who defeated her on two occasions in the British Amateur. The second of these matches was the final at St Andrews in 1929. Collett was out in 34 and seemed home and dry at five up. However, at lunchtime after 18 holes, the lead had been cut to just two up and in the afternoon the English player pulled ahead to win by 3 and 1.

GLENNA COLLETT *Greatest US amateur?*

Archie Compston

Born: January 14, 1893
Penn, England

Compston was one of the most likely British hopes in the British Open Championship from the early 1920s to the 1930s, when Americans were largely carrying all before them. In 1925 he finished a stroke behind the winner, Jim Barnes, at Prestwick's last Open, and in 1930, Bobby Jones's Grand Slam year, he went into the final round one ahead of the great man. Compston had played a third-round 68 to eliminate his five-stroke deficit. On the final afternoon, Compston fell away completely with an 82. It is said that this one round permanently dented his confidence. In the 1928 Open he had suffered a disappointment of a different kind. Walter Hagen, favourite to win in the absence of Jones, had barely stepped off the boat from American when he went into a challenge match against Archie over 72 holes at Moor Park. Compston was at the top of his form, while Hagen had not yet found his "landlegs". The result was outrageous. Compston won by 18 and 17, and went into the Open at Sandwich as the new favourite. Alas for Compston, Hagen had put in some fairly serious practice and won easily, with Compston well beaten in third place.

John Cook

Born: October 2, 1957
Toledo, Oh, USA

Since 1980, Cook has been a journeyman pro on the US Tour. His best year was 1992, when he finished third on the US money list. Otherwise, he has never been better than 16th, but has accumulated $4½ million and won six times. His moments of maximum exhilaration and despair probably came in the 1992 Open Championship at Muirfield. Cook opened with strong rounds of 66 and 67, which still left him three strokes behind Faldo's 66, 64. To the betting men it seemed to be all over when Faldo then produced a 69 to Cook's 70. But it is often said that a tournament is won and lost over the last nine holes. Cook started with a bogey on the first, but after six holes was only a stroke behind Faldo. He then dropped some strokes, but made an apparently decisive move when he birdied both the 15th and 16th. He was two strokes into the lead over the struggling Faldo, and apparently made the championship secure when he struck a three-iron to around 10 yards on the par five 17th. Another birdie here and he was almost there. Instead, having shaved the hole with his eagle attempt, he then took a couple more putts. He was still almost certain to win if he parred the difficult final hole. Having hit a poor second shot, he didn't.

Harry Cooper

Born: August 4, 1904
Leatherhead, England

Cooper, whose family emigrated to America when he was a child, is one of the best US Tour players not to win a major championship, though he came very close. He finished one stroke behind Horton Smith in the 1936 Masters after being in the lead going into the final round, and was second again two years later. His experience of close encounters with the US Open was probably even more disappointing. In 1927 he three-putted the last green while Tommy Armour holed a good one to earn a play-off, which Cooper lost. In 1936 he broke the scoring record for the same event, but the relatively unknown Tony Manero still came in two strokes better. However, Cooper, nicknamed "Light Horse Harry" because of his speed about the golf course, was an extremely successful tournament player. His total number of victories is not known but is probably about the 25 mark. His best year was 1937, when he took nine titles and was both leading money winner and holder of the new Vardon Trophy for the lowest stroke average. He is today almost a forgotten man. It's the major championships that earn immortality.

Henry Cotton

Born: January 26, 1907
Holmes Chapel, England

Cotton was the man who put the pride back into British golf, mainly by his achievements in the 1930s, when he took two of his three British Open Championship titles after a long period of American dominance in the event. Though he won the Open again in 1948, there can be little doubt that much of his golfing prime was lost to the war. Cotton was a first in British golf, a public schoolboy from a middle-class background who turned professional. The conventional course would have been to remain an amateur and do "something in the City", but Cotton wanted to be a great player to maximize his income. He succeeded in both aims. Always a prey to nerves, Cotton threw away chances of an Open title before his first victory at Sandwich in 1934. Even then, although he won comfortably enough in the end, he had a near disastrous last round of 79, having begun it with a nine-stroke lead thanks to his superb play earlier. His finest hour came in 1937, when he won the Open at Carnoustie with all the US Ryder Cup team in the field. Cotton was without doubt the greatest British player since the Triumvirate, and was knighted shorly before his death in 1987.

Fred Couples

Born: October 3, 1959
Seattle, Wa, USA

Fred Couples first began to make a name for himself on the US Tour when he took the 1983 Kemper Open, and since then he has had 12 US Tour wins and six placings amongst the top 10 money winners. He was leading money winner in 1992, when he won three US events. The most important of these was the Masters, his only major to date, though he has often featured among contenders. He has also been a very effective player for the USA in team competition. In 1995, he and Davis Love III became the first pairing to win the World Cup four times in a row, on the third of these occasions with phenomenal scoring. Couples won the individual International Trophy by five strokes after rounds of 65, 63, 68 and 69. Seemingly a very relaxed golfer, Fred no doubt has his problems like anyone else. Putting is one of them. He has lost a few events through very poor holing out at crucial stages of tournaments and came to resort, for the time being at least, to the reverse-grip method. Fred's long game is extremely fluent and long, perhaps aided by what appear to be very loose shoulder joints. If his tender back holds out, Fred is still a prospect to be the world's number one.

FRED COUPLES *Long driver*

Bruce Crampton

Born: September 28, 1935
Sydney, Australia

Nicknamed "The Iron Man" because he used to play nearly all events on the main US Tour, Crampton has continued along the same path on the Senior Tour. Playing his first full season there in 1986, he won seven events and was leading money winner. Several good seasons followed, but his career, towards the mid-1990s, seems to be petering out. Up to the end of 1994, Crampton had a total of 19 Senior victories and had won over $3½ million – more than twice the sum he won on the main tour. Crampton first came to the fore in 1956 when he won the Australian Open at the age of 20. Having joined the US Tour in 1957, he was very unsuccessful for a few years but had his first victory in 1961. More followed fairly regularly until he had totalled 14 by the end of 1975. Although he never won a major, he was twice second in the US PGA, once in the Masters and once in the US Open. In fact, in 1972, he was second in three of the four majors. After his good years his form fell away rapidly and his health gave way. He retired and went into the oil business, before making his triumphant return as a Senior.

Ben Crenshaw

Born: January 11, 1952
Austin, Tx, USA

Crenshaw was a youthful prodigy whose first success came on his debut as a PGA Tour member. In his early days he looked set to be an all-time great, but now that he is into his 40s, this no longer seems likely, though as he proved in the 1995 Masters he still had a major championship in him. Some swing analysts have thought that the weakness in his game is an overlong backswing, past the horizontal, which can mean a lack of control. Ben has certainly hit his share of fairly wild wooden club shots – as have most others. In contrast, his putting is extremely compact. Many regard him as the best putter in the game, especially after his biggest career victories, the 1984 and 1995 Masters. On the US Tour, Crenshaw has been extremely consistent with only one bad year. He has seven times been in the top eight on the money list and has 19 career victories. Crenshaw is unusual amongst Tour professionals in having a strong interest in the history of the game. Like many players, he is also becoming involved in golf course architecture, where his knowledge of traditional values should prove useful.

Fred Daly

Born: October 11, 1911
Portrush, Northern Ireland

By the age of 30 Daly was becoming consistently successful on the Irish golf scene, but as tournament play in Britain and Europe was suspended during the war, he lost what might well have been several of his most productive years. As soon as the war was over, however, Daly began to enjoy his heyday, which lasted until 1952. The biggest victory of his career was the 1947 Open Championship, over Royal Liverpool's course at Hoylake. He began with rounds of 73 and 70 in testing conditions, then sagged to a 78 on the morning of the final day. In the afternoon, he played a good 72 in reasonable weather and set a target that none of the later starters, in worsening conditions, could match – he was champion by a stroke. The following year he was second and then third in 1950. In 1952 he was third again, having led after two rounds but fallen away fairly badly on the final day. He played every Ryder Cup match between 1947 and 1953, once winning his singles by 9 and 7, and a further eight important tournaments in the British Isles came his way.

John Daly

Born: April 28, 1966
Sacramento, Ca, USA

At golf tournaments there is sometimes a buzz of expectation and a rush of spectators – usually indicating that the leaders are approaching. The exception was, till the coming of Tiger Woods, John Daly. He can still attract a crowd even when well down the field. They enjoy gasping at the distance he can hit the ball. In recent US Tour statistics he *averages* about 290 yards – his longest blows go a good deal further. The length comes from natural power, aided by a huge shoulder turn and a backswing that is absurdly long by modern standards. He is also prepared to take risks and let fly from the tee with the driver when others might be thinking about a prudent three-iron. Daly first came to attention with his dramatic appearance in the 1991 US PGA Championship at Crooked Stick, to which he drove "on spec", to find that a late withdrawal had given him a place in the field. His first chance to see the course was during his first round when he shot a 69, two behind the leader. His following series of 67, 69, 71 gave him a three-stroke victory over Bruce Lietzke. Marital or drink problems have dogged his career, though his one 1995 victory was typically spectacular, the British Open; 1996 was winless. In 1997 he entered the Betty Ford Alcohol Rehabilitation Programme, and his wife Paulette sought a divorce.

Beth Daniel

Born: October 14, 1956
Charleston, SC, USA

Daniel had a short but outstanding amateur career, making two Curtis Cup appearances and winning the US Amateur title in 1975 and 1977. She was also a member of the World Cup team. When she began competing on the LPGA Tour in 1979, she was immediately successful. She had her first win and finished 10th on that year's money list. She was soon doing much better and threatening to replace Nancy Lopez as the wonder of the age. In both 1980 and 1981 she topped the money list and increased her tour victories to eight. However, she did not top the list again until 1990, her best year, when she won seven times – a feat rarely achieved in modern times – and her winnings of over $860,000 set a new record. So far she has 10 times fin-

LAURA DAVIES *Top of the Ping world rankings 1994–95*

ished in the top eight money winners. By the end of the 1994 season she had racked up 32 tour wins, which ranks her 11th in the all-time listings. Oddly, only one of these is a major, the 1990 LPGA Championship. She has played in every Solheim Cup match to date.

Eamonn Darcy

Born: August 7, 1952
Delgany, Ireland

If quite a few Irish golfers have had stylistically entertaining swings, none have been odder than Darcy's. Perhaps the unorthodoxy accounts for his fluctuations in form. In 1975 and 1976 he seemed to be on the verge of becoming a major force in European golf with finishes of third and second on the money list. His 1975 results included a second place finish behind Arnold Palmer in the PGA Championship, in which he also reached a play-off the following year with Gary Player and Neil Coles, which the Englishman went on to win. He also had two wins in 1976, and another in 1977, but his overall level of performance fell away, a slump which continued until 1981. Then he finished ninth on the money list and earned his third Ryder Cup team place. His Cup record is poor, except for his fourth and final appearance, at Muirfield Village in 1987, when he came back memorably at Ben Crenshaw and holed a very missable putt for victory on the last hole. Darcy has four European Tour wins on his record and five more overseas. He has also played seven World Cups, and was in the winning Irish Dunhill Cup team on one of his three appearances.

Laura Davies

Born: May 10, 1963
Coventry, England

In 1994, Laura Davies became the world's leading woman golfer. Despite playing a limited schedule, she topped the US money list and produced the remarkable feat – never achieved before by man or woman – of winning on five different tours. She won three times in the USA, twice in Europe and once each in Thailand, Japan and Australia. Earlier, her greatest success had been in winning the 1987 US Women's Open when not a member of the US LPGA Tour. This caused that organization to give her exemption, after amending its constitution, from the need to qualify for Tour membership. Davies has played with great success in the Curtis Cup and the Solheim Cup, in which she has been an inspiration for her team. She is renowned for her prodigious hitting, but her great strength, she herself thinks, lies in her crisp and accurate short game. In March, 1997, she became the first player to win an LPGA tournament for a fourth consecutive time, the Standard Register Ping, at Moon Valley, Phoenix.

Rodger Davis

Born: May 18, 1951
Sydney, Australia

Many professional golfers like to identify themselves by their clothing. Davis has had two trademarks for long periods in his career: his long socks and plus-twos. He has been a strong contender in the Briish Open Championship. In Ballesteros's first year at Lytham in 1979, for instance, he held the lead with five holes left to play but, like a few others, fell back over the testing finish. At Muirfield in 1987 he started with a blistering 64, which gave him a three-stroke lead, but his following rounds of 73 and 74 took him out of strong contention. On the final day he never quite looked like winning, but his 69 was eventually good enough to earn him a tie for second with Azinger, leaving Faldo victorious by a single stroke. Davis was a winner in Australia when he first decided to try his luck in Europe in 1977. He immediately made occasional impact, sometimes fading out of contention after good starts. His first win came in 1981 and he has had half a dozen more since then, the most important being the PGA Championship in 1986 and the Volvo Masters in 1991. He has won 19 times in Australia and New Zealand.

Jimmy Demaret

Born: May 10, 1910
Houston, Tx, USA

One of the greatest players not to have won a US Open, Demaret was the first to win the Masters three times. He did this in 1940, 1947 and 1950, once managing a 30 over the second nine at Augusta, Georgia. Despite his numerous tournament successes, Demaret was noted above all for his flamboyant clothes. Walter Hagen was probably the first golfer to attire himself in, for example, two-tone shoes, a bow-tie and matching slacks and top. Demaret went much further and might grace the golf courses of America topped by a tam-o'shanter, with vivid shirt and trousers, the ensemble completed from his vast collection of shoes. If Demaret was the Payne Stewart of his time, there is no evidence that he had a lucrative clothing contract, as do Stewart and so many other modern players. As a golfer, he was very influential in his shape of shot. Before him, most top professionals favoured a draw, because of the greater run on the ball. Demaret decided that the fade was better, as that side-spin held both fairways and greens more effectively.

Bruce Devlin

Born: October 10, 1937
Armidale, Australia

Devlin began to come to the fore in 1959, when he won the Australian Open and decided he was good enough to turn professional. He then played worldwide for a while before settling in the USA. Between 1964 and 1972 Devlin won eight events on the US Tour, but continued to make appearances in Europe, most notably in 1966 when he was leading money winner. Devlin was for long considered a likely winner of a major championship, though he never came particularly close. Perhaps his best performances were two fourth places in the Masters and two sixths in the US Open. One of the latter came at Pebble Beach, in his mid-forties, when he held a two-stroke lead after two rounds but dropped back to six strokes behind winner Tom Watson. He plays a limited schedule these days on the US Senior Tour, where he has had little success. However, from his Houston base, he has worked intensively in golf course design and produced some 140 since the mid 1960s.

BRUCE DEVLIN *Consistent money-winner around the world*

Leo Diegel

Born: April 27, 1899
Detroit, Mi, USA

"They keep trying to give me the championship, but I won't take it," said Leo Diegel after yet another title had been cast to the winds. But it might all have been so different. He contended strongly for the US Open as early as 1920. A win then might well have given him the self-assurance so much needed by a young player. Though blessed with a great talent, Diegel never quite fulfilled it. Perhaps his main problems were that he lacked composure and his nerve sometimes cracked at crisis points in the majors. In the 1933 British Open at St Andrews, for example, he needed only a par four at one of the easiest last holes in golf to tie, but his putting let him down. It often did, despite endless experiments with different putters and a revolutionary method. The latter involved crouching low over the ball, club grip almost touching his chin, and pointing both elbows outwards. He hoped this would take his jerky wrists out of the putting stroke. It was much imitated. Despite his failings, Diegel was still a formidable tournament player and is credited with some 30 victories. The most important of these were in the Canadian Open, which he won four times, and the US PGA Championships of 1928 and 1929, the first of which ended Walter Hagen's great run.

Flory van Donck

Born: June 23, 1912
Tervueren, Belgium

Easily the finest golfer Belgium has so far produced, van Donck was almost a dominant figure in continental Europe and highly effective in Great Britain. The extent of van Donck's dominance in his native land can be seen from his record in the Belgian Professional Championship. Between 1935 and 1968 he won it 16 times. In 1979, at the age of 67, he was still representing his country in the World Cup, an event in which he played regularly from 1954 to 1970 and was individual winner in 1960, when it was at a peak of its prestige. In continental European Opens van Donck was for years the man you had to beat. He won the Belgian and the Dutch five times each, the Italian four times, the Swiss and the German twice and the French three times. The toughest competition, however, was then to be found in the British Isles, where he won five events and had some close encounters with the Open Championship. For nearly a dozen years from 1949 he was very seldom out of the top 10 and twice finished in second place. Van Donck had a smooth and rhythmic swing but was less elegant on the greens: he liked to putt with the toe of his putter high.

George Duncan

Born: September 16, 1883
Methlick, Scotland

Duncan emerged young on the British golf scene, and was in the Scotland team by 1906. However, it was several years later, when he beat both Braid and Taylor in the News of the World Matchplay Championship, that he really became a name. In 1913 he beat Braid again, in the final. By this time he was just about on a level with the Great Triumvirate and Sandy Herd, and was much in demand for challenge and exhibition matches. After the war, much was expected of George Duncan and Abe Mitchell, but even they could not prevent the growing American dominance of the Open Championship. However, Duncan won at Deal in 1920, and an amazing victory it was. He began with a couple of 80s, which put him right out of contention. His driving had been the main problem, but after playing his second round he picked up a driver in the exhibition tent, had a few swishes with it – and money changed hands. His game was transformed. On the final day, he had rounds of 71 and 72 and was champion by a couple of strokes.

J. Douglas Edgar

Born: September 30, 1884
Newcastle-upon-Tyne, England

Although Tommy Armour said he was "the best golfer I ever saw", and Bobby Jones called him "a magician with a golf club", Edgar is now a largely forgotten figure in the history of golf. The reason he has been forgotten is that he died prematurely – and mysteriously – in Atlanta, Georgia, as a result of a small but deep wound in his thigh. He had bled to death. Was it a mugging? Perhaps murder for an unknown reason? Or was he simply the victim of a hit-and-run driver? There were headlines for a short time and then the story became a shadowy part of golf history. The crime was never solved. Edgar became a name to be reckoned with when he won the 1914 French Open by six strokes from Harry Vardon. Then came war, after which he emigrated to

STEVE ELKINGTON *Australian globe-trotter*

America. There his greatest achievement came quickly when he won the Canadian Open by 16 strokes from Bobby Jones and Jim Barnes, still the greatest margin ever in a national Open against a top-class field. He won the same event again the next year and also reached a US PGA final. He was killed in 1921. A revolutionary feature of Edgar's game was that, like many others, he had a very full shoulder turn but, unusually, a much more restricted hip movement. He always felt he would play his best when his hands felt "thin".

Lee Elder

Born: July 14, 1934
Dallas, Tx, USA

Lee Elder is famous above all as the first black golfer to play in the Masters. There is little or no doubt that those who used to rule at Augusta hoped that no black would compete. When it was a purely invitational event this was relatively easy to achieve – there were in any case few blacks in the USA playing to a really high standard. However, once it was decided to introduce a direct qualifying system, in addition to invitations, winners on the US Tour were allowed in. Thus in 1974, when Lee Elder won his first title, the Monsanto Open, beating Peter Oosterhuis in a play-off after a dramatic last round, he qualified to play in the 1975 Masters. There, ironically, he failed to survive the half-way cut. Elder had three further wins on the main US Tour and played on the 1979 Ryder Cup team. Later on he was successful during the 1980s on the Senior PGA Tour. Between 1984 and 1988 his worst finish on the money list was 19th, and in his best year, 1985, he was second. During this period he had eight victories, in one of which he opened with a 61, a Senior Tour record.

Steve Elkington

Born: December 8, 1962
Inverell, Australia

Elkington first came to the fore in 1981, when he won the Australian Amateur Championship. The same year, while winning the Doug Sanders Junior World Championship, he was evaluated by the University of Houston golf coach and offered a "scholarship". Since then, Elkington has been mainly based in the USA. Success while at Houston showed that he was undoubtedly a promising prospect, and by 1987 he had qualified for the US Tour, immediately achieving some good results. In 1990 he won the Greater Greensboro Open, and, the following year, the Tournament Players Championship, after a tough fight with Fuzzy Zoeller. This is an event which ranks just below the four major championships. It earned him nearly $300,000 and 10-year exemption from having to qualify for the US Tour. In 1992 he took the Australian Open, another event just below major championship status. His final stride to that level came in the 1995 US PGA at Riviera, where his closing 64 for 267 equalled the lowest ever aggregate for a major (Greg Norman at Sandwich in 1993). Even this was not decisive. Colin Montgomerie tied with a 25-foot birdie putt at the 72nd hole. Elkington beat him at the first play-off hole with a birdie putt along the same line the Scot used in regulation play.

Ernie Els

Born: October 17, 1969
Johannesburg, South Africa

In 1994 Els became the most talked-about player in professional golf, earning about £1.8 million on the various world tours. He also became easily the best young player in the game of golf. His achievements that year were rivalled only by those of Nick Price. He ended his year by winning the Johnnie Walker World Championship – but this, some would say, is not actually the championship of anything, just another tournament. The same could be said of the World Matchplay event at Wentworth in the autumn, which he also won. Far more significant were his victories in the US Open in 1994 and 1997, the first after a three-way play-off. Els first came to prominence in 1992, when he won the most significant titles in his homeland – the South African Open, the PGA and the Masters. This was the first time such a hat trick had been achieved since Gary Player did it a dozen and more years earlier. Ernie Els's game seems as good as that of anyone in the world. He has huge length off the tee, great feel for pace and line around the greens – and then there's always his putting. It was in good order when he and Wayne Westner won the World Cup late in 1996.

ERNIE ELS *On his way to the US Open*

Chick Evans

Born: July 18, 1890
Indianapolis, In, USA

The Western Amateur remains one of the top events on the American circuit. Evans won it eight times, including a sequence of four in a row. However, his main target was the US Amateur. It did not come easily. In 1909, 1910 and 1911 he was defeated at the semi-final stage. The next year he got as far as the final but was heavily defeated, 7 and 6, by Jerry Travers, after having been three up early on. But Evans was good enough to defeat the leading professionals of his time, taking the Western Open in 1910. Then came a trip abroad and a win in the French Amateur – and also a meeting with James Braid, which led him to switch to the Vardon grip. In 1914 he was nearly US Open champion, finishing just a stroke behind Walter Hagen. But he did it in 1916, and in a grand manner. His 286 total brought him in by two and set an aggregate record that was to last for 20 years. That year, he also took the US Amateur at last – apart from Jones, he remains the only man to win both titles in the same year. He won again in 1920 and also reached the 1922 and 1927 finals. He still qualified for the US Amateur as late as 1953.

Nick Faldo

see Legends pp 88–89

Johnny Farrell

Born: April 1, 1901
White Plains, NY, USA

Farrell is one of the very few who beat Bobby Jones when this great American was in his peak years. It happened at Olympia Fields in the 1928 US Open. The two tied on 294, and went into a 36-hole play-off, as was then the norm. Farrell, with a 70, was three better than Jones after the first round, but Jones came back at him in the afternoon. However, Farrell held on, and a seven-foot putt on the very last hole was good enough for a one-stroke victory. That was his only major victory, though he was second in 1929 in both the US PGA and the British Open Championship. He also finished one behind the Jones/Willie Macfarlane play-off in the 1925 US Open. In the period 1923–24, he made money in every tournament he entered, but an even better spell came early in 1927, when he won seven consecutive tournaments. He had eight wins in all that year, to follow his five the previous season. Farrell played in the first Ryder Cup team in 1927 and in the next two events also. The great strength of his game was his putting.

Max Faulkner

Born: July 29, 1916
Bexhill, England

Faulkner was one of the more eccentric players of modern times. In his search for putting perfection he assembled a vast collection of putters – making most of them himself – said to have reached a total of around three hundred. He must have experienced many disappointments! Faulkner was constantly experimenting with subtle variations of the other clubs too, and seems virtually never to have played with a full conventional set. All this was because Faulkner had great feel for the shape and flight of a shot and was one of the few players who found it easy to bend the lofted irons either way. His victory in the 1951 British Open Championship at Portrush was achieved with an extremely light putter with a pencil-like shaft and grip. Faulkner went into the event with his long game in a dreadful state. That gradually improved under the influence of all the unlikely putts that were dropping. He began the final round with a six-stroke lead and was scarcely troubled in winning by two. He was the last British golfer to win until Jacklin 18 years later. Faulkner was five times in the Ryder Cup team and had 16 wins in Britain and Europe.

MAX FAULKNER *A colourful and eccentric figure, but a very successful golfer*

David Feherty

Born: August 13, 1958
Bangor, Northern Ireland

"I think I can win. I've got nothing better to do this weekend." Feherty is certainly not the best player in the world, but he is probably the most quotable. This remark was made at the British Open Championship at Turnberry in 1994, when he was in hot contention until the closing stages. That year, he had made the slightly unusual decision to compete on the US Tour instead of on the European Tour, where he has been consistently successful since early in the 1980s, winning five titles between 1986 and 1992. His 1994 US venture was a modest success, netting him nearly $200,000. Feherty has, like most but not all professionals, suffered the putting yips but, aided by a centre-shaft putter, may have conquered them. He was number one in the European Tour putting statistics in 1991, using just 28.5 putts per round, and is also one of the longer hitters in the game. He lost his US Tour card in 1995: marital problems and an arm injury hindered progress. Feherty, who forsook training as an opera singer for golf, announced he would retire, then dabbled on the European Tour again before settling down to tramping the fairways for US television.

Jim Ferrier

Born: February 24, 1915
Sydney, Australia

Ferrier came into professional golf having dominated the Australian amateur scene for several years. He won the Australian Amateur title four times in the late 1930s. Also as an amateur he won the Australian Open twice, in 1938 and 1939, and at St Andrews in 1936, became the first Australian to reach a final of the Amateur Championship. He turned professional in 1940 and, deciding that Australian golf was rather a small pond, departed for the USA the following year. He made money but no great impact on the US Tour until the mid-1940s, and scored his first win in 1944. His only major came in 1947 when he won the US PGA, then a match play event, defeating Chick Harbert in the final. Ferrier also finished second in the 1950 Masters to Jimmy Demaret – but he ought to have won. He only needed to score 38 on the final nine holes, but his game fell apart. However, as consolation that year, he was second on the money list. Altogether he had 21 wins on the US Tour, the last of these coming in 1961.

Dow Finsterwald

Born: September 6, 1929
Athens, Ga, USA

There was not much dash about Finsterwald's play. Although he was an excellent shot-maker, he always had safety in mind. Once on the green he knew his excellent putting would be the equalizer. As a result he was one of the most consistent scorers of his era. His lack of adventurousness meant he seldom had a bad round, and at one time he held the record for the most tournaments played without missing the half-way cut. He joined the US Tour in 1952 and had some very bad years, but it all went a great deal better from 1956, when he was second in the money list. The next year he won the Vardon Trophy for the lowest stroke average. He was a good performer in the majors though he won only one, the 1958 US PGA, the first year the event switched over to stroke play. He had been second, under the match play format, the year before. In 1962 he tied Arnold Palmer and Gary Player for the Masters but Palmer won the 18-hole play-off easily. Finsterwald won 12 events on the US Tour and played four Ryder Cups between 1957 and 1963. He was later non-playing captain.

Jack Fleck

Born: November 8, 1922
Bettendorf, Ia, USA

For an hour after Hogan had completed his four rounds in the 1955 US Open, he sat in the locker-room accepting the congratulations on a record-breaking fifth US Open. He was five strokes better than anyone who had finished, and there was only one still out on the course with a statistical chance: Jack Fleck, an unknown pro from a municipal course in Davenport, Iowa. He had once finished as high as sixth in a tour event and had also gone around the Olympic course in 87 in a practice round. But he was playing well enough now, and needing a birdie at the last to tie Hogan, he duly hit a very difficult approach shot to about eight feet and then holed the putt. Words failed him in the Press tent afterwards. As for Hogan, he was in peak form and no one, least of all the inexperienced Fleck, was going to beat him over 18 holes. But he did. Taking a one-stroke lead into the last hole, he took four while Hogan hooked into deep rough and took three to get back to the fairway. This was very easily Fleck's finest hour. He did win a couple of tour events several years later, but little else, and the Senior Tour came a bit too late for him.

Raymond Floyd

Born: September 4, 1942
Fort Bragg, NC, USA

Today a successful Senior Tour competitor and arguably the best player in the world for his age, Floyd was chosen for the Ryder Cup team by captain Tom Watson as recently as 1993. His professional career began in 1963, and he won in his first season on the US Tour. In later years he has added a further 21 tour wins and has totalled more than $5 million in prize money. While Floyd has had his share of moderate seasons, he has seven times been among the top nine of money winners on the US Tour. His best years were 1981 and 1982: each time he was second on the money list and had three victories. Floyd has won four major championships, the first coming in 1969, the US PGA. Perhaps his next win was the best. He dominated the 1976 Masters throughout, winning by a record eight strokes and equalling Jack Nicklaus's record 271 aggregate. In 1982, aged 40, he took his second US PGA, having started with what he called "the best round of my life" – a 63. The US Open he so much desired came his way four years later at Shinnecock Hills after a last-round 66. At 44, he was the oldest player to win the championship.

RAY FLOYD *The agony of a missed putt*

Doug Ford

Born: August 6, 1922
West Haven, Ct, USA

Not many men hole a bunker shot to win a major, but Ford did so to take the 1957 Masters. It gave him a 66, and a three-stroke margin over Sam Snead. This was his second major championship, following his success in the 1955 US PGA. Ford's swing was quite short and ugly, and although he attacked with venom, he was by no means a long hitter. However, the short hitter has a better chance of keeping the ball on the fairway and leaving a precise shot to the green. Once there, Ford was right up among the best putters of his day. He came into the game as the son of a golf club professional and, from the age of 18, had a successful amateur career, mainly in his home area. His first professional victory came in the Houston Invitational and he joined the US Tour full-time in 1950. By the end of his main career, he had won 19 events and tied in seven others where he lost play-offs. His peak years were from 1951 to 1960, when he was never worse than 10th on the money list and was twice second. Ford was on every US Ryder Cup team between 1955 and 1961. The Senior Tour came rather too late for him, but he had some good results into his sixties.

David Frost

Born: September 11, 1959
Cape Town, South Africa

Frost turned professional in 1981 and tried to play the US Tour, but with no success. Instead he tried Europe and in his first full season, 1983, finished 32nd on the money list. The following year he rose to 10th place and also won the Compagnie de Chauffe Cannes Open. Frost then qualified for the US Tour and has played it more or less full-time since then from his Dallas base. He had a quiet first two seasons but won good money before leaping to 11th place on the money list in 1987. The following year he had two victories in the Southern and Tucson Opens and moved up to ninth. In 1989 came his best win to date in the World Series of Golf, which gave him a ten-year exemption from having to qualify for US Tour events. His best tour season came in 1993, when he recorded consecutive victories in the Canadian Open and Hardee's Golf Classic. His aggregate of 259 in the latter event was just two strokes above the tour record for 72 holes. He topped $1 million for the year and was fifth on the money list. In 1994 Frost had wins in the USA (bringing his total to nine), Hong Kong and South Africa. He has also won the Sun City Challenge three times.

DAVID FROST *Will he win a major?*

Robert Gamez

Born: July 21, 1968
Las Vegas, Nv, USA

Turning professional in 1989, Gamez almost immediately became a potential star name when he won on his first entry on the US Tour – the Northern Telecom Open. He was then quiet for a couple of months before becoming one of the many who have given Greg Norman a jolt by holing an unlikely shot. This was no greenside chip. On the 72nd hole of the Nestlé Invitational at Bay Hill, with 176 yards to go to the flag, he holed a seven-iron shot for an eagle and a one-shot victory from nowhere over Norman. This unlikely feat, added to his earlier win, made Gamez a hot property, and at the end of the season, with money winnings of nearly $500,000, he was duly accorded Rookie of the Year honours. He was 27th on the money list. But Gamez has not maintained that pace, though he won around $250,000 in each of his next six seasons – not big money in the context of earnings on both the US and European tours. His other main achievements have been to lose to Fred Couples in a play-off for the 1993 Honda Classic, a first-round 61 and an eventual second-place finish in the 1991 Milwaukee Open and, in 1994, wins in the Pebble Peach Invitational (not a Tour event) and the important Casio World Open.

Al Geiberger

Born: September 1, 1937
Red Bluff, Ca, USA

Geiberger will always be remembered for being the first to break the magic 60 in a US Tour event, which he did on June 10, 1977, in the second round of the Danny Thomas-Memphis Classic. He went on to win, one of 11 successes on the main US Tour between 1962 and 1979. His most important victory came with the 1966 US PGA Championship, but others of almost equal significance were his wins in the 1975 Tournament of Champions and the Tournament Players Championship, both events which rank just below major championship status. Geiberger has always been plagued by stomach problems and found it helped him to eat little and often. His chosen snack on the golf course, famously, was the peanut butter sandwich, but even this couldn't contain the stomach problems and he has had to have several operations. When be became eligible for the Senior Tour at the age of 50, Geiberger immediately became one of the most effective competitors. Apart from being injured in 1994, he has always been among the top 20 money winners and, since 1987, has four times been in the top 10. He has won nine events. Geiberger was on the US Ryder Cup teams in 1967 and 1975.

Bob Goalby

Born: March 14, 1931
Belleville, USA

Goalby was involved in perhaps the most famous rules decision of all time. It happened at the end of the 1968 Masters. Roberto de Vicenzo having dropped a shot at the last, after a great round, glumly signed his card – marked by a fellow competitor. Alas, he had failed to notice that his score on the 17th was wrongly shown as a par, not a birdie. Roberto was not disqualified for his error, as he had merely signed for a higher score than he had actually achieved. But that score had to stand, and instead of de Vicenzo being in a play-off for the Masters, Goalby had won. This was very unfortunate – for both men. Goalby, after all, had finished with a superb 66 and would anyway have tied de Vicenzo. He had played a great tournament and, as like as not, would have won the play-off. But what is remembered is that Roberto was the real winner but that someone or other else got the green jacket. Goalby had joined the US Tour in 1957, and in 1958 was named Rookie of the Year. Usually in the top 60, he won 11 tour events in his career and was second in both the 1961 US Open and the 1962 US PGA. With a lively temper and a pronounced in-to-out swing, his great problem was a draw which could become an uncontrollable hook. Despite this, he had his very hot streaks and once set a tour record with eight consecutive birdies.

Wayne Grady

Born: July 26, 1957
Brisbane, Australia

Though he didn't win, the Troon Open Championship of 1989 was perhaps Grady's finest hour. A 67, following a first-round 68, gave him a one-stroke lead. After the third round, Grady had retained his narrow lead of one – over Tom Watson. In the final round, Grady did little wrong, but some inspired golf from Greg Norman, who had started the day seven behind, and some very good, if occasionally lucky play by Mark Calcavecchia, produced a three-way tie – and a four-hole play-off, won by the American. For Grady, it was a rare encounter with the possibility of greatness. However, a major championship did come his way the very next year when he won the US PGA. Grady had made his US Tour debut in 1984, finishing 217th on the money list, improving to 45th in 1985.The next three years were less kind, but Grady broke through in 1989 when he won the Westchester Classic and was 27th on the money list. The following year he improved to 21st, mainly a result of his US PGA win, since when he has done relatively little. Twice the Australian PGA Champion, Grady also won the 1984 German Open.

WAYNE GRADY *US PGA Champion*

David Graham

Born: May 23, 1946
Windsor, Australia

The Australian tour having limited seasons, Graham, like many of his countrymen, has had to make himself an international golfer. Indeed, he has won all over the world, though his principal efforts have been on the US Tour, where he has won eight times. He is now inactive on that tour, but if his putting remains good, he should be phenomenally successful on the Senior Tour. Putting has always been a very strong feature of his game. Graham has won two major championships. The first of these was the 1979 US PGA. This was the first success by an Australian in a major since Peter Thomson won the 1965 Open Championship. He started off four behind the leader in his final round, but got to the turn in 31 and had birdies at the next two holes. With the event in his hands, Graham then showed considerable clumsiness around the green on the last hole, and could only tie. However, he won the play-off against Ben Crenshaw with the aid of some truly remarkable putting. In 1981, he became the first Australian to win the US Open. He did it with a last-round 67, thanks largely to his precision through the green. He took 33 putts – but missed only one fairway and no greens.

Ralph Guldahl

Born: November 22, 1912
Dallas, Tx, USA

Guldahl may well be an example of a golfer ruined by writing a golf instruction book. It caused him to think about the way he himself played the game, which was extremely unorthodox. He had very little flow, with either legs or in foot roll, and compensated for a lack of cock in his right wrist action on the backswing by letting the club move in his grip. Thinking and writing about it may have ruined him, for he suffered a permanent loss of form. Guldahl himself had various other explanations, ranging from a bad back to the fact that he had done it all in competitive golf. The latter was certainly true – if only for a brief spell. He first hit the headlines in 1933 when he came within a four-foot putt of a tie for the US Open. Guldahl then disappeared for a few years but came back in 1936 as a the second highest money winner. The next spring he experienced his famous loss in the Masters, largely due to a disastrous 5, 6 sequence on the 12th and 13th holes. But his time was coming. Two months later he won the US Open and then had a rare repeat victory the following year. The Masters came his way the next year, partly because of those previously fatal holes. This time he played them 3, 3. And that was just about the end of it for Ralph Guldahl.

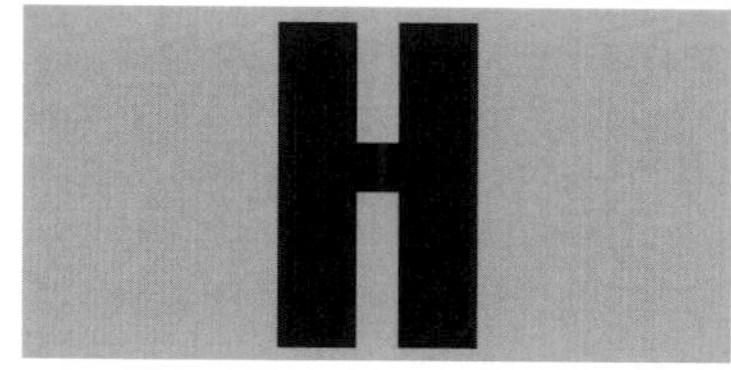

Walter Hagen

see Legends pp 90–91

Sandra Haynie

Born: June 4, 1943
Fort Worth, Tx, USA

Haynie is one of the great figures of the US LPGA Tour. In the period 1963 to 1975, her worst placing on the money list was ninth, and she had at least one victory every year. Usually, however, she was a multiple winner, 1974 being her most successful year. Then she won six times, including the LPGA Championship and the US Women's Open, two of the four majors she has won in a long career. No other player has achieved the feat of winning two majors in a single year, except for Mickey Wright (who went one better by winning three). Haynie was troubled by arthritis from the age of 33, and soon after her great years she became only an occasional competitor, playing just 17 tournaments in the space of the four years from 1977 to 1980. Yet 1982 saw her in peak form once more. She had two victories and finished second on the money list, one of the five times she has been in this position (while never being number 1). Once Haynie was into her forties she became a receding force, and has not competed since playing a full season in 1989 without any real success. Sandra Haynie was inducted into the Hall of Fame in 1977, and in 1970 won the Player of the Year award.

Clayton Heafner

Born: July 20, 1914
Charlotte, NC, USA

Displays of temper are now rare, but in earlier days on both the US and British tours, they were considered to show you had some competitive fire. One player who certainly had it was Heafner, who was quite easily upset by matters other than an unsatisfactory shot. He once stormed off the 1st tee to his car, hurled his club in, and drove off in a cloud of dust, having been angered by the announcer's introduction. Heafner just missed out on the great events. In 1942 he tied for the Tam o'Shanter, which was for some time the richest prize in American golf. He lost the play-off. In two US Opens he also came very close. At Medinah in 1949 he and Sam Snead tied for second place, just a stroke behind Cary Middlecoff's championship-winning score. Worse than this, perhaps, followed in 1951 at Oakland Hills, where most of the field were irate at Robert Trent Jones's all too successful attempt to toughen up the course. Heafner went into the last round tied with Ben Hogan and then produced a 69, which was one of only two scores below 70 throughout the championship. Alas for Heafner's chances, Hogan tamed the "monster" course with a 67, arguably the greatest round of his career.

Sandy Herd

Born: April 22, 1868
St Andrews, Scotland

Always just a notch below the standards set by the Great Triumvirate of Vardon, Taylor, and Braid, Sandy Herd outlasted them all. His long professional career began in 1892 at Huddersfield Golf Club. The same year, he won three tournaments and made a good run at the Open Championship, being held for the first time at Muirfield, finishing tied for second place behind Harold Hilton. Herd was again second in 1895, this time at St Andrews, and looked likely to win at Muirfield the following year when he started with a 72 – five strokes better than anyone and 11 better than the eventual winner, Harry Vardon – before his form collapsed. His finest hour came at Hoylake in 1902, when he won the Open by a stroke from Vardon and Braid. He was the first champion to use the "modern" rubber core ball instead of the guttie. After Herd's win, the guttie was finished. It was to be many years before Herd was. He was second in the 1920 Open, having been in the lead with a round to go, and last played 1939, 54 years after his first appearance. In 1926 he upstaged even the Great Triumvirate with what is probably the greatest feat ever performed by an "old" golfer. At the age of 58, he took the News of the World Matchplay Championship, then ranked second only to the Open.

Dave Hill

Born: May 20, 1937
Jackson, Ms, USA

Like a Hogan or a Nelson, Dave Hill has always delighted in trying to achieve perfection in his lonely vigils. "You paint pictures out there," he said, "and each good shot is a deft stroke." During the 1960s, Hill earned an outstanding reputation as a ball striker and also for being more outspoken than various authorities liked. He was particularly rude about the Hazeltine National course, site of the 1970 US Open, in spite of the fact that he eventually finished second. "All the course needs," he declared, "is 80 acres of corn and four cows." This and similar comments brought him a $150 fine. Hill joined the US Tour in 1959, and from 1960 to 1975 was 11 times in the top 30 money winners. He achieved his best placing of second in 1969, his peak season, which included three wins. Altogether Hill won 13 times on the main tour and also made three Ryder Cup appearances. Eventually, he tired of tournament golf, particularly because he felt that success depended too much on putting. When he became eligible, however, he returned on the Senior Tour in 1987 and has recorded six wins. He has been as high as third and fifth on the money list, but his career now seems to be in decline.

SANDY HERD *Just a step behind the Great Triumvirate*

Mike Hill

Born: January 27, 1939
Jackson, Ms, USA

The Senior US Tour has provided ample evidence that some golfers who have been relatively unsuccessful in their prime may last better than their peers. Mike Hill is a clear example of this. On the main tour, although he did finish in the top 60 money winners several times and also won three tournaments in the 1970s, he was never better than 28th on the money list. Regarded then as considerably less talented than his brother Dave, Mike has outstripped him as an over-50 golfer. Having won not much more than $500,000 on the main US Tour throughout his career, he came reasonably close to that in his first year on the Senior Tour. In his next year, 1990, he won five events and finished second on the year's money list with winnings of close on $900,000. Even better times were to follow. In 1991 he again had five wins and became only the second man to top $1 million in a season on the Senior Tour. In the seasons 1992–94 he did not do quite as well, but did add more than $2 million to his winnings and advanced his Senior wins to 16. He currently equals Lee Trevino as having the longest winning streak – five tournaments – on the Senior Tour.

Harold Hilton

Born: January 12, 1869
West Kirkby, England

Hilton is generally ranked alongside his fellow Royal Liverpool club member John Hall as the greatest of British amateur golfers. He may have taken only four Amateur Championship titles to Ball's eight, but he won two Opens to Ball's single victory. He remains the only British amateur to have taken the Open twice and, perhaps surprisingly, the one British amateur to have taken the American title, when he succeeded at Apawamis in 1911. Hilton's first Open Championship victory came in 1892 at Muirfield. He had not intended to play and gave himself time only for a day's practice. His start wasn't promising, but his final rounds of 72 and 74 were truly outstanding for the time. Five years later, on his home course of Hoylake, he did it again, beating James Braid by a stroke. Oddly, he found winning the Amateur Championship more of a problem, partly because his great rival, Freddie Tait, used to get the better of him. However, he won in 1900 and 1901 and then, during a revival shortly before the First World War, came two more victories.

SCOTT HOCH *Gave Faldo a Masters*

Scott Hoch

Born: November 24, 1955
Raleigh, NC, USA

Hoch came into professional golf after a good amateur career, perhaps his peak achievement being to reach the final of the 1978 US Amateur. On the US Tour since 1980, he has always made a good living, 13 times being 40th or better on the money list. On this Tour he has won six times and also been effective overseas with a Pacific Masters on his record and two Casio World Opens. Hoch was once robbed of a major victory by a putting aberration that may haunt him until his dying day. It happened in 1989, and the scene was the play-off for the Masters. He had tied with Nick Faldo and seemed to have had it won on the first play-off hole, Augusta's 10th. Faldo had hit his second shot into a bunker while Hoch was less than a dozen yards from the hole and on the green. Faldo splashed out to about seven feet. Hoch coasted his putt almost stone dead. To stay alive, Faldo had to hole out for his bogey and did so. Hoch then had to complete the formalities, with a putt of perhaps a couple of feet – but missed. As he later said, "The message between my brain and my hands got criss-crossed." Faldo holed quite a long one on the next and was Masters champion. For Hoch, history may show that this was his closest encounter with a major. The chances don't come often.

Ben Hogan

See Legends pp 92–3

Tommy Horton

Born: June 16, 1941
St Helens, England

Horton's early career was boosted by a man called Ernest Butten, who had a passionate desire to see a British player win the Open Championship. The last to do so had been Max Faulkner at Portrush in 1951. The scheme was that Butten would put some money into grooming three players with the potential to become superstars. Faulkner would teach them how to swing the club, putt and have the mental toughness to be winners. As it turned out, none of them came really close to winning the Open, but Brian Barnes and Tommy Horton did become very considerable players. Horton was twice joint leading British player in the Open Championship – in 1976 and 1977. His finest hour was probably his victory in the 1978 Dunlop Masters, then very much a top tournament. Quite a small man, Horton was somewhat underpowered and often found himself having to hit long irons into greens when Brian Barnes, for example, might have needed just a firm wedge. So Tommy Horton became one of the best long-iron players in European golf. He had eight tournament wins in Europe, was second on the money list in 1967, had three victories overseas and was in the 1975 and 1977 Ryder Cup teams. He was PGA captain in 1978.

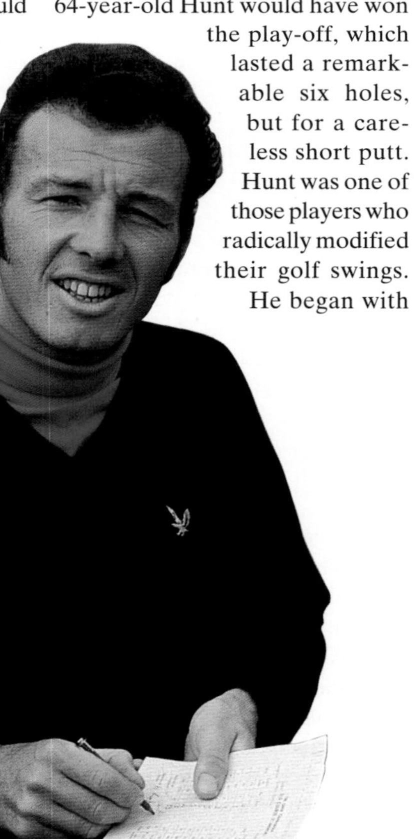

TOMMY HORTON *Success on Seniors Tour*

Bernard Hunt

Born: February 2, 1930
Atherstone, England

Seniors usually fade quietly away once past their mid-50s – but apparently not Hunt. As recently as 1994 he was competing in a senior event in Northumberland, and pulled his trolley throughout. The 64-year-old Hunt would have won the play-off, which lasted a remarkable six holes, but for a careless short putt. Hunt was one of those players who radically modified their golf swings. He began with a long backswing and was quite a wild driver at times. However, by his early 20s he had solved the problem and became a winner with a much shortened action. He was still best with the shorter irons, and was a very reliable putter. He broke through in 1953 when he won an amazing six events on what was then a very limited tour. Ironically, that year also saw Hunt's greatest disaster. Playing in the Ryder Cup at Wentworth, he needed to get down in two putts to tie the match. He failed. This was his first appearance, but in his next, at Lindrick in 1957, he beat his opponent by 6 and 5 and went on to be very effective in later matches until he bowed out in 1969. Hunt was non-playing captain in 1973 and 1975. He thrice won the Vardon Trophy for the season's lowest stroke average and won 26 tournaments.

Jock Hutchison

Born: 1884
St Andrews, Scotland

Hutchison was one of many Scots who emigrated to America to find fame and fortune and mainly developed their game there. He began to make his mark around 1910, and was fifth in the US Open the following year. His best finishes in the event were two second places, in 1916 and 1920, and he was third on two other occasions. In 1916, he came close to winning his first major, the US PGA, but was beaten in the match play final by the Cornishman Jim Barnes. However, all was well in 1920 when he defeated another English export, J. Douglas Edgar, in the final of the same event. His greatest success came on home ground, in the 1921 British Open at St Andrews. After the four rounds, he was tied with the English amateur Roger Wethered, but easily won the 36-hole play-off. There was some controversy afterwards. Hutchison's clubs were heavily scored, and it was felt that it was this factor that enabled him to stop the ball so quickly on hard and fast greens. Such designs were later banned. Hutchison won an estimated eight events of significance on the fledgling US Tour.

Juli Inkster

Born: June 24, 1960
Los Altos, Ca, USA

Inkster had a glittering amateur career which has not quite been maintained as a professional. In the years 1980–82 she became one of only three women – the others being Glenna Collett and Virginia van Wie – to have won the US Women's Amateur title three years in a row. In her last amateur season she won both her Curtis Cup matches, heading the US team, by 7 and 6 and later on went on to take the individual prize in the Women's World Amateur Team Championship by a comfortable four strokes. She was, without doubt, the world's best woman amateur. After turning professional she quickly captured her first LPGA title. In 1984 she was named Rookie of the Year and won two majors, the Nabisco Dinah Shore and the du Maurier Classic. She was sixth on the money list and went on to have her best season in 1986, when she moved up to third, winning four times. Since then, she has not been quite as successful, partly because of the demands of motherhood, but the wins have continued to pile up, including a third major, the 1989 Nabisco Dinah Shore. Two major play-offs, in 1992, were lost. At the end of 1995 she had increased her total of tournament victories to 15. She played in the 1992 Solheim Cup team.

Hale Irwin

Born: June 3, 1945
Joplin, Mo, USA

In the 1990 US Open at Medinah, Irwin played one of the most dramatic shots in the history of golf. He holed a putt of about 60 feet on the last green to tie with Mike Donald. Again they were level after a further round and Irwin then holed a birdie putt in sudden death to win. At 45, he had become the oldest winner of the US Open. Irwin has two more US Opens on his record. His first came over the very difficult Winged Foot course in 1974, where seven over par was good enough for a two-stroke victory. This win demonstrated one of Irwin's great strengths. He is by no means an outstanding putter or a genius at close range, but he does find most of the fairways and greens, so tough courses bring out the best in him. His second US Open win came in 1979 and included the shot of the year in his third round, a two-iron to a couple of feet or so. He won 20 titles and $5.6 million in 27 years on the US PGA Tour and advanced that to $8.3 million by the end of 1996 with regular Seniors wins.

Tony Jacklin

Born: July 7, 1944
Scunthorpe, England

Not many players lead a major after every round, but Jacklin did this in the US Open at Hazeltine in 1970. He cruised home to win by seven strokes, becoming the first Englishman to win the US Open since Ted Ray in 1920. Jacklin had won the Open Championship in 1969, and for a month or so was one of the select few to hold both the national championships. He was a British national hero and seemed on the verge of becoming an all-time great, but thereafter the big prizes eluded him. Lee Trevino had much to do with this, holing some outrageous and very telling shots at Muirfield in 1972, when the pair were locked in combat for the Open Championship. Playing the penultimate hole, Jacklin had victory in his grasp as Trevino struggled, but he three-putted for a six. Later that same season he played brilliantly against Trevino in the World Matchplay Championship – but again it was the American who came out on top. Though Jacklin was to play other excellent tournaments, never again did he contend in a major championship. He was a brilliantly successful Ryder Cup captain during the 1980s.

Peter Jacobsen

Born: 1954
Portland, Or, USA

This player is one of those most in demand for US golf clinics and company days. The main reason is that he is a jovial fellow who enjoys communicating. Unlike some others, he is also good copy for press tent interviews. Overall, his career has been impeded by medical problems but he suddenly found top form at 41, winning $1million in 1995. Jacobsen likes to play internationally and it is appropriate that his first win came in the 1979 West Australian Open. The following year he won his first event on the US Tour, the Buick Open. The next 14 seasons brought a meagre three wins (but $3.5 million) before his back-to-back 1995 victories

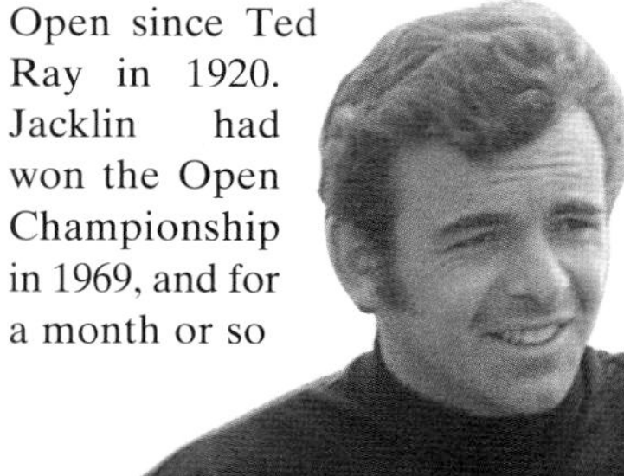

TONY JACKLIN *British hero*

raised him to his highest ranking yet, seventh. Jacobsen first broke through in 1980 in the Buick Open at Warwick Hills, MI. In 1984 he won twice and was 10th on the US money list. That remained his highest position till 1995. The strongest feature of his game is consistency through the green. He hits the fairways more than most and then goes on to find the greens. He is also thought to be the best there is at imitating the swings and mannerisms of other players.

Mark James

Born: October 28, 1953
Manchester, England

Watching Mark James play, you would think that playing professional golf is a very sad affair indeed. However, once he gets away from the office – the golf course – he is one of the most entertaining people in the international game. James had a very good amateur career, representing his country at all age levels in the first half of the 1970s, winning the English Amateur title in 1974 and reaching the final of the British Amateur the next year. In the same period he showed his toughness in match play, when he was involved in winning close on half the points the Great Britain and Ireland team won in the 1975 Walker Cup. He has shown the same qualities in the Ryder Cup, in which he has made the team seven times between 1977 and 1995, when his contribution was crucial to European success. Appropriately, his first professional success came in the 1978 Sun Alliance Match Play Championship. Since then, tournament wins have come consistently and he has often seemed on the edge of becoming a great, rather than just a very successful, player. Up to the end of 1996, Mark James had won 17 events on the European Tour. He has been in the top 20 money winners 15 times.

Don January

Born: November 20, 1929
Plainview, USA

January has been an important figure in US golf since he joined the tour in 1956. He had his first victory that year and continued to win occasional tournaments until his victory in the Tournament of Champions in 1976. In this phase of his career he was always a consistent money winner and was 20 times in the top 60 money winners. This was despite the fact that he was not a hard worker in terms of tournament entries. He left the tour in favour of course design in 1972, returning when that activity slumped to achieve ninth place in 1976. He won ten times on the main tour, including the US PGA in 1967, and subsequently gained more than a score of Senior titles.

Lee Janzen

Born: August 28, 1964
Austin, Tx, USA

There are not many people who have tied Jack Nicklaus for a record, but Janzen has. When he won the US Open in 1993 from Payne Stewart, his aggregate of 272 tied the record that Nicklaus had set back in 1980. Janzen first appeared in the US Open in 1990, but made little impact until he won his first event two years later. Then came his 1993 wins in both the Phoenix and US Opens. In 1994, he looked a good bet to repeat his US Open success, having taken the Buick Classic by three strokes over South African Ernie Els the week before. But Els went on to win the US Open while Janzen missed the cut. Like many players, Janzen looks a little anonymous because he wears a sponsor's baseball cap. Since his US Open win, Janzen has failed to reach superstar status, but his non-selection for the 1995 Ryder Cup team was greatly criticized.

Bobby Jones

See Legends pp 94–5

Steve Jones

Born: December 27, 1958
Artesia, NM, USA

The career of this son of Artesia (Pop 10,610) is a tribute to persistence. He was prospering on the US Tour, notably with three wins in 1989, till a dirt-bike accident late in 1991 damaged his left ring finger. Jones got back on tour in 1994, his long game perforce relying on the reverse overlap grip normally used in putting. A year on he was back to six figure earnings, and in 1996, inspired by Ben Hogan's "focus on each shot" exhortation, he progressed from sectional qualification to become US Open champion and "Comeback Player of the Year". Jones began 1997 with an 11-stroke win at Phoenix, his home town.

MARATHON VICTORY *Steve Jones won the US Open the hard way at Oakland Hills*

Betsy King

Born: August 13, 1955
Reading, Pa, USA

Betsy King first attracted notice at the 1976 US Open, when she finished in eighth place – a feat which has not been matched since by an amateur. However, after joining the US LPGA Tour in 1977, she found it all a very slow learning process, and her first successful season only came in 1983. That year she finished 14th on the money list, and she was on her way. From 1984 until 1995 her worst placing was ninth, and she has seven times been in the top three. She was leading money winner in 1984, 1989 and 1993. Since her first success in Japan in 1981 the victories have piled up. Her first LPGA success came in 1984. Two others followed that same year, after which she did not have a winless year until 1994. In 1989 she set a new target (broken the next year) for a season's money winnings with over $650,000. She had won six times, including the US Women's Open. This was one of her five major titles to date, the others being the Dinah Shore in 1987 and 1990, the LPGA in 1992, and the rare feat of a second Women's Open in 1990. King has 30 LPGA titles to her credit and is the first woman to win $5 million.

Sam King

Born: March 27, 1911
Sevenoaks, England

Sam King's career spanned the Second World War, and he made Ryder Cup appearances on either side of it. One of these was the disastrous first post-war match at Portland, Oregon, where Great Britain and Ireland lost every match – except Sam King's final singles. King often featured in the British Open, but had a tendency to fade in the final stages. His best performance was in the 1939 St Andrews Open when he finished third, four strokes behind champion Dick Burton. He had several other top six placings and made a very strong run as late as 1959 at Muirfield. After three rounds, he was four strokes ahead of the eventual champion, Gary Player, but his final 76 left him four behind. In 1961 and 1962 he won the British Seniors but lost to Paul Runyan in the World event. King performed well for so many years because he was not often off the fairway and had great skill with the mid to short irons. His putting was excellent in his youth, but less reliable in more mature years. He won three major events, and the Kent Championship a remarkable 12 times between 1932 and 1951 in spite of the wartime interruption.

TOM KITE *A great money winner*

Tom Kite

Born: December 9, 1949
Austin, Tx, USA

Tom appears a rather anonymous player, partly because his face is normally shielded by a very large pair of spectacles and hooded by a sponsor's eye shade. He is perhaps more famed for blowing major championships than winning them, but he is the biggest money-winner of them all, with over $9 million to his credit. Kite has achieved this by his consistency rather than by winning tournaments. After joining the US Tour in 1972, he had only three tournament victories to his credit ten years later. His strike rate, however, has greatly increased since then. He is not a long hitter but a master with the wedge, often carrying three. His peak year was 1989, when he set what was then the US Tour money-winning record at just under $1,400,000. However, having long been described as the best player never to have won a major championship, he was probably far more pleased by his victory in the 1992 US Open at Pebble Beach, and by his selection as captain of the 1997 Ryder Cup team for Valderrama in Spain.

Catherine Lacoste

Born: June 27, 1945
Paris, France

For a while Lacoste was arguably the best woman player in the world. She also has a strong claim to be ranked as the greatest French player of either sex. She had a lot to live up to, coming from a very sporting family. Her father René had been a great tennis player; her mother the first overseas player to win the British Ladies Golf Championship. Catherine's finest achievement was her victory in the 1967 US Women's Open, when a few days past her 22nd birthday. She was the youngest player to win this event, the first and only amateur, and only the second overseas player. An even better year for her was 1969, when she became only the third player to win both the British and US Amateur titles the same year. Catherine would undoubtedly have become a highly effective player on the US LPGA Tour. Instead, she married a Spaniard and competed relatively little afterwards. She did, however, add two Spanish national titles to her record following four earlier victories in the French Open Amateur. The strength of her game was her unusual power with the long irons.

Ky Laffoon

Born: 1908
Zinc, USA

Laffoon was an excellent golfer, but better known for his eccentricities, not least in his behaviour towards his golf clubs. If his putter behaved well and a long one went down, he might stroke it lovingly, but when things went wrong he was less kindly. It is said that on one occasion he attempted to strangle it. When that didn't work, he tried to produce death by drowning – not hurling it into a lake, mind you, but holding it under water. However, he usually had more respect for his equipment and liked to work on it. He particularly liked a sharp leading edge on his pitching clubs. So, while driving, he would grab a club, open his car door and grind it on the highway. You could often tell that Ky was on his way to the next tournament by the trail of sparks he left behind him. Laffoon made his main impact in the mid-1930s. In 1934 he won four times and also took the trophy for the year's low stroke average.

Bernhard Langer

Born: August 27, 1957
Anhausen, Germany

No man has conquered a putting twitch as successfully as Germany's greatest ever golfer, Langer, who is now at the peak of his career as regards all-around consistency. Even by his teens, Langer was renowned as a great approach putter but very ineffective from short range. Then he found a putter that worked, for a year or two, and later resorted to the left-hand-below-right grip. When this too failed him he had to invent another method to eliminate a convulsive breakdown, or twitch, in the left wrist. He has done so very effectively with one of the weirdest methods of putting yet seen. The left hand is placed well down the grip with the shaft well up the inside of the left forearm. The right hand then clamps the shaft to the forearm. Langer's invention seems to work and has been imitated by other players – only for Langer himself to turn to the broomhandle putter. He is the most consistent player on the European Tour. His missed cut at the PGA Championship in May, 1996 was his first in 70 events: 1996 was also his first winless year since 1979.

BERNHARD LANGER *Most consistent*

Tom Lehman

Born: 1959
Austin, Mn, USA

Lehman was 37 when, in 1996, he became the first US professional to win the British Open at Lytham, a month after tie-ing second in the US Open. In 1991 he was still seeking a way out of the mini-tours. Big Tom's career blossomed with his first PGA Tour win – the Memorial – in 1994. In 1995, despite colon surgery, he won again. His bravura finale to 1996 earned the Tour Championship by six strokes at Tulsa, made him US PGA Player of the Year, leading money-winner, second in the world rankings (he led briefly in 1997) to Norman, and confirmed his claim to the Vardon Trophy for best scoring average.

Cecil Leitch

Born: April 13, 1891
Silloth, England

Charlotte Cecilia Pitcairn Leitch was perhaps the first woman to give the golf ball an uninhibited thump. Her style was based on a broad stance and she used a palm grip with the right hand. For a few years, she was probably the best in the world – until the arrival of Joyce Wethered. Cecil won the British Ladies' Championship in 1914, 1920, 1921 and 1926.

Tony Lema

Born: 1934
Oakland, Ca, USA

Lema is remembered chiefly for two events in his career, one a triumph, the other perhaps the most remarkable defeat in the history of match play. In 1964, when the British Open still attracted only a few of the top US players, Lema decided to enter at St Andrews. Even so, he took it casually. He hardly knew the course, and mainly just tried to hit it where the caddie told him. Nevertheless, on his first appearance in the British Open, and with no previous experience of golf on linksland, he won by five strokes from Jack Nicklaus – and threw a champagne party, one of his trademarks after a win. If this was remarkable, his defeat by Gary Player the following year in the World Matchplay Championship at Wentworth was astonishing. Lema completed the first 18 holes six up and then won the first hole in the afternoon. Alas for Lema, Player then became inspired, drew level on the last hole and won the first play-off hole. That same year, Lema had been in sight of a second consecutive British Open – but Australian Peter Thomson had other ideas. From 1957 until his death in a plane crash in 1966, Lema won 16 events worldwide.

Bruce Lietzke

Born: 1951
Kansas City, Mo, USA

If Lietzke's ambitions had matched his undoubted talents he might have been a superstar. However, perhaps his limited golf workload suits his temperament. It may also have given him a longer career. He likes to spend as much time with his wife and two children as he can, to support the Dallas Cowboys and do "serious fishing". Lietzke was probably at his best when making his way up the ladder of success. His first very good year came in 1977, when for a time he played golf in a kind of trance. He didn't have any thoughts about the golf swing at all. As he put it, "I just stood over the ball and pulled the trigger." That year, he won his first two tournaments and finished fifth on the money list. The following year he was not as successful but became the Canadian Open champion, a title he repeated in 1982. This was as near as he has come to winning a major championship. But perhaps Bruce isn't much interested in the majors. He is certainly one of the now few top Americans who apparently have no ambition to win a British Open. He has won 13 times on the US Tour, most recently in 1994, and seems to win as much money as he needs – more than $5½ million in all.

Lawson Little

Born: June 23, 1910
Newport, RI, USA

This player was the first and last since the retirement of Bobby Jones who might have built a record – at least at amateur level – to have rivalled that of Jones himself. He came to the fore in 1933, reaching the semi-finals of the US Amateur and earning a Walker Cup place which took him to Britain the following year. In both his matches, the British opposition was completely overwhelmed, and Little moved on from St Andrews to Prestwick for the British Amateur. Having progressed smoothly to the final, he beat a strongly supported local man, by a landslide 14 and 13 after arguably the best stretch of golf ever produced by an amateur. He then went home and won the US Amateur, beating his opponent by 8 and 7. How do you follow that? Well, 1935 was nearly as good for Little. First he took the British Amateur, after a close fight with an English doctor, and then proceeded to win the US title again – the only time both championships have been won by the same man in two successive years. With four major championships under his belt, Little turned professional but failed to become the dominant force he was expected to be. He did, however, win the 1940 US Open, beating Gene Sarazen in the play-off.

Sally Little

Born: 1951
Cape Town, South Africa

Sally Little came to the LPGA after a successful career in South African amateur golf which included both the match play and stroke play titles. Having made a big impression in the 1971 World Amateur Team Championship, she joined the LPGA Tour. It was not until 1976, however, that she had her first victory, when she holed out from a bunker for a birdie on the final hole. After this success, she established herself as one of the leading LPGA players from 1977 to 1982 and was never out of the top 10 money winners. The last of these years was her most successful season because, as well as coming third on the money list, she had four victories. Altogether she has won 15 titles and three of them have been majors: the 1980 LPGA Championship, the 1982 Dinah Shore and the 1988 du Maurier Classic. Ill health cut her down in her prime, for in 1983 she had both abdominal and arthroscopic knee surgery and was only able to play a handful of events. She tumbled down to 139th on the money list and, despite her 1988 win, has never really regained the same form.

DAVIS LOVE III *A major breakthrough?*

Gene Littler

Born: July 21, 1930
San Diego, Ca, USA

"Here's a kid with a perfect swing like Sam Snead's ... only better." This comment came from Gene Sara-zen when Littler was a young man. The player also earned the nickname "Gene the Machine", because he made the golf swing look so effortless and the results were so predictably perfect. With his near perfect swing, really excellent putting and precision short-iron play, it is surprising that Littler did not become a superstar. Lack of a driving passion to be the best might have been the reason. He sometimes seemed content to make a good start to the season and then take things relatively easily. He first emerged in 1953, by winning the US Amateur, and his profile became more distinct the very next year when he won a US Tour event as an amateur – a very rare feat indeed. On turning professional, he continued to be successful, winning four events in his first full season, 1955. His best year was probably 1959, when he won five times. In 1961 he took the US Open and later lost play-offs for the 1970 Masters and the 1977 US PGA. He won 29 times on the US Tour, eight times on the Senior Tour, and also made seven appearances in the Ryder Cup.

Bobby Locke

Born: November 20, 1917
Germiston, South Africa

Locke was the first golfer to dominate golf on three continents – America, Europe and his native South Africa. Some of this came about because

Sam Snead won the 1946 Open Championship. Locke suggested an exhibition tour of singles match play in South Africa and Snead accepted – to his eventual regret. Locke won 12 of the 16 matches and Snead two. The American had been putted to death by a man who, to Snead, just seemed to hole everything. This success against just about the greatest player of the time persuaded Locke to try his luck in the USA, where Snead had told him he ought to be very successful. Locke won event after event and in a short 1947 season was placed second on the US money list. The following year he won three times. He then fell foul of the tour administration and afterwards played far more golf in the British Isles and Europe. His career as a winner of Open Championships now began to flourish. He won in 1949 at Sandwich, the following year at Troon and at Lytham in 1952. Though he continued to win tournaments Locke ceased to take the Open until 1957, when he had his fourth and final victory at St Andrews.

Nancy Lopez

Born: January 6, 1957
Torrance, Ca, USA

Lopez once seemed destined to be regarded as the greatest woman player ever, but it didn't quite happen. Why? One reason could be her liking for family life. Another is faulty technique – her backswing finishes in a very shut position at the top. Most of the time, however, she has it all adjusted by the time she gets the clubhead into the strike zone. She is also an outstanding putter. It was in 1978 that she set the US LPGA Tour on fire. Then she had five straight wins, which seemed to triple the gate money at US women's tournaments. Of course, it could not go on for ever, but she won nine times that year and the publicity ensured that the US LPGA has never looked back. She was also highly successful the following year with eight wins, but thereafter lost her absolute dominance. You cannot maintain an average, unless you are Bobby Jones, of winning 17 of the 50 events you enter. She remains a formidable competitor, having won 47 events and headed the US money list three times. In only four years since her debut in 1977 has she failed to win a tournament.

SANDY LYLE *Time for a change of fortune?*

Davis Love III

Born: April 13, 1964
Charlotte, NC, USA

Love was overtaken in the long driving stakes at first marginally by John Daly, then to the tune of 15 yards or so by Tiger Woods. In a similar manner to Woods, Love hits in a far more controlled fashion, and he is many people's bet to go on to be one of the great players towards the end of this century, when not a few of today's superstars will inevitably begin to fade. He joined the US Tour in 1986 and had a fairly respectable first season. In 1987, he clinched his first tournament win, in the Heritage Classic. He emerged as a major figure in world golf in 1992, taking the Heritage Classic for the third time as well as the Greater Greensboro Open and the Players Championship, and in 1993 the Tournament of Champions, another of the high prestige events just below "major" ranking. Playing with Fred Couples he has won four World Cups, and he has also represented the United States in the Walker, Dunhill and Ryder Cups. Love's outstanding driving – and long iron play – has obviously been crucial in assembling his three million-dollar years, but when it comes to majors, putting errors at the death have cost him very dear in the 1995 Masters (second to Ben Crenshaw) and 1996 US Open, second to Steve Jones, to whom he lost by a shot after bogeys on the last two holes.

Sandy Lyle

Born: February 9, 1958
Shrewsbury, England

The first of Lyle's two supreme achievements came at Sandwich in 1985, when he won the Open Championship, helped somewhat by Bernhard Langer and David Graham falling away. Even on the final day Lyle made no dramatic move until he had successive birdies on the 14th and 15th, to move into the joint lead. Disaster loomed at the 18th, when a little pitch shot from rough at the edge of the green almost came back to his feet. However, he got his bogey five and that was good enough. Lyle's greatest year was 1988. Having won the Phoenix Open and the Greater Greensboro, he enjoyed his finest hour at the Masters. He began with a 71 in high winds and then moved two strokes ahead of the field with a 67. A third-round 72 was good enough to keep that advantage. On the final day, he began to pull well away from the field but faltered on the second nine. At the last he put his tee shot into a fairway bunker along the left, but nipped a seven-iron off the sand past the flag, and his ball drifted back to about three yards. The putt went down and he was champion. Later the same year, he won the Dunhill Masters and the World Match Play. Lyle has won only three times since, and his glory days seem to be behind him. But things can change.

Mark McCumber

Born: September 7, 1951
Jacksonville, Fl, USA

McCumber seems to be one of those golfers who only occasionally emerge from anonymity, but even so he has a good and long-standing career record. US Tour earnings of more than $5\frac{1}{4}$ million attest to that. He turned professional in the mid-1970s and had little success until 1979, when he won his first tournament. It was not until 1983, however, when he won two events and finished eighth in the money list, that he was established as a player to be reckoned with. He still seems to be an up-and-down player, but when he's good, he's very very good, and he has won ten times on the US Tour, including the important Players Championship in 1988 and the Tour Championship in 1994. This last year was comfortably his best in golf. He won three times, quite a rare achievement, and was placed third on the US Tour money list, having decided to concentrate more on golf. He and his brothers have a variety of business interests, including golf-course design. McCumber played in the 1989 Ryder Cup team and has also twice been in the United States World Cup pairing, winning in 1988.

Johnny McDermott

Born: 1891
Philadelphia, Pa, USA

In 1911 MacDermott became the first native-born American to win the US Open. He had already come very close to victory the previous year, aged 19, losing a play-off to Alex Smith. He was again in a play-off situation in 1911, this time opposed to George Simpson and Mike Brady, both formidable players destined never to win their national championship. With his victory, McDermott became the youngest player, then or now, to win a major championship. The following year he won again with scores of 74, 75, 74, 71, making him still one of the select few to have achieved consecutive victories. In 1913, he proved in a US tournament that he could beat the best of the British. Harry Vardon and Ted Ray, who were until then all-conquering on a tour of the United States consisting mainly of exhibition matches, were left miles behind. Much encouraged, McDermott crossed the Atlantic to see if he could win the British Open, and came in fifth. A long and brilliant career seemed ahead of him, but instead he had a mental breakdown in 1915 and that was that.

C. B. Macdonald

Born: 1856
Niagara Falls, NY, USA

Macdonald is arguably the least great golfer in this book but, nevertheless, one of the game's most influential figures. He became fascinated by golf while a student at St Andrews University from 1872, and learned to play on the Old Course. He is said to have played against all the well-known players, including Young Tom Morris. When he returned to the United States, he had to do without golf for a few years because there were no courses. Eventually, in 1893, he solved the problem himself by designing the first 18-hole course in the country at Chicago. His monument, however, is the National Golf Links of America, where, with magnificent terrain at his disposal, he also drew on his memories of golf in Britain to design a proportion of the holes. In the meantime, Macdonald had, in fact, found open spaces where he could knock golf balls around and was reasonably well primed as competitive golf at national level began in the USA. He won the first US Amateur in 1895, by 12 and 11 in the final, having reputedly not gone to bed until five in the morning. He then played the remaining holes with a spectator friend.

Mark McNulty

Born: October 25, 1953
Bindwa, Zimbabwe

McNulty has been almost as successful over the years as his school friend Nick Price, only a major championship eluding him – though he's come close with a second place in the British Open. McNulty is underpowered by modern standards though his smooth measured swing ensures that he seldom has a bad round. The strengths of his game, however, are on and around the greens, his skill with his centre-shafted putter being legendary. Since the 1980s McNulty has been one of the leading performers on the South African circuit, where his wins include the 1987 South African Open and the Million Dollar Challenge the same year. In the two years 1986 and 1987 he had a formidable 13 wins, eight of them in 1986. In Europe too he has been a much respected competitor, with 15 tournaments to his credit between 1979 and 1994. Based in England McNulty has not prospered in the US, but began 1996 with a Sun City win in the Dimension Data Pro-Am, and ended it romping the Volvo Masters at Valderrama — by seven shots.

Lloyd Mangrum

Born: 1914
Trenton, NJ, USA

With his centre parting, thin moustache and an ever-present cigarette between his lips, Mangrum had a bit of the air of a Mississippi river boat gambler. He was indeed a hard man, hard enough to win two Purple Hearts while under the command of General Patton during the 1944 Battle of the Bulge. Apparently undeterred by his wounds, he went off to recuperate at St Andrews and won a GI tournament there before returning to the USA for the 1946 golf season. He had already made his mark there, and had in fact caused a sensation in 1940 by setting what was then an Augusta record with a first-round score of 64 in that year's Masters. In the end, he finished second to Jimmy Demaret. In 1946, he won his only major championship, a marathon US Open. He tied with Byron Nelson and Vic Ghezzi, and in the 18-hole play-off all three had 72s. So out they went again for another 18 holes. This time, Mangrum's 72 was enough for a one-stroke victory. This was the beginning of his great years, when he twice won the Vardon Trophy, topped the money list and was always up there near the top. Tournament wins piled up and he is credited with 34 on the US Tour.

Graham Marsh

Born: January 14, 1944
Kalgoorlie, Australia

This Australian is a truly international golfer who has won all over the world, from Switzerland to Malaya. He never made a prolonged assault on the US Tour, though he did win the important Heritage Classic in 1977. Elsewhere, he has won at least 56 significant events worldwide, including 24 in Japan. Marsh qualified by age for the US Senior Tour in 1994 and showed that he maintained his very consistent game by being only once out of the top 25 in 22 events. His best performance was to finish in second place in the US Senior Open. It seems inevitable that he will be a great success on the Senior Tour – if he continues to compete. However, as he paid relatively little attention to the main US Tour when at his peak as a player, this may be unlikely. The gap in Marsh's record is that he failed to win a major championship, though he has won both the European Open and the

MARK McNULTY *Consistency is the name of his game*

World Matchplay. Marsh is always meticulous in his preparations before playing a shot, particularly making sure that all the right parts are in precise alignment with the target. He then strikes neatly and with enough power and always seems to finish well balanced. He also controls his emotions and avoids histrionics, unlike his brother Rodney, the cricketer.

Phil Mickelson

Born: June 16, 1970,
San Diego, Ca, USA

Harry Vardon was once asked who was the best left-hander he had ever seen and is said to have replied that he had never seen one worth a damn. There was some justice in this, because Bob Charles is the only left-hander ever to win a major championship. But Mickelson is widely predicted to be the next. Like Charles, he is a superb putter, and his long game is perhaps even more impressive. He may also have learned that skiing is not conducive to good golf, having broken his left femur and cracked his right ankle early in the 1994 season. Mickelson seems to have most things going for him, especially as bones heal better when you are young. In 1990, he won the US Amateur (the only left-hander to do so) and that same year became the only amateur, except for Jack Nicklaus and more recently Tiger Woods, to win both that title and the NCAA in the same year. He played in the Walker Cup in both 1989 and 1991. In 1991, he was also one of the few amateurs ever to win a full US Tour event. He has had nine victories since then, four of them in 1996, when he was overtaken at the head of the money list in the last week of the season by Tom Lehman.

Cary Middlecoff

Born: January 6, 1921
Halls, USA

Middlecoff was one of the players who helped to turn golf into the slow game it is today. He took a long time to align himself to the ball, and Bobby Jones was moved to remark that it was not a visually attractive process. A serious analyst of the golf swing, Middlecoff was among the first to grasp how important the set-up can be. Another of his theories concerned getting the clubhead in the right position at the top of the backswing, where he would bring it to a careful halt before initiating the downswing. Such was his slowness, by the standards of the times, that in the play-off for the 1957 US Open his opponent, Dick Mayer, took out a camping stool on which to perch himself while Middlecoff took his time. If this was a psychological ploy it may have worked. Middlecoff went around in 79; Mayer won rather comfortably with his 72. Even so, Middlecoff's overall record was far superior. He won the US Open twice, in 1949 and 1956, and the Masters in 1955. He was also the leading US Tour player during the 1950s with a total of 37 victories, which puts him well up the all-time list. The end of his career came, as with so many great players, because of a twitch on the short putts.

JOHNNY MILLER *Brief spell at the top*

Johnny Miller

Born: April 29, 1947
San Francisco, Ca, USA

For a short span of time Miller played golf as well as it has ever been played. He was undeniably the best golfer in the world in 1974, when he headed the US Tour money list, but his peak years lasted only from 1973, when he won the US Open, to his victory in the 1976 British Open at Royal Birkdale. At Oakmont Country Club in the US Open, Miller was six strokes behind the leaders when the final round began, but a start of four birdies immediately brought him into contention. There were more birdies to come and Miller finished with a 63, at the time the lowest score ever recorded in championship golf. His putting had by no means been phenomenal. It was the supreme quality of his iron play that counted the most. In 1974 he had no fewer than eight victories on the US Tour, followed the next year by four more and a close encounter with the Masters. His 1976 British Open triumph marked the end of his great run. He lost form dramatically but did make a come-back during the early 1980s. Remarkably he won again early in 1994, having made no money in the previous year, then hardly bothered to play again.

Abe Mitchell

Born: 1887
East Grinstead, England

The Great Triumvirate of James Braid, J. H. Taylor and Harry Vardon certainly set standards that no British trio have achieved since. By the end of the First World War, the Victorian greats were all well past their prime, and the question of their successors arose. The two more obvious candidates were George Duncan and Abe Mitchell, although the latter had not established himself to the same extent. Duncan was to win a British Open; Mitchell did not. Perhaps he never quite recovered from his disappointment at Deal in 1920, when he was 13 strokes ahead of the eventual winner, Duncan, after two rounds and then three-putted the first three greens, had a seven on his card, and finished in 84. As Byron Nelson once said: "Winners are a different breed of cat." However, Mitchell was still the most effective British golfer through the 1920s and a little beyond, and had a formidable record in match play, winning the championship three times. He was also the man Americans feared most in the Ryder Cup, where, either in singles or with partners, he had such winning scores as 8 and 7, and 9 and 8 to his credit and overall took seven points out of a possible ten.

LARRY MIZE *140-foot chip won a major*

Larry Mize

Born: September 23, 1958
Augusta, Ga, USA

Mize had his finest hour in the 1987 Masters, where his birdie at the final hole produced a tie with Seve Ballesteros and Greg Norman. A play-off began in which death was indeed sudden – Seve departing in despair after just one hole. On the next Norman played a good safe shot, away from the water on the left, to the right side of the green. If he could get down in two, he looked sure to be the champion, for Mize was well off the green further right. However, from 140 feet away he played a good running pitch that seemed just a touch too strong – but down it went and that was that. It was a fluke, of course, but a highly popular one in the town of Mize's birth. The rest of his career has been less spectacular though he has been a good journeyman since he joined the US Tour in 1980. His first win came in 1983, and he has added three more Tour wins. His other great achievement was his fine winning performance in the 1993 Johnnie Walker World Championship in Jamaica – worth over $1.2 million.

Dottie (Mochrie) Pepper

Born: August 17, 1965
Saratoga Springs, NY, USA

Pepper joined the LPGA Tour in 1988 and was an immediate success, winning over $130,000 in her first season and her first event the following year. Her first three years on the Tour were very respectable, for she totalled about $500,000 in money winnings. Then her career really began to take off. In 1991 she won no tournament but was extremely consistent, rising to third on the money list and establishing herself as a leading name in American women's golf. Since then her status has remained much the same as she continued to be in the top five up to the end of 1996. Her best year was 1992, when she had four wins, of which the most important was the Dinah Shore, so far her only major championship. She was also that year's leading money winner, with close on $700,000 to her credit. A very tough competitor indeed, Pepper is well known for what some people consider to be over-aggressive demonstrations during the Solheim Cup, for which she headed the 1995 rankings.

Colin Montgomerie

Born: June 23, 1963
Glasgow, Scotland

There's that saying that you drive for show and putt for dough. However, if you can't hit the ball quite long and fairly consistently straight from the tee, you will putt in vain. Montgomerie's game is strong in both these departments. He is a long hitter who can usually be confident that his fade will "take". This means that he can rule out trouble along the left, aim more-or-less at it, and leave himself the whole width of the fairway to play with. Thereafter, he is one of the best putters in the world. One achievement that has so far eluded Montgomerie is a win in a major championship, but he has performed very well in the US Open. In 1992 he finished third to Tom Kite at Pebble Beach. He was closer still two years later, tied for second behind Ernie Els, and in 1997 second on his own by a stroke – to Els again. Steve Elkington was his nemesis in a sudden death play-off in the 1995 US PGA. On the European Tour he headed the money list from 1993 to 1996 inclusive. As a tournament winner, however, he was less dominant, with 12 European wins in 10 years' campaigning up to the end of 1996.

Gil Morgan

Born: 1946
Wewaka, Ok, USA

Most American golfers have been to university and some emerge with prefixes to their names. One example is Cary Middlecoff, who qualified as a dentist but found that golf paid even better and paid no further attention to teeth. In 1972 Morgan graduated with his doctorate from the Southern College of Optometry and fixed his eyes firmly on the US Tour, which he first qualified to play in 1973. His first big year came in 1977, when he won his first tournament, but 1978 was better still. Winning twice and finishing second on the US Tour money list, he seemed to have established himself as a name player. That has not quite happened, but he has continued to perform well: by the end of 1996 he had exceeded $5 million in money winnings, had won seven times on the US Tour, and played in two Ryder Cup teams in 1979 and 1983. His greatest triumphs and disasters, however, came in one particular event, the 1992 US Open. Here he became the first golfer to reach ten under par, and even improved that by another two – only to subside dramatically to tie for 13th place.

GIL MORGAN *Made a $5 million career switch*

Tom Morris Senior

Born: June 16, 1821
St Andrews, Scotland

Winner of the first truly Open Championship in 1861 (the first the previous year was not open to amateurs), Old Tom Morris went on to further victories in 1862, 1864 and 1867. He began playing over the Old Course at St Andrews when he was about six, and became apprenticed to Allan Robertson for the making of both clubs and feathery balls. The pair then became a formidable partnership in foursomes challenge matches for large sums of money. However they fell out when Robertson spotted Old Tom playing with a gutta percha ball at a time when these were rapidly replacing the feathery from 1848 onwards. Robertson felt they would kill his trade. Morris set up his own workshop, but in 1851 moved away to become professional and keeper of the green at the new Prestwick Golf Club. Returning later to his home town to take over a similar role, he became a revered and much-loved figure in golf. He did the original designs for many courses in the British Isles.

Tom Morris Junior

Born: April 20, 1851
St Andrews, Scotland

"Young Tommie", as he was usually called, was a brief comet on the golf scene, dying at the age of 24, just a few months after his wife in 1875. However, if only for a few years, he was the dominant player of his time. Indeed, like several players in succeeding generations, he changed the whole notion of how well the game could be played. A long hitter, he was also excellent in his recovery shots from bad lies in the rough, and his iron shots to greens were revolutionary. Where earlier players had tended to use short-shafted lofted woods, he used a rut iron. This was a small-headed club, originally intended to enable players to, literally, escape from ruts. Young Tommie used it to gain far greater backspin in his short approaches. He won the British Open for the first time in 1868, in succession to his father, at the age of 17, and retained it the next two years. Then a problem arose. The original trophy was a morocco leather belt, presented with the proviso that anyone who won three titles in a row got to keep it. With no trophy to hand, no championship was held in 1871. The following year, Tommie won the replacement, a claret cup. He remains the only man to have won four Open Championships in a row.

Kel Nagle

Born: December 21, 1920
Sydney, Australia

Nagle was one of the late developers in golf. Although he first won a tournament in his late twenties, he then almost totally disappeared from view for several years. When he again became a factor in tournament golf his game had been transformed. Formerly a long but wild hitter and a relatively poor putter, he was now shortish but one of the steadiest from the tee and a very sound putter indeed. However, he continued to be primarily an Australasia-based golfer. As he approached the age of 40 he had won the Open Championships of Australia and New Zealand, while elsewhere his record was unimpressive. Then came the British Open at St Andrews in 1960. The new hero was Arnold Palmer, making his first Open appearance, but although he played well he was left five strokes behind Nagle after two rounds. Nagle had gone round in 69 and 67 but was still given little chance. The climax came in the final round. Palmer holed out for a birdie on the last while Nagle faced a par putt on the treacherous 17th of some seven feet. He got it and went on to par the last for a one-stroke victory. After this success his confidence blossomed, and some 25 titles followed.

TOMMY NAKAJIMA *Likes to play abroad*

Tsuneyuki Nakajima

Born: October 20, 1954
Gunma, Japan

Unless "Tommy" Nakajima can manage yet to achieve international glory, it may be his sad fate to be remembered chiefly for two disasters which befell him in one year – 1978. Qualifying to play in the Masters, he managed to run up a score of 13 on the 13th hole at Augusta, where most players are thinking about eagles or at least birdies. Three months later, at St Andrews in the British Open, he earned a cruel kind of immortality. The famous Road bunker, hard by the 17th green on the Old Course at St Andrews, has almost, but not quite, been renamed "The Sands of Nakajima" following his toils there while in close contention for the championship. Nakajima was and is a superb sand player, but the shot was exceptionally demanding, with the flag close by and a narrow thread of green beyond and then the road. Trying for a delicate shot which would just clear the steep face of the bunker and gently settle on the green, poor Nakajima took four attempts to succeed, and a nine eventually went down on his card. In Japan, however, he has been prodigiously successful, with four Opens, three PGAs and three Matchplays to his credit, and has won more than 50 events.

Byron Nelson

Born: February 4, 1912
Fort Worth, Tx, USA

Between 1944 and 1946 Nelson was the greatest golfer ever. In 1944 he won seven times, but reckoned that occasional lapses of concentration were costing him something like a stroke a round. The following year he knocked a stroke and a half off his average per round. This resulted in easily the greatest winning streak ever. From March to August he played 11 tournaments and won them all. He went on to win another seven. Oddly, some might think, he was nearly burned out by the effort. In 1946 he won five more times and then, at the age of 34, announced his retirement. It is likely that there were several reasons. He disliked all the travelling involved and the constant appearances demanded of him for publicity and with sponsors. It is also claimed that competitive play made him feel physically sick. In the majors, he did not give himself enough time to build an outstanding record. Even so, he won the 1937 and 1942 Masters, the 1939 US Open and the US PGA in 1940 and 1945. Doubtless he would also have completed the professional Grand Slam had he entered the British Open more often. He played only twice, and never during his greatest years.

Larry Nelson

Born: September 10, 1947
Fort Payne, Al, USA

In terms of money winnings, Larry was only outstanding between 1979 and 1981, particularly in 1979 when he was second on the US money list. However, he has occasionally played superbly in the major championships when, after none too good a year, he has had moments of inspiration. The greatest of these came in 1983 when he won the US Open at Oakmont. He had been having a poor season and was seven strokes off the lead after two rounds. However, a 65 then brought him into contention and in the final round play was suspended because of thunderstorms with the contest really being between Watson and Nelson, who restarted on the 16th, a par three of 226 yards. He found the green and then holed out from about 20 yards. It proved the decisive shot of the championship. Nelson has also won the US PGA on two occasions, 1981 and 1987.

LARRY NELSON *You don't hear from him – then suddenly he wins*

Liselotte Neumann

Born: May 20, 1966
Finspang, Sweden

"Lotta" Neumann has been a key part of the surge in Swedish golf which could some day see them become the dominant force in Europe. This is all the more remarkable in a country which has such a short playing season. Neumann first made her mark in the early 1980s, when she twice won her country's Amateur Championship, as well as the Matchplay Championship, and represented Sweden in international events. On turning professional she achieved immediate success in Europe with wins in the German Open (three times) and the European and French Opens. Her really big breakthrough, however, came in 1988, when she won the US Women's Open during her first season on the LPGA Tour. That year she won nearly $200,000 and, unsurprisingly, took the Rookie of the Year award. Since then she has been consistently successful, especially in 1994. She was third on the money list, with just over $500,000, and had three wins. One of these was in the Women's British Open, which now rates as an official LPGA event. Neumann's earnings rose to $625,633 in 1996, when she played in her fourth Solheim Cup out of four.

Jack Newton

Born: January 30, 1950
Sydney, Australia

Newton's finest hours came in two major championships. In 1980 he came second to Seve Ballesteros in the Masters. Five years earlier he had come tantalizingly close to glory in the British Open at Carnoustie. He began with rounds of 69 and 71, and a 65 then brought him up to within a single stroke of the leader, Bobby Cole. In the final round he looked to be doing even better. With the leading pack faltering, only Newton was playing consistently. Then, two strokes ahead on the leader board with four holes to play, he began to make his own errors. After dropping a shot at the difficult 17th, he needed to birdie the last to win – and couldn't quite do it. He had, however, tied with the then little known Tom Watson. In the 18-hole

GREG NORMAN *He has lost more majors than anyone*

play-off the next day, the pair were level after 17. However, Newton bunkered his shot to the green and didn't get his recovery close. Newton won in America, Australasia, Africa and Europe, but his career ended abruptly when he walked into a airplane propeller in the dark and was very seriously injured and disabled.

Jack Nicklaus

See Legends pp 96–7

Norman von Nida

Born: 1914
Strathfield, Australia

Australian golf was a very small world when von Nida arrived on the scene. During the 1930s he had to content himself mainly with winning state titles and money games with wealthy amateurs. Having tried the Far East Tour, then in its infancy, and finished as runner-up in the 1939 Australian Open, he decided to try his luck in the United States. However, the outbreak of the Second World War put a stop to that project. It was in 1946 that he really emerged as an international golfer. He turned up in Britain with total reserves of £17 but immediately began winning money. The following year he dominated the tournament scene, taking four of the first six events. By the end of the season he had won or tied for first place seven times and was leading money winner with over £3,000. That year he had also shared the lead in the Open Championship after three rounds but faded on the final afternoon. He was never to repeat the success of 1947, but remained a force to be reckoned with for a few more years. He won the Australian PGA four times and the Australian Open three times.

Greg Norman

Born: February 10, 1955
Mount Isa, Australia

Norman must be considered one of the unluckiest golfers ever. Several major championships have slipped through his fingers. Sometimes it has been the result of lucky shots by other players at critical moments; at other times he has brought about his own downfall. By the mid-1990s Norman could have had anything up to a dozen major championships to his credit. Instead he has just his two Open Championships. Both were memorable occasions. At Turnberry in 1986 he began with a good 74 in very difficult conditions, and then on day two equalled the championship record with a 63, despite three-putting the last green. In the final round, he was never even threatened. At Royal St George's he produced one of his trademarks, a blazing final round. Often this has happened when Norman is virtually out of contention owing to the fact that his early rounds have perhaps been over-cautious: like Nicklaus, he knows that he is always a potential winner and wants a steady start. In the 1995 US Open, however, leading at five under, he shot 74, 73, and finished two behind Corey Pavin. Although he has the dubious distinction of losing play-offs in all four majors, Norman is a prodigious winner of tournaments, but how much would he not give to reverse one of his Augusta lapses – at least, surely, the $1 million he won in the 1997 Andersen Consulting final.

Andy North

Born: March 9, 1950
Thorp, USA

Of the 16 golfers to have won more than one US Open, North is perhaps the least distinguished. Oddly he has won only one other tournament on the US Tour, the 1977 Westchester Classic, and has never finished higher than 14th on the money list. Plagued by injuries, he competes rarely on the US Tour, and is able to do so only because of his exemption as a former US Open champion. His first US Open came at Cherry Hills, Denver, in 1978, where he had a four-stroke lead with five holes to play but rather staggered home. Needing a bogey five at the last to win, he only just did it. Short of the green in two, he then played his short pitch into a bunker but came out fairly close and was relieved to hole the putt. After a series of poor years he re-emerged to win the 1985 US Open by a stroke. That was a surprising year, for the runners-up were hardly great names – T. C. Chen, Dave Barr and Denis Watson. North then disappeared again but, as Walter Hagen said: "Anyone can win one US Open, but it takes a great player to win two."

Christy O'Connor Senior

Born: December 21, 1924
Galway, Ireland

Many Irish players are unorthodox, and O'Connor, nicknamed "wristy Christy", was no exception. Nevertheless, he was not only one of the greatest Irish golfers ever but was also at the top of British golf for many years. He came very close to the British Open in 1958, when his start of 67, 68 was the best since Henry Cotton's 67, 65 back in 1934. Thereafter he faltered a little, but came to the last hole at Lytham needing a par to tie. On this difficult hole, he did not quite manage it, and it was Peter Thomson who went on to win, beating Dave Thomas in the play-off. O'Connor was third, a position he repeated in 1961, and in 1965 he was second. It is tempting to speculate on what he might have achieved had his putting stroke been more solid and far less wristy. He played in every Ryder Cup match from 1955 to 1973 and also represented Ireland 15 times in the World Cup, partnering Harry Bradshaw in the winning team in Mexico City in 1958. More important for him was probably the fact that he won 24 European tournaments and dominated domestic golf in Ireland.

Christy O'Connor Junior

Born: August 19, 1948
Galway, Ireland

O'Connor first played on the European Tour in 1970, and has won four times in 27 years, including the Dunlop Masters in 1992, his best year with earnings of £249,463, plus eight other titles. His prize money then dwindled because of a painful left foot ailment "like a toothache", called Morson's Metarsalgia. O'Connor twice hit the front pages, firstly, when he led, with Seve Ballesteros, after one round of the 1976 Open at Birkdale, though his 69 included an eight. Secondly, when his two iron approach over the lake on the last hole at the Belfry beat Fred Couples in the 1989 Ryder Cup. The shot was crucial to Europe's retention of the trophy.

José-Maria Olazabal

Born: February 5, 1966
Fuenterrabia, Spain

That the career of so talented a player as Olazabal should suddenly be terminated by so banal-sounding an affliction as sore feet became a dreadful probability soon after his 29th birthday in 1995. He resisted doggedly, limping in April in defence of his Masters title at Augusta to 14th place, the highest achieved by a European. He was able to enter only eight European events in 1995. From ninth in the world he slid to 225th, brought low by what was at first diagnosed as incurable rheumatoid arthritis. Salvation came by way of a meeting with Dr Hans-Wilhelm Muller-Wohlfahrt, known as Dr Feelgood to other athletes he had helped. The German detected a spinal hernia, and specified a rugged programme of exercise and physiotherapy. Five months of this brought Olazabal, who had been forced to give up his 1995 Ryder Cup place, to Dubai in February, 1997, after two years of doubt and despair. The limp, though not all of the pain, was gone, the talent sharp as ever, proved by a 65 in round three, and 12th place overall. His comeback gained a "Golfer of the Month' award for Olazabal, who surprised even himself by winning his third event back on tour, the Turespaña Open, Gran Canaria, and inside a month finished joint 12th in the 1997 Masters. Aggressive with his irons, and armed with a short game and putting stroke comparable to that of Seve Ballesteros, Olazabal has gained twice as many Ryder Cup points (12) as he has lost in four appearances. He has won the World Series of Golf twice (once by 12 strokes), on top of 16 European events. Above all he gave proof of world class at Augusta. He was ranked fourth in Europe and seventh on the US Tour in that same year of 1994, a mighty achievement.

JOSÉ-MARIA OLAZABAL *Dazzling World Series of Golf win*

Mark O'Meara

Born: January 13, 1957
Goldsboro, NC, USA

O'Meara is a Pebble Beach (and west coast) specialist, never better than when winning there for the fifth time in 1997. He beat off an awesome surge by Tiger Woods, making his return to the Ryder Cup team almost certain. He removed all doubts by at once winning the Buick at Torrey Pines. Though he is a little underpowered compared with many players, it is likely that this great course suits him because it demands precision and imagination in shot-making. O'Meara has both of these qualities. Turning professional in 1981, it took him three years to make his mark, but he then went on to number two position on the money list in 1984, when he had his first US Tour win. That year he also had five second places and the most top ten finishes on the US Tour. Since then he has won more than a dozen times and has also lost three play-offs. O'Meara has had his moments in the majors and won the US Amateur in 1979. A US Ryder Cup player in 1985, 1989 and 1991, he likes competing internationally and has won in Japan, England and Australia.

Peter Oosterhuis

Born: May 3, 1948
London, England

This player had a meteoric rise to the top of European golf, but his descent was almost as rapid. In 1966 he began winning amateur events of significance, played in the Walker Cup team and then turned professional. For four years from 1971 he topped the Order of Merit and was easily the dominant player in Europe. However, Oosterhuis wanted to be a great player and decided that could only happen if he moved to the US Tour. He did so, particularly encouraged by his success in the 1973 Masters, where he headed the field by three strokes after the third round but dropped back to come in third, then the best finish achieved by a British player. When he left Britain he had played 200 tournaments, been in the top ten in more than half of them, won 20 and been second 26 times. In the USA he had a reasonable first year but the rest was mostly downhill. He had some high placings and eventually won a tournament, the 1981 Canadian Open. His nearest approaches to a major championship came with high finishes in the Opens of 1974, 1978 and 1982. Oosterhuis's greatest strengths were on and around the greens. When his shot in missed, he always seemed able to get down in two more. His weakness was a tendency to block his long shots out to the right.

PETER OOSTERHUIS *Meteoric rise and fall*

Francis Ouimet

Born: May 8, 1893
Brookline, Ma, USA

Ouimet became a national hero overnight when he beat the great Harry Vardon and recent Open champion Ted Ray in an 18-hole play-off for the 1913 US Open close by his home town. Oddly, it seems his victory the next year in the US Amateur Championship gave him more pleasure. Perhaps that was because his performances had earlier been poor. In his four previous entries he had three times failed to qualify and had once been knocked out in the second round. Much later, in 1931, he was to win this title again, but that was after Bobby Jones was safely retired. Despite his working-class background, Ouimet never considered turning professional. Nevertheless, he did lose his amateur status for a few years when the USGA decided he was profiting from his golfing fame by opening a sports shop in Boston. There was an ironic sequel in 1951, when the R&A decided to choose their first American captain. The obvious choice was perhaps the greatest golfer of all time, Bobby Jones, who had not broken the rules of playing golf as an amateur, but who had certainly made a great deal of money after his retirement. Yet it was Ouimet who was invited, and he performed his tasks with both grace and diplomatic skill.

Masashi Ozaki

Born: January 24, 1947
Tokushima, Japan

Japanese players seem unwilling to display their talents on the world stage. It is difficult to know why, because there is so much talent on their home tour. Perhaps, because of the language barrier abroad and the rich pickings to be had at home, there is simply little incentive to travel to places where they can be made to feel somewhat alien. "Jumbo" Ozaki is a prime example. If he turns up at, say, the British or US Open, few spectators are much interested in him, and some may even not have heard his name before – although he is the biggest tournament money winner ever. A comparison with Tom Kite is interesting. Kite's consistency in achieving high placings, even if not a large number of tournament wins, has earned him the reputation of being the highest money winner ever. So he is in terms of US and European golf – but Ozaki is miles ahead. At the end of 1994 his winnings, mostly from Japanese golf, totalled more than £8 million. In financial terms he is the most successful player in golf history and, even though in his late 40s, he seems to be getting better and better. Jumbo and his brothers Joe and Tateo won 12 Japanese events in 1988, more than a third of events played. Jumbo was first to $2 million in a season.

JUMBO OZAKI *Gets better with age*

Alf Padgham

Born: 1906
Caterham, England

There are many ways of putting and, for at least a while, Padgham found an unusual answer to his putting problems. Instead of keeping his eye over the ball, he lined up with it very much further away from his body. Padgham decided on this method because it helped him to imitate his excellent chipping stroke. The extended arm action worked for him, and for a while he carried all before him. Of course, Padgham didn't do it all on putting alone. He had one of the best swings in the British game. Vardon thought it perfect and his contemporary Dai Rees considered it the equal of Sam Snead's. In the few tournaments of his time Padgham set a record, between 1935 and 1936, of winning four consecutive tournaments. He was also very effective in match play, taking the *News of the World* event twice and reaching the final on another occasion. he won his only Open Championship, in 1936, after breaking into a pro's shop – at Hoylake. Arriving early in the morning to begin the day's final 36 holes, he found it shut and resorted to smashing the window with a brick in order to collect his clubs.

Arnold Palmer

See Legends pp 98–9

Willie Park Senior

Born: 1833
Musselburgh, Scotland

Willie Park Senior has the distinction of being the first winner of the Open Championship, in 1860. He went on to win three more times – in 1863, 1866 and 1875. For a good many years, the principal players of their time were Park and Tom Morris Senior, both eventually eclipsed by the genius of Tom Morris Junior. Park first came to notice in the mid-1850s when he challenged all and sundry to play for £100 a side, very large stakes indeed for the time. Most tended to avoid confrontation with him because he was a very long driver indeed and also an excellent putter – a difficult combination of talents to beat. Perhaps it came from his upbringing as a golfer when he used just one club for both these parts of the game of golf. Besides this, he would sometimes challenge club golfers, offering to play them standing on one leg and using just one hand. Legend has it that he lost just once.

Willie Park Junior

Born: February 4, 1864
Musselburgh, Scotland

Although golf professionals had previously been makers of clubs and balls as much as expert players, William Park Junior can be called the first businessman golfer. His success as an Open Championship winner in 1887 and 1889 (the third member of the family to win, after his father and uncle Mungo) gave him the prestige to branch out into other fields, almost certainly to the detriment of his golf. He too went into club-making but was soon tending to employ other craftsmen rather than doing the work himself as his predecessors generally had. Park had shops in both London and New York, but this business faded gradually with the development of mass manufacture. A man of imagination and energy, he then made himself the first great golf architect. He worked intensively in design and construction in Britain, continental Europe and, in his later years, North America, but Sunningdale Old is probably his masterpiece.

Craig Parry

Born: January 12, 1966
Sunshine, Australia

Nicknamed "Popeye" because of his powerful forearms, Parry began to emerge in the late 1980s. In 1987 he won both the New South Wales Open and the Canadian Tournament Players Championship; two years later, he also won in Japan. A successful competitor on the European Tour, in 1989 he took two events, the Four Stars Pro-Celebrity and the German Open, and finished third on the money list. In 1991, he won the Italian and Scottish Opens and finished fifth. Having already competed a little in the USA, he decided to increase his appearances there, but so far has been less successful than in Europe. His best results on the US Tour have been second places in 1994, 1995 and 1996, and third in the 1993 US Open after sharing the lead in the first round. In 1992 he was in strong contention for the Masters, holding the lead after the third round before subsiding to a 78 and a position well down the field. That same year he also contended for the Players Championship. In Australia he has won the Australian Masters title three times – in 1992, 1994 and 1996.

CRAIG PARRY *A winner home and away*

Jerry Pate

Born: September 16, 1953
Macon, Ga, USA

Golf is a more stressful game, physically, than many might think. Professionals often practise for hours on end, with the clubhead frequently crunching into the turf, and the results are a variety of injuries, mainly to wrists, elbows and shoulders, while the lower back suffers from the twisting motion of the golf swing. Pate seemed set to become one of the modern greats, but shoulder problems killed him off after a brilliant early career. In 1974 he won the US Amateur and also tied for the individual prize in the World Amateur Team Championship. Off he went to the US Tour qualifying school and was medalist in 1975. What better can you do than win the US Open the very next year in your first season as a professional? That is what Jerry Pate did, also hitting what many would say was the shot of the season. This was a five-iron from the rough, over water, and to a tight pin position. Pate got his ball to about two feet. He was US Open champion. That year, and until 1982, Pate was a big money winner, and at the age of 27 became the youngest player to achieve career winnings of $1 million. Then came injury.

Billy Joe Patton

Born: 1922, USA

"Hell, it ain't like losing a leg." So said Billy Joe in the press tent about his feelings after blowing the 1954 Masters, and this after arguably the best performance by an amateur in a major championship for decades. Patton, playing in his first Masters, went into the lead after two rounds – but who cared? Obviously Hogan or Snead or another great name would win. Sure enough, Patton then shot a 75 to fall five behind. But a hole in one can help, and after 12 holes on the final round the unimaginable had happened. He was back at the top of the leader board. The last nine holes at Augusta are legendary, particularly because of the shots over water, where contenders have the difficult task of judging the distance precisely and clearing the water barriers by no more than a few feet. Patton had no problem with length from the tee. He swung the club back just about faster than his downswing and was likely to win any long-driving competition. Obviously, after a dubious drive along the par five 13th, he went for the green over the creek. He took seven and soon after had a six on the par five 15th – to lose to Hogan and Snead by a stroke.

Corey Pavin

Born: November 16, 1959
Oxnard, Ca, USA

Pavin had an excellent amateur career in regional golf and made the 1981 Walker Cup team. Turning professional the following year, he had to wait until 1984 for his first title on the US Tour. He won the 1995 US Open at treacherous Shinnecock Hills, his final score of level-par 280 being a testament to solid play. Until his US Open victory, Pavin had been recognized as the best golfer to never to win a major. He had come close at Royal St George's in the 1993 British Open when, after tying Nick Faldo for the lead after three rounds, his final 70 would was overshadowed by Greg Norman's blistering 64 and Pavin finished fourth. That year he won the World Matchplay Championship. In 1994 he was eighth in the Masters and second in the US PGA. He has 14 successes to his credit on the US Tour. All this has been achieved despite not having a powerful drive. Pavin averages around 250 yards, but is accurate, and he is one of the best putters and sand players in the business. His lack of power also means that he is inventive in his shot-making. Where others will be thinking of cracking a mid-iron directly at the flag, Pavin may draw or fade a wood into the green, perfectly illustrated by the magical second shot he played to four feet in the final round to ensure his US Open victory.

Calvin Peete

Born: July 18, 1943
Detroit, Mi, USA

Peete had an unusual introduction to golf. One of 19 children, he did not take up the game until the age of 23, and even then was hampered by a broken left elbow, which means he cannot straighten that arm. At his peak, Peete had superb balance through the strike area which helps to account for his legendary accuracy from the tee. For 10 years in a row he topped the US Tour averages for finding the fairway. Perhaps more important, he was also among the most consistent at hitting greens in regulation figures. Alas, for some time his putting did not equal his other abilities, but he broke through in 1979 to win his first tournament. Peete's top years were 1982 to 1985, when he won nine events on the US Tour and was three times in the top four money winners. After 1986, his success rate dropped rapidly, partly as a result of shoulder and lower back problems. His last two victories came in the Tournament of Champions and the USF&G Classic in 1986, which brought his total of tour events to 12. Nowadays he has virtually stopped competing on the main tour but is active among the Seniors.

COREY PAVIN *Airborne at Sun City*

Henry Picard

Born: 1907
Plymouth, Ma, USA

Picard once performed the remarkable feat of beating Walter Hagen in a play-off. He must have had great character to resist the master golfing psychologist. Picard was essentially a 1930s golfer and well up among the most successful of that era. He might, for instance, have won the first Augusta National Invitational (later to become known as the Masters) and came close the second year with a 67, 68 start which put him four ahead of the eventual winner, Gene Sarazen. He put that right three years later in 1938 by producing four very consistent rounds of 71, 72, 72, 70 to win by two strokes from Harry Cooper and Ralph Guldahl. Picard won the US PGA Championship in 1939, beating Byron Nelson by 1 up in the final. Picard first became a tournament winner in 1934 and remained extremely successful until around the beginning of the Second World War when ill health virtually halted his career. By that time he had won 27 tournaments and had been leading money winner – with a little over $10,000!

Manuel Piñero

Born: September 1, 1952
Puebla de la Calzada, Spain

Piñero has always been among the best putters on the European Tour. At about 5ft 7in, it is not surprising that he is not a long hitter, but his all-round short game has made up for that. He reached the top 30 in both 1974 and 1975 and went on to produce a year of remarkable consistency in 1976 when he was never out of the top 11 and won the Swiss Open. He also made his second World Cup appearance and, with Seve Ballesteros, won the title for Spain. Piñero has appeared nine times in that event, and in 1982 he won the individual event and team prize with José-Maria Canizares. Otherwise Manuel Piñero's biggest wins came in the 1977 European PGA Championship and the 1982

European Open. He has won nine times on the European Tour and, between 1976 and 1982, was four times in the top five on the money list. Perhaps his proudest moment was playing number one in the 1985 Ryder Cup and winning his singles.

Gary Player

See Legends pp 100–101

Nick Price

Born: January 28, 1957
Durban, South Africa

In 1994 Price won six times and soared to the top of the Sony rankings. Perhaps most importantly, he won two major championships back to back, the British Open and the US PGA. With his five wins in the United States it is hardly surprising that he finished as leading money winner with just under $1½ million – roughly a repeat of his position in 1993. Though Price won the World Series of Golf as long ago as 1983 and has been a name player since 1982 he did not become a really major figure on the world stage until very much later. His performance in the 1982 British Open at Troon did cause a stir, however, and for years he probably lived with the memory of the major he should have won – but for lost strokes over the closing holes. Price lost another British Open, at Lytham in 1988, but this time through inspired play from Seve Ballesteros. He added 16 wins around the world by the end of 1996, a year spoiled by sinus problems. Two wins in Africa early in 1997 were clouded by anxiety about his faithful caddie Squeaky Medlen, struggling with leukemia.

NICK PRICE *Lines up a putt at the Turnberry Open, one of his two majors in 1994*

Ronan Rafferty

Born: January 13, 1964
Newry, Northern Ireland

Rafferty was a youthful prodigy who in 1981, having already played for Ireland as a full international, became the youngest Walker Cup player ever. He turned professional that year and qualified to play the European Tour by virtue of good performances in South Africa. He immediately made some impact, and in both 1986 and 1988 was 9th on the money list. He had previously been successful in other parts of the world, his first win coming in the 1982 Venezuelan Open. Rafferty has proved to be particularly successful in Australia, where he has four wins to his credit including the 1988 Australian Matchplay Championship. He has also won in New Zealand. In Europe, 1989 was his best year. He had three wins – the Italian Open, the Scandinavian Enterprise Open and that grand finale to the season, the Volvo Masters. He finished top of the money list, was the best at hitting greens in regulation figures and won the Vardon Trophy. He also played in the Ryder Cup that year and won his singles match against Mark Calcavecchia. Since then, he has been a little less successful, partly because of putting problems.

Judy Rankin

Born: February 18, 1945
St Louis, Mo, USA

Judy Rankin was a very early developer, winning the Missouri state title at the age of 14 and going on to finish low amateur in the US Women's Open the following year. By the age of 17 she was playing the LPGA Tour, though with very modest success – $701 in her first season. However, she made good progress and was ninth on the money list by 1965. In 1968 her stroke average came down substantially and she also had her first victory. Judy Rankin was on her way, and over the next ten years the victories piled up. In both 1976 and 1977, when she had six and five wins respectively, she was leading money winner on the LPGA Tour. From 1969 to 1979, her worst placing was 15th, and she was nine times ninth or better. By the end of 1979 she had 26 tournament wins in the USA, but that was more or less it. Rankin had a very strong left hand grip, which tends to put stress on both the left wrist and can lead to an increased twisting movement of the lower spine.Her victorious Solheim Cup captaincy in 1996 assuaged the back pains that ended her playing career.

Betsy Rawls

Born: May 4, 1928
Spartanburg, SC, USA

Rawls did not begin playing golf until her late teens but was soon winning her the Texas state title and the more important Trans-National and Broadmoor Invitational. While still an amateur, she finished second in the US Women's Open. From 1951, she played as a professional and her first win was in the US Women's Open, the most important of women's titles, which she won again in 1953, 1957 and 1960. She also won the Western and the LPGA Championship twice each. Her total of 55 LPGA victories ranks her behind only Kathy Whitworth, Mickey Wright and Patty Berg. As a money winner, she was in her prime from the mid-1950s (for which records are incomplete) until 1970. She was leading money winner in 1959 when she won a truly remarkable 10 times, and was never worse than 16th in a 14-year period. Yet in those years women's golf did not attract high prize winnings. The most she won in a season was only about $26,000. Rawls went on to become Tournament Director of the LPGA Tour during a period of rapid growth in the last half of the 1970s.

Ted Ray

Born: March 28, 1877
Jersey, Channel Islands

European success is now a common occurrence in the Masters, but not in the US Open. Only three British players, for instance, have managed to add this title to a win in the British Open: Harry Vardon (when, to be frank, it didn't matter very much), Ted Ray in 1920, when Americans were on the verge of dominance of world golf, and Tony Jacklin in 1970. Ray first really announced himself in British golf by reaching the 1903 final of the News of the World Matchplay Championship and losing to James Braid, then at the height of his powers. Ray began to contend for the British Open but had to cope with the stiffest competition from Vardon, Taylor and Braid. He finally broke through in 1912 at Muirfield, beating Vardon into second place by a comfortable four strokes. Ray was a dramatic player to watch because of his prodigious power. Even Bobby Jones was in some awe of him while watching him on a US exhibition tour. The power showed to good effect when Ray took his US Open title. On one par four hole he managed a long carry of some 280 yards over a ravine and birdied the hole in all four rounds. He excelled at thrashing the ball out of bad lies, but also had a delicate touch on the greens.

Dai Rees

Born: March 31, 1913
Barry, Wales

Rees's greatest achievement came at Lindrick in the 1957 Ryder Cup. He was in the only winning pairing on the Great Britain and Ireland side, of which he was captain, and on the second day trounced his opponent, 1954 US Open champion Ed Furgol, by 7 and 6. Equally notable was his failure to win a British Open, well though he played. Either he or Abe Mitchell must be the best British player not to win. Rees first began to make some impact in the event towards the end of the 1930s but became a really significant factor after the Second World War. He might well have won in 1946, when he had the lowest round of the championship, a 67, and went into the final round tied with the eventual winner, Sam Snead. Alas, he then had a disastrous start and could only partially recover. He was fourth. In 1950 and 1953, he outscored the eventual champions for two rounds, but they lasted better. In 1954, he needed a par on the last to tie, but his ball skipped through the green. Rees thought it had hit a small stone. His last chance came at the age of 48, when he was one behind. In compensation, he was a most consistent tournament winner with 28 to his credit.

Mike Reid

Born: July 1, 1954
Bainbridge, USA

After a strong amateur career, which included being leading amateur in the US Open, Reid has proved to be rather a journeyman pro. He wins money but not many tournaments. So far they are the important Casio World Open in Japan in 1990, the 1987 Tucson Open and the 1988 World Series of Golf, the event which gave him considerable TV exposure and which he won in a play-off with Tom Watson. Reid is one of the US Tour's shorter hitters, currently averaging something like 250 yards. This may not be as great a disadvantage as some might think, because it has made him a master with a fairway wood, and he is no worse at hitting greens than most of his fellow competitors. Perhaps his worst moments came in the 1989 US PGA Championship. After three rounds, he held a three-stroke lead and was still in the same position after 69 holes. He bogeyed the next hole and played the 71st disastrously. On this par three his ball ran just through the green into quite a dense lie. From there he took a lob and three putts to get down. Afterwards he said in the press tent: "Where can you go around here to have a good cry?"

José Rivero

Born: September 20, 1955
Madrid, Spain

Rivero started in life as a caddie and in his late teens became a club professional in Madrid. Though many good players are content with the life, most players of quality, whether amateur or professional, want to see how well they can compete against the best. So, rather late in the day, Rivero decided to attempt to qualify for the European Tour in 1980 and eventually made it. The Spanish Golf Federation gave him a loan of about £2,500 ($3,800) to enable him to compete and, after a modest year in 1983, he came through the next year with a win in the Lawrence Batley International and finished 11th on the money list. Since then he has won the 1987 French Open, the 1988 Monte Carlo Open and the 1992 Open Catalonia. This is perhaps not a great career record, but Rivero is very consistent, usually finishing well up the field, and by the end of 1994 had earned more than £1.7 million. He would probably have done far better but for occasional failures with the putter. Rivero has often represented Spain in the Alfred Dunhill Cup and the World Cup, winning the team event once. He also played in both the 1985 and 1987 Ryder Cup matches.

Allan Robertson

Born: 1815
St Andrews, Scotland

Allan Robertson may have been the reason for the founding of the Open Championship. Correctly or not, he was reputed to be the best golfer in Scotland, which, in the 1850s, virtually meant the world. When he died in 1859 it was decided that a successor should be found, and Prestwick Golf Club began its rudimentary organization of the Open Championship the following year.

As his career took place in the early days of photography, no visual evidence of his style exists. However, contemporary accounts of his playing abilities stress his accuracy, especially for shots up to the flag. For these he used an iron far more than his contemporaries, especially once the feathery ball had been displaced by the gutty – much to his disgust because of the excellent trade in the earlier ball. Robertson is the earliest known golf course architect. He was influential in the development of the Old Course at St Andrews and is

JOSÉ RIVERO *All Spaniards are in the shadow of Ballesteros and Olazabal*

believed to have designed the famous Road Hole (17th) with its wickedly difficult approach.

Chi-Chi Rodriguez

Born: October 13, 1935
Rio Piedras, Puerto Rico

Rodriguez is an even more talkative player than Lee Trevino, and in his younger days on the US Tour was known to many as "the clown prince of the Tour". Others, who disliked his chatter and on-course antics, called him "the four-stroke penalty". They felt that was about the number of strokes he cost them with his distracting behaviour. Such august figures as Arnold Palmer and Jack Nicklaus told him to moderate it, and he did so, while still remaining exuberant. Rodriguez had a successful career on the US Tour between the beginning of the 1960s and the early 1980s. His first win came in 1963, his last in 1979, and he totalled eight in all. However, he has prospered far more as a Senior since 1985 and has been one of the most prolific winners ever. In 1986 he won three times and the next year took seven events, including the PGA Seniors. That year he also managed the feat of birdies on eight holes in a row, a record, which helped him to his record fourth straight win in a single season. He continued to take a title every year until the end of 1993. Rodriguez was a member of the US Ryder Cup team in 1973 and played for Puerto Rico in 12 World Cup teams.

Bill Rogers

Born: September 10, 1951
Waco, Tx, USA

Rogers worked his way gradually to the top and then subsided rapidly. As an amateur, he made the 1973 Walker Cup team. He then turned professional and first made a real impact by winning the 1977 Pacific Masters. The following year he took the Bob Hope Desert Classic, the first of his eventual five victories on the US Tour. In Britain, Rogers attracted much attention when he won the 1979 World Matchplay Championship at Wentworth. By this time, the strengths of his game were becoming apparent. Not long off the tee, he was very accurate and his scoring average was always good. His putting, excellent, involved an action with relatively stiff arms, the stroke coming from the shoulders. In 1981, he reached his peak. He won three times on the US Tour and was named Player of the Year. More importantly, he took the British Open at Royal St George's, going into the last round with a five-stroke lead. That year he had a five wins in six entries, worldwide. Since then he has only won once, in 1983. "Then I had a very positive attitude," he said recently. "It was never the same after that."

Douglas Rolland

Born: 1860
Earlsferry, Scotland

Douglas Rolland was probably the best striker of a golf ball from the early 1880s to the mid 1890s. Many

CHI-CHI RODRIGUEZ *The crowds love his chatter; he's a big star on the Seniors Tour*

EDUARDO ROMERO *Argentina's best player, he has improved with age*

were the tales of his great length from the tee, though his putting was held in much lower regard. Although the Open Championship was quite well established by the time of Rolland's peak years, he seldom competed in the event. One reason is said to be that he faced prosecution, or a divorce case, if he returned to his native Scotland. He spent most of his life in England, where he held several golf club jobs. His fame during his best years mainly depended on his success in exhibition and challenge matches. He played the championship very little indeed but finished 13th in 1882, 10th the following year and, in 1884 tied for second place. Did this inspire him to greater efforts? Apparently not. As far as we know, he played just one more time, finishing second to J. H. Taylor in 1894. It seems his game declined shortly afterwards, perhaps because of a riotous lifestyle.

Eduardo Romero

Born: July 12, 1954
Cordoba, Argentina

Since the early 1980s, Romero has been Argentina's best player. He first won his own country's PGA back in 1983, and has repeated that success twice. The Argentine Open, however, eluded him until 1989, but he has also won the Chile Open twice. Golf in South America, however, is on a somewhat small scale and players have to make their names and earn their fortunes abroad. Romero plays mainly in Europe, with excursions to the USA and elsewhere. He began his European career in 1984 and started to make real progress in 1988 when he reached the top 50. Since then he has done a great deal better, his first big season coming in 1989 when he moved up to 13th on the money list and also won the Lancome Trophy, which has a select field. He won the Open di Firenze in 1990, and had two successes in 1991 – the Spanish Open and the French Open. These meant that he was comfortably in the top 20 money winners in the years 1989–91. In 1994, he took the Italian Open and the European Masters, earning more than £250,000/$375,000 in the season.

S

Doug Sanders

Born: July 24, 1933
Cedartown, Ga, USA

Doug Sanders won 19 times on the US Tour between 1956 and 1972, and had five wins in 1961, but his fame rests on one never-to-be forgotten shot. Unfortunately for him it was a missed putt, which cost him the 1970 British Open. By then past his prime, Sanders had had to prequalify, but he was a master of improvised shots and St Andrews was his ideal arena. He came to the last two holes needing a couple of pars to win the championship. It was not easy, because the 17th is just about the most difficult hole in world golf. With the aid of an exquisite bunker shot, Sanders got his par four. The Open then seemed to be his, for the last hole at St Andrews is as easy a finishing hole as you can find. Sanders hit a good enough drive, slightly thinned his approach so that he ended up to the back of the green, putted up to four feet or less and then contemplated that putt for the championship. You have to make up your mind. Sanders did, but then noticed a mark along the line. He paused to remove it and then did not go through the usual routine – and missed. He then lost the 18-hole play-off with Jack Nicklaus by a stroke. Never mind, he is still better remembered for that missed putt than many are for a dramatic winning shot. If you ask Doug today if it preys on his mind he is likely to reply, "No, sometimes I don't think about it for five minutes."

Gene Sarazen

see Legends pp 102–03

Peter Senior

Born: July 31, 1959
Narangba, Australia

Almost all professional golfers seem to develop a putting twitch in the end – from Vardon, through Snead and Hogan, to Watson. Today, however, solutions of a kind are to be found. The weird method of Bernhard Langer is being copied by some tour players, while others have gone for the long putter, as indeed Langer has now done. Senior too opted for the "broomstick". He had some disastrous years, largely caused by his putting problems, but then a fellow sufferer, Sam Torrance, gave him a long putter. This method, which involves tucking the club under the chin and then swinging it pendulum style, thus making demands on a different set of small muscles and nerves, has enabled him to be competitive again. His full swing shots are unusual, as he lifts up on the ball just after impact, whereas most players aim to maintain a low path into and after impact. Senior was first on the Australasia money list in 1987, 1989 and 1993. His first win came in the 1979 South Australian Open and he has 20 victories worldwide. Most of these have come in Australia, where in 1989 he won both the Australian Open and the Australian PGA Championship. Outside Australia, his most important win was probably the European Open.

PETER SENIOR *An ungainly hitter and putter … but his methods work*

Patty Sheehan

Born: October 27, 1956
Middlebury, USA

As an amateur, Sheehan won a string of state titles and climaxed her career with a win in the 1980 AIAW National Championship. She played in the Curtis Cup that same year and won all her matches. Turning professional late on that year, it was not long before she made an impression, her first win coming the following year in the Mazda Japan Classic. In the USA she first won in 1982 and had two other victories that same year. She was already a star and has remained so. Her money list placing has always been high – never worse than 14th between 1981 and 1996. The tournament victories have piled up to a total at the end of 1996 of 35 (plus a Women's British Open in 1992). These have earned her, in addition to more than $5 million, membership of the LPGA Hall of Fame. She has won five major championships (or six if you include the British Women's Open, which will surely become one now that it is an official LPGA event). These are the LPGA three times and the US Women's Open twice. Amazingly, Sheehan has won an event in 15 of her 17 years on the Tour, and starred in the winning 1996 Solheim Cup singles rally.

Denny Shute

Born: October 25, 1904
Cleveland, Oh, USA

There was little money on the fledgling US Tour of the 1930s, so Shute had to devote much of his time to his club professional's job. Even so his achievements were very considerable, notably his victory in the 1933 British Open at St Andrews. The course was playing very short, which does not mean easily, because the greens were not holding and that puts a premium on precise judgment of the pitch and run. Shute had the odd result of four rounds of 73, which gave him a total one lower than Syd Easterbrook and a tie with Craig Wood. He went on to win the play-off. Easterbrook had already featured in Shute's year at Southport and Ainsdale in the Ryder Cup. There, at the climax of the match, Shute had three-putted the last green to lose to Easterbrook, and the USA went down. Revenge was very likely sweet. In the previous Ryder Cup matches in the USA, Shute had been a great deal more successful. He and Walter Hagen won their foursomes by 10 and 9, and Shute his singles by 8 and 6. Shute won two major championships in his own country, the 1936 and 1937 PGAs, the last player to win two in a row. He was elected to the PGA Hall of Fame in 1957.

Scott Simpson

Born: September 17, 1955
San Diego, Ca, USA

After a successful amateur career, which included Walker Cup status, Simpson twice failed to qualify for the US Tour but made it in 1979. Since then, he has always made reasonable money but tends to disappear from the public view for quite long periods. His greatest season was 1987, when he finished fourth on the US money list but, much more important, won the US Open after a very close confrontation with Tom Watson. He came through by a stroke with Watson narrowly missing a long putt. All this took place at the difficult Olympic Club. Since then, Simpson has seemed a US Open specialist, though he has not won again. He tied for sixth place in 1988 and 1989, and for first place in 1991, where he lost a play-off with Payne Stewart. Simpson is regarded by some as a journeyman professional, but he is much more accurate than many from the tee, which can give him an advantage when players are confronted by the tight drive zones and dense rough that are normally part of a US Open set-up. Besides his US Open he has won five events on the US Tour and four important events overseas.

PATTY SHEEHAN *One of the most consistent players on the US LPGA Tour*

Vijay Singh

Born: February 22, 1963
Lautoka, Fiji

Singh is the only golfer of world class that Fiji has produced. Given the amount of travelling he has had to do, his achievements have been enormous. First he settled in Malaysia, and after successes there decided to compete more widely. He was particularly successful in Africa, where he won three events in 1989 and has played the European Tour since his first appearances in 1988. He was soon a winner, taking the Volvo Open in 1989. By the end of 1994 he had taken his total of victories to six, perhaps the most important being the Trophée Lancôme, which has a select field. Singh has the reputation of practising more than just about anyone else, and his results reflect this kind of dedication. In a short European career he has won more than £1.8 million. His best year was 1994, when he won about £450,000 and rose to sixth on the money list. Singh now spends more of his time in the USA, where he won the 1993 Buick Classic and two events in 1995, and has earned more than $3 million. Singh was quick off the mark in 1997, holding off Nick Price in the South African Open.

Jeff Sluman

Born: September 11, 1957
Rochester, NY, USA

Sluman's greatest achievement to date came at the Oak Tree Golf Club in the 1988 US PGA Championship. There he went into the final day three strokes behind the leader, Paul Azinger, but reversed that position with a closing 65. Surprisingly, that PGA title remained his only career victory until Steve Jones overshot the final hole at Tucson in 1997, which handed the $234,000 Chrysler Classic to Sluman. Despite seldom winning, Sluman makes a good living and gets himself into good positions. He has lost three play-offs, and in 1994 he held the lead in the BC Open for three rounds, having opened with a 63, but even a steady enough 72 saw him finish four shots behind the winner. Sluman seems to have some knack of competing well in major championships. In 1992, at

ANNIKA SORENSTAM *First foreigner to take Vare Trophy*

the tough Pebble Peach, he came second in the US Open after a 71 in his final round, one of only four below par that day, and tied for the lead in the Masters after an opening 65, when he also became the first player to have a hole in one on the 4th. Sluman finished the event tied for fourth place. He has won nearly $5 million on the US Tour.

Horton Smith

Born: May 22, 1908
Springfield, USA

Being the first to win an event gives you a better chance of entering the history books – if only because yours is the first name on the trophy. Horton Smith won the First Augusta National Invitational in 1934, the tournament which was soon to become known as the Masters. The event aroused great interest, mainly because Bobby Jones, who had retired from all competitive golf four years before, was making a reappearance in "his" tournament. But Jones never repeated his previous form in any of the Masters he played. Smith won this first event by a stroke from the ever unfortunate Craig Wood. He repeated that success a couple of years later, this time by one from Harry Cooper. Those two Masters were his only majors, but he was third twice in the US Open and once in the British. He played on three Ryder Cup teams and won some 30 tournaments.

Macdonald Smith

Born: 1890
Carnoustie, Scotland

Bing Crosby, himself a low handicap golfer, watched most of the greats over nearly half a century and considered that Smith had the best-looking swing of the lot. However, although he won over 30 times in the USA, Smith is often rated the best player not to have won a major. But how close he came. As early as 1910, for example, when only 20, he tied for the US Open and lost the play-off. He was never to come quite as close to a major again. By far the most famous failure came at Prestwick in 1925, after he took an almost impregnable five-stroke lead into the final round. The Scots turned out in their thousands to see their man from Carnoustie win. Crowd control was very poor on a course that presents difficulties in this respect. Smith sometimes had to wait too long to play his shots and occasionally, it is said, had to fire blind over spectators. As it turned out, a 76 would have been good enough but, alas, he took 82.

Jesse Snead

Born: October 14, 1941
Hot Springs, Va, USA

Jesse, or J. C., Snead is a nephew of the great Sam Snead. Both were born and brought up in Hot Springs, Virginia; both still live there. Jesse did not decide on golf as a career until well into his 20s. This was because he was a good baseball player as a youngster and became a professional on the Washington Senators farm system. When golf eventually won the day, it took him four years to qualify for the US Tour, which he managed in 1968. Success eluded him at first, but in 1971 he suddenly won the Tucson and Doral-Eastern Opens in two weeks. These and other good performances won him a Ryder Cup place that year; he also appeared in 1973 and 1975. In that first year he had an outstanding record, winning a foursomes, two fourballs and narrowly defeating the British number one, Tony Jacklin. Snead's highest placing on the US Tour money list is sixth, which he achieved in both 1974 and 1976.

Sam Snead

Born: May 27, 1912
Hot Springs, Va, USA

Whereas some would argue that Ben Hogan had the most technically effective swing of all time, Snead declared that he would take care never to watch Hogan swing. He thought the whole performance too quick and snatchy, and didn't want to be infected by the same rhythm. And rhythm was certainly what Snead had, to an almost unrivalled degree, combined with great acceleration into the ball. Although one of the greatest tournament winners, Snead never won the US Open, though he several times came close, sometimes agonizingly so. However, he won all the other majors. He was US PGA champion in 1942, 1949 and 1951, and took three Masters titles in 1949, 1952 and 1954. Reluctantly Snead also competed in the 1946 British Open at St Andrews, where he expressed his disgust with the course, his caddie, the accommodation and the food. "Whenever you leave the USA, you're just camping out", was his comment. In spite of all this he became Open champion, but did not play in the event again until long past his best. Snead is probably the most prodigious tournament winner of them all. He is credited with 81 victories on the US Tour, and his worldwide total has been put at 135, though he claims to have won 165.

Annika Sorenstam

Born: October 9, 1970
Stockholm, Sweden

Lifting the head upon impact is not recommended by the coaches. Despite this style blemish, Sorenstam climbed to the heights at the age of 24 in 1995 with a gritty last round in the US Open at The Broadmoor, high in the Rockies. She started round four two behind former champion Meg Mallon. Though Sorenstam lost two of the three-stroke lead she accumulated by the 15th, two putts from 30 feet at the 18th made her the third European and second Swede to win the Open in nine years. "For me, it is the world championship," she said – having already won the 1992 World Amateur title. Two other LPGA wins, the second in a play-off against Davies in the Samsung World Championship in South Korea, followed, helping towards Player of the Year status. Even more telling, she became the first foreign player to take the Vare Trophy for the lowest scoring average (71), and led the money list on both sides of the Atlantic, adding the most succulent cherry to the cake in 1996 by retaining her US Open title at Pine Needles, NC.

Mike Souchak

Born: May 10, 1927
Berwick, Pa, USA

How is this for nine holes of golf – 2, 4, 4, 3, 3, 3, 3, 3, 2? That was how Souchak played the second nine at Brackenridge Park during the 1955 Texas Open, for a total of 27. If he hadn't gone out in a relatively "poor" 33 he would have broken the magic 60. However, he was inspired that week, and rounds of 60, 68, 64, 65 gave him an aggregate of 257 which stood as a record low in tournament play until 1981, when Peter Tupling beat it over a 6,000-yard course. On the US Tour, only Al Geiberger and Chip Beck have bettered that first-round 60. However, it should be said that Souchak's score was achieved on a fairly easy course, while Tupling's involved putting on sand greens, which are easier than grass. Souchak played on the 1959 and 1961 Ryder Cup teams and won 16 times on the US Tour.

CRAIG STADLER *Returned to winning ways in 1996 at Riviera*

Craig Stadler

Born: June 2, 1953
San Diego, Ca, USA

Nicknamed "The Walrus" on account of his profuse moustache and a 210-pound outline, Stadler is one of the most recognizable figures in world golf. He recorded his first two victories as a professional in 1980 and shot up the money list from 55th to 8th, a position he repeated in 1981. The following year he finished as leading money winner, with close on $500,000. More importantly, he also won four times in the USA. The most significant of his victories was undoubtedly the Masters, though that was a trying experience for him. After 11 holes of the final round he held a five-stroke lead, but then dropped shots on the 12th, 14th and 16th. He came up the last hole needing a par for victory, but three-putted to tie with Dan Pohl. However, he parred the first play-off hole, Pohl bogeyed, and that was good enough. Stadler has played two Ryder Cups, won 12 times on the US Tour. He was disqualified in a 1987 event for kneeling on a towel to play a shot from under a tree for "building a stance". In 1995 he was permitted to cut down the (by now) diseased tree.

Jan Stephenson

Born: December 22, 1951
Sydney, Australia

Like Laura Baugh, Jan Stephenson has sometimes received more attention for her sex appeal than her golf. She has turned down offers to pose for both *Playboy* and *Penthouse*, but has appeared topless in a French magazine. "I'm not ashamed of my body," she said, "and I'll flaunt it if I want to." In her teens, Stephenson was phenomenally successful in Australia, winning a host of girls' and junior titles and then, after turning professional in 1973, dominating what there was of an Australian Tour. Her future obviously lay in the United States and she began to play the LPGA Tour in 1974, winning good money and being named Rookie of the Year. Her first win came in 1976, since when she has taken 16 titles on the US Tour plus two Australian Opens, the 1981 World Ladies, the French Open, and a Japanese event. Her peak years in the USA were between 1976 and 1988, when she was only once out of the top 20. She has won three major titles on the LPGA Tour doing so in consecutive years: the 1981 Peter Jackson Classic, the 1982 LPGA Championship and the 1983 US Women's Open.

Marlene Stewart

Born: March 9, 1934
Cereal, Canada

Stewart is probably the best golfer, male or female, that Canada has produced. She won her national closed championship nine times, and the total would have been higher had the event not sometimes been cancelled. The Canadian Open Amateur provided her with another record – and is a more significant gauge of her abilities, because it obviously attracted a higher class field. Starting in 1951, she won this championship eleven times up to 1973. One of her final opponents, a Miss M. Gay, must have been particularly unhappy. She played Marlene Stewart three times and lost by 9 and 8, 11 and 9, and 8 and 6. Outside her native land, Marlene did not, of course, pile up the wins as prolifically. However, in the USA she won the prestigious North and South and the US Women's in 1956, beating the great Joanne Gunderson (later Carner) in the final. She met the same opponent again a decade later, once again in the final, and this time lost on the 41st hole – at least setting a record for the longest match. The British Ladies used to be a prime target for all amateurs of stature. Marlene won it in 1953, as usual trouncing her final opponent.

Payne Stewart

Born: January 30, 1957
Springfield, USA

Though Stewart no longer stands out by virtue of the bright colours of the clothing he wore under a now-expired contract to advertise American gridiron football clubs, he has changed to a line of designer wear made on his own account. He certainly attracts a great deal of attention, though it is not quite the gear to be wearing if you have to back into a gorse bush to play a shot. Stewart may well find himself in occasional gorse bushes, because he is one of the few Americans who are fond of playing outside the US. His first professional wins came in India and Indonesia during 1981, and another followed in Australia the following year. He won in the US in both 1982 and 1983, but thereafter found it easier to win large amounts of money than tournaments. In 1993, for instance, he set a US Tour season record for money winnings – nearly $1 million – without scoring a victory. His first major event came in 1989 in the US PGA. Two years later came the US Open after an 18-hole play-off with Scott Simpson, a formidable championship player, at Hazeltine National. Stewart has won nine times on the US Tour banking in the region of $8 million.

Dave Stockton

Born: November 2, 1941
San Bernardino, Ca, USA

Stockton is one of those players whose greatest achievements have been in over-50s golf. In a long career on the US Tour, which basically lasted from 1964 to 1980, he won 11 times. This may seem a modest total, but it did include two major wins, both in the PGA Championship. In the 1970 event Arnold Palmer was one of the players he forced into second place; in 1976 Raymond Floyd and Don January were the two who came in second after Stockton holed a putt to win from several yards. Putting was, and is, the main strength of his game. He had a severe back injury in his early teens, and since then has never been able to hit full out.

He himself has claimed that he merely guides the clubhead through the ball – but he still drives 250 yards or so. Stockton twice played on the US Ryder Cup team – in 1971 and 1977 – but will be best remembered for his captaincy of the winning team in 1991, when Bernhard Langer's famous missed putt at Kiewah Island allowed Hale Irwin and the United States off the hook. Stockton was rewarded by his team tossing him into the Atlantic. On the Senior Tour he has already won nine times, earned well over $3 million, and has twice been leading money winner – in 1993 and 1994.

Frank Stranahan

Born: August 5, 1922
Toledo, Oh, USA

Stranahan, an amateur, was one of the first golfers to introduce the idea that extreme physical fitness might be important for golf. Earlier it had been thought that no excessive consumption of food, alcohol and nicotine was all you had to aim at. Stranahan caused a sensation when, shortly after the Second World War, he arrived at a famous British hotel with his weight-lifting kit. Whether or not it did his golf much good is open to question, for in golf the ability to accelerate a light clubhead counts for a great deal more than the musculature to shift inert weights. In Britain, if not America, the methods earned him the nickname "Muscles". His ideas of fitness apart, Frank was one of the great amateurs of the immediate post-war years. He won a host of US regional titles, though he never did better than reach the final of the US Amateur, when he lost on the 39th. In Britain he was much more formidable, winning the Amateur comfortably in both 1948 and 1950 and reaching the 1952 final. He was a very frequent competitor in the British Open and tied for second place in 1947 and 1953, when he was the world's best amateur.

Curtis Strange

Born: January 30, 1955
Norfolk, Va, USA

In 1988 and 1989, Strange became the first man since Ben Hogan to win consecutive US Opens. 1988 also saw him become the first to pass $1 million in a year's US Tour earnings, as well as achieving the rare feat of winning four times. If Strange's proudest achievements are his US Open victories, which are in the record books for ever, there is another that certainly won't be in the future. That is his 62 over the Old Course at St Andrews in the 1987 Dunhill Cup. This achievement is slightly devalued because the event is played as stroke match play, and over the closing holes, Strange would have been under little real pressure. Strange has had an up-and-down career, and since 1990 has not really featured as a major player. His first outstanding year was 1980, when he emerged as a significant force and finished third on the US money list. He then subsided a little before being top money winner in 1985, 1987 and 1988. Altogether he has won 17 events on the US Tour, and nearly $7 million. In his early professional days he earned the reputation of being far better at winning money than tournaments, but later became known as an "iron man" when in contention, a reputation belied by his costly slip against Nick Faldo in the 1995 Ryder Cup.

Louise Suggs

Born: September 7, 1923
Atlanta, Ga, USA

Louise Suggs ranks as one of the greatest of women players. As an amateur, she won numerous state and regional titles and capped that part of her career in some style. She won the US Women's title in 1947 and followed up by capturing the British in 1948 and playing in the Curtis Cup. She then turned professional, being a founder member of the US LPGA. As a professional, she had a great record in what were then ranked as major championships. She won the 1957 LPGA Championship, the US Women's Open in 1949 and 1952, the Titleholders in 1954, 1956 and 1959 and the Western Open in 1949 and 1953. The most remarkable of these was her first US Open victory, which she won by a record 14 strokes from Babe Zaharias. In these early years of the LPGA tournaments there were really only three players usually in contention – herself, Patty Berg and Zaharias. Louise fought very well. In her best years she was always among the top money winners and won consistently. Her last success came in 1962. It was her 50th.

Hal Sutton

Born: April 28, 1958
Shreveport, La, USA

Sutton was a player who seemed destined to become one of the stars of the modern game. He had made a big impression as an amateur, making the Walker Cup team, winning several regional events and taking the 1980 US Amateur. At Pinehurst he was the individual win-

CURTIS STRANGE *Coming out of a bunker at Brookline in 1988, on his way to the first of two consecutive US Open wins*

ner in the World Amateur team championship, winning by nine strokes while his 276 total set a record for the event at 12 under par. In 1981, he was leading amateur in the British Open and again played in the Walker Cup team. Following a very good first professional season, crowned by victory in the last event, the Disney Open, 1983 was even better. He led the US PGA from start to finish, beating Jack Nicklaus by a stroke. He also won the Tournament Players Championship. These and other results made him leading money winner for the year and saw him elected PGA Player of the Year. A no-win 1984 was followed by two titles in 1985 and 1986. Then came an eight-year drought, when Sutton "won only money". His career brightened in 1995 at the B.C. Open with a startling final round of 61, the best by a tournament winner in 20 years, since Johnny Miller at Tucson in 1975.

Freddie Tait

Born: January 11, 1870
Edinburgh, Scotland

Winner of the Amateur Championship in both 1896 and 1898, Tait was only beaten on the 37th hole of the 1899 final. It was fitting that his conqueror was an even finer amateur, John Ball. He was also a highly effective competitor in the Open Championship, being leading amateur three times in the 1890s and third overall twice. However, his forte was probably match play, in which, together with John Ball and Harold Hilton, he formed an amateur triumvirate. Tait was a prodigious hitter and also famed for his recovery play. He always seemed able to rip the ball out of the rough for great distances – disconcerting for a match play opponent. Harold Hilton, for instance, may well have been a greater player but he could seldom handle Tait. A lieutenant in the Black Watch, Tait seems to have been allowed plenty of time to play golf, but his profession was the death of him. He was killed in 1900, leading a charge in the Boer War.

DAVE THOMAS *Another vast hit*

J.H. Taylor

See Legends pp 106–107

Dave Thomas

Born: August 16, 1934
Newcastle-upon-Tyne, England

For a good spell Thomas deserved his reputation for being the longest straight driver in the world. Thomas twice came close to winning the British Open, perhaps most famously in 1958 as a young man. Several players came to the last hole at Royal Lytham and St Anne's with a chance to win, but only Thomas and the Australian Peter Thomson survived in par. Thomas had already missed his chance to win on the previous hole, the long and difficult par four 17th. Having hit a huge drive, he then did the unforgivable and missed the green with a short iron. A 36-hole play-off followed the next day. Few could beat Thomson in a play-off of any length, and so it proved this time, though Thomas put up a good fight. A new star seemed to have arrived, but his results were not as good as expected, partly becaue of a weakness in his game he could never cure – the short pitch. He was again second in an Open in 1966, to Nicklaus, and had 16 career wins. He is now a very well-known course architect.

Peter Thomson

Born: August 23, 1929
Melbourne, Australia

Thomson was probably the ultimate master of running the ball over linksland turf. These skills made him one of the greatest competitors ever in the Open Championship, which he won five times – in 1954, 1955, 1956, 1958 and 1965. During the 1950s his only serious rival was the South African, Bobby Locke. Both had a similar approach to golf: get your tee shot on the fairway and the next one on the green, and then don't three-putt. From the beginning of the 1950s until the late 1960s Thomson was the man you had to beat in Europe, Australasia and the Far East. He was less formidable in the USA. He did not much enjoy playing there, nor many of the courses on that tour. They tended to suit long, high-flying driving, and the man who putted best in a particular week was too often the winner. However, when long retired from competitive golf and more concerned with golf architecture, Thomson decided to try the Senior PGA Tour. In 1985 he was the supreme performer, breaking all the money-winning records. Then, having done what he wanted to do, he returned to golf architecture – and writing. He may be the best professional golfer writer ever.

Sam Torrance

Born: August 24, 1953
Largs, Scotland

Torrance's long and largely successful career is a testament to his long hitting and rhythm as much as anything. For a time, a twitching putter looked likely to bring his career to a premature end. Then he decided to experiment with a long putter. An avid snooker player, he practised with it on his table and the balls started to go in without that fatal tremor. He is now on his day as good a performer as any on the greens. He first played the European Tour in 1971 and made

SAM TORRANCE *Celebrates his and Europe's winning putt at the 1985 Ryder Cup*

moderate progress until 1976, when he won twice and was third on the money list. Since then, Torrance has had only two fairly poor years on the European Tour, and has proved a spirited Ryder Cup player. His highest ranking was second, in 1984, and again, by a whisker, in 1995, to fellow Scot Colin Montgomerie. His best period was 1981 to 1985, and he continues to be a very strong performer, though not at his best in major championships. He has won 20 times on the European Tour and his career money winnings surpass £3.6 million, yet it is for his Ryder Cup feats that Torrance will be remembered.

Jerry Travers

Born: May 19, 1887
New York, NY, USA

There was a time when players carried far fewer clubs than they do today – one British Open champion carried just seven! Travers was rather a different case, however. He was seldom happy with woods, and may have been the first golfer of high ability to prefer an iron off the tee. But if Travers suffered the severe problem of being erratic with his woods, he usually made up for it with his brilliance on and around the greens. He was one of the first to concentrate on this, while others thought more of excellence through the green. His putting was particularly outstanding. Travers worked on various methods to see what worked best for him. He settled on an upright stance, keeping the body still throughout the stroke and making the head of the putter follow along the line – all conventional ideas today. What made Travers unusual in his day was his emphasis on an upright stance: many used to crouch low over the ball, with legs splayed wide. Travers won four US Amateurs – more than anyone except Bobby Jones. He won the US Open in 1915 – and never played in it again!

Walter Travis

Born: January 10, 1867
Maldon, Australia

Travis, who left his native land as a youngster, did not take up golf until his mid-30s, but made up for it with the intensity of his efforts. A very reliable wooden club player, Travis compensated for his shortness off the tee by hitting accurate woods to the greens. His putting was deadly. Undoubtedly his greatest claim to fame was his performance in the 1904 British Amateur at Sandwich. In practice, Travis found his putting had deserted him, but then he was offered a Schenectady, a centre-shafted putter with a mallet-type head. Suddenly his skills came back and the putts started rattling in once again. Travis cruised through round after round to meet Edward Blackwell in the final. There were great contrasts in their play. Blackwell drove the ball way past Travis, but the American had the equalizer on the greens and won by 4 and 3. He was the first overseas player to win the title. It was not a popular success with the British, and the Schenectady putter was later banned. In the US, Travis won three US Amateurs and was second in the 1902 US Open. Later he founded *The American Golfer* and became a distinguished golf course architect.

Lee Trevino

see Legends pp 104–05

Bob Tway

Born: May 4, 1959
Oklahoma City, Ok, USA

In 1986 Tway hit one of the most famous shots in modern golf. It came on the final hole of the US PGA Championship at Inverness. After the opening two rounds, Tway lay no fewer than nine strokes behind Greg Norman, but a third-round 64 reduced the gap to four. In the final round, Tway pulled level, and then came the drama of the final hole. Norman hit a good approach which spun back into the semi-rough around the green. Tway bunkered his approach and was left with a very difficult shot to make his par. A touch too strong, and his ball would run off the green; if he came up short, he would be left with a nasty downhill putt. He played a perfect shot, the ball pitching about 20 feet short of the hole – and running in. Norman then needed to hole his chip to tie and, not surprisingly, failed. This was Tway's fourth victory of the season in his seventh year on the US Tour. He finished second on the money list, with some $650,000, and was named PGA Player of the Year. Since then he has had three more victories on the tour, the last of them, in 1995, ending a four-year drought.

BOB TWAY *Bunker shot at Inverness crowned a great year*

Harry Vardon

see Legends pp 106–07

Ken Venturi

Born: May 15, 1931
San Francisco, Ca, USA

Venturi will never forget the Congressional and the 1964 US Open. He had suffered a disastrous slump in form and had qualified to play the championship for the first time in four years. Earlier his career had been as promising as anyone's. While still an amateur in 1956 he had come very close to winning the Masters after beginning with rounds of 66 and 69, followed by a 75 in poor weather. Alas, in the final round he took 80, but had still been in the lead with two holes to play. Another Masters disaster followed in 1960. With two holes left, he had a one-stroke lead over Arnold Palmer. But the great man was unkind enough to birdie the last two holes and that was that. Even so, at this stage Venturi had the consolation of 10 wins on the US Tour, including four in 1958. Thereafter his consistency went, and he also suffered problems with his hands. In 1964, his game began to come back and he made a sound start to that US Open, followed by a 66 on the final morning. In extreme heat, he had to be accompanied by a doctor on the final afternoon but managed to make it through to victory. That was the happy end to Venturi's story, for his game soon faded because of poor health.

Roberto de Vicenzo

Born: April 14, 1923
Buenos Aires, Argentina

The greatest South American golfer ever, de Vicenzo is still probably best known for an error in checking his score card on the last day of the 1968 Masters, which also happened to be his birthday. He played the round of his life, a 65. But he failed to notice that his playing partner had marked him down for a par four on the penultimate hole, which Roberto had birdied. He was a little distracted by his bogey five on the last hole of all. He thought he had lost the event by his errors there, but it was the calligraphy on the 17th that cost him the chance of a play-off. "What a stupid I am," he said. He was less stupid at Hoylake the previous year in the Open Championship. A third-round 67 gave him a two-stroke lead over Gary Player and a three-stroke advantage over the defending champion, Jack Nicklaus. He held on to win, his round climaxed by three superb tee shots. At 44 years and 93 days he was the oldest Open champion of modern times. De Vicenzo won over 30 national titles around the world. His overall total of wins is not known, but at well over 200, he may be the most prolific of all time. Roberto, a very easy-going character, has very likely not kept count.

Lanny Wadkins

Born: December 5, 1949
Richmond, Va, USA

Wadkins plays brilliantly when the inspiration flows. Almost as quick a player as there is, he goes for the flag rather than safe parts of the green. Sometimes everything comes off; sometimes it doesn't. Perhaps this accounts for his fluctuating results in money winnings on the US Tour since his career began in 1971. He has eight times been in the top 10, but also 10 times out of the top 50. His best placings are second, once, and third, twice. His iron shots at the flag are probably the strongest part of his game, while his putting has been more variable. When his game is on song, Wadkins seizes his chances and he wants to win rather than just finish well up the field and pocket a respectable cheque. As a result, he has been a frequent winner on the US Tour and totalled an impressive 21 victories by the end of 1994. At the same stage he had won almost of $6 million. He has played on seven Ryder Cup teams, but his one turn as captain in 1995 turned sour in that while one of his personal selections, Fred Couples, did well, the other, Curtis Strange, lost all three matches as Europe regained the trophy.

LANNY WADKINS *Emotions always show*

Tom Watson

see Legends pp 108–09

Tom Weiskopf

Born: November 9, 1942
Massillon, Oh, USA

Nicknamed "Terrible Tom" by the Press, Weiskopf was sometimes his own worst enemy. A perfectionist, gifted with a magnificent swing, he didn't feel it was "proper golf" to miss greens and scramble pars by means of a chip and single putt. His play in the 1969 Masters was characteristic. He missed only four greens in the tournament but still managed to finish second, having three-putted 13 times. More dramatic was his play in the 1980 Masters. This time he came to the par three 12th having played competent golf. This shot to the green must be exact for distance: just a touch short and you are in Rae's Creek; a little long and it's difficult to salvage a par. Tom emerged with a 13. His great period was quite short. Towards the end of 1972 he won the World Matchplay Championship. The following year he won four US Tour events, and the Open Championship at Troon in generally unpleasant weather.

TOM WEISKOPF *Elegant swing remains*

Joyce Wethered

Born: November 17, 1901
London, England

Bobby Jones declared that Joyce Wethered was the best player of either sex he had ever seen and she may well have been the greatest woman player of all time. All a player can do is defeat the best of the day – and she certainly did that. Joyce first came to public notice at the 1920 English Ladies' Championship at Sheringham in Norfolk. She had entered mainly to keep a friend company. The friend was soon knocked out, but Joyce went through to the final where she beat the greatest player of the day, Cecil Leitch, after being well behind. She went on to win the event in her next four entries and apparently thought that was enough. She did not compete again. Her record in the far more international British Ladies' Championship was almost as good. She won in 1922, 1924, 1925 and 1929. In this period she lost only two matches and missed out the years 1926–28. She did not much enjoy championship golf and returned in 1929 mainly because the event was being held at St Andrews. This time she beat the great Glenna Collett in the final. For Joyce Wethered there were no more fields left to conquer and it became her final championship.

Kathy Whitworth

Born: September 27, 1939
Monahans, Tx, USA

Whitworth played the LPGA Tour from 1959 until 1991, and was consistently successful between 1962 and 1985. Her money-winning achievements were truly remarkable. She was leading money winner eight times and on another 10 occasions finished no worse than ninth. She racked up a total of 88 victories, beating Mickey Wright's record of 82.

Enid Wilson

Born: March 15, 1910
Stonebroom, Alfreton, England

Wilson got herself sacked from school (deliberately, she said, for swearing) to get down to serious golf. A relentless practiser, scornful of women who weren't, she was English champion in 1928 and 1930, and scored a hat-trick in the British 1931–1933. She lost her foursome but beat Helen Hicks in the inaugural Curtis Cup match in 1932. Declared a "non-amateur" in 1934 she retired from competition and started on a long career as an outspoken golf writer, notably for *The Daily Telegraph*. She dealt profitably on the Stock Exchange, and played Crowborough Beacon in Sussex well into her eighties.

Craig Wood

Born: November 11, 1901
Lake Placid, NY, USA

Craig Wood earned a reputation as a man who always just missed out on major championships. Easily the most famous one was the second Masters in 1935. Wood was in the clubhouse and no one on the course had a chance of catching him, unless you counted Gene Sarazen, who had to birdie three of the last four holes to tie. No one has done that in a major before or since. Playing that perilous second shot over water at the 15th, Sarazen let fly with a 4-wood – and holed out for a double eagle. Not surprisingly, Wood lost the 36-hole play-off by a wide margin – 5 strokes – the next day. By this time he had also lost the first Masters by a stroke to Horton Smith and had a close encounter with the 1933 US Open. That same year he tied Denny Shute for the British Open and, of course, lost the play-off. The US PGA in 1934 wasn't any kinder to him: he lost the final on the 38th hole, his massive driving overcome by short-game expert Paul Runyan. Wood later lost the 1939 US Open to Byron Nelson, again in a play-off. Double consolation came in 1941, with the Masters plus the US Open, from which he was persuaded not to withdraw with back trouble.

Tiger Woods

Born: 1975
Cypress, Ca

Tiger (Eldrick) Woods is Afro-American on his father's side and Thai on his mother's. He has grandparents with Caucasian and Native American blood (in old ethnic-speak, White and Red Indian respectively). Having uniquely landed a hat-trick of US Amateur titles, he turned pro at once in August, 1996. Inside two months he won two PGA events. His first tour drive measured 336 yards. Aged 20, 6ft 2in and 155lb, he outhit mighty John Daly, and began to outbox-office him too. Woods was, reputedly, paid $500,000 appearance money in Thailand, winning the Asian Honda Classic by 10 shots. He was given Thai citizenship, which involves rights not available to women, e.g. his mother Kultida. Phil Knight of Nike hinded Woods' contracts with his company and Titleist were worth tens of millions of dollars. Woods won the opening event of 1997, the Mercedes Championship, against the 1996 Player of the Year, Tom Lehman, at La Costa, where his six-iron tee-shot at the first extra hole (the short seventh) stopped four inches from the pin. Then Woods, at 21, won the 1997 Masters at his first attempt as a professional and by a record score. Father Earl's prediction of 14 majors (one more than Bobby Jones) did not sound far-fetched. President Clinton told Woods that the best shot he saw at

YOUNGEST MASTER *Tiger Woods hugs his caddie on the 72nd at Augusta, 1997*

Augusta was the one of him hugging his father.

Ian Woosnam

Born: March 2, 1958
Oswestry, England

Only 5 ft 4½ in tall, Woosnam is probably the longest-hitting short man ever. A superb striker of the ball, he hits a right-to-left shape of shot, his one pronounced weakness being with the putter. However, even on the greens he is often very good indeed – no one can have his kind of tournament-winning record without a very considerable putting talent. Woosnam has not performed as well in the major championships as his abilities would suggest. His single major was the 1991 Masters, though he came close to a US Open win. His most consistent performances have come on the European Tour, with 31 victories by the end of 1996. In 1987 he and David Llewellyn won the World Cup for Wales. Woosnam has been a Ryder Cup regular since 1983, flowering in 1993 with four and a half points – but as yet no win in singles.

Lew Worsham

Born: October 5, 1917
Alta Vista, Va, USA

There are just a few shots which enter golfing legend. Worsham was involved in two of them, even if one was actually Sam Snead's rather than his. In 1947 the great Sam Snead holed a sizable putt to tie Worsham over 72 holes. In the 18-hole play-off, the pair were level as they played the 18th. Both then had quite short putts to lose or win – or carry on. Snead saw he was further from the hole and settled down to putt. Worsham, as he was quite entitled to do, questioned the distances and asked for measurements to be made. They were; Snead was right; he putted first – and missed. Worsham then holed out to be US Open champion. They say that no one remembers who finished second, and this is almost invariably true, but Snead's miss is far more a part of golfing legend than Worsham's US Open victory. In 1953, Worsham produced an authentic great shot of his own. He was playing in the Tam o'Shanter World Championship, and approached the 18th needing to get down in two from about 100 yards to tie Chandler Harper. He holed his approach.

Mickey Wright

Born: February 14, 1935
San Diego, Ca, USA

There are few real candidates for the title of greatest woman golfer ever. Joyce Wethered, Babe Zaharias, Nancy Lopez and Mickey Wright all spring to mind, but if the quality of the swing is taken into account, then only Wethered and Wright contend. Wright proved to be as long off the tee as Zaharias and was perhaps the best long iron player of all the women. She first began to come to the fore in the mid-1950s and in 1958 won five times, taking her first US Women's Open and LPGA. The next year she again won the Open and three other events. It was 1960, however, that saw her become a great player, with six wins, including the LPGA. Then she began to fly. There were 10 wins in both 1961 and 1962, 13 in 1963 – which is still a record – and 11 in 1964. At the end of that last season she had already taken 63 events, including the Open and the LPGA four times each.

Z

Babe Zaharias

Born: June 26, 1914
Port Arthur, Tx, USA

The Babe was not the greatest woman golfer of all time but possibly the greatest athlete. Just before the 1932 Olympics she entered eight events in the US National Championships and won six of them – and all this in well under three hours. At the Los Angeles Olympics she won the 80 metres hurdles, setting a new world record, and the javelin and was second in the high jump. With her supreme athletic abilities it is not surprising that, when she took to golf a couple of years later, the Babe was soon hitting the ball a very long way. However, there is a great deal more to golf than just long hitting. It took her many years to master the game, and for some of that time she was something of a freak show in exhibitions. Her peak began around 1946, winning 16 consecutive amateur tournaments. This sequence included the US Women's, and she went on to take the British equivalent in 1947. Turning professional, she won about a third of all the events she entered, including the US Women's Open in 1948, 1950 and 1954 and was also leading money winner for four years consecutively. She died of cancer at the age of 41.

Fuzzy Zoeller

Born: November 11, 1951
New Albany, In, USA

Fuzzy Zoeller is one of the few professionals who look as if they are enjoying their day's work on the golf course. Despite playing for much of his career with severe back problems deriving from a basketball injury, he always has a jaunty lilt to his stride up the fairways and is often whistling. He must also spend less time over the ball than any other significant figure in world golf. He takes his stance quickly, glances towards his target and swings. If only there were more like him! On the US Tour, Zoeller was a consistent performer from the mid-1970s but seemed to be on his way out towards the end of the 1980s. However, he came back strongly in 1993 and 1994, in the latter year contending for the British Open Championship. His greatest achievements were his two major victories, both after play-offs. The first of these came in the 1979 Masters, the first time Zoeller had qualified to play. After a slow start, Fuzzy found himself in a play-off with Ed Sneed and Tom Watson. He birdied the second extra hole to win. His play-off win in the 1984 US Open was very different, with Zoeller cruising round in 67 to Greg Norman's 75.

FUZZY ZOELLER *His name derives from his initials, Frank Urban Zoeller*

THE GREAT HEAD-TO-HEADS

Golf creates its most compelling moments of suspense when the relentless discipline of stroke play and the cut and thrust of match play come together at the climax of a major championship. Sometimes the contenders are a handshake away, on other occasions the enemy can only be anxiously glimpsed from ahead or behind.

The struggle becomes intensely personal, a naked battle of wills, a matter of who blinks first. Here are ten of the greatest head-to-heads of all time.

Ouimet vs Vardon vs Ray
Palmer vs Nicklaus
Nagle vs Palmer
Casper vs Palmer
Trevino vs Jacklin
Nicklaus vs Miller vs Weiskopf
Watson vs Nicklaus
Watson vs Nicklaus
Ballesteros vs Price
Faldo vs Norman

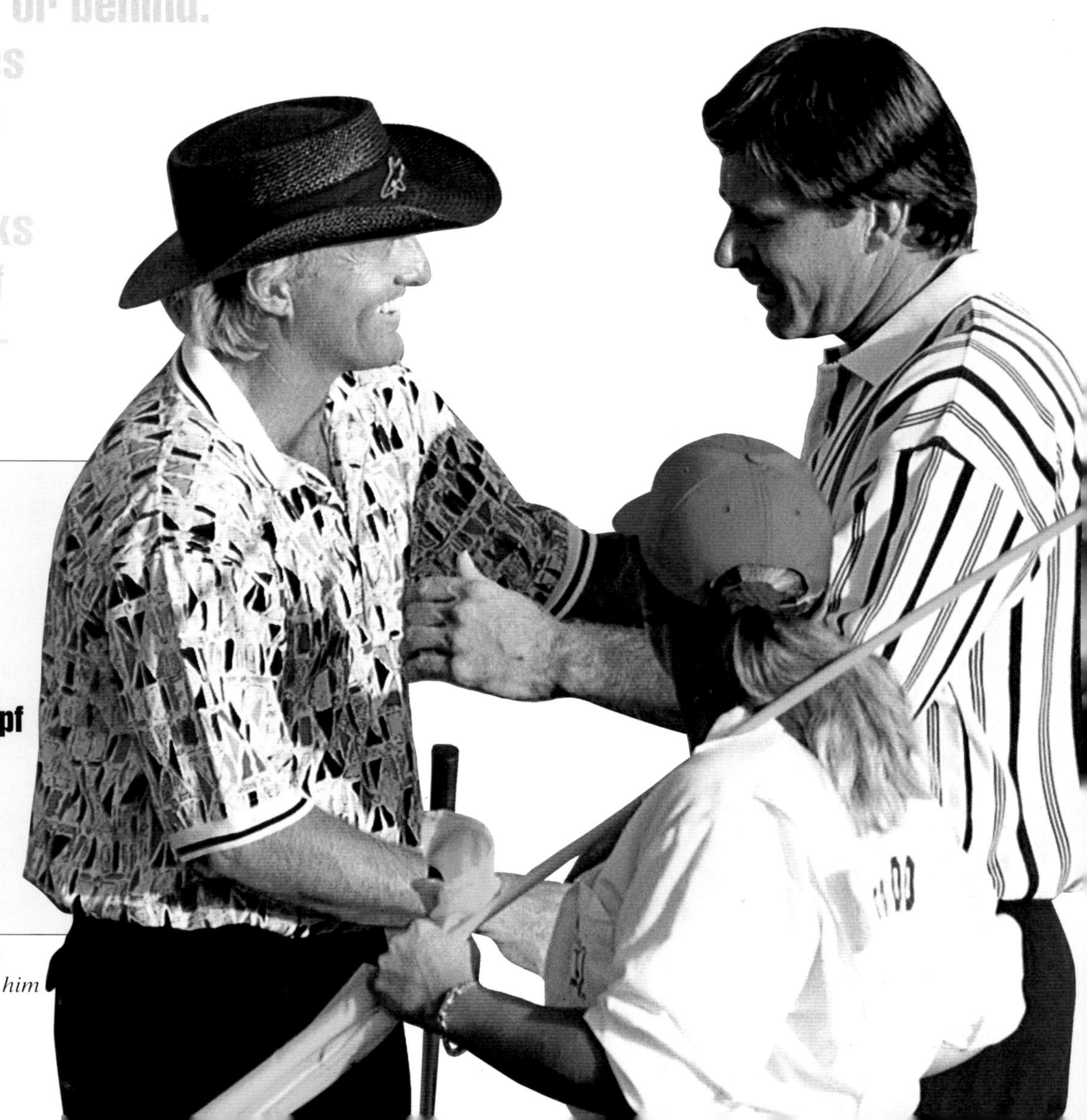

TABLES TURNED *Nick Faldo (right) consoles Greg Norman after taking the 1996 Masters from him*

OUIMET VS VARDON VS RAY
US Open, 1913

Francis de Sales Ouimet deserves to head the Great Head-to-Heads in anyone's book. He was the first amateur to become US Open Champion, snatching the title in 1913 from the master golfer of the era, Harry Vardon, and another mature and powerful British professional in Ted Ray.

Ouimet's play-off victory got golf on to the front page, at least in Boston, where the Open ended on September 20 at The Country Club, Brookline.

His triumph against all the odds had *Boys' Own Paper* romance about it, and sent the American golf juggernaut surging forward as the story of slim young Yankee upsetting invading giants sank in with the US sporting public, who, like the English, love the underdog.

Besides, Ouimet was no rich country club member, and worked in a sports shop. He had begun his golf in the fields around his home not far from Brookline's splendid clubhouse, and his credentials as the underdog were impeccable.

Though he lived close to The Country Club, he entered for the Open as a Woodland club member. Shortly before it began he had lost in the second round of the Amateur Championship to the eventual winner, Jerome Travers.

Vardon had done it all, winning the British Open five times, and the US Open with his only previous attempt. Ray had won the British Open the year before.

It was only as recently as 1911 that a native born American, J. J. McDermott, had managed to end the British-born golfers' monopoly of the US Open. He won again in 1912, so was the main hope to repel the English experts.

Ouimet, with a 77, was six strokes behind the first-round leaders, both Scots, Macdonald Smith and Alec Ross, who fell from grace on the second day, when the English pair made their move. Ray returned 70, the lowest score of the entire Championship, and Vardon, 72. Ouimet had a 74, but another 74 on the third day brought him level with Vardon and Ray, who did not fare well on the outward half of the final round.

Other players, notably Walter Hagen, had chances to catch Vardon and Ray, but only Ouimet did, playing the last four holes in one under the par of 15. He chipped dead at the 15th to get his par four, chipped and putted for his par three at the next, and got the essential birdie at the 360-yard 16th, sinking at 12-footer across and down a slope: "a masterstroke", said Ray. Another good chip and a seven-footer at the 18th meant a total 304, level with Vardon and Ray.

The crowd for the play-off was estimated at 10,000; they endured heavy rain gladly as an upset developed ... but a surprising one.

The local boy, using the less usual interlocking grip rather than the overlapping one that Vardon had made almost obligatory, most closely resembled the established pro, playing steadily from tee to green. His putting style worked well also: feet together, club swinging pendulum style from the shoulder. His opponents fell into one error after another, the clincher coming one hole from home where Vardon bunkered his drive and took five. Ouimet birdied, as he had the day before, and finished in 72, beating Vardon by five and Ray by six.

The *New York Times* awarded Ouimet the title "World's Golf Champion". Hagen, who like Ouimet was 20, shared fourth place with Long Jim Barnes, Macdonald Smith and Louis Tellier, from France.

Ouimet's caddie, Eddie Lowery, aged 10, had fought off any suggestion that he should step down in favour of an older caddie in the play-off. The logo designed for the 100th US Open of 1995 at Brookline is based on a silhouette taken from a 1913 photograph of little Lowery beside Ouimet.

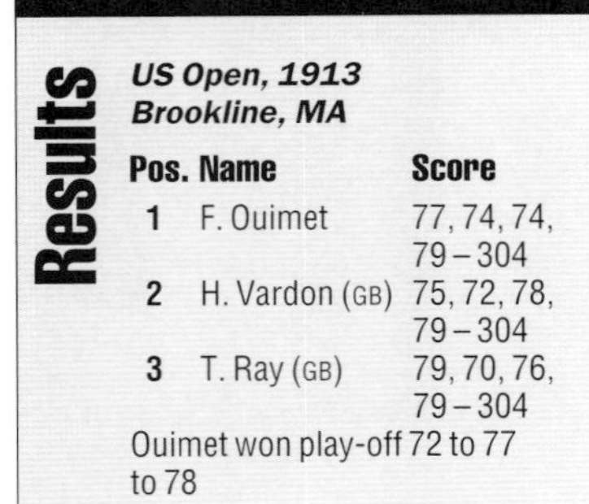

Results

US Open, 1913
Brookline, MA

Pos.	Name	Score
1	F. Ouimet	77, 74, 74, 79 – 304
2	H. Vardon (GB)	75, 72, 78, 79 – 304
3	T. Ray (GB)	79, 70, 76, 79 – 304

Ouimet won play-off 72 to 77 to 78

CONGRATS *Harry Vardon, Francis Ouimet and Ted Ray at the 1913 US Open*

PALMER VS NICKLAUS
US Open, 1960

Arnold Palmer had already won the American Amateur Championship and the Masters twice when, at Cherry Hills, Denver, on June 18, 1960, he had a slight disagreement with a Press acquaintance as he took a snack lunch, with Ken Venturi among those present, between the two final rounds of the 60th US Open Championship.

Palmer was seven strokes behind Mike Souchak, five behind Ben Hogan. Not only that, but he was four behind a large blond amateur, aged 20, from Columbus, Ohio, one J.W. Nicklaus, holder of the US Amateur Championship.

The journalist, Bob Drum, thought that Palmer was too far back, and was dismissive of Palmer's contention that if he shot 65, six under par, he could win, for it would give him a total of 280. Hogan and Mike Souchak, the holder of the world tournament nine-hole record with 27, had both managed 67s in the second round at Cherry Hills, so Palmer decided on a fast start. "280s win Opens", he told the doubters.

At 31, he was a mature golfer, and confident of his strength as a competitor, for had he not won his second Masters in the spring by slipping past Ken Venturi with birdies at the two closing holes? He had been trying to drive the first hole, a par four, all week, and got off to exactly the start he needed by at last reaching the putting surface off the tee, despite the obstacle in front of the green of a strip of long grass. His ball just made it, stopping 20 feet from the hole, and setting up a two-putt birdie; the eagle he missed by a whisker. Fireworks continued as he holed a chip for another birdie at the next hole, and he was within a foot with his wedge approach for his third in a row. An 18-footer at the fourth saved another shot, so that Souchak's seven-shot lead had been reduced to three.

Nicklaus and Hogan were playing partners well behind Palmer, now two under par. Nicklaus led briefly, until his putter let him down twice on the back nine, and Souchak was frittering away even more shots.

The news of Palmer's meteoric progress acted like a magnet for the galleries: "Arnie's Army" was becoming a numerous, if not always disciplined, force, and their commander did not fail them, for he inserted a long, twisting birdie putt on the 6th, and a six-footer at the 7th, reaching the turn in 30.

More sedate progress followed, but there was no loss of position, as he made good his declared intention: 65 for the round, and a winning 280 for the Championship, winning because Nicklaus could not make any impression on par, while Hogan, with a splendid chance of outflanking Palmer's charge, and capturing a record fifth Open, played over-aggressive shots on both the 17th and 18th, twice hitting into water hazards: he finished 6, 7. That relegated Hogan to ninth place. So ended his chances of a 10th major championship, and his first since his trio of majors in 1953.

Palmer's 65 was the lowest final round by a US champion, beaten only by Johnny Miller's 63 in 1973 at Oakmont. His outward 30 equalled the record set by amateur James McHale in 1947. Nicklaus's feat of recording the lowest total ever returned by an amateur in the Open, so beating every pro except Palmer, had to be regarded as a warning of things to come.

The Championship itself was setting records. Ouimet's Open had an entry of 165, so that the first qualifying round had to be staged. For Palmer's round the entry reached 2,453, necessitating 56 district and 13 sectional qualifying competitions. It also attracted a record gallery of more than 40,000, which enabled the prize money to be raised to more than $60,000, of which Palmer's share amounted to the sum of $14,400.

CUP WINNER ARNIE *Palmer at Portmarnock in 1960*

Results

US Open, 1960
Cherry Hills, CO

Pos.	Name	Score
1	A. Palmer (US)	71, 72, 72, 65 – 280
2	J. Nicklaus (US)	71, 71, 69, 71 – 282
3	D. Harrison, J. Boros, M. Souchak, T. Kroll, J. Fleck and D. Finsterwald (all US)	– 283

NAGLE vs PALMER
British Open, 1960

Apart from Kel Nagle and his friends and relations at home in North Sydney, the people most delighted by his win in the 1960 Centenary Open at St Andrews were the bookmakers, for Arnold Palmer was heavily backed, and came thrillingly close to crowning a third successive title charge in a major championship.

However, at least one bookmaker took a heavy hit, the one who accepted Peter Thomson's wager on his fellow Australian at long odds. Thomson had registered a first and a second in the Open at St Andrews, and did his best fully to inform Nagle of its intricacies.

Nagle had won the Australian

WARM WELCOME *Kel Nagle greets his wife in Sydney with the trophy*

Championship the previous year, to begin something of a come-back though fast approaching his 40th year. He had amended his game from long-hitter to straighter but shorter hitter, and unlike most he became a better putter with age.

His long game in the Open seldom faltered, and his idiosyncratic method of addressing the ball, with club head set inside the ball, became a familiar sight.

He faced in Arnold Palmer a player who was enjoying his hottest year as a pro. He had started out with three consecutive wins on the PGA winter tour, and travelled to Scotland to create a little history at the Centenary Open, for he was burning to equal Ben Hogan's unprecedented treble of seven years earlier, when he took the Masters, and both Opens…the British at his first attempt, as Palmer was now intent on doing.

The leader after the first round was Roberto de Vicenzo, who was 32 (four under par) for the outward nine, coming back in 35 to lead by two from Nagle and Fidel de Luca, another Argentine, with Palmer nicely placed one behind these two.

There was no catching de Vicenzo in the second round either, though Nagle was but two shots behind overall, for both men scored 67. Palmer seemed to be sliding out of the picture with a 71, for he had three putts on the Road Hole, and dropped another shot at the 18th, looked upon in reasonable weather conditions as a definite birdie chance. Palmer was now seven adrift of de Vicenzo, and five of Nagle.

While de Vicenzo blew up with a 75 in the third round, Palmer crept closer to Nagle, scoring 70 against the Australian's 71. He was two behind de Vicenzo now and, in company with Syd Scott, only four behind leader Nagle.

Then followed a frustrating interlude, for rain persisted, and forced a Saturday finish. This, it soon became clear, was to involve Nagle and Palmer, as their closest rivals began to slide down the leader board. Nagle was behind Palmer on the course, but a match play situation now began to develop. Both men were two under after nine holes, but Palmer birdied the 13th, while Nagle's indifferent approach at the 15th cost him a stroke, and cut his lead to two.

Nagle's nerves stood the grinding test of a seven-foot putt to save par at the 17th. Holing this was crucial, as Palmer persuaded the gallery of his coolness in a crisis by holing a birdie putt at the last. Nagle needed a par there, and got it safely enough, taking the Open trophy and a replica to celebrate the Centenary, together with a record first prize of £1,250. He had won by a shot with a total of 278, scoring a final 71 against Palmer's splendid but fruitless 68.

Nevertheless, this was Palmer's finest year, for he added six other tournaments to his two major victories. For British golf, his presence at the Open was to reverse the postwar trend of lack of interest by American golfers, a process his wins in the next two Opens at Birkdale and Troon were rapidly to intensify.

Results

British Open, 1960
St Andrews, Scotland

Pos.	Name	Score
1	K. Nagle (AUS)	69, 67, 71, 71 – 278
2	A. Palmer (US)	70, 71, 70, 68 – 279
3	B. J. Hunt (GB), H. Henning (SA) and R. de Vicenzo (ARG) – 282	

RAP ARTIST *Billy Casper's firm way with a putt earns an 11th hole birdie and equality with Palmer*

CASPER vs PALMER
US Open, 1966

The 1966 US Open at the Olympic Club, San Francisco, was a two-horse race. The also-rans, led by Jack Nicklaus, seven shots adrift, had no more than a distant view of the events that led to the Billy Casper vs. Arnold Palmer play-off.

The Olympic Club was an athletic and football club before members turned to golf. But it was an appropriate setting for a head-to-head contest: Gentleman Jim Corbett beat John L. Sullivan here in a battle for the world heavyweight boxing championship 74 years earlier.

The straight left is no good on the club's championship course, named Lakeside: nearly all the fairways bend to the right, so fade it and you've made it – with an important exception of which more later.

The greens are small, and though the yardage is little more than 6,700, the fairways are narrow, and lined with aggressive, ball-retentive trees.

Casper began with 69, Palmer with 71. Palmer was out in 32 next day, came back in 34 and took the lead –with Casper, who scored 68.

Palmer took a firm grip on Saturday, when he set out in company with Casper on the first hole of the 54 they were to play together. Casper missed fairways and greens and hit bunkers for a useful 73. Palmer, his Army keyed up, finished the round three ahead of Casper: 207 plays 210.

Palmer was out in 32 again on Sunday, which meant he was nine ahead of Nicklaus and seven ahead of Casper. He has not hidden the fact that at this point he thought the Open was his again, and that his target should now be the record score of 276 set by Ben Hogan in 1948.

He was still six up with six to play, and Nicklaus was heading for a 74. Palmer was calculating that level par would break the record, so in typically bravura fashion he went for a birdie to make sure. Instead, he missed the green at two short holes, which cost him a shot each time. At the second of these, the 15th, Casper got a birdie, bringing him to the relative luxury of three down with three to go.

The 16th was the exception to the Lakeside norm of left to right. It curved left, but Palmer overdid it into deep rough. His next blow, with a long iron, did not extricate his ball. A wedge did the trick, but his next was in sand, and though Palmer got up and down from there, Casper holed his birdie putt: one down.

Casper was soon level, for his celebrated, aggressive, wristy putting stroke was serving him well, saving his par at the 17th: no such luck for Palmer, who did well not to lose the day outright at the 18th, where he tried an iron from the tee, but again missed the short grass. He recovered staunchly, leaving a tough 10-yard putt, followed at once, because of the new continuous putting rule, by a six-footer. The rule, intended to speed play, added to the tension for Palmer, since Casper had not yet started to putt. Palmer got his par, but so did Casper. Taking no chances, he lagged up carefully for a two-putt four. It may have been running through his mind that golfers who have successfully played catch-up, especially long-haul catch-up, don't usually lose play-offs.

In this one Palmer was three ahead at the turn. Most of this advantage evaporated in a two-stroke swing on the 11th, he let go three more strokes in the next four holes, and lost 73 to 69, Casper keeping his nerve as the long-delayed crux was reached. Over the last nine holes on the last two days of the Open, Casper had taken 13 fewer shots than Palmer, who thereby suffered his third Open play-off defeat in five years. He never got as close again.

Results

US Open, 1966
Olympic, CA

Pos.	Name	Score
1	W. Casper (US)	69, 68, 73, 68 – 278
2	A. Palmer (US)	71, 66, 70, 71 – 278
3	J. Nicklaus (US)	71, 71, 67, 74 – 285

Casper won play-off 69 to 73

TREVINO VS JACKLIN

British Open, 1972

Lee Trevino's reputation as joker and miracle worker, especially in the pitching, chipping and putting departments, was well established when he arrived at Muirfield in 1972 for the Open. Yet only five years before he had drawn his first significant cheque, £6,000 for fifth place behind Jack Nicklaus in the US Open at Baltusrol.

Not only had he never won so much money, he had never *seen* so much, said Supermex: but then he had as many one-liners as any stand-up comedian about his family's poverty back in Dallas.

So Trevino knew "poor" and, after four years in the Marines, he also knew "tough". But since 1967 he had been getting to know "rich", with two Open victories in America and one in Britain, by a whisker at Birkdale from the Taiwanese Mr Lu, and by two from the 1969 champion, Tony Jacklin.

The favourite at Muirfield was none of these, but the recent winner of both the Masters and the US Open, Jack Nicklaus. Like Arnold Palmer 12 years before, Nicklaus was burning to land the treble Ben Hogan had, uniquely, achieved in 1953. Besides, he knew how to win at Muirfield, having done so both as an amateur and in the 1966 Open, which he dominated with the length and accuracy of his iron play.

This deserted him on the first day, and the shape of things to come was heralded at the end of round two, when Trevino and Jacklin led, a stroke clear of Nicklaus, Johnny Miller, Peter Townsend and Peter Tupling.

Trevino's third round was slow to catch fire, but patience paid off with a quartet of birdies from the 14th to 17th. He holed lengthy putts for the first two. The third, at the short 16th, was a platinum-plated fluke. He thinned his shot from a greenside trap, and his ball was scooting speedily for no one knows where until it struck the flagstick, and vanished quick as a wink.

His 66 gave him a one-stroke lead going into the final round over Jacklin, whose 67 had been distinguished by sterling play from tee to green. When Jacklin and Trevino set out last together on the final day, Nicklaus, struggling six behind the leader, gambled with his driver and was out in 32, briefly disturbing the private duel the final pair were fighting out behind him, but faltering with a bogey at the 16th and failure to birdie the long 17th.

The Trevino-Jacklin plot did not so much thicken as curdle at the 17th, where a long, well-placed drive must be followed by a second of pinpoint accuracy between the sandhills guarding the green. Jacklin was 20 yards short in two. Trevino wandered untidily from side to side, and the closest he could get with his fourth shot was on a bank of fluffy

PRIVATE EVENT *Tony Jacklin and Lee Trevino battle it out at Muirfield*

rough behind the pin. Jacklin chipped on, not very expertly.

Trevino's chip ran smartly into the hole. He compared it afterwards with the last straw that broke ... and so it seemed as Jacklin three-putted. Another bogey on the last compounded British gloom, and gave Trevino his second Open by a stroke from Nicklaus, who, like Arnold Palmer in 1960, missed his treble by a stroke, and with exactly the same total, 279.

Jacklin was third, a shattering descent after the security of 99 per cent of his play. "They" said of this reverse of Jacklin's, as they had of Palmer's defeat at Olympic by Billy Casper, that he was never the same again.

The bottom line in Trevino's victory was the bottom line – 278 for four circuits of Muirfield, held by many to be a classic without peer. His total was a record, four shots fewer than Nicklaus took in 1966. No wonder Trevino reckoned Muirfield in particular, and Scottish links in general, his preferred golf terrain.

Results

British Open, 1972
Muirfield, Scotland

Pos.	Name	Score
1	L. Trevino (US)	71, 70, 66, 71 – 278
2	J. Nicklaus (US)	70, 72, 71, 66 – 279
3	A. Jacklin (GB)	69, 72, 67, 72 – 280

NICKLAUS VS MILLER VS WEISKOPF
Masters, 1975

The outcome of the 1975 Masters tournament at Augusta depended on what might be called a two-way head-to-head. It involved Jack Nicklaus, looking for a fifth green jacket, Johnny Miller and Tom Weiskopf.

Neither Miller nor Weiskopf had won at Augusta, but both were particularly dangerous opponents. Weiskopf had been second three times, twice in the last three years; Miller had been shooting awesomely low scores on the PGA winter Tour, including 24 under par (Phoenix) and 25 under (Tucson).

There was no luck for the tournament's first black golfer, Lee Elder but plenty for the galleries, who saw what Masters regulars still recall as the most exciting finish of them all, perhaps because it concerned three golfers with a penchant for the spectacular.

Miller, seven behind Nicklaus on the opening day with 75, improved to 71 and then 65 on the third, with six birdies in a row from the second hole. That left him still three behind Nicklaus, whose grip had been loosened by his third-round 73, and four behind Weiskopf, he of the huge and stately swing arc, who had moved ahead on 207 thanks to a majestic third round of 66. Miller was in much the same course-burning vein on the final day, and close on the heels of his rivals, who were level at the turn.

The odd putt was clearly going to decide it. That seemed to have been achieved by Weiskopf, for he birdied the 14th. Now Nicklaus hears the commotion behind him, and gets down to the problem of fashioning a birdie, quick. He is standing on the fairway of the par five 15th, 242 yards from the hole. It is reachable with a wood, but Nicklaus decides to use the club he trusts best, his one iron. His ball tears straight at the pin, rolls close by the hole, but 20 feet past. He is to rate this one of the "three finest maximum pressure one irons" of his career. His two-putt birdie is timely, because Weiskopf birdies the 15th too and moves ahead. Miller almost eagles the 15th.

Both stand on the 16th tee watching Nicklaus putt for a two. Nicklaus is playing with Tom Watson, who has put two balls in the lake that makes this 170-yard hole almost all carry. Watson, three months away from his first major, the Open at Carnoustie, putts first, on the same line as the 45-footer Nicklaus faces.

Nicklaus takes in the huge swing on Watson's putt, is convinced he can see the right line with crystal clarity, and strikes firmly up the slope ... and holes out for his two, celebrating with an atypical (for Nicklaus) golfer's gavotte. This is not only a positive move for Nicklaus, but has a negative effect upon Weiskopf, who three-putts the 16th.

A roar from the 17th checks Nicklaus as he shapes up to his birdie putt on the 18th. He is anxious to know who has saved the shot there, and relieved to know it is Miller. So he lags his putt for a safe par four. His cool analysis of the situation gives a clue as to why he kept winning over so many years. Now he can only wait by the 18th green.

Both Weiskopf and Miller drive superbly. Their second shots leave Miller a 15-footer, Weiskopf an eight-footer. The putts are roughly on the same line, but Miller misses left, Weiskopf right. He is second for the fourth time, and this pressure cooker of a Masters provides Nicklaus with his fifth triumph.

Results

Masters, 1975
Augusta, GA

Pos.	Name	Score
1	J. Nicklaus (US)	68, 67, 73, 68 – 276
2	J. Miller (US)	75, 71, 65, 66 – 277
3	T. Weiskopf (US)	69, 72, 66, 70 – 277

OPPOSITE: 5 GREEN JACKETS *Jack Nicklaus on his way to the Masters title*

TURNBERRY TITANS *Nicklaus sinks his "miracle" birdie on the 72nd – but Watson has a tap in for victory*

WATSON vs NICKLAUS
British Open, 1977

The Royal and Ancient took a long time to move the Open to the Ailsa course at Turnberry, and when at last they did, in 1977, this most scenic of courses on the west coast of Scotland rewarded them with a duel between the two leading players of the day, Jack Nicklaus and Tom Watson, that for persistent quality and tension is unlikely ever to be surpassed.

Over the last two rounds, the pair were playing partners, moving further and further away from any challengers. Hubert Green robbed Lee Trevino of third place with 279 – but Green was 12 shots short of victory. For the 1977 Open produced the purest head-to-head that can be imagined in a stroke-play competition, the winner breaking the 72-hole record total by seven.

The Championship was played for the first three days in hot, humid conditions, which followed more than a month of dry weather, so the rough was not up to usual Scottish standards. The wind died away at lunch-time on the first day, so scores were low, though not until well into the gloaming did the leader come in, with 66 . . . John Schroeder, son of lawn tennis champion Ted. Nicklaus, Watson and Trevino had much earlier all gone round in 68 to share second place.

Mark Hayes, from Oklahoma, broke the Open 18-hole record next day. His 63, 13 better than his first round, included a bogey at the 18th. But Roger Maltbie's 66 for a total of 139 gave him the lead, one ahead of Green, Trevino, Nicklaus and Watson.

This latter pair, aged 37 and 27 respectively, set off on their third rounds on what might be called Furious Friday, for they both gave the course, 6,875 yards, par 70 (35=35), a severe pounding. By the 10th, Nicklaus was two ahead with 31 strokes to 33 by Watson, who was level again by the long but eminently reachable 17th, where a birdie each was disappointing for Nicklaus. He had hit his second to three feet. Six birdies and one bogey apiece left the duo level on 203 and all their rivals gasping. The Nicklaus-Watson scores were identical: 68, 70, 65.

Saturday began with more assaults on par, Nicklaus finishing off, with a birdie from 10 feet, a marvellous recovery from an awkward lie with the ball above his feet in the rough at the 2nd.

Watson dropped a shot, and fell three behind when Nicklaus reduced the well-named Woe be Tide short hole to a two from 10 yards. Watson came back at him, saving a shot at the 5th, another at the long 7th, with two drivers and two putts, and yet another at the 8th, only to reach the turn one behind when he could not get his par at Bruce's Castle, Turnberry's Lighthouse hole. Nicklaus out in 33, Watson 34.

Nicklaus stole two shots ahead on the 12th, with a sizeable putt. Watson pulled one back on the 13th, and the other with a two on the 15th from 20 yards: level again, and the form of both men holding up miraculously . . . until Nicklaus hit his four-iron approach to the 17th (500 yards) fat. He pitched up to little over a yard, but missed the putt, a tiny nod expressing his frustration. Watson's birdie put him one up.

Still the Turnberry tale had a twist: Watson's drive at the last was a cautious, straight, one-iron. Nicklaus gambled, but his driver left him in gorse. Watson, playing first, pitched almost to gimme distance. Nicklaus ripped through the gorse and left himself, improbably, a birdie putt of about 12 yards. Even more improbably, he holed it.

Watson, brisk as ever in his tempo at this searching moment, tapped his ball underground for his second Open.

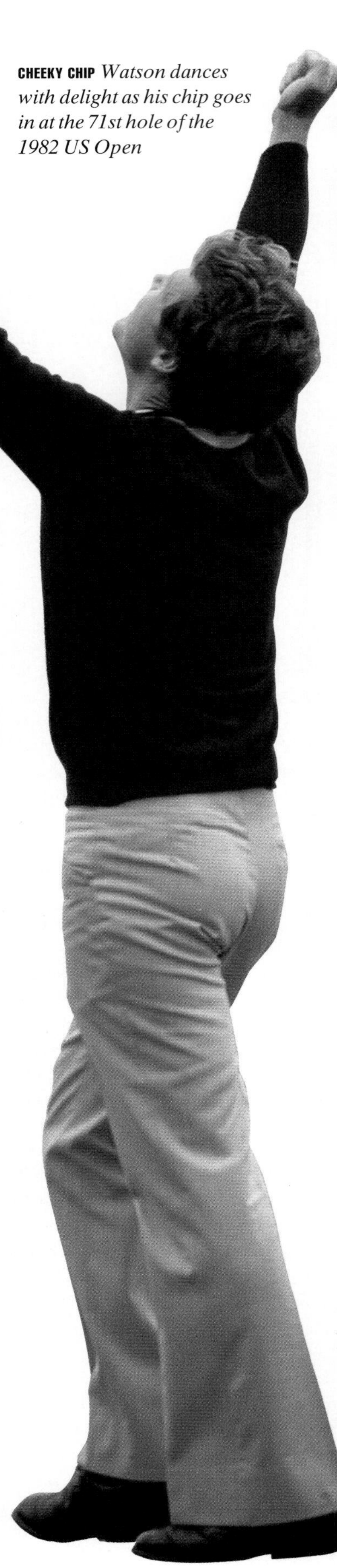

CHEEKY CHIP *Watson dances with delight as his chip goes in at the 71st hole of the 1982 US Open*

Results

British Open, 1977
Turnberry, Scotland

Pos.	Name	Score
1	T. Watson (us)	68, 70, 65, 65 – 268
2	J. Nicklaus (us)	68, 70, 65, 66 – 269
3	H. Green (us)	72, 66, 74, 67 – 279

WATSON vs NICKLAUS
US Open, 1982

Tom Watson approached the US Open at Pebble Beach in 1982 with three British Opens and two Masters to his credit, but as yet no US Open title. Jack Nicklaus's thoughts were that his unmatched career record would touch even further heights of achievement if he could win a fifth Open and move one ahead of his fellow record-holders, Willie Anderson, Bobby Jones and Ben Hogan; and his hopes were high when he considered that he had won the only previous Open held at Pebble Beach ten years earlier. Even for Nicklaus, now 42, time was running out.

Bruce Devlin shared the lead with the 1981 British Open champion, Bill Rogers, on the first day, but headed the field by two shots with a 69 for 139 at 36 holes.

Watson and Nicklaus were like prudent mountaineers, quietly working themselves into position for a dart at the summit. Watson was steadiest, though his putter had been his saviour in the first round, when his golf through the green had not been his best. But 72, 72, 68 = 212 earned him a share of the lead at 54 holes with Rogers. Devlin had faded to a 75 and stood on 214 along with George Burns, Scott Simpson and reigning champion David Graham.

Nicklaus was one under par for the Championship, a stroke behind this quartet. By the 9th in the final round on another gloomy day only Rogers was ahead of him, by a stroke: and he had caught Watson. Nicklaus bogeyed the 1st and parred the 2nd, then had five birdies in a row, including twos at the 5th and 7th, though another bogey at the 8th cut his advantage against par to four.

Behind him Watson could make no impression on par over the first half of the course, though the first six holes offer the best chance of birdies. He started back with a par that must have seemed like a birdie, for his second shot to the 10th might have bounced down on to the beach, but instead fell into spiky kikuyu grass below the green. His sand wedge left him a good eight paces from the hole, but down went the putt. A birdie from more than 20 feet at the 11th put him ahead, because his playing partner Rogers bogeyed it.

A poor bunker shot at the 12th cost him a shot, but for the moment he was one ahead of Nicklaus. Watson's birdie putt at the 13th missed by a fraction, while Nicklaus was saving a shot at the 15th, and they were level. A 35-foot putt at the long 14th was, Watson considered, the putt that won him the title.

Rogers fell away, but Watson missed a birdie chance at the 15th, and was happy, in the circumstances, with a bogey at the next. There, thanks to falling foul of a newly fortified bunker, his fourth shot was perforce a 50-foot putt with a 10-foot break. Watson managed to get it stone dead.

Relieved, he went to the 17th level with Nicklaus, who was just coming off the last green with a round of 69 and a total of 284. When he saw Watson pull his tee shot at the 209-yard 17th into thick rough 20 feet left of the flag, the odds against Nicklaus winning his fifth US Open were suddenly considerably shorter. Now Watson played the *chip* that won him the title. The sun came out, his ball was on top of the grass, and he easily sank his chip with a sand iron, landing it just on the green, a foot to the right to allow for the break.

He calmed down after a little jumping about and rejoicing, laid up cautiously at the long 18th, but pitched and putted for a final birdie for a 70, beating Nicklaus by two. No wonder Watson was the author of that definitive book on the short game, *Getting Up and Down.*

Results

US Open, 1982
Pebble Beach, CA

Pos.	Name	Score
1	T. Watson (US)	72, 72, 68, 70 – 282
2	J. Nicklaus (US)	74, 70, 71, 69 – 284
3	B. Clampett, D. Pohl and W. Rogers (ALL US)	– 286

BALLESTEROS VS PRICE

British Open, 1988

Spectators were relatively few and thus indisputably lucky as the duel between Severiano Ballesteros, from Spain, and Zimbabwean Nick Price reached its climax in the 1988 Open Championship at Royal Lytham and St Anne's on the Lancashire coast.

Smaller galleries were ensured when rain wiped out the third round, pushing the final round over to the Monday. The fortunate 15,000 had a close and uncluttered view, in greatly improved conditions, of classic stroke play. The second day's gate of 43,101 was a record for one day, and the extra day brought an overall record of 205,857.

The Saturday wash-out was a sur-

QUIET, PLEASE *Seve Ballesteros begs for silence to let his 1988 Open Championship victim Nick Price putt out for second place*

prise to all on the early holes where most of the leaders were playing. Greens 9 to 12 were worst affected by rain, two weather systems having apparently collided over the course.

The collision between Ballesteros and Price did not develop fully until Monday. Price led Ballesteros by a stroke at the half-way stage, and after his delayed third round of 69 he led Ballesteros and Nick Faldo by two. The three of them were to play together as the last group for the final 18, with Sandy Lyle, a further stroke adrift in fourth place, in the penultimate threesome with Edwardo Romero of Argentina and Larry Nelson of the USA.

Price had been in a more dominant position (three ahead with six holes to play) at Troon in 1982, when he admits he was convinced he was going to win his first major title. Tom Watson got the trophy, though, after spending nearly an hour in the clubhouse watching one player after another fail to match his total of 284, with Price proving the most fallible of his pursuers.

Two of the champions now pressing Price, Faldo and Lyle, soon found the Spanish/South African pace too hot. Lyle took 40 to the turn, and although Faldo's five at the long seventh does not sound damaging, his companions had an eagle apiece there. So the battle became a duel between Ballesteros, with two Opens and two Masters behind him, and Price, armed only with determination to avoid another Troon.

Battle was unrelenting, Ballesteros saving six shots on holes 7 to 12, with single-putt birdies on holes 8 to 11. Price had lost his two-shot lead after nine holes, having bogeyed the 2nd and failed to match the Spaniard's three at the 8th. Standing on the 10th tee, Ballesteros had taken 31 strokes, four under par. Price was two under.

They were still level on the 16th tee. Though Price dropped a shot at the 11th, so did Ballesteros as his tee shot fell short at the 198-yard 12th. Price looked good for the lead at the 13th, where he pitched close. His opponent didn't, but still got a birdie to stay level. Price missed a great chance at the 14th, where both players missed the green. Price pulled his par putt from four feet after seeing Ballesteros chip on and miss *his* par putt.

Condign punishment followed at once for this untimely lapse, Ballesteros pitching dead with a nine-iron at the 16th. Price's fighting qualities were undiminished at the 17th, where he played the bravest of recoveries from the right rough, but he was still one behind.

Chipper extraordinary Ballesteros almost holed from the back of the final green, leaving Price with a putt to tie. He was too strong, missed the one back, and lost by two.

Ballesteros's 65 was the lowest winning final round yet – "the best of my life", he said. Price's final 69 made him the only player who had broken par every round. None could say this was a chance wasted, as at Troon. He had not lost: Ballesteros had won, and never spoke a truer word than when he told Price: "Keep playing like you did today and your turn will come."

Results

British Open, 1988
Royal Lytham & St Anne's, Lancs

Pos.	Name	Score
1	S. Ballesteros (SP)	67, 71, 70, 65 – 273
2	N. Price (ZIM)	70, 67, 69, 69 – 275
3	N. Faldo (GB)	71, 69, 68, 71 – 279

FALDO vs NORMAN
Masters, 1996

The 1996 Masters made a cold start on April 11, the gates opening late to the public because of frost. The management wanted no footprints to mar Augusta's emerald perfection.

Temperatures soon soared into the 70s and 80s. Greg Norman, often an over-cautious starter here, was incandescent: out in 33 and back in 30, with birdies on nine of the last 12 holes, he equalled Nick Price's course record 63, finishing with a 24-foot birdie putt on the 18th for his best opening round at Augusta.

Phil Mickelson, who had already won twice on the '96 US Tour, also came home in 30, but was two shots behind the Australian. Nick Faldo's 69 was his best opening round since his first Masters victory in 1989. He said:"There's a long way to go yet."

He greatly improved his position with a second round of 67, Norman "slipping", so to speak, to a 69. He was still four ahead of Faldo, who joined him to make up the last pair out on Saturday and Sunday.

Norman had the better of it in their first 18 holes together, one

under par against one over by the Englishman, extending his lead to six strokes. His gritty third-round performance on the ever-faster greens, after starting badly with a miss from four feet at the second, and three-putting the third and fourth, was indeed heroic, especially the bogey putt he holed at the short 12th after hitting into Rae's Creek. Faldo bogeyed from the back edge. The pair had been cautioned for slow play at the eighth, but nothing disturbed Norman's concentration for long. He drove with passion and precision.

The last day's weather was at its Sunday best. Did Norman recall, as he and Faldo stood on the first tee, their third round together at St Andrews in the 1990 British Open, they had started level and Faldo had finished nine ahead? Ah, but he was six up now. Perhaps he did remember the Old Course horrors, for he at once lost a shot to Faldo, after finding sand by the first green. The speed at which he lost the other five strokes was astounding, often received in paralysed silence by the galleries.

The second went when he overshot the 250-yard fourth. He regained it with a birdie at the fifth, lost it again to Faldo's four foot birdie putt at the 180-yard sixth, and he was down to two ahead at the turn, for Faldo birdied the eighth and Norman bogeyed the ninth – out in 38 to Faldo's 34.

A pulled second by Norman at the 10th brought Faldo to within a shot; three putts at the 11th and they were all square. Faldo was implacable in his course management, notably at the 12th, where he resolutely turned away from risk at this little (155 yards) tester, and aimed left of the bunker just over the creek. Norman went "straight at it" but did not even clear the bunker. His ball bounced off the bank into the water. This time there was no saving bogey putt; two down.

Both men birdied the 15th, but was there a suggestion of a faster swing as Norman hooked straight into the lake at the 16th? He did not bother to watch the splash-down; four behind. Faldo's finishing touch was a reminder of Sandy Lyle's Masters – out of 18th fairway sand, a 20-foot downhill putt for birdie, a 67, a five-shot victory, a sixth major title.

He had three-putted once, in 72 holes, and achieved an 11-stroke swing in the last 18. This was the 10th Masters won by European Ryder Cup men in 17 years.

Faldo believes that Norman's collapse will be remembered longer than his 67, the best on a day when the average score was fractionally over par 72. His body language over the last few holes was clear in its expression of sympathy for the Augustan fall of Norman.

Results

Masters, 1996
Augusta, Georgia, USA

Pos	Name	Score
1	N. Faldo (ENG)	69, 67, 73, 67 – 276
2	G. Norman (AUS)	63, 69, 71, 78 – 281
3	P. Mickelson (US)	65, 73, 72, 72 – 282

EVER CLOSER *Faldo putts at the 10th, to get within a shot of Norman*

THE FAMOUS COURSES

An integral part of golf's unique charm is that the game is played in such imposing settings. The golfing landscape encompasses Florida swamplands, Arizona desert, Persian Gulf oases, English country estate parklands and the bare dunescapes of so many links courses around Britain. The most famous links course of all may be the Old Course at St Andrews, pictured below, where the R&A clubhouse stands behind the 18th green.

AUGUSTA NATIONAL

Augusta, Georgia, USA
Opened: *1933*
Designers: *Alister Mackenzie, Bobby Jones*
Yardage: *6,925* **Par:** *72*
Major events: *Masters 1934-1942, 1946-*

Not many people could tell you what the first nine holes look like. But from the 10th onwards the Augusta National is by far the world's best known course. Every hole on that last nine has become etched on the retinas of keen golf followers.

It hardly needs saying that this is because the Masters is the only major championship that keeps to the same venue every year, and Augusta the only course which hosts a major championship every year. The potent images return again and again as the contenders battle for the Masters title – not least on the crucial stretch known as Amen Corner. Will he go for a perilous flag set close to water at the left of the 11th? What will happen when the leader tries to judge the swirl of the wind above the tops of the trees on the short 12th? And then at the 13th, quite a short par five, he must surely go for the green with an eagle a possibility and a birdie almost certain if he carries the creek which fronts it... Yet many have found that creek and then been unable to get enough bite on their fourth shot.

Perhaps the most effective golf shot of all time was played at Augusta in 1935, in only the second year of what was then the Augusta Annual Invitational Tournament. With four holes to play, Gene Sarazen needed three birdies to tie Craig Wood, home and dry in the clubhouse. At the par five 15th, Sarazen hit a good drive and then let it rip with his four wood. His ball hit the bank beyond the water hazard and from there ran on and on, and into the hole for a double eagle. With that one shot he had caught Wood.

Only a handful of spectators saw the shot, but among them was Robert Tyre Jones Junior, who had taken a stroll from the clubhouse to see how his old opponents, Gene Sarazen and his playing partner Walter Hagen, were finishing off their rounds – and how the course was playing. As well as being arguably the greatest golfer of all time, Bobby Jones was also highly influential in the creation of one of the world's great courses. But Jones was a modest man. Incontestably the greatest player of the 1920s, he didn't think this in the least qualified him to design a golf course. That was a job for a specialist. However, when Jones was first taken to see the Augusta property by an investment banker, Clifford Roberts (who would become the mainstay of Masters organization until his death in the late 1970s), he immediately grasped the potential, and together they called in the British course architect Alister Mackenzie, whose work at Cypress Point in California had much impressed Jones, when he had played there in 1929.

Opinions differ as to how much Augusta owes to Jones, Mackenzie, course superintendents and later architects who were called in to undertake revisions. What is beyond dispute, however, is that Mackenzie produced the original design in consultation with Jones. In particular, Jones hit hundreds of shots to help show how a hole would play for players of high quality. Between them, they came up with a course where a club player might play to his handicap. The fairways are broad, the rough is almost non-existent, and the greens are not too fearsome until cut to Masters pace. It's this last factor, together with often fiendish pin placements, which make Augusta a terror in Masters week.

AUGUSTA 16TH *Where Jack Nicklaus holed one of his greatest putts to beat Miller and Weiskopf for the 1975 Masters*

BALLYBUNION, OLD COURSE

Ballybunion, County Kerry, Ireland
Opened: *1896*
Designer: *Anon*
Yardage: *6,503* **Par:** *71*
Major events: *None*

This course is unlikely to hold major events because, like Dornoch, it is so remote, but with the new Cashen course as well, you have here perhaps the best 36 holes of links golf in the world. The Old, by itself, ranks very high on everyone's list. As Tom Watson said during a visit: "Ballybunion is a course on which many golf architects should live and play before they build golf courses."

If the 1st hole is a comfortable enough start with a drive to a wide fairway, and downhill at that, the 2nd is more testing by far. You have to miss bunkers from the tee but also have to be long to have much chance of making it up to the green. The 3rd is 220 yards but plays downhill to a severely undulating green. At the 6th, after two relatively easy par fives, you head for the Atlantic Ocean. It is not a long par four – 364 yards – but the wind can play havoc. At the next two holes you play directly from the cliff edge and have a glorious view along the Atlantic shore, but at the 8th playing away from it with a following wind. This is no great help, as the hole is a short par three and the green will be more difficult to hold because of the reduced backspin. Apparently, on one visit Tom Watson played the hole four times and didn't once succeed in keeping his ball on the green. At the 9th, the drive is between sandhills but can be helped onwards by a couple of steps in the fairway. There is a central bunker short of the green and a steep rise to the putting surface.

This has already been outstanding golf, but many believe most of the real Ballybunion comes on the second nine. The 10th heads back towards the Ocean, bending leftwards through a valley, and at the 11th tee it is worth stopping to take in the view. Then a downhill shot confronts the player – but not an easy one. There is the beach one side and sandhills the other. Even a good shot can get into difficulties on the severely undulating fairway. If all has gone well with the tee shot, the second must be well aimed between the sandhills which protect the green.

The 12th, a par three of 192 yards, usually plays into the wind and, because the green is in the sandhills and is quite steeply sloping at the front, needs a full carry on the shot. The 13th, 484 yards, is not in the least a long par five but does demand caution. For those going for the green in two there is a stream perhaps 80 yards short. Then come two par three holes, of which the second presents an extremely testing shot to a well protected, two-tiered green.

The 17th has the most spectacular tee shot on the course, high up with dunes on either side. You are also heading straight for the United States of America. There is a sharp dog-leg left.

If the last hole is a bit of a disappointment, you can at least be sure of a warm welcome in the clubhouse.

DRAMATIC VIEW *The 7th at Ballybunion has the Atlantic Ocean crashing into the cliffs all down the right side and the prevailing wind in the players' faces*

BALTUSROL

Springfield, New Jersey, USA
Opened: *1895*
Designer: *Albert W. Tillinghast*
Yardage: *7,022* **Par:** *70*
Major events: *US Open 1903, 1915, 1936, 1954, 1967, 1980, 1993. US Women's Open 1961, 1985. US Amateur 1904, 1926, 1946. US Women's Amateur 1901, 1911*

Baltusrol's history had a somewhat macabre beginning. The club derives its name from Mr Baltus Roll, a wealthy farmer of Dutch extraction, who in 1831 was murdered in front of his wife by two thieves who believed he had a fortune hidden in his house.

The Baltusrol property eventually came to Louis Keller, a gentleman farmer and socialite, who decided to build his own course in the early 1890s. His first professional was Willie Anderson, the Scot who won four US Opens between 1901 and 1905, one of those over that original course at Baltusrol. Today there are two courses, the Upper and Lower, neither of which bears any resemblance to their predecessor. Albert Tillinghast was brought in to handle the design around 1922, at a time when golf was experiencing another boom.

While the Upper occupies the high ground, it is the Lower that has been the venue for a host of major championships, including five US Opens. Far from picturesque, it makes up for it in the challenge it presents to golfers of all standards. It is long, varied and something of an architectural anomaly in that it has only two par-fives and they are the 17th and 18th, thereby providing a sting in the tail. The 17th measures a monstrous 630 yards, which is a three-shot hole even for the long hitters. Just a few have covered the distance in two lusty blows. In the last US Open, in 1993, many were expecting John Daly to provide the fireworks, and he didn't disappoint, but Sandy Lyle did it first with aplomb.

Long before you reach the 17th there are other mountains to conquer, starting with the dog-leg par four 3rd at a cool 466 yards. Around the landing area, the fairway turns left and slopes downhill towards a creek that cuts across just in front of the green. The green is big but undulating and one of the most difficult to putt on because of its subtle rolls.

The short 4th can measure between 150 and 200 yards depending on the placement of the tee, and requires just a solid iron shot across a lake to a green that slopes left-to-right and back-to-front. When the hole was redesigned by Robert Trent Jones, members complained that it was too tough. Jones disagreed and, together with three other bigwigs, went out to test it. When it was his turn to play, he stepped up and hit a superb shot that pitched short of the flag and gently rolled into the cup for a hole-in-one. "As you can see, Gentlemen," said Jones, shrugging, "this hole is not too tough."

The straight 6th and the dog-leg 11th, both well over 400 yards and requiring two solid blows, can easily see shots surrendered, as can the 401-yard 13th, where the drive must carry the ditch which runs parallel to the fairway after crossing it. After the ultra-long 17th, the 542-yard 18th is played from an elevated tee down into the fairway then over a creek up to an elevated green protected by four bunkers at the front, left and right.

Baltusrol's US Opens have produced some famous winners as well as some daring deeds. In 1954, Ed Furgol, hooked his drive on the final hole, then played his second through the trees on to a fairway of the Upper course before playing back to the 18th green to win. In 1967 and 1980 Jack Nicklaus emerged victorious. On the first occasion he carded a closing 65 to beat Arnold Palmer by four strokes. In 1980 he opened with a record-equalling 63, matched by Tom Weiskopf, then went on to win his fourth US Open with a record aggregate of 272. This was matched by Lee Janzen at Baltusrol in the 1993 Open.

NO MARGIN FOR ERROR *With water guarding the green and almost no fringe, laying up is a safe option at challenging Baltusrol*

CARNOUSTIE

Angus, Scotland
Opened: *1842*
Designer: *Allan Robertson*
Yardage: *7,272* **Par:** *72*
Major events: *Open Championship 1931, 1937, 1953, 1968, 1975. Amateur Championship 1947, 1966, 1971, 1992. British Women's Amateur 1961, 1973*

When the Royal and Ancient Golf Club announced that the 1999 Open Championship would be held at Carnoustie, a huge sigh of relief seemed to permeate the whole of golf. The return of the world's most prestigious championship to these great links was long overdue. Also rejoicing will be the ghosts of all those past champions who have sampled the links, as well as the many sons of Carnoustie who, in years long past, went out to spread the golfing gospel around the world.

Carnoustie's spell in golf's backwaters had nothing to do with the quality of the course; more with what is required off it. The lack of a suitably large hotel in the town was given as the main reason, difficulty of access as another. The growth in popularity of the Open has made these important considerations, but a lengthy, concerted effort by the good folk of Angus and golf fans in general plus a new hotel scheme will see the world's top golfers back where they belong in 1999.

Carnoustie's history seems to have begun in 1842, when a large tract of land was bought from the Earl of Dalhousie and a 10-hole links was laid out by Allan Robertson. This was extended to 18 holes in 1867 by Tom Morris; Willie Park Junior made further alterations, but it was James Braid who remodelled the links in 1926 to what we recognize as today's supreme test.

Carnoustie has neither the deep-seated traditions of St Andrews or Muirfield, nor the breathtaking beauty of Royal County Down or Turnberry. But what it does is throw down the gauntlet, and a glance at its Open Championship roll of honour proves that only a real champion successfully takes it up. Tommy Armour, Henry Cotton, Ben Hogan, Gary Player and Tom Watson are as good a quintet as you could find and each one etched his style into Carnoustie's folklore.

Armour, one of many Scots who left for America, triumphed in 1931 at the expense of Macdonald Smith. Cotton's win in 1937, the second of his three Opens, was gained against the victorious American Ryder Cup team. Hogan's victory in 1953 on his only Open appearance was, many feel, the greatest seen at Carnoustie. Each of his four rounds was lower than the one before, and he finished with 68. Player completed his second Open success there in 1968 when the course measured 7,252 yards, the longest in Open history. The 1975 contest brought a young Watson to the attention of golf fans as he beat Jack Newton of Australia in an 18-hole play-off. Since then these giant links have seen no Open action. Happily, 1999 will change all that and provide golf with another truly great champion.

Carnoustie is basically a flat course, but don't let that fool you. It is rugged and can be brutal if you stray from its fairways. It also has some famous features which set it apart from its rivals. It has only three short holes, all far from easy, and three par fives, one of which, the 14th, is named Spectacles after the twin bunkers that stand guard in the face of the ridge that runs across the fairway less than 100 yards from the green.

Yet it is the finishing stretch that poses the greatest threat. It begins with the long 14th, then comes the 461-yard 15th, whose green is set into an attractive bowl, followed by the 250-yard 16th, a tough par three that has a well-guarded plateau green.

The Barry Burn crosses the 17th fairway three times, putting a premium on precise shot-making; and if you negotiate this par four safely, you have to do it all again on the return trip, with the Burn lying in wait ahead of the tee and the green on this 486-yard home hole. A finish to be feared.

DON'T GET BURNED *Barry Burn must be crossed several times before reaching the haven of Carnoustie's 18th green*

EMIRATES, DUBAI

United Arab Emirates
Opened: *1988*
Designer: *Karl Litton*
Yardage: *7,102* **Par:** *72*
Major event: *Desert Classic, annually*

HIGH-TECH ETHNIC *The Emirates clubhouse "Bedouin tents", in concrete, marble and glass, link past and present*

If you take the road leading north out of Dubai, with the Persian Gulf away to the right, the last thing you would expect to find is a golf course. Each year development increases, more office blocks, more hotels, more traffic, but soon it is the desert, stretching endlessly to the west, that dominates.

Yet, within some 20 minutes of the city's limits, appears the oasis that is the Emirates Golf Club, home of the Dubai Desert Classic which to many marks the serious beginning of the PGA European Tour season. It has been played there each year since 1989 (except for 1991) and has produced some outstanding champions, Severiano Ballesteros, Ernie Els, Fred Couples and Colin Montgomerie among them.

The first feature to catch the eye is the clubhouse, three inter-linked concrete, marble and glass buildings in the style of Bedouin "tents", though it is the golf course that catches the imagination. It is one of the very best on the whole European Tour circuit and one of the wonders of modern technology, which has also proved a magnet for birds of passage and native species. Before course construction began a mere 10 species of bird life were to be found there. Recently 230 have been seen, including, some never observed before in the Emirates, such as the Oriental Pratincole. In a climate of negligible rainfall in arid land, this golf oasis has been made possible by pumping 750,000 gallons of desalinated sea-water every day.

So effective is it that to stand in the middle of the course, set in a fenced rectangle to keep the drifting sand at bay, one has no conception of the desert so close at hand. There is a gentle movement to the land, the fairways are green and lush, the putting surfaces firm and true. It is also a fine test of golf. No wonder the players enthuse, enjoying in late February/early March the sort of temperature hoped for in British high summer. The two loops of nine holes both end beneath the impressive clubhouse, the green of the ninth and 18th shared in the shape of a banana with a lake at their fronts. The ninth is a par four of 463 yards, the 18th a par five of 547 yards. Both demand good shots to the green, the 18th more so since, come the final day, a birdie may be needed which means the gamble of a long second to carry the water.

No one did it better than Montgomerie in 1996. A stroke ahead of Miguel Angel Jiménez, Monte knew he would probably need a four. He faced a shot with a carry of 220 yards, took his driver "off the deck", made it and won the title. It was nominated as the shot of the year.

A year later Ian Woosnam, in contrast, played a shot which, though the date was only March 2, became a strong candidate for selection as the worst shot of the year 1997. All he needed at the 18th was a par five to win. Justifiably he therefore played the hole as a five, laying up with his second. He then mis-hit a straightforward pitch 75 yards into the water, went into a play-off and, together with Greg Norman, lost it to a little- known Australian left-hander, Richard Green.

There is water, too, at two short holes, the fourth and seventh, as well as at the fifth, but there is more to the course than that. There are more splendid holes, notably the eighth, a par four of 434 yards played from a high tee to rising fairway curving gently left to right. Played invariably into the wind, the second shot, with the flag fluttering against the sky-line, is as demanding as any.

So, too, is the golf course itself, but like many another, it needs a good wind for it to be at its best. Whatever the weather in 1997, it seems doubtful if anyone could possibly have enjoyed the Emirates more than José-Maria Olazabal. His glittering career looked for more than a year to have been ended by foot problems. New treatments brought him back to golfing life to the extent of a 65 in the third round, a £10,605 cheque for his nine under par total of 279, and joint 12th place.

MERION

Ardmore, Philadelphia, Pennsylvania, USA
Opened: *1912*
Designer: *Hugh Wilson*
Yardage: *6,544* **Par:** *70*
Major events: *US Open 1934, 1950, 1971, 1981. US Amateur 1916, 1924, 1930, 1966, 1989. US Women's Amateur 1904, 1909, 1926, 1949. Curtis Cup 1954. World Amateur Team Championship 1960*

The original Merion course, in the 1890s, was squeezed into 100 acres, formerly used for cricket, on the outskirts of Philadelphia. When the rubber-cored ball made it obsolete, the club had to look further afield.

Soon a plot of 127 acres of old farmland together with a stone quarry was bought, and the club assigned a group of young members to handle the designing. Among them was Hugh Wilson, an insurance salesman and first-class golfer. But before any work was carried out, Wilson spent seven months travelling around Britain, learning the fundamentals of constructing outstanding golf holes. On his return he set to work with the assistance of Richard Francis to build the new course at Ardmore, opened in 1912. He continued to refine the course for another dozen years, but unfortunately, it was the only complete layout to bear his name as he died prematurely in 1925 at the age of 46.

Merion is noted above all for its greens. They come in all shapes and sizes, beautifully shaped, cleverly contoured, sometimes on two levels, sometimes shelved into a shoulder of a hill, sometimes sloping away to the back. But each is protected by a bunker, a creek or a heavy rough.

A curiosity of the course is that, instead of flags, Wilson decided to mark the holes with a wicker basket atop the flagsticks. He is believed to have got the idea from Scotland where it used to be the practice to place lobster pots as markers.

Another feature of Merion is the infinite variety of its holes. There are long par fours and short par fours, two par fives, one of 600 yards, the 4th, while the short holes measure between 129 yards and 224 yards. There are right-hand dog-legs and left-hand dog-legs, while the final three holes provide what many feel is the toughest finish of any of America's US Open courses.

The 16th is the celebrated Quarry Hole of 430 yards, where the approach must carry the old quarry workings to a plateau green. The 17th is a 224-yard par three from an elevated tee back across the quarry to a green encircled by bunkers. The 458-yard 18th requires a blind drive across the quarry once again, then a medium or long iron often from a downhill lie to a green flanked right and left by bunkers. Golfers who manage par figures over that trio and can count themselves good players.

SANDY WASTES *The 10th hole is typical of the nightmare that awaits an errant shot at treacherous Merion*

One of Merion's first claims to fame was in 1930 when it was the scene of the final act of Bobby Jones's Grand Slam. On its famous 11th, a hole of only 370 yards, the drive is down a slight valley, followed by a crucial second shot up over a brook to a green flanked on one side by the same ribbon of water and a bunker on the other.

Jones, who was eight up on Gene Homans in the final of the US Amateur, drove safely, hit the green with his second and two-putted for par and a half to win 8 and 7, adding his national title to the British Amateur won at St Andrews, the British Open at Hoylake, and the US Open at Interlachen.

Merion has staged many of America's national championships. Its first US Open came in 1934 when Olin Dutra won. The 1950 event saw Ben Hogan, hardly recovered from his horrific road accident a year earlier, tie with Lloyd Mangrum and George Fazio, then win the 18-hole play-off by four strokes. In 1971, Jack Nicklaus finished tied with Lee Trevino but it was the latter who prevailed in the play-off, 68 to 71. Merion's most recent US Open, in 1981, went to Australian David Graham with a final 67 which was little short of perfection – he missed one fairway, but still got a birdie, and hit every green in regulation.

TENTED VILLAGE *Corporate sponsorship (at Muirfield in 1980) and other entertainment for spectators mean that players now have competition for fans' attention*

MUIRFIELD

Gullane, East Lothian, Scotland
Opened: *1891*
Designers: *Old Tom Morris, Harry Colt*
Yardage: *6,941* **Par:** *72*
Major events: *Open Championship 1892, 1896, 1901, 1906, 1912, 1929, 1935, 1948, 1959, 1966, 1972, 1980, 1987, 1992. British Amateur 1897, 1903, 1909, 1920, 1926, 1932, 1954, 1974, 1990. Ryder Cup 1973. Walker Cup 1959, 1979. Curtis Cup 1952, 1984*

It is often said that Muirfield was designed by Old Tom Morris, and he did indeed lay out the first course. However, his original design was by no means ideal, and little more than the site of one green seems to have survived. The Muirfield of today is largely the work of Harry Colt during the mid-1920s. It was Colt, for instance, not Morris, who produced the two loops of nine holes, each ending at the clubhouse. Since Colt's time the course seems to have little changed, which is not surprising, for Colt was an architect of genius, whereas Morris certainly wasn't.

Some say that all courses ought to begin with a hole that causes worry; others that there should be a comfortable start and that the really testing stuff should come at the end. The 1st hole at Muirfield is one that all the competitors in a British Open are very glad to leave with a par four written on their card. It is long and has threatening bunkers, but overall the most difficult holes are the par threes, each offering a tight target to a raised green, with the fall-away often being to deep bunkers, where it can be necessary to play out sideways or even backwards.

One of the best holes is the 9th, a par five. It is reachable for modern professionals in two, but there are dangers. Out of bounds lurks along the left, which seemed to have destroyed John Cook's chances in the 1992 Open when he produced a snap hook over the wall, but he then played superbly – only to throw it all away on the last two holes of the championship. On this hole, Tom Simpson, the noted architect, placed a bunker more or less in mid-fairway short of the green. It is now known as "Simpson's Folly" but greatly affects the character of the shot in.

Muirfield is one of the most popular links courses for British Open competitors. The movement of the ground is gentle, which generally means that there are very few blind shots indeed. In a press tent interview at the 1992 Open, Jack Nicklaus described the course as "just a flat field". Seriously, however, he had liked it well enough to name his most prized design in the USA "Muirfield Village", though this may partly have been due to his wish to commemorate his first British Open win here in 1966.

That year, the course was extremely testing, with the rough allowed to grow so long that Doug Sanders remarked that he didn't mind about the championship but would like to have the hay concession. Nicklaus won largely by keeping out of the rough and choosing to play irons off the tees – and at that time he was perhaps the best long-iron player in the world.

Another memorable Open came in 1972, when Nicklaus played a thunderous last round, coming from behind, while the main battle was fought out between Tony Jacklin and Lee Trevino.

As late as the 71st hole, Jacklin appeared to have the title in his grasp before he pitched a little weakly and three-putted. In the space of a very few minutes the title was Trevino's after he chipped in on the same hole.

The course is the property of the Honourable Company of Edinburgh Golfers. Founded in 1744, they initially played at Leith Links, and later at Musselburgh, before they moved to what is certainly their final home at Muirfield. Their clubhouse contains some fine paintings, a silver club and a copy of Thomas Mathison's *The Goff*, the first publication devoted solely to golf.

PEBBLE BEACH

Monterey Peninsula, California, USA
Opened: *1919*
Designer: *Jack Neville*
Yardage: *6,799* **Par:** *72*
Major events: *US Open 1972, 1982, 1992, 2000. US PGA 1977. US Amateur 1947, 1961*

Most great golf courses have been designed by acknowledged great architects. But there are exceptions, the most famous being the Old Course at St Andrews, where local golfers evolved a route through the linksland over the years. Pebble Beach was also an amateur creation, but came from the creativity of one man, Jack Neville. He was an amateur golfer of great local distinction, winner of the California Amateur on five occasions and a choice for the 1923 US Walker Cup team. The property developer Sam Morse thought he was the man to design him a golf course. It was a decision which worked out.

In later years, Neville said: "The golf course was there all the time. All I did was find the holes." And what holes they are.

Though nearby Cypress Point has been described as the Sistine Chapel of golf, and also as "the dream of an artist who had been drinking gin and sobering up on absinthe", the Pacific holes at Pebble Beach are no less dramatic.

The drama begins at the 4th, which is a short par four, usually playing at about 325 yards but with the cliffs threatening any approach shot that drifts right. The 5th, like so many par fives, is not particularly difficult and, if the golf is not going well, there is at least the reward of a splendid view along to the 10th green. The 7th is apparently an easy par three at 120 yards, but the green is set at an angle to the line of play.

Then comes one of the toughest par fours in world golf. The tee shot is blind but the real problem is that it must be precisely weighted to fall short of a chasm, but not too short, as the shot to the green will then be longer than most will prefer. Nicklaus has called this "the finest second shot on any course I have seen". The next two holes are well over 400 yards, play into the prevailing wind and call for tee shots close to the cliff edge to ease the shots to the greens.

The 17th, particularly at the close of a championship, is a very demanding par three, close on 220 yards, with a green set across the line of play and tightly bunkered. It was here, in the final round of the 1983 US Open, that one of the truly momentous shots in golf history was struck. Tom Watson had just dropped a shot at the 16th to be only level with Jack Nicklaus. Here his tee shot missed the green, leaving him a little pitch shot from the rough which seemed doomed to race past the hole. But Watson thought positively. He tried to hole it, and did so. He was back in the lead and needed only to par the final hole to win. In fact, he birdied it, to win his first and only US Open, and to deprive Jack Nicklaus of his fifth.

That spectacular last hole presents a classic tee shot situation. The bold line is along the cliff edge, having carried an inlet. To the right is less dangerous but a pine can then block the second shot. This is one of very few par 5s that have been seldom reached in two. Perhaps it has not settled many championships, but those who win have been brave.

GREAT SHORT HOLE *The Pacific Ocean crashes on to rocks behind the 7th green at Pebble Beach, where the wind may demand a five-iron for the 120-yard tee shot*

PINE VALLEY

Clementon, New Jersey, USA
Opened: *1919*
Designer: *George Crump*
Yardage: *6,765* **Par:** *70*
Major events: *Walker Cup 1936, 1985*

A beautiful monster is how Pine Valley has been described. Laid out on a huge 184-acre bunker, with forests of pine, larch and oak trees, a generous amount of water and thick, dense undergrowth, it is the most terrifying course in golf. There are no continuous fairways, just islands of green amid the never-ending sandy wasteland, plus tees and greens which can be regarded as refuges to which the golfer inevitably struggles out of the mire.

Pine Valley is the work of Philadelphia hotelier George Crump, the leader of a band of golfers from the Philadelphia Country Club who made occasional trips to play at Atlantic City. One day on their journey by train, Crump spotted a piece of land which he felt would be ideal for golf, and on investigation found virgin forest, swamps, and impenetrable bush, but all on a sandy soil.

After spending some days at the site, Crump persuaded 18 of his friends to contribute $1,000 each, and the land, reported to be the highest ground in southern New Jersey, was bought in 1912. The course took seven years to build, and Crump took to living in a small bungalow on the site, directing the felling of trees, the building of dams to form lakes, the lay-out of holes and the positioning of greens.

However, in January 1918, Crump suddenly died with only 14 holes completed. He had spent $250,000 of his own money, but there was enough left in his estate to complete the remaining four holes. Hugh Wilson, the creator of Merion, and his brother Allen were called in to direct the remaining work.

The end product drew plaudits from course designers and leading players alike. But there have been thousands of ordinary golfers who have been shattered by Pine Valley's penal qualities.

It is not so much the problems that lie in wait in the apparently endless sand as the pressure that builds up in the mind through having to hit from one green oasis to the next, with little room for error, and the increasing sense of desperation with each disaster.

The story goes that club members have a standing bet that first-timers at Pine Valley never break 80. One who did was Arnold Palmer, who went there in 1954 as US Amateur champion. As he was about to get married, he took all the bets he could find, knowing that if he had lost he couldn't afford to pay them. In the event he shot 68 and left with a sizeable wedding present.

Then there was the late Woody Platt, a good amateur, who knew Pine Valley well and started with a birdie three at the 1st, where the drive is over the inevitable sandy wasteland, followed by a dog-leg right to a green that steeply drops away. The 2nd is just 367 yards, but again the tee shot must carry 180 yards of sand, then a second to an elevated green surrounded by even more sandy wastes, Platt left nothing to chance and holed a seven iron for an eagle.

On the short 3rd, there is nothing between the tee and green but 185 yards of sand. Platt went for it and holed-in-one. The 4th measures 461 yards with a blind tee shot over more sand to an island fairway which turns right. Even more sand must be carried to the green, and Platt hit driver, four wood then holed from 30 feet for a birdie to be six under. As the 4th returns to the clubhouse, he retired to contemplate the next 14 holes, especially the 226-yard 5th across a lake. He fortified himself with a drink and never came back out.

Despite its fame and reputation, Pine Valley has never staged, nor sought to stage, a major championship, its layout being unsuitable for large crowds. Perhaps it is just as well, as it could damage many a reputation.

THE SANDMAN COMETH *The 8th hole at Pine Valley typifies the whole layout with acres of penal sandy waste everywhere*

PINEHURST COUNTRY CLUB

Pinehurst, North Carolina, USA
Opened: *1895*
Designer: *Donald Ross*
Yardage: *7,020* **Par:** *72*
Major events: *US PGA Championship 1936. Tour Championship 1991, 1992. US Amateur 1962. US Women's Amateur 1989. World Amateur Team Championship1980*

UNUSUAL SIGHT *The only water hazard at Pinehurst No. 2 is at the 16th, where the tee shot must carry a small pond*

Paradise can be a somewhat overused word when linked to golf courses, but in the case of Pinehurst it fits the bill perfectly. There are more than 35 courses in a 30-mile radius, and the club has seven of its own, designed by the likes of Ross, Fazio, Trent Jones and Maples. Little wonder that the great Bobby Jones dubbed Pinehurst the "St Andrews of United States golf".

Like so many top courses around the world, Pinehurst is situated among sandhills, thus affording magnificent terrain and, as the name implies, acres of towering pines that form majestic avenues for every hole.

Pinehurst was the brainchild of a Boston soda fountain magnate, James W. Tufts, whose idea was to set up a resort in the south where New Englanders could avoid the harsh winters in their home state. He eventually found what was then a desolate area of North Carolina. There was a natural progression to golf in the latter part of the nineteenth century, and a club was formed in 1895.

In 1900, Harry Vardon is reported to have played the original 18 holes and later that year a Scot, Donald Ross, who had been professional and greenkeeper at his local club, Royal Dornoch, was appointed as club professional.

Within a year of arriving in North Carolina, Ross started to build a second course. Opened in 1907, Pinehurst No. 2 has become the signature lay-out and has staged a number of top championships. Ross also redesigned the original course, then went on to build No. 3 (1910) and No. 4 (1919) during a 48-year stay at the resort. More recently, Ellis Maples was the creator of a fifth course (1961), Tom Fazio added a sixth (1979), and the seventh and latest was completed in 1986 by Rees Jones. But that isn't the end of the story. An eighth course, The Centennial, is being designed by Tom Fazio and will add yet another jewel to Pinehurst's glistening crown.

But it is Pinehurst No. 2 that evokes such delight and nostalgia. Ross called it "the fairest test of championship golf I have ever designed". The great Sam Snead said he rated it as his "number one course" because it constantly challenges the player. "You have to be alert and sharp for 18 consecutive holes; otherwise it will jump up and bite you. I guess that's why the experts rate No. 2 as one of the 10 greatest courses in the world." It has staged a number of major events over the years, from the US PGA and the Tour Championship to the US Amateur, Women's Amateur and the Ryder Cup. The US Open is scheduled to make its debut at Pinehurst in 1999.

It is a course where you have to drive the ball well, hit your long irons well, and, most of all, have a razor-sharp short game. The greens are small by modern standards because they fall off around the edges, allowing balls to run off into dips and swales.

Getting on to No. 2 is not easy, but it becomes a lot easier if you stay at the luxurious Pinehurst Resort Hotel, known at the Queen of the South, as tee times are reserved for guests. Access to the other courses is much easier, while staying at the New England-style village is an exercise in quiet and pristine living. Here you can enjoy wandering the sandy path from the resort to the village's quaint shops and boutiques, stocking everything from sportswear to antiques, fine wines and every gift imaginable for the golfer.

In every way, Pinehurst is, indeed, a golfer's paradise.

OAKMONT

Oakmont, Pennsylvania, USA
Opened: *1904*
Designer: *Henry C. Fownes*
Yardage: *6,921* **Par:** *71*
Major events: *US Open 1927, 1935, 1953, 1962, 1973, 1983, 1994. US Amateur 1919, 1925, 1938, 1969. US Women's Open 1992*

Oakmont, on the outskirts of Pittsburgh, is arguably the most penal lay-out in America, with hard, slick greens, bunkers everywhere, narrow fairways with thick rough, and a length of almost 7,000 yards. It begrudges low scores and these are almost impossible when it comes to major championships.

The club has also been renowned for doing its own thing, especially when it comes to staging US Opens. The 1953 and 1962 championships were marked by heated disputes between the USGA and the club over how the bunkers should be raked. This was because the rakes used at Oakmont were oversize and left wide furrows into which the ball would drop. It led to a famous remark by Jimmy Demaret, who said: "You could have combed North Africa with that rake, and Rommel wouldn't have got past Casablanca."

In 1983 there was another disagreement with the USGA – about the length of the rough. In the event, the players were greeted by thick, dense grass, some nine inches high in places, and could only hack the ball back on to the fairway. The dispute lasted two days of the championship before the mowers were summoned.

Oakmont is not the most beautiful course in the world. It was built on a stretch of flatlands at the foothills of the Alleghenies by a steel magnate, Henry C. Fownes in 1903. In those days the course was split by a railway line which curved through a gorge. In 1952 the Pennsylvania Turnpike was constructed, but as it followed the path of the railway the damage to the course was minimal.

Fownes certainly knew how to get things done. Work began in September 1903 with 150 workers and 25 teams of horses, and 12 holes were finished in six weeks; the other six holes in the spring. The whole lay-out opened that autumn with a "bogey" of 80, eight par fives, a par six, and a total of 220 bunkers. A year later it boasted no fewer than 350. Bunkers were something of a fixation with Fownes and the 8th underlines this. The hole is a par three of 244 yards but contains the Sahara bunker, which is 75 yards long and 35 yards wide and required 11 lorry loads of sand to fill it.

While the bunkers may dominate the course, it is the greens which visitors remember most. They have taken an awful toll of the top names over the years. In Oakmont's first US Open in 1927, Tommy Armour, the Silver Scot, won with 301, 13 over par; then in 1935, Sam Parks, a Pittsburgh man who knew the course like the back of his hand, won with 299, the only player to break 300.

After the Second World War, it was agreed to make Oakmont less intimidating. Some fairways were widened in the driving area and the number of bunkers was reduced to fewer than 200. In 1953, Ben Hogan came to Oakmont as Masters champion and spreadeagled the field with an opening 67. He won by six from Sam Snead and his awesome shot-making was illustrated by his covering the final four holes in 13 strokes against a par of 15.

In 1962, Jack Nicklaus won the first of his four US Opens at Oakmont, beating Arnold Palmer in a play-off; then Johnny Miller took the title at Oakmont in 1973 with a closing 63 which was no doubt helped by very wet greens. After Larry Nelson's win at Oakmont in 1983, the 1994 event promised a possible British victory when Colin Montgomerie tied with Ernie Els and Loren Roberts. But, in the three-way play-off, Els clinched his first major success after he and Roberts had tied again with 74s, four ahead of the fast-fading Scot.

WING AND A PRAYER *Oakmont's bunkers include this row called the Church Pews, separating the 3rd and 4th fairways*

ROYAL COUNTY DOWN

SIMPLY MAGNIFICENT *The Mountains of Mourne provide a breathtaking backdrop to players going around Royal County Down, but few major tournaments are held here*

Newcastle, County Down, Northern Ireland
Opened: *1889*
Designer: *Tom Morris*
Yards: *6,968* **Par:** *72*
Major events: *British Amateur 1970. British Women's Amateur 1899, 1907, 1920, 1927, 1935, 1950, 1963. Curtis Cup 1968*

In comparison to today's staggering construction fees, the cost of the course at Royal County Down was very reasonable. Back in 1889, the club's provisional committee convened in the hall of Mr Lawrence's Dining Rooms, and agreed to invite Tom Morris over from St Andrews to lay out a course "at an expense not to exceed £4".

There were already nine holes in existence, which Old Tom played, and he left recommendations for an 18-hole lay-out which was soon completed. The "outlandish outlay" probably represented his fee, but if such a magnificent piece of land became available today, many of the modern designers would arguably settle for a modest pay day.

Those who have had the good fortune to play this gem some 30 miles south of Belfast will have been enchanted by the sheer beauty of the place, never mind the splendour of the links themselves with their abundance of gorse. This is where, as it says in the song, the Mountains of Mourne sweep down to the sea, and, dominated by Slieve Donard, the highest peak in the range, they form a perfect backdrop, plunging some 3,000 feet sheer, almost to the edge of Dundrum Bay. Surrounded by such beauty, it is easy to be distracted – a grave mistake given County Down's tough reputation. In those early days, the club used the nearby railway station facilities, but by 1897 it had opened its first clubhouse. A year later, the club was affluent enough to put up a 100 guinea prize for a professional tournament between Harry Vardon, J. H. Taylor, Ben Sayers, Andrew Kirkaldy, Sandy Herd, and Willie Fernie, which culminated in Vardon beating Taylor by 12 and 11 in the final.

The course has witnessed several changes in its first century. In 1904 the then professional, Seymour Dunn, suggested some changes; Vardon did the same in 1908, the year the club was granted its Royal Charter; but its current magnificence can be traced back to Harry Colt, who made the last significant changes in 1926.

Unlike many links courses which go out and back, County Down has two nine-hole loops of different character, courtesy of George Combe, a founder member and captain in 1895–96, who spent many years as chairman of the greens committee. Its other great virtue is that each hole is separate, occupying its own valley between the sandhills, with rarely a view of the next or the adjacent hole.

The front nine, or sea nine, is uncompromising. The premium is on long, straight shot-making which means those who can handle a driver will be at a distinct advantage. Those who stray from the often narrow fairways find themselves tangling with the dunes, wild roses and heavy bunkering.

On the landward or back nine, the problems are heavy rough in the form of seaside grass, heather and gorse, while many of the greens are small, with subtle slopes and hollows that highlight the merest blemish in a putting stroke.

There are those who criticize Royal County Down because the golfer is required to play a number of blind shots, but that is a minor irritant when there is so much to admire. Best of all is the view from the 9th tee, with the Mourne Mountains towering above the rooftops of Newcastle.

Big events have tended to bypass the club. It has staged only one Amateur Championship, in 1970 when Michael Bonallack won his fifth title, and his third on the trot, romping home 8 and 7 against American Bill Hyndman after being one down at lunch. But the women have been more frequent visitors, the British Women's Amateur having been held here seven times between 1899 and 1963.

ROYAL DORNOCH

Dornoch, Sutherland, Scotland
Opened: *Unknown*
Designer: *Anon*
Yardage: *6,577* **Par:** *70*
Major events: *British Amateur 1985*

If it were not so remote, 60 miles north of Inverness, Dornoch would undoubtedly be a British Open venue. It is one of the most beautiful courses anywhere, as well as one of the oldest. Indeed it may even have a claim to be the birthplace of the game.

No one knows when golf was played here, but it was known by 1630 when Sir Robert Gordon wrote: "About this town along the sea coast are the fairest and largest links or green fields of any pairt of Scotland. Fitt for archery, golfing, ryding and all other exercises, they doe surpass the fields of Montrose or St Andrews."

There is even an earlier reference to this cathedral city which, in size, is little more than a village. A 1616 account book of the Earl of Sutherland notes expenditure on archery, golf balls and clubs. Such evidence is rare, for golf was not regarded as important, so it was seldom recorded, and we are unlikely ever to find out where golf began. Dornoch undoubtedly remains a candidate, even though the club itself was not founded until 1877. Not that this is unusual: people had wandered the linksland of Britain hitting golf balls long before any clubs were formed, and the dates of many courses are guesswork.

The whole setting of the Dornoch course is magnificent, so much so that some of those from England who "discovered" the course did not mention it for fear that too many others would hear about it and spoil the tranquillity. Dornoch remained relatively unknown until it was very highly praised by the great American golf writer, Herbert Warren Wind, in the 1960s. Since then it has been visited and played by the likes of Ben Crenshaw, Tom Watson and Greg Norman, who might well prefer to play here rather than most of the British Open sites.

The course begins comfortably enough and in fact is never a really severe test on any particular hole. Instead, it is a steady challenge all the way. The layout is the once traditional one of out from the clubhouse and then back again. The sea is in view almost all the time. The 1st is a gentle introduction, a short par four of around 330 yards, but it is followed by a more testing par three of 180 yards which features a typical Dornoch green with fall-aways on either side. Many think the 5th the first really testing hole. It is played from an elevated tee, with a mound to be carried, and the second shot is to a long but narrow green, well guarded by bunkers. By this time one is well aware of the vast bank of gorse which runs along the left but does not significantly affect play. After the 6th, a very natural looking hole, you climb up the bankside to the 7th on a ridge and play between the gorse bushes and then drive off from a height along the 8th, which features a plunge in the fairway about 200 yards out.

The homeward journey begins with the 9th, a par five of close on 500 yards which follows the curve of the bay, as do the next several holes. In this stretch many find "Foxy", the 14th, the most memorable. It demonstrates that a golf hole doesn't need bunkers, mainly because the plateau green demands both a long and precise second shot.

Every hole, however, is a delight, and even if you are playing badly there ought to be consolation in the views of the Dornoch Firth and the hills of Sutherland. At the end, there is the welcome of a very pleasant modern clubhouse.

BETWEEN THE DEVIL AND THE DEEP BLUE SEA *Playing straight at Royal Dornoch is vital, with devilish gorse on one side and the Firth of Dornoch on the other*

ROYAL LIVERPOOL (HOYLAKE)

Hoylake, Merseyside, England
Opened: *1869*
Designer: *Anon*
Yardage: *6,780* **Par:** *72*
Major events: *Open Championship 1897, 1902, 1907, 1913, 1924, 1930, 1936, 1947, 1956, 1967. British Amateur 1885, 1887, 1890, 1894, 1898, 1902, 1906, 1910, 1921, 1927, 1933, 1939, 1953, 1962, 1975, 1995. Walker Cup 1983. Curtis Cup 1992*

Hoylake is considered to be one of the toughest tests in British golf, and can be stretched to around 7,000 yards. This is largely why the Open has ten times been held here. In 1897 it was only the second English course to be used (after Royal St George's, Sandwich). Here, in 1902, Sandy Herd became the first champion to use a wound ball, and in 1924 Walter Hagen took the second of his four British Open titles. However, easily the most momentous Open came in 1930, when Bobby Jones had his third British Open win in just four entries and completed the English swing of his eventual Grand Slam of all four British and US Amateur and Open titles. The last British Open was played here in 1967, when Roberto de Vicenzo memorably outplayed Jack Nicklaus and Gary Player over the last two rounds. Hoylake is very unlikely ever to host a British Open again, for the simple reason that there isn't enough room for today's Open crowds, particularly on the closing holes. However, the course is still used for top amateur events – the Curtis Cup, Walker Cup and British Amateur, which will return for the centenary of that initial Open. It also hosts European Tour events.

The course is extremely variable in appearance. On arrival, the impression is of a flat expanse with some undulating ground in the far distance by the Dee Estuary. That bit looks the most dramatic, but in fact many players find that the flatter holes are the most testing, while the stretch from the 8th to the 11th has the most visual appeal.

The 1st is one of the flat holes but is a frightener. You have to try to keep your tee shot as close as you dare to the practice ground along the right – but that is out of bounds. You are not in much trouble going left until you play the second shot. Then you have to contend with firing directly towards the out of bounds. The 7th also used to cause much fear. There was a turf bank just to the left of the green and beyond was out of bounds. That penalty has now been removed. Judgement of distance and quality of strike, however, are just as vital as they ever were. As the course occupies a small area, out of bounds is an almost constant threat.

The course is beautifully maintained, the greens sometimes the best in Britain, and the clubhouse is full of interest, including what amounts to a museum of golf in the entrance hall.

Hoylake has seen quite a few firsts. In 1885, the club had the idea of staging a big amateur tournament, which was won by Allan Macfie. A generation later, this was recognized as the first British Amateur Championship. In 1921 the first golf international of any kind between British and American men was played over the course, and it was a forewarning of imminent American dominance that the British were trounced. In 1925 the English Amateur was inaugurated at Hoylake and, quite appropriately, was won by a Royal Liverpool member, T. F. Ellison.

TIGHT FIT *Although no longer an Open venue, Hoylake still offers one of the supreme challenges in British golf*

ROYAL MELBOURNE

WRITTEN IN THE SAND *Alister Mackenzie courses are noted for their bunkers; at Royal Melbourne there are 114 of them, in various shapes, sizes and depths, which should all be avoided*

Melbourne, Victoria, Australia
Opened: *1931*
Designers: *Alister Mackenzie and Alex Russell*
Yardage: *6,946* **Par:** *71*
Major events: *Australian Open 1905, 1907, 1909, 1912, 1913, 1921, 1924, 1927, 1933, 1939, 1953, 1963, 1984, 1985, 1987, 1991. World Amateur Team Championship 1968. World Cup 1988*

Sandy subsoils are the ideal ingredients to support golf courses as can be seen with the various Surrey clubs, those on the Lancashire coast and in many parts of Scotland. The same applies in Australia and especially in Melbourne, whose southern confines contain a 25 square mile area known as the Sand Belt. Here, the rolling terrain containing fine grasses and indigenous trees, reeds, heather and bracken, was considered the ideal site for the Royal Melbourne club to move to in the late 1920s.

The club had been founded as long ago as 1891, making it the oldest in Australia, but it had two other locations before eventually moving to its present site and building its reputation as one of the world's finest courses. The prime land was acquired in 1924, and club officials were in no doubt that they wanted "the best expert advice", irrespective of cost.

That advice was provided by Alister Mackenzie, the Scot who was later to go on to design Augusta National as well as many other top courses throughout the world. He began work in 1926 together with Alex Russell, the 1924 Australian Open champion, and the result was the West course, which many feel is a masterpiece.

While Mackenzie's name is synonymous with the course, Russell played a major role, and it was perhaps fitting that he should design and construct the neighbouring East course a little later. For championship purposes, a composite of the two courses is used, six holes of Russell's East linked with 12 from Mackenzie's West. The result is a lay-out of almost 7,000 yards and a tough par of 71.

Aesthetically Royal Melbourne leaves something to be desired because, over the years, the city's development has seen it surrounded by roads while houses back on to parts of the playing area. However, closer inspection reveals its true quality, notably in the thoughtful arrangements of humps and ridges, adding character, not to mention the odd hazard.

Apart from the overall design, another significant feature of Royal Melbourne is the large greens, which are usually extremely fast. The credit for this belongs to the former head greenkeeper Claude Crockford, who was taken on to the staff in 1934. Such were his skills and devotion to duty that there are no truer or faster greens to be found anywhere; consequently, it takes the visitor some time to acclimatize and feel at home.

Crockford also carried out some redesign work, particularly with regard to the short 7th, which Mackenzie built with an elevated green that the members felt was a blind shot. They wanted it altered, so Crockford obliged by lowering it to where it could be seen. Even now, at just 148 yards, it is no pushover, with several very deep bunkers lying in wait for the wayward shot. In fact, bunkers were Mackenzie's signature, and there are 114 of various shapes, sizes and depths to be confronted or avoided if you are to come away with a decent score.

The 11th is generally regarded as the toughest hole on the course. From an elevated tee, this 455-yard par four presents a difficult drive to the elbow of the left-hand dog-leg, the fairway sloping left towards two large, luring traps. Turning left, the approach to a sloping green also requires accuracy to avoid a gaping bunker to the right of the putting surface.

Such has been Royal Melbourne's pedigree down the years that it has been a frequent host for the Australian Open and PGA Championships. It was also the venue for the World Cup in 1988, won by the Ozaki brothers from Japan.

ROYAL NORTH DEVON

Westward Ho!, Devon, England
Opened: *1864*
Designer: *Tom Morris*
Yardage: *6,662* **Par:** *71*
Major events: *British Amateur 1912, 1925, 1931. Women's British Amateur 1900, 1910*

The Royal North Devon club, situated on the north bank of the estuary of the River Torridge, is not only the oldest club in England, still played over its original land, but can claim to possess the finest natural golfing terrain anywhere. Golf began at Westward Ho!, which took its name from Charles Kingsley's famous novel, in 1853 on common land known as Northam or Appledore Burrows, and the first club was formed in 1864. Four years earlier, Old Tom Morris had travelled down from St Andrews to advise, and when he returned in 1864, he designed two courses, one of 17 holes and another of 22. There was another significant move in 1868, when the North Devon Ladies' Club was formed, which had its own nine-hole course adjacent to the men's. In 1908 the course was totally redesigned by W. Herbert Fowler. He had earned rave reviews for his creation of Walton Heath a few years earlier, but his work on this traditional linksland lay-out was also acclaimed.

RND has another jewel in its illustrious history. John Henry Taylor, who was to win the Open Championship five times, was born at Northam in March 1871 and joined the Westward Ho! greenstaff at the age of 17. After two years as a caddie he turned professional and became greenkeeper at Burnham. He was just 23 when he won his first Open at Sandwich in 1894, the first non-Scot to do so, retaining the title at St Andrews the following year. As well as being one of golf's Great Triumvirate Taylor was also instrumental in forming the Professional Golfers' Association in 1901 and generally raising the status of the professional. He spent most of his career as pro at Royal Mid Surrey, but when he retired back to Northam in 1957, RND made him their president.

In keeping with a club steeped in history, RND has been graced by some odd customs. When Horace Hutchinson won the club medal in 1875 at the age of 16, he was automatically elected captain while taking the chair at the annual meeting. It was a custom that existed for many years, but while that has been amended, the rights of locals to graze their sheep and cattle on the course hasn't, which provides the golfer with an additional hazard.

Looking over the wild, barren landscape from the wooden clubhouse, Westward Ho! provides a slow start, but the real fun begins on the par four 4th, where your drive must carry the huge Cape bunker at around 170 yards. The 5th is the first short hole towards the sandhills before two more par fours that demand good driving. The 8th is a par three of 197 yards on the edge of the estuary at the furthest part of the course before you turn back with the long 9th that, like many holes from here on, features the famous rushes that stand like huge shaving brushes waiting to snare every shot.

The back nine starts with four more par fours, the 13th, at 440 yards being the longest on the course. The par three 14th and 16th are played in almost the same direction, while the final two holes provide a tricky finish. The 17th, the Road Hole, is usually played into a wind, and at 548 yards that can prove quite a task. The road crosses just short of the green, while a ditch must also be crossed in front of the putting surface. If that wasn't enough trouble, at the par four 18th you have two burns to contend with. Par figures at these two final holes can have you singing the praises of Westward Ho! no matter what has gone before.

DON'T BLEAT ABOUT IT *The custom allowing local famers to graze their livestock at Westward Ho! creates extra problems*

ROYAL ST DAVID'S

Harlech, Gwynedd, Wales
Opened: *1894*
Designer: *Harold Finch-Hatton*
Yardage: *6,427* **Par:** *69*
Major events: *British Women's Amateur 1926, 1949, 1960, 1967, 1987*

The Royal St David's club, which celebrated its centenary in 1994, rejoices in the most splendid surroundings you can imagine. Flanked by the Irish Sea on one side, the whole scene is dominated by the ancient Harlech Castle, which sits with medieval dignity atop its hill, no doubt surveying with a certain amount of disdain the often futile antics being played out on the links below. Beyond, the mountains of Snowdonia provide a backdrop that completes a vista of almost unrivalled beauty.

The club was established in a somewhat curious way. The story goes, although it may well have been embroidered down the years, that in 1893 a young man by the name of Harold Finch-Hatton, just returned from Australia, was out on the low-lying grazing land known as Morfa, displaying his skills with a boomerang. He was spotted from near the castle battlements by a W. H. More, who climbed down and engaged him in conversation.

Some days later they met again, while Finch-Hatton was trying out some strange implements to play a game that was all the rage across the borders in Scotland and England. "This would be a great place for a golf links," said Finch-Hatton, or words to that effect. "Let's lay one out." More knew nothing about golf, but was not about to admit the fact as they set about positioning tees and greens. Soon the club was formed and More became its secretary, a post he was to hold for 40 years.

At that early meeting, they decided to prepare 18 holes in time for an autumn competition which, despite heavy rain, was won by the famous John Ball with a score of 152 – quite a feat on a course that couldn't have been in great shape. Four years earlier Ball had captured the Open Championship and that year won the Amateur for the fourth time.

So the St David's club was established, and it is among the oldest in Wales. Among its early patrons was Edward VII, then Prince of Wales, which prompted some proud members, somewhat prematurely, to assume the Royal prefix. Fortunately, that error was rectified in August 1908 when the King sanctioned the present title. The royal connection was reinforced later when the Duke of Windsor, while himself Prince of Wales, captained the club.

The course itself is generally flat, but always has the feel of being natural. That has a lot to do with the great sandhills, and achieving a good score requires long driving as half of the holes measure 427 yards or more. But at least there is the assurance that the ultimate destinations are fine, large greens.

After starting with three successive par fours, you come to the first of five challenging short holes; the second of these completes the front nine after the only par fives, the 7th and 8th. The return is towards the sea, while the final five holes present the best part of all as they head into the hills.

The beginning of the end comes with perhaps the best of the par threes, the 14th which at 218 yards involves quite a carry from the tee to a target encircled by dunes. The 427-yard 15th is a long two-shotter, while the tee at the par four 16th provides the only view of the sea during the round. Decision time comes at the 427-yard 17th – whether to carry the cross bunker in front of the green – while the home hole is another 200-yard par three.

Once you have played Royal St David's you are hooked, whatever the season; but perhaps the time to see the links at their best is June, when you can enjoy many wild flowers in bloom and the call of a host of birds overhead.

SPLENDID SCENERY *Ancient Harlech castle, the Irish Sea and the mountains of Snowdonia make Royal St David's one of Britain's most picturesque courses*

ROYAL ST GEORGE'S

Sandwich, Kent, England
Opened: *1887*
Designer: *Dr W. Laidlaw Purves*
Yardage: *6,857* **Par:** *70*
Major events: *Open Championship 1894, 1899, 1904, 1911, 1922, 1928, 1934, 1938, 1949, 1981, 1985, 1993. Amateur Championship 1892, 1896, 1900, 1904, 1908, 1914, 1929, 1937, 1948, 1959, 1972. British Women's Amateur 1922, 1964. Walker Cup 1930, 1967. Curtis Cup 1988*

Royal St George's, on the shores of Pegwell Bay, is a great links course with an illustrious history. In 1894 it staged the first Open Championship outside Scotland, which produced the first English winner in J. H. Taylor. It also produced the first foreign winner of the Amateur Championship, Walter Travis from Australia, who won at Royal St George's in 1904, and the first American winner of the Open, Walter Hagen in 1922. Another significant first was when Tony Jacklin holed-in-one at the short 16th during a final-round 64 on his way to winning the 1967 Dunlop Masters. It was the first time such a feat was captured on television.

Royal St George's was founded in 1887, when Dr Laidlaw Purves and some 50 friends formed a syndicate called the Sandwich Golf Association, obtained a lease on the links and turned them over to the club. The story goes that Purves spotted the land from a church tower in Sandwich after a long search for such a site.

Purves is credited with the original lay-out, but Royal St George's has seen some remodelling over the years, first by Alister Mackenzie, and more recently by Frank Pennink. It has long had a reputation as a driver's course, and indeed the last two Opens there were won by Sandy Lyle and Greg Norman, two of the longest hitters the game has seen. However, it also provides some of the most testing second shots found anywhere, starting with the opening two holes, both par fours.

The 3rd is the first short hole of 214 yards, before the course progresses among the expanse of dunes along fairways that rise and fall continually to heavily guarded greens. At the 4th, a par four of 470 yards, you drive over a cavernous bunker, while the green at the 422-yard 5th is reached between two hills.

The first par five comes at the 7th, which has a slight dog-leg, while the 8th, another par four, has a belt of mounds and rough dividing the fairway from the green. After the 9th and 10th – two more par fours played in opposite directions – the 11th is another short hole of 216 yards before the dog-leg 12th around a sandy ridge heralds a loop of three holes skirting the neighbouring Prince's course.

At the 13th you have to manoeuvre between a maze of bunkers, while the par five 14th requires straight driving to avoid the out of bounds before crossing the famous Suez Canal midway down the fairway. After another testing par four at 15 comes the short 16th which, depending on the wind, can play anything from a two to an eight iron to a green encircled with traps.

The closing holes, two more par fours, again call for accurate driving and sound second shots. At 18, the front of the green is guarded by bunkers right and left which are to be avoided, but so is Duncan's Hollow, named after George Duncan, the British pro who failed to get down in two from there to catch Walter Hagen in the 1922 Open, an area of thick grass below a steep bank that is a magnet for many shots.

The 1949 Open, won by Bobby Locke, from an unlucky Harry Bradshaw, who chose – some say unnecessarily – to play his ball out of a broken bottle, was the last Open at Royal St George's for 32 years. Despite its pedigree as a course, it was felt to be unsuitable to stage the ever-expanding event, but thanks to the building of a by-pass around the old town and other improvements, its long exile ended in 1981. In 1985 Sandy Lyle became the first British winner since Jacklin in 1969. As the only Open venue south of Lancashire, and with its close proximity to London, it is unlikely to be out on a limb again.

HIT AND HOPE *Anybody driving into the enormous and steep bunker on the long 4th hole will do well to make only a bogey*

ST ANDREWS, OLD COURSE

St Andrews, Fife, Scotland
Opened: *Unknown*
Designer: *Anon*
Yardage: *7,090* **Par:** *72*
Major events: *Open Championship 1873, 1876, 1879, 1882, 1885, 1888, 1891, 1895, 1900, 1905, 1910, 1921, 1927, 1933, 1939, 1946, 1955, 1957, 1964, 1960, 1970, 1978, 1984, 1990, 1995. British Amateur 1886, 1889, 1891, 1895, 1901, 1907, 1913, 1924, 1930, 1936, 1950, 1958, 1963, 1976, 1981. Walker Cup 1923, 1926, 1934, 1938, 1947, 1955, 1971, 1975*

This is one of the world's oldest and most revered golf courses and is deservedly known as "the home of golf". It is a favourite course of many top professionals and amateurs, perhaps because it is by no means fearsome in still air but always demands good strategy and shot-making, though some of the first ten holes are easy in the extreme.

The first exciting hole is the 5th, where you need to be a little left because of a cluster of bunkers along the right. There is a steep upslope, set with more bunkers; on hard ground, with a following wind, Craig Wood drove into one of them during the 1933 British Open. The distance is about 430 yards! Even so, most professionals see this as a clear birdie chance.

The 6th is a typical links hole. When you stand on the tee, you may wonder what has happened to the golf course. Most players simply aim at the marker post, but even if all goes well that far, the second shot is difficult. There is a rise before the green, and the putting surface then slopes away from the player. The 7th is the only dog-leg on the course, and even then only a slight one. It is best to be right rather than left, because Shell bunker is on line for an approach from the left, and the green slopes from left to right.

The real tests at St Andrews come on the route back to the clubhouse. The 11th, for instance, is one of the best par threes in world golf, feared because of the deep Hill bunker to the left of the green and Strath to the front on the right. The 13th has been ranked one of the great par fours, enhanced by the skyline of St Andrews. The second shot is played over a heathery bank to a flag which seems to be perched on the top. Another great hole is the 14th, where the tee shot has out of bounds to the right and bunkers known as "The Beardies" to the left. If you succeed and get your shot down the middle, the large Hell bunker lies directly in your path to the green. For long hitters this 567-yard hole is a birdie opportunity, but few manage to get the ball close to the hole, and to be just short leaves a difficult putt or chip.

By this time, many will begin to worry about the 17th "Road Hole", a devilish par four of 461 yards. The tee shot needs to be nearly out of bounds along the right, because from the left it is extremely difficult to hit and hold the narrow, angled green, behind which are the road and a boundary wall, both potential card-shredders. Hardly any British Open competitors get past this challenge with four pars. In 1885 David Ayton took an 11 to lose by two strokes!

This is not true of the last, one of the weakest finishing holes in all of championship golf – though Doug Sanders memorably lost the 1970 Open by taking five!

Seve Ballesteros, 1984 Champion here, expressed "great sadness" at the news that five holes were to be lengthened before the Open in 2000. The Old Course, said he, is "a national monument". True enough, but it has been lengthened several times before and the changes in 2000 will bring bunkers at five holes back into play that had ceased to worry leading players armed with high-tech equipment.

NIGHTMARE SCENARIO *A visit to the Road Bunker at St Andrews is to dice with a double-figure score at the 17th hole*

SUNNINGDALE

Sunningdale, Surrey, England
Opened: *1901*
Designer: *Willie Park*
Yardage: *6,703* **Par:** *70*
Major events: *Walker Cup 1987. Women's British Amateur 1956*

Sunningdale, like its neighbour Wentworth, is a gorgeous course on the Surrey sand belt. Originally three farms surrounded by heather, gorse and pine trees, the land was owned by St John's College, Cambridge, who around the turn of the century were persuaded by their agent T. A. Roberts that the land should be turned over to golf and residential development. A committee was formed and Willie Park, twice Open champion, was commissioned to design the Old course at a fee of £3,800.

Much of the site at that time was open country with few trees. The familiar wooded outlook we know today followed a general redesign by Harry Colt, who was Sunningdale secretary for 17 years before transferring his skills to full-time course architecture.

As a result each hole is self-contained, while nature's work over the years has been instrumental in seeing Sunningdale develop into one of the great inland courses.

Colt also found time to design a second 18 holes, the New course of 6,202 yards, par 68, which opened in 1922. The two courses, both tough lay-outs, complement each other and together make Sunningdale a delight to play.

Oddly enough, the Old course starts with two par fives, but the 1st, at 494 yards and slightly downhill, can be reached in two shots during a dry summer, while the 2nd, just 10 yards shorter, is another good birdie chance with accurate shotmaking. The 3rd, a short par four, also presents the chance of picking up a shot, but the 4th, the first short hole, requires a solid shot up to a well-protected green. The next short hole, the 8th, which follows three par fours, is somewhat similar, while the 267-yard 9th is eminently drivable.

The 10th tee, at the highest part of the course, provides stunning views over the countryside. On this par five you drive down into a broad valley with bunkers to the right and left, leaving a long second shot to a receptive green. The 11th is another short par four with a drive over sand hills, and providing you avoid the trees and ditch on the right, only a short pitch is required to find the green.

The 12th is another testing par four, and after two teasing par threes and the final par five come three par fours that provide a daunting finish. The 18th is a superb finishing hole. Here, a long uphill drive is required avoiding large bunkers right and left, then a long second shot towards the big oak tree that is the club's symbol and stands between the clubhouse and green.

On the tournament side, Sunningdale has long staged its early-season Foursomes event for both amateurs and professionals, women being admitted in recent years, while it has also been a venue for the Ladies British Amateur, the Golf Illustrated Gold Vase and in 1987 the Walker Cup.

One of the greatest feats in Sunningdale's history was the famous round of 66 produced by Bobby Jones in a qualifying round for the Open Championship in 1926. It has often been described as the perfect round, because he covered each nine in 33 strokes, and he had 33 shots and 33 putts. Jones's score was also made up entirely of threes and fours, and he hit every green, except one, in regulation and was bunkered only once. He followed it with a 68, then claimed that he had peaked too early. He hadn't, of course, and he proved it by moving on to Royal Lytham and winning the title by two strokes from fellow American Al Watrous.

Sunningdale has long had a royal connection. The Prince of Wales, later Edward VIII, and the Duke of York, later King George VI, were both captains while over the years the club has become a mecca for the great and famous.

DOMINANT FEATURE *The giant oak tree behind Sunningdale's 18th green is in keeping with the beauty of the course*

TURNBERRY

Ayrshire, Scotland
Opened: *1903*
Designer: *Willie Fernie*
Yardage: *6,950* **Par:** *70*
Major events: *Open Championship 1977, 1986, 1994. Amateur Championship 1961, 1984. Walker Cup 1963. British Women's Amateur 1912, 1921, 1937*

Turnberry is one of Scotland's major golf centres. It has two fine courses – the Ailsa and the Arran – a modern clubhouse incorporating every facility, and an impressive hotel set high on a hill overlooking the complete lay-out, with the Firth of Clyde and the granite dome of Ailsa Craig beyond.

The original links course was the work of former Open champion Willie Fernie, while Turnberry, like several other resorts early this century, owed its development mainly to the coming of the railways. The line being pushed south down the Ayrshire coast required the building of a top-class hotel, and both were opened in 1906. Soon Turnberry became a mecca for the rich, and a second links course, the Arran, was opened in 1912.

However, the First World War put paid to golf. The area was used as a training ground for Royal Flying Corps pilots, while the hotel became the officers' mess. Much the same occurred in the Second World War, Turnberry becoming a base for RAF Coastal Command with much of the courses disappearing under concrete runways, hangars and other buildings.

In 1946 the then owners, British Transport Hotels, set about using the compensation from the War Office to restore the courses to their former glory. Philip Mackenzie Ross was brought in to redesign the lay-out, and the Ailsa course, most of which had to be returfed, reopened in 1951. It occupies undulating terrain, threading its way among the sand dunes along the seashore in a general north-south direction. However, the first six holes of the back nine are more east-west, which means the golfer, having got used to the wind direction, has to readjust.

BLAZING SUNSET *The sky looks on fire as the sun sets over Turnberry's Ailsa course with the lighthouse silhouetted*

Like all links courses, Turnberry's character changes with the prevailing conditions, which can vary between the docile and the stormy. It is said locally: "If you can see Ailsa Craig it's going to rain. If you can't see it, it's raining." Depending on the direction of the on-shore wind, some greens can enjoy a sheltered aspect, while others can be buffeted as if in a wind tunnel.

Apart from its majestic hotel, Turnberry's best-known feature is the lighthouse. This stands adjacent to the par four 9th hole, where the tee is built on a rocky outcrop of the cliff, requiring a drive across an inlet to the safety of the fairway beyond. The other signature hole is the 16th, another par four which presents few problems until you consider your second shot to a green perched on a knoll, below which bubble the waters of the Wee Burn. The number of shots which have found a watery grave here and the number of ruined cards are legion – for even hitting the putting surface is no guarantee of safety.

The Arran course lies inland from the Ailsa on more gently rolling terrain, but can be equally challenging, especially in the wind.

Despite Turnberry's long-established qualities, big-time golf only arrived with the Amateur Championship in 1961 and then the Walker Cup in 1963, when the home side crashed to a 12–8 defeat after leading 6–3 after day one.

But Turnberry's finest hour came in 1977 with the first of its three Open Championships. The links were at their most benign, the sun shone for all four days, and the low scoring reflected this, right up to the classic final day shoot-out between Tom Watson and Jack Nicklaus. Watson won by a stroke on 268, the lowest 72-hole aggregate in the event's history.

Conditions were almost the reverse in 1986, when Greg Norman defied wind and rain to secure his first Open; then in 1994 it was Nick Price's turn to gain his first Open after several near misses.

VALDERRAMA

Sotogrande, Cadiz, Spain
Opened: *1975*
Designer: *Robert Trent Jones*
Yardage: *6,819* **Par:** *72*
Major events: *Ryder Cup 1997*

The list of courses that bear the name of Robert Trent Jones is long and impressive, while his workmanship has become familiar throughout the world. When he designed Los Aves, in a spectacular location in the hills above Sotogrande in southern Spain, it wasn't regarded as particularly newsworthy. Most people were more familiar with Sotogrande Old, his also, and even when Los Aves became Sotogrande New, there was barely a ripple on the surface of the game. But in 1985, when a Bolivian tin millionaire and golf fanatic by the name of Jaime Ortiz-Patino, and seven of his golfing friends, acquired and improved the club, changing its name again to Valderrama, it was to have a far-reaching influence on the game, not only in Spain but in Europe and around the world.

Trent Jones was brought back in to remodel the lay-out, describing it at the time as "polishing the diamond to improve the shot values in some areas". Since then, Ortiz-Patino has made other changes on the way to making Valderrama into what he calls 'The Augusta of Europe".

There is no disputing now that Valderrama is a magnificent course in every sense of the word. Its quality is of the highest order, and such has been the refining that it has become a severe test of even the best players, while its elevation into the nearest thing to Augusta in Europe has seen it become the permanent venue for the end-of-season European tour event, the Volvo Masters. Even more stunning was the awarding to Valderrama of the 1997 Ryder Cup matches, the first time the contest will have been held outside Britain when Europe has been the host.

Thanks to its quality, its reputation for being a tough examination, and its agreeable climate, many national teams take the opportunity of going there to tune up for the season ahead. Some of Europe's leading tour professionals also use the course to hone their games, including Seve Ballesteros, one of its biggest fans, who used the facilities at Valderrama to warm up for one of his US Masters successes.

Europe's pros, almost to a man, admit that Valderrama is probably more difficult than any other course in Europe. The scoring certainly reflects that, and while its selection for the Ryder Cup was criticized in many quarters, there is little doubt that it will prove a more than suitable battleground for the best from Europe and America.

Most of the holes are memorable for one reason or another but among the most memorable is the short 3rd, which measures around 170 yards but requires a solid shot to a severely bunkered green let into a hillside. Then there is the par five 11th, where Trent Jones's redesign has left a sloping fairway with a nest of bunkers at the landing area followed by an uphill approach to the green which is difficult to judge accurately. Another testing par three is the 12th, which measures around 220 yards and is played from an elevated tee to a green set among cork trees. Anything off target is almost bound to catch one of the fearsome bunkers, while the green itself slopes from front to back and has many subtle undulations.

The 17th has also seen some changes in recent years, but this time Patino called in Ballesteros, and what used to be a long uphill par five, now has a lake guarding the front of the green. Anything short finds a watery grave, while anything too strong can leave you in clinging grass on the banking that surrounds the putting surface.

What is certain at Valderrama is that if something needs changing or improving, no expense is spared to see that it is done, so you can bet that everything will be pristine when the Ryder Cup arrives in September 1997.

RYDER CUP HOST *Valderrama will host the 1997 Ryder Cup and each hole will prove a memorable challenge the finest golfers from Europe and America*

WENTWORTH

Virginia Water, Surrey, England
Opened: *1924*
Designer: *Harry Colt*
Yardage: *6,945* **Par:** *72*
Major events: *Ryder Cup 1953. Curtis Cup 1932 (East course). World Cup 1956. Women's British Open 1980*

In the days after the First World War, developer Walter George Tarrant, who realized the potential for such facilities, and had gained considerable success in producing quality housing around a golf course at St George's Hill in Surrey, was looking for a similar site to repeat the exercise. At Wentworth he found and eventually secured 1,750 acres of prime countryside, just 21 miles southwest of London. While Tarrant set about developing the property, complete with swimming pool, tennis courts and a ballroom, his friend Harry Colt laid out two courses.

Colt was delighted with the land at his disposal. The Surrey sandbelt, with its heather, soaring pine trees, silver birch, and, in more recent times, huge banks of rhododendrons, lends itself ideally to golf courses. His handiwork has attracted worldwide acclaim, while everyone who plays Wentworth knows he faces quite a test. The East course, at 6,176 yards, par 68, is demanding in its own way. However, it is the West, completed two years later and better known now as the Burma Road, which is the more familiar, as more of the top professional events are played on it.

The West, which has always demanded accurate driving, features highly among the tour professionals' choice of top venues. Few of the holes can be seen from any other, while the conditions are seldom less than first class even in the darkest days of an English winter.

The back nine is regarded as the tougher half, and this is confirmed by the yardage and the par, 37 against the outward half of 35. The homeward run begins with a testing par three and a comfortable par four, after which the long 12th gives a chance of a birdie, if not an eagle for the leading players. But it is easy to give those shots back at the 441-yard 13th, where the line is down the right in order to open up the green to the approach. The uphill par three 14th plays every inch of its 179 yards to a two-tiered green, while the 466-yard 15th, with its diagonal ditch, requires strategy as well as a straight, long drive.

The par four 16th provides a lull before the storm which starts with the dog-leg 17th, one of the great par fives of British golf. The 571 yards is downhill from the tee for about 300 yards and the best line is to hug the trees down the left if you don't want your ball to spill off the sloping fairway into the right rough. Then the hole turns left uphill before descending to a generous green, but beware the private gardens down the left which are out-of-bounds. The pros hope to pick up a shot here, as they do at the 18th, another par five, but this time a dog-leg right. Here the drive should be to the elbow of the dog-leg, thereby providing another long shot to a green well guarded by bunkers at the front.

Although a comparatively young course, Wentworth has played its part in golfing history. It was here in 1926 that an informal match was played between the professionals of Great Britain and those of America, which the British won comfortably. This was to prove the forerunner of the Ryder Cup which began a year later.

In 1953 Wentworth played host to the Ryder Cup, with the United States scraping home by a single point, then three years later the Canada Cup, now the World Cup. The occasion provided Ben Hogan with his one and only appearance in England. He and Sam Snead carried off the trophy by a massive 14 strokes, both players shooting final round 68s. The World Match Play Championship has been played at Wentworth every year since its inception in 1964, and the Volvo PGA Championship has been resident at Wentworth since 1984.

In 1978 Wentworth acquired another 150 acres of land so it was decided to build a third 18-hole course, the South. The design of John Jacobs, with Gary Player and Wentworth professional Bernard Gallacher, it opened in July 1990 and was renamed the Edinburgh, in honour of the Duke, who performed the opening ceremony.

A GREAT COLT COURSE *Wentworth's rebuilt clubhouse, refurbished in original turretted style, overlooks the first tee, but would look just as good on a wedding cake*

WINGED FOOT

Mamaroneck, New York, USA
Opened: *1923*
Designer: *Albert W. Tillinghast*
Yardage: *6,980* **Par:** *70*
Major events: *US Open 1929, 1959, 1974, 1984. Walker Cup 1949. US Women's Open 1957, 1972. US Amateur 1940*

When Albert Tillinghast was commissioned to design a new lay-out in Westchester County, not far from New York City, he was tersely instructed: "Give us a man-sized course." The message was delivered by the gentlemen of the New York Athletic Club, from whose emblem the golf club takes its name, and the end result was the best golf course in Westchester County.

To create his masterpiece, Tillinghast had to move 7,200 tons of rock and cut down almost 8,000 trees. In fact, he created two courses, but it is the longer and more treacherous West course which has played host to four US Opens.

The key to Winged Foot is its 12 gruelling par fours, 10 of which measure 400 yards or more. These require long, straight driving, then a controlled second shot, often with a long iron, to greens that are fiercely contoured and guarded by deep bunkers.

Tillinghast's thinking was that "a controlled shot to a closely guarded green is the surest test of any man's golf". By the standards of some of America's top courses, Winged Foot's total of 60 bunkers is on the conservative side, until you consider that every green has at least two deep ones.

The club has not only produced a lot of low handicap players with excellent bunker skills; it has also had more than its fair share of national champions. At one time in the early 1940s it had both the US Open and Amateur champions in Craig Wood and Dick Chapman. Claude Harmon, who became pro six years later, won the US Masters in 1948; his assistants included Jack Burke and Dave Marr, both major winners, while Dick Mayer, the US Open champion in 1957, was a Winged Foot member before turning professional.

Winged Foot comprises two nine-hole loops, extending like two parallel arms. There are two 400-yard-plus holes to start followed by the 216-yard 3rd to a green flanked by two bunkers that run the length of the putting surface. Another long par four heralds the first of two par fives, the dog-leg 5th of 515 yards that is again heavily trapped near the green. After a shortish par four and a moderate par three, the front nine finishes with two more long par fours completing an outward 3,446 yards. The back nine starts with the par three towards a house, prompting Ben Hogan to describe it as "the 3-iron into some guy's bedroom", and finishes testingly with five successive par fours, all over 420 yards.

Bearing that in mind, it isn't surprising that of the four US Opens held there, only one has seen a winning score under the par of 280 for four rounds. Bobby Jones won the first US Open there in 1929. He tied with Al Espinosa on 294, then won the 36-hole play-off by a stunning 23-stroke margin.

The championship didn't return for 30 years, but in 1959 Billy Casper took the title with 282, single-putting 31 greens in the process. In 1974 Hale Irwin won with 287; then in 1984 came the memorable tie between Fuzzy Zoeller and Greg Norman. The Australian produced some amazing recovery shots over the final four holes, including holing a 30-foot par putt on the last, to finish on 276, four under par. Zoeller, waiting down the 18th fairway, thought the putt was for birdie and waved a white towel in surrender. Moments later he holed out for the same score. In the following day's 18-hole play-off, Zoeller won comfortably by eight shots.

That championship, perhaps more than any other, proved that Tillinghast did indeed produce a man-sized course.

FOUR IS NOT ENOUGH *Greg Norman lost to Fuzzy Zoeller in the 1985 US Open after tieing on a Winged Foot record 276*

THE GOLF INDUSTRY

Golf is big business. The top professionals are among the wealthiest sportsmen and women in the world, at the head of an immensely rich industry. If money talks, then golf is indubitably the most loquacious of sports.

Big bucks for a growing sport

Four distinct periods can be discerned in the growth of US and British golf. First came the pioneer days of the 1890s, a decade which began with a handful of clubs and finished with hundreds in both countries. The second period of growth following the First World War was inspired by amateur and tour stars, notably Bobby Jones, Walter Hagen and Gene Sarazen; the third wave, after the Second World War, by Byron Nelson, Ben Hogan and Sam Snead. Both post-war surges were in any case periods of rapid economic growth and great wealth.

The fourth wave arrived and golf became a mass market – the global estimate is 40 million – once television hypnotized the stay-at-homes, seized the attention of the sponsors, and pushed tournament prize funds into seven figures. Ryder Cup star Chip Beck had a "bad" year in 1994, slumping to 68th on the US money list – with $281,131.

Yet the prize money offered is only part of the total cost of staging a tournament. It is generally accepted, that on top of the cash to be earned by the players, the tournament sponsors have to budget additionally for at least the same amount for controlling the event, preparing the course, and providing score boards, catering facilities, transport, media, medical staff, fitness centres, and even crèches.

The bigger the event, the greater the attendance, the bigger the on-costs, and for some tournaments the operating costs swell to far more than double the total purse. The main US Tour, together with the "feeder" secondary tour (now the Nike Tour, but which started under Hogan's name in 1990) and the Senior Tour, put on well over 100 tournaments a year. The TV deals signed in 1997 ensure regular purses on the main PGA Tour of $3 million by the millennium – more for "majors". Dozens of players have enjoyed million dollar seasons. So it cannot be long at the present rate of progress (bearing in mind that the Senior PGA Tour took only 14 years to grow from four events in 1980 to an annual average of more than 40 tournaments) before the tours cost $500 million. This does not include the Ladies Professional Golf Association Tour prize budget of $30 million. Karrie Webb (in 1996) was the first to win £1 million in a season.

The European Tour's purses of nearly £28 million suggest cash needs of twice that amount. The Japanese Tour also pays out huge winning dividends, with first prizes well up to standards in the West, and total purses in excess of $20 million.

On the professional tours worldwide, there are now approximately 400 events (men, women and seniors), with purses totalling in the region of $250 million. There are more than 200 men's tournaments, paying out in excess of $150 million, and nearly 80 per cent of that goes to the top 300 golfers. Senior golfers in the US have already passed $5 million. All these figures are approximate, and they do not include extras such as skins games, shootouts and the like.

A magazine study of a week in 1994 when there were five major events (on the American and European PGA Tours, the US Senior, the American and European Women's tours) showed the total purse money was over £2 million, and combined attendance 250,000.

Tour finances are not concerned simply with the running of tournaments. The capital projects of the US PGA are spread far and wide. Their Golf Course Properties include more than a dozen Tournaments Players Clubs, and more are planned. During the 21 years Deane Beman was Tour Commissioner, the assets of the US PGA grew from $730,000 to more than $200 million.

The most extraordinary aspect of these Players Clubs is that they have enabled American tour players to become the only professional sportsmen in the world who own the stadiums upon which they play. Fans who can't make the tournaments have the benefit of the videos and TV magazine programmes from PGA Tour Productions.

The tour's charitable achievements are impressive too, for $300 million was disbursed country-wide between 1938 and the end of 1996.

PROS' PERKS *While amateurs insure themselves* against *a hole-in-one, for pros they can be very lucrative*

PEUGEOT
PEUGEOT 205

Footing the bill

PRODUCT AND PLAYERS *Sandy Lyle (second left), Tommy Horton (in hat) and Nick Faldo at the 1989 Volvo Masters in Spain*

American Express safeguarded the future of the Women's Professional Golfers European Tour (WPGET) with a three-year deal worth at least $3 million, starting in 1995. So "Amex" become the headline tour sponsors ... this after the company rejected approaches from the men's tour as "not value for money", which, in relation to the sort of treatment women all too often suffer in the game of golf, amounts to reverse discrimination. Soccer and a symphony orchestra fared no better in getting Amex money. Tour chief executive Terry Coates expects a £10 million prize fund by the end of the decade. No wonder the tour, with an 18-event 1997 programme, holds a qualifying school, from which there is no better chance that one in three of gaining a tour card.

WPGET's growing reputation was demonstrated at their first qualifying school at La Manga in Spain by the presence of the 1993 US Amateur Champion, Jill McGill. The tour had many uncertain early years, mainly owing to the damning bottom line that the players were not good enough to attract public or sponsors. Rapid improvements took place, with Laura Davies leading the way as the win-anywhere star and first Briton to reach the top of the Ping world rankings. Yet the tour would not have survived at one point without a £50,000 subsidy from the R&A, nor would it be in its present buoyant state without the Solheim Cup win of 1992 which demonstrated a remarkable enthusiasm for European togetherness among players and fans.

US RECRUIT *Jill McGill, WPGET card-seeker, on 1994 Curtis Cup duty*

The sources of the wealth funding the US men's tour, which since 1983 includes a pension fund for players, began with a few thousand dollars put in by the "Jaycees" (junior chambers of commerce) in southern US resorts back in the 1920s, the formative years of the US Tour; in Britain it all started with events set up after the foundation of the PGA, with prize money donated by club members. The Jaycees still do put on golf for local causes, but in the world of big-time pro golf millions flow in now from the modern headline or corporate sponsors of a tour, as with the Swedish carmakers Volvo and their major role in the European Tour.

It is a counsel of perfection for sponsors that they should never plunge into sport just because the board chairman or the chief executive is a 15-handicapper who would like to treat customers (and himself) to a few days out with the stars. It sometimes happens, though, and there are other ways in which a sponsorship proves to be flawed, as when a tobacco company found their event secured good UK publicity, but their main market was in Africa.

Equally wrong-headed is any attempt to alter the format of a sporting event to suit sponsor and guests. In other words, the performance in the market-place of the sponsorship should be the primary concern.

Sponsorship is not necessarily support of a single event, as seen with Volvo, who in 1996 added to their eight years of headline sponsorship with four further years as "principal sponsor". PGA European Tour players will compete for the Volvo Rankings, while guarantees are in place to the end of the century for the Volvo PGA Championship, Scandinavian Masters, German Open, and Masters at Valderrama. Volvo are clearly satisfied customers – the Tour, they say, remains the bedrock on which their sponsorship programme is based – tailor-made for their ABC1 consumers.

Sponsors' Eastern promise

Volvo have quite different reasons for sponsoring the China Tour, which begins with only six Chinese touring pros, in a five-year deal centred on the China Open in Beijing. The field will consist mainly of Asian and Australian players, plus whoever Volvo can tempt away from Europe and the US. Volvo can as yet sell few cars in China, but many elsewhere on the

Pacific Rim: besides, no one can afford to ignore trade openings in such a fast-growing economy.

Golf has proved a useful marketing tool for companies who wish to establish a new service or product or, as in the case of the financial management company NM, a business which has changed its name, and needed to increase public awareness of the fact quickly. NM sponsored the English Open for three years for that purpose.

Johnnie Walker Scotch is another major sponsor. Though they gave up their season-ending World Championship in Jamaica, into which they sunk £20 million ($32 million) over five years, their love-affair with golf goes on. It is a long term liaison, going back 80 years. The distillers will continue to support their other major event. the Ryder Cup, and the Classic in Asia. Overall, J.W. pledges £11 million ($17,050,000) a year, a great deal of it at grass roots level (as with their hole-in-one awards from club level upwards) with over 100 events in more than 60 countries.

Performance of sponsorships is carefully monitored. Television exposure is the key, plus how many mentions the event wins in the other media. The bottom line must be what happens to group sales.

The US Tour also has marketing contracts with multinationals such as soft drink makers and airlines. Any number of products can be adopted and their manufacturers endorsed as tour suppliers.

A point consistently agreed by the game's rulers and sponsors is that golf is seen as a clean sport: not too many spectator seats are thrown at tour or amateur events, and those who throw clubs in anger may find the practice expensive. It is well known that Volvo withdrew from tennis sponsorship because they considered the players got too much money and behaved badly.

Finally there are the fees for television rights, for this medium and the cash it raises are the key to the threefold rise in prize-money in a decade (200 per cent in seven years in Europe), and the knock-on effects enthusing newcomers to golf and consequent course construction.

Tapping the global market

The virility of the game is well demonstrated by the fact that since the first exhibition of golf merchandise at the close of the 1920s, the attendance has always increased year by year, so much so in America that it is necessary to hold one show on the East coast and one in the West. The Las Vegas version at the Sands Convention Centre attracted 900 exhibiting companies and more than 18,000 visitors. Significantly the space-age materials feel of golf equipment as the millennium approaches was underlined by the fact that every major manufacturer displayed some form of a titanium metal wood. The metal, whose lightness and strength is the key to the vogue for over-sized clubs, had been the headline-making material at the earlier Orlando show, and also made its presence felt at the Eurogolf Trade Show at Birmingham in England.

BEAUTY IN DEMAND *Jan Stephenson*

A recent Orlando show had trade stands shown by close circuit TV in hotel bedrooms at the resort. But shows are mainly about business, and that is spreading world-wide: travel grants are offered by Britain's Department of Trade and Industry to encourage exhibitors to seek Pacific rim customers at Singapore Golf Asia.

The effort and expense put into these shows, replicated in every major golfing nation, is explained by the extent of the global market, with its target of an estimated 40 million players world-wide. Yet clearly, on the basis of the US figures which show that half the nearly 24.7 million American golfers do not play at all regularly, it is reasonable to suppose that many players get by with the minimum of equipment, or rent, borrow or share clubs.

The US Golf Foundation state, however, that 43 per cent of players in the US come from households headed by professionals or managers. This prosperous group must put up the lion's share of the estimated $15 billion spent each year on golf gear, and the playing fees for a US total of 477 million rounds. Well-heeled retired folk in the sun belt states are good customers for clubs that compensate for the ravages of age.

Persuading golfers to part with rather more than the minimum necessary to propel a ball around the local nine-holer requires a proof that the new product will genuinely help the customer's game. The use of space-age materials, the unending search for a bigger "sweet spot" on the face of the club so as to make a not quite perfect shot into a reasonable one, and production of a ball that flies furthest, are all part of the trade's effort. Temptation has to be strong, however, when a set of graphite shafted irons – and this applies to goods of pro-

BAHT MILLIONAIRE *Mats Lanner's 1992 hole-in-one in Bangkok paid him £25,250/$39,000 or 1 million baht*

shop quality, not the specialized equipment used by many top pros – can cost £1,300 ($2,000), and still leave the purchaser in need of a putter and woods.

Yet since the manufacturers must abide by the restrictions imposed by the USGA and R&A on the liveliness of the ball, and they do in the vast majority of cases, it is still the nature of the ball which rules the golfing roost, as it always has.

Recent moves by the golf industry's boffins have concentrated on the sweet spot, and occasionally a manufacturer will get a sales-swelling boost thanks to an heroic exploit or two.

When part-time tour player Johnny Miller, aged 46, won the AT&T National Pro-Am at Pebble Beach at the beginning of 1994, his first Tour win since taking the same prize seven years earlier, he did it in rough weather with the aid of Callaway's new big-headed driver.

Shortly before the company's new irons were officially launched the following year, Colin Montgomerie, the Scottish Order of Merit winner of the previous two years, began his defence of top spot on the European Tour in the Emirates, Dubai, and scored 68, 63 in his first two competitive rounds with the new clubs.

Taylor Made and Cobra provide plenty of competition for Callaway, who have responded by technological leaps and bounds to what sounds like the ultimate weapon: the Biggest Big Bertha Titanium Driver. Net income went up 25 per cent in 1996 to $122.3 million, and the company claim that their drivers are used more than any others on the five main professional tours, where in the opening 1997 events they claimed 70 per cent use of titanium drivers.

However, customer loyalty is strong. Karsten Solheim's original putter concept of weighting the heel and toe of the club has countless adherents, to the extent that the original Anser series is collectable and examples reportedly command four-figure prices.

Arnold Palmer's meat packers

Arnold Palmer gets more popular with every passing year, and his farewell appearances, while not nearly as frequent as those of some singers one could mention, are widely discussed with regretful sighs. There are frequently jokes among the fans, like the one about the spectator who was booed because he made a poor throw sneaking Palmer's ball back on to the fairway.

Anyone that popular, whose dogged army of supporters was forming up while he was still in his twenties, has to be among the most marketable professional sportsmen of all time.

Yet Mark McCormack, at one time manager of the big three, Palmer, Player and Jack Nicklaus, who so dominated the 1960s, had to wait a long time before he was able to turn Palmer's promise into wads of dollars. This was because Palmer could not break free of a contract he signed with Wilson Sporting Goods Co. soon after becoming a professional in 1954.

The representatives of golf gear makers are ever on the look-out for the player who is one day going to pay off in huge endorsements and autograph club-making deals for all the golf balls, clubs and assistance put his way while in the apprentice stage. A good many amateurs are accorded much the same treatment, which in many cases is illegal but not too easy to check. Most of the reps' guesses are wrong, but Wilson was right about Palmer and certainly loath to let him go, definitely not after his second Masters win in 1960.

As a rookie on the tour he could not reasonably hope to appear as a good catch to the parents of his girlfriend Winnie Walzer, so he eloped with her and, as McCormack says, no doubt found the $5,000 a year he was getting from Wilson very use-

BIG AND BEAUTIFUL? *Johnny Miller's AT&T trophy and $225,000/£145,000 cheque at Pebble Beach in 1994 were a testament to big clubs*

ful. Moreover in 1957 he had, rashly in McCormack's view, renewed the contract he signed in 1954. By 1958 he was winning nearly six times as much as in his first year ($7,958). McCormack's difficulty in selling Palmer's name, which was soon, figuratively speaking, blazing up there in lights, derived from the fact that he could do so only where Wilson's products were sold: not, for example, in Australia. Added to this, the royalties for Palmer's Wilson autograph clubs were not generous.

In 1960 it became clear that Wilson, a subsidiary of a meat packing company that had initially gone into the sports business using animal gut for tennis rackets, was not going to release Palmer from a clause in the 1957 contract that gave them an automatic renewal option until 1963. This was a disappointment to Palmer, who believed that he had shaken hands with Wilson executives on a promise that they would not want to keep him if he was unhappy. So, no release ... but almost at once Palmer mounted his most famous charge and won the US Open. He became, in his manager's phrase, "an immortal in alligator shoes."

TOP MANAGER *Mark McCormack at the 1991 World Match Play at Wentworth; his first client, Arnold Palmer, won in 1961*

After long negotiations with Wilson, whom Palmer was still loath to abandon, a 10-year contract was drawn up which suited everyone, though it fell far short of McCormack's marketing projections for Palmer. Everyone, that is, except, Judge James D. Cooney, head of Wilson. He said no deal, because no Wilson executive had a deferred-income plan or an insurance policy as stipulated in the contract.

McCormack wrote to Wilson to the effect that its decision would end up being the most expensive it had ever taken. However, Wilson even rejected Palmer's offer to pay back all monies he had earned from them, and buy out unsold Palmer clubs to a total of half a million dollars. So he and McCormack had to wait out the final days of the contract in 1963.

Ten years after his unfortunate renewal in 1957 of the original Wilson contract, Palmer's annual earnings were into six figures, and products from insurance to dry cleaning, as well as his own-firm autograph clubs, were bringing in sales of $15 million a year. Later NBC paid millions for a piece of the Palmer enterprises.

The Palmer-McCormack bond has proved unbreakable to date. Not so McCormack's management of Nicklaus, who began in the marketing stakes with a grave disadvantage. He was bulky, and upon his crew cut descended all manner of imprecations because he beat Palmer. After leaving McCormack in 1971, he became a rep's delight, looking slimmer in build, with his fair hair profiting from a new, softer haircut. He became more comfortable in his relations with the Press. His "Golden Bear" motif fitted, and his businesses boomed, including an increasing involvement in golf architecture when, at long last, he stopped winning tournaments. Then he started winning again, on the Senior Tour.

The same magic was worked on John Miller, a Mormon who was induced to become Johnny Miller, though he preferred John. One wonders how much this can have helped the marketability of a player who had it all: huge distance off the tee, steepling mid-irons, plus a tall athletic figure, blond hair and rugged good looks.

McCormack's International Management Group (IMG) looks after a large number of sports stars, and finds ways of advising event organizers, right up to R&A/USGA level, of mutual profitability. The R&A Open logo, which is registered throughout the world, is sold on sweaters and other products, and brings in much revenue, was an IMG notion.

Perhaps the most marketable golfer in the world today is that rare bird, a left-hander – tall, personable Phil Mickelson, who performed an even rarer feat – winning a professional tournament, the 1991 Northern Telecom Open at Tucson, while still an amateur. Mickelson had first come to international notice in the 1989 US Walker Cup team. That team lost, but in 1991 Mickelson, with three points out of four, played a strong role in the US team that snatched the Cup back. One of the men who has helped Greg Norman to profit from his golfing skill and powerful charisma, watched Mickelson at the Masters giving out balls to children whose fathers he addressed as "Sir". This marketing man's opinion was: "You couldn't sit down with a blank piece of paper and create something better. He will make millions". As well as being the PR man's dream, Mickelson is the only golfer to equal Jack Nicklaus's record of winning four times on the US Tour before reaching the age of 24.

Fuzzy Zoeller, the rich runner-up

Few sporting contests allow the 100th finisher to pull up with $178,501 as his reward, but such was the luck of the Irish in the list of official money winners at the end of the 1994 US Tour. David Feherty's first year on the tour also left him in secure possession of his player's card for 1995.

Even more remarkable in a year awash with dollars was Fuzzy Zoeller's unprecedented feat of earning more than a million dollars – without ever winning a tournament. One is reminded that Jack Nicklaus has been heard to criticize US golfers for being less than focused on winning, and being content with earning a good living ... a possible source of Ryder Cup failures.

This accusation can scarcely be brought against Zoeller. He had been squeezed into second place four times before coming to the Tour finale at the demanding 7,005-yard Olympic club course at San Francisco. He finished 10 under the par of 284, returning three scores in the 60s, yet was second again. It required a 40-foot putt by Mark McCumber on the first hole of their play-off to beat Zoeller for the Tour Championship, total purse $3 million. That's how hard McCumber was focused on winning the $540,000 first prize, and why Zoeller ended the season still winless since 1986.

Nothing is likely to block the flow of cash going to banner events like the Tour Championship, but the recession born in the 1980s is still having its effects on sponsorship. Torrey Pines, near San Diego, was in the days of the Andy Williams Open a magnet for southern Californians, and had an attractive showbiz touch lent by the singer.

Many changes of sponsorship followed, and a decline in the condition of the two courses cast a shadow, before Buick came to the rescue. Both North and South Courses have now been brought up to scratch, and the venue's future seems assured.

Sponsorship in Scotland, despite its standing as the home of golf, is a problem for both the men's and women's tours. Only six months before the male and female versions of the 1995 Scottish Open neither tour had found a backer.

The determining factor is usually television, without which sponsors are loath to invest. Yet offers were slow in coming in Scotland, despite the fact that the women's Open had three days of BBC coverage promised: the men would have to rely on satellite coverage.

Sponsors were there none when championship golf got under way in 1860, apart from the Prestwick Club and their Championship Belt. No money was offered in the Open until 1863, when Willie Park Senior got £10, a not inconsiderable sum in those days.

Prize money was forced past the £100 mark by the Musselburgh "revolt" of 1892. It went down to £100 the following year, and took another half century to get into four figures. But from £10,000 in 1965, it took only 28 years to reach £1 million, at the 122nd Open. US prize cash has usually kept a step ahead.

Today prize money is but a minor part of the story. The opportunity to profit from endorsements runs a long way down the money list, and at the top level the rewards are spectacular. A second Masters for Bernhard Langer in 1993 earned him an immediate $306,000, but like Palmer he is in the financial care of McCormack and his International Management Group. The endorsements IMG had gathered for him already included Adidas shoes, the American Express card, Hugo Boss clothing, Ebel watches, Lufthansa Airlines, Mercedes-Benz, and Palmer's erstwhile associates, Wilson. As a good-looking family man Langer is a commercial treasure, especially at home in Germany. Guesses at what all this means in cash terms go as

OPEN MEETING *David Feherty and (right) Fuzzy Zoeller shake on it during the Open at Turnberry*

high as $3 million.

Greg Norman is reputed to do even better, his second Open at Sandwich bringing additions to his list of endorsement contracts that had reputedly already been worth $12 million, thanks in particular to Australian, Japanese, and US admirers of his dashing style – and the fact that, as was once said of Palmer, it is often more thrilling to see Norman lose than to see others win. He has a winning way of losing.

FAMILY VALUES *Marketable Master golfer Bernhard Langer, with his wife and children at Augusta in 1993*

The emancipation of the pro

The leading pros of the late Victorian/Edwardian generation, led by Harry Vardon, J. H. Taylor and James Braid, the tall Scot who came down to London in the role of a club-maker, can have pocketed less than £2,000 between them all told for their 16 Open wins. But they ascended to the dignity of the complete playing professional: indeed, while admitting that on hot days in America he had taken off his coat, Taylor adds, a trifle stuffily to our ears: "In England it is only the novice who plays in the style."

The golf boom of the 1890s had, in Taylor's words, disproved the erroneous impression that the task of manufacturing golf club heads by means of machinery would be an impossible one. Club pros were slowly being freed from the toil of club-making, though the pro incapable of rewhipping or regripping a club is very much the product of the era of the touring pro in the second half of the twentieth century.

"For today [1902] it is the simplest of simple matters to turn out heads to any required model in the course of a few minutes," Taylor added. He particularly dwelt on the excellence of the machine-made clubs he saw in America – "far the neatest in finish".

Taylor clearly had no high opinion of American home-bred professionals and felt that caddies there were not encouraged sufficiently with facilities to practise. Golf was more expensive in America than in Britain, and members did not like their fairways to be cut up or clogged up by youngsters. For all that, his prescient conclusion was that "ere long American players will be able to hold their own in the best company."

Even Taylor must have been surprised by the speed at which his prediction came true, culminating in golfers who win nothing but a million dollars.

Kindly transatlantic tyrants

It is a moot point whether the authorities administering golf do or do not make a better job of it than their counterparts in other sports. However, they certainly make less noise and fewer compromises.

What success they have managed is rooted in two achievements. Firstly, despite the odd tiff over the years, the major powers, the USGA and the Royal & Ancient, have produced between them a body of rules which, for once in a sport, is more honoured in the observance than the breach.

Secondly, they have come close to rigid control of the form of the clubs and the performance of the balls with which the game is played.

The degree to which they have managed to control professionalism and keep the pure flame of amateurism burning bright is rather less clear. The distinction between the two is sharper in golf than in most other sports, for some of whom the term "shamateur" was mockingly invented. Among these are most notably athletics, lawn tennis and soccer, in former times. Finally even rugby union has "come out".

The USGA, which is almost exactly a hundred years older than this book, was founded to some degree because of Charlie Macdonald's impatience with the inadequate attempts made in 1894 to stage championships. He had a vested interest in this, for he had failed to become champion in these events which he condemned, if not in so many words, as not proper golf – and he had seen proper golf, in Fife. For all that, he and the other USGA pioneers brought a spirit of selfless service to the task of furthering golf.

Not only did Macdonald refuse to profit from his work in course design; he told Coburn Haskell, when the inventor of the rubber-cored ball offered him an interest in the project, that he had made it a principle never to receive any profit from his association with the game.

As we have seen elsewhere, the USGA could raise hackles with the Draconian punishments it inflicted at the first hint of a violation of the letter of the amateur status law. It should never be forgotten, however, that the amateur game far outweighed the professional in importance well into the present century, and that the modern Olympic movement, which held its first Summer Games a few months after the USGA's inaugural championships, had similar attitudes.

The temptation to depart from the rules set forth by the R&A was not always resisted in America, on the grounds that differing conditions demanded change. Macdonald the traditionalist did resist a suggestion by USGA president R. H. Robertson that the rules should be Americanized, though as first chairman of the Rules Committee he did suggest minor departures from R&A orthodoxy.

Transatlantic journeys began to codify the rules. An early attempt at defining an acceptable club held that it should have a plain shaft and a head with no mechanical devices, such as springs. Relations ebbed and flowed across the ocean, co-operation becoming ever closer after the great coming together of the 1951 rules conference. A joint committee regularly reviews the rules, striving to make them proof against technological advance and changing conditions of play across the globe.

An enduring difference between golf in the old country and the new is the American love of pencil and card golf, that is, stroke play, at all levels of expertise, contrasted with the British focus on match play. This US obsession rules most professional events, and acceptance is general of the American practice, long since sanctified by rule, of picking up, marking and (horrors) *cleaning* balls on the green. This is anathema to the old school, which abhorred touching the ball from tee to holing out – except with a club.

When the USGA was barely seven years old, and with the start-up of the US PGA still 14 years in the future, J. H. Taylor, who had just playing a leading part in the creation of British PGA, declared that "Americans have thrown themselves into the pursuit of the game with such determination and goodwill that at the present time they know more about the game than we do ourselves" ... this in 1902!

Which is why America has forced the pace in the development of the game, never afraid to make a profit from it, and never afraid to follow and finance new ideas. The USGA has had to steer a middle course, identifying and restraining excess, encouraging research, as with their Green Section, begun in 1920. Both USGA and R&A have been much empowered by television revenues.

Their policeman's role, as every sporting administrator knows, is a walk on a knife-edge. Though the USGA started bravely with respect to the admission of black players to competition, they did not always maintain that stance; and they had governed for very nearly a century before a woman, Judy Bell, was allowed to play a part in the inner councils of the Association.

STAR SILHOUETTES *Francis Ouimet (left) and Glenna Collett mark Centennial*

No issue has divided the R&A and USGA, and in recent years united them, as much as the legality or otherwise of club manufacture. We have seen how the centre-shafted putter was a metallic bone of contention for the early part of this century. There was considerable British disquiet about the R&A ruling against it, a decision opposed among others by Vardon, Hilton and Herd, and in any case a centre-shafted mid-iron made by Anderson of Edinburgh about 1870 had not been banned.

A united front was the watchword after the atmosphere at a celebration dinner attended by USGA and R&A members was somewhat chilled when both organizations were served with writs from Karsten Solheim. His Ping Eye 2 irons with square grooves instead of the usual V-shaped grooves had been ruled illegal. The Ping Eye 2, it was held, offered unfair advantages, at least to the expert player.

An American judgment in 1990 that an Arizona court had no jurisdiction over the R&A let Michael Bonallack, the secretary, off the hook. Caution was the watchword for the USGA, who had recently had to pay out several million dollars to a ball manufacturer. In the end they and Karsten Manufacturing settled out of court. Compromise was reached on the crucial issue: existing Ping Eye 2 irons might be used for a period, but clubs henceforward must conform to USGA specifications. In the long term, the USGA and R&A retain control of the tools of the trade.

Taming the landscape

Nearly a century ago, pioneer American architects showed that the most unappetizing terrain could be turned to golfing account. This was done with increasing ease once earth-moving equipment replaced horse and scoop. Charles Macdonald's recreation of celebrated British golf holes on his National Links of America, on a windy site near Southampton on Long Island, was achieved and the course opened in 1909 by virtue of having moved enormous quantities of material and bringing in thousands of tons of topsoil. His masterpiece was complete with turf nursery and watering system.

Similarly, the building by George Crump of Pine Valley in New Jersey, cut through the middle of thick woodland and again requiring the re-siting of great amounts of mate-

PING CREATOR *Karsten Solheim, with three early examples of his innovative putters*

rial, produced a superb course wrested from a difficult site.

Elsewhere the demand for courses had been met rather more peremptorily. Tom Bendelow left his job as a New York newspaper compositor in 1895 and is reputed to have laid out 600 courses. This sounds unlikely until his methods are discussed.

He had a fine Scottish accent, which helped in any golf dealings in the early days of US golf, and could lay out two courses a day. First he would use a stake to mark the first tee, then march a hundred yards and stake a spot for a bunker, onward to mark where a mound should go, and on again to mark the green: all of his greens were either round or square, and were bereft of bunkers. Then lunch, one supposes, and on to the next town. At least he charged only $25 a time.

Nowadays the fees of big-name designers like Jack Nicklaus and Arnold Palmer, backed up by experienced course builders, can amount to as much as 25 per cent of the overall cost. But employing them pays off because the star's involvement helps sell the homes that go with so many courses. Meanwhile, course maintenance has become ever more expensive, because golfers, especially in America, demand fairways of a standard that at a quick glance can be mistaken for a green, and the greens must be perilously fast, which is what the professionals prefer also.

Costly search for pastures new

Pressure on course builders became intense as boom times in the eighties raised the tempo again. Europe and Asia in particular have kept and are keeping the architects busy. However, supplies of natural golfing land, such as Scottish links created by tide, wind, birds and animals, wild and domesticated, and the heathland of Surrey and Berkshire, are finite. Despite the availability of earth-moving equipment, designer seeds to suit the turf to the environment of soil and climate, and machinery that reduces the toil and labour costs of course maintenance, new courses cost more and more to complete.

VALDERRAMA REVAMP *Robert Trent Jones on the course he reshaped*

Major course developments on reasonable ground add up to £2.25 million ($3.5 million). Draining a swamp in China, however, or building a course on a Japanese mountainside, and inserting the water hazards which are popular there, is a different matter altogether. But then merely refurbishing Penina reportedly cost £2.5 million.

Even a long-established club such as Ballybunion (1893) in County Kerry, on the west coast of Ireland, can run into construction problems on the choicest golfing linksland. The Old Ballybunion course has long been a favourite stop for British and American golfing tourists in general and for more distinguished Tourists like Tom Watson in particular, who will travel across from the US to play there before going on to a major event elsewhere in the British Isles.

During the building in the 1980s of an additional 18 holes to a design by the doyen of architects, Robert Trent Jones, Ballybunion encountered a major problem: large amounts of sand, not in the characteristic clover-leaf shaped bunkers that are a hall-mark of Robert Trent Jones designs, but smothering one of the new holes.

The project had come about as a financial by-product of the enormous response of Irishmen and Ballybunion lovers world-wide to the club's appeal for funds to restore their celebrated short 7th, which the Atlantic had eaten away. An Italian system of stones in mesh baskets was used to underpin the restoration.

Surplus funds were deployed towards a new course, a highly desirable acquisition for the members, since their well-drained course was sometimes in great demand when neighbouring clubs were weatherbound.

As this new course, recently renamed Cashen after the river reaching the sea at its far end, was taking shape, a sizeable sandhill overlooking the beach was removed by the river authority in the course of drainage works. Soon sand from the beach, no longer restrained by the mound, was sweeping inland, just as the final fairway grass was coming up, protected by the "shelter" grass which allows it to develop, then itself dies off. The sandhill had to be restored, and the fairways cleared – a penalty exacted, no doubt, for the crime of interfering with the natural topography.

This has not ended coastal erosion problems at Ballybunion. The restored sandhill is being kept in place by plantings of marram grass, and this is but a small part of the club's activities in defending their coastline from the Atlantic Ocean. They spend £100,000 every year on this work: 28,500 visitors a year, reports secretary/manager Jim McKenna, help to pay the bills at about £35 a round on the Old Course, £25 on the Cashen.

Financial difficulties with new lay-outs start when several hundred housing units are added to the equation, the property is slow to move and the cash rewards only start to flow after debts are being called in. How often in recent years has such a development been picked up for a relative song when it turns out to be break instead of break-even.

Environmental concerns pose further problems for course builders. Informed opinion is that an average of as much as 10 per cent of total outlay may be spent on finding how best to avoid damage to flora, fauna, water supplies and the landscape in general. The following pages enlarge on these concerns.

Welcome for golf no longer sure

Until the 1990s the global spread of golf seemed to be virtually unrestrained. now countries such as those on the Pacific Rim, which have gone through a period of massive economic growth, are beginning to consider the question of priorities. Some

SWEDISH SURVEY *Joakim Haeggman checks his line at the 1993 Dunlop Masters at Woburn*

are pausing, to rethink the balance between increased economic activity and poorer quality of life, as flowers, trees, animals, birds, water to drink and irrigate, and even air to breathe are sacrificed to what might or might not be progress. The result is that not everyone is overjoyed to see the bulldozers move in, shaping the landscape into a golf course.

Though Tiger Woods quickly became Thailand's favourite sporting son, alongside snooker player James Wattana, human rights activists accused him of irresponsible action when in 1997 he accepted a huge appearance fee to play in his first Asian tournament in Bangkok (an inducement that would not, said Tobin Prior of Sun International at the time, be held out to Woods if ever he were to be asked to play in the Sun City million dollar challenge). Woods was, into the bargain, made a Thai citizen. Roger Bunn, of the Anti-Apartheid Golf Campaign in Britain, said that two million Thais could not plant a second rice crop because of golf club irrigation, and added: "People have been evicted from their homes to clear the way for golf courses to be built". He urged top golfers to stay away.

The contrast between haves and have-nots was starkly presented during the European PGA Tour's first foray to Manila, where Fred Couples took first prize. Correspondents remarked on the close proximity of slums and poverty to the enormous clubhouse, offering all the comforts of the modern country club, that ran about one-third of the length of the final fairway. Leading players, whisked by helicopter back to their hotels, can have seen little of the "other" Manila.

Respecting the environment

In both Europe and the USA efforts are now being made to meet the concerns of maintaining the environment and strike a balance between recreational needs and possible despoliation of nature.

In America the USGA have striven to help preserve wildlife habitats and make clear the environmental benefits conferred by golf courses: among other projects they have co-operated with the Audubon Society and granted money for a Sanctuary Programme, encouraging clubs to show the way. Jim Snow and his USGA Green section have also been of great help as studies intensify in Europe to identify the criteria by which the wisdom of building upon a particular site can best be judged.

Touche Ross management consultants prepared a report for the European Commission entitled "How Green is the Fairway?" that began with the daunting thought that if a similar supply of golf courses as exists in the United Kingdom (there were 3,678 at the beginning of the 1990s, or one 18-hole course per 25,000 inhabitants) were to be built in Europe, 10,000 courses would be needed – four times the present number. They would involve an additional five million players.

French construction reached a 10 per cent rate of annual increase between 1985 and 1991. In some areas, notably tourist regions, the figure was about 25 per cent. The UK figure for the 1983–93 period was 2 per cent. Rates of increase on the continent are now likely to slow because of rising public disquiet about such rapid change in land usage. Legislators, pressed by environmental groups, tend to ensure that protesters shall have ample time to examine and object to projects.

Planning permission is now difficult to obtain in Austria, Germany, Switzerland and Belgium, mainly on environmental grounds. Much earth-moving, big changes in the landscape, and loss of flora and fauna, added to accusations – here too – of golf's perceived elitism, produce an atmosphere hostile to construction. Two recently constructed courses serving Swiss urban areas, Golf de Bossey (near Geneva) and Golf de Basle, are sited mainly or wholly in France because planning permission could not be obtained inside Switzerland.

German clearances for building can take seven years, and there are strict controls: courses must be spacious enough to allow buffer zones for natural habitats; earth-moving and bunkers are closely monitored; greens and tees must be undersealed to permit water recycling.

Elsewhere course builders are less hobbled, though in southern Spain water shortage is a problem. It has been less acute during the tourist recession, but likely to return unless recycling and better water economy can be made to work.

In Sweden, whose leading professionals include names such as

Joakim Haeggman, Jesper Parnevik and Annika Sorenstam, and are doing much to make the game fashionable, the scale of growth in demand for golf can be gauged from recent annual rates of increase in the numbers of players ... up to 15 per cent. No nation is more aware of environmental issues, so that the golf union provides appreciation of the conflicting claims of use for the land in question. Land is limited in Sweden, and pressure upon existing golf facilities severe.

That is also very much the case in the Netherlands, where the authorities make a point of involving all interested parties in the environmental field when course construction is mooted.

It would seem logical to suppose that more golfing land has become available because of the Common Agriculture Policy payments of "set-aside" money to farmers who agree not to cultivate all their fields. (The UK rate is £200 per hectare, about £81/$126 per acre.) Many courses have indeed been the result, but not without criticisms about land being lost to food production forever. Golf courses designed for derelict sites are much more likely to get the planner's nod.

The EC report offers a chart of a succession of judgments to be made in deciding whether a project should or should not go ahead. Environmental damage or an unsound business plan would be immediate reasons for cancellation. If the environmental flaws can be righted in time, and if the social benefit exceeds the costs, the plan may win approval.

The accuracy of the initial judgements can only be assessed by regular monitoring, for instance, of the crucial link between the finished course and wide water usage, that is to say, grass. Rainfall apart, British courses need 100 cubic metres of water a day in July; Mediterranean littoral courses need all-over irrigation in summer, at 25 times the British volume. Thus the choice of grass is central to success. Native grasses in Britain need less water, but do not give the brilliant, lush colouring of US-style courses that have proved so attractive to leading European players, notably Nick Faldo.

As in southern USA, Mediterranean courses do well with Bermuda grass, and water can be saved with hybrid varieties. Water demand nevertheless remains high in summer, which may lower the water table and encourage saline intrusions into the supply, with possible deleterious effects on drinking water further down the drainage system.

The course architect must therefore be aware of what grasses will ease or exacerbate water problems. This is a subject upon which the Americans are having second thoughts, which may possibly lead to less use of the varieties of grass which produce the deeply attractive green tones on the fairways.

At a French course on the Mediterranean a neat solution was found to the problem of its turf being affected by a change in its water source. The villain was algae, so algae-eating fish were placed in the storage lake.

The way towards coexistence

Failure to confront the conflicting claims of leisure, the environment, and food production leads to golf schemes going off at half cock. Sometimes the construction stage is reached before any analysis has been attempted of the imperatives involved – even the elementary issue of what demand exists for a course in the first place. A 1995 poll of English clubs by the EGU showed that waiting lists totalled only 80,000 country-wide. Advertising for members is not uncommon.

AGADIR INCIDENT *Robert Karlsson on a right royal course – the King's – for the 1994 Morroccan Open, an early season stopping point on the European Tour*

In Europe conservationists, and not just wildlife movements, are working hard to provide a set of guide-lines for course builders and maintenance staff. Michael Harvey, chairman of the trustees of the Golf Course Wildlife Trust, chaired a meeting in Brussels several years ago attended by representatives of 20 nations.

Many Continental golf organizations expressed the feeling that there was a negative image of golf. A rational strategy was needed to destroy that image, which was encouraging, as we have seen, a whole raft of obstructive legislation.

The meeting was attended by David Stubbs, Director of the European Golf Association Ecology Unit, based in Brussels and Dorking in Surrey. He subsequently led a study which early in 1995 resulted in the publication of *An En ironmental Strategy for Golf in Europe*, a companion study to the massive USGA work on the subject.

Workers in many different disciplines have played a part in its production, among them Dr Anne-Marie Brennan, a wildlife consultant from Kent University, Bob Taylor, of the Sports Turf Research Institute, and archaeologists. The English Golf Union have published *Li ing Together – Golf and Nature in Partnership*.

Michael Harvey would like to see an extension of the idea, already test-marketed, of a Golfers' Conservation Club, with its members spreading into clubs across the land, leading to the appointment of club conservation officers. There are many fairly cheap measures that can be taken to improve landscape values, especially if members are prepared to contribute a few hours of labour or gardening expertise.

A happy example at Wentworth

A fine example of how the manifold difficulties involved in course construction can be overcome is to be found just to the west of London, at Wentworth. Here the club's pride in their third 18-hole course, the Edinburgh, is not founded merely on its popularity with professionals and members and the way in which it has eased pressure of use on the two famous existing courses. The West Course is the home of the Volvo PGA Championship and the World Matchplay Championship, while the East Course has also staged important professional and amateur events.

The third lay-out was at first to be called the South Course. The design of John Jacobs, teacher, Ryder Cup captain and European Tour pioneer, was accepted, while the club professional, Bernard Gallacher, and Gary Player were retained as consultants. The course was renamed in August 1990, when the Duke of Edinburgh opened it.

Since it was carved out of Surrey's Great Wood, just off the A30 road that links London with the south-west of England, it was bound to become a difficult planning proposition, because the site was not only in an area designated as green-belt, but was also recognized as one of outstanding natural beauty.

The 150-acre site was bought in the late 1970s for a most reasonable £80,000, considering its position in one of the region's most desirable residential districts. The land was heavily wooded, and the original plan for its use by the club involved the construction of a course and golf centre surrounded by high-class housing.

Planning permission was initially refused, but the central idea of golf course use was not the main sticking-point, so all was not lost. Richard Doyle-Davidson, one-time managing director of the club, was a leading figure in the campaign to meet all

WENTWORTH PRIDE *The tree-lined majesty of the Edinburgh course, a model for meeting wildlife and botanical concerns: this is the par-4 fourth hole*

the concerns involved in building the course, and likes to think other clubs can learn from the way in whichthe club conducted that campaign.

It was based on the idea that the course could work with the environment, and not against it. A report commissioned from Liverpool University assessing how the new course would affect the local environment cost £10,000, but it favoured construction, and impressed environmental and wildlife groups who were in any case consulted. The Surrey Wildlife Trust were invited to manage particularly sensitive areas on the club's behalf. One such area is designated as of Special Scientific Interest.

Wet woodlands are a vanishing habitat in Britain, so that areas of that type, which supported flowers, toads and insects peculiar to Surrey, were given extra protection. Specimen trees were chosen, and the lines of fairways adjusted to protect them. A South Course Environmental Committee was formed. Doyle-Davidson represented the club's owners, and sat with the planning consultants and representatives of Wentworth Residents Association, Surrey Wildlife Trust and Runnymede Borough Council. Doyle-Davidson says that the initial fears that restricted access to areas of interest to naturalists were dispelled, because footpaths were retained through the woodlands.

COURSE CONFERENCE *Gary Player (second left), John Jacobs (centre) and club professional Bernard Gallacher (right), map out Wentworth's third course*

Long-term care of the club's estate was the end purpose of an overall Environmental Audit undertaken in 1990, by a group comprising landscape architects, experts in the field of ecology and landscape management from Liverpool and London Universities, and experts in forestry.

The stated aim is to improve conditions for golf while caring for the beauty of the landscape, protect and improve a wide range of habitats for wildlife, "establish long term semi-natural woodland cover which will be self-sustaining with limited maintenance and management, and develop woodland edge and off-fairway areas easy to maintain and manage."

The range of wildlife in the area revealed by the audit would surprise 99 per cent of the galleries and television audiences of Wentworth's chief events. Chobham Common nearby has two nationally rare items of vegetation, marsh gentian and marsh club moss, as well as marsh orchids.

The Wentworth area has spider species found only in Surrey and the New Forest in Hampshire: 40 per cent of all British spider varieties live there. Rare birds, including small falcons called hobbies, breed on the Edinburgh course, and there are green and great spotted woodpeckers. Adders and great crested newts also breed there, and there are badger, deer, fox and (too many) rabbits.

The club also employed a PR man and a traffic consultant who looked at the increase in road use involved. All in all, it is estimated that £200,000 was spent on studies, PR and an explanatory video before planning permission was eventually obtained. The money proved to have been well spent.

It seems almost an afterthought to record that the third Wentworth course turned out well, and may host a European Tournament once it has matured. The first significant event played on it was the Peugeot Cup for assistant professionals, some of whom pronounced the course better than Wentworth's older ones. It is certainly a better viewing course than the West; its culminating feature, around the 18th, is an amphitheatre which could hide a battalion. With tall trees as a backdrop, this natural arena is sure to enhance the drama of a close finish.

A boon during construction was that a great deal of earth-moving was not required as the fairways were fashioned through the trees, avoiding the protected areas. Because of its sandy soil, the Edinburgh has proved playable when bad weather has closed down its more elderly neighbours.

THE RULES OF GOLF

Golf is a target ball game of stark simplicity, but it is governed by a wide-ranging and detailed set of rules and circumscribed by a code of conduct and an etiquette that are throw-backs to a more gentlemanly age.

In the beginning, and for several centuries after the game emerged as a cross-country sport, match play was the only form of golf. The object was to strike a ball with a club from point A (called a tee) into a hole at point B in fewer strokes than one's opponent. The contest was played over a stipulated number of holes in a set order. It could be single combat, or between pairs of players.

Games were organized person to person, on a private and individual basis, on the common land of such courses as Leith links and St Andrews. The idea of the club, as a sporting institution, is far younger than the game of golf: before the founding of the Gentlemen Golfers of Edinburgh (now the Honourable Company of Edinburgh Golfers) just over two and a half centuries ago, clubs were political in function.

There came a time when golfing man's competitive instincts reached a stage when a search for the best player became imperative. Hence the gift of the Silver Club by the City of Edinburgh to the Gentlemen Golfers of that city. The winner of the Silver Club was to become Captain of the Golf: in modern parlance, champion. As such he was to settle all points of dispute concerning the rules.

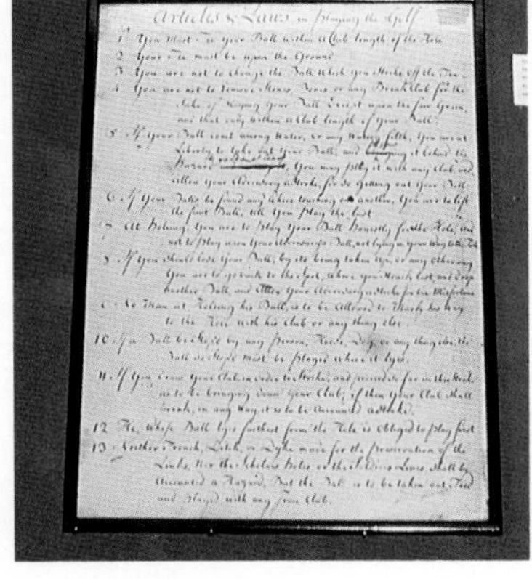
Articles & Laws in Playing the Golf

SHORT AND SWEET *An 18th Century version of the Rules at St Andrews Museum*

John Rattray, winner of the first two Silver Club contests (1744-45), was undoubtedly concerned with the first code of rules, copied in 1754 by the St Andrews men away to the north in Fife.

To lift, or not to lift

These rules are simple and unequivocal. Though the player is never adjured in so many words to play the ball as it lies, the underlying thrust of the rules is unmistakably to that effect. Only if the ball landed in water or "watery filth", or shots came to rest so close together that strokes were impeded, could the ball be lifted. A player must, for the privilege of lifting his ball out of water, dropping it behind the hazard and playing on towards the hole, give up a stroke to his opponent. Obstructions, termed "break clubs", such as stones, were not to be removed, except upon "the fair green" – the putting surface. A lost ball cost a stroke too, the substitute to be played from the location of the errant shot.

St Andrews golfers played for their Silver Club from 1754 until 1759 not by a knockout process but on the basis that he who won more holes in his match than anyone else in theirs was the victor. This would clearly not do: a weak opponent, rather than a brilliant winner, might settle the issue.

So it was decreed that the trophy would go to "whoever puts in the ball at the fewest strokes over the field, being 22 holes" ... for not until 1764 did St Andrews amend their course to the now universally accepted 18 holes for a round. This invention of stroke play brought its problems.

The old play-it-as-it-lies rule of thumb could not survive in all circumstances. It was slow to die, however. Charles Macdonald, the first US amateur champion, a pupil of Old Tom Morris in the 1870s, wrote: "Touching a ball in play without penalty was anathema to me, a kind of sacrilegious profanity."

Provision had to made in stroke play for golfers to complete their rounds and submit a score no matter what difficulties they ran into. So

TREE TROUBLE *Rules man John Paramor can offer no relief for Seve Ballesteros in the 1994 Volvo Masters*

punishments for hitting into trouble, penalties for escaping from it, and definitions for every facet of play had to be minted and, over the years, reminted and refined. So varied is the nature of courses throughout the world that conundrums for the Rules of Golf Committees of the USGA and the R&A will never cease to present themselves. So their work is never done: for it is their joint responsibility to exercise authority worldwide, keeping the rules up to date amid changes in conditions and equipment and responding to the curious scrapes that golfers get into.

Modern terminology

There is plenty of variety in the forms golf can take. On top of the linchpins of single combat at match play and stroke play, there are threesomes, in which one plays against two, and each side plays one ball; foursomes (two against two, each side playing one ball); three-ball (three playing one another, with a ball apiece); best-ball (one plays against the better ball of two or the best ball of three); four-ball (two play their better ball against the better ball of two other players). In the foursome format, the partners play tee-shots at alternate holes, thereafter playing alternate shots; playing out of turn costs the hole in match play, two strokes in stroke play.

Disqualification follows in stroke play if the error is not corrected before teeing off at the next hole, or, where the last hole is concerned, leaving the putting green without declaring intention to correct the error.

American terminology is accepted world-wide where scoring is concerned: par means the score expected on each hole of a first class, i.e. scratch player. Birdie (one under par), eagle (two under), the rare double eagle or albatross (three under) developed from the day in 1899 at Atlantic City after George Crump's second shot at a par four fell close to the hole after hitting a bird in flight. There is an alternative version, that the origin is a comment about "a bird of a shot". Bogey is one over par (double and triple bogey, etc. being self-explanatory).

Bogey used to mean the score achieved by the mythical Colonel Bogey, who made no mistakes, and therefore turned in the perfect score. The American system is clearly far more explicit, though the Colonel lingers on in older dictionaries.

The variations of the golf game are infinite, especially where the myriad betting formulas are concerned. Rules Committees have an opinion on betting too; it is frosty. Since private wagers are beyond the reach of the game's rulers, they make no attempt to police such gambling, and bookmakers take bets world-wide on professional tournaments. Where amateur play is concerned, the authorities frown on large-scale Calcutta sweepstakes and, on days of major club competitions, the purchase of shares in competitors with a view to receiving a dividend if investment has been made in the winning player.

UNGENTLE SARCASM *René Vincent's drawing, "Gardening", in* L'Illustration, *1933*

"Vive la politesse"

Almost alone among sports, golf demands, but does not always elicit, total respect for opponents. Generally speaking, the better the golfer, the closer he or she comes to the USGA/R&A ideal. Etiquette comes first in the book of rules, the concept wedded to safety and consideration for others.

Players must be alert lest their practice swing injures a bystander, while absolute silence and immobility is demanded when a player prepares to hit the ball. Players must not dawdle, strike the ball before players in front are out of range, or fail to call following players through when a ball is being sought; three- or four-ball matches must let two-ball matches through, and golfers must not delay in leaving the green (by inference, this means also not standing about filling in score cards before moving off.) A group losing more than one clear hole on the players in front should invite the following group to go through.

It would be folly to suggest that all these counsels are followed with saintly forbearance, or even that the vast majority of players are aware of every one of the foregoing, not to mention further points of etiquette, such as that "Any match playing a whole round is entitled to pass a match playing a shorter round" and "A single player has no standing and should give way to a match of any kind."

There is also the matter of consideration for the course, in that players should smooth over marks they make in sand bunkers, repair pitch-marks (dents made in greens by approach shots), replace "divots" (portions of fairway turf dislodged in play ... though turf damaged on tees should *not* be replaced, lest a tee peg shift in a loose divot) and avoid damage to the holes themselves. Damage caused on greens by shoe spikes should be repaired only *after* putting is completed. However, repairs to old hole plugs and turf damaged by ball impact can be repaired before putting out.

In the writer's experience, one point of etiquette that is seldom ignored is that the great majority of players do take care not to walk on the line of other players' putts.

Professionals in general and top-class amateurs in particular will go further than the rule book on etiquette. On the tee, they will not drive off while a player is putting on a nearby green. This may lead to minor delay, but seldom causes ill feeling. The major cause of high blood pressure on golf courses is the failure to yield to other groups on the basis of the rules of precedence outlined above.

A basic cause of slow play, especially where groups of three or four are concerned, is the disinclination of players to get ready to play as soon as it is their turn. No. 2 of a quartet will delay his pacing out and surveying of his putt until No. 1 has performed the same sequence.

The rules are not the same for stroke play and match play. Suppose a player thinks his ball is damaged and unfit for play when he reaches his drive. Before lifting his ball to check, he must "announce his intention to his opponent in match play or his marker or a fellow competitor in stroke play." Then he must mark the position of the ball. He must not clean it (mud on the ball does *not* make it unfit for play) He must allow opponent, marker or fellow-competitor the chance to examine the ball.

The ball can be changed if it is found to be unfit for play. (When a ball breaks into pieces the stroke is cancelled, and another ball played from the same spot.) Any deviation from this procedure is punished in match play by the loss of the hole; in stroke play by a two-stroke penalty.

Since the usual penalty in stroke play for breaking a rule is two strokes, and in match play loss of hole, it is not permitted to indulge in both forms of the game at the same time: so a player keeping count of his opponent's strokes for submission for handicap purposes, of which more later, while also competing with him at match play has, according to the letter, and spirit, of the law, lost at match play and compiled an inadmissible card at stroke play.

It's no handicap

Golf has unique charms for spectator and player. It is possible to get a close-up view of players even in major championships. Furthermore, while an overweight, none-too-fit business man of 45 would never survive on a lawn tennis court even with the world's 100th-ranked player, or do more than just get in the way as a linebacker with the Dallas Cowboys, he could enjoy a game of golf against a top-class amateur, or a leading professional, and even hope to win if he played to his handicap. By which is meant the number of strokes that his ruling body consider to represent the difference between our plump businessman's golfing skill and that of the expert.

In principle, a player's handicap is, or should be, an accurate assessment of his ability to play to the standard scratch score (SSS) of a course. Great minds have been applied to the intricate and thankless task of making these judgements which affect a golfer's prospects every time he enters a competition, or even plays a friendly match. Until 1983, a great many British players could not, consistently, play to their handicaps because they were awarded on the basis of their best scores.

Since 1983, performances are reckoned against the SSS of courses, after a model developed by the Australian Golf Union. The SSS computation starts with the length of a course. At 7,001 yards the provisional SSS is 74; at 4,100 it is 60.

The final SSS might be increased or lowered on consideration of general layout, sizes of greens and whether watered or unwatered, difficulties imposed by hazards, width of fairway, trees, rough, and prevailing weather conditions, together with the degree to which the ball runs on landing. Therefore the total *par* of a course will not necessarily equal the SSS, which must not be allocated hole by hole, but given only as a total for the course.

In the first place a player can obtain a handicap by submitting score cards. The national union or a delegated area authority is responsible for ratifying the handicaps of players with low or plus handicaps.

A player's handicap is effective wherever he plays, and can only be obtained by a member of a club affiliated to the national union. The USGA operates a patented system that depends on evaluation of 20 scores against two assessments of a course's playing difficulty, one for scratch players and one for players inferior to that standard.

The player in receipt of strokes from his betters on a golf course cannot choose where he will take them. The card of the course includes a stroke index, which will decree that if two strokes are to be given, they will be, for instance at Royal St David's, Harlech, taken at the 10th hole (stroke index 1) and third (SI 2). If 14 strokes were to be given, the receiver would get them at every Royal St David's hole except the 2nd, 9th, 11th and 18th. The SI figure is not an indication of a hole's degree of difficulty.

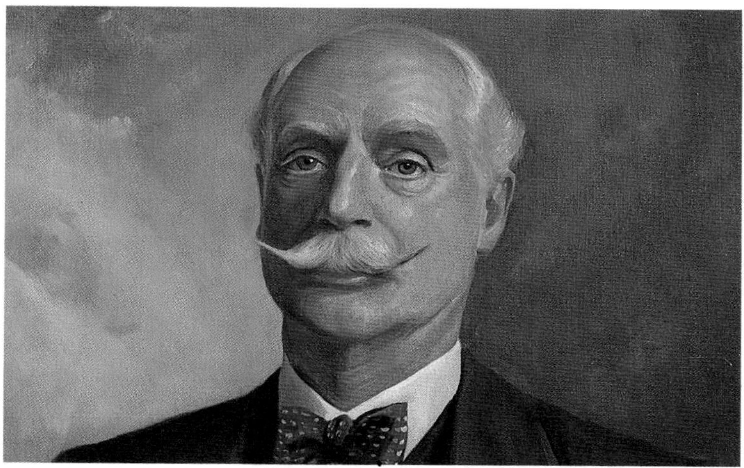

WINNER ON POINTS *Dr Frank Stableford, golfing "saint"*

Point scoring

One of golf's principal benefactors was Dr Frank Stableford, who has been called the patron saint of club golfers. His eponymous points system not only allows single matches to involve players of varying ability in a meaningful contest, but any number of players on a course – or courses. His system was first used at Wallasey on Merseyside in the early 1930s. A scratch player receives four points for an eagle, three for a birdie, two for par, one for bogey, none for double bogey. A player who has a stroke on any particular hole receives an extra point at each stage of this progression, so a par brings him three points, a birdie four.

Recent converts to golf cannot fully appreciate it, but those who were playing before 1952 may consider that the 1951 R&A/USGA rules conference included a majority of saintly figures. The conference was the first of its kind between the two ruling bodies, and issued uniform rules effective world-wide from 1952. One conference decision ended a hoary, old, and bitter controversy: the "stymie" was abolished.

A player was "stymied" on the green if he was unable to putt to the hole because his opponent's ball lay in the way. Unless the balls lay within six inches of each other, the only solution was either to loft the ball, or use the contours of the green to circumvent the obstacle: Old Tom Morris had remarked how skilful Allan Robertson had been at finding the crumbling edge of a hole in such circumstances.

Traditionalists wanted to keep the stymie, to some degree because it had been part of the game for so long, but also because ending the stymie rule offered another opportunity to lift the ball, anathema to the old school of play-it-as-it-lies. Abolitionists considered that the essence of golf was that players should never be baulked in this way.

The USGA, among others, agonized about the matter, and polled the larger associations about it: 22 said keep the stymie, which had been in force since 1812, apart from one year. That was when the R&A abandoned the rule in 1833, but re-imposed it the following year. Twenty-four associations said the stymie should be abolished.

Controversy was periodically renewed when famous matches were decided by stymies, as in Bobby Jones's 19th-hole win over Cyril Tolley on his way to the first leg of his Grand Slam in 1930, and the defeat, six years later, of the Scot, Jack McLean, in the US Amateur final by Johnny Fischer from Kentucky. English hackles were raised when the final of the English Close Amateur Championship in the crucial year of 1951 ended at the 39th hole where G. P. Roberts of Southport and Ainsdale beat H. Bennett of Buxton with the cruellest of stymies.

Seventeen years later the conference outlawed croquet putting: players may not putt with one foot on either side of the line of putt, as

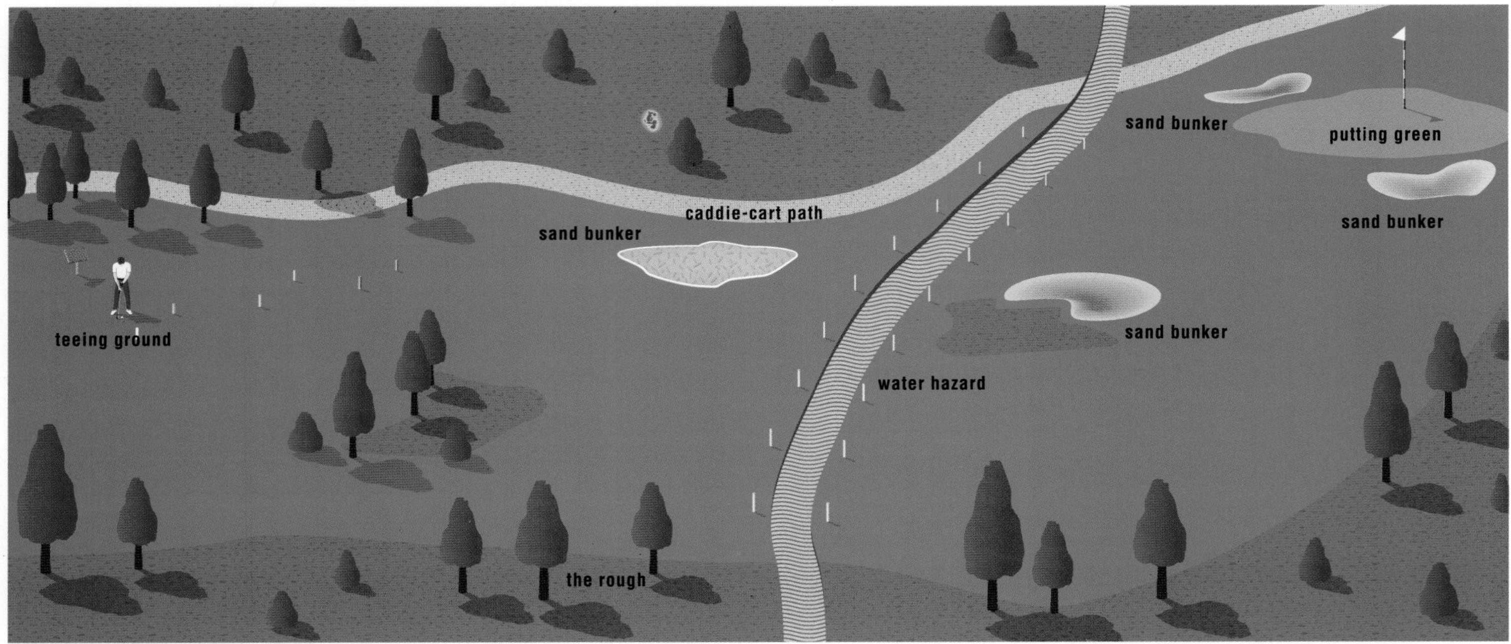

FEATURES OF A GOLF COURSE *A standard golf course consists of 18 holes, each usually between 100 and 600 yards (91 and 549 metres) in length*

if with a croquet mallet. Like many other players, especially older ones who had developed a twitch using the traditional stance, Sam Snead had to resort to a posture known as the "side-winder", holding the top of the shaft with the left hand, then stroking the ball forward with the right hand lower down the shaft. Few believed croquet putting was golf.

One waive and you're out

Anyone who has served in the military will recognize the third section of Rule 1 (The Game) for what it is ... golf's version of that service charge prohibiting conduct prejudicial to good order and discipline which, as every soldier, sailor or flying officer knows, means any conduct of which the Service disapproves in the slightest degree.

Golf's version is entitled "Agreement to Waive Rules", and says: "Players shall not agree to exclude the operation of any Rule or to waive any penalty incurred."

Rule 1 has already, in section two, brought the players to the realization that they are on their own. It makes clear that no player or caddie shall take any action to influence the position or the movement of a ball except in accordance with the rules. Nor are players to give advice on play, or choice of club, to anyone except a partner, or their caddies ... nor seek it, with the same exceptions. Penalty, loss of hole in match play, two strokes in stroke play. Penalties henceforward will be given in that order: first for match play, then stroke play.

Man is a litigious animal, and legislators are frequently outflanked by the expertise of the general public, aided by sharp-eyed lawyers, in finding loopholes in statutes. After more than 260 years of refinement, the rules of golf present a brick wall to the cheat. Admittedly, this is a strange claim to make of a game where cheating is easy, because the player is often out of sight of his fellows.

Here is the inner appeal of the game for in effect, as the totality of the rules make clear, the golfer's only opponent is himself. If he cheats, he has lost and the game has won: it usually does whether he cheats or not, but the difference is between honourable and dishonourable defeat. The stigma attached to the latter is a destroyer of character, and a quick way to lose club membership. Henry Beard has written, tongue in cheek one assumes, "The Official Exceptions to the Rules" with a sub-title of "at last a rule book that makes cheating legal" – but the *official* rule book accepts no exceptions to observing the rules.

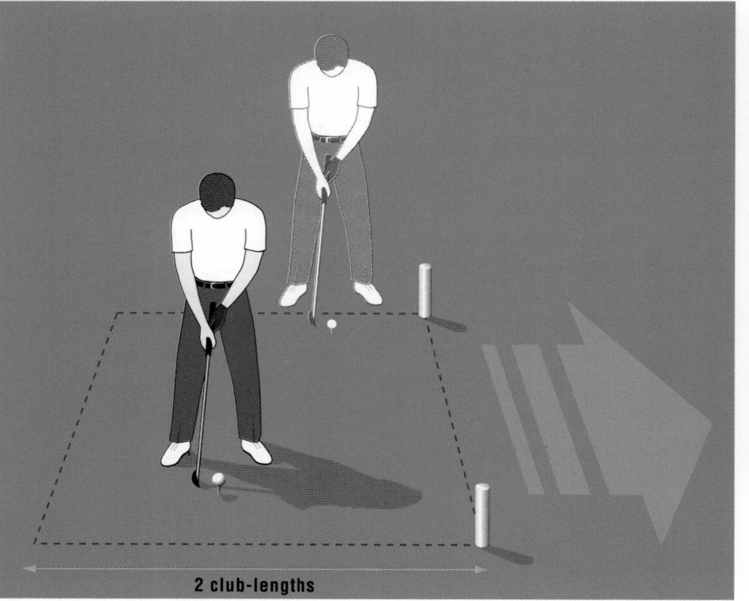

TEEING GROUND *Tee-shots must be struck from within a rectangle two club-lengths in depth – but players can stand outside it to hit their shots*

OUT OF BOUNDS *The out of bounds line is that which joins inside points of fence posts at ground level. Therefore, the ball on the left is out of bounds; the other two are in bounds*

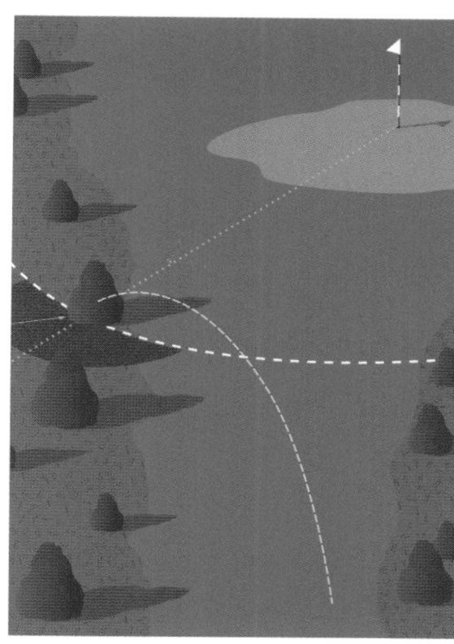

UNPLAYABLE BALL *If a ball is declared unplayable in a bush, the player can (under penalty of one stroke):*
1 *Go back to play from where the previous stroke was played*
2 *Drop a ball within two club lengths of where the ball was declared unplayable, not nearer the hole, as shown in the shaded area in the diagram*
3 *Drop a ball behind the point where the ball lay, keeping that point directly between the hole and the spot on which the ball is played, with no limit to how far behind that point the ball may be dropped*

Playing by the rules

Let us now start at the beginning, on the tee. The player must arrive there with no more than 14 clubs. Six or seven was the usual complement for Harry Vardon and his rivals in the days of wooden, usually hickory, shafts. With the coming of steel clubs (legalized by the USGA in 1924, but not until 1929 by the R&A) and particularly with the refinement of matched sets, the temptation to carry a club for every length and variety of shot was powerful.

Lawson Little, winner of both British and US Amateur Championships in 1934–35, carried as many as 25. Opponents always of excess, and eager to encourage shot-making skills (veteran golfers were scornful of players who couldn't play a half shot with a six-iron to make up for lack of a seven-iron), the authorities called a halt at 14 clubs in 1938. Penalties are heavy for the unwary: one hole for each hole at which the infraction occurred to a maximum of two holes, or two strokes per hole, maximum four strokes per round. The clubs too must conform to strict regulations as to configuration.

The ball must conform to USGA/R&A specifications, and much money and effort are expended to make sure that it does. Briefly, its weight must be no more than 1.62 ounces (45.93 gm), and its diameter no less than 1.68 inches (42.67 mm). Crucially, the initial velocity of the ball must be no greater than 250 feet (76.2 m) per second, within a tolerance of 2 per cent.

Suitably equipped, which means without "artificial device or unusual equipment" and certainly without means of measuring distance or gauging the conditions, the golfer makes a start, mindful always that "the ball shall be fairly struck at with the head of the club and must not be pushed, scraped or spooned". Hitting the ball twice in the execution of a stroke costs a penalty stroke, i.e. the one blow counts as two. The golfer must be careful to take his rightful turn on the tee according to the rules of precedence. In a competition, that means following the draw order issued by the Committee, in the absence of which the order "should be decided by lot".

Low handicap golfers do not gain the honour, as the right to strike the first blow is called, because of respect for their greater expertise, though they often do by custom in friendly matches. Thereafter the honour falls to whoever last won a hole.

Our man should be equally careful not to place his ball nearer the hole than a line joining the twin tee-markers. Nor can he play from more than two clubs' lengths behind that line. At last, he steps up to make a start, only to find his ball has toppled off his tee-peg (not an essential item for teeing off) before he could make a swing at it. He is at liberty to replace the ball, and carry on: this happening involves no penalty, since no attempt to hit the ball was made.

If it falls off during the downswing, and the golfer cannot check his swing, too bad – it counts as a stroke, even if the club makes no contact.

A tee shot struck from outside the proper teeing ground can be recalled by your opponent. You must play again: apart from this there is no penalty, but in stroke play the penalty is two strokes, and play again.

That would make three off the tee, which is also the answer when a ball is lost, or flies out of bounds. The score card tells what the boundaries of the course are, and what marks them: a line, itself out of bounds (OOB), a ditch, a fence, wall or stakes, in which last case the OOB line is the nearest inside points of the stakes or fence posts at ground level, excluding angled supports. The principle follows the soccer model: the ball is out of bounds when all of it lies out of bounds.

The player who fears his ball is lost can, to save time and an irritating walk back after a fruitless search, play a provisional ball. This constitutes the stroke and distance rule, in this case being provisionally followed in case the ball cannot be found in the statutory five minutes allowed. Opponent(s) or marker must be informed of the intention to play a provisional, which must be done before searching for the first ball starts: normally, that is before leaving the tee. The provisional can be played again, up to the point where the player believes his original ball might be.

If that stays lost, the provisional ball becomes the ball in play. A second ball can also be played when a disagreement occurs between players in a group about the right way to proceed, for example, what

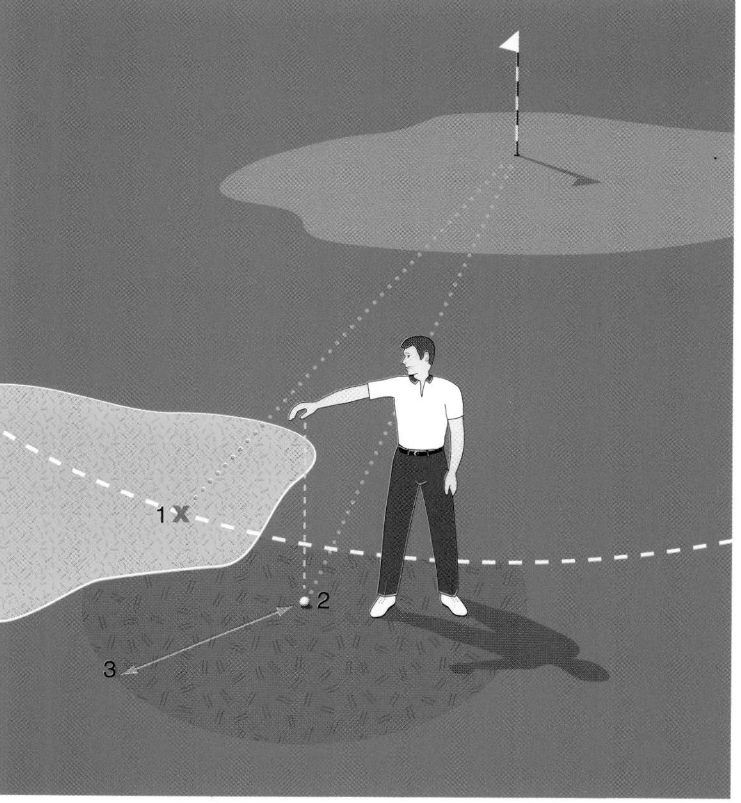

WHERE AND HOW TO DROP *A ball lying in ground under repair (GUR) at 1 must be lifted and dropped (without penalty) within one club-length of the nearest point of relief (2), and not nearer the hole (i.e. not between the dotted line and the hole). The ball is still in play as long as it rolls to no further than 3, two club-lengths from 2. If the stance to dropped ball is inside the GUR, the ball must be redropped. To drop the ball stand erect with arm outstretched to front or side and release the ball. The ball must not be dropped over the shoulder*

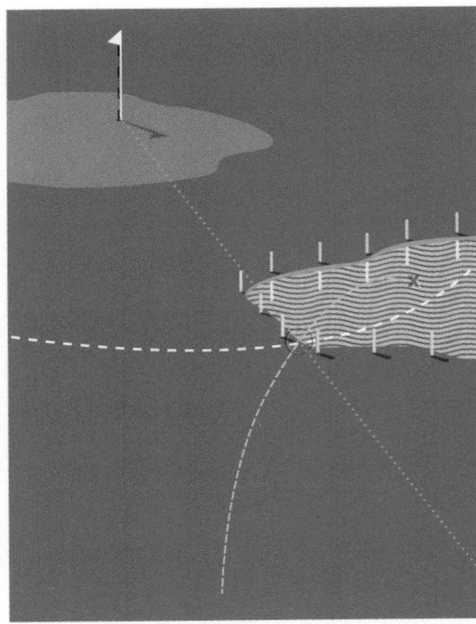

WATER HAZARD OPTIONS
1 *Play ball as it lies without penalty*
2 *Drop, not nearer the hole, on an extension of line from hole through the line of entry: penalty, one stroke*
3 *Return to point where previous stroke was made: penalty, one stroke*

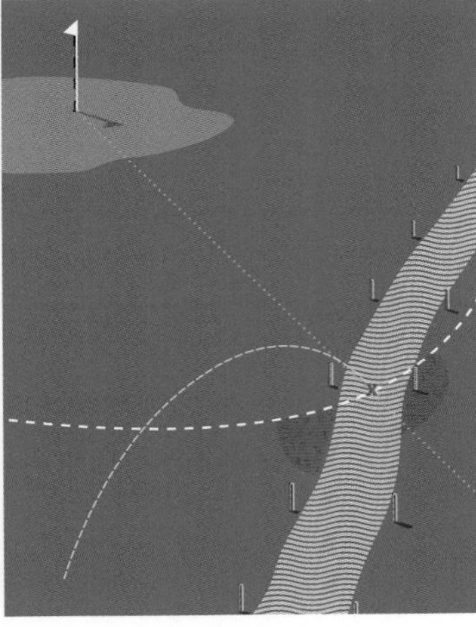

LATERAL WATER HAZARD OPTIONS
1 *Play it as it lies*
2 *Drop behind hazard on a line through hole and point of entry*
3 *Play from point of previous stroke*
4 *Play from shaded area, i.e. within two club-lengths of point of entry, no nearer hole or* **(5)** *shaded area on opposite side of hazard. Options 2, 3, 4 and 5 cost one stroke*

penalty should be imposed if any, or relief received. The player whose position is in doubt may play the first ball as it lies, the second with a drop, make a note of the score from both, and seek an official ruling at the end of the round, remembering not to sign the card until the issue has been settled.

The rules allow golfers to declare their balls unplayable at any time, except in a water hazard. The "unplayable" decision is entirely up to the golfer's sense of fair play. First, at the cost of a stroke, the golfer can follow the stroke and distance procedure, taking the ball back to where it was last struck. Second, the golfer can drop the ball, again with a stroke penalty, within two club-lengths, but not nearer the hole. Finally, the ball may be dropped any desired distance behind the unplayable spot, keeping that spot between the new position of the ball and the hole. This too costs a shot. "Drop" means releasing the ball while standing erect with ball at arm's length.

The revised rules effective from 1996 have been expanded to state that: "if a dropped ball rolls back into the pitch-mark from which it was lifted, the ball shall be re-dropped."

The most frustrating misfortune in golf is undoubtedly playing the wrong ball: which is why a distinguishing mark on a ball is a good and potentially match- or card-saving precaution. The penalty for playing the wrong ball, except in a hazard, is loss of hole, or two strokes. Disqualification follows in stroke play if the error is not put right before the miscreant tees off at the next hole. If the wrong ball played in stroke play belongs to an opponent, it must be replaced as nearly as possible to the position of the first stroke played in error.

The golfer is at liberty to lift a ball to identify it, if it is not in a hazard, and to replace it, but may not clean it. If was found in deep grass or mud, thence it must be returned.

Since lifting a ball to identify it in a hazard is not permitted, the golfer may play a ball in a hazard (defined below) when it cannot definitely be identified. This carries no penalty.

Next the golfer must be aware of penalties and rights attaching to hazards, defined as any bunker (usually termed a trap in America) or water hazard. Grassy ground near a bunker is not part of a bunker, which is basically a hollow filled with sand. Grassed areas within a bunker are not part of it. Little dells lined with grass are not bunkers and not hazards.

A water hazard is "any sea, lake, pond, river, ditch, surface drainage ditch or other open water course (whether or not containing water) and anything of a similar nature".

There are options in both types of hazards. Play it as it lies is always an option, though the club must not touch the hazard except when the ball is being struck: so the club must not be grounded before the stroke is made. It is a good precaution never to ground a club in the rough either, for the grass, being disturbed, may move the ball, for which there is a one-stroke penalty.

A ball in a bunker which is also lying in casual water, ground under repair (usually delineated with a white line and labelled GUR by the greenkeeper) or in casts made by a burrowing animal can be dropped in the bunker without penalty, or outside it with a penalty stroke. It is sometimes impossible to find a spot clear of water in a bunker. Casual water is defined as an temporary accumulation of water visible before or after the player takes his stance.

Water hazards marked with yellow stakes or lines differ from lateral water hazards, which have red markings. Islands within a water hazard are part of it. First option

PLAYING THE BALL AS IT LIES *Don't improve the lie of the ball (e.g. by pressing the foot into long grass behind the ball). Principle: play the ball as it lies. Penalty for violation: match play, loss of hole; stroke play, two strokes*

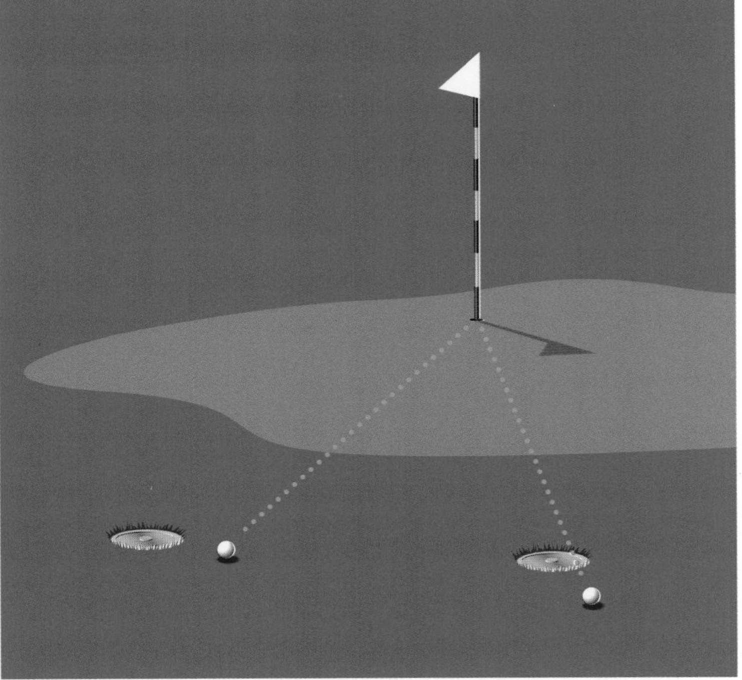

SPRINKLER BLOCKAGE *The ball shown on the right must be played as it lies, as the sprinkler head is not interfering with stance. The ball on the left can be lifted as sprinkler head is interfering with stance (though not in the case of a left-hander). No penalty*

INDICATING THE LINE OF A PUTT *A caddie or partner may indicate line of putt, but must not touch the green or mark it. Penalty: loss of hole, or two strokes*

with a ball in either is to play it as it lies ... easier when the area is dry, but not impossible when wet. The club must not be grounded.

If there is "reasonable evidence" that the ball is lost in the hazard, the player may, at cost of a stroke, play a ball as nearly as possible at the spot from which the original ball was last played; or "drop a ball behind the water hazard, keeping the point at which the original ball last crossed the margin of the water hazard directly between the hole and the spot on which the ball is dropped, with no limit to how far behind the water hazard the ball may be dropped". In the case of a lateral water hazard procedure is different; it lies along the general direction of play, so if it is not possible to drop behind it, a ball may be dropped within two club-lengths of either the point where the original ball last crossed the margin of the water hazard or a point on the opposite margin of the hazard equidistant from the hole.

Loose impediments (natural objects such as leaves and stones) and obstructions (artificial, man-made) present different options. The former may be moved, as long as they and the ball are not in a hazard: boundary fences and the like are not obstructions. Movable obstructions are what their name suggests ... the rules are highly literal in their wording ... but where immovable obstructions are concerned, relief without penalty is the general rule, unless the ball is in a water hazard.

The over-riding instruction is still to play the course as you find it, avoiding any temptation to improve lies or "moving or bending or breaking anything fixed or growing except in fairly taking your stance or making your swing".

Having finally reached the green, the golfer must never make a mark upon it to indicate a line for his putt, nor hit the flagstick with his putt, which costs the hole or a two-stroke penalty. Sand and loose soil are loose impediments *only on greens*, and can be brushed aside (but not pressed down), and balls may be cleaned before putting.

When a putt overhangs the hole, the golfer, having reached the hole "without unreasonable delay", is allowed 10 additional seconds to make sure the ball is at rest. If it falls in after that, the player is deemed to have holed out with his last stroke, but a penalty stroke is added.

Golfers must be men of their word to the last. If a putt is conceded, the offer may not be refused. The offer, once made, may not be withdrawn.

A golfer who seeks to absorb golf's 34 rules by competing at a board game called Masterstroke can be secure in the knowledge that this is by no means a Trivial Pursuit. Masterstroke has been put together by an acknowledged rules expert, Bruce Adams.

Caning for slow coaches

Golf's legislators anxiously sought an effective procedure for eradicating slow play for about as long as they agonized about abolishing the stymie. The nettle was grasped by radically expanding Rule 6–7, which required players to play without undue delay.

From 1996 this must be done, "in accordance with any pace of play guidelines which may be laid down by the Committee." Penalty: loss of hole or two strokes, and "for subsequent offence – disqualification". This, think some, is a sure-fire source of bad blood at club level, especially if "pace of play" is not clearly set out and impartially enforced – an error avoided to great effect at the celebrated Sunningdale Foursomes in 1997, when the draw sheet was accompanied by set time limits for shots, holes and courses: the rounds had to be completed in 3hr 32min for both the Old and New courses.

The professionals' rulers are also now being very specific. For instance the PGA European Tour have been empowered to impose a one-stroke penalty and a fine of £500 on players who are guilty of three "bad times". A "bad time" is acquired by a group spoken to by a Tour official once they got out of position, which means more than 10 minutes behind the group in front. Further monitoring follows, with specific timings allowed for playing a shot or putting. There is a penalty schedule in place for those who offend: one bad time = no action, two = a warning, three = a stroke plus £500 fine, and so on till five costs two strokes plus £1,000 fine. Seven brings a £1,000 fine and disqualification.

There is absolutely no pity or waiting on the US Tour, where officials stroll over to the offending party and say, "That'll be a thousand dollars."

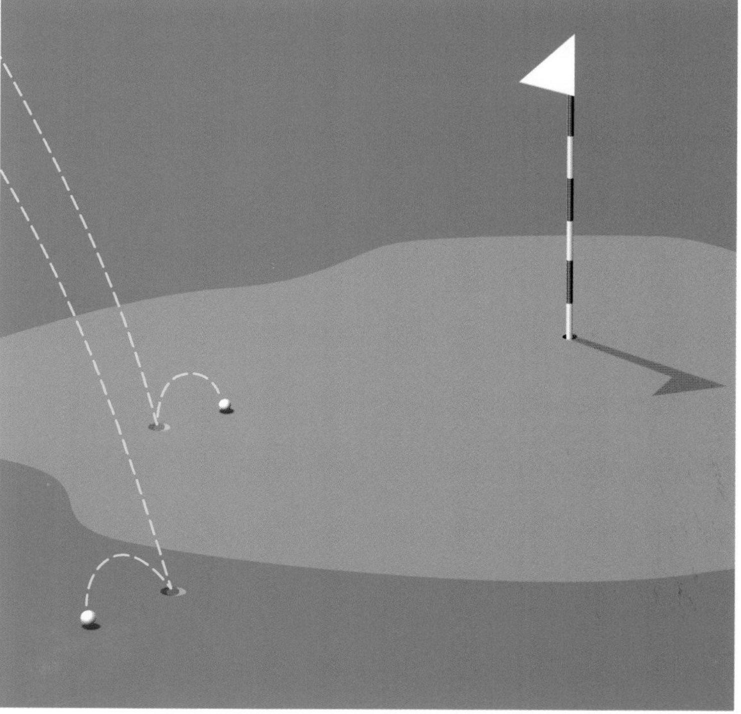

RUNNING REPAIRS *Repairing pitch marks on the green (top) is legal – repairing spike marks is illegal. Repairing ball marks off green is a violation, but permitted after putting out (below)*

THE HISTORY OF THE SWING

Some players, such as Bobby Jones and Sam Snead, are born great; some achieve greatness by sheer persistence, such as Ben Hogan and Henry Cotton; lesser mortals, short on both counts, labour in between.

The ball shapes the swing

Every bat and ball game is at the mercy of the men who make the ammunition, the ball, and the men who fashion the playing arena or, in the case of golf, amend what nature has provided.

Cricketers chat away endlessly about the ball's hardness, resilience, ability to retain shape, and the height of the seam; and that's quite apart from the question of how to keep the shine on the ball, legal and illegal aids thereto, and the state of the pitch. Tennis reformers want a bigger projectile, so that the power of the big servers is reduced and the public can watch rallies of more than two or three strokes again.

The golf ball has gone through even more radical changes, notably with its composition: boxwood, feathers stuffed into a leather sphere, gutta percha, wound rubber bands, liquid cores, solid cores, two-piece, three-piece, constant improvement of dimple patterns on the cover ... and at every stage different demands, complicated by wind and weather, have been made on the mechanics of making the ball fly. Books defining these flow ceaselessly from the printing presses, and it is a safe bet that the majority of golf books in any public library will be of the "Play Golf the Whatsisname Way" variety. Refusing to supply such a market would be unbusinesslike for publisher, teacher and (frequently) the teacher's ghost-writer, though wise golfers and reputable teachers know that personal instruction by a professional is the best way to success in the quest for a reliable swing.

One thought about the golf ball and how to propel it has remained a favourite through the years. As expressed by Harold Hutchinson in his classic and comprehensive 1891 study of the game in the Badminton *Golf*, and in various ways since by books, videos, magazines, and pros without number: it's a swing, not a hit ... very short and simple words containing a truth universally admired but, all too often, forgotten.

IN THE GROOVE *The unmistakable and reliable swing of Lee Trevino*

Hutchinson held that "hit" means a jerk with tensed muscles, whereas the golf swing involves gradual acceleration with flexible muscles. This does not preclude the application of great strength, but does preclude its misapplication.

Hutchinson played in the era which started with the solid gutty ball, which arrived in the middle of the nineteenth century, and finished with the lively Haskell, patented in 1898, with its wound rubber interior. Before these innovations the light and responsive feathery ball made its own swing rules. It fairly sprang off the club face, performing best in the dry. In the wet, especially when clumsily hit, the feathery would burst its stitches, and a careless iron shot would cut it.

Therefore it was necessary to sweep the ball away, so what is thought of as the old St Andrews swing was flat, and sent the ball flying away over the wide open spaces of what is now the Old Course. The favoured stance was closed, that is, with left foot in advance of the right, which had the additional advantage on windswept links courses (there were few of any other type) of keeping the ball low and running.

This method contrasts sharply with the model swing of the late twentieth century, which has become more and more upright, though Lee Trevino's swing, while scarcely a throw-back to Victorian times, has resisted the trend, and won him a fortune. Jack Nicklaus, himself an exemplar of the upright swing, defines Trevino's as "effective in that it is wonderfully well grooved". In other words, it is an action Trevino can repeat exactly and almost endlessly, an action that has stood the test of time deep into Senior status. He had the best stroke average five times on the PGA Tour. It is the repeatability of the swing that counts, rather than its beauty and technical orthodoxy or the strength of the player. This is what

STEADY STEVE *Steve Elkington's much admired swing is a big earner*

Henry Cotton implied in his comment that anyone watching top class professionals setting off from the tee would rapidly realise there was more than one way to strike a golf ball with power and accuracy.

The coming of the solid gutty ball called for immediate adjustments, especially for such players as Allan Robertson, the champion of the 1850s, both in his play and his business, since he was a feathery maker. Though he and noted feathery makers like Gourlay felt threatened by the new ball, Robertson proved himself a true professional by mastering the art of clipping the gutty into flight, which called for accurate timing of the shot and firm wrists, and increased the value of iron club shots that came down hard on the ball, enabling the player to pitch the ball positively and stop it on the greens.

Every golfer has a friend who, once in a while, will excitedly make the claim that he has discovered the "secret" of golf. For Hutchinson, whose steadiness under pressure made him such a fine match player, the secret was accuracy in bringing the club back to the position it was in when addressing the ball. This, he wrote, "can best be accomplished by keeping under firm control all parts of the body whose free movement is not essential to speed of swing."

Thus there should be no swaying to the right (the movements of a right-handed player are specified throughout this section) involved in turning the body on its own axis. This simple idea of building up power by means of the body swivelling around the axis of the spine was scarcely challenged in essentials for half a century until refined by American researches into the full impact, and potential, of the Haskell and its derivatives as propelled by steel-shafted clubs. These researches are continuing, computer-aided, at USGA headquarters in New Jersey.

Hutchinson was not the first to publish an instruction manual. H. B. Farnie's *A Keen Hand*, which appeared in 1857, was described the clubs involved and their purpose, but fell far short of an attempt to analyse the mechanics of the swing.

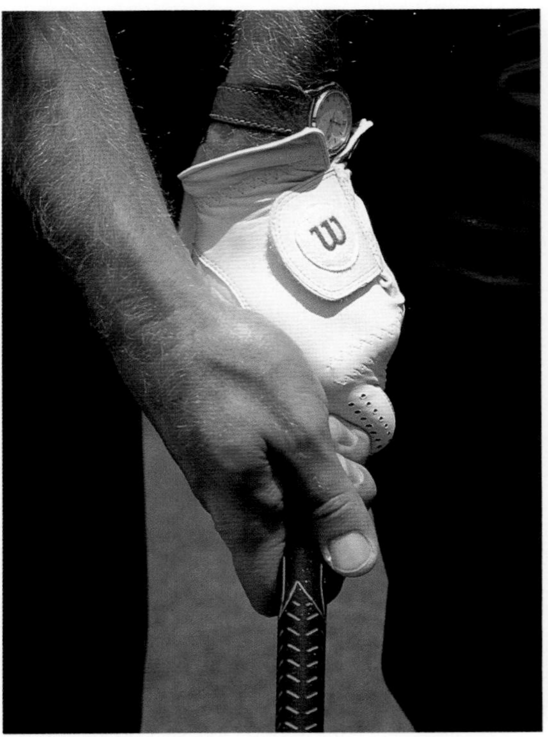

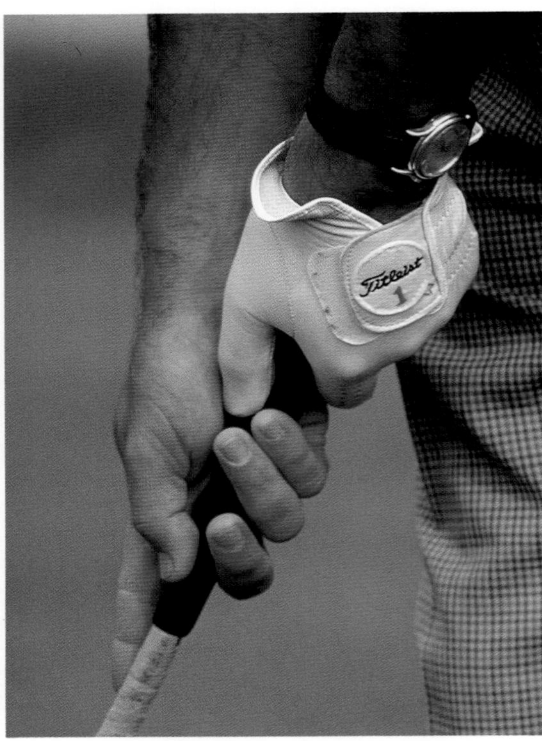

GRIP VARIATIONS *Orthodox overlapping grip and (right) the now almost obsolete split-handed baseball grip*

Hutchinson's work, in contrast, was a bold and specific analysis. His starting-point was a closed stance, with the right foot two to three inches behind the left, as was the method of the feathery players, with their long-shafted, long-headed clubs that swept the ball away. This, he wrote, was the practice of most fine players, who lifted their left foot on to the toe at the top of the backswing, with the sole of the left shoe facing towards the green.

Though he did not speak of posture as often, or rate its importance as highly, as modern teachers, he was making a related point when he insisted that the upward swing was important because it must forecast the nature of the downswing to the ball. He held that the left hand provided power, the right guidance, so that the grip should be tight with the left hand, lighter with the right.

John Ball, the Hoylake champion, changed all this with a more upright, open stance that proved a winner, because it allowed a plane of swing that got the gutty up in the air. Ball was a ball-manoeuvrer supreme, and he would have been scornful of the modern professional practice of carrying wedges for all occasions, sometimes as many as three or more.

He was able to open or close the club face to achieve his ends, which included keeping the ball low into the wind, or getting it up, with backspin, to pull it up quickly on the green. Bernard Darwin considered Ball's swing even more pleasing to watch than Bobby Jones's.

J. H. Taylor, first of the Great Triumvirate to win the Open, added significantly to the golfer's armoury with the spin he imparted to his iron shots, and his control over the ball in bad weather, in which he was a dangerous opponent. The story is told of him that while giving a playing lesson on course to Tommy Armour, he was asked how he contrived to get so much "stop" on the ball. Taylor replied that he would instruct Armour on that art as soon as he showed some signs of being able to hit his ball up to the hole.

Vardon officiates at a marriage

Harry Vardon was the next great innovator. He made a successful adaptation of the overlapping grip, with the little finger of the right hand crooked over the index finger of the left, first employed by Johnny Laidlay, the Scottish amateur. By this means it was possible, in Vardon's phrase, "to wed the hands." The highest and lowest points at which the club is grasped are well separated, the thumb and first finger of the right hand at the lowest point of the hands, and the third, fourth and fifth fingers of the left at the highest.

Adding this to matchless timing, for he was said never to force a shot, Vardon created a classic model admired on both sides of the Atlantic. A contemporary account has it that the outstanding impression of watching Vardon play was of "utter ease and lack of physical effort."

The inescapable conclusion about Vardon's career is that he never thought about his swing until he had developed it. He had reputedly played only 20 full rounds of golf by the time he was 20. His writings confirm that it was not until he turned 21, and was established in his second professional post and five years short of his first Open win, that he began to think about why he had taken up an open stance, with upright posture.

Vardon put many a golfer on the right track, inveighing always against the straight left arm, which he considered to be the ruination of a golfer.

He certainly did not advise a tight grip with either hand, which "creates a tautening of the muscles ... the chances of executing a perfect stroke are remote." He began his swing in a fashion not taught today, dragging the club back and the hands inward: at the top of the backswing his arm was not merely bent but at a right angle. He held that the force of the swing would cause the arm to straighten at impact, which refutes accusations that he "hit from the top". Further proof is in pictures of Vardon taken at an advanced stage in his downswing. They show he was as late a hitter as the golfing world has seen, bringing his wrists into the equation at the last fraction of a second.

The only other player to attract as much veneration and fulsome praise as Vardon was Bobby Jones. Jones's instructional films and the flick books of his swing, which are now eminently collectable, display an upright swing with an effect of unbroken, rounded symmetry. This is as different as can be from pictures of golfers in the late gutty days.

Dick Aultmann points out in his work on outstanding swingers of the club that a picture of Jones, aged seven, at the top of the backswing shows no difference in essentials of posture from how he appeared as a mature player.

Like Sam Snead, Jones had natural rhythm and outstanding eye-hand co-ordination, so much so that a crack shot who was with Jones when he made his first attempt at trap shooting reported that Jones, unused to firearms, was soon regularly hitting the targets. But Jones was wise enough not to interfere with these natural gifts.

A search for means to control the lively Haskell-type ball quickly became a top priority as the new century dawned. Americans supplied the best answers, especially in approach shots, though Jock Hutchison's deeply grooved clubs that brought him the Open in 1921 also brought action from the authorities.

Henry Cotton's doctrine of the crucial importance of hand action, and training the fingers by practice to take up the correct tension on the club, helped him become the envy of all for his straightness off the tee. He believed teachers inflicted damage on their pupils by their (to Cotton's mind) injurious emphasis on body action. He did not need a full swing to send the ball enormous distances, and his swing attracted the epithet "grooved" before the American development of the notion.

Byron Nelson's great contribution to the swing, as he ran down one prize after another before and after the Second World War, was his ability to make best use of the firmer and more obedient steel shafts by virtue of using his legs, both of them, to drive through the ball. Hitting against the braced left side had long been the accepted gospel of the swing, ever since the days when Hutchinson was insisting that there should be no lateral swaying.

Vardon had implied that the use of the legs was part of the required swing sequence, in his practice of bringing the left heel back to the ground as he began his downswing. Now Nelson went further, and harnessed the power of his legs, yet achieved a straightness few could rival, and runs of tournament success no one has ever equalled.

Ben Hogan progressed from youthful hooker, by way of prodigies of practice, to perhaps the most complete master of ball control from tee to green that the game has seen. Tommy Bolt once remarked that Nicklaus watched Hogan practice; he never heard of Hogan watching Nicklaus practice. Hogan's slight fade and low flight were an insurance policy that paid off handsomely.

Nick Faldo remodelled and tightened technique in three years of hard labour, though not, as yet, with the same reward in major events. Comparing photographic studies of Hogan's action in the early years of his domination with its full flowering in the early 1950s, the impression is inescapable that everything became tighter, less flamboyant (if such a canard can ever be aimed in Hogan's direction) ... leg action and all other physical movements a paradigm of economy. The impression was that the whole production was so compact, there was so little left to chance, that very little *could* go wrong.

"Grooved" was indeed the name of his game, and of American teacher-technology since the Second World War. Jack Nicklaus and Tom Watson in particular have carried on in that grooved tradition, Watson with one of the most upright swings of all, sharp, speedy, yet compact.

John Jacobs, the English coach whose greatest contribution to golf is undoubtedly the major part he played in the creation of the European Tour, sums up the swing by reminding the player that "the grip largely determines clubface alignment at impact, that body alignment at address can directly affect the clubhead's path, and that posture before swinging largely determines its angle of approach."

Seve Ballesteros would get most people's vote as the player who has put this together most beguilingly as the possessor of the smoothest of all swings: harmony is the name of his game, allied to tremendous power. He also pleases the swing doctors, with his model posture at address. There has been no finer examplar of Hutchinson's insistence

FILIAL REFLECTION *Jackie Snead, aged 12, surveys the grace of father Sam Snead's swing, 1956 vintage*

that it's a swing, not a hit. Ernie Els and Fred Couples are currently the next best.

Shedding light on putting

Frank Thomas and his USGA team of researchers are brave, or foolhardy, enough to be going into the mystic business of putting. At the 1994 US Open at Oakmont, and at certain 1995 PGA events, laser beams were used to take exhaustive measurements of putts as to length, slope, speed and borrow. Pro tour statistics over the last 20 years also come into the equation. Yips sufferers the world over will hope there is a cure in all this for those soul-destroying missed three-footers.

Early tees were, by rule, so close to holes that putting surfaces could scarcely be velvety in texture, and putting was sometimes better tackled as a chipping manoeuvre, a useful skill in any case in the days of the stymie. There is therefore a fine irony in the fact that it was largely through his putting supremacy that Willie Park Senior became the first winner of the Championship Belt back in 1860. He also won the Open on three other occasions, despite a tendency to foolhardy gambles through the green. Once on it, he usually proved the master. The historian Robert Browning tells how, as a boy, Park spent his evenings on a practice green of four holes, 25 to 30 yards apart. His best effort was five putts for the four holes.

Nowadays it is a useful putter who gets round, consistently, in less than 30 strokes on the greens. Pros on majors tours must aspire to around 28. The coming of better greens made it clear that putting is a game within a game. It still is, and one at which success has suddenly eluded even the greatest players, from Harry Vardon to Nick Faldo and Tom Watson. When it happened to Watson, he had already written one of the most useful of all instructional books, *Getting Up and Down*, subtitled *How to Sa e Strokes from Forty Yards and In*. It is a genuine stroke-saver. It is rather sad to read, in Jack Nicklaus's foreword to the book: "He [Watson] knows he isn't going to

ROLL ON *Putts went further and straighter when Bob Charles struck them*

miss many short putts, so he can be aggressive and take a run at a long putt or chip. Someday maybe he'll start missing some short putts and come back into the real world ..." This last conjecture is exactly what has happened to Watson, who would otherwise have added several majors to his tally.

This suggests that, however good the putting method, it will fail unless nerve and inspiration support it. Park believed in a pendulum stroke principle, using hands and arms. Watson's major points are keeping the eye over the ball, hands locked with forearms so that the putter is moved with the arms, which are locked to the shoulders, and (a crucial point) a consistent angle of bend in left elbow. Extending the arm, he believes, must break the bond with the shoulders.

Watson uses the term pendulum, but only as a tip to maintain a good rhythm: after hitting the putt, he advises, count one before looking up. As with all other strokes, deceleration of the clubhead as it reaches the ball is a cardinal sin, often caused by taking the putter back too far.

In between Park and what might be called the classic American "straight-line" putting technique espoused by Watson there were all sorts of contrivances, notably croquet putting, banned in 1968, and the Sam Snead side-winder style: a development of croquet putting but with left hand high on the shaft, right hand much lower, this involved pushing the putter head through the ball while both feet remain the same side of the line of putt, i.e. in a legal position.

Desperate measures have been taken to combat putting failures. Henry Longhurst's cure, most radical of all, ensured he never missed another short putt: he retired from the game. Faldo has tried left hand below right, gone back to orthodoxy, then returned to left hand below right, and so on. Others have garages packed with putters, and many have gained comfort from the broomstick putter, long enough to cuddle under the chin, with one hand acting as a fulcrum, while the other pushes the putter head through.

Bernhard Langer's valour in the face of putting terrors is unrivalled. He has twice been in the depths, but rebuilt his game on the greens with his much copied ploy of gripping well down the shaft with his left hand, while holding his left forearm against the upper part of the shaft with his right hand. The shaft is thus made to act as a splint for his left wrist.

The far from encouraging fact for each and every struggler on the green is that the list of consistently great putters is much shorter than that of golf's "Legends". The six giants of the putting game are Walter Travis (once described as "a killer" on the green), Walter Hagen, Bobby Jones (who had no weaknesses, least of all perhaps when it came to a "must" putt), Billy Casper, Bobby Locke and Bob Charles, he of the inexorably rolling putt ... that is, four Americans (though Travis was born in Australia), the South African Locke and a left-hander, the New Zealander Charles.

Hagen's strength as a putter was two-fold. His hands, firstly, were those of a musician, with long slender fingers. Wrapping these around the grip, and with his weight on his left foot, he stroked through the ball in the approved US style of the straight-line putter, continuing the clubhead's path towards the hole for as long as possible.

Secondly, his mental toughness was renowned. Who else would have asked for his closest rival at the climax of a US Open to come out and watch him putt for a win? Hagen rimmed the hole, went out on the town for most of the night, then beat his man in a play-off next day. Who else would provoke fate by saying there was no chance of his missing an eight-footer, because it was for several thousand dollars, and then sinking it?

Casper's method was almost frightening to watch: his stroke was the antithesis of Hutchinson's swing-not-hit gospel, for he gave his putts a thorough-going rap with an action that was almost all wrist. His putting average in winning the 1959 US Open was 28, and at Winged Foot too, notorious for its slopes.

Locke is held by many to be the greatest putter of them all. John Reece tells the story of how Norman Sutton gave an off-form and worried Locke a putting lesson just before the 1949 Open. Sutton had spotted that Locke was moving his body at impact. By the end of the lesson Locke had holed 50 putts in a row from four feet without moving any part of his body apart from his hands, with which, Sutton diagnosed, Locke had been gripping too tightly. Locke won that Open, after single-putting eight of the nine holes at which he had to escape from sand.

He won the following year, too, when at Troon he became the first Open champion to break 280. Locke is renowned, like Hogan, as a hooker who made good: but Locke, who stuck to his right to left flight, and was famed for his banana shots with wooden clubs that unerringly sought out the green, also reputedly hooked his putts, over which he took a long time, taking particular note of the nature and grain of the grass. But then his second putts, and he had fewer of these to play than most of his rivals, were usually tap-ins.

It is worth noting that the greatest putter took a lesson. Watson puts a question to the weekend golfer: "How many do you know who've ever taken a putting lesson?"

GOLDEN RAPPER *Bill Casper's putting put out the fire of Winged Foot's greens*

GOLF EQUIPMENT

From tee-peg to flagstick, golf can be one of the most expensive sporting journeys in the world. For all golfers, arming themselves with the right equipment is a vital prerequisite to the happy and successful pursuit of their game, and for many of them looking the part is a pretty serious business, too.

Never in the field of human recreation has so much been spent by so many to so little effect. The members of many a handicapping committee must think along these lines as they survey the sad and stratospheric figures returned in the monthly medal by fellow-members employing the most up-to-date and terrifyingly expensive confections of steel, carbon-fibre, exotic woods, rubber, leather and ceramics known as golf clubs, to belabour to no great effect a small dimpled spheroid that is itself a technological marvel, the result of approaching a thousand years of tireless search for the perfect projectile. But the viability of the whole subscription and green-fee lifeblood of a club, not to mention profitability of the bar and professional's shop, is a by-product of the restless search for improvement by average golfers, "the dogged victims of inexorable fate", as they have been called. Encouraged by the PR men, the golfer's watchword is that if spending a few hundred will do the trick, then let's go. Even playing well is not enough, for excepting always old whatshisname who has worn those velvet trousers and much-darned sweater since the days of the 1.62 inch ball, the golfer must look the part, and so must the bag that holds the clubs, the natty gloves that protect them and the trolley or cart that brings it along …

LEFT: IT'S NOT JUST ROUND *The three-piece ball of today is a technological marvel*
RIGHT: GOLF'S *DERNIER CRI* *Expensively cast in search of more consistent striking*

Callaway
BIG BERTHA
WAR BIRD
USA

3
Callaway
5
BIG BERTHA
WAR BIRD
USA
HEAVEN
WOOD

Callaway
BIG BERTHA
WAR BIRD
sole plate

Callaway
BIG BERTH
WAR BIRD
sole plate

Callaway
GOLF
THE
TUTTLE
USA

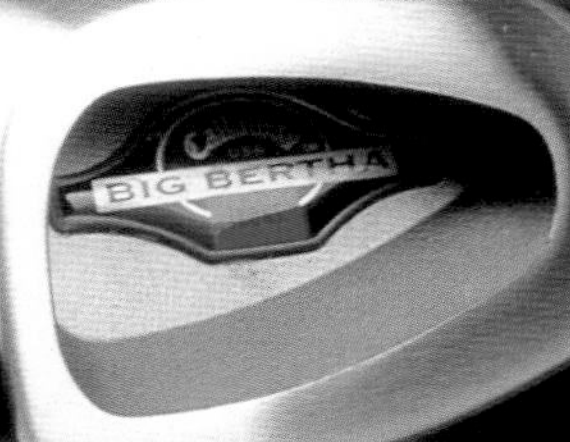
BIG BERTHA

Callaway
BIG BERTHA

GOLF BALLS

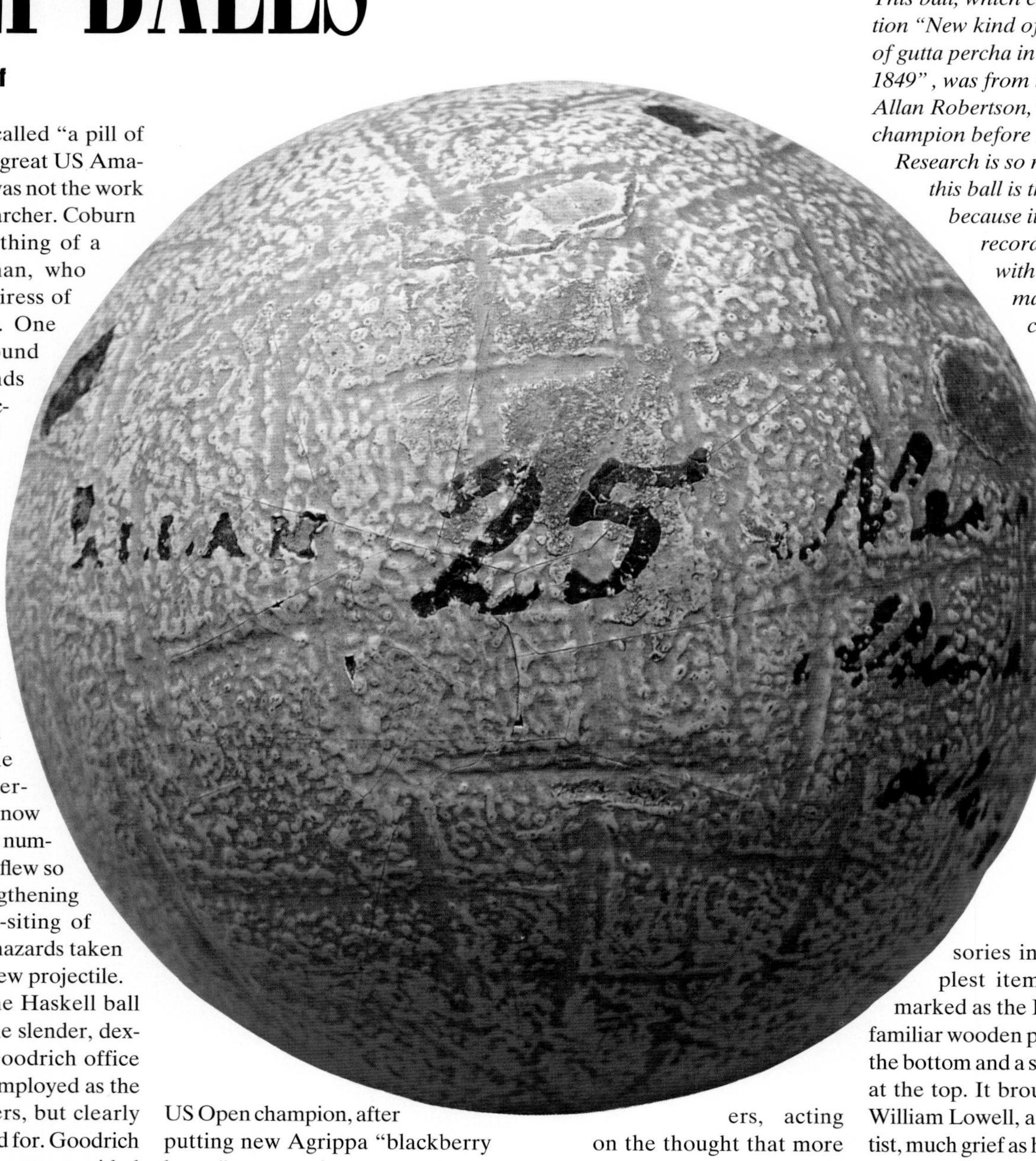

A CHAMPION'S MARK

Collectors' enthusiasm for antique golf equipment knows few bounds. This ball, which carries an inscription "New kind of golf ball made of gutta percha in the ... year 1849", was from the workshop of Allan Robertson, the last great champion before the Open began. Research is so meticulous that this ball is the more valued because it is the first recorded "Robertson" with random hammer marks; others all carry longitudinal marks

Defying the laws of aero-dynamics

The Haskell ball, called "a pill of quicksilver" by the great US Amateur Chick Evans, was not the work of a dedicated researcher. Coburn Haskell was something of a dilettante sportsman, who had married an heiress of the Hanna family. One day Haskell wound some rubber bands into a ball at the factory of his friend Bert Work, President of Goodrich Rubber. When his plaything slipped out of his hand, its liveliness gave Haskell the notion that changed the game. Just as the resilient, but costly, feathery ball had been ousted by the cheap, if stodgy, performer, the gutty, so now the gutty's days were numbered. The Haskell flew so far that it led to lengthening of courses, and re-siting of bunkers and other hazards taken out of play by the new projectile.

Progress with the Haskell ball was slow at first. The slender, dexterous fingers of Goodrich office girls were initially employed as the rubber-band winders, but clearly machinery was called for. Goodrich engineer John Gammeter provided it, and Patent 622834, granted on April 11, 1899, was made over to the firm. His complex machine wound two threads round a core, providing a balanced, homogeneous and highly resilient centre to the ball. David Stirk and his co-author Ian Henderson have gone so far as to say of Gammeter's machine: "If one single invention revolutionized golf, it was Gammeter's."

This was not an obedient ball, however, until James Foulis, the 1896 US Open champion, after putting new Agrippa "blackberry bump" patterned covers on a batch of (so he thought) gutties, found that one of them played wonderfully well. Curious, he cut it open. He found he had re-covered a Haskell and had found a cure for its flight problems.

Research has greatly improved the flight control exerted by the cover pattern, i.e. an arrangement of dimples, up to 500 of them covering 70 per cent of the ball's surface, usually based on the icosahedron pattern, with 20 repeating triangles. Spalding designers, acting on the thought that more dimples would give more lift and control, made space for them by making the ball bigger.

Oversize balls at 1.72 or 1.74 inches in diameter have contradicted one of the laws of aero-dynamics ... that a larger body moves more slowly through the air, just as the dimpled ball earlier disproved the law stating that smooth surfaces provide least wind resistance. The modern golf ball is *not* a simple spheroid.

It has encouraged in its train endless expansion of a mighty accessories industry: the simplest item, at first trademarked as the Reddy Tee, is the familiar wooden peg with a point at the bottom and a small concave cup at the top. It brought its inventor, William Lowell, a New Jersey dentist, much grief as he tried to protect his patent.

Haskell had varying fortunes as he tried to protect his invention. He was successful in America, but in Britain his 1905 suit failed because Capt. Duncan Stewart showed his design for a wound rubber ball with gutta percha cover which had been tried – unsuccessfully – 30 years earlier. Haskell must justifiably have thought the law an ass: his ball worked, made the game easier and pleasanter to play, opening its delights to millions.

FEATHERY SURVIVORS

Balls of leather and feather are often sold for thousands of pounds/dollars. The first (right) is still protected by its original paint. The second has lost most of its white paint, revealing the untanned hide that has been fashioned into an almost perfect sphere: it will have cost five shillings to buy 150 years ago. The third, though damaged, can still command large sums today.

SPOT THE ODD ONE OUT... *The ball in the middle of the third row is made of wood and was used during wartime rubber shortages. The rest are gutties. The wooden ball has aiming spots because they have to be struck on the end grain to avoid splitting. The first gutty in the first row is a fine example of a hand-cut gutty; it has red marks to its poles. The variety of gutty balls starkly contrasts to the gleaming uniformity of the modern Titleist balls below.*

GOLF CLUBS

Club-making runs in the genes

Ironically, the best early clubs command higher prices than the most high-tech modern variety; clubs by Hugh Philp, who was made clubmaker at St Andrews in 1819, are especially prized. His family and Robert Forgan's were linked by marriage, and Forgan, reputed to be the first to hand-hammer patterns on to gutty balls when it was found that smooth gutties performed poorly, carried on the club-making business after Philp died. Many famous makers began as Forgan apprentices. Forgan and Co. were based in Fife; other celebrated makers such as the Dickson and McEwan families, in the Lothians near Edinburgh.

David Stirk, in his study of the great club-makers, says they were born, not made. Family members who did not inherit the right genes usually left the business. The sheer volume of demand ended the era of the creators of the refined and beautiful club. George Cann was one such, and produced clubs for J. H. Taylor, whose playing success publicized Cann's products. But Cann soon became manager of a factory.

Wooden- and iron-headed clubs, with hickory, ash or bamboo shafts, remained the norm until the late 1920s, when metallurgical progress ushered in the steel shaft, and the production of matched sets of clubs, which began to lose their tradition names and be known by numbers.

Brassie	No. 2 wood
Mashie	No. 5 iron
Spoon	No. 3 or 4 wood
Spade mashie	No. 6 iron
Driving iron (cleek)	No. 1 or 2 iron
Mashie-niblick	No. 7 iron
Midmashie	No. 3 iron
Pitching niblick	No. 8 iron
Mashie iron	No. 4 iron
Niblick	No. 9 iron

Note: "Cleek" was also a generic term for an iron club, while a "jigger" was an iron approach shot club.

The steel shaft, now replaced in turn by graphite, began to bring scores down because it behaved in a much more predictable manner than the wooden shaft, and gave better control over the new Haskell ball.Huge titanium-headed metal woods became the vogue in the nineties, offering an extra (highly expensive) millimetre or so of "sweet spot" – with which the expert connects so often that a small, worn, black spot appears, usually on his favourite approach iron.

FUNCTIONAL DESIGN

The early rules of golf were a good deal less forgiving than they are today, with not many free-drops available, so a rutting iron (right), with long hosel and small head, was useful for extracting the ball from cart-tracks and other desperate lies. Equally handy, when a better opportunity for progress presented itself, was this square-toe iron (left) or a lofting iron (far right), also with a long hosel, current in the early part of the nineteenth century

CLUB MASTERS (TOP ROW)

Beechwood playclub by Dunn with leather face insert is shown with a driver, brassie and putter by the great Forgan, and a Morris playclub. Auchtlerlonie made the persimmon baffing spoon (bottom left); the remainder are by Ashford, two by Anderson, and the last is a rare Brand's Bulger driver. The top half of the Bulger grip was conventional, the lower part was equipped with a swivelling cyclinder to make the back-swing easier

THE WONDER OF WEDGES

Many professionals and leading amateurs carry more wedges than woods, for in their ceaseless quest for control over their ball, a major difficulty is stopping it on the green, especially when the target is close by, and back-spin may not be an option. Phil Mickelson's lob shot has done the marketing of wedges no harm. Mickelson, even from a bare lie, can with a club like these chrome alloy Howson wedges (available with lofts of 55, 60 and 64 degrees) execute a full swing and get the ball up almost vertically, landing it softly a few yards away next to the hole, if not in it.

PRETTY PUTTERS

The ingenuity of putter designers knows no bounds. Nor does the size of the putter collections of leading players who find greens unreadable and unbearable but are willing to try anything. These Fazer Millennium putters have a polymer insert on the club face to give a better "feel", and the golfing equivalent of a gunsight (sight alignment markings) to help square the club face to the line of putt. Larry Nelson carried two putters: his caddie said this was just to let the other one know it could be replaced.

FAIRWAY FASHION PARADE

Men's fashions in golf began gaudily, continued plain, but are tending of late toward what the Victorian guardians of the game would have regarded as dandyish.

Red or blue tail-coats, cocked hats and buckled shoes were the thing when the first clubs held their competitions. Whether impelled by the need for economy or a Victorian distaste for show, players opted for knickerbockers and tweed jackets as the 19th century grew old: the average mid-century pro, to judge from pictures of the eight competitors for the Championship Belt in 1860, were a dowdy lot. Hats were still in favour, but cocked no longer, as prosaic flat caps and bonnets became the norm. Harry Vardon and the rest of the Triumvirate were most soberly clad. Plus twos and plus fours developed after knickerbockers fell out of favour, and are practical garments still much in evidence in fashionable clubs in Britain. Turn-ups in wet heather are a mistake.

Walter Hagen tended to flat caps, white slacks and shirts with bowtie at the time of his first US Open but, after the First World War, he set new trends. He soon became jacketless and hatless, with a short, carefully pomaded, centre-parted hair-style, set off by bright trousering and sweaters, and glittering two-tone brogues. Yet Hagen was seldom as brightly garbed as the Tour peacock, Jimmy Demaret, but then who was? The most famous single accessory of the 1940s and 1950s was the flat white cap Ben Hogan wore (and which he ordered by the dozen).

Looking good on TV

Television has empowered the manufacturers to sell modern styles in ever greater volume, since the advertising men have made leading pros, and not a few amateurs, into walking clothes-horses and billboards, kitting them out in the season's latest shade and style of trousers, shirts and sweaters, together with multicolour umbrellas and hats emblazoned with marketing messages. Payne Stewart, clad, until lately, in outfits based on the colours of American football teams, succeeded Demaret as latter-day peacock of the links. It all means big business, in which one of the world's great retailers of clothing, Marks and Spencer, felt it worth their while to challenge the established suppliers. They burst on to the scene at the 1993 Royal St George's Open, after a six months' planning and production campaign ending in a scrum around their section of the main Exhibitors' tent, and lined foreheads elsewhere.

Upmarket, Nick Faldo's bright sweater styles decorated with colourful golfing images are to be seen on every course: so are high-crowned straw hats carrying the names of club-makers and so, to the chagrin of the traditionalist, is golf's version of the baseball cap. Fierce competition abounds in the wet weather gear market; even here, colour and fashionable cut are key weapons of the makers, who wage war with TV commercials.

From the fairway to the cat-walk

It would be interesting to compare the weight of clothes worn by Victorian women golfers with that of the short skirts of the 1920 flappers and the (apparently) featherweight shorts and tops that suffice, but only just, these days. They wore hats with huge brims, boaters, lace blouses, starched leg of mutton sleeves, long skirts, substantial undergarments that included whale-bone corsets, and were shod in button boots. The skirts were a bother in a breeze, especially when putting. The solution was the "Miss Higgins", a band of elastic material slipped over the knees and designed to restrain the skirt from billowing out at crucial moments.

The first woman, between the wars, to wear trousers caused more than a ripple. Grace Minoprio's play, in the 1933 English championship, made less of a stir. More modern players should pause before donning shorts or slacks, and take to heart the poet's lament about how his "sweeting" looked when retreating. Versace trousers, cashmere sweaters, designer blouses and shoes in pastel shades enliven the scene, though Alan Shepard has an irrefutable claim to have been the most expensively kitted-out golfer of all time. To hit shots on the moon as he did with a sawn-off 6-iron during the 1971 Apollo 14 mission, the first essential was a spacesuit.

FASHION SECONDARY
Stylishly dressed as the young couple on the right may be, the point of René Vincent's 1933 illustration is that the bald gentleman with his caddie – and his nose haughtily in the air – is to be envied because he possesses "a handicap".

PRETTY BUT...
Gracefully swaying ankle-length skirts and extravagant millinery fascinated magazine illustrators yet frequently frustrated the wearers. Joyce Wethered, the great British champion, pointed out that such encumbrances did not help in efforts to observe the game's golden rule: "Keep your eye on the ball." Many players resorted to the "Miss Higgins", a restraining band tied round the skirts which was useful when putting on a windy day.

TECHNICOLOR TRAVELLER
Payne Stewart (below) who has a US Open Championship and a US PGA title to his name, and several high finishes in the British Open, added to the fame and fortune he earned with his golfing skills by means of a clothing contract to wear outfits based on club colours of National Football League teams. He would normally wear the local team's colours during the final round of PGA tournaments in America. Here he is resplendent in scarlet and tartan, and NFL logos.

SURPRISE SURPRISE
One of Michelle McGann's sponsors is Sonni Hats. A striking, tall blonde, she has won well over $2 million, so can generously indulge her love of shopping, especially for spectacular millinery, her trade mark. Three 1996 tournament victories and a Solheim Cup win against Laura Davies, closely followed by her sixth LPGA title early in 1997 (her fourth in a play-off) suggest there is more to come from Michelle, whose life style is as up-market as her birthplace: West Palm Beach, Florida.

COMPUTER-AIDED DESIGN

The thought that such instinctive grace as Seve Ballesteros displays when swinging a golf club could possibly be evaluated, let alone improved upon, by a box full of transistors sounds like a heresy punishable by a St Andrean thunderbolt. But in 1991 the USGA granted $2 million for their South African-born technical director, Frank Thomas, to expand their Research and Test Centre.

Part of the money is being used in a computer programme in which glass marbles attached to the club and to key points of a golfer's anatomy – shoulders, hips, elbows, wrists, knees, and ankles – are used as markers whose movements during the swing are picked up by infra-red cameras and fed into a computer. A model is produced on the monitor screen that shows precisely the path of each moving part, of players and equipment, that makes up the swing, from start to finish. The swing record is shown milli-second by milli-second.

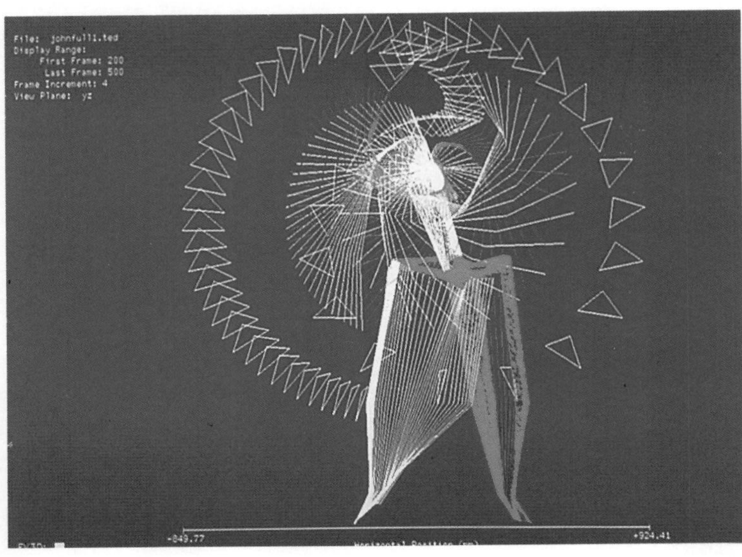

SWING TRUTHS ... *revealed by computer, milli-second by milli-second*

Critics of photographic sequences of famous swings have pointed out that inadequate shutter speeds can falsify the position of various components of the swing at any given moment. Andy, the USGA Android, who on a monitor screen looks like a cross between the Michelin Man and a peacock displaying his tail feathers, overcomes these difficulties. What golfer *think* they are doing, and what Andy knows and records they are doing, can obviously be two entirely different things.

Thomas, as design engineer for a club-maker before joining the USGA in 1974, took the industry into the space age by his innovative use of graphite shafts. Not that he is about to tell people how to swing a club: this is not, he thinks, the business of the USGA. Teachers, however, are alert to the possibilities of using the Android to analyse and instruct.

What drives on Thomas's team is the opportunity for original research. His assistant is Bernard Soriano, a Hawaiian with impeccable space-age credentials. After reading mechanical engineering at the University of California, Soriano worked on satellite guidance systems for Hughes Aircraft before joining the USGA, who co-operate with academics from Princeton, LeHigh and Brooklyn Polytechnic Universities in the study of the flight of golf balls and the efficiency of clubs in propelling them. Space-age materials, for example thermo-plastics, are already important ingredients in ball cores and covers.

A major strand in research as far as the day to day traffic on a golf course is concerned is the routine, long-established checking of balls submitted by makers, which must conform to R&A/USGA standards. The size (1.68 inches) test is carried out at 23°C (±1°), and to pass it a ball must fall through a 1.68-inch ring gauge under its own weight in fewer than 25 out of 100 randomly selected positions. It must be symmetrically spherical, a property measured by comparing the flight when speed (238 feet per seond) and differing spin are imparted by a system of rubber rollers after the ball has been fired out of an airgun.

The balls are propelled down an indoor range, breaking through light screens as used to measure the velocity of a bullet. Computer evaluation follows. The use of a wind tunnel for this work was discontinued because creating the necessary laminar (smooth) flow of air was not possible, and the results were therefore flawed; hence the invention of this Indoor Testing Range (ITR) which turns the problem around and solves it by monitoring ball performance through the air.

A ball's initial velocity must not exceed 250 feet per second, and the average distance covered by the ball in carry and roll must not exceed 280 yards, plus a tolerance of 6 per cent, which will be reduced to 4 per cent as test techniques are improved. Testing for this is done on an outdoor range, with a centre-line within 2½ inches of level. The balls have been fired down it for many years by a driver-wielding mechanical device famously nicknamed Iron Byron, after that scarcely less reliable human swinger of that ilk, Nelson. As soon as the test ball comes to rest, the distance it has travelled is immediately transmitted to researchers by sensing devices known as geophones, buried the length of the test range.Iron Byron now has a clone beside it. Possibly, in this innovative age, the son of Iron Byron should be named Graphite Kite, after another model of consistency.

Soriano says that few balls are rejected, which means that the struggle to protect the skill factor is not without its successes. Despite the money and hype devoted to late twentieth-century golf gear, the balance between golfer, his or her gear, and the golf course has not changed very much. Thomas pointed out to the World Scientific Congress of Golf at St Andrews that the driving distances of the best professional players have increased only 12 yards since 1968 (he was no doubt excluding John Daly). Average *winning* scores improved by only one in 21 years.

CAD does the game a good turn

Computer analysis is also being used to determine how different clubhead designs perform, though the researchers are not yet ready to do more than make comparisons. The truth is that club design, despite all the manufacturers' claims made on behalf of their innovations, is not wholly based on scientific principle, because the type of pure research now being carried out has not previously been performed.

Once the best formulation has been established, Computer-Aided Design (CAD) will presumably do the rest. CAD is already being used, for example, in the highly successful perimeter-weighting of club heads: successful in the market place, at least. Duffers still need to practise, however, for they cannot be sure of buying success with money alone. That is a situation which golf's ruling bodies are watchful to prolong.

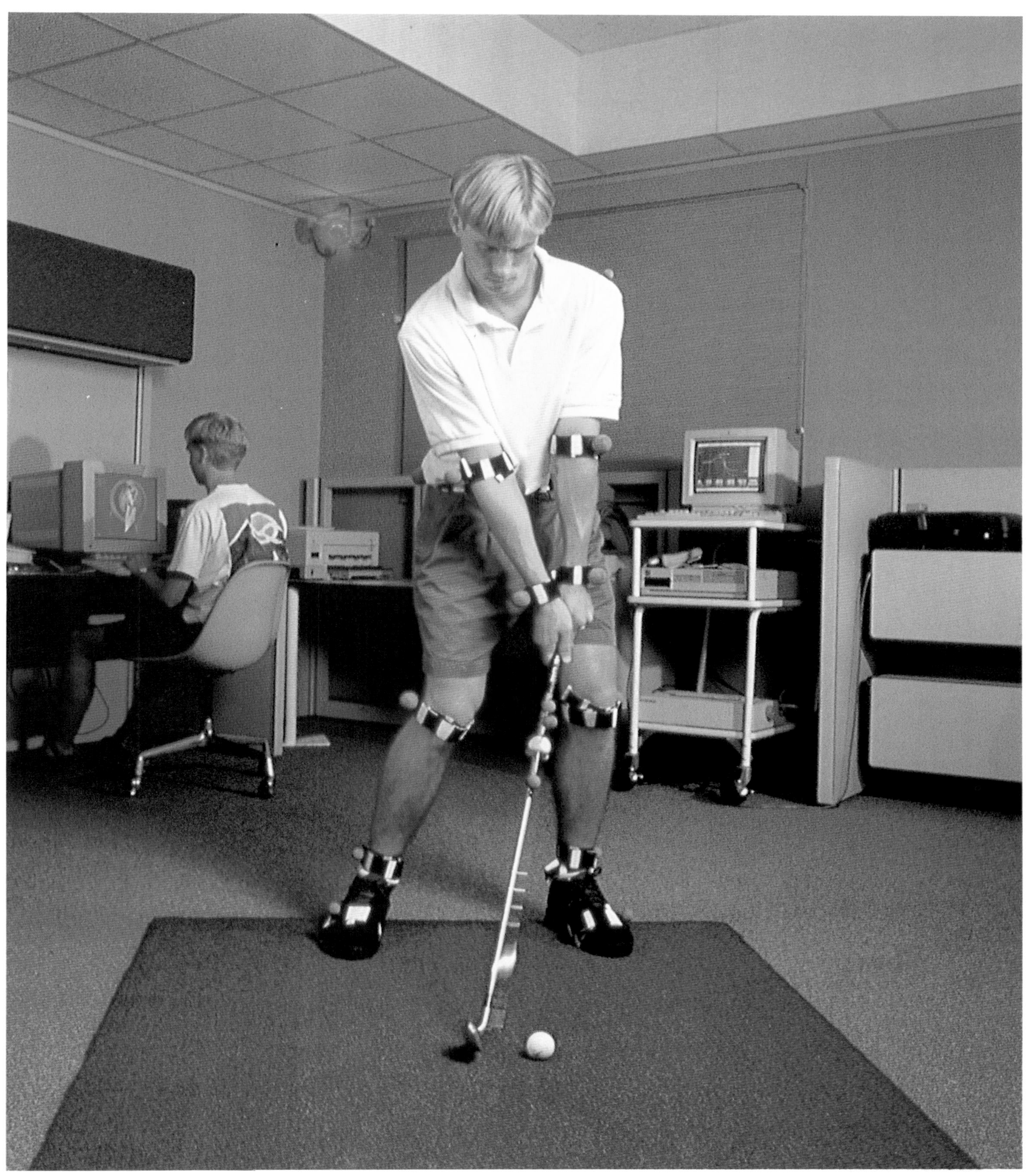

TELL-TALE KINEMATICS *Infrared cameras track the markers attached to the golfer and club, producing the computer image*

GOLF CULTURE AND GOLF POLITICS

Golf's inexorable conquest of Planet Earth has been hampered by wars, revolutions and charges of elitism, but never halted. Golf inspires the adulation of the crowd and fires the obsession of the collector, but it also harbours vestiges of racism and male chauvinism that continue to prove resistant even to the zealots of political correctness.

THIS GOLFING LIFE

John Hayes did his training on the roof of Bloomingdale's department store in Manhattan before winning the 1908 Olympic Marathon. Roof training is the *only* way many a Japanese golfer can practise the royal and ancient game, since the admission fees to clubs are in telephone numbers of yen, and space being limited in Japanese cities, some driving ranges (and there are about five thousand of them in Japan) are perched on the top of buildings. The Shiba driving range, reputedly the biggest, is on terra firma in Tokyo, if such a thing exists in Japan: it has three tiers.

For the Japanese, being a golf club member is a great source of "face". Here, obviously is a privileged, influential, not to mention well-heeled person. Japan's golfing population is uncertain, yet must be moving up towards 20 million, given that well over 20 million use either courses or driving ranges – and the sad fact is that more visits are made to driving ranges than to courses. It's cheaper, by far, and it is still a sign of some affluence, and provides a fair amount of face, if you are seen to be in possession of a set of clubs.

Reliance on driving ranges for golf technique can have its drawbacks to judge by the actions of a group of competent-looking Japanese players observed recently on the Old Course at St Andrews. They were fine off the tee, but on turf they were in trouble. Could it be they had never hit a ball off a yielding surface of that nature?

Golf in the West can demand uncomfortable personal disciplines, such as getting up in the dark to reach a public course long before dawn, then to book a tee-time and wait until one's number comes up. It is just as onerous in the East: Jakarta in Indonesia has courses with a queue forming at 3.30 a.m. But it is not necessary to wait for daylight: there are floodlit courses for the super-keen and the insomniac from Los Angeles to Dubai.

Nothing new about a loud crowd

The present writer, after watching a Worplesdon Foursomes final late in September 1991, adjourned to the club's television set just as the Ryder Cup was reaching the climax of Bernhard Langer's final errant putt amid the sandy wastes of Pete Dye's Kiawah Island course in South Carolina, watched by a huge, brightly dressed, be-flagged crowd.

The difference in atmosphere was like a blow in the face. It was almost like watching a bar-room brawl after a scene from *The Importance of Being Earnest.* Only an occasional "Good shot" or restrained applause disturbed the autumnal peace of Worplesdon (off-line shots received the gentle therapy of silence); at Kiawah tribal howls of dismay or triumph bore witness to the effectiveness of the pre-Cup hype about the "War on the Shore" .

It must be said that excesses of hero-worship have not diminished to any great extent over the years. Young pros playing with Arnold Palmer, with his army in vociferous attendance, could find it daunting. If Palmer could arrange it, he would make his putt the last, for if it was not, an opponent would have to putt to the accompaniment of the army thundering off to the next fairway: they had not come to see tyros.

Macdonald Smith was less sympathetically treated at the 1925 British Open, when inadequate stewarding at Prestwick is held to have cost him the championship as he was buffeted by the crowd and lost the five-stroke lead he had taken into the final round.

Golfing relics for the aficionado

Golf is a wonderfully versatile advertising medium, which also makes it a collector's dream. Much of the ephemera connected with golf is collectable on aesthetic grounds, notably posters and art work on a wide range of objects – blotters, travel advertisements, pottery, any number of oil paintings, calendars, postcards and bookplates. There are few areas of human endeavour into which golf cannot be dragged to boost some product or other, and it has been a staple, until recently,

THE WONDERS OF MODERN TECHNOLOGY *Floodlit golf at the Emirates GC, host to the Dubai Desert Classic Tournament, an early-season stop on the European Tour*

SWINGING PARTY *American supporters raise voices and flags in triumph as the 1991 War on the Shore is won and the Ryder Cup regained at Kiawah Island*

for the tobacco trade. A mint set of golfers' cigarette cards issued by Cope Brothers of Liverpool in the 1900s will set you back £2,600 ($4,030). Postage stamps are a particular feature of golfing interest.

Phillips of Chester are among the acknowledged leaders in auction sales of historic golf equipment. Anything pre-dating 1800 is of immense value. Phillips issued a note of caution in one of their catalogues. they believe that no more than six or seven dozen clubs can safely be attributed to the eighteenth century. Two-thirds of these are irons, and the rest "play clubs", or drivers. Few putters of the period have survived: such clubs have, typically, square heads with no undercut at the toe, and the top and bottom lines of the clubs are parallel. Lucky finders of such a club can expect to raise far more than say the £1,800 made in 1994 by an early nineteenth-century lofting iron.

Members of a Highland club, Fortrose and Rosemarkie near Inverness, had a valuation done on a collection of old clubs which had lain for years in an unlocked cabinet beside the members' bar. The answer was a quarter of a million pounds; one club alone, a square-toed, dish-faced heavy iron, dating from the seventeenth century, was valued at £100,000 ($155,000). The collection was put in a bank, and replicas made.

Championship medals are in a class way above gold dust. Bobby Locke's four Open medals raised £82,000 ($127,000) – the 1949 Sandwich medal the costliest, at £24,150 – in a 1993 auction. The lovely Spode bowl in Imari, Japanese style, won by a Bow of Fife golfer in 1814, was bought for the magnificent collection being assembled in the Valderrama clubhouse on the Costa del Sol. Sir Henry Cotton's personal archive made £155,000 at Sotheby's in 1996, including £17,250 for his 1934 miniature Open claret jug. His 1934 Open medal had gone to the R & A by private sale – estimated at more than £20,000.

Other striking sales were of a book of rules from Musselburgh GC, which went for £30,000. Prices are generally lower now than in the 1980s, partly owing to the absence of Japanese collectors, which is likely to be the more marked following the Kobe earthquake.

MOST VALUABLE MEDAL *(middle bottom) from short-lived Caledonian Club, 1811–13*

Satisfying the thirst for figures

Among modern golf's most praiseworthy developments, certainly at the top level of the game, are the excellent scoring systems that keep galleries in touch with tournament progress. Bob Harlow started the trend on the nascent US Tour in the 1930s, and they can be seen at their best at the Opens. Not only is there a giant board at the 18th, showing the leaders' scores and those of the players approaching the green, but at every green there is a board giving the position of the players approaching.

All has been brought to a fine simplicity, with red figures indicating that a player is beating par, black for over par. At Opens no detail is allowed to escape the media, whose working desks are faced with huge boards detailing every score at every hole. Shortly after every notable round, there is a conference starring the player concerned, and documents detailing every stroke taken and with what club are circulated.

Every Monday since 1986, Sony have issued their world golf rankings. (Ping perform a similar service for women's golf.) This was the first serious attempt to set the performances of golfers worldwide in order of excellence. Bernhard Langer was the first to head the "Sony", but has never been at the top since, for Greg Norman, Nick Faldo, Seve Ballesteros, Ian Woosnam and Nick Price had much the best of it over the rankings' first decade.

Points are awarded on the basis of official events from the various tours, and are related to the quality of the players involved.Sony employed a three-year roll-over period for a decade until, in 1996, the rankings took account of results over only two years, so as to increase emphasis on current form. Major titles command most points, and points earned in the most recent 52-week period count double.

Performance statistics (length and accuracy of driving, greens reached in regulation, number of putts per rounds and "saves" from sand – getting "up and down" in two shots) can mislead; players near the top of the money list are sometimes not all that close to the top of any performance rating.

Winning at any level is all a matter of getting it all together at the same time. For those who fail, there is always the consolation of the 19th hole, where the barman will (sometimes) be prepared to lend a sympathetic ear. One thirsty landlord, unwilling to wait that long for consolation, adapted his golf trolley to transport a fair selection of drinks. Traditionalists would call this cheating.

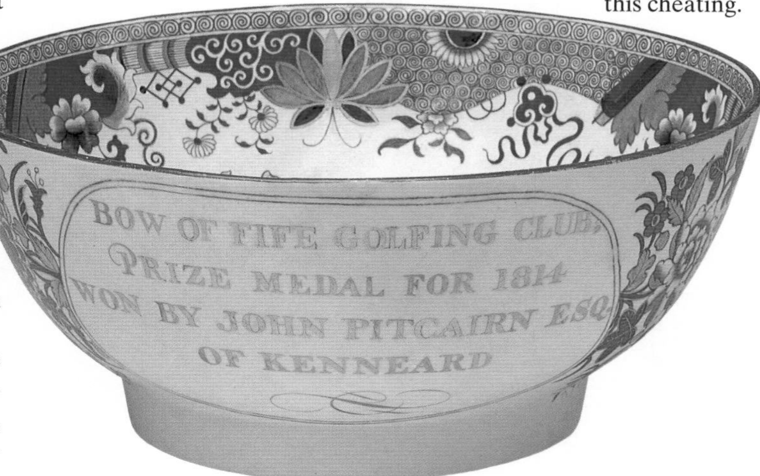

PITCAIRN'S POT *Golf's first-known prize, the Bow of Fife Bowl*

GOLF AND POLITICS

Racialism in Golf

Race has been the greatest source of friction in golf. Racial problems started for the USGA right away. Their first president, Theodore Havemeyer, donor of the original US Open trophy, was faced with player rebellion at the second ever US Open, at Shinnecock Hills, on Long Island, in 1896.

The field was all white, except for two players. Both were entered from the host club. One was John Shippen, who worked at the club as a caddie. He had a black West Indian father and a Shinnecock Native American mother. The other was Oscar Bunn, and he was a full-blooded Shinnecock.

Shippen's testimony, to the writer "Red" Hoffman, many years later, was to the effect that Havemeyer told the white pros that the Open would proceed with them or without them. Result: all present teed off for the 36 holes, over which the (one-day) Open was then played.

James Foulis, from the Chicago Club, became the first Scot to take the title. He won by three strokes from the defending champion, Horace Rawlins, thanks mainly to a second round of 74, a score not equalled until the coming of the Haskell ball, in the development of which Foulis was to play a significant part.

Shippen shared the first-round lead, finishing joint fifth in company with H. J. Whigham, Charlie Macdonald's son-in-law, who had won the Amateur title the previous day. No black man has come closer in the following hundred years. Shippen did play again twice, but did not make the top 20 either time.

Chances of black success were sharply curtailed by two factors. The first was economic, though there was, from 1928, a black equivalent of the PGA, the United Golf Association. When a black tour started up, even more intermittent and a good deal poorer than the PGA circuit, good crowds (of blacks) turned up, for not many had seen any of their race playing golf, certainly an elite sport where the black masses were concerned. White golfers played in these events, but there was no cross-fertilization, so to speak, in the other direction, for a compelling reason.

This was the second factor, namely a clause in the 1916 constitution of the US PGA stating that non-Caucasians could not be members. It was not deleted until 1961, and very few black pros managed to jump the gun and appear in PGA Tour events before that.

Charlie Sifford was the most notable of these. Born in 1923 in Charlotte, North Carolina, he began as a caddie, served in the US Army, later acted as private pro for the singer Billy Eckstine and won, almost routinely at one stage, the Black Open. He also won the Long Beach event, which was over 54 holes, and the Puerto Rican Open.

Like many other blacks, he was barred from this hotel and that restaurant, and he even received death threats when he began to play on the tour. He was heckled when he was the first black to play in the South (in the Greensboro Open), and withdrew.

Money talks; golf listens

The end of the PGA's Caucasian clause came, in one sense, because of financial considerations. The Los Angeles Open always showed a laudable disregard for the clause, while George S. May took no notice of it, and carried on with his independent "World Championship" in Chicago, offering large purses and staging pro-ams with such black heroes as Joe Louis. Here and there states began to legislate against exclusion of blacks from courses.

But mostly the PGA clause stuck, Sifford usually having to omit the southern leg of the tour. The clause came under attack in the run-up to the 1962 US PGA Championship arranged for Brentwood, Los Angeles. In the previous year a letter from a black pro, Bill Spiller, to a lawyer about black exclusions from the pro tour led to a California state statute making it illegal to stage PGA tournaments on public courses from which blacks were excluded. Stanley Mosk, the State's Attorney General responsible for this, told other State's attorneys what he had done.

TRAIL BLAZER *Charlie Sifford, who challenged the Caucasian clause*

TIGER ON THE PROWL *Three times US Amateur champion Tiger Woods reconnoitres Augusta's 17th in 1996*

Now the PGA were faced with purse losses on a grand scale. Totally without fanfare, they did the despised clause to death in November 1961. It made front-page news in the *New York Times*.

Sifford won the Hartford Open in 1967 and, appropriately, the LA Open in 1969. It was not enough to get him a place at the Masters, however, then the decision of past Masters. Lee Elder got in by winning a tournament after the Masters entry gate had been enlarged a little.

Sifford was turned down several times for club pro jobs at the end of his tour career, but was able to play on the Senior Tour.

Lucius Bateman, who died in 1972, was not so lucky. While his talent as a player can never be assessed, it is clear that he could teach. Tony Lema and Dick and John Lotz were among the boys he instructed who became tour players, a privilege denied to Bateman.

Shoal Creek gives an inch

Money, in the form of vested interest, had helped to expunge the Caucasian clause. It proved an irresistible force in support of the anti-discrimination front in 1990. Shoal Creek in Alabama, which had hosted the US PGA Championship once before, in 1984, had been chosen again, but this time the club was the focus of media attention long before the first player teed off.

Indeed, any teeing off at all seemed unlikely after the publication of a newspaper article by Shoal Creek's founder, Hall Thompson, which included the statement: "I think we've said that we don't discriminate in any other area except the blacks."

The wrath of black America and their supporters in the white community was at once directed at the club, and the PGA must have had visions of Shoal Creek staging scenes comparable to those surrounding the desegregation of schools in the recent past.

It did not happen, because the threat of being involved, however remotely, in messy demonstrations, the danger of a boycott of their products and hence a costly loss of market share, prompted most sponsors of the ABC telecasts of the championship to pull out – which automatically meant no TV coverage.

Moreover, it was made clear by the USGA, PGA and tour administrations that none of their events would be staged by clubs who held to Hall Thompson's line. A positive PGA declaration, ostracizing "any club that has membership practices or policies that discriminate on the basis of race, religion, sex or national origin", had taken 29 years to arrive after the abolition of the Causasian clause.

On the regular tour the PGA moved the Centel Western Open from Butler National to Cog Hill, where it still is, sponsored now by Motorola. Poppy Hills replaced Cypress Point for the AT&T Pro-Am, and on the Senior Tour the Southwestern Bell Classic moved from Old Warson in St Louis to Loch Lloyd in Kansas City. Skokie, near Chicago, was replaced as site of the Ameritech Senior Open by Newby Stonebridge. There was also a move away from Amarillo Country Club on the Ben Hogan (now the Nike) Tour. Interlachen acquired the 1993 Walker Cup match when Chicago GC withdrew following the anti-discrimination rulings. Later, Tom Watson resigned from the Kansas City Country Club when a Jewish applicant was blackballed.

Finally, Shoal Creek enrolled Louis Willie, a black Alabama businessman, as an honorary member just two weeks before the 1990 US PGA Championship, so battle commenced after all. No one was more grateful than Queenslander Wayne Grady, who won by three shots from Fred Couples for his one and, so far, only "major". In September 1990, Augusta National enrolled its first black member.

Four years later Eldrick "Tiger" Woods, America's first black Amateur Champion (and the youngest too), led Stanford University to victory in the Jerry Pate National Intercollegiate tournament at Shoal Creek. Woods, aged 18, was best individual, 10 under par. Hall Thompson was moved to tell Woods, who also has Thai, Chinese and Cherokee blood, that he was a great player, and that he was proud of him.

Louis Willie is still the only black member at Shoal Creek.

Discrimination on ethnic grounds has ever been more than just a matter skin colour. Delicate shades of discrimination have clouded US membership issues ... for instance, German Jews OK, East European Jews not OK. Italians (as Gene Sarazen discovered), and Roman Catholics were also in discrimination's shadow.

Gender Wars rage on

Discrimination against women in golf has rarely had such a high profile or raised temperatures as readily as discrimination against non- Caucasians, yet the degree and what might be termed the effrontery to which it still exists is scarcely less eyebrow-raising. Publicity is the oxygen that has done female emancipation most good, and the 1996 election of the first woman USGA president, Judy Bell, cannot be without significance. Yet, as Marcia Chambers makes clear in her study of gender discrimination, a good deal of what goes on in the United States has not until recently been dragged out into the open.

Not that golf is the only culprit on either side of the Atlantic. When institutions as august (and often as adversarial) as Oxford and Cambridge Universities jointly dissociate themselves from what they feel is "discriminatory and offensive" it makes front page news. Both seats of learning made clear, in 1995, their dislike of the membership policy of the Pall Mall London-based United Oxford and Cambridge University Club. Women were excluded from full membership, though 40 per cent of Oxbridge graduates are female. A vote on the issue, overwhelmingly in favour of change, was declared void under the original admission rules which were nearly 200 years old. All but one of the 70 Oxbridge heads resigned from the club, including Lord Jenkins of Hillhead, a former Cabinet minister. So did scores of other members. The club ran into cash problems, making a loss for the first time in 16 years.

What might be termed the Shoal Creek effect now intensified (though David Fay, executive director of the USGA, has said that the guidelines that came after Shoal Creek focused on Afro-Americans. The women's issue was "tricky." Rules hampering women were "internal club policies"). Pall Mall peace was sought through a policy of appeasement. Women were to be allowed to become "lady associates": this status included permission to climb almost to the top of the staircase, beyond which women could penetrate only to visit (a new privilege this) the second-floor library. They were not to be admitted to the smoking room or morning room bar, but were to be charged an extra £100 each year for these extra rights. A further (postal) vote, with 85 per cent of the 3,000 members in favour of full membership for women, swept aside the old rules early in 1996. The Club, said the chairman, would enter the new millennium with renewed vigour, and the great and the good prepared to rejoin the Oxford and Cambridge University Club.

Reforms in such high and influential circles are unlikely, on recent form, to inspire universal change in favour of women's rights in golf clubs: this stricture applies mainly to sinning private clubs, since local authorities that own public courses do not run the risk of being accused of discriminatory practices at property they control.

In late Victorian times, when the cheap gutty ball was hastening the expansion of the game in Britain, the chances of women becoming full members of a club were remote. Men of substance founded golf clubs: there were few women who could find the time or cash to play. In Victorian eyes, women were homemakers. Scottish women were more fortunate, here and there, because there were no restrictions against play on common land where the public links lay. As early as 1810 there was a competition at Musselburgh for the wives of the fishing community. At private clubs, springing up everywhere as 1900 approached, the outlook for women golfers was bleak. It did not mean there was no place for them in golf: Tom Dunn, the professional at Royal Wimbledon, had a daughter who made and mended clubs in his shop. Westward Ho! was among the few enlightened clubs who allowed women on their links. Musselburgh and Wimbledon founded ladies' clubs in 1872.

In America, country clubs have long recognized only the state of marriage, and have not had a category for single women, including divorcées and widows, regardless of their standing in the community, from judge to captain of industry. A man, once he acquires a membership, whatever the colour of his skin or his religious persuasion, gets full rights. The traditional entry for women, enforced by club by-laws, is as the wife of a member. The same privileges do not, in many clubs, extend to both partners – the women does not have a vote in club affairs: bear in mind that when many clubs were formed, women had no vote for state or national legislatures, or the right to own property. If the male is widowed or divorced, his membership is unaffected.

Divorce can cost a woman club membership. Her former husband gets a new wife, who inherits, so to speak, the membership of the parted wife. One such sufferer had to make way for her marital successor who did not even play the game. Another strand in this tangled web is that men in some clubs can bequeath memberships to their sons, but not their daughters.

The 19th Amendment, 1920, emancipated American women politically, but it is fruitless to plead the 19th when seeking membership of private clubs. The disinclination of many women members to campaign against injustice or to support those who are willing to do so is based on apprehension that the resultant friction may make things worse. (A nickname for them is WORMS – Wives Of Regular Members). Even more appalling, Marcia Chambers reports the case of a recently divorced woman told to clear out her locker who was given to understand that she was thought to be too attractive in her new, unattached state, to be around without a husband.

Marian Carr, secretary of the English Ladies' Golf Association, says the problem is receding, especially as new clubs tend to start out on the right foot. Restrictions on playing times are a particular irritant for the growing band of women executives in America who may find they cannot, as men do, take a customer for a round and lunch.

Indeed, not only does the country club tradition, which is largely White-Anglo-Saxon-Protestant, restrict entry and privileges to courses, but certain other facilities are defended to the nth degree by male members. Some states, though not all, forbid discrimination on grounds of race, gender and the like in hotels, clubs, and other facilities.

The State of Michigan legislated in 1992 against discrimination in private clubs, which lead Oakland Hills male members (whose Donald Ross/Robert Trent Jones course staged the 1996 US Open) to a cunning strategy to keep the grill room to themselves – and bear in mind that top-class women professionals, such as Jane Blalock, have been turned out of grill rooms. The solution: make the grill room part and parcel of the men's locker room. Naturally no women could enter the locker-room-cum-grill, not even the six grill waitresses, who objected to this loss of employment, and went to law.

Their lawyer found the club had no full women members, and no blacks. By the time he filed lawsuit for the waitresses, one woman and one black had received admission. A Senator implied that the grant of a liquor licence to a lavatory was unlikely. The waitresses got their jobs back, and received compensation.

Television can also change minds quickly. The producers of a fly-on-the-wall documentary shown by Britain's Channel 4 in 1994 were clearly on the look-out for a club with discriminatory tendencies. In choosing Northwood, a London suburban club, they hit upon a propaganda jackpot for women golfers. Not only did the club chairman have to resign after denying at the annual general meeting that he had threatened a [male] member with expulsion, which he clearly did in the TV film, but the second-class-citizen plight of women members was brutally exposed. They paid subscriptions, but could not so much as speak at the AGM, let alone vote; nor could they play at weekends. The board resigned, and the new one granted full voting rights to all members over 21 with two years' membership.

Britain's Equal Opportunities Commission seek an amendment to the Sex Discrimination Act which would close the private clubs' loophole. Such clubs may still discriminate against women. A successful case against the practice went to appeal, and the club's appeal was allowed, although it has been pointed out that the 1964 Licensing Act states that all members entitled to use club premises must be entitled to vote and must have equal voting rights.

The EOC seek an amendment to section 29 of the Sex Discrimination Act making it unlawful from 1998 for anyone providing goods, facilities or services to the public or a section of the public to discriminate by refusing or deliberately omitting to provide them. Section 29's list of facilities includes those for "entertainment, recreation or refreshment." Liz Kahn, doughty fighter for women golfers' rights and a former Press Golfing Society captain, claims that at most clubs in Britain she is a second-class citizen, with no voting rights, restricted tee times, and prevented from paying an equal subscription. Her letter to the *Daily Telegraph* attracted charges that her allegations were over the top. Others held that conditions were exactly as she described for example at Wigan Golf Club. In short, equal opportunities are not universally available. The fact that Lottery money is not available to discriminatory organisations may help to accelerate change.

The World Tour

The managements of the game's most powerful, prosperous and complex tours, the American PGA Tour and the PGA European Tour, have maintained strong and effective opposition to the plan put forward late in 1994 by Greg Norman and backed by media magnate Rupert Murdoch, for World Tour of about eight events with fields composed of the world's top 40 players. Many found it hard to see what good Norman's circuit would contribute to the well-being of golf, in the US, Europe, or anywhere else for that matter, though it would clearly be of vast financial benefit to the fortunate 40 and to Mr Murdoch's satellite and Fox TV companies, who would show the events.

Furthermore, it was felt anything that would weaken the viability of golf's four major events must be resisted. The recent action of the controllers of the three majors played in America, in widening the entry to include more overseas players, was a wise move, aimed at protecting those events, because it heightens their world-class standing.

Norman's sales pitch for a World Tour went like this: "I want to finally see the Seve Ballesteroses, Nick Faldos, José-Maria Olazabals and Nick Prices playing against each other, week in, week out." One wonders if Norman has thought out just how lacking in variety this would prove. The 40 would be made up of the world's 30 top golfers, plus 10 invitees. A prize of $600,000 (£387,000) would go to the winner, out of a prize fund for each tournament of $3 million, and a $1 million bonus to the leading player at year's end.

Four tournaments would be staged in the US, starting at Atlanta

US PGA ULTIMATUM *US Tour boss Tim Finchem: "Players must choose."*

the week before the Masters down the road at Augusta, one in Mexico, one in Canada, one in Scotland at Gleneagles, and one in Spain.

Jack Nicklaus seemed to be in favour, saying he had wanted it to happen in America. Arnold Palmer counselled caution: think about the new tour, "but ... protect the US PGA Tour as it is today." Olazabal faxed his support; Bernard Gallacher did not. As Ryder Cup captain and member of the European Tour Board he had perhaps a more global view than most: "The World Tour is wrong," he said, "... it would send the wrong signals to long-term sponsors ... it wouldn't help young players to come into the game. It's a power struggle within management companies, backed by television."

Lanny Wadkins, the 1995 US Ryder Cup captain, concurred: "I think the public has seen enough greed from athletes." Wadkins spoke at a time when player power had blacked out part of the US baseball and ice hockey seasons.

For the Norman camp it must be said that the rise in standards outside the US has made clear the extent to which the free movement of players between one tour and another has been restricted. Ken Schofield, executive director of the European Tour, recognized this when he agreed that the top players want to play more internationally, adding, "but that is the route the game is taking."

The immediate appeal of the Norman plan looked less than intoxicating when a poll revealed that none of the American players in the Sony top 30 would commit themselves to the World Tour.

Tim Finchem, a former White House aide, who had recently been promoted to PGA Tour Commissioner to succeed Deane Beman, quickly came down on the Norman plan with a warning to his players that they would have to choose to play on one tour or the other. Tour rules are basically the same either side of the Atlantic: members must play in at least 15 events in America; 11 in Europe. This does not mean that US PGA Tour men can sign up for any foreign event that takes their fancy outside those 15. The Federal Trade

WORLD TOUR ALLIES *Nick Price is a supporter of (right) Greg Norman and his – so far still-born – plan for a world tour for the superstars*

Commission investigation into the extent Tour policies were in violation of trust laws lost urgency when Finchem showed greater flexibility in granting releases for card-holding members to perform abroad. He also pointed out that the Tour is more than mere tournaments, but contributes massively to charity and golf development.

This is undoubtably true, but there is a history of courts being totally unimpressed by sporting bodies who imagine they can set up a body of rules which runs counter to common or statute law. Fine examples of this are the consternation among major European soccer clubs at the Jean-Marc Bosman court decision making players free agents when their contracts end, and cricket authorities' inability to prevent Kerry Packer from signing top players and staging international games.

The World Tour will not lie down

Despite its initial lack of progress, the concept of the World Tour is not dead by any means. The new tour appointed an executive director, John Montgomery, and at the Johnnie Walker World (*sic*) Championship in Jamaica, a month after Norman's scheme was unveiled, Montgomery gave leading players further details about it. Nick Price and Seve Ballesteros were among the supporters of the concept, but Nick Faldo's conclusion was that it was not going to happen. He had one particularly awkward question to ask of its would-be organizers: "How do the tournaments rate when it comes to selection for the Ryder Cup team?"

Deciding how many Cup points should go to the winner of a 40-player "World" event, and how many to the victor in a US or European Tour event with the usual 150 field, might be a contentious business, especially where the players warring for the last Cup place were concerned.

Price and Norman, the top two in the Sony rankings at the time, left Mark McCormack's International Management Group in 1994. McCormack's opposition to the World Tour may or may not have been magnified by their defection, but his case against a scheme to fold such a tour into the existing major tours is strong.

The idea is to designate four events in each tour which all players good enough to qualify would be free to enter. McCormack thinks it would be unfair to the 30-odd tournaments on each tour *not* chosen, whose sponsors and supporters had built up their events only to have them inescapably demoted in class. These events would inevitably become weaker.

The US, European, South African, Australasian and Japan tours have resolutely circled the wagons against the Murdoch/Norman take-over raiders, not only by increasing the admission of "foreign" golfers to the major championships, but with regular "World Golf Forum" meetings. These reflect, says Schofield, "our healthy relationship with all governing bodies of the game." The recent launching of the Andersen Consulting World Championship is not perhaps the strongest tactic to disarm the World Tour camp, but does show the PGAs are alive to golf's would-be corporate raiders.

How significant that not a word was said after the crucial 1995 PGAs get-together about what must have been the burning topic, Norman's global bombshell. But like company directors threatened by asset-strippers – which is what the World Tour really is – the PGAs are undoubtedly wise to set out their own agenda.

SCANDALS, DISASTERS AND TROUBLE-MAKERS

Golf is a game involving a projectile which may (legally) be dispatched at a velocity of up to 250 feet per second. Accidental death and destruction would seem unavoidable, while bad shots bring on suicidal tendencies.

In an age scarred by great suffering and slaughter in racial and religious conflict, words like tragedy and disaster, applied to strokes of ill fortune on a golf course, will seem to many to be inappropriate, incongruous, wild overstatements.

Yet the world must, for a giddy, disoriented and stomach-churning moment, seem to be coming to an end when a long-fought-for triumph is at the finger-tips, and then dashed away by a chance happening, or a Draconian punishment for a moment of carelessness, like Roberto de Vicenzo's card error that ruled him out of a Masters play-off.

Consider the thoughts of Richard Boxall, a European touring pro, as he was being carried off Royal Birkdale during round three of the 1991 Open Championship. Only three strokes behind the leader, perhaps 24 hours from immortality, his chances were suddenly ended when his left leg fractured as he drove off the 9th tee. He had won his first European Tour event the previous year; now his playing days might be over. They weren't, but he has not been so close to glory since.

GRIP IT AND RIP IT *John Daly applies his unvarying formula at the 1992 Open*

Bobby Cruickshank from Granton-on-Spey never won a major, though this 5 foot 5 inch battler looked good at the Merion Open in 1934 when his ball hit a rock and bounced on to the green instead of sinking into a water hazard. Cruikshank joyfully threw his club in the air – and it came down on his head. Dazed, he finished joint third.

The slings and arrows

Fatal accidents are not all that uncommon, some of the most harrowing caused by clubs breaking, sometimes as the terrible result of a fit of ill-temper, as when Richard McCulough banged a club against a golf cart. The shaft broke, and flew up, cutting his carotid artery. Ian Cornwell may properly be recorded as the most unfortunate of golfers: he was struck twice, first on the leg and then on the head – which knocked him out – by the same player, two groups behind, on the same round at Tehidy Park.

His fate was at least preferable to that of John Mosley, who in 1972 got into an argument about a green fee with a guard at Delaware Park, Buffalo. The dispute ended with a bullet from the guard's gun in Mosley's chest and he was "dead on arrival". His wife got more than a hundred thousand dollars in compensation from the City of Buffalo, and the guard got seven and a half years for second-degree manslaughter.

CRUTCH PUTT *Richard Boxall makes an early start on golfing rehabilitation*

Tony Lema's death in 1966 is the only instance of a world-class professional being killed at the height of his powers. He and his wife Betty, and two other people, were killed when their light aircraft, flying them from the US PGA Championship at Akron to an exhibition near Chicago, crashed on to the 7th green of a course at Lansing, Illinois, and slid into a lake. At least Lema had lived to enjoy an Open Championship triumph. John White, the slim Scot who was one of the most delicately skilful footballers ever to don the white shirt of Tottenham Hotspur, enjoyed a Championship too - of the English Football League – before his career was cut short by lightning in 1964 as he sheltered under a tree when a storm interrupted his practice at a north London club. Lee

Trevino, Jerry Heard and Bobby Nichols were luckier when struck in 1975, during the Western Open at Medinah near Chicago, though Heard was never a force in golf again, and Trevino required surgery on his back and was out of the game for many months.

It's an ill wind though - Harry Vardon must have felt that the illness that prevented his setting sail for America in 1912 could scarcely have come at a more frustrating time in his career. The name of the liner on which he had booked a passage was the Titanic. Two years later he won his record sixth Open.

The game has seen many mighty falls - none more so in recent years than that of Ian Baker-Finch, who quelled the rest of the field on the final day of the 1991 Open at Royal Birkdale so majestically. His only win in the next four years, troubled among other things by back and shoulder injuries, was the Australian PGA Championship (1993). He has gone as long as 16 months without winning a cent. The cash drought ended with £1,250 for 33rd place in Sydney early in 1996. But he qualified for the final two rounds in only one of the eight majors in 1994 and 1995. All too often he has, as the Tour pros say, been "slamming his trunk on Friday."

IAN BAKER-FINCH *From Birkdale riches to years of missed cuts*

Marion Hollins had, in a way, even further to fall. She was a powerful hitter who became US Champion in 1921, beating Alexa Stirling, who was trying for her fourth title in a row, by 5 and 4 in the final. Her father, formerly a partner of J. P. Morgan, lost a fortune setting up his own firm. His daughter made one.

She was a leader in the building of the Women's National Club on Long Island, which was not only an all-women club, but also entirely financed by women. An even bigger concept, the Pasatiempo club in the hills near San Francisco, rejoiced in a course designed by Alister Mackenzie. The club's opening day in 1929 offered an exhibition match comprising Marion and three legends of amateur golf, Glenna Collett, Cyril Tolley and Bobby Jones.

The following year the oil prospecting company she put together, with the help of Chrysler and Whitney money, hit the jackpot with its first well. Marion made $2.5 million, a vast amount in the depths of the Depression. Pasatiempo acquired a steeplechase course, race horses and polo grounds and a guest list that included leading financiers from the east, and Hollywood's finest, such as Mary Pickford, Jean Harlow and Will Rogers.

The Depression and the fact that she stepped a little too heavily on the champagne pedal at Pasatiempo led to money troubles, and Marion's health suffered when she refused medical attention after a severe concussion in a 1937 road accident. She had to sell her beloved Pasatiempo, and though she made an appearance in the 1940 Amateur, cancer killed her in 1944.

A candle-lit memorial service early in 1994 on the 18th green at Moon Valley, Phoenix, mourned the passing of a more recent cancer victim, LPGA tour player Heather Farr, who was 28. A lone piper's lament was a reminder of how Heather had enjoyed the national music of the Scots at the closing ceremony of the Curtis Cup at Muirfield in 1984.

Yet, while they have breath in their bodies, golfers play on, as did the 43 competitors who entered, in 1933, for the first event for one-armed golfers; 37 of them had lost an arm in the First World War. The event has been held every year since.

Daly, the demon and the drink

Like many other sports, golf is blessed, or beset, depending on their mood, by players whose talent is undeniable but whose temperament is not ideal. One such is John Daly.

One clue to his box-office appeal is his long sojourn at the top of the long driving statistics. Had he played one more round in 1994 he would have qualified to lead for the fourth year in a row. He did lead again in 1995, with a figure of 289 yards, the best in any of the 16 years for which this statistic has been collated, and more than four yards better than Davis Love III. He won $574,783, 17th place on the money list in his first full year on the tour, 1991, and won Rookie of the Year.

Daly is big, and hits his weight – a fact he proved right away in commandeering the US PGA title at Crooked Stick in 1991. He went there as an unknown; four days later it was "Who's that playing with John Daly?" This Indiana course, one of Pete Dye's longest and most difficult, is well supplied with railway sleepers supporting pond banks, lots of rough toughened by heather, and greens with complicated, deceptive slopes.

The course is so long that David Feherty, who was seventh to Daly in the 1991 US PGA, said of it: "It's the first time that I've had to take the curvature of the earth into my shot-making calculations." Ray Floyd's conclusion about Daly's tee-shots there was: "I don't even drive that far when I go on vacation."

Add in a confident short game, and you have a golfer to reckon with: there is also a demon to reckon with inside the man, that prevents him from, so far, making the best use of the exemption to tour events that his US PGA title confers.

He began 1992 with the threat of a paternity suit from his girlfriend: they had split up before Christmas. They were reconciled by the summer, and daughter Shyna Hale Daly was born. Not long afterwards, Daly and his caddie Greg Rita, who had consumed "a few beers", were invited to leave a Newark-bound flight from Denver before take-off. Daly withdrew from the next tournament, the Buick Open, accusing a Buick official of starting rumours about his being drunk, and announcing that he would never buy a Buick. He managed to beat the 36-hole cut when he began his defence of his PGA title, but only by a stroke, and was 20 over par for the 72 holes at Bellerive, St Louis.

In September of 1992 Daly was back on top, taking the BC Open at Endicott, New York, by six shots. "The first tournament is not the hardest one to win. It's always the second one," said he. His marriage to Bettye Fulford lasted only a year, and Daly was put on probation by the PGA Tour following an alleged assault on her at Christmas, 1992.

Daly really cut loose at Greg Norman's Open in 1993, by which time he had given up his excessive drinking and also got over a chocolate addiction. He drove the 421-yard 5th hole in practice, his ball stopping four feet from the pin. The 5th got its own back later, though Daly finished with a creditable tie for 14th place.

Complete with new girlfriend, Paulette Dean, Daly was back in Britain for the Dunhill Cup at St Andrews in October. He, Fred Couples and Payne Stewart carried off the trophy and £100,000 each ($155,000), only Couples scoring better than Daly. Next month Daly was suspended indefinitely from the PGA Tour, after walking out midway through the second round of the Kapalua International in Hawaii.

So "Wild Thing" Daly – a not inappropriate nickname for a player whose watchword was "Grip it and Rip it" – did not start the 1994 Tour until March. He soon made two top-10 finishes, followed by a one-stroke victory in the BellSouth Classic. Again he drew the crowds, particularly at Augusta, where the netting at the end of the 260-yard practice ground had been raised to 65 feet in his honour, so to speak. It was raised further after Daly, at his third attempt, got a ball over the top of it ... but he finished tied for 48th place, with a last round of 78.

As in 1993, competition in 1994 ended early for Daly, who had in any case been hampered by lower back pain, after an unseemly car park scuffle with the father of a fellow competitor at Akron's World Series in August. Daly had been accused of driving into the group in front of him but Fuzzy Zoeller thought the accusation misplaced: "What we didn't read was that John was the second guy to hit ... Neal [Lancaster] hit first." Despite going through a drink rehabilitation programme early in 1993, Daly seemed to be finding it hard to adjust without his previous prop, the bottle. A month after Akron, Daly withdrew voluntarily from the Tour, and Wilson Golf and Reebok suspended his contracts.

The 1995 season amounted to a miniature of Daly's career; 57th on the US Tour, and only one win anywhere ... the British Open. Feherty's verdict was that as there were five courses at St Andrews, "he's bound to hit one of them." Yet Daly got the better of the blustery Old Lady not by a display of brute strength, but by keeping the ball lower off the tee with a new club. Daly's undistinguished 1996 (one top ten finish) was followed by his admission the following spring that he had "1,000 addictions" – the most damaging, clearly, a return to drinking, so he went back into rehabilitation.

Even Daly has seldom generated so much heat as the deal struck in the year of his Open victory by the Links Trust, who administer the Old Course. Two years on it became clear that the scheme to sell £1,300 packages by travel agents Keith Prowse to play at the Old Course was not going to raise the revenue expected. John Lindesay-Bethune, the Trust chairman, said that in the first 12 months of the deal, only 60 per cent of the expected £500,000 return was received. St Andrews' clubs, hoteliers and a multitude of others were angry about this national treasure being connected with corporate golf packages. There was also the matter of the American financial backers of the scheme being

YEAR OF TURMOIL *John Daly had trouble in 1992 both on and off the course*

investigated in the US for breach of gun sale regulations in their shops – highly unattractive so soon after the massacre at the Dunblane school.

The days of the scheme seemed numbered. There were demands for a less ostentatious scheme which would be more beneficial to the prosperity of the area and more in keeping with its traditions.

Brown meets "Thunder" Bolt

Players of uncertain temper are not confined to the US Tour. Eric Brown, whose fiery spirit of competition helped create a Ryder Cup record far above the British average, was quite ready to trade psychological punches with the leading American club-thrower of his time (or any other, probably) Tommy Bolt.

Here is a small tragedy: Bolt was considered by some to be among the top half-dozen at his profession, yet his skill has always been submerged in the public's consciousness by his tantrums. Salty, not to say toxic, legends attach to both these players. The truth of Brown's greeting to Bolt when they met in the 1957 Ryder Cup has been attested, however (though not Jimmy Demaret's assertion that the pair of them had been throwing clubs at each other from 50 paces). Once on first tee, at Lindrick Brown's invitation to Bolt to hit first was couched thus: "Your beat, sucker." Brown won 4 and 3.

"Thunder" Bolt, however, won the US Open the following year at 39, in his native Oklahoma, four ahead of Gary Player (aged 22). He led every round in heat and strong winds, and later passed the acid test of quality by keeping his game together in Senior competition.

If logos had been current in the 1950s, Bolt's would have resembled a javelin thrower, a reputation he nurtured by advising imitators to throw clubs *forward*, so as to avoid having to retrace one's steps. Golf's favourite chestnut ends with Bolt's caddie explaining why the next shot is an easy two iron, not a nine iron as decided by Bolt: "There's only the two left in the bag."

A fulminating gallery of US golf's malcontents is presented in Al Barkow's books on the tour: notably Clayton Heafner, who would walk off the first tee if his name was wrongly pronounced by the starter, and Lefty Stackhouse, a Texan, who once beat a whole set of clubs into pieces against a tree stump, and another time refused help when he had thrown himself into a thorn hedge.

As the Irish-American satirist and golfer, F. P. Dunne, aptly put it: "...it's the kind iv game iv ball that ye play wit ye'er own worst inimy, which is ye'ersilf."

When is a scandal a scandal?

The scandal meter deep within us is an untrustworthy instrument. The prejudices that control it vary from generation to generation and by class, race, sex and a few other items.

When Maurice Flitcroft, a crane driver from Barrow-in-Furness, managed to finagle his way into the qualifying rounds for the British Open in 1976, scored 121 first time out and then withdrew, saying he had no chance of qualifying, all agreed: that *was* a scandal, and all the beleaguered R&A's fault too. So it had been in the same event in 1965, when Walter Danecki from Milwaukee (who said he was "after the money") scored 221 for 36 holes.

Golfers' cries of "bandit" are usually accompanied by a rueful smile, but the Pebble Beach Golf Foundation made it clear that they had found one of Japanese origin when they stripped Masashi Yamada of the 1995 amateur title he won by three strokes in partnership with Bruce Vaughan, a US pro, with better ball rounds of 63, 65, 64, and 59. Yamada (aged 72) had entered the event with a certified handicap of 15. Dean Knuth, senior director of handicapping for the USGA, ruled his scores "statistically impossible". Besides, Yamada had handicaps of six and four at other clubs. So David Duval's partner Hughes Norton, of Mark McCormack's organization, got the prize.

American spectators tend to accept the extreme partisanship of leading US Tour player Dottie Pepper (formerly Mochrie) with rather greater equanimity than the British. She is reported to have made her pleasure plain when Laura Davies missed in the 1994 Solheim Cup. "I don't really care," she said. "I know what it takes to play well and I know I am professional about it ... I have to be happy with myself."

How far is her behaviour calculated, and therefore scandalous, or spontaneous, and therefore merely regrettable? Either way, it was effective – and good box-office. Her attitudes were not copied by any other player on either side in a match of generally good humour and (although the word risks accusations of scandalous political correctness) sportswomanship.

A startling confession from New Zealander Michael Campbell elicited "unsporting" charges ... and sympathy too; frustration at loss of form led him, so he said, to miss a putt so as to miss the cut in a 1996 tournament. He retracted when the resultant storm blew up.

The whole business seems to have been born of anxiety. He may simply have wished it on himself, since examination of scores did not provide an occasion when it had been possible for him to avoid qualifying by missing a putt.

The punishment fits the crime

The American novelist Henry James lived at Rye, England, close to a gem among links, but was so prejudiced against golf that his term for a course was "a series of beflagged jampots". Golfers are a forgiving lot, and tend merely to smile benevolently at such asinine jibes.

The depth of prejudice against what many folk think of as a suburban, middle-class, bourgeois pastime becomes clear when a plan for a £40,000 ($62,000) nine-hole course is scrapped, and approval is given

TALENTED OKIE *Tommy Bolt's skills were obscured by his petulance*

Double-edged verdict

Cheating has ever been the worst scandal in golf, because it is an honour game, and no one is there to see you use the shoe wedge to ease your ball out of trouble. Some cheats seem to have a death wish as far as golf is concerned, like the young and skilful Scottish pro who, in full view of his fellow competitors trying to qualify for the Open, respotted his ball nearer the hole. His sentence of suspension was a heavy one.

Just as heavy, in its way, was the Nottingham Crown Court verdict reached in a libel case brought by John Buckingham against Graham Rusk and Reginald Dove, who reported him to the Sherwood Forest club's committee for cheating. Dove's evidence included expressions of disbelief at seeing Buckingham move his ball with his foot after his shot became stuck behind a tree.

The committee cleared Buckingham, who then sought to eradicate any lingering stain by suing for libel. The jury returned a verdict that was as palatable as Snow White's apple ... poisonous in places. They found libel not proved because there was no evidence of malice on the part of the defendants in reporting Buckingham. The jury did not, however, want the verdict "to be perceived as proof that Mr Buckingham had definitely cheated".

He left Sherwood Forest, and could not afford to take further legal action against a newspaper that said an act of cheating would in future be known as a "Buckingham".

for a £75,000 ($116,250) all-weather football pitch. The link is that both facilities were planned for inside the walls of British prisons.

The golf course was intended for Swaledale on the Isle of Sheppey in the Thames Estuary, and was "completely unacceptable" according to the Director General of the Prison Service; the Astroturf football pitch, full sized with landscaped flower gardens behind each goal, is for Parkhurst on the Isle of Wight, a maximum security prison for some of Britain's worst and most dangerous offenders.

Elmley prison in Kent, a category D, low-security gaol, not far from Swaledale, has a 13-hole pitch and putt lay-out, but it was not a burden on the tax-payers, having been built by the prisoners with waste materials. A prison spokesman added a no doubt unwitting touch of disdain by saying: "This golf course provides exercise for the elderly and less fit prisoners."

Not so happy families

A family foursomes competition conceived in good fellowship and played in the best sporting spirit, which had attracted unfailingly for more than half a century and from a wide area hundreds of amateurs (long handicappers to internationals) ... surely such a fun event could never be accused of discrimination, and cited as an example of the élitism golf's enemies believe to be lurking behind every club's front door.

Yet such was the unhappy fate of Burhill, a private proprietary club in Surrey, two months after two of the host club's members, Ann Croft and her son Michael, won the 52nd annual Family Foursomes.

The controversy centred upon Audrey Briggs, four times a Welsh champion, and her son Laurie, aged 13. After rallying to bring off last ditch wins in the first two rounds, they lost in the third, after which Mrs Briggs wrote a thank-you letter to the club.

The response of the secretary, Dick Richards, was to say that the competition was open only to mothers and fathers with natural sons and daughters. Laurie, he went on, was adopted (correct, in Brazil 13 years before). The entry form, Richards further pointed out, ruled out stepchildren, and it was his error that adopted children were not mentioned, an omission which would be corrected for 1997.

It never was, the club's action brought down a fire-storm of criticism, re-heated by a follow-up letter from the club captain, condemned by Mrs Briggs for "an attitude to adopted children ... wholly outmoded in today's society." R & A secretary Michael Bonallack deemed it against the whole spirit of family foursomes.

Though it is clear that many Burhill members were convinced that blood relationships were obligatory, nothing written could be produced to that effect, an indication perhaps of the informal beginnings of the event. Even if set in stone, the ban would still have been unacceptable in an age when discrimination is keenly hunted down, though not always with success in the fields of gender and race.

Happy outcome: the Briggs were invited to tee it up again at Burhill.

GREENBRIER HIGH JINKS ... *and high-fives too as Brandie Burton and Dottie (Mochrie) Pepper (right) celebrate US progress in the Solheim Cup of 1994*

GOLF ECCENTRICS, COURSE CURIOSITIES AND BIZARRE HAPPENINGS

Oddballs abound in golf's literature, from P. G. Wodehouse's Oldest Member, by way of the hilarious Ring Lardner's diabolically truthful caddies and his hapless Mr Frisbie, to the country club satire of John. P. Marquand: these writers are outdone only by real-life characters, such as ...

A MOTLEY CREW

Dame Ethel Smyth

Creative talent often comes with a powerful urge to swim against the tide. Dame Ethel Smyth was one such swimmer, making her mark as composer, writer, and equal rights campaigner (with the accent on votes for women) and, to a lesser degree, golfer. Her musical works have long been neglected, though one of her operas *The Wreckers*, was revived at the 1994 Promenade Concerts at London's Albert Hall. Having studied music at Leipzig, she turned from symphonies and operas to compose a battle-song, "The March of the Women", for the Women's Social and Political Union founded by Emmeline Pankhurst in 1903.

Just before the union began a window-smashing campaign in 1910, the two women practised stone-throwing, it is believed, on the 13th fairway at Woking GC. The practice was much needed, for the 13th almost lived up to its reputation for ill-luck as far as Ethel

ORDER & CONFLICT *Dame Ethel brought both*

Smyth's dog was concerned: Mrs Pankhurst's first throw narrowly missed the animal. She and Ethel Smyth were soon scoring satisfactory hits on Government windows, and were briefly imprisoned in London's Holloway prison.

Ethel Smyth's rehabilitation with the establishment came with surprising speed. She was made Dame of the British Empire in the New Year's Honours of 1923. The new Dame was convinced that this turnabout was the result of her adroit handling of a skirmish in the war of the sexes at Woking, and the fact that Woking club member Lord Riddell was a friend of the prime minister, Lloyd George, who had evidently decided to let bygones be bygones, as far as militant women's movements were concerned: a house being built for him at Walton Heath had been blown up in 1913. Greens were dug up, and insurance cover had to be organized for the St Andrews clubhouse.

The Woking skirmish concerned male objections to women members (still temporary) taking a short cut leading past the men's changing-rooms. There was disquieting talk of no weekend tee times for women. A touch of humour from Ethel Smyth helped persuade the ladies to vote against using the short cut in future, a concession that was necessary, as she put it, "given the modesty of the British male".

Her attitude to the rules was not all it might have been, to judge from the report that when she lost her ball in a patch of heather, she sent to the greenkeeper's yard for a sickle to trim the offending vegetation. This is all of a piece with Victoria Sackville-West's valedictory judgment of Dame Ethel, who died in 1944 at 86: "Blinkered egotism could scarcely have driven at greater gallop along so determined a road. But although often a nuisance, Ethel was never a bore."

Denys Finch-Hatton

Another free spirit with an equally unorthodox life-style, and a far more adventurous one, was Denys Finch-Hatton. Like his brother Harold, the prime mover in the foundation of Royal St David's (*see* p182), Denys, a big-hitting golfer, was a son of the Earl of Winchilsea and Nottingham. He is the original of the big game hunter and pioneer aviator character in Karen Blixen's *Out of Africa*, based on her experiences as a planter

CHARITY CAPERS *Mark Roe (in drag) and Robert Lee at a fund-raising event*

THE ENGLISHOPEN
GOLFCHAMPIONSHIP

in Kenya. She shared his enthusiasm for flying, which eventually cost Denys his life.

Not long before the First World War, Denys captained the Oxford University golfers in the Varsity Match. He achieved one of the greatest put-downs in the game's history when chided for conceding putts to a Cambridge player: "Do remember, Finch-Hatton, you are playing for your side and not for yourself." Finch-Hatton replied: "And do remember you are playing for neither."

Crows the bogey

A teacher in a Sydney, New South Wales, school playground saw three crows flying over, and one of them, she remarked, had something round and white in its beak. Next instant a golf ball struck a fellow teacher, Karen Gilles, over the left eye. The ball caused a wound that needed stitches. It took some time for Karen to convince nurses at the hospital as to how she came by the cut. There it is in the Admissions Book: "Patient struck in left eye by golf ball dropped by passing crow." So it must be true ... mustn't it?

Jeannine Pelletier

Jeannine Pelletier wishes she hadn't found a ball at a Maine, New England, golf club, or rather that the ball hadn't found her. So do the club now, for the ball hit her on the nose after ricocheting off an abandoned railway. The court's ruling was that: "Although the tracks are not under the club's control, the club's duty extends to land which it has invited golfers to use." Mrs Pelletier got $40,000 (£25,800), but the jury found no evidence to support her husband's claim that he had suffered "a loss of consortium with his wife."

Count John de Bendern

The difference between an eccentric and a card is a matter of judgement: Count John de Bendern qualified as a card, if one accepts the definition given by Arnold Bennett at the end of his eponymous novel as being "identified ... with the great cause of cheering us all up". He played top-class amateur golf despite the intermittent, but still dreadful handicap, more usually suffered on the putting green, of being unable to take back the club.

Instead, in the same way that bowlers at cricket have felt unable to release the ball, he would stand waggling club over ball on tee or fairway for what seemed an age before he could strike it. He still managed to capture (as John de Forest) the British title in 1932 at Muirfield.

SPIRITED PERFORMER *James Balfour of the Honourable Company of Golfers*

He was invited to play in the Masters at Augusta, and achieved immortality when deciding to step into the water to play a recovery shot at the 13th. Carefully taking off one shoe and sock, he took up his stance ... placing his bare foot on dry land, the other, still shod, in the water.

Dress and Undress

Rules on proper golfing attire have always been contentious, never more so than when, at the Ridgeway Club, Cardiff, Wales, Dr Stephen Glascoe lost his membership because he would not discard his earring, never a problem, he said, at other courses.

At La Jenny Domaine Residentiale Naturiste, near Bordeaux, he would have been asked to play without a stitch, never mind an earring.

"Singing Jamie Balfour"

The legends about James Balfour, better known as "Singing Jamie Balfour", secretary and treasurer of the Honourable Company of Edinburgh Golfers, elevate him to supercard and eccentric. Balfour was not only renowned as a singer of Scottish songs, but as a toper. It is said he had only to hear a cork being withdrawn to ask for "a glass o' that", whatever it might be.

Hence the tale about his fall into a pit on a building site. He asked a passer by to pull him out, but was refused, on the grounds that, once out, he would be unable to stand. Balfour then offered to run a race to the Tron Kirk for a bottle of claret. His rescuer must have thought this an easy way to obtain a bottle of claret, but Balfour set off at great pace and was waiting on the church steps, seemingly incapable of further progress, by the time the also-ran got there. "Another run to Fortune's for another bottle of claret," challenged the indomitable Balfour. He won that too; his two-bottle benefactor needed a sedan chair to get home.

THE RUB OF THE GREEN

Happy Valley

Golf began in Hong Kong in 1889, on a course which had no holes: tees, fairways and greens, yes; but holes, no. Foundation of the club, soon to be Royal Hong Kong, was mainly down to the enthusiasm of the Harbour Master, Robert Rumsey RN, and Gershom Stewart, who most fittingly became MP for Hoylake.

The inaugural course had no bunkers either, and for the explanation of this Chinese puzzle it is necessary to look to the military, who held the land. The course was laid out on the infield of the Happy Valley racecourse. Polo, football and hockey were played on it, and parades were held there too, though it was a marshy area, with a large pond in the middle, and the soldiers could foresee horses (and others perhaps) breaking their legs in holes.

Instead of bunkers, close mesh netting was laid down to catch errant shots. In place of holes, granite setts were placed on the greens which the players were required to hit in lieu of holing out. The research facilities of the USGA boffins would not be required to work out that hitting these setts was a far easier proposition than persuading putts to drop into a hole less than five inches across.

This happy (putting) state of affairs did not last long. The club acquired land at Deep Water Bay on the other side of Hong Kong Island. When the first course, complete with holes, was laid out there, it could be reached only by launch. It was improved, and re-opened in 1898. Later, golfers arrived by ponies, caddies making the steep trek over the hills from Happy Valley complete with tiffin. This, says the club historian Spencer Robinson, was always the same: cold saddle of mutton, cold gooseberry pie, and Watson's dry sherry...cost, HK$1.

Busy Fanling

Now the club's main area of activity is on the mainland in the New Territories, which were annexed without canvassing Chinese opinion, soon after the club was founded. Royal Hong Kong's three courses at Fanling are among the world's busiest.

The Hong Kong Open, thanks to the development of the Asian Tour, now facing competition from the Asian PGA Tour, has a most impressive list of winners. The first was Lu Liang Huan (Mr Lu), who later became pro at Fanling. Greg Norman, Peter Thomson, Kel Nagle and

Ian Woosnam also won the Open, always played at Fanling, whence Joe (the Pro) Hardwick has just retired. He succeeded Mr Lu, and among his pupils was former Governor Chris Patten.

Between 11,000 and 12,000 Fanling golfers use the courses every week, including more than 100 Japanese a day, served by an army of 600 registered caddies. The register (popular since it involved having a photograph taken) was introduced to solve a rash of caddie troubles, including the time when a deputation of village elders came to request that an increase to 30 cents a day should be cancelled, because 30 cents was more than the average farm worker's pay.

Control was essential to ward off caddie strikes, during one of which 100 Sepoys were sent to act as caddies. Then there were difficulties at the nearest railway station, caused by crowds of would-be caddies fighting to get hold of members' bags.

View from the East

Visitors to China's first international tournament, the 1995 World Cup at Shenzhen, were treated to a startling re-examination of the game's origins. Dutch and Scots claims as originators were ignored in a Beijing sponsored Propaganda Handbook of the Cup, according to which Scotland took up the game in 15 AD, 2,000 years after a Chinese version was current. Scots shepherds are given some little credit, though the handbook says they took up the game with wood clubs while their cows were wandering around. The explanation of why 18 holes is the norm is as picturesque: the winter was cold, and the shepherds took one mouthful of wine with the cap of the bottle while they hit a ball. When they hit 18 balls with their clubs all the liquor was gone and so ... The rule of 18 "made the British Royal House interested very much". This at least is not too wide of the mark.

"Île Flottante de Golf"

Anyone who thought an île flottante was ice cream swimming in liqueur in a Parisian restaurant should visit Idaho, where the par three 14th hole at the Cœur d'Alène club is a movable feast – or beast if you miss it – because it is a floating green, surrounded by water. It is made of expanded polystyrene and is moved around daily, so that it can be a mere 100 yards from the tee, or as much as 175. *Flottante* also means vacillating and undecided, a state of mind easily induced by this novelty.

The only way players can reach it is by ferry. The designers actually had the nerve, as if all that water did not pose enough of a threat, to put a bunker each side of the putting surface. An enraged member may well have it torpedoed one day. The course was chosen as the most beautiful resort course in 1992 by *Golf Digest*. The ball-hunting concession for the lake must be worth a fortune.

McDERMOTT'S REST *Kilkenny Churchyard, reachable from Ballybunion's first tee*

ARBORIAL ANTICS *Nick Faldo trying a Spanish tree in 1993*

Tree irons and ladder of the law

Nick Faldo was very upset to find that "his" tree by Pebble Beach's 14th hole was missing, the victim of a storm, when he returned to the course in 1995 for the first time in three years. "I loved that tree," said Faldo, who had climbed it during the 1992 US Open in a vain attempt to find his ball, and raised a laugh by asking, when aloft: "Where's Jane?"

Bernhard Langer did find his ball up a tree in a European Tour event, and played it down on to the nearby green, but didn't get his par.

Sir Simon Brown used a ladder when his partner Nigel Wilkinson, QC, put their ball on the Woking clubhouse roof: the intrepid Appeal Court judge, aged 57, used a putter and moved the ball to within a few feet of the pin. But he and Wilkinson lost the match for the Middle against the Inner Temple.

Death didn't part him

Nearly every golfer who has played at all often at beautiful Ballybunion near Limerick on the west coast of Ireland, has sliced his opening tee shot one time or another into the village churchyard. Martin McDermott, of Los Angeles, who died aged 43, loved the course so much that in 1987 he had his body flown over to rest in that same churchyard.

Ever onwards

A Texan has invented (and patented) the "Reversibly Elevated Golf Cup". His device is secreted inside each golf hole. It comprises a battery-powered telescopic piston, topped by a cup. A ball falling into the hole activates the gadget. Up comes the cup, lifting the ball to waist height. Risks of damage to lumbar regions are averted. But what does the lumbago sufferer do when offered a gimme?

STRANGE BUT TRUE

Prof. Treasure's dream putt

David Talbot paced about nervously as he lined up a putt for his amateur partner Professor John Treasure on the sloping green of the long 18th at Penina in the third and final round of the National Pro-Am in 1981. There was no mistaking the air of unease demonstrated by Talbot, at that time Captain of the British PGA.

Treasure, one time chairman of the giant advertising agency J. Walter Thompson, and a lecturer in business studies, had not taken up golf till he was past 50, but soon became a methodical and tidy golfer with a handicap in the mid teens.

Earlier in the week he had told Talbot of a dream in which he reached this final hole in three, and knew it was important to hole the putt: why, he didn't discover, for the dream ended before he could strike the putt.

Now, in reality, playing with the last group out on the course, Treasure had reached the same green in three with driver, fairway wood, and six iron. He faced a 15 foot downhill putt for a net eagle that would force a play-off against Steve Harrison, a Cumbrian pro, and his young, left-handed amateur partner Peter Hetherington.

Talbot pointed to a spot just outside the left lip of the hole. Treasure struck the putt perfectly. "We knew it was going in" is Harrison's fatalistic memory – and sure enough, in it went.

"At least we know now why you had to hole the putt," said Talbot to his partner. Perhaps the dream had been prompted by a conversation during the practice round, when Talbot recalled to the professor how Great Britain and Ireland had needed a birdie putt on the 18th while beating Japan for the Eisenhower Trophy (the World Amateur Team Championship) in 1976.

There was still a twist or two still to come in the story. Talbot flashed into the huge trees on the left of the first fairway, on a hole of well over 400 yards which dog-legs to the left. Treasure hit a respectable shot down the middle, but their opponents nailed their drives far beyond his.

INDOOR CHAMPION *Enid Wilson tees off at the Grosvenor House Golf Ball, 1931*

Talbot hacked out from a dreadful place onto the fairway. His third shot, a fairway wood, flew 230 yards and pulled up three feet beyond the pin. It was the second best shot of its kind he had ever struck, Talbot thought, considering the urgency of the situation, and remembering a blow he had struck during his PGA Championship victory of 1968.

Talbot was not called upon to putt, for his opponents, possibly shaken by Talbot's mighty strike, took an embarrassingly large number of shots to reach the green. So Treasure, still a member at Royal Mid-Surrey, and Talbot, still professional there, were National Pro-Am champions, dream-struck survivors of the original entry of well-over a thousand club Pro-Am pairs.

Watch the birdie

Birdies, eagles and albatrosses are all very fine, but birds can be provoking: members of a Surrey club took to setting out on a different kind of round, armed with small-bore rifles, with which to cut down the number of feathered ball-thieves. The hunt gave rise to a neat headline, "Crows the Bogey". Three times British Champion Enid Wilson reported that visits to a small island off the St Enodoc course in Cornwall could be fruitful: birds nesting there sometimes had golf balls as well as eggs in their collections.

The increasing number of urban foxes can be a problem: one almost brought on apoplexy when a society member at a London suburban course who gave a candy to a (begging) fox during the morning round saw the same animal make off with his ball in the afternoon.

Four-legged friends

Among golf's most unusual caddies are surely the ones with four legs, a well-fitting white fur coat and a tendency, when piqued, to spit: llamas from South America. They carry two bags and cost $100 per round (llama handler included). The llamas are available for hire at Talamore at Pinehurst, North Carolina. Talamore is a Gaelic word meaning "land of great value".

Call the USGA stuffy if you like, but their contention that the use of llamas as caddies is not within the rules is indisputably correct. "Caddie" is defined as "one who carries or handles a player's clubs during play and otherwise assists him in accordance with the Rules". To start with, llamas have no hands. Their rating at club selection is not known to the present writer.

From One Generation...

The death early in 1996 of George Selbach, the game's oldest golfer at 109 was a reminder of how golfing lives can link one age with another. Selbach held a course record at an Ohio club with a 64 – an honour of which he was relieved by Jim Barnes US Open Champion of 1921. Or to put it another way Selbach's father fought at the battle of Gettysburg long before many Americans had even heard of golf. Also in 1996 Raul Ballestestors aged 15, who had lifted the Spanish under-18 title at 14 played for his old school Cranleigh at Royal St George's and doubted uncle Seve would make the cut the same weekend at the Masters. But Seve did qualify on the Friday at Augusta and, well as Raul played, Cranleigh didn't.

That's the way to do it

TV cameras called at Trentham, Staffordshire, early in spring, 1997, for pictures of Suzan Toft and her friend Gill Dyke who had scored consecutive holes in one. Suzan, 72, posed for an action shot and, swinging an easy five wood, bingo, another ace. Bookmakers said they could not begin to calculate the odds against that happening again.

Yet there is a precedent – of sorts. Well before the days of TV, Irish international Lionel Munn was asked to pose for a still picture at the short 14th of the Royal Cinque Ports course in Kent. He was not playing at the time, so borrowed a club and a ball. His picture is still there on the club wall. Cigarette in mouth, he is casually swinging and – (you've guessed it) he holed out – no mean feat on this brute of a linksland hole, which then measured 195 yards.

CROCODILE HAZARD *Ball hunters may find the 13th at Sun City very unlucky*

CHRONOLOGY

"Tour guides," said John Betjeman, leave their clients "shipwrecked on a sea of facts." In case the dates listed below inflict similar sinking feelings upon readers, they should take comfort in the fact that there are only 10 truly significant dates in golf history. The first is not included hereunder, since painstaking research has failed to reveal when a Scottish shepherd invented the game. 1502: when James IV of Scotland stopped trying to stop people playing the game and took it up himself. *Circa* 1600: the invention of the feathery. 1848: gutta-percha ball. 1744: first club founded and rules codified. 1860: British Open begins. 1888: United States fuse lit in Yonkers. 1898: Haskell ball, and Gammeter's winding machine. 1926: steel shafts legalized. 1947: TV coverage of US Open.

1457, 1471 and under James IV of Scotland in **1491**: Parliament forbids golf and football for hindering military training
1502 Anglo-Scottish Perpetual Peace Treaty
James IV, first recorded golfer, buys clubs and balls
1513 James IV killed at Flodden
1553 Archbishop of St Andrews confirms right to play over links
1567 Mary Queen of Scots accused of playing golf a few days after the murder of her husband Lord Darnley
1592 Golf at Leith forbidden for interfering with worship on Sunday
1603 James I (and VI of Scotland) ascends English throne: he appoints a royal club-maker and encourages both his sons to play
1600 *(circa)* Feathery ball is introduced
1618 James I approves Sunday play ... after worship
1637 Boy is hanged in Banff, Scotland, for stealing golf balls
1646 Charles I, prisoner of Scots, plays at Newcastle-upon-Tyne
1650 Charles II plays after being crowned King of Scotland
1689 Royal link with golf is broken as William III succeeds James II
1744 John Rattray, Edinburgh surgeon, wins first club competition for Hon. Co. of Edinburgh Golfers' Silver Club
First recorded code of rules
1754 St Andrews men set up similar Silver Club contest
1759 St Andrews men change Silver Club knock-out to stroke play
1766 Foundation of Blackheath club, first in England
1786 First mention of golf in US: Charleston club is founded
1834 Royal and Ancient title is conferred on St Andrews Club
1848 Gutta-percha is ball introduced
1856 Continent of Europe's first club is founded at Pau, France
1857 Inter-Club foursomes, first Championship Meeting, is suggested by Prestwick; won by Blackheath
1858 Robert Chambers wins individual Championship
1859 Death of leading professional Allan Robertson
1860 Willie Park wins Championship Belt offered by Prestwick for annual Championship, beating seven other professionals
1861 Tom Morris Senior wins first "Open" as Championship is widened to admit amateurs
1864 Westward Ho! (Royal) North Devon Club, founded
1869 (Royal) Liverpool Club formed at Hoylake, former race-track
1870 Young Tom Morris lands hat-trick of Opens at 19 and retains Championship belt
1872 Silver claret jug offered by Prestwick, St Andrews and Honourable Company of Edinburgh Golfers as perpetual trophy for Open. Young Tom wins again
1875 Young Tom dies, aged 24, soon after wife's death in childbirth
1878 Oxford beat Cambridge in first University match
1885 Royal Liverpool organize first British Amateur Championship, won by Hoylake member, A. F. Macfie, from Scotland
1888 Formation of St. Andrew's Club, Yonkers, New York, nicknamed the "Apple Tree Gang"
1890 John Ball is the first amateur and Englishman to win Open, at Prestwick
1891 R&A rule hole width at 4½ inches, minimum 4 inches deep
1893 Ladies' Golf Union founded in Britain
Lady Margaret Scott wins first Championship
1894 J. H. Taylor first English pro to win Open, played in England for first time, at Royal St George's, Sandwich
1894 United States Golf Association formed
1895 USGA stages first Amateur Championship, won by Charles Mac-

donald from Chicago; Open won by Horace Rawlins, an English pro; and Women's Amateur, won by Mrs Charles Brown

1896 Harry Vardon, Channel Islander, wins British Open

1898 Coburn Haskell patents ball with gutta-percha cover over rubber bands wound under tension around core

1900 Vardon tours US and wins US Open by two shots from Taylor
Freddie Tait, former Amateur Champion, killed in Boer War

1902 Sandy Herd pioneers Haskell "Bounding Billy" ball to win British Open from Harry Vardon and James Braid by a stroke
Rib-faced clubs introduced to gain control over lively "Haskell"

1904 Walter J. Travis lands first US victory in British Amateur at Royal St. George's using Schenectady centre-shafted putter

1905 British women's team beats US 6–1 at Cromer, Norfolk

1907 Frenchman Arnaud Massy is the first foreigner to win Open

1908 Old Tom Morris dies at St Andrews, aged 87

1909 Dorothy Campbell from North Berwick is the first to gain British and US titles in one season

1911 Johnny McDermott is the first American-born winner of US Open

1912 Jamie Anderson, Open winner 1877–8–9, dies in Perth Poorhouse

1913 Bostonian Francis Ouimet, aged 20, is the first Amateur to win US Open, beating Harry Vardon and Ted Ray in play-off at Brookline

1914 Walter Hagen wins his first US Open

1916 PGA of America founded: Jim Barnes wins first USPGA title

1919 R&A take over management of major British Championships

1921 Jock Hutchison is the first to take the British Open trophy to US
R&A and USGA rule ball must be not more than 1.62 ounces in weight and 1.62 inches in diameter
US beat Britain 9–3 in unofficial amateur international, Hoylake
British pros bt US 10½–4½ in unofficial international at Gleneagles

1922 Walter Hagen first American-born player to win British Open
US win inaugural Walker Cup match, National Golf Links

1924 Joyce Wethered wins fifth English Ladies' Amateur in a row

1926 Britain defeats US 13½–1½ in unofficial professional international at Wentworth
Bobby Jones wins British Open at Lytham
Jess Sweetser first American to win British Amateur title

1927 Hagen wins his fourth USPGA title in a row, his fifth in all
US beats Britain in the first Ryder Cup match at Worcester, MA

1929 Hagen wins his fourth British Open
R&A legalize steel shafted clubs, following USGA lead of 1926

1930 Bobby Jones Grand Slam: wins US and British Opens, British and US Amateurs, in same year

1932 Inaugural Curtis Cup match: US beat Britain 5½–3½

1934 Henry Cotton is first Briton to win the Open since 1923

1937 First US Ryder Cup away win, by 8–4, at Southport and Ainsdale
Harry Vardon, record six times winner of British Open, dies

1938 Britain and Ireland scores first Walker Cup win at St Andrews

1940 Johnny Laidlay, true inventor of the "Vardon" grip, dies aged 80

1943 Pam Barton, first Englishwoman to win the British and American Amateurs in same year (1936), dies in RAF air crash

1945 Byron Nelson wins 19 events in 31 starts, 11 of them in a row

1947 Lew Worsham beats Sam Snead in play-off for US Open at St Louis in first Championship to be televised (locally)
Babe Zaharias first American to win British Women's Amateur

1948 Ben Hogan wins first US Open, at Los Angeles

1949 Ben Hogan is almost killed, legs crushed, in road crash in Texas

1950 Ben Hogan recovers to win second US Open
James Braid, five times British Open winner, dies aged 80

1951 USGA/R&A Rules conference to rationalize golf throughout world: major decision abolishes stymie

1952 Britain and Ireland gain first Curtis Cup win over US

1953 Ben Hogan becomes the first (and only) golfer to win Masters, US and British Opens in one year

1955 Last day of Open at St Andrews is televised; Peter Thomson won

1956 Babe Zaharias, "Athlete of the Century", dies aged 42

1957 Dai Rees leads Britain and Ireland to first Ryder Cup win over US in 34 years at Lindrick, Nottinghamshire

1958 Arnold Palmer wins his first major, the Masters at Augusta: US Tour prize-money reaches record $1 million
Britain and Ireland retain Curtis Cup (won in 1956) with tied match, the best showing yet by the visiting team in the US

1959 Sam Snead's team regains Ryder Cup by five points in California

1960 Palmer wins Masters and US Open, the latter with a final round 65, then fails by a shot to catch Kel Nagle in Centenary British Open

1961 Bernard Darwin, greatest of golf writers, dies aged 85

1962 Jack Nicklaus, aged 22, beats Palmer in US Open play-off

1963 Bob Charles is the first left-hander to win a major – British Open
J. H. Taylor, last survivor of "Great Triumvirate", dies, aged 91

1965 Peter Thomson wins his fifth British Open at Royal Birkdale

1966 Tony Lema, 1964 British Open Champion, dies in air crash

1967 Francis Ouimet dies, aged 74

1968 Tour pros win fight for new USPGA division to run own affairs
Croquet putting banned

1969 Tony Jacklin becomes first Briton to win his national Open since 1951
Walter Hagen dies, aged 76

1970 Jacklin is US Open Champion by seven strokes

1971 Lee Trevino wins US, Canadian and British Opens in 3 weeks
Bobby Jones dies, aged 69
John Hudson holes successive tee shots at 11th (195 yards) and 12th (311) in Martini Tournament at Royal Norwich, Norfolk

1972 Britain and Ireland's second Walker Cup win in 50 years
European Tour gets under way

1974 Gary Player wins Open, with now obligatory 1.68 inch ball, at Lytham

1975 British Tour pros gain large measure of autonomy in separate PGA division

1979 Seve Ballesteros wins British Open, via BBC parking lot
US Ryder Cup foes now Europe, who lose, 17–11, in West Virginia

1980 Ballesteros becomes the first European to win the Masters

1985 Europe beat Trevino's US team in Ryder Cup at The Belfry

1986 Nicklaus is oldest Masters' winner, aged 46. Sixth win also a record

1986 Britain and Ireland women score first European win by any team in US, winning Curtis Cup 13–5 in Kansas

1987 Nick Faldo wins his first British Open with final round of 18 pars
Ryder Cup further revitalized with European victory in Ohio
Sir Henry Cotton dies, aged 80
Bobby Locke, reputedly best of all putters, dies, aged 69

1989 Europe retain the Ryder Cup with the second-ever tie in the series
Britain and Ireland score their first Walker Cup success in the US

1990 Faldo wins second successive Masters, then wins Open at St Andrews
US gain revenge in the Curtis Cup: 19–4 in New Jersey

1991 Europe lose Ryder Cup "War on the Shore" at Kiawah Island
US regain Walker Cup at Portmarnock

1992 Europe's women make it one-all in Solheim Cup at Dalmahoy

1993 Greg Norman's Sandwich Open is "the greatest" – Gene Sarazen
US take knife-edge Ryder Cup battle at The Belfry 15–13

1994 Nick Price (British Open, USPGA), Ernie Els (US Open), and José-Maria Olazabal (Masters) leave US without "major" winner
US women regain the Solheim Cup

1995 Europe regain the Ryder Cup

1997 Tiger Woods, aged 21, becomes the youngest winner of the Masters

INDEX

Note: Page numbers in **bold** refer to illustrations.

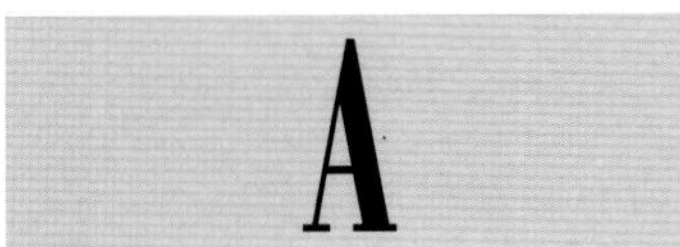

accidents 237–8
Adair, Rhona 60
Adams, Bruce 211
administration 197–8
Africa 84
Alcott, Amy 110, **110**
Alison, Charles 71
Allenby, Robert 71, **71**
Alliss, Peter 110
Amateur Links Championship 61
amateurs
  drug testing 241
  full-time 69
  status 62, 197
American Express 192
American Golfer, The 62
American Professional Golfers 50
Americas Cup 113
Anderson, Willie 21, 110–11, 168
Andrew, Duke of York 10
Aoki, Isao 79, 111, **111**
APGA see Omega Asian PGA Tour
Apple Tree Gang 58
Archer, George 111
Argentina 77
Armour, Tommy 22, 111, 169, 176
Asian Order 77
Asian Tour 79
Asquith, Henry 68
AT&T National Pro-Am 194
Auchterlonie, Willie 26
Augusta Invitation 16–17
Augusta National 16–17, 121, 166, **166**
  Daly, John 239
Augusta National Invitation 166
Australasian PGA Tour 79
Australia 12, 71
Australian Open 53
Austria 75
Azinger, Paul 26, 30, 30, 33, 111, **111**

B

Bailey, Diane 43
Baker, Peter 34
Baker-Finch, Ian 111–12, 238, **238**
Balding, Al 63
Balfour, Arthur James 68
Balfour, James (Singing Jamie) 244
Ball, John 35, 66, 112, 182, 214
Ballesteros, Severiano 74, **74**, 85, 86–7, **86**, **87**
  1994 Masters 204
  British Open 26, 87, 161–2, 161
  Japanese Open 53
  Masters 19
  Ryder Cup 31, 32, 33, 34, 87
  swing 216
  Valderrama 187
  World Tour 235
balls 220–1
  cleaning 206–7
  earliest 13
  feathery 13
  gutta-percha (gutty) 13, 214
  Haskell 60, 68–9, 220
  lifting 210
  lost 209–10
  research 226
  rules 204, 206–7
  sales 54
  specifications 208, 212, 226
  unfit for play 207
  unplayable 11, 209–10, **209**
  Vardon Flyer 60
  Wilson **218**
  wooden 13
Ballybunion, Ireland 70, 167, **167**, 199, 245, **245**
Baltusrol, New Jersey 168, **168**
Barbados 78
Barber, Miller 112
Barnes, Brian 33, 112, **112**
Barnes, (Long) Jim 28, **48**, 112, 246
Barr, Dave 63
Barrett, Thomas 16
Batam 80
Bateman, Lucius 232
Bean, Andy 33, 112–13, **112**
Beard, Frank 113
Beck, Chip 22, 33, **33**, 113, **113**
Beck, John, Walker Cup 40
Bedford Club, Cape Province 84
Belfry, The 32–3, 34, 77, **205**
Belgian Professional Championship 120
Belgium 73–4
Bell, Judy 198, 233
Belton Woods and Country Club, Lincolnshire 64
Beman, Deane 113
Bendelow, Tom 198
Bendern, Count John de 244
Bennett, H. 207
Bentley, Harry 40
Berg, Patty 42, 113
best-ball 206
beta-blockers 241
betty 206
birdie, history 206
birds 246
Black Open 231
Blackheath 11, 66
Blackwell, Ted 35
Blalock, Jane 234
Blue Canyon club, Thailand **82**
bogey, history 206
Boit, Florence 60
Bolt, Tommy 52, 113, 239–40, **240**
Bonallack, Michael 24, 35, 35, 41, 113–14, 177
Boros, Julius 52, 114
Bothwell Golf Club, Tasmania 71
Boxall, Richard 237, **237**
Bradley, Pat 45, 114, **114**
Bradshaw, Harry 114
Braid, James 24, 48, 107, 170
Brand, Gordon Junior 77, 114–15, **114**
Brazil 77–8
Brews, Jock 53
Brews, Sid 53
British Amateur Championship 12, 35–6, 113–14, 116, 179
British Golf Museum 107
British Open Championship 24–7
  Ballesteros, Severiano 161–2, **161**
  Carnoustie 109, 169
  Daly, John 118, 239
  Feherty, David
  Hagen, Walter 91
  history 12, 13
  Hoylake 67–8, 118
  Jones, Bobby 95
  Muirfield 172
    1970 97
    1972 127, 157–8, **157**
    1987 89, 111
    1992 89, **236**
  Palmer, Arnold 99, 155–6
  Player, Gary 101
  Portrush 1951 122
  Prestwick 1925 112, 145
  Price, Nick 161
  prize money 26
  results 27
  Robertson, Allen 141
  Royal Birkdale 87, 109, 111
  Royal Lytham 87, 148, 161–2
  Royal St Georges **14**, 128, 183
  Royal Troon 124
  Royal Troon 1989 115
  St Andrews 184
    1921 127
    1933 144
    1939 115
    1960 155–6
    1964 130
    1970 25–6, 143
    1984 87
    1990 89
    1995 239
  Sandwich 114, 131
  Turnberry 136, **159**, 160, 186
British Women's Amateur Championship 42, 177
British Women's Open 46
Broadhurst, Paul 33
Brown, Billy Ray 22
Brown, Eric 239
Brown, Sir Simon 245
Bruen, James 36, 40
Buick Open 127
Bunn, Oscar 231
Burke, Jack 115
Burma *see* Myanmar
Burns, George 21, 160–1
Burns, William 56
Burton, Brandie **241**
Burton, Dick 115
Butten, Ernest 126

C

caddies
  Augusta National 19
  carts 56

Eddie Lowery 154
Fanling 245
history 12–13
llamas 246
Sunesson, Fanny **89**
Calcavecchia, Mark 33, 115
Callaway, Ely 56
Campbell, Dorothy 63, 115
Campbell, Michael 69
Campbell, Willie 20
Campell, Michael **72**
Canada 63
Canadian Open 63, 137
Canadian Women's Amateur 63
Canizares, José-Maria 31, 32, 115, **115**
Caribbean 78
Carnegie, Andrew 59, **59**
Carner, Joanne 44, 115–16
Carnoustie, Scotland 25, 169, **169**
Carr, Joe 36, 116
Carr, Marian 234
Carter, David 84
Cashen course, Ballybunion 167
Casper, Billy 116, **116**, 156, 189, 216, **217**
casual water 210, 211
Cerda, Antonio 25, 77
Challenge Tour 69
Chambers, Robert 12, 66
championships 14–53
Chapman, Dick 189
charity, US PGA Tour 190–1
Chark, Howard 34
Charles, Bob 25, 72, 116, 216
Charles I, King of England 9, 10
Charles II, King of England 9
cheating 208, 240
Chemapol Trophy Czech Open 76
China 81, 82
China Tour 192
chole 8, 9
Clark, Howard 31, 116, **116**
Clark, Robert 12
clothing 224–5
1798 **10**
club uniforms 17, 66
Davis, Rodger 119
Demaret, Jimmy 119
Hagen, Walter 119
Stewart, Payne 146
women 60
clubs **219**, 222–3, **222–3**
Anser series 194
Calloway 194
collectors 230
drivers 194
early history 13
Faulkner, Max 122
Laffoon, Ky 129
long putter 143, **143**
machine made 197
manufacture 198
marketing 193–4
names 222
PGCA 68
prices 54–5
research 226
restrictions 197–8, 209
Sarazen, Gene 103
Schenectady putter 35, 149
scoring 127
Solheim, Karsten 56
steel 68, 209
titanium 193, 222
clubs and members
captains 66
early development 10–11
racism 231–3
Scotalnd 10–11
Scotland 65
sexism 233–4
uniforms 66
US 56
Coe, Charles 38
Coeur d'Alene, Idaho 245
Coles, Neil 31, 116–17
collecting 228–9
Collett Vare, Glenna 43, 117, **117**
Colt, Harry 172, 177, 185, 188
Coltart, Andrew **66**, 77
Coltewah, Tennessee **192**
Combe, George 177
Compston, Archie 117
computers 226–7
Condie, George 12
Cook, John 117, 172
Cooper, Harry 117, 145
Corcoran, Fred 42, 49, 62
Cornwell, Ian 237
Cotton, Henry **25**, 117
British Open 24, 169
Golf Foundation 69
Penina 75
swing 215
Walker Cup 40
Country Club, Brookline 60
country clubs, US 58
County Championship 69
Couples, Fred **4**, 33, 34, 82, 118, **118**
courses 164–89
boundaries 209
CAP 201
construction 198
England 64
environmental impact 199–203
etiquette 206–7
grass 201
history 12
maintenance 198
pars 207
planning permission 200
prisons 240–1
Scotland 9, 64
Spain 74
SSS 207
US 54
Crampton, Bruce 118
Creavy, Tom 29
Crenshaw, Ben 30, 31, 33, 34, 118, 119
Crockford, Claude 180
Crooked Stick, Indiana 30, 238–9
croquet putting 207–8
Crosby, Bing 39
Crosby, Nathaniel **38**, 39
Cruikshank, Bobby 95, 237
Crump, George 174, 198, 206
Cummings, Edith 44
Curtis Cup 43
Curtis, Harriot **43**
Curtis, Lawrence 43, 60
Cypress Point, California 173
Czechoslovakia 76

D

Dalhousie, Earl of 169
Daly, Fred 118
Daly, John 26, 29, 30, 46, 71, 118, **236**, 238–9, **239**
Danecki, Walter 240
Daniel, Beth 118–19
Darcy, Eamonn 3, 31, **32**, 119
Darwin, Bernard 40
Davies, Laura 42, **43**, 46, 119, **119**, 192, 240
Davis, Rodger 119
Demaret, Jimmy 17, 119, 224
DeMoss, Grace 43
Denmark 76
Derby, Earl of 31
Devlin, Bruce 119–20, **120**, 160–1
Dey, Joe 234
Dickinson, Gardner 50, 52
Didrickson, Mildred see Zaharias, Babe
Diegel, Leo 28, **28**, 120
Dinah Shore Tournament 45
disabilities 238
divots, etiquette 206
Donck, Flory van 74, 120, 121
Dowie, J. Muir 66
dress *see* clothing
drugs 241
du Maurier Classic 45
Dubai Creek 83
Dubai Desert Classic 83, 170, **229**
Duncan, George 120
Dunedin, New Zealand 72
Dunhill Cup 63, 77, 119
Dunhill Masters 79, 126, **200**
Dunlop Phoenix Championship 53
Dunn, Seymour 177
Dunn, Tom 233
Dunn, Willie 20
Dwyer, Robert F. 75
Dye, Pete 238–9
Dyke, Gill 246

E

Edgar, John Douglas 28, 63, 120–1
Edinburgh see Honourable Company of Edinburgh Golfers
Edward VII, King of England 182
Edward VIII, King of England 185
Eisenhower, Dwight **57**, **61**
Eisenhower Trophy 72, 113
Elder, Lee 19, 121, 159, 232
elitism 200
Elkington, Steve 30, 121, **121**, **212**
Ellison, T.F. 179
Els, Ernie 121, **121**
British Open 1994 162–3
Dunhill Cup 63
Dunlop Phoenix **53**
Grand Slam 52
US Open 22, 176
Emirates Course 83, **83**, 170, **170**
English Closed Amateur Championship 207
English Golf Union 64, 69, 70
English Ladies' Golf Association 234
environment, course development 199–203
Epson Singapore Open 79
Espinosa, Al 29
etiquette 206–7
European Challenge Tour 51
European Commission, *How Green is the Fairway?* 200
European Golf Association, Ecology Unit 202
European PGA Tour 51
Apollo Week 69–79
Brand, Gordon Junior 114
Canizares, José-Maria 115
prizes 190
sponsorship 192
Evans, Albert 65
Evans, Chick **37**, 38, 40, 121–2

F

Faldo, Nick **18**, **19**, 85, 88–9, **163**, **192**
1996 Masters **153**
British Open 26, 111
1988 162
clothing 224
Masters 19, 126
Masters 1996 162–3
Pebble Beach 245
putting 216
Ryder Cup **31**, 32, 33, 34
swing 215
US Open 22
Falkenburg, Bob 77–8
Fanagan, Jody 41
Fanling, Hong Kong 81, 244–5
Far East Circuit *see* Asian Tour
Farr, Heather 238
Farrell, Johnny 29, 122

Faulkner, Max 122, **122**
Faxon, Brad 34
Fay, David 233
Fazio, George 21
Fazio, Tom 175
Feherty, David 122, 195, **196**, 238
Fernandez, Vicente 77, **77**
Fernie, Willie 186
Ferrier, Jim 30, 122
Fetes, Raul **78**
Finch-Hatton, Denys 242–4
Finch-Hatton, Harold 182, 242–4
Finchem, Tim 50, 234
Finsterwald, Dow 122–3
Fischer, John 40
Fite, John 75
Fleck, Jack 123
Flitcroft, Maurice 240
Floyd, Ray 238
Floyd, Raymond 19, 31, 32, 52, 123, **123**
Foot, Henry 66
Forbes, Duncan 11
Ford, Doug 123
Forest, John de 244
Forgan, Robert 222
Foulis, James 220, 231
four-ball 206
foursomes, rules 206
Fowler, W.Herbert 181
Fownes, Henry C. 176
Fownes, William Junior 40, **40**
France 73
Franco, Angel 77
Franco, Carlos 77
Fretes, Raul 77
Frost, David 123, **123**
Furgol, Ed 168

Gallacher, Bernard **31,** 32, 33, 34, **34**, 188, 202, **203**, 234
Golf Foundation 69
Gamez, Robert 123–4
Gammeter, John 220
Gann, Michelle 46
Gardner, Robert 36, 38, 40
Garrido, Antonio 31
Geddes, Jane 45
Geiberger, Al 124
Gentleman Golfers of Edinburgh see Honourable Company of Edinburgh
Germany 75
Gibson, Rick 63
Gilford, David 33, 34
Glascoe, Dr Stephen 244
Glennie, George 12
Goalby, Bob 124
Goalby, Greg 19
Goetze, Vickie 44
Golf Course Wildlife Trust 202
Golf Foundation 69
Golf Illustrated Gold Vase 185
Golf magazine 59
GOLF Magazine 62
Golf World 62
Gonzales, Jaime 78
Gonzales, Mario 78
Goodman, Johnny 16, 40, **40**
Goosen, Retief 84
Gosen Tour 69
Grady, Wayne 115, 124, **124**
Graham, David 21, **21**, 26, 30, 124, 160–1
Graham, Jack 66
Grand Slam 52, 95
grass, courses 201
Great Britain 64–70
  addresses 70
  County Championship 69
  match play 198
  professionals 68
Great Triumvirate see Triumvirate
Greater Greensboro 131
Green, Hubert 31, 32, 160
Green, Robert **83**
green, rules 211, **211**
Grey Oaks 59
Griffin, Ellen 42
Groom, Arthur 80
Guldahl, Ralph 17, 124
Gunderson, Joanne see Carner, Joanne

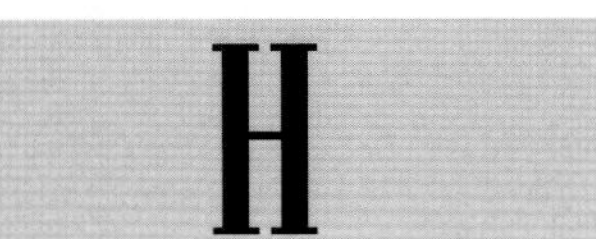

Haas, Jay 32
Haeggman, Joakim 34, **200**
Hagen, Walter 85, 90–1, **91**
  British Open 24, 61, 179
  clothing 119, 224
  Masters 16, 17
  putting 216
  US Open 48, 154
  US PGA 28, **28**
Hall, Caroline 44
Halldorson, Dan 63
Hamilton, Bob 29
handicaps 207
Happy Valley, Hong Kong 244
Hardstaff, Joe 79
Harlow, Bob 49, **49**, 62
Harmon, Claude 189
Harper, Chandler 49
Harrington, Padraig 41
Harris, Robert 40
Haskell, Coburn 220
Havemeyer, Theodore 37, 231
Hayes, Mark 160
Haynie, Sandra 125
hazards 210–11
Hazeltine National 125
Heafner, Clayton 125, 240
Heard, Jerry, accidents 238
Herd, Alex 48
Herd, Sandy 68, 125, **125**, 179
Heritage Classic 111
Herreshoff, Fred 38
Hicks, Helen 43
Higuchi, Chako 46
Hill, Dave 125
Hill, Mike 126
Hill, Opal 43
Hilton, Harold 35, 38, 66, 126
history 8–13, 56–7
Hoch, Scott 19, 36, 89, 126, **126**
Hogan, Ben 85, 92–3
  British Open 25, 35, 93
  clothing 224
  Masters 17
  Oakmont 176
  swing 215
  US Amateur Championship 38
  US Open 21, **93**, 155
  US PGA 14, 29
  World Cup 188
hole in one 246
Holland 74
Hollins, Marion 238
Hong Kong 12, 81, 244
Hong Kong Open 244–5
Honourable Company of Edinburgh Golfers 11, 65, 68, 172
Hopkins, John Mark, Walker Cup 41
Horton, Tommy 126, **126**, **192**
Hotchkin, Neil 70
housing developments 199
Howden, Charles Richie 72
Howell, David 41
Hoylake, Cheshire 35, 66–8, 179
Hoyt, Beatrix 60, 61
Hudson, John 246
Hunt, Bernard 126–7
Hutchinson, Horace
  British Amateur 35
  Royal North Devon 66, 181
  swing 212, 214
  women golfers 42
Hutchison, Jock 28, 127
Hyndman, Bill 41

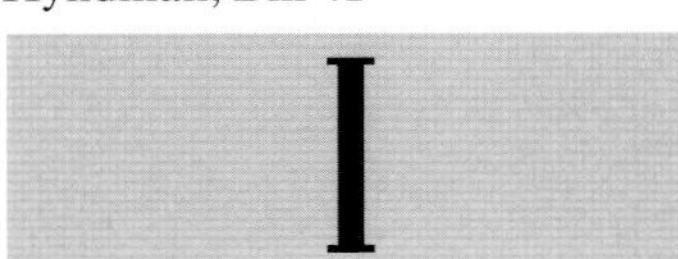

India 82
Inkster, Juli 127
Innes, William **11**
instruction manuals 214
Inter-Club Foursomes 12
Interlachen 21
Ireland 12, 64–70
Irish Closed Amateur Championship 116
Irish Open Amateur 116
Irwin, Hale 31, 33, 87, 127, 189
Israel 83
Italy 76
Ivory Coast Open 84

Jacklin, Tony 127, **127**
  British Open 25, **25**, 157–8, **157**
  Royal St George's 183
  Ryder Cup **31**, 32, 33, 34
  US Open 21
Jacobs, John 31, 51, 70, 188, 202, **203**, 215
Jacobsen, Peter 34, 116, 127–8
James I of England 9
James II of England 9–10
James IV of Scotland 8
James, Mark 31, 33, 34, 128
Jameson, Betty 44, **44**
January, Don 128
Janzen, Lee 128, **128**
Japan 79–80, 228
Japanese Open 53
Japanese Tour 190
jeu de maille 8
Johansson, Per Ulrik 76, **76**
Johnnie Walker, sponsorship 193
Johnnie Walker Asian Classic **193**
Johnny Walker World Championship 78, 121
Johnson, Trish 46
Jones, Bobby 66
Jones, R.T. Junior (Bobby) **16**, 85, 94–5, **95**
  Augusta National 16–17, 166
  British Amateur 36
  British Open 24, 179, 185
  Grand Slam 14, 16, 171
  putting 216
  stymie 207
  swing 215
  US Amateur 38, 171
  Us Open 21
  US PGA 29
  Walker Cup 40
  Winged Foot 189
Jones, Steve 128, **128**
Jones, Tom 69
Jurado, José 77

Kapalua International 52
Karlsson, Robert **201**
Keiser, Herman 17
Keng-chi, Lin 79
Kenya Open 84
Kiawah Island, South Carolina 33–4
King, Betsy 46, 128
King, Sam 128–9
Kinloch, Sir David 12
Kirk, Peggy 45
Kite, Tom 31, 32, 129, **129**
Kocsis, Charles 40

kolven 8–9, **9**
Kuehne, Trip 39
Kukup, Malaysia 80–1

Lacoste, Catherine 129
Ladies British Amateur 185
Ladies' Golf Union (LGU) 42, 65
Ladies Professional Golf Association (LPGA) 42, 50, 190
Laffoon, Ky 129
Laidlay, Johnny 35, 107, 214
Langer, Bernhard **75**, 129, **129**, **197**
  earnings 196
  Masters 19
  putting 216
  Ryder Cup 31, 32, 33
  trees 245
Las Vegas Invitational 113
Lawson Little, William 36, 38, 130
Leadbetter, David 56, **56**, 79, 89
Learmouth, Lennie 246
Lee, Robert **243**
Lee Smith, Jenny 46
left-handed players 25, 39, 116, 133, 195
Lehman, Tom 129
Leitch, Cecil 63, 129
Leith Links 10, 11
Lema, Tony 237
Lema, Tony 129–30
Lietzke, Bruce 30, 31, 130
lightning 237–8
Little, Sally 130
Littler, Gene 38, 130
Littlestone 68
Liverpool Club see Royal Liverpool Club
Locke, Bobby 24–5, 53, 84, 130–1, 216
Lockhart, Robert 57–8
loose impediments 211
Lopez, Nancy 45, **45**, 131
Love, Davis III 82, **130**, 131
Low, Carrie 60
Lowery, Eddie 154
LPGA see Ladies Professional Golf Association
Lu Liang Huan (Mr Lu) 79, 244–5
Lyle, Sandy 31, 131, **131**, **192**
  British Open 26
  1988 162
  Masters 19, 115
  Ryder Cup 32, 33
  Safari Circuit 84
  US Open 168

McCormack, Mark 194–5, 196, 235
McCready, Sam 36
McCulough, Richard 237
McCumber, Mark 22, 131–2
McDermott, Johnny 20, 61, 132
Macdonald, Charles 56–7, 132
  course designs 58
  golf rules 204
  National Links of America 198
  US Amateur 37
  US Open 20
  USGA 197
McEvoy, Peter 41, **41**
Macfie, Allan 35
McGann, Michelle, clothing **225**
McGill, Jill 192, **192**
McGimpsey, Garth 41
Mackenzie, Dr Alister 71
  Augusta National 16, 166
  Littlestone 68
  Royal Melbourne 180
  Royal St George's 183
MacKenzie, Keith 24
Mackenzie Ross, Philip 186
McLeod, Fred 28
MacNamara, Tom 61
Macneil, Hugh 72
McNulty, Mark 26, 132, **132**
Malaysia 80–1
Maltbie, Roger 160
Mangrum, Lloyd 17, 21, 25, 132
Maples, Ellis 175
March, Graham 132–3
Markes and Spencer 224
Marr, Dave 31
Marsh, David 41
Martin, Blanche 42
Mary Queen of Scots 8, **8**
Massy, Arnaud 68, 73
Masters 14, 16–19
  1996 162–3
  Augusta National 166
  Ballesteros, Severiano 87
  Burke, Jack 115
  Faldo, Nick 89, 126, **163**
  Goalby, Bob 124
  Hoch, Scott 126
  Lyle, Sandy 131
  Miller, Johnny **158**, 159
  Mize, Larry 133
  Nichlaus, Jack **158**, 159
  Player, Gary 101
  racism 232
  Vicenzo, Roberto de 19, 124, 150
  Weiskopf, Tom **158**, 159
  Woods, Tiger 151, **151**
match play
  ball unfit for play 207
  Britain 198
  foursomes 206
  history 10, 11, 204
  penalties 208
Matheson, Donald 170
Matthew, Catriona 44
May, Bob 36
May, George S. 49
Mayer, Dick 189
Mazda LPGA Championship **193**
medals, collectors 230, **230**
Mehlhorn, Wild Bill 28, 47, **47**
Merion, Pennsylvania 21, 171, **171**
Mexico 78
Mickelson, Phil 39, **39**, **53**, 133, 162, 195
Middle East 83
Middlecoff, Gary 133
Mike Tour 190
Miller, Johnny 31, 133, **133**
  AT&T National Pro-Am 194
  British Open 1972 157–8
  Dunlop Phoenix 53
  Masters 1975 **158**, 159
  sponsorship 195
  US Open 22
Minoprio, Grace 224
Minoza, Frankie 79
Mitchell, Abe 133
Mize, Larry 19, 33, 133, **133**
Monterey, Pebble Beach **54**
Montgomerie, Colin 22, 30, 33, 34, **51**, 134, 176
  US PGA 121
Montgomery, John 235, **235**
Moodie, Janice 44
Morgan, Gil 134, **134**
Morgan, Wanda 43
Morris County, New Jersey 61
Morris, George 66
Morris, Jack 66
Morris, Tom Junior 24, 57, 134
Morris, Tom Senior 134
  Blackheath 66
  British Open 24
  Carnoustie 169
  Muirfield 172
  Royal County Down 177
  Royal North Devon 181
  US Amateur 37
Mosley, John 237
Motu, Nga 35
Mourino Club, St Petersburg 75
Muirfield, Scotland 26, 68, 157–8, **157**, 172, **172**
Muirfield Village 33, 172
Murdoch, Rupert 234
Murphy, Bob 39
Murphy's Open 77
Musselburgh, Scotland 11, 68
Myanmar (Burma) 82

Nagle, Kel 25, 134–5, 155–6, **155**
Nakajima, Tsuneyuki (Tommy) 53, 135, **135**
National Cape Schank 71
National Golf Links of America 40, 198
Nause, Martha 46
Nelford, Jim 63
Nelson, Byron 135
  Masters 17
  swing 215
  US Amateur 38
  US PGA 29
  US Tour 115
Nelson, Larry 135, **135**
  British Open 162
  Ryder Cup 31, 33
  US Open, 1962 176
Netherlands 74
Neumann, Liselotte 46, **46**, 76, 135
Neville, Jack 173
New South Wales Golf Club 71
New Zealand 72
Newton, Jack 135–6, **135**
Nichols, Bobby, accidents 238
Nicklaus, Jack **52**, 85, 96–7
  Australian Open 53
  British Open 25, 26
    1967 179
    1972 157–8
    1977 **159**, 160
  Masters 19, **158**, 159
  Muirfield, Scotland 172
  Muirfield Village, Ohio 33, 172
  Ryder Cup 31, 32, 33
  Senior Tour 52
  Shenzen Mission Hills Club 81
  sponsorship 195
  swing 212, 215
  US Amateur 38–9
  US Open 21, 22, 168
    1960 154–5
    1962 **20**, 176
    1966 156
    1982 160–1
    1983 173
  US PGA 30
  US PGA Tour 50
  World Tour 234
Nida, Norman von 136
Niddry, Lothian 64
Nomwa, Mawonga 84
Norman, Greg 18, 71, 136, **136**, 149, **163**
  British Open **14,** 22, 26, **26**, 115, 124
  earnings 196
  Grand Slam 52
  Masters 19
  Masters 1996 89, **153**, 162–3
  US PGA 30, 121
  Winged Foot **189**
  World Tour 234–5, **235**
North, Andy 21, 33, 136
Northwood, sexism 234
Norton, Hughes 240

Oak Hill, Rochester **15**
Oakland Hills 30
  sexism 234

Oakmont, Pennsylvania 22, 176, **176**
obstructions, rules 204, 211
O'Connor, Christy Junior 33, 136–7
O'Grady, Mac 241
Okamoto, Ayato **46**
Olazabal, José-Maria 74, 137, **137**
  Grand Slam 52
  Masters 17, **19**
  Ryder Cup 33, 34
Olympic Club, San Francisco 156
Olympics 241
O'Meara, Mark 33, 137
Omega Asian PGA Tour 79
Oosterhuis, Peter 63, 70, 89, 137, **137**
  Ryder Cup 31
Oporto, Portugal 74
Orcutt, Maureen 43
Ortiz-Patino, Jaime 187
Ouimet, Francis 137–8
  amateur status 62
  US Amateur 38
  US Open 20, 48, 61, 154, **154**
  Walker Cup 40
out of bounds **208**, 209
Ozaki, Masashi (Jumbo) 53, 79–80, 138, **138**

Padgham, Alf 138
Page, Paul 36
Palmer, Arnold 52, **52**, 85, 98–9
  British Open 24, 25, 155–6
  Canadian Open 63
  fans 228
  hole in one 246
  marketing 194
  Masters 17
  Pine Valley 174
  television 54
  US Amateur 37, 38
  US Open 20–1, 97, 99, 116, 154–5, 156
  US PGA 29–30
  World Tour 234
Panton-Lewis, Cathy 46
Paraguay 77
Paramor, John **204**
Park, Willie Junior 138, 169, 185
Park, Willie Senior 24, 138, 216
Parks, Sam 22
Parnevik, Jesper 26
Parry, Craig 138, **139**
pars, SSS 207
Pasatiempo, California 238
Pate, Jerry 31, 139
Pate, Steve 33
Patton, Billy Joe 40, 139
Pau, France 12, 73
Pavin, Corey 22, 30, 33, 34, 111, 139, **139**
Pearson, Issette 43
Pebble Beach, California 160–1, 173, **173**
Pebble Beach, Monterey **54**
Peete, Calvin 139, **139**
Pelletier, Jeannine 244
penalties, advice 208
Penina, Algarve 74–5, **75**
Pennink, Frank 183
Pepper, Dottie **44,** 133–4, 240, **241**
Peters, Richard 62
Philp, Hugh 222
Picard, Henry 139
Pine Valley, New Jersey 174, **174**, 198
Pinehurst Country Club 175, **175**
Pinero, Manuel 31, 32, 139–40
Ping, golf rankings 119, 230
Pirce, Nick 84
Platt, Woody 174
Player, Gary 85, 100–1
  Australian Open 53
  British Open 25
  British Open 1967 179
  Masters 19, 101
  South Africa 84
  US PGA 30
  Wentworth 188, 202, **203**
  World Match Play 130
Players Championship, Queensland 79
Poe, Henry, Ryder Cup 31
point scoring 207
Portugal 74–5
Portuguese Open 75
Posson, Chet 49
Prestwick Golf Club 24, 68
Price, Elizabeth 43
Price, Nick **6**, 7, 26, 140, **140**
  British Open 161–2
  Grand Slam 52
  US PGA 30
  World Tour 235, **235**
prisons, courses 240–1
prize money 190, 196
Professional Golfers' Association, establishment 68, 161
Professional Golfers' co-operative Association 68
professionals
  club-making 197
  earnings 197
  Great Britain 68
  history 47
  status 197
  US PGA 28
prohibition, Scotland 8
Public Links Championships 54
Purves, Dr Laidlaw 183
putters **227**
  Schenectady 35, 149
  Solheim, Karsten 194, 198
putting
  croquet 207–8
  Diegel, Leo 120
  etiquette 206
  Faulkner, Max 122
  Langer, Bernhard 129
  long putter 143, **143**
  rules 211
  technique 216
Pyman, Iain 36, 41

Qualifying School 69

racism 19, 121, 231
radio reporters 62
RAF Coastal Command, Turnberry 186
Rafferty, Ronan 33, 140
Rankin, Judy 140
rankings 80, 230
Raphael, Fred 52
Rattray, John 10–11, 204
Rawlins, Harold 20
Rawlins, Horace 231
Rawls, Betsy 45, 140
Ray, Ted 20, 140–1, 154, **154**
Rees, Dai 25, 32, 141
Reid, Alex 71
Reid, John 57, 58, **58**, 60
Reid, Mike 141
Relagado, Victor 78
research 226–7
Rice, Grantland 16–17
Riley, Polly 43, 45
Rivero, José 141, **141**
Roberts, Clifford 16–17, **61**, 166
Roberts, G.P. 207
Roberts, Loren 22, 34, 176
Robertson, Allan **12**, 13, 24, 141–2, 169, 207, 214
Rocca, Costantino 26, 34
Rodriguez, Chi-Chi 142, **142**
Roe, Mark **243**
Rogers, Bill 31, 142, 160–1
Rolex Player of the Year 114
Rolland, Douglas 142–3
Romero, Eduardo 77, **142**, 143
  British Open 1988 162
Roosevelt, Franklin Delano 61
Rospoli, Prince 61
Ross, Alec 154
Ross, Donald 175
Ross-on-Wye, Herefordshire 65
Royal & Ancient Club
  administration 197–8
  Bonallack, Michael 114
  British Amateur 35
  British Open 24
  captains 66
  club manufacture 198
  clubhouse **13**
  logo 195
  Rules of Golf Committee 206
  Walker Cup 40
  Women's European Tour 70
Royal Adelaide Club 12, 71, **71**
Royal Birkdale 87
Royal Bombay club, India 82
Royal Calcutta club, India 82
Royal Canadian GA 63
Royal Cape Club 12, 84
Royal County Down, Northern Ireland 177, **177**
Royal Dornoch, Scotland 178, **178**
Royal Liverpool Club (Hoylake) 35, 66, **66**, 179, **179**
Royal Lytham and St Anne's 25, 161–2
Royal Melbourne 71, 180, **180**
Royal North Devon Club 66, 181, **181**
  see also Westward Ho!
Royal St David's, Wales 182, **182**
Royal St George's, Sandwich **14**, 128, 183, **183**
Royal Thai Army Course 81
Royal Westmoreland, Barbados 78
Ruangkit, Booncha 79, 82
rules 204–12
  agreement to waive 208
  clubs 197–8
  history 11
  obstructions 204
  play it as it lies 204–5
Rumsey, Robert 244
Russell, Alex 180
Russia 75
Ryder Cup 31–4
  Brand, Gordon Junior 114
  Canizarez, José-Maria 115
  Clark, Howard 116
  Hunt, Bernard 127
  Jacklin, Tony 127
  James, Mark 128
  Kiawah Island **229**
  Kite, Tom 129
  O'Meara, Mark 137
  over-50s 52
  PGA European Tour 51
  Sarazen, Gene **103**
  Souchak, Mike 145
  Stockton, Dave 147
  Torrance, Sam 149
  Valderrama 187
  Wadkins, Lanny 150
  Wentworth 188

Safari Circuit 84
St Andrew's Golf Club, New York 20, 57–8
St Andrews, Scotland **164–5**, 184, **184**
  British Open 25–6, 26, 115, 143

earliest golfers 9
Inter-club Foursomes 12
links 10
sale of start times 239
Silver Club 11, 204
swing 212
St Pierre Hotel Country Club Resort 70
sand traps 103, 210
Sander, Anne 44
Sanders, Doug 25–6, 143
Sands, Charles 37
Sandwich Golf Association 183
Sandy Lane, Barbados 78
Sarazen, Gene 16, **17**, 48–9, 85, 102–3
Augusta National 166
British Open 24, **26**
clubs 103
Masters 17
professionalism 61
Ryder Cup **103**
US PGA 28
scandals 237–42
Schenectady putter 35, 149
Schofield, Ken 234
scholarships, US 62
Schroeder, John 160
scoreboards 230
Scotland
clubs and members 65–6
courses 64
prohibition 8
Scott, Lady Margaret 42
Scottish Golf Union 64
Scottish Open 196
Seignious, Hope 42
Selbach, George 246
Semple, Thompson 44
Senior, Peter 46, 143, **143**
Senior Tour 52
Archer, George 111
Barber, Miller 112
Geiberger, Al 124
Hill, Mike 125
prizes 190
Trevino, Lee 105
Sewgolum, Sewsunker 84
sexism 233–4
Shade, Ronnie 41
Sheehan, Patty 46, 143–4, **144**
Shenzen Mission Hills Club 81
Shenzhen, China 245
Shepard, Alan 224
Sherry, Gordon 41, **41**
Shinnecock Hills **56**, 58, 59
shinty 9
Shippen, John 231
Shoal Creek, Alabama 232–3
Shute, Denny 29, 144
Sifford, Charlie 19, 231–2, **231**
Sigel, Jay 36, 39, 41
Silver Club
Blackheath 66
Edinburgh 10, 204
St Andrews 11, 204
Simpson, Scott 144, 160–1
Simpson, Tom 172
Singapore 80
Tanah Merah **66**
Singh, Vijay 144, **145**
Skibo Castle 59
Skins Game 52
Slaly Hall, Northumberland 64
slow play 240
rules 211
Sluman, Jeff 144–5
Smith, Frances 43
Smith, Horton 17, 145
Smith, Macdonald 112, 145, 154, 228
Smith, Reynolds **40**
Smith, Willie 78
Smyth, Dame Ethel 242, **242**
Smyth, Des 31
Snead, Jesse 145
Snead, Sam 52, 145, **215**
British Open 24
putting 208, 216
US PGA 29
US PGA Tour 50
Snow, Jim 200
Solheim Cup 42, **44**, 46, 70
Daniel, Beth 119
Mochrie, Dottie 134
Rankin, Judy 140
Solheim, Karsten 42, 56, 194, 198, **198**
Somerville, J.A. 72
Sony World Ranking 80, 230
Sorenstam, Annika 46, 145, **145**
Souchak, Mike 145, 154
soule 9
South Africa 12, 84, 101
South African Open 53
South American Tour 77
Spain 74
Spalding, Albert Goodwill 60
Spanish Open 89, **191**
sponsorship 49–50, 70, 192–3
SSS *see* standard scratch score
Stableford, Dr Frank 207, **207**
Stackhouse, Lefty 240
Stadler, Craig 146, **146**
Stanahan, Frank 25, 147
stance 214
standard scratch score (SSS) 207
Stephenson, Jan 146, **193**
Stewart, Gershom 244
Stewart, Lieutenant J.C. 12
Stewart, Marlene 146
Stewart, Payne 146
British Open 26
clothing 224, **225**
Stewart, Ray 63
Stockton, Dave 146–7
Strange, Curtis **15**, 22, **22**, 34, 89, 147, **147**
Streit, Marlene née Stewart 63, **63**
stroke play
ball unfit for play 207
foursomes 206
history 11, 204–6
penalties 208
US 198
stymie 11, 36, 207
Suggs, Louise 45, 147
Sumitomo Visa Taiheiyo Masters 53
Sun City **247**
Sun City Classic 84
Sunesson, Fanny **89**
Sunningdale, Surrey 185, **185**, 240
Sunshine Tour 84
Sutherland, Earl of 178
Sutton, Hal 147–8
Sweden 76
Sweeney, Bob 36
swing
history 212–17
St Andrews 212
teeing off 209
Switzerland 76

Taft, William Howard **60**, 61
Tait, Freddie 35, 148
Talleyrand-Perigord, Marquise de 61
Tallmadge, Henry 59
Tam O'Shanter National Open 49, 125
Tareha, Kurupo **72**
Tarrant, Walter George 188
Tataurangi, Phil 72, **72**
Taylor, J.H. **64**, 107, **107**
British Open 24, 48
professionals 68, 197
Royal County Down 177
Royal North Devon 181
technique 214
teaching, swing 212
technique
Daly, John 118
Edgar, J. Douglas 121
Ford, Doug 123
Guldahl, Ralph 124
Middlecoff, Gary 133
Player, Gary 101
Sarazen, Gene 103
swing 212–17
Taylor, J.H. 107
Trevino, Lee 105
Vardon, Harry 107, 214
tees
etiquette 206
Reddy 220
rules **208**, 209, 211
television
Alliss, Peter 110
clothing 224
earliest coverage 49–50
Golf Channel 54
US PGA Tour 49
terminology 206
Texas Open 49
Thailand 81
Thomas, Dave 148, **148**
Thomas, Frank 226
Thomson, Peter 24–5, 72, 148
three-ball 206
threesomes, rules 206
Tillinghast, Albert W. 168, 189
Toft, Suzan 246
Tolley, Cyril **35**, 36, 207
Tooting Bec Cup 68
Torrance, Sam 31, **31**, 32, 33, 34, 82, 148–9, **148**, 241
Tournament Players Championship 112, 121
tournaments, costs 190
Towns, Jerry 246
Townsend, Peter 40, 70, 157–8
trade shows 193
training, Great Britain 69
Travers, Jerome 38
Travers, Jerry 149
Travis, Walter 35, 37–8, 62, 149, 216
trees 245
Trent Jones, Robert
Ballybunion 70, 199
Baltusrol 168
Pinehurst 175
Royal Westmoreland 78
Russia 75
Walderrama 74, 187
Trevino, Lee 85, 104–5, **105**
accidents 238
British Open 26, 157–8, **157**, 160
Ryder Cup 31, 32
Senior Tour 52
swing 212, **212**
Triumvirate 85, 106–7
Tshabalala, Vincent 84
Tucker, Sam 59
Tufts, James W. 175
Tunesa, Joe **28**, 29
Tunesa, Willie 36
Tupling, Peter 157–8
Turnberry, Ayrshire 26, 159, 160, 186, **186**
Tutweiler, Edgar 41
Tway, Bob 30, 149, **149**
Tze-Chung Chen 21

United Arab Emirates 83
United Distillers, sponsorship 193
United Golf Association 231
United Oxford and Cambridge University club 233
United States 54–62
addresses 62
amateur status 62
newspaper reporters 61–2
scholarships 62

stroke play 11, 198
women 60
United States Amateur Championship 20, 37–9, 62
United States Golf Assocation (USGA) 11, 20, 37
environmental concerns 200
Green section 200
professionalism 197
racism 231
Rules of Golf Committee 206
United States Golf Association (USGA), championships 62
United States LPGA 114, 125
unplayable balls 209–10
US Open Championship 20–3
Anderson, Willie 110
Barber, Miller 112
Barnes, Jim 112
Boros, Julius 114
Casper, Billy 116, 122, 156–7, **156**
Fleck, Jack 123
Hagen, Walter 81
Heafner, Clayton 125
Hogan, Ben 93, 123
Irwin, Hale 127
Jacklin, Tony 127
Jones, Bobby 95
MacNamara, Tom 61
Merion 171
Nicklaus, Jack 154–5, 160–1
Oakmont 176
Ouimet, Francis 154, **154**
Palmer, Arnold 97, 99, 156–7, **156**
Pebble Beach 173
Pinehurst 175
prize money 48–9, 240
racism 231
results 23
Sarazen, Gene 103
Strange, Curtis **15**
Vardon, Harry 60, 154, **154**
Watson, Tom 160–1
Winged Foot 189
US PGA Championship 28–30
1979 124
assets 190
Boros, Julius 114
Daly, John 118
Elkington, Steve 121
Hagen, Walter 91
January, Don 128
Montgomerie, Colin 121, 134
Norman, Greg 121
racism 231
results 29
US PGA Tour 47–50
Beman, Deane 113
charity 190
Chip Beck 113
costs 190
Daly, John 239
Elkington, Steve 121
Finchem, Tim 50, 234
marketing contracts 193
sponsorship 192
World Tour 234–5
US Professional Golfers Association (US PGA) 28, 47
racism 232–3
US Women's Amateur Championship 61, 113
US Women's Open 44–5, 125
US Women's Tour 113

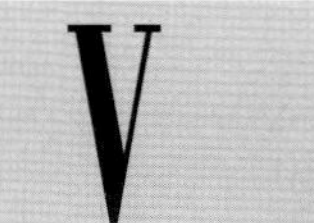

Vagliano Cup 43
Valderrama, Spain 74, 187, **187**
Valentine, Jesse 43
Van Courtland Park 59
Vardon, Harry 48, 107
British Open 24, **24**
clothing 224
grip 122, 214
hole in one 246
Pinehurst 175
Royal County Down 177
US Open 20, 60, 154, **154**
US Tour 60
Vare, Glenna *see* Collett, Glenna
Vare Trophy 114
Varndon, Harry, accidents 238
Vaughan, Bruce 240
Venturi, Ken 149–50, **149**
Vicenzo, Roberto de 52, 150
British Open 25, 155–6, 179
Masters 19, 124, 237
Volvo, sponsorship 193
Volvo Masters **192**
Volvo PGA Championship 188

Wadkins, Lanny 32, 33, 34, 150, **150**, 234
Wales 65
Walker Cup 40–1, 113
Wall, Art 52
Walt Disney Magnolia 245
Walton, Philip 34, 244
Wanamaker, Rodman 28
Ward, Harvie 62
Ward, Marvin 40, **40**
water hazards 210–11, **210**
Watrous, Al 185
Watson, Tom 46, **52**, **80**, 85, 108–9, 160–1, **160**, 173
Ballybunion 70, 167
British Open 24, 26, 160
Gleneagles 170
putting 216
Ryder Cup 31, 32, 33, 89
swing 215
US Open 21–2
Way, Paul 32
Wedges **227**
Weiskopf, Tom 150, **150**, 159
Wentworth Golf Club, Surrey 188, **188, 202–3**
West Australia Open 127
Westner, Wayne 53, 84, **84**
Westward Ho! 66, 181, **181**, 233
Wethered, Joyce 43, 150–1
Wethered, Roger 36
Whigham, Jim 62
White, John 237
White, Ronnie 40
Whitworth, Kathy 45, 151
Wilder, Edmund 72
wildlife 203, 246
Williamson, Tom 68
Willie, Louis 233
Willock, Curtis 56
Wilson, Enid 43, 151, 246, **246**
Wilson, Hugh 171, 174
Winged Foot, New York 189, **189**
Wolstenholme, Gary 36, **36**, 41
women
championships 11, 42–6
clothing 224, **225**
sexism 233–4
US 60
Women's European Tour 70
Women's National Club 237
Women's Professional Golfers European Tour (WPGET) 192
Wood, Craig 17, 145, 151, 184, 189
Woodhall Spa 70, **70**
Woods, Tiger 19, **19**, 39, 41, 50, 151, **151**, **232**, 233
Woosnam, Ian 19, 22, 33, 34, 70, 151–2
World Cup 63, 112, 114, 180, 188
World Match Play 53, 101, 130, 188
World Open 52–3
World Tour 234–5
Worsham, Lew 49, **50**, 152
Wright, Mickey 152

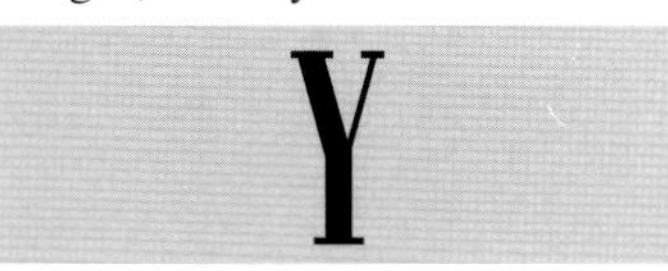

Yamada, Masashi 240
Yancey, Bert 105
Yugoslavia 76

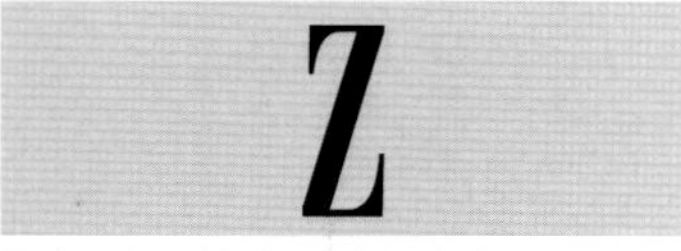

Zaharias, Babe 42, 45, **45**, 152
Zoeller, Fuzzy 31, 32, 52, 152, **152**, 189, 195–6, **196**

ACKNOWLEDGEMENTS

The publishers would like to thank the following sources for their kind permission to reproduce the photographs in this book: **Allsport**/Howard Boylan, Simon Bruty, David Cannon, Russell Cheyne, Phil Cole, Mike Cooper, J.D. Cuban, Stephen Dunn, Matthew Harris, Phil Inglis, Rusty Jarrett, David Leah, Bob Martin, Stephen Munday, Gary Newkirk, Mike Powell, Steve Powell, Gary M. Prior, Andrew Redington, David Rogers, Pascal Rondeau, Richard Saker; **Allsport Historical**/Hulton Deutsch Collection, Mirror Syndication International; **Ted Barrett; Bridgeman Art Library**; **Callaway**; **John B. Carnett/Popular Science Magazine**; **Colorsport**; **E.T.Archive**; **Mary Evans Picture Library**; **Hobbs Golf Collection**; **Phillips - Chester**; **Popperfoto**; **Range Bettmann UPI**; **Phil Sheldon Golf Picture Library**; **USGA**.